THE JIM CROW ENCYCLOPEDIA

THE JIM CROW ENCYCLOPEDIA

Volume 2: K–Z

Edited by
Nikki L.M. Brown and
Barry M. Stentiford

Greenwood Milestones in African American History

GREENWOOD PRESS
Westport, Connecticut • London

Library of Congress Cataloging-in-Publication Data

The Jim Crow encyclopedia : Greenwood milestones in African American history /
    edited by Nikki L.M. Brown and Barry M. Stentiford.
      p. cm.
    Includes bibliographical references and index.
    ISBN-13: 978–0–313–34181–6 ((set) : alk. paper)
    ISBN-13: 978–0–313–34183–0 ((vol. 1) : alk. paper)
    ISBN-13: 978–0–313–34185–4 ((vol. 2) : alk. paper)
1. African Americans—Segregation—History—Encyclopedias. 2. African Americans—
Segregation—Southern States—History—Encyclopedias. 3. African Americans—Civil
rights—History—Encyclopedias. 4. African Americans—
Civil rights—Southern States—History—Encyclopedias. 5. United States—Race relations
—History—19th century—Encyclopedias. 6. United States—Race
relations—History—20th century—Encyclopedias. 7. Southern States—Race relations—
History—19th century—Encyclopedias. 8. Southern States—Race relations—History—
20th century—Encyclopedias. I. Brown, Nikki L. M. II. Stentiford, Barry M.
E185.61.J53 2008
305.896′07307503—dc22   2008013645

British Library Cataloguing in Publication Data is available.

Library of Congress Catalog Card Number: 2008013645
ISBN: 978–0–313–34181–6 (set)
        978–0–313–34183–0 (vol. 1)
        978–0–313–34185–4 (vol. 2)

First published in 2008

Greenwood Press, 88 Post Road West, Westport, CT 06881
An imprint of Greenwood Publishing Group, Inc.
www.greenwood.com

Printed in the United States of America

The paper used in this book complies with the
Permanent Paper Standard issued by the National
Information Standards Organization (Z39.48–1984).

10 9 8 7 6 5 4 3 2 1

CONTENTS

K

Kansas Exodusters

The Kansas Exodusters were the thousands of rural working-class African American men and women who tried to emigrate from the states of the Deep South to Kansas in 1879. "The Kansas Fever Exodus" pointed to African Americans' rejection of the new status quo in the Redeemer South following the collapse of **Reconstruction**. Rural blacks voted with their feet in opposition to rampant political and economic injustice: the violent intimidation of black voters and political leaders, persistent white terrorism, and ongoing economic exploitation and debt peonage at the hands of white plantation owners and shopkeepers. The mass departure to Kansas represented African Americans' hopes to build new a future where they could own land, cast their ballots, hold offices, and move about freely. The Kansas Exodusters hoped to be governed by the principles of the Thirteenth, Fourteenth, and Fifteenth Amendments, not the whims of Southern whites who wanted to destroy the legacies of Reconstruction and impose new systems of oppression that too closely resembled antebellum slavery.

The migrants came from **Louisiana, Mississippi**, and **Texas**. In these states, as well as the other Southern states, many years of white intimidation and terrorism shattered the constitutional and political promises made to African Americans during the years of Reconstruction. As blacks became free persons and citizens during the 1860s, whites in the South responded with violent hostility. For them, the idea that African Americans were equal under the law defied the most fundamental premise of white Southern culture: that white men could command and control the labor and status of African Americans. Initially in the spring of 1865, during the era of Presidential Reconstruction, whites in Southern state legislatures imposed "**Black Codes**" that were intended to constrict the newly freed's rights. Whites wanted to force blacks into strict labor contracts with Southern planters, curb their political activities, and preclude African Americans from testifying against whites in court. Whites wanted to build a new South that closely resembled the old. Radical Reconstruction, however, destroyed the Black Code regime. Angered by Southern whites' actions, the Republican Congress imposed military rule, gave blacks the vote and the right to hold office, and promised equality under the law. Southern whites continued to fiercely resist black empowerment, however. They deployed extralegal tactics such as nightriding and "bulldozing," and formed terrorist organizations such as the **Ku Klux Klan** and the White League, to intimidate and murder black Republican voters, candidates, and organizers. In election after election during the 1870s, Southern whites undermined the political process by stuffing ballot boxes, scaring away voters, forcing black candidates into exile, and murdering blacks who stood up to injustice. The terrible corruption and violence that overshadowed the 1878 elections in Louisiana convinced many blacks in the Gulf region that the South held no future for African Americans. In fact, some Louisiana parishes passed laws in 1878 that required blacks to carry passes when they traveled on public roads—distressing reminders of the days of slavery and the absence of democracy in the Redeemer South.

Unremitting poverty was the second major factor that gave rise to the exodus. In the years after the Civil War, poor blacks and landowning whites struggled to define the terms of labor and land use in the South. African Americans refused to submit to whites' demands that they become landless laborers, struggling to distance themselves from any labor system that resembled Old South slavery. Black men and women wanted to possess their own land and live independently. Rural whites, however, opposed black landownership, which would have signified equality among whites and blacks. During the 1860s and 1870s, sharecropping and tenant farming emerged as the predominant labor and landholding arrangements that were available to blacks. As renters, African American families farmed a specified portion of a planter's land, perhaps between 15 and 20 acres, paying an annual rent with a portion of the cotton crop they produced. While tenancy allowed blacks to distance themselves from their former masters, the workings of tenant farming created a cycle of debt peonage. White planters, shopkeepers, and creditors forced black farmers into a state of permanent debt by setting high prices for the "ginning" of cotton bales, overpricing tools and supplies at local stores, and establishing high rents for land. Black families had to remain on the land as renters in order to work towards paying off their outstanding debts. They seldom made a profit, sinking deeper into debt every year. To make matters worse, contracts between landowners and tenants often stipulated that the landlord could seize a tenant's personal property—including farming tools, supplies, and mules—as payment. Whites never allowed African American farmers to climb out of poverty and tenancy to become landowners themselves, enforcing their will with the threat of violence. In 1879, after many years of struggle on Southern plantations, the Exodusters viewed emigration to Kansas as a way to finally achieve economic independence.

In the 1870s, Benjamin "Pap" Singleton, an aging former slave who once worked as a carpenter in Tennessee, popularized the notion of emigration to Kansas. Singleton viewed himself as a deliverer who would bring the oppressed of the South to the Promised Land. While Singleton called himself the "Father" of the migration, the Kansas Fever Exodus arose from the rural black working class itself. Between March and the end of the year, thousands of black men and women departed from Louisiana, Mississippi, and Texas. Despite their shortage of funds, the migrants determinedly made their way north and westward—doing so without the aid of a centralized leadership. Newspapers reported that 75 black men and women reached St. Louis in the early spring of 1879. The migration from the South rapidly expanded, much to the surprise of white observers. Between March and May, observers noted that the banks of the Mississippi River were crowded with Southern black families, all trying to secure passage to St. Louis and points beyond. The Kansas Exodusters reported to curious journalists that they were leaving the South for the land of John Brown. An estimated 4,000–5,000 migrants arrived in Kansas during 1879. Despite the groundswell that pushed the migration forward, the movement slowly began to fade. Many steamships refused passage to the migrants, and the poor black families who led this great migration quickly began to run out of money and could not complete the journey. Those who made it to Kansas found more opportunity than in the South, purchasing 20,000 acres of land, acquiring more than $40,000 in assets, and securing an average yearly income of $363. The migration would continue into the 1880s, but on a smaller scale.

The Kansas Fever Exodus was the high point of a broader pattern of grassroots emigrationism that unfolded in the post-emancipation South. In response to the racial violence and injustice of the post–Civil War years, African Americans looked abroad to Africa and the Caribbean, as well as domestically to Kansas and Indiana, in the hopes of finding freedom and new opportunities to own land. For instance, hundreds of black Americans in **Georgia**, Tennessee, **Virginia**, and the Carolinas applied to the old American Colonization Society for transportation to the African nation of Liberia. Between 1865 and 1868, 2,232 African Americans relocated to Liberia from the South. The average number of those who emigrated to Africa in the 1860s (558 per year) was more than double the rate during the years between 1820 and 1861. During the 1870s, emigration sentiment intensified because of the efforts of a U.S. Army veteran, black civil rights advocate, and former slave named Henry Adams, who helped create the grassroots Colonization Council. Adams and the other members of the Council tried to organize poor black farmers for emigration to Liberia, collecting the signatures of more than 69,000 rural black men and women. While a lack of funds prevented the organization from sending migrants overseas, the group popularized the idea of leaving the South and paved the way for the 1879 exodus to Kansas.

White reactions to the Kansas Exodusters varied. Early on, many white Southerners claimed the migrants had been duped into leaving by demagogues, while others expressed hopes that Southern labor might be more productive now that these quitters had left. However, as the migration intensified, whites in the South and North began to worry that the South would experience a labor shortage that would injure its fragile economy. African Americans generally endorsed the migration. However, some prominent blacks, including Frederick Douglass, criticized the migrants. Douglass believed the Exodusters had implicitly abandoned the struggle for citizenship in the South. While only a fraction completed the journey to Kansas, the fact that so many tried indicated that African Americans firmly opposed the political and economic practices that defined the post-Reconstruction South. *See also* Disenfranchisement.

Further Readings: Foner, Eric. *Reconstruction: America's Unfinished Revolution, 1863–1877.* New York: Harper & Row, Publishers, 1988; Hahn, Steven. *A Nation under Our Feet: Black Political Struggles in the Rural South from Slavery to the Great Migration.* Cambridge, MA: Harvard University Press, Belknap Press, 2003; Painter, Nell Irvin. *Exodusters: Black Migration to Kansas after Reconstruction.* New York: Alfred A. Knopf, 1977. Reprint, New York: W. W. Norton & Company, 1992.

Gregory Wood

Kennedy, John F. (1917–1963)

As president, John F. Kennedy overcame initial reluctance to expend political capital on civil rights to make the issue integral to his administration. Kennedy evolved from a focus on symbolism to substance in addressing the persistence of the **Jim Crow** South and struck a major blow on behalf of equality under the law.

Enjoying a life of privilege in a *nouveau riche* family, "Jack" Kennedy was most familiar with the sort of prejudice directed at Irish Roman Catholics like himself in private schools and related settings. Forming the "Muckers Club" (named for Irish American laborers) while a senior at the Choate School, he reveled in defying pretentious authority figures with pranks committed by students whose wealth precluded expulsion. The fate of African Americans struggling to achieve full citizenship rights held no emotional relevance for Kennedy over much of his political career. Although progressive in his personal views on race, he cast two votes as a senator in 1957 that endangered a civil rights bill endorsed by most Northern Democrats.

More of a centrist than is commonly remembered, he had little interest in making social activism a prominent feature of his agenda, particularly if it compromised his prospects for the White House. Angling for a presidential run in 1960, Kennedy courted both civil rights leaders and segregationists in pursuit of a reputation for moderation. An opportunity for a politically advantageous gesture to African Americans presented itself when **Martin Luther King, Jr.**, was sentenced to several months of hard labor after attempting to integrate an Atlanta department store eatery. With King destined for a rural **Georgia** prison camp, the environment seemed tailor-made for the sort of "accident" that could remove one of the most inspiring figures from the movement. Kennedy comforted a pregnant Coretta Scott King and used the influence of his brother, Robert (recent Senate counsel), to secure King's release. Meanwhile, the Republican nominee, Vice President Richard M. Nixon, remained silent on the matter lest he face accusations of pandering (a concern shared by the Kennedy camp). In a close election in which Kennedy took the popular vote by roughly 120,000, the impact of this *faux pas* by Nixon was crucial. African Americans still provided considerable support to Republicans, to the extent that they could vote in an era of widespread disenfranchisement in the former Confederacy, for the party's legacy of emancipation under President Abraham Lincoln. But King reversed his previous endorsement of Nixon, who belonged to the NAACP, in a move that may have decided the election for a candidate now praised for moral courage by the reverend.

African Americans comprised a constituency that would increasingly favor Democrats as the 1960s unfolded.

Despite the spirit of optimism and eagerness for social change generated by the Kennedy campaign, the newly elected president proved skittish about taking dramatic steps to address racial inequities in the South. Segregationists carried tremendous weight in the **Democratic Party**, as it had long enjoyed a virtual monopoly on political power in the South that rendered its legislators among the most senior in Congress. Kennedy knew that his economic initiatives could face obstruction, particularly in the Senate with its allowance for filibustering, if he designated civil rights a top priority. The leader of the Southern Caucus, Senator Richard Russell (D-Georgia), had not even endorsed Kennedy in 1960 and remained pointedly absent from the country during the final stage of the campaign. The hawkish president appreciated the like-minded views on national security typical among Southern Democrats and suffered from the period's most overwhelming political anxiety: fear of being labeled as ''soft'' on communism. The Kennedy White House consequently offered little more than lip service as Southern communities were convulsed by violence amidst the rise of the modern **Civil Rights Movement**. The president might have integrated the **National Guard** or highlighted the indignities suffered by African diplomats at restaurants in Virginia and Maryland, but instead he merely emphasized the enforcement of existing laws.

Yet federal oversight on race-based discrimination proved far from vigorous. The plight of the ''Freedom Riders'' of 1961 belied the rhetoric of Kennedy's vaunted New Frontier. Justice Department agents failed to protect **Congress of Racial Equality (CORE)** activists from beatings in Anniston, **Alabama,** while escaping from a bus set ablaze by segregationists resisting the integration of interstate transportation. As with similar incidents, these officials seemed content to take notes and liaison with state and local authorities without interjecting themselves into jurisdictional disputes. The president had no political cover in light of the fact that **Robert F. Kennedy** supervised the agency as attorney general.

Jack and Robert Kennedy harbored profound ambivalence over the Civil Rights Movement. To his credit, Robert labored tirelessly to impress upon Southern leaders the need to safeguard civil rights workers. Jack utilized federal troops and marshals to ensure that **James Meredith** could begin classes at the all-white University of **Mississippi**. He drew the ire of a powerful senator on the Armed Services Committee, John Stennis (D-Mississippi), for a Defense Department policy of discouraging military personnel from frequenting establishments that practiced segregation. But whenever the central issue was no longer the legitimacy of federal authority, their commitment waned. Robert betrayed a dislike for the political and social outlook of civil rights workers by characterizing them as dangerous radicals best kept at arm's length by the White House. He sanctioned illegal wiretaps of King's phones to investigate the possibility of Communist influence within King's entourage. Seeking a presidential term of his own in 1968, Robert would evince a conversion on political protest that transformed his standing with marginalized groups in America.

Jack Kennedy experienced an epiphany of sorts in the spring of 1963 when the focus of the civil rights struggle turned to Birmingham, Alabama. King vowed to make this city the proverbial Gettysburg of a new civil war as he marched with supporters to call for economic opportunity and an end to Jim Crow laws. Police chief "**Bull**" **Connor** employed tactics completely out of proportion for civil disobedience. When confronted with images of teenage demonstrators subjected to attack dogs and high-pressure water hoses, Kennedy was reportedly sickened and outraged. Galvanized into action, Jack and Robert lobbied national business leaders to pressure their Southern facilities to integrate. The president federalized soldiers from the Alabama **National Guard** to guarantee the admittance of two black students at the University of Alabama in Tuscaloosa despite the theatrics of Governor **George Wallace**. While many black leaders remained angry at the administration's tepid track record, the White House was producing more results. In May, Kennedy supplied his first public address with unequivocal, impassioned support for the Civil Rights Movement. Working largely without a script, he emphasized the hypocrisy of a nation priding itself as unique and reformist on the international stage without tackling the clear failure to live up to the promise of its Constitution. Kennedy had received admonitions from African statesmen for efforts to apply a distinctly American solution to the war-torn Congo while newsreels ran Birmingham footage worthy of a tinhorn dictatorship. Kennedy introduced a civil rights bill in 1963 that aimed to eradicate employment discrimination and augment the legal assault on the segregation of public facilities. His assassination in November left Americans wondering what might have been if Kennedy had lived to continue his relatively activist approach, particularly with a second term in office. Marketing the bill as a final tribute to a fallen president and his legacy, President Lyndon B. Johnson ushered the legislation through Congress in 1964, in a complicated move for a Southern chief executive. Kennedy's newfound commitment to civil rights has contributed to an ongoing scholarly debate over whether a longer presidency would have spared the United States much of the contentiousness and polarization of the 1960s in military, social, and economic affairs.

Further Readings: Chafe, William. *The Unfinished Journey: America Since World War II.* New York: Oxford University Press, 1995; John F. Kennedy Presidential Library and Museum Web site. http://www.jfklibrary.org (accessed May 23, 2008); Matthews, Christopher. *Kennedy & Nixon: The Rivalry That Shaped Postwar America.* New York: Simon and Schuster, 1996.

Jeffrey D. Bass

Kennedy, Robert F. (1925–1968)

Robert F. Kennedy, as attorney general under his brother, President **John F. Kennedy,** and as a presidential candidate himself, contributed to both the frustration and the promise of the **Civil Rights Movement** as it attempted to transform race relations in the 1960s. Kennedy mirrored his brother John in adopting a more substantive approach to social justice as his career progressed.

Raised in an ambitious family where his older brothers were groomed for higher office, Robert dutifully played the role of political lieutenant by running Senate and Presidential campaigns for John in 1952 and 1960, respectively. During the latter race, he employed his influence as a former Senate counsel to facilitate the release of **Martin Luther King, Jr.,** from incarceration in **Georgia** for civil disobedience. This maneuver helped sway black allegiance towards Democrats in a tight race and enhanced the image of John Kennedy as a socially progressive candidate. Appointed as his brother's attorney general, Robert presided over a Justice Department that earned little goodwill with the Civil Rights Movement. In 1961, federal agents stood by as members of **Congress of Racial Equality (CORE)** suffered beatings upon fleeing from a bus torched by segregationists hostile to these "Freedom Riders." Such laxity was not uncommon given concerns in the White House over antagonizing powerful Southern Democrats who could stymie presidential legislation in Congress. Although the two men never got along, Robert approved the illegal wiretapping of civil rights activists conducted by J. Edgar Hoover as head of the **Federal Bureau of Investigation**. The attorney general entreated Southern officials to refrain from violence even while regarding civil rights workers as dangerous radicals unworthy of full-fledged administration support. Only in the spring of 1963, with the horrific treatment of demonstrators in Birmingham, **Alabama**, did the White House confront squarely the question of race relations. On the night that President Kennedy delivered his first major speech on civil rights, National Association for the Advancement of Colored People (NAACP) activist **Medgar Evers** was murdered outside of his **Mississippi** home. The Kennedys were deeply moved by the conduct of the Evers family, and Robert provided his personal phone numbers so that federal authorities could be summoned quickly at any hour. John and Robert continued to view the Civil Rights Movement with some trepidation for its potential to alienate the administration from middle-class whites and to associate it with the excesses of black militants impatient with the integrationist approach of leaders such as King. But these two politicians recognized that the campaign for racial equality must press on regardless of its impact on reelection prospects. The assassination of President Kennedy in November left new initiatives and a sense of momentum in limbo.

Robert remained attorney general until September 1964 in an uneasy relationship with President Lyndon B. Johnson, who perceived him as a threat both intellectually and politically. Hoover cut him out of the loop on civil rights wiretapping with the exception of an instance in which King and his staffers had commented luridly on the sexual activities of the fallen president and his wife. Kennedy resigned his post for a successful run at a Senate seat from New York. By the late 1960s, his image was decidedly more progressive based upon a growing advocacy of social issues and his questioning of hawkish assumptions on the Cold War.

In 1968, a presidential campaign moved into high gear amidst a series of shocks to the U.S. political process and collective psyche. The Tet offensive in South Vietnam laid bare the extent to which government officials had underreported the strength of resistance in the region. After only narrowly winning the New Hampshire primary over antiwar senator Eugene McCarthy,

Johnson found his political base rapidly eroding. Meanwhile, Kennedy agonized over whether to enter the contest. Fearful of touching off internecine warfare among Democrats in what could be judged as a personal vendetta against Johnson, he could only content himself that the president remained obsessed with his potential candidacy. But the political landscape created by the Tet offensive paved the way for Kennedy to enter the campaign in March with a focus on disengagement from Vietnam and a comprehensive assault upon poverty and racism. Later that month, Johnson announced suddenly that he was abandoning his campaign to concentrate on the war effort. Kennedy was left to compete in the primaries against McCarthy and Vice President Hubert Humphrey.

As he joined the presidential race, Kennedy had begun a process of convergence with King despite minimal personal contact. The two had suffered dramatically for their causes and reached the conclusion that America's limitations ran far deeper than moderate reform could address. Neither crusader could tolerate that deteriorating race and class relations were fostering a society more likely to emphasize its differences than common bonds. Both men went out on a limb in a period of virulent anti-Communism to argue that the premises of the Vietnam War were faulty and that the conflict was tearing the nation apart at home by exacerbating racial tensions. Kennedy had become more compassionate than evident in his earlier days as political enforcer in his brother's White House, and King had developed greater pragmatism for translating his vision of racial cooperation into a tangible agenda. These fellow travelers in the quest to transcend the bitterness of their times would soon share the distinction of paying the ultimate price for their convictions.

Adding to the tumult of an extraordinarily bleak year, King was gunned down in April on the eve of what was anticipated as a radical speech in Memphis on the interrelation of poverty and racism. In the immediate aftermath of the slaying, Kennedy was en route to Indianapolis to speak to a ghetto audience unaware of the news. At a time of such racial polarization, few white politicians would have risked the potential hostility of a black crowd shocked by the loss of one of its most charismatic leaders. But Kennedy forged ahead with oratory both candid and inspiring. Referencing the loss of his brother to politically based hatred, he urged Americans to reject violence as a solution to any of the problems that plagued the nation in domestic and foreign policy. Soon, his presidential campaign grew more focused as he found a niche as the champion of the disenfranchised and dispossessed. Blacks, **Latinos**, and working-class whites rallied behind his banner of attacking the twin scourges of racism and poverty. His early campaigning bore the mark of a loose cannon, but he learned to channel intensity in a way that roused citizens to a sense of duty and action without losing their moral bearings in the process. A difficult road still lay ahead as McCarthy appealed to the antiestablishment vote as well. Yet Kennedy's emotional and confrontational style appeared to resonate more effectively than the professorial temperament of McCarthy.

California offered the greatest test yet with its numerous delegates and absence of a clear frontrunner. Activists such as Charles Evers and John Lewis of the **Student Nonviolent Coordinating Committee** worked on Kennedy's behalf. But the candidate continued his grassroots approach of facing angry black militants and converting many into backers. Kennedy triumphed with a 5 percent margin over McCarthy in what appeared to be a tremendous momentum shift propelling him towards the Democratic nomination. Just moments after addressing supporters at a Los Angeles hotel, he was shot in the head at close range by a Palestinian extremist, Sirhan Sirhan, and America lost another potent voice for change.

The abstract, intellectual McCarthy could not strike the same chord with Democratic voters, and most of the party turned to Humphrey. Though sporting a strong reform record of his own, Humphrey adopted a generally pro-war stance that alienated younger Democrats. The scenario that developed during the Democratic convention in Chicago was everything that Robert Kennedy had worked to prevent. Thousands of disenchanted youth descended upon the Democratic stronghold to protest the Vietnam War, the "safe" choice of Humphrey by party leaders, and other perceived features of a moribund status quo. The resulting clashes between demonstrators and law enforcement fractured the Democrats and helped secure the triumph of Richard M. Nixon.

Although a latecomer to the crusade for social justice, Robert Kennedy ultimately devoted himself to building a coalition across racial and class boundaries to make the political process work for all Americans. Ever cognizant of the odds, he preferred this uphill struggle to watching U.S. society lapse into apathy or revolution. Many of his contemporaries have argued that only his election in 1968 could have sufficiently unified the nation to avert the waning of the Civil Rights Movement, growing stagnation in Vietnam, and the petty political partisanship that lay ahead in the near future.

Further Readings: Chafe, William. *The Unfinished Journey: America Since World War II.* New York: Oxford University Press, 1995; John F. Kennedy Presidential Library and Museum Web site. http://www.jfklibrary.org (accessed May 23, 2008); Thomas, Evan. *Robert Kennedy: His Life.* New York: Simon & Schuster, 2002.

Jeffrey D. Bass

Kentucky

The Commonwealth of Kentucky was admitted in the Union on June 1, 1792, becoming the nation's first state west of the Appalachian Mountains. Isaac Shelby was elected the state's first governor, and Frankfort was chosen the capital. During the first half of the nineteenth century, Kentucky was primarily a state of small farms rather than large plantations. In 1833, the state's General Assembly passed a law that made the importation of slaves into the state illegal. In 1850, however, the legislature repealed this restriction, and Kentucky, while slave trading had began to redevelop during the mid-1840s, was converted into a huge slave market for the lower South. At the same time, the overall population of African American Kentuckians began to increase. For example, in 1800, of the 220,955 people who resided in the Bluegrass State, 41,084 were black Americans who lived mostly in the state's major urban centers. Thirty years later, in 1830, the number of African Americans throughout the state had increased to 24.7 percent of the overall population (170,130 of the 687,917 inhabitants of Kentucky were black Americans).

Antislavery and abolitionist sentiment began in the state as early as the late eighteenth century. In various churches and other civic organizations, people such as John G. Fee, James G. Birney, Delia Webster, Calvin Fairbank, and Cassius M. Clay worked vigorously throughout Kentucky to eliminate the system of human bondage. This group was joined by a cadre of African Americans, like Eliza Harris, Henry Bibb, Lewis Hayden, John Rankin, John Parker, and Margaret Garner, who set out to prove that slavery could not stand in a state as well as a nation that rested on the principles stated in the Declaration of Independence. Soon Kentucky, like other border states, was torn by conflict over the issue of slavery. With the onset of the Civil War, with 30,000 Kentuckians fighting for the Confederacy, and about 64,000 serving in the Union ranks, including some 23,000 African Americans, the institution of slavery came to an end.

In 1865, as a result of the passage of the Thirteenth Amendment, black Americans in the Bluegrass State gained citizenship. However, many white Kentuckians, retaining their racist views about African Americans, sought to prove that they still were in charge. More specifically, with the help of various white supremacist groups like the **Ku Klux Klan**, the enormous gains African Americans made in Kentucky during **Reconstruction**, as well as nationwide, came to an unceremonious end. Very quickly, the state began to enact a series of **Jim Crow** laws such as the 1892 Separate Coach Law, which required separate coaches for blacks and whites on interstate railroads. Although a group of African American Kentuckians tried to challenge the constitutionality of this law in court, in 1900, the **U.S. Supreme Court** ruled that the law was valid.

During the early 1900s, state politicians continued to enact Jim Crow laws to curtail the educational accessibility and limit the mobility of African American Kentuckians. For example, in 1904, the state passed the Day Law, which required the segregation of all public and private schools. Ten years later, in 1914, the Louisville Board of Alderman passed an ordinance designed to promote residential segregation. This law declared that if the majority of a specific community was one race, than only members of that race could purchase a home in the area. Despite the overturning of this law by the U.S. Supreme Court in *Buchanan v. Warley* (1917), residential segregation unremitting characterized most of the Bluegrass State until the late 1960s. However, the stern walls of legal segregation had started to crumble during the late 1940s.

In 1949, a federal court ordered the University of Kentucky to admit African Americans to its engineering, graduate, law, and pharmacy schools. A bill was defeated in the Kentucky General Assembly to rescind the Day Law in 1954, however, the landmark ***Brown v. Board of Education*** on May 17, 1954, made this challenge moot. Most educational facilities throughout the state quickly complied with this ruling, thus avoiding the harsh battles that erupted throughout the Deep South. Although unwritten discrimination practices continued in Kentucky during most of the 1950s and early 1960s, most of the overt forms of residential segregation gradually disappeared mostly as a result of the pressure garnered by civil rights–led boycotts and marches throughout the state. For example, in March 1968, Kentucky became the first state to enact a statewide anti–housing discrimination law.

Further Readings: Harrison, Lowell H., and James C. Klotter. *A New History of Kentucky.* Lexington: University Press of Kentucky, 1997; Klotter, James C. *Our Kentucky: A Study of the Bluegrass State.* Lexington: University Press of Kentucky, 1992.

Eric R. Jackson

King, Martin Luther, Jr. (1929–1968)

Martin Luther King, Jr., was a theologian, social activist, lecturer, and author. Born into a middle-class family in Atlanta, **Georgia**, King, during the decades of the 1950s and 1960s, first represented the social, moral, and political aspirations and struggles of black Americans during the age of segregation and would become the leader of the **Civil Rights Movement** generally organized in black **churches** and supported largely by middle- and working-class blacks throughout the South. Later, as white resistance in the South organized to oppose desegregation on all levels and violence against blacks and Northern whites who traveled to the South to support desegregation, the movement took on national as well as international importance.

King was a precocious youngster, both mentally and physically, and grew up in a Christian home. His father, Martin Luther King, Sr., was the pastor of Ebenezer Baptist Church, the largest black church in Atlanta, and his mother, Alberta Williams King, was the organist. At home, the young King was doted on, was loved and told that he was special, and enjoyed middle-class comforts. Though his parents, especially his father, railed against racism and segregation, they made it a point to remind him that it was very important to transcend hate, even from those who publicly humiliated you. King joined the church when he was five, received his first experience of racism when he was six when his white friend, with whom he had played since King was three, suddenly informed him that he could no longer play with him. At eight, he was slapped by a white female on whose feet he accidentally stepped. Before enrolling in Morehouse College at the age 15, King would witness and experience many examples of racial and social injustice that prevailed in Atlanta. He was mostly undaunted by such examples, and all visible and overt examples of racism he experienced in the world outside of the home were largely negated by the expressions of love and devotion directed towards him by his parents and others who recognized his talents: he won the an oratory contest when he was 14 on the theme "The Negro and the Constitution."

Enrollment at the all-male Morehouse College (1944–1948) for a BA in sociology and Crozer (1948–1951) for his BD threw King into an intellectual and academic world that, he claimed, shattered his fundamentalist upbringing. For in these worlds, he rediscovered Thoreau and discovered Hobbes, Marx, Locke, Mill, Nietzsche, and the writings of Christian theologians, **W.E.B. Du Bois,** and the Satyagraha theory of **Mahatma Gandhi**. This exposure prompted King to reflect on two features of religion he would seek to attain: the infusion of more intellect, not just emotion, in black sermons, and his view that religion should be used to challenge and change the existing society, not

Martin Luther King, Jr., removes a burned cross from his lawn in 1960. Courtesy of Library of Congress, LC-USZ62-126560.

simply adapt to its ongoing values and norms. He later attended Boston University (1951–1955), where he received a doctorate in theology. There, he met Coretta Scott, who was studying to become a concert singer. They were married in Marion, **Alabama**, in June 1953.

In April 1954 King accepted an offer to become the pastor at Dexter Baptist Church in Montgomery, Alabama, while completing his dissertation at Boston University. He was installed as pastor in October of that same year. King, however, was indecisive with respect to his future career. He was torn between a career in education and a career as a pulpit minister, just as he was once torn between living in the North or living in the South. He chose living in the South because he pledged himself to work to resolve racial and human rights problems in the area. On December 1, 1955, **Rosa Parks** was arrested for refusing to give up her bus seat to a white man, though no other seats were available in the bus. After her arrest, the ministers assembled and elected King president of the Montgomery Improvement Association (MIA). After a judge deemed Parks guilty and fined her $100, the MIA agreed to launch a bus boycott. The news of the boycott spread like wildfire throughout the South; the boycott was successful, and it was the beginning of King's problems with justice in the South. Between the beginning of the boycott and November 1956, when the **U.S. Supreme Court** struck down the segregation law as unconstitutional, King was arrested for speeding—30 miles per hour in an area with a 25 MPH speed limit—and received more than 40 death threats, and, on January 30, 1956, his home was bombed. During this time, King was solidifying two approaches that would be a part of his strategy in resolving social issues: a Christian approach that emphasized Christian love and forgiveness, and Gandhi's method of winning through nonviolence. He visited Gandhi's India in February 1959, where he got a close look at the world of the Untouchables, those at the bottom of the Indian caste system. King's leadership was recognized by many in the Civil Rights Movement, for he was elected president of the **Southern Christian Leadership Conference (SCLC)**.

As demonstrations against racial segregation in the South began to spread, King was called upon to lead these demonstrations and to help organize the protests. The demonstration against segregation in Birmingham, Alabama, would be the next test case after Montgomery. It was here after his arrest in April 1963 for protesting racial segregation in the city that King wrote his famous "Letter from a Birmingham Jail."

This letter, written on the margins of old newspapers, scraps of paper, and legal pads, was first of all a castigation of the Christian ministers who criticized King for leading the protest in the city. It was also the beginning of King's assertion that there were just laws (God's Laws) and unjust laws (human laws), and citizens had an obligation to disobey unjust laws. In August

1963, King made his famous "I Have a Dream Speech" to the more than 300,000 people asscmbled on the Mall in Washington, DC. King reminded the nation that it was time to put an end to segregation, that Americans had to be conscious of the importance of the Declaration of Independence and the Constitution in the making of the nation, and that blacks have come too far to give up or permit the freedoms they had won to disappear. The speech was an often stern message to both whites and blacks: for whites, to judge Americans not by their color but by their character; for blacks, the advice was to stay strong and remain disciplined in their protests.

In 1964, King was honored as *Time* magazine's Man of the Year, published the book, *Why We Can't Wait,* and, in December of that year, received the Nobel Peace Prize in Oslo, Norway. Then overt racial strife began to break out in the North, the Vietnam War was heating up, and critics of the war began to overtly question the government's war policy. Young blacks, more impatience than their elders, began to utter the cry of Black Power as a new approach to power and diversity in American life. Younger members of the movement had long expressed their discontent with older leaders, withdrew from their association with older members of the movement and formed the **Student Nonviolent Coordinating Committee (SNCC)** in April 1960.

The Vietnam War and Human Rights

King began to compare the war in Vietnam as an example of the attempt by the large Western nations to colonize Third World nations of color. First, he raised the issue of spending billions for war while the poor were not being sufficiently cared for at home. King's public antiwar declarations strained the racial alliance he had formerly created to addressed issues of poverty and discrimination, for there were whites who favored the war as a necessary war against Communist aggression, while supporting all efforts to abolish segregation in the United States. King also raised the issue of "guns vs. butter" and whether it was possible for the nation to spend billions abroad and not neglect its problems at home. King opposed the war on moral and economic grounds. Like **Malcolm X** before his death, King wanted to move from civil rights to a more universal human rights movement and struggle, and he saw nothing wrong in linking the American Civil Rights Movement to international political and war matters.

Black Power

King understood the importance of the idea of Black Power for black youth given the historical legacy of slavery and segregation. He believed the slogan "Black is Beautiful" to be positive and asserted the right of any group to be proud of itself. He was simply afraid of "excessive" racial or ethnic pride, one that might short-circuit attempts to forge social and political alliances with others. He was particularly concerned that young blacks were raising the cry of race precisely at the moment the rest of the world was focusing on the changing world economy and the impact of automation on all aspects of life. Above all, King hoped to forge alliances between all segments of American society—poor whites, Hispanics, Asians, and Native Americans.

That he was unable to forge such alliances would be one of his greatest disappointments.

The year 1967 was one of massive urban devastation as riots occurred in a number of large American cities, and King's last book, *Where Do We Go from Here? Chaos or Community,* seemed to mirror some of his disappointments due to notable progress in racial and human relations and the lack of great progress in alleviating abject poverty in the nation. Despite these shortcomings, King continue to believe that the nation would right the wrongs perpetuated against blacks and other minorities. He was a moral leader who believed white Americans could and would step up to the plate and do the right thing, and he also believed that blacks would not give up their quest for greater freedoms in the nation. He also believed that black Americans would link their struggles at home to the struggles of others abroad, and thereby strengthen the politics of one type of power confronting another power, but with love, patience, and forgiveness in the forefront.

When King agreed to travel to Memphis, Tennessee, to join others in support of the striking sanitation workers, he was warned to be careful, and he, himself, had a degree of uneasiness, though he did go. His speech in the Memphis Masonic Temple, "I've Been to the Mountain Top" was revealing in that he vowed to fight on and to look death in the face and remain unafraid and unbowed. On April 4, 1968, he was shot and killed on the balcony of the Lorraine Motel in Memphis by James Earl Ray. *See also* March on Washington; Montgomery Bus Boycott.

Further Readings: King, Coretta Scott. *My Life with Martin Luther King, Jr.* New York: Holt, Rinehart and Winston, 1969; King, Martin Luther, Jr. *Letter from Birmingham City Jail.* Philadelphia: American Friends Service Committee, 1963; King, Martin Luther, Jr. *Where Do We Go from Here: Chaos or Community?* New York: Harper and Row, 1967; Lincoln, C. Eric, ed. *Martin Luther King, Jr.: A Profile.* New York: Hill and Wang, 1984; Walton, Hanes. *The Political Philosophy of Martin Luther King, Jr.* Westport, CT: Greenwood Press, 1971.

Rutledge M. Dennis

Ku Klux Klan

The Ku Klux Klan (KKK) is the name of various terrorist organizations originally created in late 1865 to restore white Democratic rule to the recently defeated states of the former Confederacy. In order to realize their goal, the KKK used violence and the threat of violence to prevent blacks from exercising their civil rights, and to cower or drive out whites who assisted blacks or in any way supported Republican rule in the South. The original Ku Klux Klan can be interpreted as a continuation of the Civil War by insurgency. The original Klan and other white supremacist terrorist groups such as the White League were able to drive blacks away from the voting booth in large enough numbers to allow the legal disenfranchisement of blacks. The original Klan largely disappeared by the mid-1870s. It revived in 1915, and reached new heights of influence in the 1920s, when the Klan became politically strong in several states, particularly in the Midwest. The new Klan focused on Jews, Catholics, and immigrants as much as blacks. After declining into obscurity in the 1930s, new, more violent organizations calling themselves the KKK began to thrive in the 1950s, ostensive defending traditional American values against communism, but in practice attempting to use violence to prevent integration and black voting.

The original Ku Klux Klan was created by six former Confederate soldiers on Christmas Eve in 1865, in Pulaski, Tennessee. According to later accounts, several former Confederates dressed in white sheets pretending to be the ghosts of Confederate dead and rode around in the night to frighten the local black population. After seeing the effect of their actions, the night riding continued. The men, all college educated, chose the name *Ku Klux Klan,* based on the Greek word *kyklos,* meaning circle, and the word *Clan,* which reflected the commonly held idea that white Southern culture was transplanted Scottish Highlander culture. Originally, the Klan focused on terrorizing blacks who attempted to change their social, economic, and political subordination. However, the Klan also targeted white Republicans who assisted blacks.

The Klan relied on grassroots organization and newspapers stories of Klan activities to spread its message across the occupied South. From 1866 until 1869, many groups with little or no formal coordination between them referred to themselves as the Ku Klux Klan. Their tactics were similar, including face coverings, the use of horses, and the tendency to attack during the night. While the original group dressed in white, other groups began using a wide variety of costumes to conceal their identity Soon almost all areas of the South under federal control had at least one group claiming to be part of the KKK, although some groups were more bent on theft, revenge killing, or general mayhem than restoring white Democratic rule to the South.

Despite attempts to create a hierarchy, the movement remained decentralized and not subject to any central direction. Most KKK groups agreed broadly on ending Republican rule over the South. To accomplish that goal, the Klan used extra-legal means such as murder, arson, whipping, and intimidation to keep blacks from voting, and assuring that blacks remained socially inferior to whites. Most victims were black and white Republicans. **Arkansas** congressman James M. Hinds and three members of the South Carolina legislature were only the most prominent Republicans killed by the Klan. Enraged by this lawlessness and flagrant attacks on its political base, Republicans in Congress passed the Civil Rights Act of 1871, also known as the Ku Klux Klan Act, which empowered civil and military authorities to use federal power to destroy the Ku Klux Klan. President Ulysses S. Grant backed the Radical Republicans and used the act to bring the Klan to bay. However other forces also worked against the Klan. Middle- and upper-class Southern whites increasingly feared the lack of control over the Klan by the "better" elements in society. Additionally, Reconstruction was drawing to an end, and some areas had been returned to civil control. Once Klan activity helped white Democrats to assume control of all elected offices, extra-legal methods to keep Republicans from voting were no longer needed. Indeed, some Democrats began to argue that the continued violence and even existence of the Klan only served to keep federal troops in the South longer. By 1873, the original Ku Klux Klan was largely defunct. However, it had largely fulfilled its purpose. With the declining federal presence in the South, white Democrats increasingly gained control of state and local governments. Thus state laws, state courts, and sheriff's departments could increasingly be used to oppress blacks lawfully.

The rebirth of the Ku Klux Klan came as part of a general romanticization of the Civil War era. The novels *Leopard's Spots* (1903) and *The Clansman* (1905) by **Thomas Dixon** presented a heroic interpretation of the Klan as chivalrous gentlemen who fought blacks, carpetbaggers, and scalawags to return civilization to the South during Reconstruction. The novels introduced the concept of the burning cross as a symbol of the Klan, something that was never used by the original Klan. The burning cross borrowed on Scottish highlander traditions of using burning crosses on hilltops as a way to call together the Highland clans in the event of invasion or other crisis, although the Scots used a diagonal St. Andrews cross. Dixon probably got the idea of the Scottish Highlander clans burning crosses from Sir Walter Scott's 1810 poem the *Lady of the Lake,* which had been popular among white Southerners. The images of the Ku Klux Klan in the novels became even more entrenched in popular culture as a result of **D. W. Griffith**, who used the novels as the basic of one of the first truly modern motion pictures, ***The Birth of a Nation*** in 1915.

The Klan was reborn in 1915 in a wave of nostalgia, nativism, and anti-Semitism. The immediate cause for the revised Ku Klux Klan was the trial and conviction in **Georgia** of a Northern Jewish factory owner named Leo Frank for the rape and murder of a young factory worker named Mary Phagan. Although little evidence connected him to the crime, he was a Northerner, wealthy, and Jewish. After his appeals in the trial failed, the governor commuted his death sentence to life in jail. However, the threat of mob violence had surrounded the case from the beginning, and after the commutation, a group of vigilantes calling itself the Knights of Mary Phagan took Frank from the prison farm where he was being held and lynched him.

Many Southerners, especially in Georgia, saw the death of Phagan at the hands of a Northern Jew as synonymous with the suffering of white womanhood under Reconstruction as depicted in the film *The Birth of a Nation.* Although blacks in the South remained relatively powerless through **Jim Crow,** some white Southerners believed a revived Klan was needed against a new host of perceived enemies, such as Catholics, Jews, immigrants, and the decline of sexual morality. The new Klan was inaugurated in 1915 at a meeting led by William J. Simmons on top of Stone Mountain, Georgia. Along with the Knights of Mary Phagan, some men attending claimed to have been members of the original KKK. The new group, calling itself the Knights of the Ku Klux Klan, was more organized than the original Klan, but still had little central control and no one executive leader. New terms and offices were invented, and Klan attire became more regular. While the members of the original Klan wore a variety of costumes, often in colors other than white, members of the new Klan tended to wear the familiar white robe with pointed top.

While Southern Klansmen could act more openly, the Klan found its most fertile recruiting grounds in the Midwest, areas in which the black population was increasing due to the **Great Migration**, but without formal Jim Crow laws to oppress blacks. In the South, the Klan orchestrated lynches, or members participated as individuals, but much of the Klan's attacks were in the form of arson, beatings, or whippings. Most Klan activity was more psychological, using the burning cross or simply announcing their presence to instill fear. With blacks in the South excluded from government and the judicial process, Klansmen could act with a sense of impunity. Klan groups seldom participated in overtly violent acts together, and unlike the former KKK, almost never wore Klan regalia during acts of racial violence. Instead, through rhetoric and public spectacle of the rally and mass meeting that featured a burning cross, Klan leaders spread their message of using violence against blacks, Jews, Catholics, or whoever angered the local group. Then Klansmen, working in small groups, would carry out specific acts of violence. In the case of an allegation of rape or murder of a white by a black, Klan members often acted in concert with non-Klan members in lynching suspects. Outside of the South, secrecy was more important, as courts were often less sympathetic. In the Midwest and West, the Klan was often more overtly antiblack, although Catholics, Jews, and other enemies were also targets of Klan activity.

The new Klan grew as a for-profit fraternal organization, pitching itself as the friend of the common man. Klan support for Prohibition made it many friends among rural Protestants, but its real strength came from urban areas, where many old-stock whites saw themselves awash in new peoples, new ideas, and new morality. Many people who did not join the Klan at least tolerated it and even admired it for the Klan's purported support for sexual morality, Protestant Christianity, and opposition to corruption and Communism. The new Klan had dominated some state governments during the 1920s, specifically in Oklahoma, Oregon, and Indiana. In the South, Klan support for honest government and assistance for poor whites against big city corruption also brought it much popular support.

In 1928, the Klan made a showing of its power by a large march down Pennsylvania Avenue in Washington, DC, but in retrospect, the Klan had already peaked and its influence was on the wane. Klansmen's sense of their own power caused several serious missteps. Their attempt to take control of the Democratic Party in 1924 alerted many who had been ambivalent in the past to the political threat of the Klan. The Klan's use of overt violence against whites believed to be acting immorally in the South lost it much of its political support. Several sexual and financial scandals, including one particularly salacious rape and murder by Grand Dragon David Stephenson of Indiana, destroyed the Klan's claim to represent integrity and morality. The Klan declined in strength and influence throughout the 1930s. By the end of the 1930s, the Ku Klux Klan was again a spent force. Scandals, a recovering economy, and the example of Nazi Germany all helped bring a decline in numbers so that the Klan was negligible as social or political force.

The Klan did not remain fallow for long. Following the ***Brown v. Board of Education*** ruling in 1954, new Ku Klux Klan groups formed, taking advantage of white fears of integration. While the Klan in the 1920s drew heavily from the lower middle class, the new Klan was more working class, and its growth reflected the anxiety many poorer whites felt at their relative loss of status and privilege as Jim Crow was dismantled. While not as numerous or as politically powerful as the Klan in the 1920s, the Klan in the 1950s and 1960s used murder, bombs, and arson to spread fear though the **Civil Rights**

Movement. The Klan in the 1950s was not unified in any meaningful sense. Several distinct organizations claimed to be the "true" Ku Klux Klan, with the largest, the Invisible Empire, Knights of the Ku Klux Klan, controlling only a minority of Klansmen. While the Klan in the 1950s and 1960s continued to list the old enemies of Catholics, Jews, and immorality, in practice it was more focused on opposing integration as its main goal. In much of the South during the Jim Crow era, courts and police did an effective job of enforcing segregation. But with the crumbling of Jim Crow, the Klan assumed that mission. The Klan advertised itself as a patriotic organization, dedicated to protecting America against Communism. The Klan used broadsheets, billboards, posters, and speeches to equate integration with Communism, thus taping into Cold War fears about the Soviet Union and Communism to gain a measure of respectability. In reality, the existence of the KKK and similar groups, as well as racial violence as a whole, were powerful propaganda issues for the Soviets, who often used the term "Negro lynchers" to refer to non-Communist white Americans. The Soviets publicized throughout the world, especially in the newly independent nations in Africa, **lynchings**, bombings, and other incidents of American race violence.

The Civil Rights Movement struck directly at white supremacy, and the Klan reacted with increased savagery. One of the most horrific acts of the new Klan came on the early morning of Sunday, September 15, 1963, when a bomb set by Bobby Frank Cherry, Thomas Blanton, and Robert Chambliss, all members of United Klans of America, exploded at the Sixteenth Street Baptist Church in Birmingham, Alabama, killing four girls and wounding another 22. Although some whites in Birmingham, including police chief **"Bull" Connor**, blamed the bombing on blacks themselves, or on the **U.S. Supreme Court** for its *Brown* decision, many moderate whites throughout the nation were horrified by the attack. Political pressure built for the **federal government** to become more involved in protecting blacks and prosecuting terrorists at the federal level. Beginning with Attorney General **Robert F. Kennedy**, and increasing after the passing of the **Civil Rights Act of 1964**, the federal government increasingly took an active role in persecuting people who attempted to use violence or the threat of violence against blacks and whites who attempted to ensure that blacks were able to vote. Although deprived of the de facto immunity offered by all-white juries in state courts the Klan had long enjoyed, Klan members continued to use violence in an attempt to maintain white supremacy in the South. In January 1966, a group of white men, led by Samuel Bowers, an Imperial Wizard of the Ku Klux Klan, firebombed civil rights leader **Vernon Dahmer**'s home, killing him.

Although the violence of Klan groups and individual Klansmen in the 1960s and into the 1970s could often be bloody and shocking, their power, as limited as it had been, was again on the wane. With the ending of Jim Crow, blacks in the South formed a formidable voting bloc, which would hold Southern governments accountable for prosecuting Klansmen involved in violent acts. Black voters meant the end of sympathetic all-white juries for Klansmen accused of crimes. The legacy of Klan violence during the Civil Rights Era left the Klan with a poor reputation among middle-class and even most working-class whites. Klan groups that continued to exist increasingly drew from the most marginalized whites in the South, and had little political power. *See also* Communist Party.

Further Readings: Carr, Cynthia. *Our Town: A Heartland Lynching, a Haunted Town, and the Hidden History of White America.* New York: Three Rivers Press, 2007; Chalmers, David. *Backfire: How the Ku Klux Klan Helped the Civil Rights Movement.* Lanham, MD: Rowman & Littlefield, 2005; Jackson, Kenneth T. *The Ku Klux Klan in the City, 1915–1930.* Chicago: Elephant Paperbacks, 1992.

Barry M. Stentiford

L

Labor Unions

Labor unions in the United States are affiliated organizations that function as the legal representatives for a multiplicity of workers in various industries. The history of labor unions during the era of **Jim Crow** is the history of struggle to overcome racism and discrimination within labor unions and the labor movement. It is also a history spotted with episodes of biracial activism. Because racial exclusionary policies are a very effective way to control the labor supply and, consequently, exercise bargaining power over the wages of workers, labor unions, particularly during the era of Jim Crow, have a long history of racial discrimination on their hands. Racial discrimination is fundamental to understanding labor unions during the era of Jim Crow, and, conversely, labor unions are fundamental to understanding racial discrimination in the Jim Crow era. Discrimination within unions during the Jim Crow era is unique given the fact that a majority of union leaders' rhetoric and theories were are always quick to include, or at least not explicitly exclude, African Americans by arguing that working-class consciousness would ultimately trump racism. However, in practice and organization techniques, they often fell short and were quick to embrace exclusionary policies that stemmed from Jim Crow policies.

Slavery and Free Labor

The budding relationship between black workers and organized labor movements began to take form during the periods of the Civil War and post–Civil War **Reconstruction**. The Civil War not only freed three and a half million people of African descent from a life of bondage and oppression by dismantling the institution of **slavery**, but also transformed millions into free laborers, and resurrected union activity that had been static since the depression of 1837. However, it has been noted that was not until the post–Civil War era that the United States completed abolition and had defined civil rights. The politically established principles of free labor had to confront the first nationwide labor organization by the late 1860s.

Unions, arguably, were from the start not concerned with the plight and struggle of Africans Americans. That labor unions and early working-class peoples' opposition to slavery rarely rested on the claim that slavery was a moral injustice imposed upon bond(wo)men is testament to their peculiar strand of racism. Indeed, working-class people of the Midwest and the West became aware and raised concern over the pro-slavery 1854 Kansas-Nebraska Act—an act that would soon allow the expansion of slavery to proceed and expand into the open Midwestern and Western territories—and the Dred Scott decision—a court decision that declared that people of African descent, slaves and nonslaves alike, could never become citizens and declared that Congress had no authority to prohibit slavery in federal territories—not as an expression of the immorality of slavery or commiseration for those enslaved, but rather, expressed outrage over the fact that the expansion slavery might affect their working-class status. To be sure, working-class opposition to slavery was not so much against slavery per se, but against the expansion of slavery that would ultimately jeopardize their status as workers.

Knights of Labor

While the National Labor Union (NLU) and the National Colored Labor Union (NCLU) fought unsuccessfully to preserve their respective unions during the devastating depression of 1873, the Noble Order of the Knights of Labor (KOL) successfully avoided the union-crushing depression and survived to see the early beginnings of Jim Crow. Uriah Stephens, a Philadelphia tailor and antislavery Republican, formed the KOL in 1869. Blacks were loyal to the **Republican Party** due to its abolitionist past. Originally, the KOL was formed as a secret union that embraced both trade and industrial unions. Moreover, the KOL's rhetoric of racial inclusiveness, Christian evangelicalism, and abolitionist heritage, backed by an unwavering appreciation for class unity, ultimately made the organization acceptable to black workers

Although the Knights of Labor at their birth practiced exclusionary policies vis-à-vis the black worker, they did lift their ban on black workers during the early shaping of Jim Crow in 1883. The fact that the Knights of Labor boasted an agenda of racial inclusiveness may have led to the dramatic increase in their union membership. By putting worker dissatisfaction, low wages, and class unity across racial lines at the front of their agenda, the Knights of Labor's membership increased dramatically throughout the 1880s. By the mid-1880s, the KOL had won several important strikes and saw its membership increase to approximately 750,000 official union members, of which 60,000 to 90,000 were black. The KOL's commitment to interracial activism trickled down to the workers and created cooperation across the color line. Due to the efforts of the KOL, throughout the Jim Crow South, episodes of interracial working-class unity were at work. Indeed, in the mid-1880s, the heyday of the KOL, the KOL and other unions saw a dramatic increase in the amount of interracial class unity experienced. While KOL District Assembly 194 sought negotiations with the nearby black Louisiana Sugar Planters Association in an effort to increase wages and better methods of pay, white and black miners of Alabama, under the auspices of the KOL, stood unified in strike against wage cuts for mine operators. In the end, prison laborers and Italian immigrants broke the miner's strike.

Although the Knights of Labor's rhetoric preached about racial inclusiveness, and while at times they even practiced racial inclusiveness, they too practiced a major policy that defined the Jim Crow South: separatism. While union leaders stood at the pulpit recommending black-white worker unity, they constantly and consistently advocated separate but unified black and white local organizations. Moreover, the Knights of Labor were ardent supporters of the anti-Chinese movement and refused to admit Chinese workers. In 1885, in Spring Rock, Wyoming, the Knights of Labor led a riot that resulted in the deaths of 28 Chinese railroad workers. They also did not support European immigrants.

In retrospect, the KOL's racial inclusiveness may have been as much responsible for the union's increase in membership in the mid-1880s as much it was responsible for its decrease in the late 1880s. By 1890, 100,000 members remained in the KOL; few of whom were black. The violence of the Knights' strikes caused a decrease in support from blacks, who were once attracted to their peaceful revolutionary style. Despite the Knights' efforts, the period put blacks and the labor movement at further distance.

American Federation of Labor

That the more racially restrictive American Federation of Labor (AFL) replaced the Knights of Labor and took control of the labor movement during the nadir of race relations—a racially complex time period starting in 1890 and enduring throughout the Jim Crow era until 1930, when blacks were forced back into noncitizenship and race relations, indeed, got worse—is evident in their workings as an organization. AFL delegates took their cue from the KOL's broad social vision of racial inclusiveness by focusing their efforts on securing higher wages, shorter working days, and improved working conditions for the unions and union members they represented across racial lines. Throughout the early 1890s, the KOL and AFL engaged in bitter disputes around the country as to what the goals of labor movement should be. The AFL rejected the KOL's favoritism of workers' cooperatives, and criticized their simply defined economic agendas. By the 1890s, the AFL became the dominant national labor organization.

While open to socialist and Marxist thought concerning the economic structure and the direction of the labor movement, AFL leaders, like the KOL leaders before them, remained perplexed about the race issue within the labor movement during the racial hostile period of Jim Crow. The AFL was an umbrella organization with which separate trade unions were affiliated. The AFL's constitution was quiet on race issues and implicitly included African Americans. AFL founder Samuel A. Gompers initially opposed the inclusion of racially exclusive organizations under the AFL's umbrella. However, due to the fact that the AFL focused on skilled labor, many African Americans, who were barred from such jobs and relegated to perform "unskilled" labor due to racial discrimination, received very little attention from the AFL.

Like the KOL leaders before them, AFL leaders were quick to spout rhetoric in favor of racial egalitarian ideals. Gompers, who led the AFL from 1886 until his death in 1924, affirmed his commitment to racial egalitarianism at the 1891 annual convention. Although the AFL's commitment to racial egalitarianism remains suspect, there were episodes of biracial activism. In 1892, white and black longshoremen of New Orleans rallied behind the AFL banner and supported each other's strikes at substantial risk to themselves. Gompers would constantly herald the event as a landmark case of biracial union activism. More scattered episodes of interracial union activism carried on throughout the **World War I** era and into the 1920s. During the war, in Little Rock, **Arkansas**, the white-controlled labor council supported black women who worked in the city's steam laundries that served a nearby army base. Meanwhile, the black longshoremen labored on the docks of Philadelphia and became attracted to and strongly affiliated with the radical, Marxist, and, above all, racial egalitarian **Industrial Workers of the World (IWW)**, African Americans and their white counterparts struggled, with varied success, to form unions that rose above the color line in places such as, Chicago, rural **Louisiana**, and Memphis. For example, AFL carpenter unions in rural 1919 Bogalusa, Louisiana, struggled together in an effort to preserve their biracial union. In the South Side of Chicago's packinghouses and stockyards, World War I–era interracial unity reached its peak. Fifty thousand men and women, both black and white, rallied behind the AFL's Amalgamated Meat Cutters (AMC), a very powerful AFL organization of skilled workers that did not ban blacks, side by side with the AFL's Chicago Federation of Labor (CFL) between 1916 and 1922 in a long-drawn-out struggle for equal rights and better working conditions in Chicago's meat packinghouses.

The president of the CFL, John Fitzpatrick, and a Railway Carmen Union organizer, William Z. Foster, both radical syndicalists who dedicated their efforts to turn the AFL on to socialism, led the Chicago labor activists and workers' struggle to effectively organize industrial unions and stockyards across the color line. Together they formed the Stockyard Labor Council (SLC) in an effort to unite all packinghouse workers regardless of color and gender. As a result of other, less-skilled unions segregating and banning blacks, the SLC and AFL became locals that blacks could join. The successful organization of meat industry workers was vital to the success of the labor movement as a whole. It presented the opportunity for the AFL to enlarge its influence by expanding from craft unions into one of the country's largest mass production industries. AMC affiliates, one of the AFL organizations that did not ban black workers, were ardent supporters of organizing across racial lines and continually, with mixed success, advocated the importance of nondiscrimination in the labor movement. The AMC, in an effort to show their commitment to black workers, created a black local. In fact, all the AMC locals representing workers in the South Side of Chicago included African Americans. The SLC shared the AMC's commitment to African American workers. The SLC pressed for dramatic changes, such as their call on the **federal government** to nationalize the meatpacking industry, the implementation of the eight-hour workday, and increased pay for unskilled workers, a category into which most African American workers fell. As the end of the Great

War approached its demise, the SLC started pressing for a 100 percent union agreement with the packers, with blacks being the primary hurdle. Ninety percent of white workers and a meager 25 percent of African American workers were members. However, black gains in union membership and wages came at the cost of increased racial hostility between blacks and native-born and immigrant whites, which culminated in the vicious **Chicago Race Riot of 1919**.

The Chicago race riots might, indeed, be reflective of the collective consciousness of the American public at large during the racially daunting years of Jim Crow. Although a causal claim between the SLC's effort to organize black workers in Chicago cannot be verified, there is, no doubt, information that makes such a causal connection attractive. On the packinghouse floors, where native-born and immigrant whites toiled side by side with their African American coworkers and fellow union supporters, whites expressed their hostility and contempt for African Americans. European immigrant laborers who were "working toward whiteness" by reminding their native-born white coworkers that African Americans were, indeed, the "other" and the real problem, met African Americans with intense racial tension. In the summer of 1919, racial tension erupted onto the streets and an all-out riot ensued. The riot was sparked when a black boy was drowned for crossing into a white neighborhood on Lake Michigan beach. The event triggered racial violence that would last for weeks. Most of the mayhem was attributed to gangs of Irish immigrants. In the end, 23 blacks and 15 whites lay dead. The July race riots, arguably, ended the hope of the SLC to successfully organize black workers. Racist policies, although not explicitly written in the constitution, was a tradition for the AFL and its affiliated organizations from the beginning.

As Jim Crow policy tightened its grip on everyday life in the South, and newly arrived immigrants began competing with native-born whites and black for jobs, exclusionary policies vis-à-vis immigrants and African Americans increased. Immigrants were not welcome into the AFL or any affiliated organizations from the start. Gompers, a Jewish immigrant from Great Britain and once a supporter of racial egalitarianism, stated that the AFL's policy was to protect whites from the "evils" of the Chinese invasion. Chinese immigrants who toiled on the railroads were banned from unionization outright. While white workers led vicious, bloody massacres and anti-Chinese riots, writers and editors of union and labor newspapers were busy constructing the Chinese and other immigrant groups as "savage" and "uncivilized." As early as 1897, AFL leaders urged the adoption of a draconian literacy test in an effort to curtail immigrant labor. They argued that the plethora of early European immigrants who emigrated had not proved themselves assimilable or fit for union organization ultimately posed a threat to the American worker whose wages they undercut.

The AFL's putative commitment to racial egalitarianism was a sham. They, like much of American society had elements of both de jure and de facto segregation along with a history of violence against African American and Chinese laborers. The railroad unions proved to be the least accepting of African Americans and Asian immigrants. Blacks were often barred from unions or were forced to form separate unions. In fact, the early radical **W.E.B. Du Bois**, in a publication on union activity, revealed that of the one million AFL members, 40,000 were black. Moreover, 43 unions practiced Jim Crow policy to the point that they had no African Americans at all. The National Association of Machinists, an umbrella organization affiliated with the AFL, is a case in point to the AFL's ultimate commitment to party building, not to racial egalitarianism. The National Association of Machinists was founded in 1889 in Atlanta as an organization dedicated to organizing skilled railroad laborers. For five years, the AFL denied the admittance of the National Association of Machinist into the organization to do its constitution declaring white only membership. However, in an effort to build union membership, AFL officials backed down from their commitment to racial egalitarianisms and biracial activism and admitted the National Association of Machinists in 1895. In the 1890s, firemen stood with the Brotherhood of Railway Trainmen in an effort to organize against the admittance of African Americans into their unions on a national scale. In 1899, the trainmen's union voted for the exclusion of African Americans from railroads worldwide.

Violent means were often used to ensure that railroad unions remained as segregated and off-limits to African Americans as possible. Violent outbreaks against African American railroad workers often sprung from strikes advocating white-only hiring policies. In an effort to maintain the color line, white workers in 1911 organized a strike against New Orleans, Cincinnati, and Texas Pacific railroads for employing African Americans. In the end, 10 African Americans were murdered. As a result, the strikers and the railroad companies decided that African Americans would not be employed north of Oakdale and Chattanooga, Tennessee. More still, is that the railroad companies concurred that the overall percentage of African American firemen would not rise on a national level. The AFL continued to ignore, or at least place secondary to increasing union numbers, African Americans and their complaints of racial discrimination into the 1920s. When union officials refused to make the Railroad Brotherhood of Railway Carmen strike the words "white only" from its constitution, and when they refused to grant international charter to the black Railway Coach Cleaners, blacks took the jobs of whites during the 1922 shopmen's strike. The results were tragic. Over 1,500 cases of attempted murder, kidnapping, dynamiting, and vandalism occurred in an effort to curtail blacks from acting as strikebreakers. African Americans' willingness to act as strikebreakers increased the AFL's hostility toward them. The AFL often blamed their lack of attention to African American workers on the African Americans themselves. As the Depression began to take a grip on the economy, and as racial tensions increased due to the lack of job opportunity, increased competition, and Jim Crow laws, African Americans made up only 50,000 of the nation's 2.25 million union members. However, as the Congress of Industrial Organization (CIO), arguably the most egalitarian significant union to emerge since the Knights of Labor, emerged as the primary labor organization in 1935, African Americans saw increased racial tolerance, and labor unions saw a dramatic increase in the number of African American affiliates.

The Congress of Industrial Organization

The Congress of Industrial Organization was, no doubt, the most racially egalitarian and radical labor organization to emerge since the Knights of Labor. While Jim Crow laws began to cripple the South, the CIO presented a viable opportunity to organize African Americans within a largely racist labor movement. CIO leaders took a divide-and-conquer, radical, Marxist approach to the racial question vis-à-vis the labor movement by contending that racial division was created by bourgeois employers who wished to disrupt working-class solidarity so as to keep wages low and create "super profits." Thus, the CIO's primary goal was to organize industrial sectors of the labor force, which, they realized, necessitated the inclusion of African American workers who by the 1930s made up a significant portion of the industrial labor. In the South, where labor union representation was comparatively weak to that of the North, unions desperately needed the support of African American workers if they wished to succeed in mining, steel, and a multiplicity of agriculture sectors of which African Americans dominated. As such, the CIO sought to reach out to African American workers and civil rights groups to create interracial, working-class solidarity. And reach out they did. The CIO, in a remarkable effort to preserve and create racial harmony, formed the Committee to Abolish Racial Discrimination, and encouraged blacks to reject and speak out against the American Federation of Labor and other independent unions.

The congress took its cue from the United Mine Workers Association (UMWA), which had been promoting and practicing racial egalitarianism under the presidential leadership of John L. Lewis since the late nineteenth century. By the turn of the twentieth century, African Americans made up one-quarter of UMWA's membership and enrolled at a much higher rate than their white comrades. The UMWA consisted of more than 20,000 black miners, approximately half of the AFL's black membership. In the depths of the Great Depression in 1934, the United Mine Workers boasted 90 new locals and 20,000 men, of whom 60 percent were African Americans. Even in the hostile time and space of Jim Crow Alabama in the 1890s, the United Mine Workers struggled to create interracial unity in the union locals of Alabama and other Southern states. Furthermore, Irish immigrants along with British immigrants made up a significant portion of union leadership. To be sure, the UMWA did, indeed, have its share of racial turmoil, but it was their effort to forge class unity across racial lines that caused the CIO to adopt the UMWA's organizing techniques. For example, UMWA organizers in Alabama made it clear that their commitment to African American workers did not embrace the idea of social equality, simply better wages and working conditions. At one point in 1920, white mine workers bombed the houses of a dozen black strikebreakers. Despite a few episodes of interracial hostility, the United Mine Workers Association proved its commitment to black workers.

Indeed, the CIO's efforts and commitment to African American workers did not go unnoticed. Unlike the AFL, which practiced Jim Crow policy if not in rhetoric or theory then in practice, the CIO transcended racial lines in its organizing process and made its way into Piedmont region—southern Virginia to northern Alabama—and had organized 200,000 cotton textile workers. From the early stages of the **Great Depression** to the end stages of **World War II**, African American union membership increased radically from 60,000 to an impressive one million. African Americans became the CIO's main supporters. Other unions such as the Knights of Labor and AFL tried to organize across racial lines but ultimately fell pray to Jim Crow practices. The CIO represented the first massive effort to organize workers across racial and ethnic lines for a common movement This was indeed the case in Chicago's meatpacking industry, in which African Americans made up 20 to 30 percent of the labor force. Thanks to the efforts of CIO and other, mostly Communist activists, the Packing House Workers Organization Committee brought together several unions to reach out to blacks by promising designated seats for blacks on the executive board, and by mandating a quota equivalent to the local population.

As World War II emerged, the labor movement more broadly, and labor unions in particular would again have serious consequences for African American workers. Blacks were direly needed in the industrial sector to produce goods for the war effort; however, their employers were very hesitant to hire them due to long-standing Jim Crow practices within the industrial sector. By the end of 1944, it is estimated that at least 1.25 million African American workers, a quarter of which were women, were performing industrial work, a 150 percent increase from 1940. During the time period of World War II, both the AFL and the CIO grew dramatically. The AFL had expanded its union affiliates from 4.2 million to just shy of seven million. The CIO grew to four million members from two million members from 1940 to 1945. In all, union membership doubled from 1940 to 1945 to fifteen million.

However, Jim Crow policies that pervaded the labor movement and unions would tighten their grip during the war effort, and blacks were forced to overcome racism and discrimination on a multiplicity of levels. Their struggle in the railroad unions and craft brotherhoods is a case in point. Railroad unions have a history of Jim Crow policy under the tutelage of the AFL, and they continued this tradition during the course of the war. While railroad employment increased to meet the demands of the war effort, so too did discrimination against black workers in labor unions. Black workers faced severe forms of discrimination, including contracts that limited the number and locations where blacks could work. The Brotherhood of Locomotive Firemen, for example, pushed to rapidly accelerate the removal of black workers. This culminated in the Brotherhood successfully winning Southeastern Carriers agreement, which limited the employment of "unpromotable" firemen to 50 percent and ended the increased hiring of blacks. While the Brotherhood of Locomotive Firemen practiced a strict form of Jim Crow by virtue of job elimination, the International Boilermakers Brotherhood (IBB) did admit blacks, albeit in a Jim Crow fashion that separated black and white union members into separate locals. Black workers paid dues to the union but were denied membership. Additionally, the hierarchal structure of the union did not allow all black unions to exercise autonomy and set up "parent" all white unions to dictate their organization techniques and behavior. In short, the IBB openly practiced Jim Crow policies.

AFL-CIO *at the End of Jim Crow*

The postwar effort to organize across racial lines in the Jim Crow South proved fruitless. The *Taft-Hartley Act*—an amendment passed in 1947 to amend the National Labor Relations Act of 1935—provided little protection for black union members who were already in unions. The act permitted Jim Crow segregation in union locals and weakened the efforts of the AFL and the CIO to organize across racial lines. The act was effective. Black and white union members in the South remained largely segregated despite the fact that the AFL had sixty percent of its seven million African American members located in the South. Soon after Jim Crow began to loosen grips on the policy and consciousness of the United States with the **Brown v. Board of Education** case in 1954, the AFL and CIO merged in 1955.

Both AFL and the CIO strongly and openly endorsed the black **Civil Rights Movement** that emerged in the South in response to Jim Crow. The AFL-CIO led charges in favor of Civil Rights Acts throughout the late twentieth century, and played a significant role in bringing civil rights to fore of national consciousness. Indeed, the **Civil Rights Act of 1964**—an act that outlawed school public school, public workplace segregation, and guaranteed fair employment practices—and the **Voting Rights Act of 1965**, were all endorsed by the AFL-CIO, who now began to understand the Civil Rights and labor movements as organically linked phenomena, and acknowledged that biracial activism is the life's blood of the labor movement. *See also* Fair Employment Practices Commission (FEPC); Freemasons; Veterans Groups.

Further Readings: Bernstein, David. *Only One Place of Redress: African Americans, Labor Regulations, and the Courts from Reconstruction to the New Deal.* Durham, NC: Duke University Press, 2001; Honey, Michael. *Southern Labor and Black Civil Rights: Organizing Memphis Workers.* Urbana: University of Illinois Press, 1993; Moreno, Paul. *Black Americans and Organized Labor: A New History.* Baton Rouge: Louisiana State University Press, 2006; Nelson, Bruce. *Divided We Stand: American Workers and the Struggle for Black Equality.* Princeton, NJ: Princeton University Press, 2001; Obadele-Starks, Ernest. *Black Unionism in the Industrial South.* College Station: Texas A&M University Press, 2000; Roediger, David. *Working Toward Whiteness: How America's Immigrants Became White: The Strange Journey from Ellis Island to the Suburbs.* New York: Basic Books, 2005; Zieger, Robert H. *For Jobs and Freedom: Race and Labor in America Since 1865.* Lexington: University Press of Kentucky, 2007.

Jack A. Taylor III

Latin America

Latin America occupies a southern portion of the Americas and refers to countries where Romance languages (particularly Spanish and Portuguese) are spoken. Such countries include Venezuela, **Mexico**, Argentina, Costa Rica, and Brazil, among others. While the presence of **Jim Crow** segregation in the United States alludes to numerous forms of public and private segregation, few of these legally sanctioned practices migrated into Latin America. The discrepancy in defining Jim Crow in Latin America rests on the premise that few forms of de jure segregation exist. Although race remains a topic of inequality in the Americas, the presence of Jim Crow practices becomes even more distinctive in Latin America, where the social codes of racial identification impose de facto forms of discrimination. The term Jim Crow is synonymous with the southern United States, yet the range of varying practices becomes even more familiar when crossing the water into Latin America. Since the practice of Jim Crow as defined by law fails to exist, a look into the similarities of racial discrimination will shed light on the appearance of this phenomenon in Latin America.

The presence of Jim Crow segregation in the United States refers to a period of systematic discrimination of, violence toward, and alienation of African Americans. Since Jim Crow laws were adopted after **Reconstruction**, the significance of **slavery** plays a great role in understanding the impact of these laws upon the lives of African American citizens. As slavery was officially abolished by the United States in 1865, numerous steps were taken to ensure that further generations of African Americans would remain dependent upon the white majority whose fears of retribution rose because of emancipation. Using a logic of mental and physical inferiority, state governmental authorities openly established laws that discriminated against African Americans in the form of education, housing, employment, and placed restrictions upon most public facilities under the guise of "**separate but equal**," which sought to stifle African American social, economic, and political participation. The most significant wave of African American opposition erupted during the 1960s **Civil Rights Movement**, as numerous laws were established to counteract blatant acts of racism. Although acts of racial discrimination continue across the Americas, the transference of Jim Crow to Latin America is not clearly delineated. While strains of Jim Crow appear visible in Latin America, the replication of this systematic oppression takes numerous forms while offering an interesting look into modern modes of racial discrimination.

While the prevalence of Jim Crow in the United States rested on the premise of racial inferiority, specific attention to racial attitudes in Latin America exposes the role of racial categories that continues to plague Latin American countries. In Latin America, the act of **miscegenation**, or *mestizaje*, is the focal point for understanding racial tensions. Mestizaje is defined as the mixing of races, or more specifically, the mixing of European and indigenous cultures. Due to nineteenth- and twentieth-century European colonialism in Latin America, a preoccupation with color defined the contours of Latin American countries, whose citizens were cast into hierarchies of racial identification. In part, these classifications sought to stigmatize peoples of African descent and others whose color complexion deviates from whiteness. Because of racial mixing, mulattoes were often granted special privileges from which other minorities were excluded. While the United States outlawed racial miscegenation in many states until the late 1960s, such practices in Latin America have become a way of life. Despite the complexities surrounding mestizaje, the hierarchies of racial identification in Latin America continue to suppress and mimic features prevalent during Jim Crow's rein in the United States.

One important distinction that becomes apparent when discussing mestizaje is the role of the mulatto. While individuals of European descent most often assume the top positions of racial hierarchy, mulattos occupy the second senior positions in Latin America. In the United States, Blackness is defined by African ascendency and in opposition to Whiteness, whereas ideas of Blackness in Latin America operate through more rigidly defined distinctions of color complexion. For instance, a light-skinned complexion garners more access and opportunity in both the United States and Latin America, yet the latter perceives such color distinctions as a badge of convenience for individuals who are considered and treated as acceptable members of society. Mulattoes in Latin American countries often receive better treatment in terms of access to education, employment, and housing than their darker counterparts. The reason such discrepancies exist is due to the privileging of European features and complexions that mulattoes can easily claim. When such divisions arise, racially defined members are pitted against one another as claims to whiteness make impressionable distinctions that allow greater freedoms and access in Latin America.

Jim Crow segregation in the southern United States was a direct result of emancipation in an attempt to confine and restrict the activities of African American citizens. Similar practices of exclusion in Latin America were not intrinsically similar because race was often employed as social codes rather than governmental laws. In Brazil, for instance, racial classifications consist of five categories: Whites, Blacks, Browns (mulattos), Asians/Yellows, and Indigenous. These monikers serve to distinguish and label different racial groups of the country, and they provide meaningful ways to analyze racial hierarchies of the country. While racial distinctions serve as the focal point of mestizaje in Latin America, the appearance of class must be considered as well.

The exploration of race and class are appropriate methods for analyzing the significance of racial hierarchies in Latin America. While class most often derives its own set of characteristics based primarily on economic factors, the inclusion of racial undertones makes class assume a different function for identification. It should come as no surprise that members of the elite class wield most, if not all the power in a given society, but the opportunities for such inclusion are most often tied to race. Those who exhibit European features and skin tone are more likely to be embraced by the dominant group who control access to education, economic, and political influence. Mulattoes wield an enormous amount of power in Latin America as members pass to fit in with the given status quo. While passing among African Americans in the United States served a viable means for some to secure education and employment during Jim Crow segregation, it also placed a stigma upon those individuals who openly chose such acts, which were considered a betrayal to the race. In Latin America, the racial landscape allows a greater flexibility for passing. Although critics argue over the perceptions of passing in Latin American countries, it provides a viable means for individuals to escape poverty and make a better life for themselves.

Despite the absence of laws governing racial segregation, Latin American societies are plagued with equally trying forms of racial discrimination. Since the advent of European colonization, indigenous groups have struggled to control land and resources across Latin America. In Mexico alone, there are over 60 indigenous groups who practice cultural and linguistic traditions that differ from the dominant society. As a result of colonial rule and the continued disavowal of indigenous populations, numerous organizations were created to give voice and support for these communities across Latin America. In addition to the formation of organizations and political parties, literature plays a significant role in raising awareness about indigenous lifestyles and resistance.

In terms of Jim Crow discourse, Latin America seems an unlikely match; however, it helps to consider how the different implications of racial identification affect individual lives across the globe. In Latin America, the emphasis on skin color ultimately determines the course of an individual's life, whereas a similar focus on race in the United States equates to a life of undue suspicion. While remnants of Jim Crow segregation linger in the United States, the exploration of Latin American racial politics sheds light on continuing disparities for people of color who struggle to navigate worlds that rely solely on skin color as markers for identification. *See also* Caribbean.

Further Readings: Miller, Marilyn Grace. *Rise and Fall of the Cosmic Race: The Cult of Mestizaje in Latin America.* Austin: University of Texas Press, 2004; Winn, Peter. *Americas: The Changing Face of Latin American and the Caribbean.* 3rd ed. Berkeley: University of California Press, 2006.

Lauren Chambers

Lawson, James Morris, Jr. (b. 1928)

James Morris Lawson, Jr., was a minister, teacher, and activist who performed an influential role during the **Civil Rights Movement**. As an officer in the **Student Nonviolent Coordinating Committee (SNCC)**, Lawson changed the tactics by which Americans fought for integration and racial equality. As a leading proponent and theorist of the resistance tactics of Indian leader **Mahatma Gandhi**, Lawson trained hundreds of young people to use nonviolence as a tool of mass protest. A close confidant of **Martin Luther King, Jr.**, and other important leaders, Lawson led the lunch counter **sit-ins** in Nashville, Tennessee, participated in the 1961 Freedom Rides, and advised the Memphis sanitation workers strike in 1968.

Born on September 22, 1928, in Uniontown, Pennsylvania, Lawson was the oldest son of a preacher who was heavily involved with the National Association for the Advancement of Colored People (NAACP). Lawson grew up in Massillon, Ohio, and attended schools with mostly white students. Just out of high school, Lawson got his first license to preach in 1947 and traveled a good deal for Methodist training and prayer meetings, soon coming to see race and poverty as the major divisive elements in American society. As a freshman at Baldwin-Wallace College in Berea, Ohio, Lawson joined the pacifist Fellowship of Reconciliation (FOR) in 1947. Lawson began to learn more about Ghandian resistance, or using nonviolent means to struggle against oppression, from the FOR's executive director A. J. Muste. Increasingly committed to pacifism, Lawson refused to comply with the military draft at the start of the Korean War and spent 13 months in federal prison beginning in 1950.

Following his parole, Lawson graduated from Baldwin-Wallace and became a professor at Hislop College in Nagpur, India, in April 1953. In India, Lawson studied Ghandian tactics and considered their usefulness for combating segregation, while reading eagerly of the **Montgomery Bus Boycott** (1955–1956) in Indian newspapers. Lawson returned to the United States to begin graduate work in theology at Oberlin College and met Martin Luther King, Jr., in February 1957. The two men connected instantly over discussions of nonviolent mass action, and King urged Lawson to move to the South. At Lawson's request, the FOR made him a field secretary in Nashville, Tennessee, where he also joined the **Southern Christian Leadership Conference (SCLC)**. Upon his arrival in Nashville in January 1958, Lawson became the second African American student ever to enroll at Vanderbilt University's divinity school. Soon after Lawson's arrival, he met Dorothy Wood, whom he would marry in 1959.

If moderate by Tennessee standards, Nashville remained largely segregated in 1958, which included restaurants, the bus station, lunch counters, restrooms, hotels, cabs, neighborhoods, and schools. Lawson began holding workshops in nonviolent philosophy in November 1959 in the basement of Kelly Miller Smith's First Baptist Church. Sponsored by FOR, Lawson's workshops stressed the importance of complete pacifism in order to provoke a moral crisis in their opponents. Lawson trained students in actual protest tactics as well as the philosophy of peace. Students also began to test policies in different stores in late 1959 to choose targets for a sit-in protest. Among Lawson's mentees were Diane Nash, James Bevel, Bernard Lafayette, Marion Barry, and John Lewis, all of whom went on work for civil rights through the 1960s with the SCLC, SNCC, and other organizations. The Nashville movement relied primarily on young people because they would be less vulnerable to pressure or stricture from white employers once they began protests against segregation.

When students in Greensboro, North Carolina staged a sit-in on February 1, 1960, the Nashville Students sprung into action. One hundred twenty-four students, all trained and prepared by Lawson, staged an initial sit-in at downtown Nashville lunch counters on February 13, 1960. On February 27, Nashville police allowed mobs of angry whites to physically assault the activists and then arrested 81 demonstrators. However, the sit-ins had been organized such that replacements stood ready to fill empty seats at lunch counters. Lawson's strategy of "jail, no bail" meant that protestors remained in overcrowded jails for some time, financially costing the city of Nashville and forcing the local government to become involved in the conflict. Segregationists on Vanderbilt's Board of Trustees, including *Nashville Banner* publisher James Stahlman, demonized Lawson in the press and in private meetings. Vanderbilt chancellor Harvey Branscombe subsequently expelled Lawson on March 3, 1960, and Nashville police arrested Lawson the next day for his involvement in the demonstrations.

Lawson and the Nashville leaders soon called for an Easter boycott of downtown stores that depended on African American business but refused access to restrooms and lunch counters, which heightened the pressure on Nashville mayor Ben West to intervene. On April 19, 1960, reactionaries bombed the home of Z. Alexander Looby, the attorney representing the arrested students. The Loobys were unharmed, but the furious Nashville students and ministers initiated a silent march towards the courthouse downtown. Confronted by Diane Nash on the courthouse steps, West publicly acquiesced that downtown lunch counters should be integrated, effectively ending the symbolic reign of Jim Crow in city restaurants. By May 10, 1960, six downtown stores had integrated, and more gradually followed. Over the next two years, the Nashville Movement built by Lawson integrated movie theatres and restaurants in Nashville as well.

A few days before the Looby bombing, on April 15 and 16, Lawson delivered the keynote address at a conference organized by SCLC member Ella Baker in Raleigh, North Carolina. Baker had called the meeting to build upon the work of students activists in Nashville and throughout the South. On the podium, Lawson criticized the NAACP for being too conservative and timid in its methods, and pointed to direct action as the only way to defeat Jim Crow. The Shaw University conference marked the birth of SNCC, and also began a period wherein Lawson advised ever greater numbers of activists. In 1960, the SCLC made Lawson its director of nonviolent education. At the same time, Lawson finished his master of divinity degree at Boston University (1960) and accepted an appointment to tiny Green Chapel Methodist Church in Shelbyville, Tennessee, just south of Nashville.

When the **U.S. Supreme Court** banned segregation in interstate travel facilities in *Boynton v. Virginia* (1960), the **Congress of Racial Equality (CORE)** organized "Freedom Rides" to test the integration of transportation facilities throughout the Deep South. Leaving Washington, DC, on May 4, 1961 the Freedom Rides nearly dissolved in Anniston, Alabama when the bus was firebombed. Activists from SNCC and CORE chapters reinforced the original riders in Birmingham and Montgomery after additional attacks. Lawson joined the riders in Montgomery, where he was made spokesperson for the initial bus sent to Jackson, Mississippi. Authorities in Jackson arrested Lawson and many others, and sent them to notoriously brutal Parchman State Penitentiary. Waves of Freedom Riders followed to attempt to integrate the Jackson bus station and nonviolently resist arrest. After repeated violence and national attention, Attorney General **Robert F. Kennedy** ordered the desegregation of bus terminals in November 1961.

In 1962, Lawson assumed the pastorship of Centenary Methodist church in Memphis, where segregation was more ingrained than Nashville. In June 1966, King asked Lawson to organize a replacement march after **James Meredith** was shot by a sniper on his solo walk against fear from Memphis to Jackson. During the march, Lawson became dismayed by increasing factionalism between SNCC and the SCLC and wary of the separatist strain adopted by SNCC under Stokely Carmichael's leadership. Lawson thought that greater militancy belied a turn away from nonviolence, a shift that Lawson could not support. Lawson also served as a counselor for King in Chicago, where he saw increasing weariness among nonviolent activists struggling to fight more complicated forms of Jim Crow that existed outside of the South.

Lawson also helped to fight racial injustice in Memphis as an advisor for the Memphis Sanitation Workers strike in 1968. Long underpaid, denied access to higher paying jobs, and without benefits, African American sanitation workers' frustration boiled over on February 1, 1968, when two workers were killed due to a short circuit in a garbage truck's crushing mechanism. Under

Lawson's guidance the workers commenced a strike on February 12, making their slogan "I AM A MAN" as visible as possible. Lawson reached for national exposure by inviting King to Memphis, suggesting the sanitation strike fit perfectly with King's burgeoning Poor Peoples Campaign against poverty. After a March 28 demonstration fell apart due to a number of disruptive elements, King agreed to return to lead another march. Fatefully, King was assassinated the day before he was to lead the second march. City officials and the sanitation workers settled the strike one week later.

Lawson moved with his wife and three sons to Los Angeles in 1974, and became pastor of Holman Methodist Church. Lawson continued to work for peace education and racial justice throughout the latter decades of the twentieth century, and retired from the ministry in 1999. In the fall of 2006, Lawson returned to Vanderbilt University as a visiting professor.

Further Readings: Ackerman, Peter, and Jack DuVall. "The American South: Campaign for Civil Rights." In *A Force More Powerful: A Century of Nonviolent Conflict.* New York: St. Martin's Press, 2000; Halberstam, David. *The Children.* New York: Random House, 1996; Inskeep, Steve and James Lawson. "James Lawson: An Advocate of Peaceful Change." Radio interview, National Public Radio Web site. http://www.npr.org/templates/story/story.php?storyId=6676164&sc=emaf (accessed July 2007); Lovett, Bobby L. *The Civil Rights Movement in Tennessee: A Narrative History.* Knoxville: University of Tennessee Press, 2005.

Brian Piper

Legislation

The practice of **Jim Crow** has always been supported by legislation at the federal, state, and local levels. The wording, intent, enforcement and impact differed in various areas of the country, but it is generally thought that it was most damaging in the southern United States. The former states of the old Confederacy developed a myriad of laws to restrict the civil rights of blacks, perpetuate the customs of Southern life, and return Southern society as closely as possible to the days when **slavery** was legal. These laws touched on every area of life, from social discourse to employment to the rights of blacks to attend public schools. Jim Crow laws began to be passed during the middle to late 1870s and remained in place until 1968.

The stage was set for the development of Jim Crow in the late eighteenth century when the Declaration of Independence and the Constitution, the so-called charters of American freedom, were written. The incendiary rhetoric of the Declaration—"We hold these truths to be self evident, that all men are created equal"—did not protect the rights of free blacks, nor did it settle the issue of slavery. Furthermore, Thomas Jefferson, principal author of the Declaration, wrote a stinging indictment of King George III of Great Britain, blaming him for the slave trade in the colonies. It was dropped from the final document lest the Southern colonies, especially **South Carolina** and **Georgia**, refuse to sign it and the grand experiment at independence was scuttled.

Moreover, when the Constitution was written in 1787, several sections underscored the importance of slavery and the reluctance of the **federal government** to tamper with the peculiar institution. Article I, Section 2 decreed that blacks would only count as three-fifths of a person for the purpose of apportioning taxes among the states; Article I, Section 9 forbade Congress from interfering with the international slave trade before 1808. The comity article, Article IV, Section 2, required the governments of the several states to assist in the return of runaway slaves.

From the early nineteenth century through the Civil War, the legislative process was used primarily to define slavery, punish runaways and those who harbored them, and ensure the return of runaway slaves who were considered to be property. At the federal level, the Missouri Compromise, passed in 1820, admitted the territory of Missouri as a slave state and Maine, which had been part of Massachusetts, as a free state. It also banned slavery from any new state with territory north of the southern border of Missouri. The Compromise of 1850 forced the federal government to guarantee the return of runaways to their masters, denied blacks the right to jury trials and banned them from testifying in legal proceedings. Neither of these compromises satisfied the North and the South; they merely postponed the day of reckoning over the spread of slavery.

By the 1860 presidential election, the country was sliding inexorably to war, and the election of the Republican Abraham Lincoln sealed its fate. South Carolina, Georgia, **Florida**, **Alabama**, **Mississippi**, **Louisiana**, and **Texas**, located in the lower South, seceded that year; **Virginia**, **North Carolina**, Tennessee, and **Arkansas**, located in the upper South, seceded in 1861. In that same year, Lincoln signed his preliminary Emancipation Proclamation allowing for the gradual end of slavery, compensation for slave owners and colonization, and the Confiscation Act declaring runaway slaves as booty in the war. The final Emancipation Proclamation, freeing the slaves in the states of rebellion, was signed in 1863, and Lincoln, certain the war would end soon, began working on how to reunite the Union when war ended. Reelected in 1864, he supported the creation of the Bureau of Refugees, Freedmen and Abandoned Lands, and championed the passage of the Thirteenth Amendment to the Constitution, which abolished slavery. Lincoln did not live to see the Union restored; he was assassinated on April 1865. It was left to Vice President Andrew Johnson, a Southerner, to reconstruct the Union.

Soon after the assassination of Lincoln, President Johnson gave speeches that seemed to indicate he would follow the plans developed by the martyred president. However, he quickly changed his mind and decided that the most important task was bringing the former Confederate states back into the Union. To this end, he decided not to punish the states for leaving the Union and waging war. He also turned his back on newly freed African Americans, vetoing legislation to extend the life of the Freedmen's Bureau. Johnson also vetoed the Civil Rights Act of 1866, designed among other things to protect blacks' rights and ensured they would be afforded the equal protection of the laws, in effect repudiating Lincoln's plans for Reconstruction. Johnson also vetoed the Reconstruction Act of 1867, which provided that the South be divided into five military districts that were placed under the authority of Northern military officers. They were to be responsible for assisting the South in reestablishing republican governments as guaranteed by the Constitution. Congress, where the Republicans had garnered a two-thirds majority in the previous election, overrode the president's vetoes, but the damage was done: Johnson had sent a clear message that protecting the rights and aspirations of African Americans would not be a priority of his administration.

Simultaneously, de jure segregation had begun in the South almost immediately after the end of the war. Prior to the Civil War, there had been no need to formally segregate the races—although some states had done so—while slavery existed and the free black population was small. Once slavery had been abolished, Southern officials, almost all former Confederates, quickly began to exclude blacks from virtually every phase of public life. Fearing a nation in which blacks would be equal to whites, Southern states quickly established **Black Codes**, which were designed to keep blacks from owning property, using the court system in any manner, and proscribing the occupations in and conditions under which they could work. The Codes differed from state to state, but all had the same impact: they trapped blacks into a life of poverty and prohibited them from taking full advantage of the freedoms for which many of them had fought. It should come as no surprise that the **Ku Klux Klan** (KKK) was formed at this same time. A fraternal organization of Confederate veterans established in Tennessee by Nathan Bedford Forrest in 1866, its purpose was to resist the advances of Reconstruction. It quickly turned into a vigilante group still operating today and went to work intimidating and terrorizing blacks who dared assert their rights.

As Reconstruction developed, Johnson and Congress continued to wrangle over the best way to guarantee full rights for blacks. In the meantime, Congress, led by the Radical Republicans, continued to pass legislation in an effort to define and secure those rights. In 1868, it passed the Fourteenth Amendment, which defined citizenship and guaranteed due process and the equal protection of the law to all Americans. Thus, it overturned *Dred Scott v. Sandford* (1857), which had stated that "the black man who no rights the white man was bound to respect." The Fifteenth Amendment, which outlawed discrimination in voting based on race, color, or previous condition of servitude, was passed in 1870. It brought thousands of black men into the political process. But it angered Southern whites who had begun to fight back, literally and figuratively, to quash black rights. Whites, including members of the KKK, harassed and intimidated black voters with impunity; they also killed several Republican candidates. Southern state governments, led by the former planter elite, failed to protect Republican candidates and black voters. To force compliance with the Fifteenth Amendment, Congress passed the Enforcement Acts of 1870 and 1871. The first protected the civil rights of blacks at the federal level and outlawed the use of disguises and masks. The 1871 law, also known as the Ku Klux Klan Act, made it a federal crime to interfere with an individual's right to hold office, serve on a jury, vote or enjoy the equal protection of the law. In extreme cases, the KKK Act of 1871 also authorized the president to suspend the writ of habeas corpus and send in federal troops to protect black rights and restore order. That same year, President Ulysses S. Grant declared martial law in several counties in South Carolina, sent in army troops, and suspended the writ of habeas corpus. Even these actions, however, had little impact, as the federal government lacked the will and resources to bring hundreds of Klansmen to trial.

A last spasm of federal lawmaking designed to protect African Americans occurred when Congress introduced another Civil Rights Act. The law sought to ensure that blacks could enjoy public accommodations. Passed in the Republican-led House, it was stripped of bans on discrimination in schools and in private accommodations such as churches and cemeteries by Democrats in the Senate. The law passed in 1875. It mattered little, however. The federal government refused to enforce the Act, and the **U.S. Supreme Court** declared it unconstitutional in 1883.

It would be the last major piece of federal civil rights legislation for almost 100 years. All but four of the Southern states—Mississippi, Louisiana, South Carolina, and Florida—had returned to home rule, and much of the country seemed weary of the arduous task of protecting black rights. The increasing intransigence of Southern state governments controlled by Democratic Redeemers ensured that the federal government would have an increasingly difficult time guaranteeing black rights. Several government scandals at the federal level, the Panic of 1873 and the resulting depression stole the attention of Congress. Conflict between black and white Republicans coupled with the death of several highly influential Radical Republicans who served in Congress made it all but impossible to maintain Reconstruction. State elections, especially in the four states that had yet to be redeemed by Democrats, grew increasingly violent, and President Grant publicly declared his weariness with the battles over Reconstruction. When Mississippi Governor Adelbert Ames asked for federal assistance, Grant opined that the federal government was tired of rescuing the South from election-year violence and refused to send troops. All this was played out against the backdrop of the presidential election of 1876.

The election was one of the most confusing and hotly contested in American history. Samuel Tilden, the Democratic candidate, won the popular vote by a large margin and was ahead of his Republican challenger, Rutherford B. Hayes in the Electoral College, 185 votes to 167. Twenty electoral votes from South Carolina, Florida, and Louisiana were being claimed by both parties. A special commission split along party lines, and Hayes let it be known that he would not support Republican governments in the unredeemed states. This so-called compromise ensured that Hayes was the victor. Very shortly after being inaugurated, he withdrew the last federal troops from the South, and Republican governments collapsed. Reconstruction was over.

The promise of emancipation and Reconstruction was reduced to ashes. Of course, African Americans were no longer slaves, had won some basic freedoms and had begun to build strong families and communities. But in spite of a formal legislative apparatus, thousands of blacks had been terrorized and killed in the aftermath of the Civil War. Most whites, especially in the South, were determined that blacks would not be given even a modicum of freedom and civil rights. White Republicans, Northerners, and even some Radical Republicans began to believe that Reconstruction was a mistake; they no longer looked at African Americans as a people who deserved their protection. The failure of Reconstruction augured the success of Jim Crow.

White Southerners and Democrats moved quickly to strip blacks of one of their most important rights: the right to vote. The ink was barely dry on the

Fifteenth Amendment to the Constitution when whites began to develop schemes to circumvent it. A campaign of economic intimidation, threats, and violence kept thousands of black men away from the polls. When this was not enough, whites sought quasi-legal means to suppress the black vote. South Carolina passed the Eight Box Law, which required voters to place their ballots in separate boxes for separate races. Voters in Mississippi were required to demonstrate they could understand the Constitution before they were allowed to cast their votes. Louisiana instituted a grandfather clause that allowed black men to vote only if their grandfathers had voted. All of the Southern states instituted poll taxes, and voters were required to verify their place of residency and change polling locations if they moved. People convicted of theft or bigamy or other offenses deemed to be black crimes were disfranchised. So successful were these tactics that by 1890, no blacks were elected to office and black voters, especially in the deep South, had virtually disappeared.

Southern whites had been so successful in disfranchising blacks that they turned their attention to developing strategies to legally separate the races. By the 1880s, blacks and whites rarely mingled, although the term segregation was seldom used until the early twentieth century. In spite of the **Civil Rights Act of 1875**, blacks and whites had separate institutions, including hospitals, schools, and cemeteries. It is the case, too, that many blacks were content to sit in separate areas in public places as it was an improvement over the total exclusion they had experienced during slavery.

While no one knows how the term *Jim Crow* came to define the practice of segregation, it is patently clear that it allowed whites to exercise almost total control over blacks, and this control allowed them the illusion of living much as they did during slavery. Whites next went to work to ensure they would have little or no contact with blacks in public spaces, and their first target was public transportation.

The confined spaces on passenger trains was especially galling to whites. By 1881, Southern states began passing laws which relegated blacks to the separate cars or separate sections within cars. Tennessee passed a law mandating segregation of railroad cars in 1881; Florida passed similar legislation several years later. In Louisiana, railroad officials, black politicians, and other black leaders also protested against segregated transportation, but to no avail; the state segregated its passenger trains in 1891.

In 1892, a full scale attack on segregated transportation was launched by Homer A. Plessy, a fair-skinned black man. Having purchased a first-class ticket, he boarded the train and attempted to sit in the section reserved for whites. He was arrested and charged with violating the new segregation law. His case, ***Plessy v. Ferguson***, was heard by the U.S. Supreme Court in 1896. Counsel for Plessey argued that by requiring him to sit in a blacks-only car, the state was violating his Fourteenth Amendment right to equal protection of the law. In an eight-to-one decision, the Court ruled that separation of the races did not imply blacks were inferior, nor did it deprive Plessy of his rights as long as the facilities in question were equal to those of whites. Justice Herbert Brown, writing for the majority, made a clear distinction between political and social equality. Justice **John Marshall Harlan**, the lone dissenter whose grandfather had owned slaves, warned that in ruling against Plessy, the Court was condoning a practice that would be of great harm to American society. His dissent proved prescient; the highest court in the land had paved the way for a dual society based on racial prejudice and false claims of white superiority. By the end of the nineteenth century, hundreds of laws all over the country had created a web that ensnared most blacks and virtually guaranteed they would live lives of crushing poverty and brutal oppression.

In addition to being racially segregated, African Americans were forced to dance an elaborate minuet of racial etiquette that always found them at a severe disadvantage. Whites would not shake hands with blacks, and blacks were taught to never look whites in the eye, especially when addressing white women. When blacks were permitted to enter white establishments, it was through the back door, and they could not be served in those establishments. They were expected to always speak in a deferential manner when addressing white people. Furthermore, blacks were not given honorific, but whites were. It was not uncommon for whites to refuse to learn or use the names of blacks; instead, blacks were addressed as "boy" or "girl"; "auntie" or "uncle."

It was in the area of sexual relations that the racial etiquette was most damaging. black girls and women had no control over their bodies and were often the victims of forced sexual relationships with white men. Black men could do nothing to protect their wives and daughters from these assaults, and most white women pretended that black women's forced sexual relationship with white men did not exist. Black parents often disciplined their children harshly over the slightest violation of racial etiquette; especially discouraged was speaking freely to or around whites, as it could mean the difference between life and death.

The penalty for violating racial etiquette was often administered at the end of a rope. The National Association for the Advancement of Colored People (NAACP) defines **lynching** as the murder of someone by three or more people who claim to be serving the causes of justice or tradition. Lynching was a common means of dealing with people who violated laws or community norms. Indeed, between 1890 and 1930, more than 3,700 people had been lynched in the United States; this figure includes women and whites. The practice was especially prevalent in the West, which during this time period often had no established criminal justice system. By the late nineteenth century, however, lynching became the preferred way that whites used to oppress and dominate blacks, and most lynchings were performed in the South, where black men made up most of its victims. Whites liked to claim that lynching was needed because the justice system could not be counted upon to punish black criminals, and those who were lynched were guilty of serious crimes, such as the rape of a white woman or murder. However, statistics do not bear this out. Black activists **Ida B. Wells-Barnett** and **Walter White** conducted careful empirical studies and reported that while whites often accused blacks of various crimes, the main reason for lynching was race hatred and the fear of blacks' advancement. Whites used lynching as an instrument of war in their campaign to crush black economic aspirations, maintain white supremacy, and squelch black political activism. Indeed, a black man could be lynched for any or no reason.

Whites defended lynching as a much-needed tool that helped to uphold Southern honor, communal values, and democracy. Moreover, it was a premeditated crime, often tacitly supported or openly condoned by people considered pillars of their respective communities, including law enforcement officers, politicians, and judges. Indeed, few whites condemned lynching unless it was carried out in an exceptionally brutal manner.

Lynchings during the era of Jim Crow were public spectacles. It was not uncommon for lynchings to be scheduled so that the public could be on hand, infusing lynchings with a carnival-like atmosphere. Sometimes, special excursion trains were run to deliver people to the event, and families sometimes brought picnic baskets. Women and children were often present at lynchings, and items such as postcards or recordings were sold to commemorate the event. Some victims were doused with oil or gasoline, set on fire, and allowed to slowly burn to death. Bodies were often mutilated after the victim died either by riddling the dead with bullets, or cutting off extremities and sexual organs was often done to provide participants and onlookers with souvenirs of the crime.

Just as they had during slavery, black activists, politicians, and whites in sympathy with them worked valiantly to stamp out lynching. In addition to Wells-Barnett and White, William Monroe Trotter, Mary Church Terell, and William Pickett worked assiduously to end lynching. Organizations such as the National Association of Colored Women's Clubs and the NAACP were involved with the decades long effort to make lynching a federal crime. White women in the Progressive movement formed the Association of Southern Women for the Prevention of Lynching to battle the attitudes that led to lynching and ensure its demise. The efforts of these groups, although not entirely successful, bore some fruit. The number of blacks lynched in the United States declined from a high of 155 in 1893 to 20 in 1930.

In spite of the fact that whites had been phenomenally successful in creating and maintaining the dual society, their obsession with ensuring that blacks remained at the bottom of society bordered on the pathological. A number of state and local lawmaking bodies had gone to extremes in their efforts to maintain Jim Crow. Florida and **Kentucky** required that schoolbooks for blacks and whites be stored in separate facilities. The races were not allowed to play board games together in Alabama, and Mississippi passed a law making it a criminal offense to publish materials that considered or advocated racial equality and intermarriage. Oklahoma permitted its Conservation Commission to segregate fishermen and boaters based on race.

The 1905 **Niagara Movement** gave birth to the most famous of black uplift organizations, the NAACP. While a number of organizations had used various methods such as protests and boycotts to dismantle Jim Crow, the NAACP developed a two-prong approach that proved to be extremely effective. The first was the use of lawsuits to force the courts to end Jim Crow. The organization won its first major victory in 1915 in the case of *Guinn v. United States,* when the Supreme Court overturned the grandfather clause that had kept black men from voting in Oklahoma. Two years later, the organization won another victory when the Supreme Court ruled unconstitutional a Louisville law that enforced residential segregation through restrictive covenants.

In 1918, the NAACP joined black activists and their white allies in its most important fight to that date: attempting to secure a federal antilynching law. Along with several organizations, prominent black activists The Dyer Bill, named after its sponsor white congressman **Leonidas C. Dyer** of St. Louis, first passed in the House of Representatives in 1922; it was blocked by the Senate. The bill continued to be introduced into the 1930s, but it never passed the Senate.

Jim Crow reared its ugly head during **World War I**. As in previous wars, African Americans volunteered in large numbers. White officials, fearful of arming thousands of black men who were training at Southern army posts, did everything they could to discourage black soldiers. In every branch of the service, black men were assigned to the most menial tasks, and they were blocked from serving in the Marine Corps at all. When black men were permitted to see combat, it was in segregated units under the supervision of white officers. Black soldiers generally acquitted themselves well, and three regiments distinguished themselves so that they were awarded the Croix de Guerre from the French government. Most white Americans, however, refused to afford African Americans their rights in spite of their sacrifices in the war. Indeed, almost two dozen black men were lynched while wearing the armed forces uniforms. Yet, black men were emboldened by their experiences in Europe, and their return marked a turning point in blacks' efforts to overturn Jim Crow.

From 1906 through 1923, African Americans sometimes engaged in armed resistance to protect their families and secure their rights as race riots broke out in large cities, from Atlanta to East St. Louis to Chicago. While each riot had its own personal circumstances, there was a common denominator: whites' inability to treat blacks as equal. Simultaneously, black Americans protested with their feet and engaged in a mass migration from the rural South to the urban North. Between 1910 and 1940, the black population outside the Southern states doubled; more than 1.75 million African Americans fled the South. The migrants were primarily young people who had no personal memories of slavery, and they were responding to a number of factors that made migrating not only necessary but desirable. Natural disasters in the form of boll weevils and the great Mississippi River flood destroyed crops throughout the South, leaving agricultural workers without employment. Northern labor shortages, advertisements in black-owned newspapers and labor recruiters lured blacks to Northern cities with promises of better paying factory jobs. On the one hand, white planters and businessmen were happy to rid themselves of African Americans; on the other, they worried about the loss of cheap labor. They tried a variety of methods to cope, from requiring Northern labor agents to get licenses to operate, to urging a cessation of violence against blacks.

By the 1930s, black activism had greatly matured. Multi-prong efforts by black organizations, the legal system, and individual activists were slowly chipping away at Jim Crow. Walter White, now with the NAACP, led the fight to defeat the nomination of John J. Parker, a committed white supremacist, to the U.S. Supreme Court. The organization hired the Harvard-trained black lawyer Charles Hamilton Houston, to head its legal attack on segregation. Houston, along with his former student **Thurgood Marshall**, first focused on forcing the Southern states to equalize public facilities as stated in *Plessy v. Ferguson.*

The duo met with several important victories. The state of Missouri was ordered to provide blacks the opportunity to study law in state-supported schools in the case of *Gaines v. Canada* (1938). A similar case, *Sipuel v. Board of Regents of the University of Oklahoma* (1947) required the state to provide blacks the opportunity to attend the university's law school; previously the practice had been to provide black students with an out-of-state tuition award. In *Sweatt v. Painter* (1950), the University of Texas Law School had created a separate law school for black students, but Marshall argued that its facilities and faculty were inadequate. The Supreme Court agreed. These cases paved the way for the landmark case of ***Brown v. Board of Education*** (1954), which formally declared Jim Crow in public schools a violation of the equal protection clause of the Fourteenth Amendment.

The year 1954 is often recognized as the beginning of the modern **Civil Rights Movement**. Within 10 years, the movement and its followers had ensured that racial discrimination was at the top of the political agenda. In 1957 Congress passed a civil rights act—the first since Reconstruction—that created a commission that would monitor and report violations of blacks' civil rights and propose remedies for disfranchisement of African Americans. The 1960 Civil Rights Act was primarily an administrative directive aimed at forcing local officials to protect black voting rights and giving the federal government the ability to monitor compliance.

Fervent civil rights activities, the assassination of President John F. Kennedy and the kidnap and murder of three young civil rights workers in the summer of 1964 provided the impetus for the **Civil Rights Act of 1964**, which ended Jim Crow practices in public accommodations. The movement then turned its attention to obtaining the ballot in the states of the Old Confederacy. A massive march from to Selma, Alabama, to the capital in Montgomery and the murder of several civil rights activists convinced Congress to pass the **Voting Rights Act of 1965**, which guaranteed the rights of all Americans to vote. Finally, President Lyndon B. Johnson signed into law the Civil Rights Act of 1968, also known as the Fair Housing Act, which banned racial discrimination in housing and provided protection for civil rights workers. Unlike the previous acts, however, it contained no enforcement role for the federal government. *See also* Civil Rights Act of 1957 and 1960; Discrimination.

Further Readings: Ayers, Edward L. *The Promise of the New South: Life after Reconstruction.* New York: Oxford University Press, 1992; Litwack, Leon. *Trouble in Mind: Black Southerners in the Age of Jim Crow.* New York: Alfred A. Knopf, 1988; McMillen, Neil R. *Dark Journey: Black Mississippians in the Age of Jim Crow.* Urbana: University of Illinois Press, 1989; Woodward, C. Vann. *The Strange Career of Jim Crow.* New York: Oxford University Press, 1955.

Marilyn K. Howard

Levittowns

Created in 1947 by William Levitt, Levittowns were standardized, large-scale suburban developments. Levitt emphasized efficiency and mass-production methods, which put the cost of home ownership within reach of middle-class America. Designed to accommodate the housing needs of returning **World War II** veterans, Levittowns served as a symbol of the postwar American dream. However, Jim Crow practices and housing policies kept African Americans out of this utopian community. Levittowns are the exemplar of innumerable American developments that prohibited black suburbanization.

The first of many Levittowns was built in Long Island, New York. Thousands of modest houses in these subdivisions mirrored one another. Levitt's goal was to provide affordable, not designer, homes. Often known as "cookie cutter communities," similarities did not end with the architecture. Most of the Levittown residents were young, married with children, and held similar jobs. Possibly one of the most obvious and shared characteristics among Levittowners was race. The Levitt organization openly stated that Levittowns were solely Caucasian communities and made every effort to keep Levittowns segregated. Thirteen years after its inception, not one African American resided in a Levittown. Levitt and residents of Levittown worried that integrating the communities could cause the property values to plummet. Additionally, attitudes of white supremacy encouraged segregation to endure.

When African Americans slowly began to break Levittown's race barrier in the mid-1960s, it was not an easy feat. White realtors and financial institutions made it almost impossible for African Americans to move into all-white communities. Banks would refuse to lend money or offer only the most expensive rates to black families. White residents joined together to form homeowners' associations with the common goal to prevent integration. Many homeowners refused to sell or rent their home to African Americans. Moreover, desperate white segregationists resorted to threats, violence, and arson in hopes of scaring black families away. Even **Jackie Robinson**, one of the greatest baseball players of all time, had so much difficultly finding a home near New York that he and his wife eventually decided to reside in Connecticut.

These prejudicial practices became illegal in April 1968, when President Lyndon B. Johnson signed the Civil Rights Act of 1968, also known as the Fair Housing Act. This legislation prohibited "discrimination based on race, color, religion, sex, and national origin in the sale or rental of housing" and banned well-known discriminatory practices such as blockbusting, redlining, and real estate steering. Ironically, according to the 2000 census, Long Island, New York, the first home to a Levittown, is the most racially segregated suburban area in the United States. *See also* Housing Covenants; Neighborhood Property Owners Associations; Segregation, Rural.

Further Readings: Civil Rights Act of 1968, Public Law 90–284, April 11, 1968, 82 Stat. (Title VIII, Fair Housing). *U.S. Statutes at Large, 90th Congress, 1968,* Leif and Goering, "The Implementation of the Federal Mandate for Fair Housing," 235, 261; Jackson, Kenneth T. *Crabgrass Frontier: The Suburbanization of the United States.* New York: Oxford University Press, 1985; Wiese, Andrew. *Places of Their Own: African American Suburbanization in the Twentieth Century.* Chicago: University of Chicago Press, 2004.

Emily Hess

Liberia

Liberia is a coastal West African nation that covers a geographic area about the size of Ohio, sharing borders with Sierra Leone, Guinea, and Cote d'Ivoire. Before the founding of the country in 1822, indigenous peoples belonged to 16 main ethnicities further categorized into three linguistic sets. Most of these people lived in polygynous, patrilineal societies organized first into households, which conglomerated to form villages. The political structure of the village most resembled a central chieftaincy state or a decentralized governing system based on age sets, gender, and kinship networks. The diversity of ethnic groups impeded unified resistance to outside forces and further fed the success of colonizers. Although the region was not conflict-free prior to colonization, the arrival of American ships in the early nineteenth century marked the beginning of intense pain and suffering for the 1.5 million Africans that came to be ruled by Americo-Liberians.

Free blacks, newly emancipated slaves, and recaptured slaves traveled to the west coast of Africa seeking a haven from the racial oppression these groups faced in the United States. The American Colonization Society (ACS) spearheaded the movement and first worked to acquire land in Sierra Leone. Ultimately, the society shifted southeastward in the areas that later became Liberia, where they established coastal settlements that were eventually grouped into five counties. Many of the ACS leaders owned slaves and sought to rid the United States of free blacks to strengthen the bonds of slavery. Other members embraced colonization as a way to spread Western civilization to the indigenous peoples of Africa. Free blacks and former slaves sought a better life. While most African Americans snubbed repatriation because they considered American their rightful home, some believed settlement in Africa would accomplish the dual goal of guaranteeing black Americans' civil rights along with the redemption of Africa through racial uplift.

The first Americans to try to colonize present-day Liberia met more failures than successes. Prior to departure, there were no training or educational sessions about the new climate, land, or population. Many of the passengers and crew on the *Elizabeth,* the first ship to set sail, died from disease and battles with the indigenous coastal residents soon after arriving. Some emigrants considered their flight from America an opportunity to embark on work arrangements that did not entail the physically taxing types of labor they experienced in the States. Although conditions forced the new Liberians to do some farming, the men and women worked to distinguish their labor from that of the indigenes. Many held on to mythic conceptions of Africa that developed among many enslaved in America. This Africa, a utopia of plenty in which Africans worked collaboratively to build a black nation, contrasted greatly with real-life conditions.

The joining of African and European cultural norms, values, and beliefs that developed into African American identity did not translate into an appreciation of traditional African culture. Paradoxically, former slaves and free black emigrants had internalized the negative caricatures and stereotypes of Africa and her people that pervaded Western thought. They did not try to bridge the communication gap between themselves and the Dey, Via, Bassa, Kru, and Grebo peoples they met along the coast and did little to assimilate into existing social systems. Rather, they worked to spread "civilization" to a continent that Western circles described as barbaric and primitive. Settlers degraded traditional African customs and beliefs while teaching the superiority of the European worldview. Christianity played a major role in their civilizing mission, and many traveled as missionaries to spread Western religion and education to the Gold Coast.

In 1824, the colony took the name Liberia and became an independent African republic. Before 1832, the ACS was the only emigration organization involved in Liberia, after which a number of organizations sent pioneers to the new country. In 1839, the groups established a commonwealth to unite the various branches that settled along the coast. Mulattoes in Liberia reaped real benefits from their skin tone, since lighter-skinned blacks often held higher political positions than those of a darker hue. These ideas held significance for those Americo-Liberians, as the immigrants from their United States and the descendants were called, who withstood the experience of slavery in the United States. During the height of the Atlantic Slave Trade, U.S. slave-owners made note of their preferences for captives from certain areas of Africa, which led to job specialization among certain ethnicities. As the American-born population of slaves in America began to supersede the African-born, owners used distinctions in skin color for job assignments, favoring lighter-skinned blacks for the work with the most contact between whites and blacks. Slaves who had the most contact with whites were more likely to adopt Eurocentric values. Although this group gained better resources and did not usually perform the more strenuous jobs of field laborers, they were often ostracized by the black community and, as those always under the gaze of whites, endured a different type of oppression. Settlers transplanted this hierarchy of color to Liberia.

Americo-Liberians soon established a caste system and governed the indigenes from the capital city of Monrovia. The ruling elite treated Africa's people as whites in America treated African Americans. Although there was no explicit segregation policy, Americo-Liberians forced the indigenous to enter through back doors, sit in separate pews at church, and limited citizenship rights to exclude many peoples of the hinterland. By the second decade of the twentieth century, indigenes of Liberia outnumbered Americo-Liberians by a ratio of about 100 to one. In 1906, leaders oversaw the organization of the Liberian Frontier Force, a military unit formed to protect the Liberian government from the majority. Their role would expand to include the collection of taxes after they were institutionalized in 1916. The collection of taxes provoked the ire of West Africans and led to conflicts with the government.

Although the constitution forbade forced human labor, governmental officials sanctioned *pawning*, denying its strong resemblance to slavery. Under this system, a person or guardian could lease his labor to an employer in exchange for a set number of years for an agreed payment. The system of pawning and labor export deals made with the Spanish heightened divisions between the government and the indigenous peoples. The Liberian government demanded so much from the indigenous peoples in the hinterland that some had to pawn themselves or others in order to pay hut taxes. In 1914, the Liberian government made a deal with the Spanish to send laborers to Fernando Po, an island of plantations to the west of Liberia. To gain these laborers, the Liberian Frontier Force sacked local villages demanding payment of taxes in cash or in the form of young boys. When these frequent instances of forced labor gained national and international attention, governmental officials in America and Europe criticized those in power. In spite of public chastisement, those responsible usually remained in office. Labor exports to Fernando Po ended legally in 1930 but continued illegally for a number of years. Colonial powers mounted long and somewhat successful attacks against slavery, but their calls to end coerced labor were few. Many noted the irony of the United States speaking out against forced labor in light of their inaction in ending the similar types of coercion toward African Americans. Like sharecroppers in the American South and prisoners laboring in convict leasing systems, indigenous peoples of Liberia at Fernando Po worked for promises of payment never fulfilled.

During the height of **Jim Crow**, some black leaders in America supported **Back-to-Africa** initiatives, of which **W.E.B. Du Bois** and **Marcus Garvey** were the most popular. Du Bois, organizer of the fifth Pan African Conference, appreciated Africa's gifts, but also spoke from a more mythic conception of the continent. Garvey, the leader of the **United Negro Improvement Association**, envisioned a nation ruled by indigenous Africans and was quickly rejected by the Liberian ruling party. African Americans proved to be an unwelcome presence in Liberia. Liberian governmental officials did not want the threat of a growing body of black entrepreneurs and community builders in Liberia.

Economic and militaristic interest led to U.S. involvement in Liberian politics. The Liberian government made an agreement with Harvey Firestone in November 1926 for land to build a rubber manufacturing plant. When Firestone began to face labor shortages, the United States stepped in as a voice against the forced labor shipments to the Spanish. American intervention helped mend Firestone's labor problems, and he soon organized a segregated society around the rubber plantation. Like the black/white segregation that defined Jim Crow in the United States, the community of whites that came to Liberia with the Firestone business also developed separate lives. A segregated white community grew to include schools, churches, and golf courses. Even the ruling apparatus of Liberia could not gain entrance into this white metropolis without permission until the late 1950s. Du Bois would come to attack the color line that defined the company's relations to Liberia, although he originally supported the rubber baron's investment in the debt-ridden nation.

An investigation of Liberia's labor abuses headed by Charles Johnson, an African American sociologist, led to the fall of President C. B. King's administration. Unfortunately for the indigenous Liberians, his political party remained in power. Although many saw the election of Edwin Barclay in 1930 as a turn for the better, the new president adamantly opposed international involvement in Liberian affairs and thus blocked humanitarian attempt to address the continued exploitation of the indigenes by Americo-Liberians.

The government did not see itself as an exploiter of a people with little economic and no political power. This would all come to a head in January 1980, when the Progressive People's Party staged a coup d'état that dismantled the Americo-Liberian True Whig Party. The new regime empowered continental Africans, but governmental abuses continued. *See also* Black Nationalism; Ethiopia; Racial Stereotypes.

Further Readings: Fredrickson, George M. *The Black Image in the White Mind: The Debate on Afro-American Character and Destiny, 1817–1914.* New York: Harper and Row, 1971; Ham, Debra Newman. "The Role of African American Women in the Founding of Liberia." In *Global Dimensions of the African Diaspora,* edited by Joseph E. Harris, 2nd ed., 369–85. Washington, DC: Howard University Press, 1993; Stone, Verlon L. Liberian Collections Project. Indiana University Archives of Traditional Music. http://onliberia.org/urls.htm (accessed August 1, 2007); Sundiata, Ibrahim. *Brothers and Strangers: Black Zion, Black Slavery, 1914–1940.* Durham, NC: Duke University Press, 2003.

Christina L. Davis

Lincoln Memorial

The Lincoln Memorial is a U.S. presidential memorial authorized in 1911, started in 1914, and dedicated in 1922. It occupies a site on the western extreme of the National Mall. The memorial honors the 16th president, Abraham Lincoln. The memorial was designed by Henry Bacon in the style of a Greek Doric temple, with an interior statue of a seated Lincoln by Daniel C. French. The statue gazes down the Mall past the Washington Memorial toward the Capitol building. The memorial celebrates important contributions to the nation by Lincoln; preserving the Union, reconciling North and South, and freeing the slaves. His preservation of the Union is marked by an engraving of his Gettysburg Address. The reconciliation is represented by his Second Inaugural Address, while his role as emancipator is show by a series of murals by Jules Guerin above showing an angel freeing a slave.

While President Lincoln was widely lionized in the North after the war, white Southerners held more ambivalent feelings about him. His election in 1860 touched off the succession crisis that started the Civil War, and during the war he was hated across the South as a tyrant who resorted to race war to crush the Confederacy. However, in the decades after his death, his reputation in the white South had been modified to an extent. By the turn of the century, white reconciliation had been built in part on the diminution of slavery as a cause of the war. As **Jim Crow** laws kept blacks as oppressed as the institution of slavery once had, the sting of abolition had largely abated in the white South. Lincoln's moderate reconstruction plan and his generosity to the defeated South contrasted sharply with later Radical **Reconstruction** enacted after his death, which white Southerners saw as a terrible period and a crime perpetrated against the South. Acceptance of Lincoln by the white South was based on his status as the man who kept the nation together, which, by the early twentieth century, most of the white South agreed was a good thing.

Black Americans, whether Northerners or Southerners, however, still held Lincoln in high regard. Lincoln was the Great Emancipator, the leader of the abolitionist party who finally ended slavery. Thus Lincoln himself held a high position in African American culture, and his memorial became the site for several important large gatherings of blacks.

The memorial became linked with large gatherings of blacks in 1939, when the Daughters of the American Revolution (DAR) refused to allow one of the most talented singers of the period, Marian Anderson, to perform at Constitution Hall, which they owned. While the DAR claimed that the hall was unavailable due to a previous booking, most understood that she was turned down because she was black. Thousands of liberal members of the DAR, including First Lady **Eleanor Roosevelt**, resigned over the incident. After the District of Columbia Board of Education refused to allow Anderson to use the auditorium in a white school for a concert, Roosevelt intervened and pressured her husband to find a suitable spot for her performance. With the president's urging, Interior Secretary Harold L. Ickes arranged for her to perform from the steps of the Lincoln Memorial. A live audience estimated at 70,000 people, black and white, crowded on the Mall to hear her, while a national radio audience of millions listened in. The image of one of America's greatest singers, who happened to be black, singing in front of a statue of the Great Emancipator, became a powerful symbol for blacks and liberal whites. The DAR, deeply embarrassed by the incident, invited Anderson to sing at Constitution Hall in 1943, in the middle of **World War II**.

However, the Anderson concert was only a preview of an event of much more import that would occur more than 20 years later. On August 28, 1963, during the height of the **Civil Rights Movement**, a rally was held at the Lincoln Memorial as the climax of the **March on Washington** for Jobs and Freedom. The march, which occurred just over 100 years since Lincoln issued the Emancipation Proclamation, underlined how far the nation had yet to go in fulfilling the promises of Abolition, as well as the principles of the Declaration of Independence and the Constitution. With an estimated quarter of a million people gathered around the memorial, **Martin Luther King, Jr.**, delivered his "I Have a Dream" speech, one of the seminal speeches of American history. The setting of the speech, on the steps of the Lincoln Memorial, added to the dignity of the occasion, and emphasized just how long the struggle for equality had been for African Americans. The National Park Service later placed a marker on the spot where King stood as he delivered his famous speech. *See also* March on Washington Movement.

Further Readings: Thomas, Christopher A. *The Lincoln Memorial and American Life.* Princeton, NJ: Princeton University Press, 2002; Williams, Juan. *Eyes on the Prize: America's Civil Rights Years, 1954–1965.* New York: Viking, 1987.

Barry M. Stentiford

Little Rock Nine

The term "Little Rock Nine" refers to the group of nine students who in September 1957 became the first African Americans to attend Central High School in Little Rock, **Arkansas**. The nine students were Melba Pattillo, Minnijean Brown, Elizabeth Eckford, Ernest Green, Gloria Ray, Carlotta Walls, Thelma Mothershed, Terrence Roberts, and Jefferson Thomas. The Nine, who had been carefully selected for their role, submitted themselves to humiliation and physical danger in order to help desegregate the public schools of Little Rock.

On May 24, 1955, the Little Rock School Board unanimously approved a plan drafted by Virgil Blossum, the superintendant of schools, for the gradual integration of the city's schools, in compliance with the **U.S. Supreme Court**, which had ruled in the 1954 decision ***Brown v. Board of Education*** that segregated schools were unconstitutional, and that all schools were to be desegregated. The initial phase, when nine black students would begin attending classes at the previously all-white Central High School, would begin in September 1957. Local civil rights leaders and the Little Rock School Board understood that the first black students to attend the school would be under intense scrutiny, with any deficiency in academics or conduct used as an excuse to label the entire movement to integrate the schools a failure. The nine students were carefully selected by the local chapter of the National Association for the Advancement of Colored People (NAACP) for their high grades, solid attendance records, and lack of discipline problems in their previous school records. **Daisy Lee Bates**, a journalist and publisher who was active in the **Civil Rights Movement** in Little Rock, provided continual advice and support to the Nine. The students were instructed to dress neatly, not to overreact to provocation, and in general to give segregationists no excuse to use them as an argument against integration.

White residents of the city formed "citizen's councils," which pledged themselves to uphold segregation, with force if necessary. Governor Orval Faubus, a former liberal who had come to support segregation, promised white voters that he would keep Central High an all-white school. By inclination, President Dwight D. Eisenhower disliked heavy-handed government approaches, and preferred to remain aloof from the Civil Rights Movement. However, he saw a crisis building in Little Rock, as segregationists rallied and planned during the 1956–1957 school year. Hoping to avoid a showdown between state and federal authorities, Eisenhower met with Governor Faubus to discuss the approaching integration. While Faubus remained noncommittal, Eisenhower apparently believed that although Faubus might speak against integration, he would ensure that federal laws were obeyed.

The initial attempts of the Nine to attend classes at the school on September 4, 1957, brought out large crowds of white adults, mostly parents of students attending the school, bent on maintaining segregation. The crowds had assembled around the school in the early morning to keep the black students out of the school. Governor Faubus mobilized part of the Arkansas **National Guard** with the mission to physically block the nine black students from entering the school. Faubus explained his actions as stemming from his concern for maintaining law and order, but the white mobs were the people violating the law, not the black students. Photographs of the day's events were published nationally, with the image of a row of white armed Guardsmen and the mobs of angry adult white adults blocking the small group of neatly dressed black students, all of whom were in their mid-teens, making a powerful impression throughout the nation. Eisenhower was furious at the actions of Faubus, seeing his stance as a direct challenge to federal authority. Eisenhower had the U.S. Department of Justice request an injunction against the use of the National Guard in U.S. District Court for the Eastern District of Arkansas. The injunction was granted, and Faubus was ordered to withdraw the National Guard or face contempt of court.

Faubus, having shown his commitment to his political base while holding himself and his city up to national ridicule, complied and withdrew the Guard on September 20, and city police took over the mission of ensuring the safety of the Nine. However, the situation at Central High was still tense, as a large crowd of whites, estimated in the hundreds, kept a vigil at the school in an attempt to ensure that the Nine did not enter the school. On September 23, the police were able to sneak the Nine into the school to begin attending classes. However, when the surrounding mob learned that the Nine were in the school, order began to break down. The police, seriously outnumbered, feared for the safety of the Nine, and escorted them away from the school.

Supporters of integration, as well as people who supported the rule of law and not the rule of mobs, realized that a stronger show of authority would be needed, or else the mobs around Central High would continue to keep the Nine away from school. Woodrow Mann, the Democratic mayor of Little Rock, formally requested that Eisenhower use federal soldiers to maintain order and ensure that the Nine were able to attend classes. On September 24, Eisenhower sent in the U.S. Army's 1,200-man 327th Battle Group of the 101st Airborne Division to Little Rock to take control of the campus. At the same time, he federally mobilized the entire Arkansas National Guard, about 10,000 Guardsmen, mainly to prevent Governor Faubus from attempting to use the Guard to oppose the federal soldiers. With this overwhelming show of disciplined soldiers, the threat from the mobs abated, although the shouting continued. The Nine were able to enter the school and begin attending classes on September 25.

The federal soldiers were deployed for the immediate crisis, but Eisenhower and the army wanted them returned to Fort Campbell, Kentucky, as soon as the situation allowed it. Originally, most of the National Guardsmen were ordered to remain at the armories. However, the army began organizing some of the federalized National Guardsmen into what became Task Force 153 on Camp Robinson, in North Little Rock, with the long-term mission of ensuring order at the school, while demobilizing most of the remainder of the Arkansas National Guard. By the end of November, the 101st soldiers were all withdrawn, and Task Force 153 assumed full control of the campus.

Although the Nine attended classes under tight security, they were still subjected to a host of threats, harassments, and even assaults, from white students throughout the year. Despite the hostile environment, the Nine remained at the school though the fall semester. Minnijean Brown was the only one of the Nine not to complete the school year. In December, a group of white male students began hassling her in the cafeteria. In the confrontation, she dropped her tray, in the process splashing some of her chili on one of the white students. For this, she was expelled from the school. Melba Pattillo suffered injury when acid was thrown in her face by a white student, but continued to attend Central and finished the school year.

However, the opponents of integration were not finished. With the support of the governor and the state legislature, the school board closed all public high schools in Little Rock after the end of the 1957–1958 school year. The public high schools remained closed only for one year, though. Under pressure from the Little Rock Chamber of Commerce, as well as the enormous negative publicity the city and state received nationally over the crisis, the school board reopened the high schools, as integrated schools, in the fall of 1958.

Of the eight black students who completed the first year, Earnest Green was the only senior, and at the end of the 1957–1958 school year, became the first African American to graduate from Central High. Elizabeth Eckford moved to St. Louis in 1958 and completed her college preparation there. Jefferson Thomas returned when Central reopened, and graduated from Central High in 1960. Terrence Roberts moved to Los Angeles after the end of the first year, and graduated from Los Angeles High School in 1959. Carlotta Walls, the youngest of the nine, also returned to Central High School when it reopened in 1959 and graduated in 1960. Thelma Mothershed completed most of her coursework by correspondence during the year the public schools were closed. She received her diploma from Central High by mail. Melba Pattillio moved to California after the first year and completed her high school program there. In 1999, each of the Little Rock Nine was honored with Congressional Gold Medals presented by President Bill Clinton, in recognition of their courage and their important role in knocking down segregation. *See also* Federal Government; White Citizens Council.

Further Readings: Fitzgerald, Stephanie. *Little Rock Nine: Struggle for Integration.* Mankato, MN: Compass Point Books, 2006; Freyer, Tony. *The Little Rock Crisis: A Constitutional Interpretation.* Westport, CT: Greenwood Press, 1984; Jacoway, Elizabeth, and C. Fred Williams, eds. *Understanding the Little Rock Crisis: An Exercise in Remembrance and Reconciliation.* Fayetteville: University of Arkansas Press, 1999.

Barry M. Stentiford

Louisiana

Louisiana holds an important place in the history of **Jim Crow**. It is where the landmark case ***Plessy v. Ferguson*** originated. The *Plessy* case established the doctrine of "**separate but equal**," which legalized Jim Crow in America. According to the **U.S. Supreme Court**, it was constitutionally permissible to maintain a regime of racial segregation if the services a state provided were equal. This ruling justified several Jim Crow laws, while opposition to it began the modern **Civil Rights Movement**.

The city in Louisiana responsible for the *Plessy* case was New Orleans. New Orleans had a unique history that made it one of the most interesting places in Louisiana and the entire South. Its unique demography began to take shape as early as 1720 with the first mass importation of African slaves. By the end of the eighteenth century, New Orleans was home to several ethnic groups and had the largest free black community in the Deep South. Most of the free black population in New Orleans considered themselves Creoles of Color. They were Catholic, educated, born in New Orleans, and could trace some family ties to white Creoles of the city. Their wealth, social standing, education, and unique history set them apart not only from slaves, but from free persons of color elsewhere. Most were descendants of unions between Native Americans, French, Spanish, and Africans. Before the Civil War, they owned property and dominated skilled crafts like bricklaying, cigar making, carpentry, and shoemaking. The Creoles of Color provided the leadership for the black community in Louisiana after the Civil War. They were instrumental in bringing about the *Plessy* case.

At the end of the Civil War in 1865, the **federal government** had to come up with a plan to govern former Confederate States, reunite the nation, and recover from the destruction of the war. The 1865 passage of the Thirteenth Amendment to the U.S. Constitution ensured that blacks would no longer be held in bondage by abolishing the institution of slavery in America. Newly freed slaves dreamed of a new South that would allow them their basic rights as freedmen, while white Southerners looked for ways to retain as much control over former slaves as possible. After the passage of the Thirteenth Amendment, former slave states, including Louisiana, implemented the infamous **Black Codes**. The Black Codes consisted of a series of laws aimed at restricting the rights of freedmen by making them second-class citizens. The Black Codes enraged Northerners, who pushed for radical changes in the South. In 1866, Congress began a new phase of reconstruction, called Radical **Reconstruction**. Under Radical Reconstruction, all Black Codes were repealed and the South was put under military rule. To ensure that nothing like this could ever happen again, Congress granted all freedmen citizenship rights by drafting what became the Fourteenth Amendment to the Constitution and pressuring the states to pass it. In 1870, Republicans continued their Radical Reconstruction by pushing the Fifteenth Amendment through the states, which gave blacks the right to vote. From 1870 to 1875, Southern blacks voted in record numbers for Republicans. In 1875 this changed with the adoption of the **Mississippi Plan**, which was made by the **Democratic Party** to overthrow Republican rule in the South. The plan relied on organized violence, intimidation and fraud.

Louisiana was one of the first Southern states to adopt the Mississippi Plan. Redeeming Louisiana government was very important to the Democratic Party. In 1872, Louisiana had for the first time ever a black governor, courtesy of the **Republican Party**. P. B. S. Pinchback became governor of Louisiana after the impeachment of Henry Clay Warmoth. Pinchback served as governor of Louisiana for 35 days, from December 9, 1872, to January 13, 1873. With the help of the Mississippi Plan and the Compromise of 1877, which ended reconstruction in the South, the Democratic Party had taken over in Louisiana and proceeded to reverse the constitution of 1868 and all of the work of the Creoles, including integrated schools, integrated public accommodations, and voting rights. Reconstruction was over, and the nation was united once again. The national Republican Party was tired of the problems in the South and had abandoned blacks, leaving them powerless to white redeemers.

Between 1877 and 1900, racist politicians in the South gained control of Southern governments and began infringing on the rights of black citizens. Southern redeemers believed in the ultimate supremacy of the white man, especially in matters concerning social and political equality. It was accepted as a fact to many white people that blacks were inferior to whites, and incapable of any real social or political equality; however, Southern whites more so than Northern whites were committed to making racial policies reflect that belief. Although, their beliefs rested upon prejudice, emotion, and ignorance, they acted upon the assumption that they were correct, and made sure that their premises justified their policies of social segregation, economic discrimination, and political subordination. In 1890, the state of Louisiana took things a step forward by passing the Separate Car Act, which stated that railroad companies provide separate but equal train cars for blacks and whites. This act provided for the basis of several Jim Crow laws.

In 1891, two Creole of Color leaders, Rudolph L. Desdunes and Louis A. Martinet, began a grassroots attempt to form a committee of black citizens to fight against the Separate Car Act. Desdunes and Martinet believed that there could be no accommodating the rights of a United States citizen. They saw the Separate Car Act as the first of many acts that would hinder those rights. Through their efforts, the Citizens Committee was formed. The goal of the committee was to end the infringing practice of racial segregation in the South. In 1892, the committee chose **Homer Plessy** a light-complected Creole of Color who worked as a shoemaker in New Orleans, to test the validly of the Separate Car Act. The committee instructed Plessy to board a designated white train car of the East Louisiana Railroad. Officials of the East Louisiana Railroad told Plessy that he could not ride on the white train car because he was not white. They asked him to take a seat on the black train car. Plessy refused to do so. He was arrested and jailed.

Once Plessy was arrested the Citizens Committee began to work on his defense. At his trial, *Homer A. Plessy v. State of Louisiana,* lawyers argued that the railroad company denied Plessy his constitutional rights under the Thirteenth and Fourteenth amendments. The judge presiding over the case, John Ferguson, ruled that Louisiana did not infringe on Plessy's rights. According to Judge Ferguson, the state of Louisiana had the right to regulate railroad companies that operated in their state. Judge John H. Ferguson found Plessy guilty of violating the Separate Car Act and fined him $300.

Many members of the Citizens Committee were not pleased with the verdict of Judge Ferguson. They decided to take the case to the Supreme Court of Louisiana, where the ruling was upheld. In 1896, the committee tried one last time to have the ruling overturned by bringing the case all the way to the U.S. Supreme Court. The U.S. Supreme Court ruled the same way as Judge Ferguson and the Louisiana Supreme Court. According to the U.S. Supreme Court, it was constitutionally permissible to maintain a regime of racial segregation if the services a state provided were equal. The *Plessy* case became the landmark case that established the doctrine of "separate but equal," which legalized Jim Crow in America.

"Separate but equal" was the law. Even though the doctrine specified that all facilities and accommodations were to be equal, generally the facilities for blacks were inherently unequal. The National Association for the Advancement of Colored People (NAACP), founded in 1909, tried from its beginning to destroy the constitutional doctrine that the *Plessy* case established. They gradually began to develop a plan for coordinating litigation to fight against Jim Crow laws. Unequal education systems provided the NAACP with the first cases it needed to challenge the *Plessy* decision. The fight to overturn the *Plessy* decision began the modern Civil Rights Movement.

Further Readings: Fairclough, Adam. *Race & Democracy: The Civil Rights Struggle in Louisiana, 1915–1972.* Athens: University of Georgia Press, 1995; Foner, Eric. *A Short History of Reconstruction 1863–1877.* New York: Harper & Row, 1984; Hirsch, Arnold R., and Joseph Logsdon, eds. *Creole New Orleans: Race and Americanization.* Baton Rouge: Louisiana State University Press, 1992; Medley, Keith Weldon. *We as Freemen: Plessy v. Ferguson.* Gretna, LA: Pelican Publishing Company, 2003.

Sharlene Sinegal DeCuir

Lowery, Joseph (b. 1924)

A confidante of **Martin Luther King, Jr.**, and prominent pastor in the **Southern Christian Leadership Conference**, Joseph Echols Lowery played a key role in the peak years of the **Civil Rights Movement** in **Alabama**. He was born in Huntsville, Alabama, in 1924, and spent part of his youth in Chicago. He attended Knoxville College and Alabama A&M College in the late from 1939 to 1942. Lowery was an avid student of divinity and Christianity, studying theology at Paine Theological Seminary in Augusta, **Georgia**, and the Chicago Ecumenical Institute. In 1952, he was ordained as a pastor in the United Methodist Church, a denomination that partnered with thriving African American congregations since the nineteenth century. As pastor of the Warren Street Methodist Church of Mobile, Lowery used his position to advance a program of social justice and civil rights for African Americans in the South.

Alabama stood as one of the most racially divided states in the South, as nearly every aspect of life, including public accommodations, cemeteries, political parties, and education, were strictly segregated. After the *Brown v. Board of Education* decision, political leaders in Alabama had pledged to resist desegregation for as long as they could. Despite the ruling, throughout Alabama, blacks were routinely threatened with violence or were victimized by police action for challenging **Jim Crow**.

In 1957, Lowery was asked to join Martin Luther King, Jr. and **Ralph Abernathy** in the founding of the Southern Christian Leadership Conference (SCLC). Based in Alabama, Lowery served as the vice president of the organization, and his leadership was vital to its early success. Lowery and Abernathy knew the political landscape better than most black preachers, as they had been born, raised, educated, and lived in the state for much of their lives. Lowery helped the SCLC navigate the most contentious aspects of Jim Crow in Alabama, understanding that some cities and constituencies were more open to nonviolent civil action than others. Lowery's public role as the vice president of the SCLC led to the consolidation of political power in black congregations, direct challenges to diffident white ministers, petitions to the city governments of Montgomery and Birmingham, and the long-term organization of the nonviolent protests of black residents of the state.

Lowery's leadership in the SCLC also put him at considerable risk of retaliation from the white institutions he challenged. Most notably, Lowery and three other preachers, Abernathy, Fred Shuttlesworth, and S. S. Seay, were the defendants in a lawsuit initiated by the attorney general of the state of Alabama in 1962. At issue was an advertisement appearing in the *New York Times* urging readers to donate to the Martin Luther King Legal Defense Fund in April 1962. The city government of Montgomery claimed that the four preachers, whose names appeared in the margins of the ad, had libeled the city for targeting King with racist intentions. In a landmark case, *Sullivan v. New York Times* (1964), Lowery and the other ministers were vindicated by the **U.S. Supreme Court**, which had overturned an earlier ruling for the plaintiff, Police Commissioner L. B. Sullivan. Though the original judgment was upheld by the Alabama State Court, the Supreme Court found that the ruling violated the free speech rights of the four ministers and the First Amendment rights of the *New York Times*. The state of Alabama returned to Lowery all of his personal assets and property, which totaled nearly $100,000.

His position in the SCLC provided critical moral and logistic support to the Birmingham campaign in 1963 and the Selma marches in 1965. In order to expose the injustice of segregation in Birmingham, Lowery was joined by Shuttlesworth, E. D. Nixon, King, and other prominent ministers in the SCLC, who made the crucial decision to launch Project C, the Children's Crusade, in the spring of 1963. Project C organized African American youth for nonviolent marches challenging the segregation in Birmingham. With segregation viciously enforced by Sheriff **"Bull" Connor**, the nationally broadcast images of police dogs and water canons turned on teenagers were critical to public condemnation and Birmingham's eventual capitulation to the desegregation efforts.

In 1965, Lowery moved to Birmingham, where he served as the pastor for the St. Paul's Methodist Church and an organizer in the Alabama Christian Movement for Human Rights. He then moved to Atlanta in 1968, and for the next 18 years, he was the head pastor at the Central Methodist Church, a predominantly black congregation whose donations raised enough funds to establish its own housing complex for low-income residents. After a divisive battle over the aims and future development of the SCLC, in 1977, Lowery became the president of the organization. With Lowery as its leader, the SCLC confronted ongoing problems left in the wake of Jim Crow, such as lackluster interest in voting, economic disempowerment, and Apartheid.

Lowery has maintained his steady commitment to civil rights and social justice issues. He founded the Lowery Center for Justice and Human Rights at Clark Atlanta University. He maintains a rigorous schedule as a lecturer and activist in Atlanta. *See also* Preachers.

Further Readings: Branch, Taylor. *Parting the Waters: America in the King Years, 1954–1963.* New York: Simon and Schuster, 1988; Fairclough, Adam. *To Redeem the Soul of America: The Southern Christian Leadership Conference and Martin Luther King, Jr.* Athens: University of Georgia Press, 1987; Russell, Thaddeus. "Joseph Lowery." In *Encyclopedia of African-American Culture and History,* 1344–45. Detroit, MI: Thomson Gale, 2006; Lowery Institute for Justice and Human Rights. http://www.loweryinstitute.org (accessed May 24, 2008).

Nikki Brown

Lucy, Autherine (b. 1929)

Autherine Lucy was the first African American to attend the University of **Alabama**. Born in October 1929 and raised in Shiloh, Alabama, Autherine Juanita Lucy was the youngest of 10 children born to Minnie Maud Hosea and Milton Cornelius Lucy. The Lucy family resided on a 110-acre farm in Shiloh, and escaped much of the desperation of the **Great Depression** by raising cotton, watermelons, and sweet potatoes. Lucy attended public school in the Shiloh area, and graduated from high school shortly after **World War II**. She continued her education at two historically black institutions, Selma University and Miles College. She graduated from Miles College in 1952 with a BA in English. Lucy's tremendous feat of desegregating university education in Alabama began when she decided to pursue another BA in 1952, in library science.

She applied in 1952, with her friend from Miles College, Pollie Myers, a student and civil rights activist. The University of Alabama initially accepted the two women for admission, apparently without realizing they were African American. The University of Alabama, however, maintained a policy of rejecting the applications of African Americans solely on the basis of race. When the university realized its mistake, under pressure from the Alabama **White Citizens Council**, it withdrew its offer of admission. Lucy and Myers approached the National Association for the Advancement of Colored People (NAACP) with their case, and they were assigned its top attorneys, **Thurgood Marshall**, **Constance Baker Motley**, and Arthur Shores. The NAACP team sued the university, and three years later, Judge Harlan Hobart Grooms of the federal District Court ruled on *Myers and Lucy v. Adams* (1955) in favor of the plaintiffs. It was just two months after the **U.S. Supreme Court** desegregated public schools in the ***Brown v. Board of Education*** decision. The University of Alabama reinstated its acceptance to Lucy, but denied admission to Myers. Lucy enrolled in February 1956.

However, Lucy's matriculation at the University of Alabama was not the end of her journey. Indeed, the most troubling part of her experience lay ahead when she began attending classes. The University of Alabama gave her little help in securing room, board, and books. White students resented her presence in the classroom, while hate groups and white supremacists phoned in bomb threats and burned crosses on the university campus and on her attorney's lawn. In some of her classes, the other students were also of little help. Some declined to sit next to her, and angry mobs of students followed her to her class. In other classes, such as children's literature, she was politely, and sometimes warmly, greeted by fellow students. Eager to chronicle the story, reporters and photographers also trailed Lucy, adding to the chaotic atmosphere. Lucy's first day had ended without serious incident, but trouble mounted, as parents, students, and groups not associated with the university grew increasingly hostile.

On February 6, Lucy's third day as a student, she required a full-time police escort to walk her to and from classes. After each class, a violent and angry mob awaited her, throwing rotten eggs and gravel at her. One mob chanted, "Let's kill her!" Another mob vowed to lynch her to "Keep 'Bama white!" Fueled by the **Ku Klux Klan** and other hate groups, crowds swelled across the campus, threatening Lucy's education at the school and, eventually, her life.

The University of Alabama suspended Lucy on the evening of February 6, for her protection and for the protection of the other students. On February 29, the NAACP filed a lawsuit against the University of Alabama, arguing that the university had not shielded Lucy from danger. In effect, the lawsuit claimed that the university acted in collusion with the mobs to drive Lucy out of the school. The NAACP was unable to prove its case and later withdrew the lawsuit. In retaliation, the university expelled Lucy for slander. Though the NAACP could have contested the decision, the entire episode exhausted Lucy, and she declined to pursue it. In March 1956, her attorney, Thurgood Marshall, invited Lucy to stay with his family in New York to recover from the ordeal.

Lucy married Hugh Foster in April 1956, and moved with him to **Texas**. In the first year of their marriage, she remained active in the **Civil Rights Movement**; she traveled the country and frequently lectured about her time as a student at the University of Alabama. She was unable, however, to find a teaching position for many years. Her family settled first in Texas, but they later moved to **Louisiana** and then **Mississippi**. In 1974, Lucy Foster, her husband, and her five children relocated to Birmingham, Alabama, where she worked as a substitute teacher.

Her fortunes took a surprising turn in early 1988. Invited to speak at the University of Alabama about her experience 35 years earlier, Lucy was asked afterward whether she would ever pursue her education again at the university. She answered that she would consider it, but the expulsion on her record had virtually nullified the possibility. An emergency petition to the university, then the Board of Trustees, resulted in the overturning of her expulsion in spring 1988. She entered the University of Alabama in fall 1989 as a graduate student in elementary education. In May 1992, Lucy graduated with an MA in elementary education; she was joined in the commencement ceremonies by her daughter, Grazia Foster, who earned a BA in corporate finance.

The University of Alabama named an endowed professorship in honor of Lucy, and a portrait is on display at the Ferguson Center, the student union of the university. The 40 years between Lucy's initial enrollment and her eventual graduation signify two important themes in **Jim Crow**: the tremendous courage of ordinary citizens who challenged institutionalized racism, and the time it takes to rectify the damages caused by decades of Jim Crow.

See also Historically Black Colleges and Universities; NAACP Legal Defense and Education Fund.

Further Readings: Clark, E. Culpepper. *The Schoolhouse Door, Segregation's Last Stand at the University of Alabama.* New York: Oxford University Press, 1995; Carter, Dan T. *The Politics of Rage: George Wallace, the Origins of the New Conservatism, and the Transformation of American Politics.* Baton Rouge: Louisiana State University Press, 2000.

Nikki Brown

Lynching

Scope

Mark Twain (1835–1910), the prolific writer and observer of American life and culture, once sarcastically noted that America had become the "United

Men preparing to lynch African American man, 1920s. Courtesy of Library of Congress, LC-USZ62-35741.

States of Lyncherdom" and other social commentators observed that "America's national crime was lynching." Lynchings were extralegal murders carried out by a mob or a group of vigilantes. It functioned to summarily and severely execute individuals accused of heinous crimes. Depending upon the period and region, individuals were lynched for both trivial and serious allegations, such as whistling or sexual assault.

Historians have been extremely skeptical of any attempt to define, reconstruct, or accurately measure the scope of lynching given the geographical, racial, and ethnic variations. For example, black Southerners were lynched for almost 100 offenses; however, on the whole, Southern lynch mobs primarily lynched blacks suspected of murder or rape. While lynching served to punish particular criminals and crimes, it also functioned as a kind of mass communication in which the objective was to produce and enforce social conformity with respect to racial hierarchy, social status, and gender norms. Lynching constituted state- and community-sanctioned violence for which federal, state, and local governments and courts rarely prosecuted the individuals involved, and even those prosecutions seldom resulted in fines or prison sentences. Lynch mobs and vigilante groups murdered with impunity because lynching occurred within a culture of violence that embraced popular conceptions of repressive violence.

Lynching in the United States has a long and tragic history. Lynch mobs expeditiously executed alleged criminals and perceived social deviants from the colonial period (1619–1781) through the Civil Rights era (1955–1975). While present throughout all periods of American history, lynching occurred sporadically prior to the American Civil War (1860–1865). In post–Civil War America, lynching increased dramatically, so that by the end of the nineteenth century, it had engulfed virtually every region in the nation. Between 1882 and 1930, approximately 4,760 men, women, and children fell pray to lynch mobs. No individual or group was entirely safe from lynching. White Americans, Mexicans, Chinese, Italians, and other racial-ethnic groups were all victims of lynching.

Lynching was indeed a national crime, but it was also a Southern hysteria that targeted African Americans, who represented approximately 70 percent of all lynching victims. Lynching was so pervasive and commonplace in the South that ten Deep South and Border South lynched more individuals than all other states and regions combined. During the peak of Southern lynching (1882–1930), approximately 2,800 Southerners perished as a result of lynch mobs, accounting for nearly 60 percent of all lynching victims in the United States. Moreover, Southern lynching stretched far beyond punishing particular individuals for heinous crimes and became a systematic and constitutive component within **Jim Crow** segregation—an expansive system of racial subordination and oppression.

Between 1882 and 1930, African Americans constituted 94 percent of lynching victims. Lynching came to symbolize black oppression within the system of American race relations. Regardless of region, lynch mobs desired to swiftly and brutally punish individuals who violated seemingly sacred community norms and provided a mechanism by which communities could collectively participate in apprehending and punishing criminals. In this way, lynching was as much a form of community-building as it was extralegal violence.

Geography

While lynching occurred in every region and period in American history, it was concentrated within particular subregions and social groups. Generally speaking, in the South, lynching functioned as an instrument for racial control and terror; however, depending upon the Southern subregion in which lynching occurred, African Americans perished "at the hands of persons unknown" at varying rates and for differing reasons. Southern lynching was concentrated and occurred most frequently within Black Belt counties, a contiguous cross section of several Deep South states (**Louisiana, Mississippi, Alabama,** and **Georgia**) with dense black populations, cotton monocultures, and plantation economies. The Southern agricultural elite employed lynching to exploit and manipulate black sharecroppers and tenant farmers, whereas lynching beyond Black Belt counties were generally targeted at African Americans who ostensible violated the labyrinth of racial taboos of Jim Crow etiquette. For instance, lynching in Louisiana and Georgia was most prevalent in their respective cotton-producing regions. Louisiana's cotton producing regions accounted for 60 percent of lynching incidents in the state between the years 1878 and 1946. Between the years 1880 and 1930, 458 lynchings occurred in Georgia, of which 84 percent were concentrated in Georgia's Cotton Belt region. White planters did not always resort to mob violence to punish unruly black workers, particularly when racial demographics did not work in their favor. Within Louisiana's black-dominated Mississippi River Delta parishes, white elites employed state-sanctioned executions because they believed African Americans' numerical superiority made the outcome of lynching unpredictable. State-sanctioned executions took the form of legal trials in which African Americans were unable to offer testimony and were at the mercy of all-white jury pools who often were unconcerned with the rules of a fair trial. Extralegal executions could lead to widespread quitting, work stoppages, or even retaliatory violence. White planters believed sham trials with legal executions or imprisonment were the most effective means to control black labor. In plantation regions, where large numbers of blacks and whites labored as sharecroppers and tenant farmers, plantation elites less frequently employed lynching as a means to intimidate and control black laborers for fear of retaliation by blacks and the perceived threat of poor whites and blacks uniting against the wealthy plantation owners.

Lynching in the Northeast and Mid-Atlantic states was virtually nonexistent and accounted for less than 10 percent of total U.S. lynching incidents. The relative small number of lynchings in the Northeast can be mostly attributed to a civic culture that respected the rule of law. Although lynching was relatively scarce in the Northeast and Mid-Atlantic regions, lynchings could eerily resemble those in the South. For instance, in 1911, Zachariah Walker, a black steel worker, was burned alive in Coatesville, Pennsylvania, for murdering a white man. It is estimated that 5,000 men and women witnessed the spectacle and, in the lynching's aftermath, several onlookers mutilated Walker's body, including taking his fingers and bones as souvenirs. Between 1882 and 1930, only 41 individuals were lynched in the Northeast and Mid-Atlantic states. The vast majority of persons lynched, though, were African Americans such as Walker, who accounted for roughly 87 percent of lynching victims in both the regions. Of the 41 lynching victims, 30 lynchings occurred within Maryland, and the state with the next highest total (Pennsylvania) had only six total lynchings.

In contrast to the Northeast, Midwestern and Western lynching activity was much more prevalent and more evenly distributed throughout the region. For instance, between the years 1882 and 1930, 588 lynchings occurred within the Midwest, for which Oklahoma (160 lynchings), Missouri (116), Nebraska (60), Indiana (52), and Kansas (52) had the highest number of lynching incidents. In addition, Western lynch mobs killed 415 individuals, and at least seven out of 10 Western states had in excess of 30 mob murders during the height of the lynching epidemic. Unlike Southern lynch mobs, Midwestern and Western lynch mobs primarily lynched whites, who constituted roughly 67 percent of lynchings in the Midwest and 93 percent in the Western United States. Lynching was never entirely utilized for the purpose of controlling a particular ethnic or racial group, but rather to punish individual acts of social deviance such as horse theft, counterfeiting, murder, and rape. In addition, Midwestern and Western lynching was more concentrated in rural areas. For instance, lynching occurred more frequently in rural southern Iowa than the urban centers of northern Iowa because of the lack of influence of capitalist culture and the relative weakness of legal institutions.

Typology of Lynch Mobs

Lynchings were cultural performances that legitimated the values of mob participants and translated its cultural significance through social rituals or patterned practices designed to broadcast their message. However, the form and content of lynching varied significantly and impacted its overall meaning. The key differences between lynch mobs were their organization, planning, longevity, and the extent to which they engaged in ceremonialism or lynching rituals. Private mobs, terrorist mobs, posses, and mass mobs represent the four persistent patterns of mob behavior.

Private and terrorist mobs were composed of 50 or fewer individuals and were most prevalent in Western and Midwestern lynching. Private mobs murdered 75 percent of lynching victims in California, 63 percent of lynching victims in Iowa, 61 percent of lynching victims in Washington State, and 44 percent of lynch victims in Wyoming. In the South, private mobs claimed the lives of less than half of all lynching victims. For instance, in Georgia, private mobs accounted for 30 percent of lynching victims and 46 percent of lynching victims in Virginia. In addition, private mobs were organized several days or even weeks after an alleged crime occurred. They usually became disillusioned with the legal system and the broader community's failure to lynch an alleged criminal, and consequently they used their anger and disappointment as impetus for their organization. Private mobs were usually comprised of friends and family members of the victim, and their participation was motivated by their desire to exact revenge due to their sense of collective loss. Since private mobs generally did not seek community support, the lynching was carefully premeditated, secretive, and less preoccupied with ritualism associated with other lynchings. Despite private mobs' penchant for premeditation and secrecy, their vengeance killings were usually discovered; however, very few private mobs were ever prosecuted or received jail sentences. Similar to private mobs, terrorist mobs operated clandestinely and rarely gained community support for lynching. Extensive or broad-based community support guaranteed personal anonymity for mob participants and immunity from criminal prosecution. When private and terrorist mobs believed community support was negligible, they wore masks in order to conceal their identities. Unlike private mobs, terrorist mobs did not disband after an accomplished lynching. Rather, their modus operandi was to use lynching as a means of achieving a broader social agenda. The **Ku Klux Klan,** arguably the most famous and long-lived terrorist organization, is one example of a terrorist mob that used lynching and other forms of repressive violence. While these groups and organizations boasted hundreds or even thousands of members, the impact upon lynching was fairly minimal. In the South, terrorist mobs were responsible for 59 of 460 lynchings in Georgia and only 3 of 86 lynchings in Virginia between the years 1880 and 1930.

Posses and mass mobs usually received the broadest community support. Unlike private mobs and terrorist mobs, posses had quasi-legal status and operated with near immunity. In most communities, posses were respected and viewed as heroes because they were central to apprehending and punishing dangerous criminals. Often, they had the support of local elected officials, including the sheriff and mayor as well as community leaders. Mass mobs occurred most frequently during the 1880s and 1890s and consisted of hundreds or even thousands of participants and spectators. White men dominated leadership positions within mass mobs, while women and children often occupied supporting roles, such as cheering and gathering rope used in the lynching. Despite their sheer size, mass mobs often displayed sophisticated organization, planning, and ritualism. During the zenith of mass mob activity in the American South, it was routine for mob leaders to advertise an impending lynching so as to guarantee a "festival of violence." Furthermore, mob leaders orchestrated these large gatherings with the intention of demonstrating the lynching's cultural significance as well as the community's collective support. Mass mobs encompassed 34 percent of lynchings in Georgia and

40 percent of lynchings in Virginia. Southern mass mobs were usually reserved for African Americans who were accused of rape or murder of white men, women, and children. These lynchings placed a premium upon performing racial domination, humiliation, and eliciting excruciating pain. Typical ritual aspects of Southern mass mobs included taking the lynching victim to the scene of the crime, forcing them to confess or pray for forgiveness, mutilating their body parts, and burning the lynching victim's corpse. Individuals who evaded or resisted capture were often pursed by mobs. Posses killed 11 percent of lynching victims in Louisiana, 51 lynching victims in Georgia, and 31 persons in Virginia. Importantly, the families of accused individuals were also subjected to threats and violence as mobs pursed the accused.

Lynching and Identity

If lynchings were indeed cultural performances that legitimated the values of mob participants, sexuality, race, class, and gender identity were cornerstones of those cultural performances. Lynch mobs were organized and carried out by men who believed lynching was an honorable masculine duty that demonstrated their mastery over inferior men and by extension the home, the workplace, and community institutions. Lynching as a ritual of masculine domination and authority was at its root a critique of the legal system and its inability to effectively dramatize or perform collective notions of crime, punishment, and justice. In the Midwest, West, and South, proponents of lynching espoused a "rough justice" ethos that embraced and valorized extralegal vigilantism and violence. Rough justice advocates favored lynching because the legal system seemed remote, abstract, and ineffective in punishing criminal behavior. They tended to emanate from rural working-class communities in the West, Midwest, and South, and in many cases, working-class social ties facilitated lynchings.

While Midwestern, Western, and Southern lynch mobs were informed by a working class "rough justice" ethos, racial, gender, and sexual cultural scripts more heavily influenced Southern lynch mobs. Southern lynchings were often gendered performances that criss-crossed racial lines. With respect to black Southerners, the ritual of lynching served as a dramatization of unequal racial and gender power relationships. Through lynching, white lynch mobs asserted and enforced white masculine dominance. It confirmed for white men their right to emasculate black men by demonstrating their impotence as public citizens. Black women were also targets as white men employed sexual violence against black women as a means to demonstrate black men's inability to protect black women and their combined racial and masculine authority over black men as patriarchs. Lynching's ability to efficiently communicate racial and gender subordination constituted "lynching's double message."

Racial and gender mythologies structured rationalizations for lynching black men and sexual violence against black women. In the Southern racist imagination, black women were viewed as naturally sexually promiscuous, and therefore sexual relationships between white men and black women were always consensual. Moreover, lynching apologists persistently trumpeted black men as lustful and sex-crazed rapists who only desired to rape virginal white women. The black male rapist syndrome represented an "emotional logic of lynching," which meant that only swift and sure violence, unhampered by legalities, could protect white women from sexual assault. Some lynching proponents so vehemently believed black men were innate rapists that they suggested black genocide! Even though Southern whites tirelessly clung to the rape myth as the basis for lynching, contemporary scholarship has overwhelming demonstrated that murder rather than rape was the most frequent accusation for lynching black men and women. *See also* Costigan-Wagner Anti-Lynching Bill; Till, Emmett, and Mamie Till Mobley.

Further Readings: Brundage, W. F. *Lynching in the New South: Georgia and Virginia, 1880–1930.* Urbana: University of Illinois Press, 1993; Dray, Philip. *At the Hands of Persons Unknown: The Lynching of Black America.* New York: Random House, 2002; Hall, Jacqueline D. "The Mind That Burns in Each Body": Women, Rape, and Racial Violence. *Southern Exposure* 12 (1984): 61–71; Hall, Jacqueline D. *Revolt Against Chivalry: Jesse Daniel Ames and the Women's Campaign Against Lynching.* New York: Columbia University Press, 1979; Pfeifer, Michael J. *Rough Justice: Lynching and American Society, 1874–1947.* Urbana: University of Illinois Press, 2004; Tolnay, Stewart E., and Beck, E. M. *A Festival of Violence: An Analysis of Southern Lynchings, 1882–1930.* Urbana: University of Illinois Press, 1995.

Karlos K. Hill

M

Malcolm X (1925–1965)

Malcolm X, or El-Hajj Malik El-Shabazz, was the charismatic religious leader, a relentless activist for black liberation, a brutally honest public speaker, a social scientist, an international revolutionary, and an unequivocal cultural icon during the mid-twentieth century of the United States. He ascended to prominence through his public speaking appointment with the **Nation of Islam** (NOI, or "The Nation"), the heterodox religious black nationalist/separatist North American organization, during the mid 1950s and early 1960s. He traveled the nation, and the globe, speaking on behalf of the NOI, and its spiritual leader, Elijah Muhammad (d. 1973), while critiquing the remnants of white supremacy, questioning "Civil Rights," and advocating black self-defense. Along with speaking to ethnically mixed audiences in public forums, Malcolm participated in countless interviews and debates, which appeared on numerous popular **television** programs and in print media, such as newspapers and magazines, at the time. His oratory abilities affected reputed his notoriety, though his eloquence and terse way of speaking did not translate into prolific writing. Indeed, Malcolm was not known as an author, but he was very involved in the publication of the once-popular NOI newspaper, *Muhammad Speaks*.

He was born Malcolm Little on May 19, 1925, in Omaha, Nebraska, to a Baptist minister, the Reverend Earl Little, and his wife, Louise Little, who were members of the "**Universal Negro Improvement Association** and African Communities League" (UNIA). The organization was founded in the early twentieth century by the provocateur of rights for all people of African descent in the United States, **Marcus Garvey**. The seventh child of 10, Malcolm spend his early life growing up in foster homes, and with family members, after the murder of his father at the hands of the local **Ku Klux Klan**. Subsequently, Louise was institutionalized years later on the diagnosis of insanity.

Once older, he worked menial jobs amidst traveling between to Lansing, Michigan, Boston, Massachusetts, and New York City during the early 1940s, but was eventually lured by the desire for bigger profits through criminal means in the street life of the big city. Influenced by lack of opportunity sanctioned by a Northern version of Jim Crow, and the survivalist mentality born from a environment of criminality, Malcolm experimented with peddling dope, larceny, running numbers (gambling), and *pimpin'* (procuring prostitution). Consequently, he was arrested in 1946, and served a brief period of imprisonment as a young adult. While serving an eight-year prison term for larceny and burglary, Malcolm was introduced by his brother Reginald to the teachings of Elijah Muhammad.

The NOI, or the "Black Muslims" as the press called them, was an organization founded in Chicago during the **Great Depression** of the 1930s by Elijah Poole. He was taught "Islam" and the "legacy" of blacks by a mysterious man, Wallace D. Fard, who appeared in the Chicago slums. Fard was a silk peddler who claimed to be a messenger of God from the East, and would "convert" would-be followers to **Islam** for a nominal fee. However, when law enforcement officers began to question neighborhood inhabitants for information on Fard, he fled. Poole, who was a staunch believer in Fard's rhetoric, recognized an opportunity, and developed a palatable theology for the growing numbers of uneducated former Christian-turned-Muslim followers. Now as Elijah Muhammad, he began to spread the message to blacks that Fard was God incarnate, and that he was to be considered God's (Fard) prophet. Thus, the then "Lost-Found Nation of Islam in the American Wilderness" was founded, which was essentially an amalgamation of three other preceding movements: Marcus Garvey's Pan-Africanism, Noble Drew Ali's Moorish Science Temple, and, to a lesser extent, the Ahmadiyyah Movement. The confluence of these three movements was important, because they served as "pillars" for the NOI's religious-based **Black Nationalism**. For example, the Moorish Science Temple was more religious than political in its ideologies, while Garvey's program through UNIA was strictly political. A considerable number of followers from both organizations were among those who joined the NOI at its inception during the 1930s. Both organizations, and their leaders in particular, prioritized agendas for "escape" from the "implications of being black in a white-dominated society."

Noble Drew Ali founded the Moorish Science Temple of America, which was a sect of Islam influenced by Buddhism, Christianity, and the Freemasons. The Moors, as they were often called, maintained the reactionary ideology that whites were naturally demonic, and expressed the only way for minority salvation was through conversion to Islam. Drew Ali decided to change the mental condition of blacks by introducing a new nomenclature of Arabic names and new cultural symbols such as "Nationality and Identification" cards for his followers—i.e., Black Moors—while Garvey believed in secession in, or complete emigration, from predominately white America.

The Ahmadiyyah Movement came to the United States during the late nineteenth century from the Punjabi region of British-ruled India, and was led by spiritual leader and Indian Muslim Mirza Ghulam Ahmad. As a studious young man, Ahmad was convinced he was a prophet and a messiah sent to earth to receive and disseminate, what he believed to be, revelations from God. This claim drew tremendous criticism from orthodox Punjabi Muslims, who believed that the descention of revelation was completed when the final verses of the Holy Qur'an came down from Heaven to the Arab prophet, Muhammad ibn Abdullah, during the later years of his life in seventh-century Arabia. Thus, Ghulam Ahmad and his followers, who would later spread their teachings to America's shores, were violently persecuted for their heretical beliefs.

The introduction to the NOI was pivotal in young Malcolm's life considering the context of the United States at the time. Affronted with a system that infringed on their inclusion in cultural and political participation within America, historically blacks had found solace in the Christian church. The black church was a refuge from the misery of white racism, a cornerstone of any black community, and a crucial, relatively safe haven for public discussion. And as Malcolm would often point out through his later speeches, what was surprising to him was that Christianity was a religion given to blacks by their enslavers, and yet they clung to it tightly.

The dilemma was that in the church, some black Americans discovered an equivalent difficulty to challenge oppression in American Christianity, because it remained dominated by a similar white supremacy to that of the secular society. Thus, in a race-conscious society in which blacks were disproportionately imprisoned, openly discriminated against by Jim Crow laws in the Southern, as well as Northern states, unprotected by a biased legal system, collectively held the least amount of property, and terrorized by the Ku Klux Klan with the constant threat of death, American Christianity's appeal as the path to liberation was contested.

Growing weary of the treatment they received from their Christian brethren, some black Christians debated whether Christianity was a source of liberation or oppression for their peoples. Few black Americans decided to challenge the white supremacy in Christianity from within, while others "took a leap of faith," and left Christianity completely. As other black Americans before him sought an alternative path to cultural and political equity, the teachings offered by the NOI ignited something in Malcolm, and served as a catalyst for his program of self-education on subjects, such as world and U.S. histories, literature, and philosophy.

Once released from prison on early parole in 1953, Malcolm began to attend NOI temples and, shortly after, was given responsibility as a minister under the guidance, and personal attention, of Elijah Muhammad. After spending time in NOI temples in New York City, Philadelphia, and Chicago, Malcolm later ascended to the position of national representative for the NOI from the late 1950s until 1963, which allowed him to further the organization's black separatist rhetoric. Through the heterodox interpretation of the religion of Islam, blacks sought out an alternative cultural and religious experience not to become honorary Arabs or whites, but truer, more authentic black men and women. The author of the seminal book, *Black Muslims in America*, C. Eric Lincoln, had the opportunity to conduct firsthand research on the Nation during the height of its popularity, and conducted personal interviews with Elijah Muhammad and Malcolm. Lincoln wrote that the NOI espoused ideas such as self-reliance, economic empowerment, and high morality, and was an exemplar of black social protest for social change. Malcolm, with the teachings of Elijah Muhammad, and the NOI as his base, exemplified these characteristics.

Further, the NOI promoted ideas such as: "getting equality now instead of salvation in heaven later"; prohibition of consuming harmful food products, e.g., pork, alcohol, cigarettes, and other narcotics; refrain from gambling; chastity, responsibility, and honesty, which were all the ills that plagued the black community. Additionally, the NOI offered a discourse of black superiority to challenge white supremacy, and they firmly believed that Islam was the natural religion of black people.

Along with the rather docile empowerment concepts, there were two theories that distinguished Malcolm and the NOI. One of the most disturbing theories asserted by Malcolm was the race-tinged generalization of white Americans based on the world history that all white peoples were "devils," as taught to Elijah Muhammad by his teacher, W. D. Fard. The second was their call for a separate area in North America for blacks, because they rejected the idea of integration as a ploy to re-subjugate blacks. This was a departure from the ideas of Garvey's **Back to Africa Movement**, and was an obvious break from orthodox Islam's historical tradition of leaving a home to establish a society that would abide by justice, or egalitarian principles not available. Due to the persecution they experienced in their home city of Makkah (Mecca), Allah (God) commanded His believers through the Prophet of Islam, Muhammad, to establish a truly Muslim community in Madinah in 622 CE.

In a move to emulate tradition, the NOI prioritized connecting Black Muslims in the West to the broader Muslim world community. Their slant was that they emphasized "brownness" of the larger community, who had been, in most cases, oppressed like blacks on the North American continent. In a constructed prophesy, Elijah Muhammad "foretold" of America's destruction for its treatment of the darker humankind. Likewise, he tried to make the case for black non-Muslims to see their condition in America as a microcosmic representation of what was happening globally wherever the "white man" went. Earlier, Muhammad even admonished his followers to not fight against Japanese military forces in **World War II**, because they were victims of white racism also.

Continuing this rationale, the analysis of the political infrastructure of the United States' government by the NOI, and Malcolm in particular, was a lucid interrogation of U.S. history, U.S. domestic policies, and the claim of democracy in the United States for its citizens. Malcolm, in his eloquent manner of oration, took the government to task, delivering now infamous speeches, such as "The Message toe the Grassroots," "A Declaration of Independence," "The Ballot or the Bullet," and "The Black Revolution." Through his words, whether speaking to audiences in Detroit, Harlem, Cleveland, or London, Malcolm also questioned the intellectual coherence of blacks who desired to be in the political establishment, and spoke suspiciously of the loyalty of white liberals.

In terms of political philosophy, he considered Democrats to be identical to Republicans in that they supported the white supremacist infrastructure. It made no difference whether the discussion was on the Northern or the Southern states, because where the North provided more economic opportunities, there was unemployment and disparate housing. Alternatively, in the South, blacks faced those conditions in addition to threats of being terrorized by the Ku Klux Klan, or even lynched, or murdered, for no serious reasons. Being a critic of the altruistic tactics of protesting nonviolently, Malcolm advocated the constitutional right to bear arms for all blacks in the United States as a means to protect their bodies, families, and communities where the government had failed to do so.

For these reasons, Malcolm argued that Democrats, or as he called them, "Dixiecrats," were most often "Southern" in political orientation, and not really friends of blacks. In numerous speeches, he directly referenced the absence of voting rights for Southern blacks as an abomination to democracy, being that the **Civil Rights Act** had been signed in 1957. Malcolm continuously emphasized being aware of the words by white liberals (Dixiecrats) in Washington, D.C., and the actions of the Republicans and their constituents in the Southern states, because white liberals kept blacks disenfranchised with no hope of casting votes in the best interest of themselves. As the **March on Washington** took place in 1963 where **Martin Luther King, Jr.,** gave the famous "I Have a Dream" speech, Malcolm only witnessed a ploy to appease the frustrated blacks around the country with no real gains.

In early 1964, he left the NOI after being silenced for making unauthorized comments about the assassination of President **John F. Kennedy**, and over confirmed reports that the person who saved his life, his father-like figure, Elijah Muhammad, had fathered several children with young secretaries within the Nation. He formed a new organization, Muslim Mosque, Inc., in Harlem, New York City, to support the smaller Muslim community outside of the Nation of Islam. In the spring of 1964, through the financial generosity of his sister Ella, he traveled to Makkah, Saudi Arabia to perform the *hajj* (the required pilgrimage of all orthodox Muslims). Also on this extended trip, he was able to make contacts in foreign countries such as Egypt, Morocco, Algeria, Nigeria, Ghana, and Lebanon.

While on hajj, Malcolm was struck by the sense of "brotherhood" he experienced, as he witnessed no racial divisions among men and women, but saw only a unity of being for the worship of Allah (God). By observing, and sharing quarters with white European Muslims, Malcolm, now identifying himself as Malik El-Shabazz, concluded that the race problems of the United States could be, potentially, solved by Christian, white America's conversion to Islam. Additionally, the experience of hajj solidified his decision to increase the call for Black Nationalism in black communities in the United States, and to replace efforts for civil rights with a more internationalized consciousness towards human rights for blacks.

Through the contacts he made on his extended trip abroad, Malcolm felt certain that with a Pan-Africanist perspective, his people in the United States could receive more support from partners within United Nations if the focus was on obtaining human rights instead of civil rights. Upon his return to the United States, he formed a new secular group, Organization of Afro-American Unity (OAAU), to complement Muslim Mosque, Inc., and address social, political, and economical issues facing the broader, disenfranchised, non-Muslim black community in the United States.

Malcolm would never see his plan materialize, as an unexplained chain of events began to happen in his life. He was attacked by assailants, was to be evicted from his family home by the NOI, and his house was under constant surveillance by the **FBI**. In early February 1965, Malcolm's family home was firebombed with Molotov cocktails thrown by assailants in the early morning hours as he, his wife, Betty Shabazz, and their four daughters slept. This was an obvious attempt on his life by assassins, though who was responsible for sending them was left to speculation. However, while giving a speech before an audience of supporters in the Audobon Ballroom in Harlem, New York City, assassins infiltrated the crowd, and fatally shot Malcolm several times. El-Hajj Malik El-Shabazz, posthumously called the "Black Prince" and "our manhood" by film actor, playwright, poet, activist, and friend, Ossie Davis at his funeral, died from those wounds on February 25, 1965.

Further Readings: Breitman, George. *Malcolm X Speaks.* New York: Grove Weidenfeld, 1990; Chapman, Mark. *Christianity on Trial: African-American Religious Thought Before and After Black Power.* New York: Orbis Books, 1996; Haley, Alex, and Malcolm X. *The Autobiography of Malcolm X: As Told to Alex Haley.* New York: Ballantine Books, 1964; Jackson, Sherman. *Islam and the Black American: Looking toward the Third Resurrection.* New York: Oxford University Press, 2005; Lincoln, C. Eric. *Black Muslims in America.* Boston: Beacon Press, 1961; Strum, Philippa, and Taratolo, Danielle, eds. *Muslims in the United States.* Washington, DC: Woodrow Wilson International Center for Scholars, 2003; Turner, Richard Brent. *Islam in the African American Experience.* Bloomington: Indiana University Press 1997.

Mika'il A. Petin

March on Washington Movement (1940–1941)

The origins of the March on Washington movement can be traced to a September 27, 1940, meeting between **A. Philip Randolph**, the president of the Brotherhood of Sleeping Car Porters; Walter White, head of the National Association for the Advancement of Colored People (NAACP); T. Arnold Hill of the Urban League; and President **Franklin D. Roosevelt**. Randolph urged Roosevelt to promote equal employment opportunities and to desegregate the armed services. When the meeting did not produce a positive response from Roosevelt, Randolph decided that he would bring the case directly to the American people by staging a march on Washington, DC.

African Americans had benefited less than other groups from **New Deal** programs during the **Great Depression**, and continuing racial discrimination was excluding them from the job opportunities in the defense industries that were expanding as the world plunged into the **World War II**. At a September 1940 union convention held at Madison Square Garden, Randolph discussed the problem of discrimination in the defense industry. Government training programs excluded blacks; defense contractors announced that they would not hire blacks or would only hire them for menial positions, and that despite the shortage of construction workers, contractors would not hire experienced blacks. During this time, the **armed forces** were segregated: in an army of half a million men, there were only 4,700 blacks. There were no blacks in the Marine Corps or the Army Air Corps, and even the Red Cross blood supply was segregated. In the audience the evening of Randolph's speech was First Lady **Eleanor Roosevelt**, who was going to speak to the convention the following evening. She learned from Randolph that the president's staff had refused to set up a meeting between Roosevelt and Randolph. Through her efforts, the September 27 meeting took place.

At the meeting, Randolph pointed out the discrimination in the defense industry; the refusal of skilled labor unions to admit blacks, and the discrimination in the armed forces. Roosevelt responded that progress was being made, although his secretary of the navy, Frank Knox (who also attended the meeting), asserted that it would be impossible to desegregate the navy. Roosevelt told the black leaders that he would consult his cabinet and military leadership and respond to their concerns. The response they received was not from the president, but was instead a statement by Roosevelt's press secretary, Stephen Early, who announced that the military would not be desegregated, and implied that the black leaders Roosevelt had met with agreed with decision. Randolph and the others publicly announced that this was not the case, and the requested another meeting with the president, which was not forthcoming.

This led to a change in tactics. Randolph had sought change through letter writings and meetings with government officials. He now believed direct action was essential, and started making public statements to this effect. Randolph, along with **Bayard Rustin**, the youth director of the Fellowship of Reconciliation, and A. J. Muste, the executive director of the Fellowship of Reconciliation, proposed a march on Washington to protest discrimination in government and the defense industry as well as segregation in the armed services. They established a March on Washington Committee (MOWC) to organize the march. Their slogan was: "We loyal Negro Americans demand the right to work and fight for our country." By late 1940, Randolph had established a National March on Washington Committee with chapters in 18 cities.

Randolph made his formal proposal in January 1941, and spent months gathering support for his plan and preparing for the march, which was scheduled for July 1, 1941. His union, the NAACP, the Urban League, and the black press played major roles in generating interest in the march. In "The Call to March," which appeared in the May 1941 issue of *The Black Worker*, he wrote that "[o]nly power can effect the enforcement and adoption of a given policy. Power is the active principle of only the organized masses, the masses united for a definite purpose."

Roosevelt, who had continued to refuse to meet with Randolph, became concerned about the political impact of the march, which had originally promised to bring more than 10,000 marchers to the nation's capital and had grown to where more than 100,000 marchers were expected. Randolph had indicated that all the marchers would be black, and Roosevelt feared that there might be violence, and that such a march would then become a precedent for other groups. Also, given the Roosevelt administration's opposition to the fascist regimes in Europe, a march by blacks against discrimination would be embarrassing to the country, which presented itself as a model of democracy. Also, Roosevelt was concerned about the reaction of Southern Democrats to such a march.

At the president's request, Eleanor Roosevelt wrote to Randolph asking him to call off the march. Randolph refused. Randolph then met with the first lady, who concluded that the only way to stop the march would be for the president to meet with Randolph. President Roosevelt met with Randolph and White on June 18, 1941, to urge him to call off the march. Roosevelt told them that the **armed forces** would remain segregated, but that he would consider an investigation of discrimination if the march was called off. Randolph's response to the president was that the march would be called off only if Roosevelt issued an executive order. Roosevelt agreed, and Randolph worked with Roosevelt's staff to draft the order.

On June 25, 1941, Roosevelt issued Executive Order 8802, which made discrimination based on race, creed, color, or national origin illegal in the defense industry, and establishing the **Fair Employment Practices Committee (FEPC)** to investigate charges of racial discrimination. This was the first executive order concerning the rights of African Americans since President Abraham Lincoln issued the Emancipation Proclamation during the Civil War. In response, Randolph announced in a radio address from Madison Square Garden on June 28, 1941, that he had agreed to suspend the march. In his speech, Randolph said that he had not cancelled the march, but had only suspended it. By leaving open the possibility of a march, Randolph asserted that this was the movement's "ace in the hole" to ensure that the government would not backtrack on its commitment.

The decision to suspend the march led Rustin, who believed that Randolph had "sold out" by not holding out for desegregation of the armed forces, to break (temporarily) with Randolph. In 1942, Rustin would help found the **Congress of Racial Equality (CORE)**.

While suspending the march, the effort continued. By December 1941, the MOWC had become a dues-paying organization in order "to help create faith by Negroes in Negroes." During 1942, the MOWC mounted rallies in New York, Chicago, and St. Louis. The goal of the organization was to mobilize African Americans into an effective pressure group. Nearly two million African Americans worked in the defense industries by the end of 1944. However, the FEPC did not effectively tackle discriminatory practices in the South, and following Roosevelt's death, the FEPC was abolished as Congress refused to fund the agency. It ceased operation in 1946. Randolph and Rustin would initiate the effort that would culminate in the **March on Washington of 1963**.

Further Readings: Garfinkel, Herbert. *When Negroes March: The March on Washington Movement in the Organizational Politics for FEPC.* Glencoe, IL: Free Press, 1959; Goodwin, Doris Kearns. *No Ordinary Time.* New York: Simon and Schuster, 1994; Pfeffer, Paula F. *A. Philip Randolph, Pioneer of the Civil Rights Movement.* Baton Rouge: Louisiana State University Press, 1990.

Jeffrey Kraus

March on Washington of 1963

The emotional high point of the first half of the **Civil Rights Movement**, the 1963 March on Washington for Jobs and Freedom brought together nearly 250,000 Americans to the nation's capital, all pledging their support of a transformation in race relations. It was a triumph in rhetoric, compassion, and civil rights, heralding the approaching demise of **Jim Crow**. The March on Washington also marked the end of the first, nonviolent stage of the modern Civil Rights Movement; the second half of the Civil Rights Movement, ranging from 1963 to 1970, took a decidedly more militant turn. The gathering of nearly 250,000 Americans also signaled to the administration of President **John F. Kennedy** that the time had come for the **federal government** to make its allegiance to the Civil Rights Movement plain.

The 1963 March on Washington was influenced by an earlier attempt to gather African Americans for protest in the nation's capital. Led by **A. Philip Randolph**, the 1941 March on Washington Movement was intended as a peaceful demonstration against the widespread problem of racial discrimination in defense work during **World War II**. Randolph, a well-respected labor leader and president of the Brotherhood of Sleeping Car Porters, had spoken directly with President **Franklin D. Roosevelt** about the problem of African American exclusion from lucrative employment in the defense industry, which provided aircraft and munitions for the war in Europe. When Roosevelt balked, saying that he could do nothing to prevent private contractors from employing whomever they chose, Randolph called on 10,000 blacks to stage a "March on Washington" and to use the slogan, "We Loyal Negro-American citizens demand the right to work and fight for our country." Roosevelt eventually gave into to some of Randolph's demands, and in June 1941, he created the **Fair Employment Practices Committee** to police the desegregation of defense industry in a presidential decree, Executive Order 8802.

In the years between the end of World War II and the 1963 March on Washington, several civil rights organizations had gained a considerable membership supporting their challenge of Jim Crow using nonviolent tactics. The National Association for the Advancement of Colored People (NAACP) and its **Legal Defense Fund** won several key **U.S. Supreme Court** decisions, including *Brown v. Board of Education*, that gravely wounded the institution of segregation. The **Southern Christian Leadership Conference (SCLC)** and the **Student Nonviolent Coordinating Committee (SNCC)** staged successful **sit-ins** and boycotts of cities, transportation systems, and department stores. The **Congress of Racial Equality (CORE)**, formed by peace activist **James Farmer**, led a series of Freedom Rides in the summer of 1961 that tested the application and enforcement of **desegregation** laws. The National Urban League's plan for economic growth and independence provided an avenue of support for African American businesses. Together, these five organizations coordinated a one-day mass movement that spoke to Randolph's vision of African American empowerment by way of peaceful, yet urgent protest.

The events of the spring and summer of 1963 also revealed the national urgency for an awareness of the vicious backlash to the Civil Rights Movement. In early 1963, **Martin Luther King, Jr.**, and SCLC went to Birmingham, leading boycotts of stores in downtown Birmingham and protest marches through the streets of the city. Though the demonstrations were peaceful, the televised images of African American children and adults attacked by police dogs and fire hoses, ordered by police chief **"Bull" Connor**, horrified the nation. In April, King and his confidant, **Ralph Abernathy**, were arrested and placed in solitary confinement in Birmingham; King used the time to write his moving polemic, "Letter from a Birmingham Jail." In May, the A. G.

Gaston Motel, the headquarters of the SCLC in Birmingham, and the home of King's brother, Alfred Daniel King, were bombed by the **Ku Klux Klan**. In June, **Medgar Evers**, executive secretary of the Mississippi NAACP, was shot and killed by Klan sympathizer Byron de la Beckwith. Just one day earlier, President Kennedy had proposed a strong civil rights bill that would have made such hate crimes federal offenses. Yet, the legislation was having difficulty garnering support in Congress, as the Southern bloc of the Democratic Party strongly resisted any usurpation of states' rights in favor of a federal mandate.

By the summer of 1963, the five main civil rights groups—the Urban League, SCLC, NAACP, SNCC, and CORE—had decided to pool their efforts and organized a March on Washington. A. Philip Randolph, in a nod to the march called off in 1941, inaugurated the march as the March on Washington for Jobs and Freedom. Randolph was joined by **Bayard Rustin** as chief organizers of the march. Rustin, a Quaker and a Freedom Rider for CORE, drew upon his wide network in peace activism to raise funds and awareness of the event. With a budget of $120,000, Rustin, the chief coordinator, collected donations from African American celebrities, churches, and business, as well as through selling buttons and posters for as little as 25 cents.

On the morning of August 28, 1963, hundreds of chartered buses from across the country arrived in front of the **Lincoln Memorial**. Marchers also traveled over thousands of miles by chartered train and cars. One group of CORE volunteers walked over 200 miles from New York to Washington, DC, to show their solidarity. Eventually, nearly 250,000 people crowded the national mall for the march, the largest political assembly in American history.

With 17 components of the program, the 1963 March on Washington unfolded over eight hours. Marian Anderson, who had once been denied the opportunity to sing at Constitution Hall, sung the national anthem. Randolph gave the opening remarks, and the program included a tribute to the struggles of African American civil rights workers **Daisy Lee Bates**, Diane Nash Bevel, **Rosa Parks**, Merlie Evers, and others. As president of SNCC, John Lewis denounced the passivity of the Kennedy administration in securing a civil rights bill. Gospel singer Mahalia Jackson sang "I've Been 'Buked and I've Been Scorned"; folk singers Bob Dylan and Joan Baez later joined Jackson on stage. Other speakers included Whitney Young, president of the National Urban League; Roy Wilkins, executive secretary of the national NAACP; Joachim Prinz, president of the American Jewish Congress; and James Farmer, national director of CORE.

The March on Washington is best remembered for King's "I Have a Dream" speech. King had delivered the speech as a sermon on several occasions in the early 1960s, but it was his experience in solitary confinement during the Birmingham campaign that honed the finer rhetorical points. In his earlier version of "I Have a Dream," King stressed a number of social justice issues of the period—a federal promise to supersede states' rights; prosecution of **police brutality**; the elimination of Jim Crow; and the passage of Kennedy's proposed civil rights legislation. These previous drafts were intended to nudge the national conscience into recognizing the debilitating effects of violent repression on the peaceful movement.

At midpoint in the speech, however, King abandoned the policy initiatives that had weighed down the language of the speech in favor of the passionate sermon that he delivered in churches and rallies across the South. Calling for freedom and equality, King's most famous words still resonate: "I have a dream that one day even that one day even the state of Mississippi, a desert state sweltering with the heat of injustice and oppression, will be transformed into an oasis of freedom and justice. I have a dream that my four little children will one day live in a nation where they will not be judged by the color of their skin but by the content of their character." By granting a vision and mission to the Civil Rights Movement beyond boycotts and sit-ins, King's language of hope and change ushered in a phase of clear-focused determination on the greater goals of social justice. The peaceful end to the march helped Kennedy win victory for a number of his social programs. The astounding success of the 1963 March on Washington, coupled with his steadfast support of nonviolence in the Civil Rights Movement, led to the conferral to King of the Nobel Peace Prize in 1964.

However, the success of the 1963 March on Washington did not spell an end to the violence. In September 1963, a bomb left at the Birmingham Baptist Church killed four African American girls, Addie Mae Collins, Denise McNair, Carole Robertson, and Cynthia Wesley. In November 1963, President Kennedy was shot and killed in Dallas while on a campaign stop. Assassinated before he could see his Civil Rights Bill reach fruition, Kennedy was followed by Lyndon B. Johnson, who made the passage of the **Civil Rights Act of 1964** a priority.

The 1963 March on Washington, ultimately, heralded the urgent need for a second **Reconstruction** for African Americans. It also served as a harbinger of hopefulness in the 1960s, before assassinations of political and spiritual leaders, the war in Vietnam, and the free speech movement lent the patina of turbulence. In front of a national audience, Americans across generations and racial lines pledged their support for the moral objectives of the Civil Rights Movement. As much a success for the entire nation as it was for the Civil Rights Movement, the 1963 March on Washington spelled the death of Jim Crow through peaceful, orderly, and steadfast affirmation.

Further Readings: Branch, Taylor. *Parting the Waters: America during the King Years, 1954–1963.* New York: Simon and Schuster, 1988; Branch, Taylor. *Pillar of Fire: America during the King Years, 1963–1965.* New York: Simon and Schuster, 1998; Carson, Clayborne, et al., eds. *The Eyes on the Prize: Civil Rights Reader: Documents, Speeches, and Firsthand Accounts from the Black Freedom Struggle.* New York: Penguin, 1991; Lewis, John. *Walking with the Wind: A Memoir of the Movement.* New York: Harvest Books, 1999.

Nikki Brown

Marriage, Interracial

Laws in many states made illegal the marriage between adults of different "races." Specifically, these laws were intended to prevent marriages between whites and nonwhites. State laws banning interracial marriages aimed to keep the "races" separate and identifiable, and sought to buttress white privilege, especially of sexual access to white females. Differences among the states in their laws regarding marriages between whites and nonwhites made being married under the laws of some states a criminal act in others.

Laws preventing marriages between whites and nonwhites predated **Jim Crow**, dating back to the colonial period, appearing in colonial statutes in the late seventeenth century. Jim Crow simply gave support to such laws, particularly but not exclusively in the South. By 1950, about 30 states still carried such laws, although they were increasingly ignored outside the South. While almost all states of the South had such laws, many Northern and Western states also carried them. No uniform definition of what constituted a nonwhite person existed, and standards varied from state to state. Usually such laws specifically banned marriage between a white person and a person of the opposite sex with at least one black great-grandparent, although occasionally the "**one-drop rule**" was used. While most such laws were specifically aimed at black-white couples, marriages between whites and other nonwhites such as Asians, Native Americans, and South Asians were also affected by such laws. However, marriages between whites and **Hispanics/Latinos** were usually not banned under the law, as most state laws regarding racial classification considered Hispanics as white. However, if a Hispanic person looked black, officials usually refused to issue a license.

State laws varied considerably. On one extreme was Virginia, with a 1922 law that made being married itself a crime for black and white couples, regardless of where the marriage occurred. Other states simply refused to issue marriage licenses to couples of different races but did nothing officially against couples who were married in other states. However, local customs and hostility often prevented mixed-race couples from residing in most areas of the South. Western states, especially California, Arizona, and Oregon, focused on preventing unions between whites and Asians and Malays as much as between whites and blacks. Enforcement of anti–interracial marriage laws tended to be less stringent when neither partner was white.

In American territories, such laws either did not exist or were seldom enforced. However, in those situations, the overwhelming majority of white Americans were male, making such unions perhaps inevitable. However, prejudices against such unions usually resulted in the ostracizing of interracial couples from the polite society, which meant white couples. In the Panama Canal Zone, men who married local women were referred to as "squaw men," and became social outcasts. American soldiers who were stationed in the Philippines or Hawai'i and married local women often continued to reenlist in the army to stay out of the continental United States, where they would be unable to take their wives.

Such laws and customs reflected white society's fears of **miscegenation,** and were specifically aimed at preventing sexual relationships between white women and black men. In a society that depended in part on easily definable categories of "race," children of such unions presented problems that law against interracial marriage attempted to prevent. Children of such illicit unions were often raised by the mother if she were the nonwhite partner, or aborted or given to a black family to raise if the mother were white. However, popular culture abounded with the concept of the "tragic mulatto," indicating that such people were doomed to live miserable lives and thus their creation should be avoided. Of course, that such misery was caused by racism seems to have not occurred to many people. The rise of so-called scientific racism buttressed the belief that the offspring of unions between people of different "races" were genetically inferior, and should be avoided. Such pseudoscientific nonsense found its way into court rulings and legislative debates for decades.

Despite officially being banned in many areas, sexual relationships between white males and nonwhite women were tolerated if kept discreet, and such couples did not seek legal sanction. Many of the states with anti–interracial marriage laws also had laws that defined any sexual contact between black men and white women as rape regardless of the circumstances. Such laws made any indication of sexual activity between black men and white women dangerous for black men. White women caught in a compromising position could always claim rape, which often resulted in the **lynching** of the black man involved, or any black man as a warning to all, especially in the South. Even when state laws did not specifically define interracial sexual relations as rape, an allegation of rape against a black man commonly resulted in a lynch mob.

The end of anti–interracial marriage laws began with the marriage of Richard Loving, who was white, and Mildred Jeter, who was black, in 1958. Unable to wed in their native Virginia, the couple wed in Washington, DC. Upon their return to Virginia as a married couple, they were arrested and faced up to five years in prison for their crime. Under a plea, the couple agreed to leave the state and not return for 25 years. The couple moved to Washington, DC, and, in 1963, began court action against the Commonwealth of Virginia. The lawsuit eventually led to the **U.S. Supreme Court**, which ruled in 1967 in *Loving v. Virginia* that state laws banning interracial marriages were unconstitutional. At the time, some 16 states still had such laws, as many states had been repealing them in the two decades before the Supreme Court ruling. By the end of the 1950s, an estimated 51,000 mixed black and white marriages existed in the United States, compared to almost half a million by the end of the century.

Such laws could not prevent interracial marriages among committed couples, who traveled to states without such restrictions to marry. But these laws did force interracial couples to choose their state of residence carefully, and made travel in states with such laws problematic and even deadly. Such laws made interracial couples, even in states that permitted such unions, not quite respectable. Official disapproval of such marriages limited their acceptance, and the numbers of interracial marriages only began to swell after such laws were nullified by the Supreme Court. *See also* Asian Americans; Civil Rights Movement; Jews in the South.

Further Readings: Gay, Kathlyn. *The Rainbow Effect: Interracial Families.* Danbury, CT: Grolier Publishing, 1987; McNamara, Robert P., Maria Tempenis, and Beth Walton. *Crossing the Line: Interracial Couples in the South.* Westport, CT: Greenwood Press, 1999; Moran, Rachel F. *Interracial Intimacy: The Regulation of Race and Romance.*

Chicago: University of Chicago Press, 2001; Robinson, Charles Frank, II. *Dangerous Liaisons: Sex and Love in the Segregated South*. Fayetteville: University of Arkansas Press, 2003.

Barry M. Stentiford

Marshall, Thurgood (1908–1992)

The lead attorney for the National Association for the Advancement of Colored People (NAACP) in the 1954 ***Brown v. Board of Education*** case and the first African American to sit on the **U.S. Supreme Court**, Thurgood Marshall was born in Baltimore, Maryland, on July 2, 1908. Named for his great-grandfather, Thoroughgood, who had escaped slavery, Marshall grew up comfortably in middle-class, but segregated, black Baltimore (Marshall shortened the name himself to Thurgood as a child because he found his name too long to write out). His father, William, was a Pullman porter and a waiter at a white club, while his mother, Norma, was a schoolteacher.

In 1925, Marshall followed his older brother, Aubrey, to Lincoln University in Pennsylvania, one of the nation's most prestigious black universities. At Lincoln, Marshall was not an exceptionally serious student and was suspended from school for his involvement in hazing freshmen. When he returned to school, his racial consciousness was stoked by a fellow Lincoln student, the poet **Langston Hughes**, who was leading the charge to have Lincoln's all-white faculty integrated. Marshall, like most Lincoln students, initially opposed to integrating the faculty, but he eventually became a supporter of the idea, and took over the campaign when Hughes graduated. As a senior, Marshall pushed a student referendum to force the administration to integrate the faculty, and the school's first black faculty member was hired the following year.

Marshall married Philadelphia native Vivian "Buster" Bury, a University of Pennsylvania student, in 1929. He graduated from Lincoln the following year but was relegated to working as a waiter at Maryland's all-white Gibson Island Club, with his father, as the onset of the **Great Depression** had left jobs scarce. Marshall, who had been an excellent debater in college, then decided that he wanted to go to law school. He and Buster lived with his parents in Baltimore, so he applied to the all-white University of Maryland Law School, but was rejected because of his race, bringing him face to face with the Jim Crowism that he had mostly avoided growing up in black Baltimore and at Lincoln University. Angered at the rejection, his only other option seemed to be to apply to the historically black Howard University Law School in Washington, DC. Howard's reputation at this time was poor, as the law school was not accredited by the American Bar Association or the Association of American Law Schools.

Marshall was admitted to Howard Law in the fall of 1930, at a fortuitous time in the school's history. Harvard-educated Charles Hamilton Houston, who had joined Howard's faculty in 1924, had recently been promoted to dean of the Law school, and, along with Howard University's first African American president, Mordecai Johnson, was determined to increase Howard's academic standards and become a fully accredited law school. Despite some opposition to his rigorous policies, Houston succeeded in toughening admission requirements to the school, and by 1931, it was accredited by both the American Bar Association and the Association of American Law Schools. Most importantly, Houston was committed to using Howard Law School to develop a cadre of black lawyers to fight racial injustice. It was into this vigorous academic environment that Marshall entered in 1930.

At Howard, Marshall quickly became a disciple of Houston and fellow Howard faculty member William Hastie. Along with fellow student and future NAACP attorney Oliver Hill, Marshall developed as Houston's protégée, accompanying him to court and sitting in on strategy sessions for NAACP cases. Through Houston's tutelage, Marshall became aware of the power that lawyers could wield in bringing about change, and he wanted to be a part of it. Following his graduation from Howard in 1933, first in his class, Marshall traveled South with Houston to examine the state of black elementary schools throughout the region. The trip was part of Houston's research in developing a legal strategy for the NAACP to challenge segregated education; it was the basis of what would eventually culminate in the *Brown* decision.

Marshall was offered a scholarship to pursue an advanced degree at Harvard Law School in 1933, but instead decided it was time for him to begin his own practice and earn some money for his family, so he opened his own firm in Baltimore. However, the clientele available for a black attorney in Depression-era Baltimore was slim, and Marshall had a very difficult time making ends meet. The clients he did have often had a tough time paying his fees, but he developed a reputation of not turning anyone in need away. His reputation also brought him to the notice of the Baltimore branch of the NAACP, which retained him as its counsel, and in December 1933, Marshall began preparing his first civil rights case, what became *Murray v. Maryland*.

As Marshall knew all too well, the University of Maryland's law school refused to admit black students on account of their race. Marshall and the local NAACP wanted to challenge the legality of this segregationist policy but they were hampered by the Supreme Court's 1896 **Plessy v. Ferguson** "**separate but equal**" decision, which ruled that segregation was constitutional. This decision was the great hurdle for black lawyers like Marshall and Houston to overcome, as once the Supreme Court has ruled on a decision, it rarely overturned itself, a practice known as *starre decisis* ("Let the decision stand").

Houston, however, had been working on a different approach to challenge school discrimination, and when Marshall informed him that he planned to sue for the right of Donald Murray to attend the University of Maryland Law School, Houston sought to put his strategy to the test and join his former pupil on the case. He and Marshall would not challenge the *Plessy* decision, they would embrace it. Houston and Marshall argued not that Maryland had to admit Murray to its law school because segregation was unconstitutional (overturning *Plessy*), but instead that Murray had to be admitted under the "separate but equal" statute, because there was no public law school open to African Americans in the state of Maryland. Houston's strategy was relatively simple: in the *Murray* case, he did not have to prove the inequality between black and white law schools (the way he would have to with black and white elementary schools, for instance), because there was no black law school in the state; it was a question of exclusion, not equality, and therefore not allowed by *Plessy*.

Houston and Marshall prevailed in the *Murray* case when the Maryland Court of Appeals upheld the lower court's decision to admit Murray to the law school and the state decided not to appeal the case to the U.S. Supreme Court. It was Marshall's first civil rights victory, and it began a strategy that he and Houston would pursue in attacking school segregation for another 15 years, in cases such as *Missouri ex rel. Gaines v. Canada* (1938), *Sipuel v. Board of Regents of the University of Oklahoma* (1948), and **Sweatt v. Painter** (1950). In all of these cases, Marshall and/or Houston focused on graduate educational facilities and did not challenge the legality of separate but equal, but instead on the lack of education programs provided for black citizens. With each victory, the NAACP lawyers chipped away at the legitimacy of school segregation and laid the groundwork for the eventual assault on *Plessy*.

While Marshall is most famous for his work on school desegregation during this era, he was involved in a host of other cases for the NAACP as well. In 1936, he closed his unprofitable one-man firm in Baltimore and became a full-time employee of the NAACP, focusing on cases in Maryland and Virginia. Many of the cases he pursued successfully were pay-equalization cases for African American public school teachers and employees. In 1938, he took over as head of the NAACP's legal division, replacing Houston, who was in ailing health. Two years later the **NAACP Legal Defense Fund**, Inc., was founded as a organization separate from the NAACP to focus on civil rights litigation, and headed by Marshall from its inception until 1961, when he became a federal court of appeals judge.

With Marshall at the head of the NAACP's legal wing, the organization flourished. In addition to continued work on school integration and pay equalization, he instituted successful litigation which eliminated the white primary (*Smith v. Allwright*, 1944) and restrictive **housing covenants (*Shelley v. Kraemer***, 1948). Marshall even traveled to Japan and Korea in 1951 to investigate discrimination by the U.S. Army against black soldiers, who were being court-martialed at much higher rates that whites, mostly on vague charges of "cowardice" and "incompetence." Between August and October 1950, 32 black servicemen in Korea were convicted under the 75th Article of War—"misbehavior in front of the enemy"—in comparison to only two white soldiers; blacks also got harsher penalties for being convicted for the same crimes as whites. Marshall's investigation revealed a pattern of discrimination in the court-martial process, going back to **World War I**. Marshall blamed the army high command, specifically General Douglas MacArthur, for continued discrimination against African American soldiers, as the army leadership continued to resist integration two years after President **Harry S. Truman**'s **Executive Order 9981** mandating the end of discrimination in the **armed forces**.

In 1950, Marshall also believed that the time had finally come for a frontal attack on *Plessy*, and the NAACP announced that it was looking for plaintiffs who would be willing to challenge school segregation. For almost 15 years, the

NAACP had pursued the legal strategy developed by Houston of using *Plessy* to gain equal educational facilities for African Americans (with the hope that the cost of making schools truly equal would force school integration). Now, Marshall decided that the Supreme Court was ready to hear a challenge to the constitutionality of school segregation itself. His team compiled five cases—from Kansas, **Virginia, South Carolina**, the District of Columbia, and Delaware—which became known as *Brown v. Board of Education.*

The cases came before the Supreme Court in 1952. Marshall's strategy in arguing *Brown* was controversial, in that he based much of his argument on evidence provided by psychologists Kenneth and Mamie Clark and their famous doll experiment. The Clarks' study of three-to-seven-year-old children reveled that white superiority was so ingrained in society that young black children preferred while dolls (which they identified as "pretty" or "nice") instead of black dolls (which they described as "ugly" or bad"). While derided as sociological garbage by opposing counsel, Marshall's use of the "doll test" proved to be powerful evidence that school segregation caused a sense of inferiority in black children that was a violation of their Fourteenth Amendment right of equal protection of the laws. The justices agreed with Marshall's arguments, and in 1954, the Supreme Court overturned *Plessy*, ruling that "separate is inherently unequal in the area of education."

While the *Brown* decision was a dramatic victory for Marshall and the NAACP, the culmination of almost two decades of legal attacks on segregation in education, it did not bring about the immediate desegregation of the nation's schools. At the conclusion of *Brown*, the Court asked lawyers from both the NAACP and the states to return the next year to present their plans for a timetable on how *Brown* should be implemented. In his brief for the high court, Marshall recommended that integration plans go into effect in 1955, with complete school integration by the fall of 1956. Lawyers for the states asked instead that the court set no timetable for integration, but to leave the decision on how and when to integrate to local school boards. In what became known as *Brown* II, Chief Justice Earl Warren sided with the gradualist approach of the states in 1955 by refusing to set a timetable for integration, ruling instead that integration should processed "with all deliberate speed." This infamous order set the stage for massive resistance against school integration, as many school districts throughout the South simply refused to integrate until finally forced to by the **federal government** following the passage of the **Civil Rights Act of 1964.**

The same year as his professional setback with *Brown* II, Marshall suffered a personal loss when Buster, his wife of 25 years, died of cancer. His personal fame, however, in 1955, was at an all-time high. Known even before Brown in the African American community as "Mr. Civil Rights," he became well known throughout the nation as a result of the Brown decision, even appearing on the cover of *Time* magazine. As black protests regarding **Emmitt Till's** murder in **Mississippi** and the **Montgomery Bus Boycott** in **Alabama** developed, Marshall also emerged as a lighting rod in the **Civil Rights Movement.** He believed that the best way for African Americans to enact change was through the courts, not the streets; he was not always totally supportive of the protest movement, and was highly critical of black separatist organizations.

Despite some of his reservations over public protests, Marshall and the NAACP did provided legal assistance to the protesters. Marshall was directly involved in the Montgomery Bus Boycott case, working with local NAACP attorney Fred Gray as the case was eventually settled in their favor by the U.S. Supreme Court in 1956. He also continued to work for school integration, including representing **Autherine Lucy** in her fight to integrate the University of Alabama. Marshall, who remarried in 1955 to Cecilia ("Cissy") Suyat, an NAACP secretary, enjoyed a personal joy when his first child, Thurgood, Jr., was born in 1956. The couple later had a second son, John.

In 1961, Marshall left the NAACP after a quarter-century of service when President **John F. Kennedy** appointed him as a federal appeals judge. As counsel for the NAACP, Marshall had argued 32 cases before the U.S. Supreme Court, winning 29 of them. Four years after his appointment as a federal judge, President Lyndon B. Johnson appointed Marshall as U.S. Solicitor General. As the nation's top litigator, Marshall won numerous other decisions before the Supreme Court on behalf of the United States. After less than two years in that post, Johnson appointed Marshall to the U.S. Supreme Court, becoming the first African American to serve on the nation's highest court in 1967.

During Marshall's 24-year term on the Supreme Court, he consistently supported civil rights, voting with the court's liberal majority in the 1970s on landmark cases regarding affirmative action, abortion, defendant rights, and school desegregation. As the court took a conservative turn in the 1980s, Marshall increasingly found himself arguing with the minority, and many of his written opinions became angry and bitter, especially in regard to cases in which he believed that the court was trying to turn back the clock on civil rights. Frustrated by the conservative nature of the court and in failing health, Marshall retired in 1991. The decision to appoint Clarence Thomas, a conservative African American with little experience as a litigator or a judge, hurt Marshall, but he accepted it with dignity, meeting with the new justice for more than two hours when Thomas joined the Court. Thurgood Marshall died the following year, at age 84. *See also Brown v. Board of Education, Legal Groundwork for.*

Further Readings: Davis, Michael D., and Hunter R. Clark. *Thurgood Marshall: Warrior at the Bar, Rebel on the Bench.* New York: Carol Publishing Group, 1992; Tushnet, Mark V. *Making Civil Rights Law: Thurgood Marshall and the Supreme Court, 1936–1961.* New York: Oxford University Press, 1996; Williams, Juan. *Thurgood Marshall: American Revolutionary.* New York: Times Books, 1998.

Thomas J. Ward, Jr.

Masculinity, Black and White

A concept traditionally associated with the appearance and behavior of men, masculinity serves as a defining characteristic of maleness in many cultures. Masculinity refers to the meaning that a culture attaches to being male rather than the physical or biological category itself. Although recent scholarship reveals ways in which biological sex is also subject to societal definitions, masculinity is culturally constructed and can be interpreted differently by disparate groups. Cultural definitions of masculinity have changed and continue to change over time and between regions and cultures, and it is impossible to classify all black or white men under a particular definition of masculinity.

The gender concept of masculinity is often tied to economic, familial, and spatial issues. Men are often considered to be the primary economic forces in society. Masculinity can be defined through space. Since men can control access to certain types of work and leisure places, they therefore can control what type of work women can perform. Masculinity is typically differentiated from that of femininity. Throughout the history of the United States, different economic classes, ethnic groups, and religious and political organizations have defined family and gender roles for men and women in various ways. A "traditional" family was frequently defined as a man who made important decisions and provided financial resources and physical protection for his family, a feminine woman who cared for the home and children but was not necessarily responsible for the family's economic well-being, and children who were subordinate to the demands of both father and mother. Although societal reality did not always conform to a true gendered division of labor in the home and workplace, this concept is pervasive in American culture. Masculinity and manhood were intimately tied to male domination over the family structure, as well as in economic and political affairs.

Men have also frequently defined masculinity or manhood in relation to what men are not, or what society says men should not be. The opposite of masculine is not only feminine, but also childish, brutal, or animal-like. In the United States, homosexual, unmarried, unemployed, or pacifist men may be considered less masculine than other men. Although a cultural definition of masculinity includes particular types of men, it excludes many others. Control over women or other men was never complete, nor did all men support the same ideals.

In the earliest years of North American colonial settlement, issues of race and gender intertwined. White patriarchs controlled labor systems, property rights, and sexual access to both black and white women. Since white men had the power to define the rights of all people, they used discourses of race and gender to solidify their own economic and political authority. The importation of African slaves as laborers was a recent development, and **slavery** was not yet defined as the status of only black workers. Since they did not want black men to have access to white women, white patriarchs discredited the masculinity and intellectual abilities of black men. Conversely, elite white men guaranteed their own sexual access to black women by classifying them as morally weak. White women needed the moral protection of white men, but black women did not merit physical protection.

Colonists created their households based on the English assumptions of patriarchy and female domesticity. White men chose to maintain social control by placing women, children, and all people of color in subordinate roles. White women were spatially restricted to the home and domestic labor, while black women were forced to work as slaves. Since communal standards dictated that white men had to control their own households and white women had to adhere to their assigned gender role, aggressive women and weak husbands were publicly humiliated through customs such as *charivari*. Elite white men solidified control over working-class white men and black workers by feminizing dissent and severing ties between laborers who might otherwise join in solidarity. By emphasizing race as an important division, elite white men enlisted the support of poorer white men against black slaves. Free white men defined masculinity as the opposite of both female and slave. Since all white men could be potential patriarchs over their homes, whiteness and masculinity were closely tied to the colonial endeavor in North America.

As racialized slavery became more pervasive in the colonial era and solidified during the early years of the United States, black men found it more difficult to attain traditional masculine roles. Enslaved men had to endure the knowledge that white slaveholders held power over themselves and their families. Not only did white owners dictate the types of labor slaves must perform, but also had control over housing, food, travel, religious gatherings, and other freedoms. The threat of sale away from one's family was ever present. Enslaved families were not always able to live together as a unit. At times, the father was located on another plantation, or was sold away entirely. Children could be sold at the discretion of the master. In a society in which protecting one's family was a sign of masculinity, black men were unable to protect their wives or daughters from the sexual advances of white men. This vulnerability undermined the patriarchy and masculine roles of enslaved black men.

Free black men in the antebellum period were subject to discrimination in jobs and housing. Those men who managed to save wages and purchase their own freedom often worked to free the rest of their family, but they faced tremendous difficulties in doing so. In the years leading to the Civil War, many states passed manumission laws that prevented white slaveholders from freeing their slaves, or required that freed slaves had to leave the state immediately. Whether free or enslaved, black men confronted challenges to their masculinity.

Race played an important part in the antebellum discourse of masculinity. Elite white men in the colonial era had established patriarchy through the control of the household and property ownership. They maintained this masculine dominance through paternalism. Slaveholders believed that they were benevolent and were "civilizing" their enslaved workers. They believed that their actions were honorable and benefited society, and used the rhetoric of honor to glorify the system of enslavement. Both Southern slaveholders and abolitionists often adopted fatherly attitudes toward black Americans, which allowed them to believe that they were acting in the best interests of enslaved people.

Although far from wealthy, Southern yeomen farmers also had a vested interest in maintaining a system of slavery. These farmers could not prove their paternalism by dominating a large number of slaves, and they were often ashamed that their wives had to work alongside them in the fields rather than serve in a purely domestic role. Yeomen, however, conceded political power to the planter class in order to maintain patriarchal authority over their families. White yeomen farmers not only claimed equality with planters because they were all white, but also because they exerted authority over women and black men. In exchange for a measure of public influence, Southern yeomen supported the system of slavery as an extension of their own white, masculine authority.

In urban areas of the early nineteenth century, few white men could afford to own property and control their own livelihood. As wage labor became more common, white workers feared that they were being reduced to "wage slaves," or men enslaved to the capitalist system. These workers invoked the language of slavery to argue for the masculine ideal of free labor. They considered themselves men as long as they owned their own labor. In order to justify their jobs and find pride in their circumstances, white workers intentionally distanced themselves from black slaves. Once again, a system of racial slavery was solidified by the lack of solidarity between workers.

The Civil War provided the opportunity for both black and white men to prove their masculinity. Most men were greatly motivated by issues of home, family, and protection. Union soldiers emphasized the Victorian ideals of manly restraint, virtue, self-discipline, and loyalty, while Confederate soldiers abided by Southern codes of honor and protecting one's home. Both sides of the conflict placed great importance in displays of courage and valor. Soldiers feared that they would be branded as effeminate or cowards if they ran away from battle. At the same time, other soldiers feared that killing would make them brutal and inhuman. Soldiers were angry at pacifists or civilians who refused to fight. Many young men, away from home for the first time, experienced vice and a sense of adventure, but feared that their families would disapprove.

Black soldiers, especially former slaves, were anxious to fight for their own freedom and that of other enslaved people. They equated manhood with the ability to direct one's own destiny, which slavery had denied them. White politicians and soldiers on both sides of the conflict argued that black soldiers were unfit for warfare and would run at the first sign of danger. With the ongoing threat of slave rebellions in mind, Southern slaveholders viewed regiments of armed black men as their greatest fear. White Union officers often assumed that black soldiers were docile and childlike, traits bred into them through years of slavery and oppression. Black soldiers directly challenged these assumptions as they exhibited courage in battle. In time, many white officers grew to respect their black regiments, finding them strong, well disciplined, and fearless under fire. Members of the United States Colored Troops had to endure unequal pay, fatigue duty, dangerous assignments, and the threat of death or enslavement at the hands of Confederate troops. The courageous performance of black men in battle had a profound impact on the Union's fight for emancipation and racial equality.

Following the Civil War, black men throughout the country experienced a renewed sense of hope and manhood. With the passage of the Thirteenth, Fourteenth, and Fifteenth Constitutional Amendments, African American men secured the right to vote and access to full citizenship in ways they had previously been denied. Black politicians sought to secure land, educational support, and equal legal protection for former slaves. Many men left their former employers and chose their own occupations for the first time. Once free to protect and control their families, some black men implemented patriarchal power in their homes. Black men and women legalized their marriages, although some women were subject to coercion or abuse as a result. Many men adopted middle-class notions of domesticity and family roles and urged their wives to stay at home. Not only did they want to be the primary breadwinner for their family, but they also hoped to protect their wives and children from abuse by white employers. Under the system of slavery, white men had free sexual access to black women, and black men wanted to end this practice.

The hopes of **Reconstruction** were short-lived. White men throughout the country feared the potential backlash of free black men. White laborers continued to use the rhetoric of race and wage slavery to distance themselves from black workers. With so many black workers no longer under the economic control of white men, former white planters feared physical and economic repercussions. Black people were not able to purchase large amounts of land, and white landowners still needed black labor to run their farms. A system of sharecropping and tenant farming was the solution. Although black laborers technically worked for themselves, they were still economically dependent on white people. Black workers throughout the country experienced job discrimination and low wages. African American freedom was undermined by racial injustice.

In order to reclaim masculine control in the South, white men formed organizations such as the **Ku Klux Klan** to intimidate black men politically, economically, and physically. Although black women had always been susceptible to white men's sexual access and violence, white men did not want black men to have sexual access to white women. White men exerted control through the invented myth of the "black beast rapist," a hypermasculine black man with animalistic and brutal sexual impulses who preyed on innocent white women. Implementing a process of torture and murder called **lynching**, white men used the reality and threat of violence to control black behavior. Black men were frequently physically emasculated, and their cultural and political activities were limited.

As years since the Civil War passed and veterans aged, regional hostilities became less important in light of economic and cultural similarities among white people. Northern industries had economically invested in the New South, and veterans of both armies wanted to celebrate their wartime heroism and courage rather than their differences. Across the country, veterans emphasized their manliness and valor while undermining challenges from independent black men and suffrage-seeking women. Northern

Ku Klux Klan parade in Washington, DC, 1926. The Klan drew its membership from angry white men, playing on fears that white masculinity was under attack from an unknown black menace. Courtesy of Library of Congress, LC-USZ62-96154.

cities, fearing the effects of so many black residents, looked to the South for a solution to the "Negro problem."

The South's answer to controlling black people continued to lie in violence, disfranchisement, economic marginalization, and segregation. White southern politicians appealed to the ideal of white supremacy and white fears of black brutes to undermine any attempts for interracial political organization. Democratic political victories at the end of the nineteenth century resulted in the loss of black men's right to vote. Since manhood and citizenship had been linked throughout American history, black men were excluded from male privilege, and thus citizenship, by their inability to participate in the political system. In order to avoid violence, black men often had to adopt a servile demeanor rather than a public masculinity.

As black men's masculinity and patriarchal control was undermined in the Gilded Age and **Jim Crow** era, white men articulated a new type of masculinity. Fearing that the Victorian ideals of self-discipline and restraint were having a feminizing impact, white men placed great emphasis on a vigorous, aggressive masculinity. White men claimed to share the virile, primitive, "masculine" qualities of black men while maintaining a superior moral, civilized "manliness." Many white men believed that experiences with nature and violence would regenerate their moral character. Since white men controlled many of the economic and intellectual resources of society, they could spread this particular idea of masculinity to many people and advocate for a "strenuous life." Progressive Era reformers condemned aggressive sports such as prizefighting and football, arguing that such activities taught children to be brutal. Even as black soldiers once again proved their manly courage in the Spanish-American War, white men continued to argue that black men could never claim the civilized manliness of white men.

With the onset of **World War I**, many black people migrated to Northern cities. They not only hoped to escape the financial difficulties of **sharecropping**, but also desired to leave behind disfranchisement and lynching violence in the South. Expanded economic opportunities allowed them to provide for their families, and they were not subject to such extensive abuse at the hands of white men. Many black men believed that they could attain true citizenship in the North, where they would be allowed to vote, and through their military service. Black soldiers once again proved their courage and equality in battle, but encountered racism and competition for jobs and housing when they returned to the United States.

Men in the black middle class urged newly arrived workers to prove their equality through good behavior. Reformers tried to educate migrants in the dominant cultural ideals of thrift, sobriety, cleanliness, efficiency, and respectability. The middle class advised black men to be the sole breadwinners for the family and indicated that women should stay at home rather than enter the workforce. However, it was financially impossible for many black families to meet this ideal. The black middle class was also critical of how black workers spent their free time and money. The reformers recommended that working-class African Americans refrain from disreputable or excessive forms of leisure. Middle-class leaders did not want the whole race to be judged poorly by the behavior of some.

Black migrants were often limited to particular types of jobs in Northern cities. Although black men did not want to be viewed as either brutal or servile, they were often forced into roles, such as Pullman porters, that recreated the master/servant system of slavery. Better-paid industrial workers faced threats from white unions and returning veterans. In the **Red Summer** of 1919, tensions between black and white people erupted in brutal race riots. Many people, mostly black, died in the violence. Unlike racial violence under slavery or white supremacy, black people were willing and able to fight back. Organizations such as the National Association for the Advancement of Colored People (NAACP) and many black publications like the *Chicago Defender* advocated that the "New Negro" assert his rights and race pride. Although white men tried to maintain cultural and economic dominance, there were continual challenges.

Segregation and racial violence continued throughout much of the twentieth century. Black men fought for their rights to provide for their families and be treated as societal equals, and white men asserted their dominance at every opportunity. All men experienced threats to their masculinity during the **Great Depression** as they found it more and more difficult to act as breadwinners. Although black men could gain employment through some **New Deal** programs, discrimination continued to impact their economic situation.

Black men were forced to serve in segregated units during **World War II**, but once again hoped that their military service would translate into equal citizenship. Through the **Double V Campaign**, black people demonstrated their patriotism and their demands for civil rights. This initiative called for military victory abroad and civil rights victory at home. Although the campaign was a step toward the future civil rights movement, black veterans continued to experience discrimination when they returned to the United States. Black soldiers did not receive equal treatment under the **G.I. Bill**, which hampered their access to housing and education benefits. Segregation and discriminatory practices at times thwarted notions of black masculinity.

As the **Civil Rights Movement** gained strength through the 1950s and into the 1960s, both white segregationists and black civil rights leaders articulated their arguments in terms of masculinity. The defense team of the white men accused of killing **Emmett Till** in **Mississippi** in 1955 argued that the men had the right to protect their families, especially white women. They tried to invoke the image of the black beast to divert attention from the fact that Till was a 14-year-old boy. Although some white Southerners rallied to the defense, most white people throughout the country were sickened by the murder. Discomfort with racial mixing still existed, as evidenced by the turmoil following the *Brown v. Board of Education* decision, but changes were on the horizon.

As consumption became more important in the twentieth century, white industrialists and landowners tried to maintain economic dominance. Housing segregationists claimed that they were protecting their economic investment rather than acting as racists. Both black and white men felt some threat from the rise of second-wave feminism and women's greater role in the workplace and civic culture. Black men viewed the Moynihan Report of 1965 as yet another challenge to their manhood and their ability to provide for their families. At times, black women were able to make political statements in ways that men were not, which some thought was a challenge to black masculinity. The Black Power movement advocated a shift from nonviolent protest to a more aggressive type of masculinity. Manhood was articulated in a variety ways among both black and white men.

Concepts of black and white masculinity continue to be relevant in the late twentieth and early twenty-first centuries. Events such as the Million Man March highlight a particular type of black manhood, while gangsta rap conveys another. Issues of race and masculinity are prevalent in social and religious organizations like the Promise Keepers, and continue to be addressed in political forums on job discrimination, military action, welfare, and inner-city violence. Just as ideas of family, honor, and economics were expressed early in the history of the United States, they are still relevant to masculinity today. *See also* Great Migration; Homosexuality; New Negro Movement.

Further Readings: Bederman, Gail. *Manliness and Civilization: A Cultural History of Gender and Race in the United States, 1880–1917.* Chicago: University of Chicago Press, 1995; Brown, Kathleen M. *Good Wives, Nasty Wenches, and Anxious Patriarchs: Gender, Race, and Power in Colonial Virginia.* Chapel Hill: University of North Carolina Press, 1996; Clinton, Catherine, and Nina Silber, eds. *Divided Houses: Gender and the Civil War.* New York: Oxford University Press, 1992; Estes, Steve. *I Am a Man!: Race, Manhood, and the Civil Rights Movement.* Chapel Hill: University of North Carolina Press, 2004; Gilmore, Glenda Elizabeth. *Gender and Jim Crow: Women and the Politics of White Supremacy in North Carolina, 1896–1920.* Chapel Hill: University of North Carolina Press, 1996; Glatthaar, Joseph T. *Forged in Battle: The Civil War Alliance of Black Soldiers and White Officers.* New York: Meridian Free Press, 1990; Kantrowitz, Stephen. *Ben Tillman and the Reconstruction of White Supremacy.* Chapel Hill: University of North Carolina Press, 2000; Roediger, David R. *The Wages of Whiteness: Race and the Making of the American Working Class.* New York: Verso, 1991; Summers, Martin. *Manliness and Its Discontents: The Black Middle Class and the Transformation of Masculinity, 1900–1930.* Chapel Hill: University of North Carolina Press, 2004; Wood, Amy Louise. "Lynching Photography and the 'Black Beast Rapist' in the Southern White Masculine Imagination." In *Masculinity: Bodies, Movies, Culture,* edited by Peter Lehman. New York: Routledge, 2001.

Shannon Smith Bennett

Mays, Willie (b. 1931)

Willie Mays was one of the greatest stars in the history of baseball. The ultimate "five-tool player," Mays could run, hit, hit with power, field, and throw, and he played the game with energy, style, and charisma. In his extraordinary career, the "Say Hey Kid" was named to the National League All-Star team 24 times, more than any other player in history. Younger than **Jackie Robinson** and Satchel Paige, Willie Mays was, nevertheless, a product of **Negro League Baseball.** But he played into the 1970s, tracing an arc from Jim Crow segregation to acceptance as an icon of major league baseball.

Mays was born in in Westfield, **Alabama,** outside Birmingham, where his father and grandfather had played for black baseball teams in the Tennessee Coal and Iron League. His mother had been a high school track star. At age 16, in 1948, Mays joined the renowned Birmingham Black Barons of the Negro National League. Two years later, after he had graduated from high school, he was signed by the New York Giants in the wake of Jackie Robinson's initial success with the **Brooklyn Dodgers**. Mays became known for his spectacular ability as a center fielder before he established himself as a hitter. By the 1954 season, though, he was topping the league with a .345 batting average, hitting 41 home runs, and leading the Giants to the world championship. From that time, through the late 1960s, he was one of the brightest stars in baseball and, for a time, the game's highest paid player. Over the course of his career, Mays hit 660 home runs and batted .302. Most of his contemporaries commented that the most impressive thing about Mays was not his raw power or ability. What impressed them was his reckless and breathtaking style of play.

His success was unlikely. In a family with 11 children in rural Alabama, Mays grew up with poverty and segregation. He attended a vocational high school and trained to work in a laundry. He was a phenomenal athlete in high school, though, starring in football and basketball, and he played semipro baseball. With the Birmingham Black Barons, he played against Negro League legends Satchel Paige, Josh Gibson, and Buck Leonard. Following the success of Jackie Robinson, major league ball clubs were looking to develop young black talent, and within a couple of years, Mays was batting .330 and slugging .547 for Birmingham. Giants scout Eddie Montague wrote manager Leo Durocher, "this was the greatest young player I had ever seen in my life or my scouting career."

After signing him in 1950, the Giants wanted to send Mays to its minor league affiliate in Sioux City, Iowa, but the city would not accept a black player, so he was assigned to Trenton of the Interstate League. "I was the first black in that particular league," he would write. And we played in a town called Hagerstown, Maryland. I'll never forget this day, on a Friday. And they call you all kinds of names there, 'nigger' this, and 'nigger' that. I said to myself, 'Hey, whatever they call you, they can't touch you. Don't talk back.' "

His first year in major league baseball, at the age of 20, Mays led the Giants to the World Series. He was voted National League Rookie of the Year, and his manager, the legendary Leo Durocher, claimed that "just to have him on the club, you had thirty percent of the best of it before the ball game started. In each generation, there are one or two players like that, men who are winning players because of their own ability and their own ... magnetism." Nevertheless, when Mays returned to the Jim Crow South after the season was over, he tried to patronize a Woolworth's lunch counter and was refused service.

Mays served in the U.S. Army during the Korean conflict, although he spent most of his time playing with a stateside army baseball team. When he returned to the Giants in 1954, he began a dozen years of unbroken excellence. He won the batting title in his first year back, and he hit 51 home runs the following year. He led the National League in stolen bases four years in a row. And he won 12 consecutive Gold Gloves, awarded to the top fielder at each position. His talent and drive prompted historian Jules Tygiel to comment that, "Mays, with his indisputable excellence, convinced all but the most stalwart resisters to integration of the need to recruit African-Americans."

When the Giants moved from New York to San Francisco before the 1958 season, Mays was not warmly welcomed, in part, because he was black. Soon after he moved into his new home, a brick crashed through his living room window. By 1963, though, Mays was the highest paid player in baseball, making $105,000, and his personal stature provided the impetus for integration. When the Houston Astros were formed in 1965, for instance, team ownership wanted to make certain that the city would not force the great Willie Mays to sleep in a Jim Crow hotel.

Mays was a pragmatic thinker and urged moderation in race relations. During the 1964 season, when manager Alvin Dark publicly expressed the view that Spanish-speaking and black players were not as mentally alert as white players, many of the Giants' Latino players threatened to boycott their games unless Dark was immediately fired.

Mays argued that such a move would be disastrous for their season and told a team meeting that Dark had always given everyone a fair chance to play, no matter his racial views. "I'm telling you he helped me," Mays told his fellow players. "And he's helped everybody here. I'm not playing Tom to him when I say that. He helps us because he wants to win, and he wants the money that goes with winning. Ain't nothing wrong with that." Mays urged the Latino players, "Don't let the rednecks make a hero out of him." At the same time, Mays himself continued to play, but he did not speak to Dark for the rest of the season, after which Dark was fired.

Mays was voted the National League's Most Valuable Player in 1954, and again 11 years later, in 1965, a testament to his consistency and drive. Although his skills had diminished by the end of the 1960s, Mays was voted Player of the Decade by the *Sporting News*. He was traded to the New York Mets in 1972, then retired the following year, his skills eroding fast, in the city where he began his major league career.

By the time he finished playing, Mays was acclaimed by everyone in the world of baseball, black and white. Home run legend Hank Aaron said Mays was the better player. Ted Williams commented at his own Hall of Fame induction that the All-Star game was made for Willie Mays. And Joe DiMaggio claimed that Willie Mays came as close to perfection as any ballplayer he had ever seen.

Elected to the Hall of Fame in his first year of eligibility, Mays again demonstrated moderation in the racial views he shared during his induction ceremony. In spite of his Jim Crow upbringing, at his induction ceremony, Mays was gracious. "This country is made up of a great many things. You can grow up to be what you want. I chose baseball, and I loved every minute of it. I give you one word. Love." *See also* Sports.

Further Readings: Durocher, Leo. *Nice Guys Finish Last.* New York: Pocket Books, 1975; Einstein, Charles. *Willie's Time: A Memoir.* New York: J. P. Lippincott, 1979; Linge, Mary Kay. *Willie Mays: A Biography.* Westport, CT: Greenwood Press, 2005; Mays, Willie. *Willie Mays: My Life in and out of Baseball.* New York: E. P. Dutton, 1966; Mays, Willie, and Lou Sahadi. *Say Hey: The Autobiography of Willie Mays.* New York: Simon & Schuster, 1988; Negro League Baseball Players Association, "Willie Mays," http://www.nlbpa.com/mays_willie.html (accessed July 2007); Saccoman, John. "Willie Mays." The Baseball Biography Project, http://bioproj.sabr.org/bioproj.cfm?a=v&v=l&bid=388&pid=9039 (accessed July 2007); Tygiel, Jules. "The Negro Leagues." *Organization of American Historians Magazine of History* 7 (Summer 1992).

Louis Mazzari

Meredith, James (b. 1933)

James Howard Meredith was a reluctant civil rights pioneer known for his integration of the University of **Mississippi,** but he always eschewed such honorific labels as well as the public spotlight.

Meredith was born on June 25, 1933, in Kosciusko, Mississippi. After graduating from high school, Meredith enlisted in the U.S. Air Force, in which he served from 1951 to 1960. During his service, he spent time overseas. Additionally, Meredith began to take college courses offered through military outreach programs. Upon his honorable discharge from the air force, he returned to Mississippi and attended historically black Jackson State College, completing two years of study. On January 31, 1961, Meredith applied to the University of Mississippi. From the outset, university officials stalled the admission process by using, what Meredith would describe in his letter to the U.S. Justice Department in which he appealed for assistance, as "delaying tactics."

Anticipating the struggle he faced in his attempt to be admitted to the University of Mississippi, Meredith also wrote to **Thurgood Marshall,** seeking representation from the **National Association for the Advancement of Colored People (NAACP) Legal Defense and Education Fund.** Near the end of May 1961, the NAACP proceeded with litigation to have Meredith admitted, and the case eventually ended up in the **U.S. Supreme Court.** On September 10, 1961, the Supreme Court decided that Meredith should be allowed to attend the university.

What followed was a showdown between the state of Mississippi and the **federal government** over states' rights and opportunities for equal education. Segregationist governor Ross Barnett took active steps to prevent Meredith from registering for classes by physically blocking Meredith's entrance into the appropriate university office. Tensions grew in the area and boiled over with riots that encompassed the entire campus. In response to Barnett's defiance of the Supreme Court, President **John F. Kennedy** ordered the mobilization of federal marshals and federal troops to Mississippi to enforce the order admitting Meredith. This step only further riled the segregationists in the area, and there were several violent clashes between the protesters of Meredith's admittance and the federal authorities. The conflicts were bloody, with two deaths and scores of serious injuries. Finally, the violence abated after pleas from all sides, and Meredith attended his first class on October 1, 1962. He went on to graduate from the University of Mississippi, pursue further studies in Nigeria, and receive an LLB from Columbia University.

Meredith took a leadership role in the March Against Fear in 1966. He was shot by Aubrey James Norvell while participating in the march from Memphis, Tennessee, to Jackson, Mississippi. He recovered from the wound and was able to complete the journey. Meredith then retreated from the limelight and became a businessperson who seemed to want to put his contributions behind him. After this period, he relocated to Washington and worked on the staff of Senator Jesse Helms on matters of domestic policy. He made several unsuccessful runs for Congress as a Republican and wrote a number of books and articles.

As the 40th anniversary of Meredith's entry into the University of Missis- sippi approached, his attendance at the ceremony remained in doubt. In the end, Meredith reluctantly attended the ceremony, but he again expressed his desire to be viewed only as a humble U.S. citizen who sought the protections and opportunities offered by the government and not as a civil rights hero. Nonetheless, many still view Meredith as a significant contributor to the **Civil Rights Movement** and, at the same time, respect his wishes to be thought of as just another American standing up for himself and others through action. *See also* National Guard; Segregation, Suburban.

Further Readings: Klarman, Michael. *From Jim Crow to Civil Rights: The Supreme Court and the Struggle for Racial Equality.* New York: Oxford University Press, 2004; Meredith, James. *Three Years in Mississippi.* Bloomington: Indiana University Press, 1966.

Aaron Cooley

Mexico

With the Spanish imperial ambitions in the New World satisfied by the con- quest of the Aztec Empire, Spain set in place a racial system that endures to this day. The racial caste (casta) system that existed in Mexico in the eigh- teenth century was developed by the Spanish crown to refer to the racial mix- tures that comprised Mexican Society. At the top of the racial caste system were the Spaniards born in Spain. Since the Spaniards did not prohibit **interra- cial marriages**, the racial paradigm became blurred and ambiguous. The Brit- ish colonies, on the other hand, maintained a rigid system of segregation. This difference can be explained in part by the influence of religion in Spanish colonialism, and the lack of it in North America. In the late 1500s, a Mestizo classification was often the result of an illegitimate offspring between an indigenous person and a Spaniard. Since the slave population was at the lowest end of the caste system, it became necessary to deny African connections.

"Mixed race people" is what Mexican intellectual Jose Vasconcelos pro- posed in his book, *The Cosmic Race,* written in 1925. This contribution was a continuation of the Spanish racial paradigm that was developed earlier under Spanish rule. Jose Vasconcelos also proposed a more subtle form of rac- ism embedded in his racial proposal when he said that blackness could be elim- inated in a few generations through intermarriage.

Though the long-held belief that the racial paradigm of "Mestizaje" is non- racist, it cannot be sustained when viewed from the perspective of it calling for the absorption of racial phenotypes into a "whiter" version of humanity. Interestingly, it was nevertheless viewed negatively by the white settler popula- tions who rejected any form of intermarriage. What Vasconcelos wrote of was not exactly white, but implied a twist on the Anglo "**one-drop rule**" of racism, which says that any percentage of African ancestry makes an individual black. Notwithstanding the argument that the one-drop rule is racist, and implies that only "black blood" somehow contaminates, Vasconselos reversed the argument so that the opposite becomes true. The opposite of the one-drop rule, as applied by racial models in the United States, was applied in Mexico, and lays claim to another racist model that says that "white blood purifies."

In the United States, the one-drop rule was used to enforce a racist outlook designed to perpetuate slavery and segregation. The Mexican reverse of the one-drop rule was used to create a national identity devoid of its Indian and African past. This twist of racism is linked to "beauty," or lighter skin, which, according to Vasconcelos, blacks cannot have, but some "lighter"-skinned individuals can. Here, Vasconcelos defended the racist Spanish hierarchical structure and saw it as superior to the segregated policies of British Protestant colonialism that generally existed in the United States since its inception.

The Spanish method of removing black and Indian features was the desired outcome. This may explain why some Mexicans attempt to deny African connections and prefer a "Latinized" version of racial identity. This assimilation is carried over into the term "Hispanic." Arguably, the modern-day use of the term "Hispanic" is the continued remnant of colonialism and the racial agenda of "blood purification," in that it includes all persons who are descendents of Spanish culture regardless of racial classifications developed by North Americans. Thus, "Spanish linguistic superiority," the inverse of English language chauvinism, is but the remains of the colonial conflicts for world supremacy between English and Spanish slavers. Vasconcelos wrote that the Spanish language is "the language of one of the most illustrious races in the world." Such racist Hispanocentric constructions places Spain at the top of all other cultural-racial constructions and leads to the purposeful extinction of the Indian and the African influences.

When Mexico abolished slavery in 1829, it became a haven for runaway slaves and *Mascogos,* or Black Seminoles. The slaveowners on the Texas side of the border often crossed over to capture blacks to sell, or to return runaways. This tension between the two countries was exacerbated by the belief that Mexicans, or Spaniards, were not white by American standards, though the Mexican Creole elite tried very hard to be. Mexico also had an Afro-Mestizo president, Vincente Guerrero, who abolished slavery, creating even more tensions for the slaveowning class in **Texas**.

The national identity created in Mexico accomplished a light-skinned paradigm, but unlike the extreme racial polarization inherent in British colonial thought. Racism in Mexico was a "blending" that approaches racist forms of whiteness. It could be argued that Spanish racism sanctioned the belief that the more "drops of white (Spanish) blood" one had, the closer one came to the accepted racial hierarchy. This difference meant confrontation between the United States and Mexico. Intermarrying that resulted in lighter-skinned babies allowed for cross-cultural paths to be chosen that would increase the probability of being accepted into whiter identities. But this applied in Mexico only and was rejected by the Anglo view of race. Those who were ethnically vague began to pass into either Indian or Spanish culture in Mexico. The visible racial features, however, did not completely disappear, as is evidenced by the Afro Mexicans in Veracruz and in western coastal areas of Mexico today. However, these racial underpinnings would serve to develop the Mexican national identity in the form of a light-skinned ruling class, but would also cause racially minded whites in the United States to view Mexico as a country of nonwhites.

On the surface, when races are compared in Mexico with the U.S. definition of what constitutes "blackness," one might be tempted to conclude that the Mexican construction is more progressive. However, contortions of racist concepts do not enjoy acceptance. But these differences produce racial tensions despite agreement on the concept of racial inferiority between Mexican paradigms and Anglo ones. A mixed-race person who would be described as black in the United States could be described as Mexican (with white underpinnings) in Mexico. *See also* Hispanics/Latinos.

Further Readings: Carrera, Magali M. *Imagining Identity in New Spain.* Austin: University of Texas Press, 2003; Carroll, Patrick J. *Blacks in Colonial Veracruz: Race, Ethnicity, and Regional Development.* Austin: University of Texas Press, 1991; Krauze, Enrique. *Mexico Biography of Power: A History of Modern Mexico, 1810–1996.* New York: HarperCollins, 1997; MacLachlan, Colin M., and Jaime E. Rodriguez O. *The Forging of the Cosmic Race: A Reinterpretation of Colonial Mexico.* Berkeley: University of California Press, 1980.

Mario Marcel Salas

Minstrelsy

Minstrel shows were the first form of musical theater that was uniquely American, based on American history and featuring uniquely American social relations. Minstrelsy began in the 1820s and went on to become America's most popular form of entertainment for nearly a hundred years (although blackface depictions date back to the 1750s, before the American Revolution). The very phrase "**Jim Crow**" came into existence by **Thomas D. Rice**'s depiction of a black man who "Jumped Jim Crow" and later became *the* image of African Americans in the United States. For these shows, whites used burnt cork to darken their skin and lipstick to enlarge their mouths to depict a stereotype of Africans and African Americans in a wide variety of American settings

General Description

Minstrel shows used stereotypes for white profit by simultaneously constructing black and white identities in the national imagination. Minstrel shows represent the most provocative and, perhaps, revealing form of entertainment in the late nineteenth and early twentieth centuries. Their enticing use of black bodies and representations created, enforced, and disseminated ideas about whiteness and white privilege, and, conversely, black inherent inferiority and subservience. By both portraying blacks a certain way, generally in line with racial stereotypes of the time, as well as articulating statements that voiced political, social, and economic concerns, minstrel shows became both a principal site of struggle in and over the perceived culture of blacks.

The image of blacks that appeared in minstrel shows, Jim Crow, was based on a caricature of a black homeless man, dressed in ragged clothes, singing and dancing on stage. Though a gross misrepresentation of blacks, these depictions were perceived as reality and taken as truth when depicted by working-class whites in blackface. During minstrel shows, white audiences witnessed blacks in a wide variety of settings, ranging from slave ships to plantations to the urban North. Nearly all included (mis)representations of "authentic" black dancing styles. To attract large audiences, minstrel shows featured popular American music, most notably "Dixie," a nostalgic song dreaming of the "good old days" of white aristocracy rooted in blacks' plantation life. Contributing to these shows were many famous American songwriters, including Stephen Foster, who wrote lyrics to accompany blackfaced actors performances.

The content and subjects of minstrelsy changed with each historical epoch in America. The largest shifts appeared after **slavery** and emancipation and then again during the early part of the twentieth century, which coincided with both the **Great Migration** of blacks northward and out of the South and mass migration of Southern and Eastern Europeans into America. This inexpensive entertainment for the masses provided many urban dwellers who spent their evenings watching minstrel shows with sufficient information about blacks to develop racial (and racist) attitudes about many of the men and women with whom they often lived in close proximity and/or competed with for jobs. However, traveling minstrel shows, which were extremely popular, brought these forms and ideas to countless Americans in the Midwest who never had any contact with blacks, thereby allowing them to participate in both American cultures and ideologies.

Popular image of Jim Crow as a minstrel, 1860s. Courtesy of Library of Congress, LC-USZ62-13935.

After the Civil War, minstrel shows featured nostalgically longing depictions of the "good old days" of slavery, when slaves were happy and content on the plantations. The new content of minstrel show also resulted in the introduction of new characters into the shows. Prominent characters included Zip Coon, Sambo, the mammy, and the brute. Characters were depicted as whites' conceptions of good blacks (Sambo and Mammy), the "brute nigger" who delighted in carrying knives and starting fights, and the dandy, who attempted to imitate upper-class white styles of dress and speech. The inhumanity and cartoon-like nature of these characters distanced real blacks from being perceived as equal to whites. Finally, black children, often referred to as "pickaninnies," were ignorant youths often prone to thievery and other forms of deviance with little potential aptitude for the new public education system in America that few wanted to extend to blacks.

Particularly fearful to whites was the black brute intent on raping white women. These depictions of these rapacious black men fueled a century of lynchings that took countless lives of innocent black men and women oftentimes only on the whispered rumor of a rape, or even a sideways glance, deemed inappropriate, at white women. Deeply embossed in American culture, the nation's first feature-length film, *The Birth of a Nation* (based on **Thomas Dixon**'s book, *The Clansman*), featured the black brute, a white man in blackface depicted as chasing after a white woman who would rather jump from a cliff to her death than lose her chastity and virginity to a black man.

Throughout their long history, minstrel acts reflected an admiration and longing for values and characteristics of blackness in line with racial ideologies of the time period. Childish, emotional, and musical and rhythmic characteristics of blacks conveyed to white audiences that blacks were intellectually inferior to whites and lacked the intelligence and other mental resources to succeed in any profession beyond servile positions. In this way, caricatures of blacks in minstrel shows also embodied the past for which whites longed, thus voicing a conscious wish for black social and economic inequality implicit in slavery.

Ideological Functions

Minstrelsy is a useful example of how race was learned and perpetuated through popular culture, entertainment, and media forms. Minstrel shows, like **lynchings**, focused on a black otherness that unified whites and led to the creation of a unique American identity. These images of blacks supported, dispelled, and reinforced ideologies of white superiority ranging, depending on the time period, from environmental causes for degradation, inherent inferiority, romantic racialism, paternalism, social Darwinism, and progressivism. These images then provided whites, many of whom in the North likely knew few blacks, with the knowledge necessary to shape their own identity to the contrary of this perceived black inferiority.

As black culture developed, whites appropriated parts and pieces of it to use for their own economic advantage and political purposes, thereby shaping their own culture in turn. When blackness was vague and uncertain whites took what they saw and assumed that it was authentic, combined these visions with previous stereotypes, prejudices, and images about savages in Africa and created a blackness they could use to their advantage. In this way, blackness became integral to both the American identity and culture, even though most whites rarely maintain any kind of sustained relationship with their black counterparts.

As the first true and realized white entertainment in the nation, and in the world, minstrel shows emphasized the white identity of its audience and actors, and their difference from those whom they were imitating. In line with the racial ideologies of the time, particularly Romantic racialism, minstrel shows usually portrayed blacks as emotional characters who, although they had qualities whites often lacked, had a number of others that made success in America impossible—they were shiftless and lazy, brutish and sex-crazed, dirty and incompetent. In other words, they were everything whites were not, and thus something against which whites could use to measure themselves. Minstrel shows thereby educated Northern whites and new immigrants who may have rarely encountered blacks in their daily lives, as to these characteristics, thereby disseminating a highly damaging and long-lasting racial ideology of white supremacy.

Unskilled immigrants from Europe, particularly Ireland, during the second half of the nineteenth century were flooding America's shores and competing with blacks for the lowest paying jobs in the North. Mocking blacks through minstrel shows in the late nineteenth and early twentieth centuries ensured that blacks would be considered neither citizens nor workers on the same plane as whites. Instead, minstrelsy further identified the presumed differences between blacks and whites, even among those working in similar positions in the North. The license with which blackface provided whites allowed them to make statements about their own social circumstances that reflected the longing, fears, hopes, and prejudices enmeshed with being among the white working class in the nineteenth century. Minstrel shows inhibited cross-racial coalitions by ideologically suppressing black workers and obscuring any similarities between the two groups.

Lasting Legacies of Minstrel Shows

In addition to existing on the historical stage, minstrel figures continue to exist in many popular forms. For example, the vast majority of television programs and movies lack depictions of blacks in middle-class and professional roles and instead often appear as sidekicks, clowns, or criminals. Advertising, historically, drew on America's longing for the ideal and "simple" days of the plantation era. For generations, stereotyped caricatures of blacks have appeared on a wide variety of popular brands (such as the Gold Dust Twins and Nigger Brand oysters, tobacco, and toothpaste) and household products (ashtrays, piggybanks, kitchen accessories, etc.). A trip to a modern supermarket will find the legacies of these products and images in Aunt Jemima and Mrs. Butterworth's (classic examples of the Mammy figure) and Uncle Ben (an Uncle Tom figure) remain on store shelves.

Minstrel figures have also appeared in popular cartoons, particularly Bugs Bunny cartoons by Warner Brothers and a variety of cartoons by Walt Disney (including *Brer Rabbit and the Tar Baby*), through the 1980s. These cartoons often featured happy, smiling, banjo-playing, watermelon-eating, big-lipped, barefoot, blacks in the South in a plantation setting or in Africa, as comic savages, roasting the hero in a pot, alluding to cannibalism. Therefore, while these images appeared from stage shows prior to **World War II** their lasting legacy continues to influence new generations of youth, including the current one. *See also* Children's Literature.

Further Readings: Dates, Janette L., and William Barlow. *Split Image: African Americans in the Mass Media.* 2nd ed. Washington, DC: Howard University Press, 1993; Fredrickson, George M. *The Black Image in the White Mind: The Debate on Afro-American Character and Destiny, 1817–1914.* New York: Harper & Row, 1971; Hale, Grace Elizabeth. *Making Whiteness: The Culture of Segregation in the South, 1890–1940.* New York: Vintage, 1999; Lott, Evan. *Love and Theft: Blackface Minstrelsy and the American Working Class.* New York: Oxford University Press, 1993; Roediger, David R. *The Wages of Whiteness: Race and the Making of the American Working Class.* Rev. ed. New York: Verso Books, 1999.

Melissa F. Weiner

Miscegenation

"Miscegenation" refers to the mixing, interbreeding, sexual union, marriage, or cohabitation of people of different races or ethnic groups, especially whites and nonwhites. Given the pejorative and racist implications of its historical application, the term is considered offensive and has largely dropped from contemporary usage. From **Thomas Dixon** to **Gunnar Myrdal**, two poles in the evolution of mainstream American racial thought, it was expressed as common knowledge that the primary reason for segregation during **Jim Crow** was the fear of the ultimate taboo of miscegenation. Ostensibly, the issue of miscegenation can be considered the linchpin of racial antipathy during the Jim Crow era.

The term first appeared during the war election of 1864 as the title of an anonymous pamphlet, *Miscegenation: The Theory of the Blending of the Races, Applied to the American White Man and Negro.* While the term "amalgamation" had been used previously, the anonymous author explained his need to invent a new term from the classical Latin *misc,* "to mix," and *genus,* "race," in order to be more specific. The pamphlet, which sold on newsstands for 25 cents in the summer of 1863, turned out to be a hoax concocted by copperhead journalists David Goodman Croly and George Wakeman in order to sabotage President Abraham Lincoln's reelection campaign and Republican control of Congress. The treatise, pretending to represent the radical Republican goal of "social equality," argued in favor of race mixing, stating not only that all races originated from one type and are therefore equal, but, even more controversially, that racial mixing would actually strengthen the human race and should be adopted as national policy. In actuality, these views represented the polar opposite of what appeared regularly in scientific and popular literature from the mid-nineteenth century through the first few decades of the twentieth century.

The History of Racial Mixing in the New World

Unlike in the West Indies and **Latin America**, the attitude toward miscegenation as one of reprobation appeared in written legislation during the early colonial period in the late seventeenth and early eighteenth centuries. One of the earliest surviving colonial records from Virginia shows that in 1662, the Virginia colony established a law that imposed additional punishment for fornication between whites and blacks. Other legislation of the period already referred to the "mulatto" offspring of interracial sexual relations as "mongrel" and "spurious" and attempted to formally bastardize such progeny. Through such legislation, the mulatto came to be legally characterized as black and thus faced the same slave codes as blacks of predominantly African heritage.

The difference in the history of white treatment of mulattoes among the European colonies in the New World largely depended upon the ratio of white men to black and Indian women in the population. To a lesser degree, but a significant one, the status of white women and attitudes toward the family played a role in white attitudes toward miscegenation, or more properly, how to classify mixed progeny. In the United States, where there came to be a high ideal placed on the white family and likewise the purity of the white race and its dominance, it became more important to distance mulattoes from the master class.

Through antimiscegenation law and the legal classification of mixed-race offspring as black, illegitimate, and, if enslaved, property, the white male ruling class was able to have it all: increased slave labor supply, indulgence of sexual fantasies and desires, maintenance of white purity, and maintenance of white power. The classification of mulattoes as black also allowed white men to deny that miscegenation ever occurred and thereby allowed them to relieve, to some degree, their guilt over their inability to control their sexual desire. However, despite legal classification, mulattoes remained an ostensible reminder of their actions, and whites attempted to cover their tracks with particular rhetorical stringency against the practice.

Before the Revolutionary War, only two states, **Virginia** and **North Carolina**, bothered to write the taboo of miscegenation into law, although for all states (except **Louisiana**), common attitudes and regulation prevailed. After the Revolutionary War when the free black population increased, however, slave states began coming up with their own laws. These laws often defined the percentage of black "blood" present in one's heritage to determine one's race. Over time, these laws would become more stringent and morph into the so-called "**one-drop rule.**"

In the antebellum lower South, where demographics more closely resembled those of the **Caribbean** and Latin America, free mulatto classes did develop, particularly in the cities, but also in rural areas. Louisiana, and the city of New Orleans in particular, with its more recent history of Spanish and French colonialism, exhibited a more overt likeness to the southern part of the hemisphere with its general acceptance of interracial relationships and its intermediary mulatto class. While concubinage was prevalent throughout the Cotton Belt, it was practically institutionalized in Louisiana through the practice of *plaçage* and the related "quadroon balls." Likewise, before the Civil War, attempts to legalize blood quantum usually failed in Louisiana. South Carolina, especially Charleston, was a close runner-up in terms of the prevalence of a free and accepted mulatto class, although all of the lower South exhibited this phenomenon to some extent. Savannah, Georgia and Mobile, Alabama, are two other major examples of cities with a history of thriving free mulatto communities.

The mulatto communities of the lower South maintained only a fraction of the population, yet they comprised a large percentage of the free black population. They were often property owning and sometimes even well off. Nonetheless, they were consistently distinguished from whites, despite the groups' cultural similarities. This situation created an atmosphere of color discrimination within the black population whereby lighter-skinned mulattoes would employ racialist justifications for their superiority over darker-skinned blacks.

Whites in the lower South achieved a degree of loyalty from the free mulatto class which they saw as a level of security, a buffer, between the planter class and the slaves—a view much like that held by white planters in the Caribbean and Latin America. However, the free mulatto class represented just a fraction of mulattoes in the United States during slavery. Most mulattoes were enslaved.

Approaching the Civil War, attitudes toward the free mulatto class began to change. The discourse of racial purity and the unnaturalness of interracial sex began to permeate the (lower) South from the North, particularly as the idea of race gained currency apart from the condition of servitude, and as the United States witnessed increased attention toward the biological and social scientific disciplines as authorities for explaining folk impressions about racial differences.

Racial Science and the Era of Jim Crow

Within 50 years after emancipation, the "one-drop rule" emerged alongside increasingly popular scientific classifications and explanations of race. Whereas during slavery, there was a relatively unsophisticated correlation between skin color and status of enslaved or free, after emancipation, various scientific endeavors sought biological evidence of racial differences. In 1758, Swedish botanist, zoologist, and physician Carl Linnaeus developed a simple classificatory system of races—Caucasian, Ethiopian, Mongolian, and American—based largely on external, visible factors. A short while later in 1775, German anatomist and naturalist Johann Friedrich Blumenbach recovered this system and added a fifth category—Malayan—to complete the schema, which inaugurated the modern notion of race.

Anthropology in the nineteenth century drew upon this classificatory system in the attempt to link race to intelligence and behavior. The practice of phrenology, which consisted of taking cranial measurements, weighing brains, and charting head shapes and sizes, served as the precursor to evolutionary psychology and social evolution introduced by Herbert Spencer, and later, the eugenics movement of the Progressive Era.

The Civil War marked a turning point in popular conceptions of racial scientific theories. The Provost Marshall-General's Bureau and the U.S. Sanitary Commission both engaged anthropometric studies that used soldiers as subjects to gather cranial measurements and other racial data. These studies added "scientific evidence" to folk claims of racial difference. As well, this "war anthropometry" marked the beginning of the popular scientific notion that so-called mixed-bloods are weak and inferior to pure "breeds." Miscegenation was thought to be a serious social error, not simply for its effects in creating a physically and morally weak hybrid species, but mainly for its role in degenerating the white race.

The language of blood, breed, and racial species that gained such powerful ideological currency from the Civil War years through the Jim Crow era begins with the debate over the monogenetic or polygenetic origins of the various races. Monogenesis refers to the idea that all races have the same human origin, while polygenesis implies that all of the races evolved independently. This latter notion was considered by many to be heretical in that it goes against a literal reading of Biblical creationism, which links all humans to the Adamite family. Still, this view eventually prevailed in the scientific community and in the public consciousness since it correlated with prevailing folk understandings of race. As emerging scientific disciplines attempted to prove polygenetic theories in the middle to late nineteenth century, religion in general had to make room for the dominance of science as the master narrative of the social. Thus, while folk theories about race pervaded in the era of piety in the United States, race as it is known today, and as it came to be enforced in the Jim Crow era, was inextricably linked to the scientific age.

By the late nineteenth century, polygenist notions inherent in the Great Chain of Being were replaced by more contemporary strains of thought, namely Jean-Baptiste Lamarck's environmentalism, and Charles Darwin's hereditarian determinism. Nevertheless, the core of polygenist thought permeated both schools and shaped racial theory between **Reconstruction** and the **World War I**—and beyond.

It was the polygenist notion of separate "species" that effected conversations on "amalgamation," or what came to be termed "miscegenation." The interbreeding of species was considered unnatural and counterproductive to the advancement of human civilization and the preservation of the so-called superior race. The tripartite logic of the polygenist view rested on the notions of mulatto infertility and sterility, the unnaturalness of race mixing, and the importance of racial purity. Despite advances in the biological and social sciences into the twentieth century, the impressionistic and anecdotal bases of polygenist racial theory continued to shape academic and popular theories about race and race mixture.

Darwin's theory of evolution became very influential on scientific thought in the late nineteenth century, even though it is based on the idea of monogenesis. Nevertheless, it was easily adapted to popular notions. Lamarckianism—the doctrine of the inheritance of (environmentally) acquired characteristics within a racial group over time—on the other hand, did not contradict the polygenist view. Lamarckianism and Neo-Lamarckianism (post-Darwinian recuperations of evolutionary psychology) conflated culture and biology and suggested that the social was reified in the biological. Additionally, Lamarckianism put forth the notion that race prejudice had biosocial origins developed for the preservation of the species. In other words, while race mixing did occur, the subconscious instinctual aversion to other groups would eventually predominate to maintain a healthy species. This view justified race prejudice as natural and desirable. Though at odds with Darwinian hereditary variation, Lamarckianism succeeded in its ability to incorporate Darwinian evolutionism and polygenist ideas. In any case, the three strains of thought together dominated the discussion of racial difference far into the twentieth century.

Franz Boas's anthropological work between 1890 and 1910 eventually developed the notion of culture as distinct from race. Boas' work in this regard helped to shape a more progressive and contemporary view of race which competed against the polygenist view and its legacy. Boas stressed the importance of accident and environment over the biological in cultural development, and eventually paved the way for the notion of human equality (of cognitive capacity). *The Mind of Primitive Man* (1911) noted a turning point in anthropological thought, ushering in the notion of cultural relativism and the ethnological method. By 1910, due in large part to Boas's advances in racial theory, Lamarckianism was largely dead and the notion of culture as separate from biological race was adopted. However, the predominance of intelligence testing in the social sciences and eugenics in the biological sciences continued with success to try to put scientific fact with racialist impression.

The American eugenics movement gained popular attention in 1912 after the first of three International Congresses on Eugenics; the second two were in 1921 and 1932. However, the interest in the scientific movement traveled over the Atlantic from the teachings of Sir Francis Galton as early as the late nineteenth century, about three decades after the publication of Darwin's *Origin of Species*. In the first three decades of the twentieth century, the founding of several U.S.-based journals including, *Eugenics and Social Welfare Bulletin* (1906), *Eugenical News* (1916), and *Eugenics: A Journal of Race Betterment* (1928), in addition to the American Breeders Association (ABA) in 1905, J. H. Kellogg's Race Betterment Foundation in 1906, and the Eugenics Record Office in 1910 officially established eugenics as a reputable field of study. Once in the United States, the American eugenics movement metamorphosed into a unique and elaborate state project.

The state and the science collided in their shared concept of rights—the right to *eugenes,* "good genes," or the right to be "well born" was the mantra of the movement, which could be heard just as frequently from scientists, statesmen, and welfare officers. With genes, or "gene plasm" (the common term), as an organizing concept, eugenics policies of immigration restriction, sterilization and race segregation were juridically enacted at a time when the United States had to decide the shape and character of American identity. By the second decade of the twentieth century, the eugenics movement and a concern with genes had taken root in the scientific community. One of its primary concerns was to address the ongoing "problem" of miscegenation. Eugenics specifically sought political and cultural ends to its academic products, particularly in the form of changing law and public sentiment.

Eugenicists were convinced—or convinced themselves—that the "mongrel" was the living embodiment of why the mixing of races should never occur. Reports in eugenics journals attempted to pile up the ways in which the racial hybrid was considered a "bodily maladjustment" based on the quasi-Mendelian idea that "racial" traits are linked traits and that to unlink these traits is to undo years of evolution and to unleash unnatural and harmful genetic combinations into the general population. In other words, the condition of miscegenation was a type of congenital disease. It is interesting to observe that eugenicists relied on Mendelian genetics to support their claims about the disharmony of miscegenation, yet actively ignored Mendel's discovery of "hybrid vigor," or the claim that the mixing of alleles from parents of different "breeds" can produce more vigorous offspring. Instead, they saw the mongrel as a particular abomination who should be kept from the general population.

Race Theory in the Public Sphere

Those involved in propagandizing the notion of racial inferiority relied upon the testimony of the academic community to justify their claims to a public. In the mid-nineteenth century, popular writers and scientists were often hard to distinguish, since either title had more to do with reputation among the scientific community then about training in a given field. However, even when, at the turn of the century, the scientific community became more discriminating, folk knowledge of race and race theory changed little. The professionalization of the academic disciplines and the establishment of academic journals in mid-century began to isolate the intellectual community from the public so that popular writers became the primary interlocutors between racial theory and popular consciousness. Ironically, these writers relied on claims to scientific fact in order to convince a public increasingly shaped by science's dominant authority. Since actual scientific advancements were often involved in disproving older folk claims, popular writers would cite any scientific source—old or new, accepted or not—to justify their claims.

Also at this time, religious arguments proclaimed the blasphemy of miscegenation. Despite popular interest in the authority of science, the United States remained a highly religious nation that paid particular attention to its consecrated leaders. Extreme clerical contributors to popular race theory attempted to use the Bible to prove miscegenation as inherently evil. Some, such as William H. Campbell, writing toward the end of the nineteenth century, argued that the great catastrophes of the Bible were all God's punishment for human attempts to mix pre-Adamic species of the genus homo with homo sapiens, the direct line of Adam and Eve. Much of the propaganda coming from the religious community paradoxically incorporated insights from the scientific community that contradicted a literal interpretation of the Bible, the polygenist thesis being a prime example.

Popular themes of the mulatto in the late nineteenth century reflected those of the scientific literature, but were often elaborated in the context of racialist propagandizing. Miscegenation was considered an "abnormal perversion" of the "instincts of reproduction" which threatened white civilization culturally, morally, and genetically. Products of miscegenation were described as physically and genetically weak, fragile and incapable of hardships, prone to consumption and venereal disease, unlikely to live into old age, sterile like the hybrid mule (from which the term *mulatto* originates), and in this way anomalous, monstrous, or diseased in condition. Mulattoes were also described as immoral, cruel, vicious, lazy, malignant, treacherous, criminal, sensual, brutal, innately depraved, the epitome of moral degradation, and the embodiment of the sin that begat him or her. Mulatta women were seen as especially lewd and hypersexual, seductive threats to white men's moral willpower, and men as especially mischievous, carnal, and indecent.

Despite the belief that products of miscegenation would inherit the worst traits of both parent races, it was assumed that mulattoes inherited an enhanced mental faculty from their white parents. This cognitive advantage, however, was seen as a dangerous threat. Racialist logic reasoned that the bestial nature of the Negro and the audacity and intellect approaching the white man present in the mulatto made for the most dangerous form of criminality. Mulatto mental superiority to the so-called pure Negro, it was believed, made him a likely instigator of revolution. With all this, the mulatto was considered a burden to the integrity of the Negro race, but far more importantly to this logic, a threat to the white race and the American nation. Many foresaw that increased miscegenation within the United States would render the nation vulnerable to the superior, pure white civilizations of Europe. In other words, American sovereignty depended on its racial purity.

The escalation of fear and paranoia over the threat of miscegenation stemmed in part from the popular concern in the South at this time about "Negro retrogression," the notion that blacks were retrogressing to a more savage state. Popular race theorists justified this notion by citing statistics demonstrating a spike in crime, particularly the rape of white women and girls. Panic over this issue was deeply linked with a sense that miscegenation was burgeoning out of control. The idea that black men were on a quest for "social equality," a term euphemistically understood as a rape-quest to miscegenate America, reached the level of popular hysteria and can explain the culture of the Jim Crow South

In the decades surrounding the turn of the century, the South witnessed a hysterical, frenzied radicalization of racial attitudes defined by these popular notions that resulted in many an effort to combat the so-called yellow peril. Solutions to the problem of miscegenation circulated within the public sphere often came down to a tripartite answer: send the Negroes back to Africa, re-enslave them, or exterminate them. A combination of legal apartheid and disenfranchisement, an economic system of indentured servitude that closely resembled slavery, and campaigns of white pride coupled with racial terror organized largely by the leadership of the **Ku Klux Klan** became the immediate solution under Jim Crow.

Lynching appeared as a regular practice of extralegal justice in the United States as early as the Revolutionary War. However, lynching developed a distinctly racial and regional character by the twentieth century. The majority of lynchings occurred in the South, perpetrated by whites on black victims. The first major spike in the 1890s coincided with the rise of the Ku Klux Klan, and by the Klan's second incarnation in the late 1910s and early 1920s, lynchings became public affairs organized by mobs and drew crowds of up to 10,000 spectators. Daytime lynchings were attended by men, women, and children in plain clothes who came, at times, with picnic lunch in hand to enjoy the brutal spectacle. Victims were tortured in ritualistic fashion, often sexually mutilated for symbolic import, and body parts were cut off and passed around as souvenirs. Nearly 5,000 people, most of whom were black, were executed in this brutal fashion during the Jim Crow era in the United States.

The ritual of lynching was propelled by many possible anxieties regarding interracial sex embedded in white patriarchal culture. These include that black men stood in for the repressed desires of white men, which they had to kill off in ritual sacrifice; that only white men had privileged access to interracial sex; that the keepers of racial purity, white women, needed actual and symbolic protection; and that white women should be frightened into a position of docility, vulnerability, and subservience to maintain white men's proprietary relationship to them. With all these possible psychological motives driving the peculiar nature of the ritual, the primary impetus for lynching black men, as discussed previously, was the purported tendency of black men to rape white women and the dire consequences of a miscegenated America.

This pernicious myth was indelibly captured on screen in **D. W. Griffith**'s landmark film *The Birth of a Nation*, which in its blockbuster success single-handedly rekindled a spike in racial violence in the South and in Ku Klux Klan membership nationally. The film, based on Thomas Dixon's novel *The Clansman,* celebrates the rise of the Ku Klux Klan as a response to advances in "social equality" during Reconstruction and an antidote to a war-torn nation. Vividly bringing to the popular imagination the major notions of race theory, the film features three villains, a black rapist, a hypersexed mulatta temptress, and the mulatto conspirator of the black takeover of the South.

While popular representations of the anxieties surrounding miscegenation appeared in films such as Griffith's in the first few decades of the twentieth century, those same anxieties eventually prompted censorship under the miscegenation clause of the Motion Picture Production Code of 1930 (the Hays Code). The trend in the representational ban on interracial relationships was unofficially lifted with the release of Stanley Kramer's acclaimed film *Guess Who's Coming to Dinner* in 1967, the same year as the *Loving v. Virgina* case that would undo an epoch of antimiscegenation legislation.

Miscegenation and the Law

While extralegal "lynch law" cropped up as a method of enforcing racial barriers in the Jim Crow South, the institution of statutory law worked to regulate intermarriage and the racial status of individuals of mixed heritage in nearly all states. Under the so-called miscegenation laws, all interracial marriages and the offspring of those marriages were considered illegitimate, and rights commonly extended to blood relations were denied.

The criminalization of miscegenation, namely **interracial marriage** and sexual relationships, had begun in the colonial period. Maryland passed the first miscegenation statute in 1661, which criminalized marriage between white women and black men. During slavery, all Southern states and many Northern ones had antimiscegenation statutes on the books. Although they were enforced almost universally in the case of white women and black men, they were ignored nearly universally in the case of interracial sex between white men and black women. The children of interracial relationships between white men and black women under slavery were bastardized, denied the usual rights of relation, and became the property of the slave master who was also oftentimes the father. Slave statues that declared that the mulatto children of slaves were also slaves both helped to create clear demarcations between slave and free, black and white, and also granted white masters and overseers the dual benefit of unrestricted sex and an increased slave labor supply.

Legislators and judges paid increasing attention to miscegenation from the mid-nineteenth century through the Reconstruction period. The Civil War amendments (1865–1870) and the Civil Rights Acts of 1866 and **1875** threatened to legitimatize interracial sex and marriage, and as a result, state courts and legislators acted more aggressively to police interracial relations. After Reconstruction, however, the **federal government** became equally interested in the enforcement of antimiscegenation legislation.

In *Pace v. Alabama,* the major precursor to the landmark **Plessy v. Ferguson** decision, the U.S. Supreme Court decided that the state of Alabama's antimiscegenation statute was constitutional. In 1881, Tony Pace, a black man, and Mary Cox, a white woman, were both charged and convicted to two years in prison for "adultery and fornication" under Section 4189 of the Code of Alabama. The couple appealed their sentences with the Alabama Supreme Court, which upheld their convictions. Upon bringing their case to the U.S. Supreme Court, the plaintiff's charge that the statute violated the equal protection clause of the Fourteenth Amendment to the U.S. Constitution was denied. The opinion of Justice Stephen J. Field argued similarly to the Alabama Supreme Court case that since both the white and black parties involved in the crime of miscegenation are punished equally, equal protection under the law is upheld. While the federal court more or less reiterated the state decision, Justice Field did not comment on the State's argument that Section 4189 did not aim to discriminate against the person involved in the crime, but rather against the offense itself, whose "evil tendency" threatens to bring forth a "mongrel population and a degraded civilization."

By the second decade of the twentieth century, in most of the states, the penalty for participating in one of these prohibited marriages involved a fine of up to $2,000 and up to 10 years in jail. Particularly into the twentieth century, it became clear that the "evil" behind antimiscegenation legislation was not so much the act of fornication, which has its own legislative history, as it was the tendency of the offense to lead to a mongrel population that threatened white purity and white dominance in the United States.

Antimiscegenation laws and the prohibition on interracial relationships were originally targeted at African American and white marriages. However, the discourse on miscegenation in the United States applied to other races as well, albeit with great variation. In the case of the American Indian, antimiscegenation law was enforced but with notable leniency. For example, while "quadroons" and "octoroons" were generally treated under the law as "black," persons one-quarter or less American Indian were considered white, depending on the state and the year in history. Evidence of a more lax attitude toward Indian-white mixing is exemplified in the Pocahontas exception of the Virginia Antimiscegenation Act of 1924, which states that those white persons who could trace there ancestry back to the union of John Rolfe and Pocahontas were considered by law to be fully white. Long before the rising fear of miscegenation reached its pinnacle in the early twentieth century, claiming lineage to the legendary Powhatan princess was a privilege withheld for Virginia's aristocratic families. Racial visibility played a crucial role in identification as well, and American Indian lineage, as well as the lineage of the other nonwhite races, was considered harder to detect than "Negro blood."

The One-Drop Rule

In 1850, the federal census first began taking note of "mulattoes," but in 1890, the census became more specific, designating mulattoes, quadroons, and octoroons. The accuracy of these records, of course, is dubious, considering the inability of the record taker to determine blood quantum by appearance. At different points in history, it was possible to possess a black lineage so "diluted" by white "blood" as to be legally insignificant. However, by the twentieth century, the "one-drop rule" deemed that any evidence whatsoever of Negro ancestry determined black identity. Despite the laws that dealt with percentages, there are no cases that show attempts to prove white identity through them. In reality, identification was made through visual appearance. In *Hudgins v. Wright* (Va. 1806), the court made the decision that three generations of women with straight black hair were Indian, not black, and therefore free. This decision legally established that racial appearance, even more than calculated percentages, determined a person's race.

The particular obsession with racial appearance and the one-drop rule, which distinguished race relations in the United States (and Canada) from those in Latin America and the Caribbean, brought on the common practice among light-complexioned persons of color of "passing," or identifying as white. During slavery, racial passing was often employed as a strategy for escape. In the years after emancipation, some chose to pass in order to experience the benefits of being part of the racial majority. Passing was often considered a risky endeavor in that the discovery of one's true racial identity could result in dire, sometimes violently fatal, consequences. Such has been the theme of many works of literature from the Jim Crow era. Some notable examples include Frances Ellen Watkins Harper's *Iola Leroy*, Mark Twain's *Pudd'nhead Wilson*, Nella Larsen's *Passing*, James Weldon Johnson's *The Autobiography of an Ex-Colored Man*, George Schuyler's *Black No More*, Jessie Faucet's *Plum Bun*, and William Faulkner's *Light in August*.

Loving v. Virginia *and After*

It was not until 1967 that the opinion in *Pace v. Alabama* was overturned in the case of *Loving v. Virginia,* in which Chief Justice Warren observed that "the fact that Virginia prohibits only interracial marriages involving white persons demonstrates that the racial classifications must stand on their own justification, as measures designed to maintain White Supremacy." The opinion thus states that "there can be no doubt that restricting the freedom to marry solely because of racial classifications violates the central meaning of the Equal Protection Clause." However, the California State Supreme Court Case *Perez v. Sharp* actually made a similar decision in 1948, nearly 20 years earlier.

Further Readings: Courtney, Susan. *Hollywood Fantasies of Miscegenation: Spectacular Narratives of Gender and Race, 1903–1967.* Princeton, NJ: Princeton University Press, 2005; Croly, David Goodman, and George Wakeman. *Miscegenation: The Theory of the Blending of the Races.* New York: H. Dexter, Hamilton, 1864; Dailey, Jane, Glenda Elizabeth Gilmore, and Bryant Simon, eds. *Jumpin' Jim Crow: Southern Politics from Civil War to Civil Rights.* Princeton, NJ: Princeton University Press, 2000; Johnson, Kevin R., ed. *Mixed Race America and the Law: A Reader.* New York: NYU Press, 2003; Lemire, Elise. *"Miscegenation": Making Race in America.* Philadelphia: University of Pennsylvania Press, 2002; Mencke, John G. *Mulattoes and Race Mixture: American Attitudes and Images, 1865–1918.* UMI Research Press, 1979; Zack, Naomi, ed. *American Mixed Race: The Culture of Microdiversity.* Lanham, MD: Rowman & Littlefield, 1995.

Danielle C. Heard

Mississippi

Jim Crow practices were arguably more deeply entrenched in Mississippi than in any other state. The roots of this lie partly in the large number of slaves in the state before 1865. In 1860, there were over 436,000 slaves in Mississippi, who accounted for more than 55 percent of the population, second only to **South Carolina**. Following emancipation, many freedmen remained in Mississippi and gained the franchise under the 1868 **Reconstruction** state constitution, the first constitution of Mississippi not to limit voting to whites. Black Mississippians registered to vote in large numbers: in 1868, 96.7 percent of those eligible to register had done so, compared with 80.9 percent of eligible whites. Several blacks held high political office during this period: among others, Hiram Rhodes Revels and Blanche Kelso Bruce were both U.S. Senators, while A. K. Davis served as lieutenant governor. Most black office holders held minor local positions.

Despite the large number of registered black voters, black Mississippians made little mark on the state's politics during Reconstruction. This was largely because of white efforts to prevent blacks from taking advantage of the franchise. In 1875, the First Mississippi Plan gerrymandered black majorities into irrelevance, a move that was supported by intimidation and violence to discourage blacks from voting. The results were obvious and immediate: in 1880, 66 percent of registered blacks did not vote in the presidential election. By 1890, when the Second Mississippi Plan redrew the state constitution, black disfranchisement was almost complete. This was achieved by a range of measures that, although they did not expressly mention race, were clearly designed to exclude blacks from the vote. This was particularly true of the understanding clause, which required an individual to read any section of the state constitution, or to be able to understand it, or give a reasonable interpretation of the section, when read to him. While this clause allowed illiterate whites to register, the function of the 1890 constitution was primarily to deny the franchise to black Mississippians. Although some blacks still managed to register, by 1896 only 8.2 percent of eligible blacks were registered.

The large-scale exclusion of blacks from the vote was matched by increasing restrictions on their freedom and rights in other aspects of Mississippi life. Before Reconstruction, Mississippi had introduced a series of repressive **Black Codes,** and many of these were carried on when home rule returned. In 1888, the first Jim Crow law was passed, segregating railroad coaches. In practice, however, Jim Crow had been in place in Mississippi for many years. Even before it came into law in 1888, most railroad coaches were already segregated, as were many other public facilities, including steamboats, hotels, and restaurants. Biracial education was virtually nonexistent; interracial marriage was forbidden, and in their leisure time, the races were separate. Increasingly, blacks and whites lived in different parts of towns by law, while in some towns' curfews defined when blacks could be on the street.

Indeed, while Mississippi did pass other Jim Crow laws, fewer were required than in other states, because the custom of racial separation was so entrenched. There are examples of apparent integration throughout Mississippi in this period (for example, a soda fountain in Indianola remained integrated until the 1930s), but the subordinate position of blacks was never in doubt and was rarely challenged. Even where blacks and whites shared personal space—such as in working situations—long-established Jim Crow customs made it clear that whites were always superior. The custom of white supremacy was as effective a tool as legal segregation.

Black employment opportunities were severely limited by Jim Crow. In urban areas, blacks worked in a variety of occupations, which tended to be limited to low-paid domestic and manual jobs. In such occupations, blacks could be paid less than whites and worked harder and longer; black labor was less likely to be organized and could more easily be fired. While there were black professionals, they were few in number and tended to exist solely for the black community. The respect afforded white doctors and lawyers was rarely directed towards black professionals: indeed, they were often regarded with suspicion as race agitators.

For many black Mississippians, however, agricultural work was all that could be expected. Few blacks could afford to buy land, and when they were able to do so, such land tended to be on poorer soil: in the Delta region, black landowners were scarce, although they were more numerous in the southwest part of the state. Most black agricultural workers were tenant farmers and sharecroppers. In the first half of the twentieth century particularly, this system bore more than a passing resemblance to slavery in a number of ways. Black tenants relied on white landowners for employment and shelter, were subject to the whims of their landlord, and were vulnerable to punishment for transgressing racial codes. Sharecroppers were routinely swindled by landlords who paid them less than their share; while blacks were often aware of this, they had little recourse. Tenants who sought to leave or to break employment contracts were often forcibly returned to the land, sometimes being punished to serve as peons. Through **sharecropping**, the Delta planter elite was guaranteed a cheap, pliable and easily-replaceable workforce.

Sharecropping also did much to perpetuate Jim Crow as a means of social control. The planter class was powerful financially and politically, and many prominent Mississippi politicians relied on the support of working-class whites. Blaming blacks for Mississippi's ills and ensuring that the potential power of a united black and white labor force never came to pass helped Delta planters to protect their position. Race-baiting became a regular tactic on the stump, and politicians like Theodore G. Bilbo and James K. Vardaman were renowned for engendering race hatred among their supporters.

Clear lines of racial etiquette existed in Mississippi, and these were well-known to blacks, who were careful to adhere to expected standards of behavior. The punishment for transgressing racial codes were also well-known: between the 1870s and 1930s, **lynchings** were more common in Mississippi than in any other state. The brutality of lynching was matched often by its seeming randomness. While white mobs regularly lynched alleged criminals before they could be tried legally, countless individuals were lynched based on rumor, suspicion, or mistaken identity. Moreover, as much as lynchings were used to punish blacks who had crossed racial lines, they also served to send a message to the black community; thus, few lynch mobs were concerned if their victim was innocent. It was not uncommon for a crime to be punished

Farmers in a Mississippi cotton field, 1908. Courtesy of Library of Congress, H118685.

by the indeterminate lynching of several black people. Lynching was often a method through which whites reasserted their dominance over blacks and lynching tended to be more frequent during times of economic difficulty.

The second-class nature of black life in Mississippi extended to **education**. Throughout the Jim Crow period, schools were segregated. State spending on black schools was a fraction of that on white schools. Based on assumptions that black education was an unnecessary and expensive luxury, the proposition that only black taxes should be spent on black schools was popular in the early years of the twentieth century, although never enacted. Black education was also considered a threat to the state's social structure, and many whites feared that educated blacks would challenge Jim Crow; in particular, planters were concerned that black education would reduce the agricultural labor force.

While some black Mississippians believed that education was pointless in a state that denied black people access to jobs where it might be required, many blacks were convinced that education was a cornerstone of black uplift, and money for black schools and teachers' salaries often came from black community efforts and privately owned buildings like churches and stores often served as schools. Few schools, whether private or public, had the resources to provide a high school education, and eighth grade was as far as many black children were able to attend, although many did not reach that mark. Private institutions, whether elementary, high school, or further education colleges, were often supported by Northern benefactors, but many still struggled to survive.

While black teachers were noted for their diligence and enthusiasm, they were faced with seemingly unending challenges. Attaining the appropriate training was difficult for potential black teachers. For much of the first half of the twentieth century the only teacher training available at a public college of higher education was at Alcorn Agricultural and Mechanical College; otherwise, private institutions like Tougaloo College, or unaccredited summer schools were the only means of obtaining training. Black teachers' salaries were routinely significantly smaller than those of white teachers, and resources were scarce. Such difficulties were compounded by the tendency of many black children to attend school for only part of the year, particularly in rural areas where they assisted in the fields, or to attend only until they were old enough to became full field hands.

Black higher education was rare, but private institutions like Tougaloo and Alcorn represented efforts to provide the education that white Mississippi sought to deny. These institutions counted many prominent black Mississippians among their alumni. Eventually, in the 1940s, Mississippi created two state black teacher training institutions, Jackson State College for Negro Teachers and Mississippi State Vocational College. For many blacks, however, particularly in rural areas, Jim Crow ensured that higher education was not a viable option by denying a quality elementary education and regarding blacks as little more than cheap labor.

World War II marked a watershed in race relations in Mississippi. Blacks were offered opportunities that allowed them to escape the restrictions of Jim Crow. Many black men left Mississippi, many for the first time, to serve in the military; financially, this meant that their families no longer needed to work on the land. Others were able to leave agriculture through better-paid factory employment supporting the war effort. By breaking their economic dependence on whites, blacks were less curtailed by Mississippi's social structure. In the Delta, planters attempted to counter this by offering higher wages, but few blacks were tempted, and the Second World War was a time of relative freedoms for many black Mississippians.

These freedoms gave rise to a new determination to challenge racial subjugation. This was complemented by the return of black veterans, many of whom were all too aware of the irony of fighting for freedoms in Europe that they themselves did not have in Mississippi. During the late 1940s and early 1950s, a statewide network of black activists, organizers, and leaders grew up, often through membership in the National Association for the Advancement of Colored People (NAACP), but also through homegrown organizations such as the Regional Council of Negro Leadership, founded by T. R. M. Howard. Many of these leaders were business owners, giving them the independence and financial security to participate in such activity. These efforts helped to raise the number of registered black voters. Atrocities like the murder of 14-year-old **Emmett Till** were accompanied by open condemnation from the black community. The number of black people who came forward as witnesses in such cases was unprecedented, and represented the first large-scale challenge to the orthodoxy of Jim Crow since Reconstruction.

Mississippi whites reacted to this in a number of ways. Massive white resistance was a reaction not only to increased black defiance, but also to the **U.S. Supreme Court**'s ruling in **_Brown v. Board of Education_** (1954). The two main instruments by which whites reasserted their dominance were the Mississippi State Sovereignty Commission and the **White Citizens Councils**. While the Sovereignty Commission operated mainly as a means to monitor activity that was considered to endanger the sovereignty of Mississippi, these councils were primarily responsible for disrupting the network of black activism that had developed. Eschewing the brutality of lynching, the Citizens' Councils used other means to assert its power. Black leaders were particularly targeted, often economically: loans were recalled and credit lines stopped, while business owners found that their customers were taking their business elsewhere. Intimidation and (less often, although not rarely) violence, saw NAACP membership dwindle and the number of registered black voters fall sharply. During this period, many prominent black leaders, including Howard, left the state.

By the early 1960s, Mississippi was known as the most brutal enforcer of Jim Crow values in the South. Black life was governed almost entirely by Jim Crow, and whites felt secure in their domination of the state. Signs of black defiance were quickly suppressed, usually without any fear of punishment. In every sphere of public life blacks were cowed by white supremacy. The extent of Mississippi's defiance is illustrated by **James Meredith**'s attempt to integrate the University of Mississippi. Meredith had initially tried to enrol in 1961, only to be physically prevented from doing so by Governor Ross Barnett. When Meredith arrived to enroll in September 1962, after a federal court had ordered his admission, Barnett once again prevented him entering. Meredith's admission was achieved only with the assistance of federal marshals and the Mississippi **National Guard**, which had been federalized by President **John F. Kennedy** to quell a riot in which two people were killed. During his time at the University of Mississippi, a constant troop presence was maintained on campus.

However, the very depth of black subjugation in Mississippi made it a focus for the burgeoning **Civil Rights Movement**; while Jim Crow was challenged throughout the South, Mississippi received particular attention. Much of this was led by young activists, especially those belonging to the **Student Nonviolent Coordinating Committee (SNCC)** and the **Congress of Racial Equality (CORE)**, the two organizations that would be most active in Mississippi.

Many activists gained their first experience of Mississippi during the Freedom Rides of May 1961. The Kennedy administration struck an agreement that would allow Governor Barnett to jail the freedom riders, but required that he guarantee their safety. The activists confounded Kennedy by refusing bail and remaining in jail until July. Such intransigence and single-mindedness would mark the attitude of civil rights activists in Mississippi. Another key development in the Mississippi movement was the establishment by SNCC of a voter registration project in McComb. The project was run by Bob Moses of SNCC, who had been directed to McComb by Amzie Moore. The McComb project, particularly the tactics used by Moses, along with the experience of the Freedom Rides, would crucially inform the Mississippi movement.

SNCC soon became the leading civil rights organization in Mississippi. Working at the grassroots level, SNCC activists assisted communities to organize to challenge for equal access to the vote. SNCC's strategy was to encourage the development of local leadership and an activist infrastructure that could sustain a prolonged, community-led challenge to Jim Crow. The role of SNCC was to facilitate, rather than lead, such activity. This approach reached its apogee with the Mississippi Summer Project (often known as Freedom Summer).

During the summer of 1964, thousands of civil rights activists, many of them white northern college students, entered Mississippi to participate in Freedom Summer, the main focus of which was to increase the number of registered black voters. This was done under the banner of the Council of Federated Organizations (COFO), which included several national civil rights organizations, as well as Mississippi groups. The Mississippi Freedom Democratic Party was formed to challenge the seating of the regular Mississippi delegation at the Democratic National Conference (a challenge that ultimately failed). Freedom Summer addressed many of the problems that had been caused by successive generations of blacks being subjugated by Jim Crow: as well as voter registration, citizenship education classes, community centres and a range of other projects were created to help black Mississippians access and make full use of the vote.

Freedom Summer provoked strong support from black communities, but also a fierce backlash from whites. Civil rights workers were particularly vulnerable during their time in Mississippi, as were local blacks who participated. Evictions, intimidation, beatings, and bombings were all widespread, and membership of the **Ku Klux Klan** increased. Perhaps the most notorious incident of Freedom Summer was the murder of three civil rights workers, Andrew Goodman, Michael Schwerner and James Chaney; they disappeared in June but their bodies were not found until August. The national interest in this case brought an unprecedented federal presence into Mississippi and signaled that Mississippi would no longer be able to exercise Jim Crow justice with impunity.

The precise effect of Freedom Summer is hard to gauge: in some communities, it had long-lasting effects and helped the emergence of local leaders (such as **Fannie Lou Hamer** in Sunflower County); elsewhere, it had almost no impact. The poverty that had blighted black Mississippi for so long continued, and for much of the remainder of the 1960s, poverty relief and access to welfare were key campaigns for black communities. Gradually, however, the effects of civil rights legislation, as well as the cumulative impact of the civil rights movement, both in Mississippi itself and more widely, began to erode Jim Crow in its last stronghold. In 1969, *Alexander v. Holmes County* effectively desegregated public schools, and social customs that had separated blacks and whites weakened. Many public facilities that had traditionally been separated became gradually integrated, although often without any single sweeping blow. Nonetheless, in *Ayers v. Fordice* (1992), the Supreme Court held that Mississippi had not yet eradicated fully Jim Crow from higher education.

Crucially, by the end of 1968, 60 percent of eligible blacks were registered to vote, perhaps the most important achievement of the civil rights movement in Mississippi. In the face of such large numbers of registered blacks, and in line with political shifts elsewhere, notably the election of racial moderates in several states, Jim Crow could no longer dominate Mississippi life. As blacks gained the vote, they were able to use it to leverage concessions from white politicians. Even more significantly, increasing numbers of blacks began to run for office. Across Mississippi, black office holders were elected to a variety of posts, including to the Mississippi state legislature, and, in 1986, for the first time since Reconstruction, a black Mississippian, Mike Espy, was elected to Congress. *See also* Alabama; Dixiecrats.

Further Readings: Dittmer, John. *Local People: The Struggle for Civil Rights in Mississippi.* Urbana: University of Illinois Press, 1995; Kirwan, Albert D. *Revolt of the Rednecks: Mississippi Politics, 1876–1925.* New York: Harper Torchbooks, 1965; McMillen, Neil R. *Dark Journey: Black Mississippians in the Age of Jim Crow.* Urbana: University of Illinois Press, 1990; Parker, Frank R. *Black Votes Count: Political Empowerment in Mississippi after 1965.* Chapel Hill: University of North Carolina Press, 1990.

Simon T. Cuthbert-Kerr

Mississippi Plan (1890)

The Mississippi Plan was a pioneering strategy for African American disenfranchisement that endured well into the twentieth century. The Mississippi Plan helped build the "Solid South" with its monopoly of white political power situated largely within the **Democratic Party**.

The Mississippi Plan of the **Jim Crow** era was less violent than proscriptive when compared to its 1875 forerunner. Previously, angry Southern whites (Redeemers) had taken to the streets with paramilitary forces to terrorize Republicans of both races and wrest control of state and local governments. The new approach relied upon statutory manipulation interlaced with the tacit threat of physical coercion. In 1890, white Mississippians convened a constitutional convention that subverted the intent of the Fifteenth Amendment to guarantee that race, color, and previous condition of servitude not determine voter eligibility. Poll taxes, literacy tests, and residency requirements were established that facilitated the targeting of blacks without overt employment of racial language or standards. A predominantly poor, uneducated, and transient population would soon feel the full force of these arbitrary requirements.

Other Southern states did not immediately follow suit due to the soul-searching engendered by the rise of the Populist reform movement in the early 1890s. With a platform celebrating the aspirations of the common man, Populists faced an uphill struggle in an age in which corporate elites and political machines openly cooperated to protect narrow interests. Challenging this oligarchy required mobilizing new constituencies and utilizing the discourse and tactics of inclusion. Some Populists genuinely hoped to forge an enduring biracial alliance, while others at least judged pragmatically that black support was instrumental for a third party's survival. Perceiving the Populists as a legitimate threat, some Democrats reluctantly courted the black vote as a form of inoculation against this political insurgency. The possibility of reformers galvanizing Northern public opinion against the injustice of the Mississippi Plan further encouraged Southern caution. The next state to employ the measure, **South Carolina**, would not do so until 1895.

Once the Populists were defeated in the 1896 presidential election, the Southern political landscape better favored blatant disenfranchisement. Democrats had nominated the Populist favorite, William Jennings Bryan, as their own standard-bearer and co-opted enough of the Populist platform to dilute the movement's appeal and splinter its organization. Consequently, the "reform" impulse in regional politics manifested itself strictly in efforts to widen the franchise for whites under the aegis of the Democratic Party. Figures such as embittered Populist Tom Watson argued that only by denying blacks the vote could the integrity of the electoral process be ensured. This argument signified a crass attempt to manipulate legitimate outrage over a nationwide epidemic of electoral fraud and coercion into tolerating a racially motivated vendetta. The **U.S. Supreme Court** decision *Williams v. Mississippi* (1898) validated the Mississippi Plan and highlighted the sort of reactionary thinking in political and social affairs that dominated the Gilded Age. Between 1898 and 1910, the rest of the former Confederacy (as well as Oklahoma) had enacted some facsimile of the Mississippi Plan.

Successful implementation of this measure in its early years owed as much to the lethargy of its opponents as to the audacity of its backers. Segregationists counted on the prevailing Northern view that racial questions were just too divisive anymore following the carnage of the Civil War. Sectional healing was paramount while the black population served as a convenient whipping-boy around which to cement a new alliance; a pathetic example of a "blame the victim" mentality. Developments in U.S. foreign policy only reinforced this trend. Angling to join the colonial powers of Europe, authorities engineered a conflict with Spain in 1898 whose rationale rested largely upon a hierarchy of race with embedded notions of dominance and paternalism. The heady expansionism of the times was often expressed in terms of spreading Anglo-Saxon civilization to "mongrel" and benighted peoples of color. The rise of eugenics and social Darwinism provided superficial rationalizations for exploitation as though a versatile, "scientific" template could be superimposed over any scenario. Soon, the denizens of Cuba, the Philippines, Guam, Puerto Rico, Samoa, and Hawai'i fell under the paradoxical influence of a republic that behaved like an empire. With the anti-imperialist movement at the turn of the century failing to elicit a fundamental reassessment of foreign policy assumptions and objectives, the liberation of the permanent underclass at home remained unlikely. Even white Republicans could not unify against the Mississippi Plan, since many saw it enabling the GOP to compete for the white vote without the need to cater to blacks or contend with race-baiting.

The movement behind the Mississippi Plan reflected not only the desire to retain the antebellum status quo in race relations, but also a struggle over precisely which whites would dominate regional politics. Those whites residing in the Black Belt counties tended to be the strongest advocates for disenfranchisement against others from predominantly white communities. The latter group was often placated by favorable redistricting (gerrymandering) in the state legislatures. A perversion of the U.S. Constitution was thus sanctioned through the most banal form of political horse trading.

Poorer whites rightfully feared that the Mississippi Plan would be employed as an instrument of class warfare, despite assurances to the contrary by political leaders. Most states did not allow property ownership as a substitute for literacy in determining voter registration. As yeoman farmers expressed their anxieties in the 1890s, safeguards were enacted to protect their status. Mississippians fashioned an "understanding clause" whereby anyone who demonstrated a command of the state constitution could forego the literacy test. This highly subjective examination would be administered by white officials free to let their prejudices dictate their assessments. Louisianans adopted a "grandfather clause" stipulating that anyone whose father or grandfather could vote as of January 1, 1867 (before the Fourteenth Amendment went into effect guaranteeing equal protection under the law—i.e., whites only), could avoid both the literacy and property tests. Although various forms of special dispensation proliferated among the Southern states, the poll tax remained in effect. Yet, without a receipt or payment well in advance of an election, one could still be disqualified.

The response of the African American community did little to threaten the Mississippi Plan. In keeping with what he deemed a realistic philosophy, **Booker T. Washington** merely contended that any restrictions upon voting should be applied equally to all races. His 1895 **Atlanta Compromise** called for black disengagement from political affairs in favor of concentrating upon economic self-improvement. In what seemed to be an acceptance of white stereotypes on some level, he argued that blacks must use their occupational performance to demonstrate their worthiness for full citizenship. Although sometimes mischaracterized as a toady to the white power structure, Washington unwittingly facilitated a silencing of African Americans that would last for generations. Although a much younger man not yet at the height of his influence, **W.E.B. Du Bois** argued conversely to fellow blacks that the dignity and self-respect desired by Washington could never be achieved through submission, regardless of how it was justified. A New England native, Du Bois commented more bluntly on the reality of Southern society as a caste system with its nearly immutable class boundaries. His call for an appreciation of the higher aspirations in life that transcended materialism was underappreciated amidst crushing poverty. A combination of apathy and oppression ensured the absence of a large-scale, grassroots campaign among Southern blacks to defeat the Mississippi Plan.

In a final act of disrespect for democratic principles, all but one state convention that composed a version of the Mississippi Plan avoided using a popular vote for ratification. Meanwhile, the white primary replaced the old convention system as a vehicle to allow party officials at the state and local levels to marginalize and exclude any undesired voters who had navigated the obstacles inherent to the new registration process. In conjunction with tenant farming, sharecropping, Jim Crow laws, and lynching, the Mississippi Plan demonstrated that the promise of Reconstruction had gone unrealized.

These repressive techniques helped mire the South in a state of moral and cultural stagnation that the modern **Civil Rights Movement** would confront at its peril. The **Voting Rights Act of 1965**, promoted by President Lyndon B. Johnson, sounded the death knell of the Mississippi Plan, though subsequent legislation over the following two decades was necessary to augment this initiative. *See also* Tillman, Ben; Watson, Tom.

Further Readings: Kousser, J. Morgan. *The Shaping of Southern Politics: Suffrage Restriction and the Establishment of the One-Party South, 1880–1910.* New Haven, CT: Yale University Press, 1974; McMillen, Neil. *Dark Journey: Black Mississippians in the Age of Jim Crow.* Urbana: University of Illinois Press, 1989; Williamson, Joel. *A Rage for*

Order: Black-White Relations in the American South since Emancipation. New York: Oxford University Press, 1986; Woodward, C. Vann. *Origins of the New South, 1877–1913.* Baton Rouge: Louisiana State University Press, 1971.

Jeffrey D. Bass

Montgomery Bus Boycott

Starting in December 1955, the African American community of Montgomery, Alabama, boycotted the city bus system for over a year. Demanding equal and fair treatment, blacks refused to ride until their requests were met. Organized by the Women's Political Council (WPC) and Montgomery's National Association for the Advancement of Colored People (NAACP) branch, this boycott is often referred to as the beginning of the modern **Civil Rights Movement**.

In the 1950s in Montgomery, the city bus system was segregated. African Americans were not hired as drivers, rode in the back of the bus, and were expected to surrender their seat at a white passenger's request. Black passengers entered the front of the bus to pay the fee, exited the bus, and reentered at the back entrance. At times, bus drivers would leave black passengers standing at the sidewalk after paying the bus fee. Although 75 percent of passengers were African American, they were constant victims of public degradation and humiliation.

For several years, the WPC, led by Jo Ann Robinson, and Montgomery's NAACP branch, formerly led by E. D. Nixon, had discussed the inequalities of the city bus system and possible resolutions. In 1954, Robinson sent a letter to Montgomery mayor W. A. Gayle requesting the buses' Jim Crow practices be put to an end and warned of a potential boycott if the demands were not met. Gayle paid no attention to Robinson's warning.

Even though the WPC had been organizing a possible boycott, the challenge of rallying the entire black community remained. A successful boycott required full participation. Due to fear of losing jobs, harassment, and racial violence, few African Americans publicly acknowledged their discontent of second-class citizenship. These organizations waited for the right person who would stand up against the ways of the south. That day came on Thursday, December 1, 1955, when **Rosa Parks** stepped on one of the city buses. It had been a long day of work, the bus was almost completely full, and Parks sat in the first row of the black section. At the next stop several white passengers entered the bus. A white male wanted Parks's seat. Parks refused. The bus driver ordered her to move or he would call the authorities. Parks did not move. Parks was arrested, and the inspirational story Nixon and Robinson had waited for arrived. The soft-spoken, respectable Parks served as the perfect symbol to mobilize African Americans for the bus boycott.

Days following the arrest, over 200 volunteers passed out 30,000 flyers calling for a one-day boycott of the Montgomery bus system on Monday, December 5, 1955. The one-day boycott was successful and that evening the black community gathered in Holt Street Baptist Church to decide if the boycott should continue. Thousands attended the meeting. The church overflowed to the outside stairs and sidewalks.

Jo Ann Gibson Robinson, *The Montgomery Bus Boycott and the Women Who Started It*

The black Women's Political Council had been planning the boycott of Montgomery City Lines for months, but the plans had been known publicly for the past three days. The idea itself been entertained for years. Almost daily some black man, woman, or child had had an unpleasant experiences on the bus and told other members of the family about it at the supper table or around the open fireplace or stove. These stories were repeated to the neighbors, who re-told them in club meetings or the ministers of large church congregations.

At first the ministers would soothe the anger of the congregations with recommendations of prayer, with promises the God would "make the rough ways smooth," and with exhortations to "have patience and wait upon the Lord."

The member had been patient and had waited upon the Lord, but the rough ways had gotten rougher rather than smoother. As the months stretched into years, the encounters with some of the bus drivers grew more numerous and more intolerable.

Very little or nothing tangible had ever been done on the part of the darker race to prevent continuous abuse on city transit lines, except to petition the company and the City Commission for better conditions. Ten years before, when Mrs. Geneva Johnson, in the latest of a long string of similar incidents, was arrested for not having correct change and "talking back" to the driver when he upbraided her, nothing was done. Charged with disorderly conduct, she paid the fine and help on riding. A representation of Negro men complained the bus company about the matter and about other mistreatments as well, but nothing came of it.

During the next few years, Mrs. Vila White and Miss Katie Wingfield were arrested, as well as two children visiting from New Jersey. All had committee the same offense—sitting in the front seats reserved for whites. The children were a sister and brother, twn and twelve years old, respectively, who had been accustomed to rising integrated transportation. They got on the bus and sat down buy a white man and a boy. The white youngster told the older black youth to get up from beside him. The youngster refused. The driver commanded them to move, but the children refused. The driver again commanded them to move, but the children continued to sit where they were. They were not in the habit of getting up out of their seats on a public vehicle to give them to somebody else. The police were called, and the two children were arrested. Relatives paid their fines, sent the children home, and the case became history. People kept on riding the bus, and in all probability, those two children carried and will continue to carry that bitter experience with them forever.

Three years later, in 1952, a white bus driver and a Negro man exchanged words over the dime the passenger put into the slot. The Negro man, Brooks, was not afraid, for he had been drinking. He never quavered when the driver abused him with words and accused him of not putting the money into the meter box of the bus. Instead, he stood his ground and dispute the driver. The "bracer" gave him confidence to confidence to stand there, and to sit down, and to talk back in his own defense.

What followed was never explained fully, but the driver called the police, and when the police came they shot and killed Brooks as he got off the bus. Newspaper reports stated that the coroner had ruled the case justifiable homicide because the man had resisted arrest. Many black Montgomerians felt that Brooks was intoxicated and had gotten "out of his place" with the white bus driver. Others wondered if any man, drunk or sober, had to be killed because of one dime, one bus fare. Each had his own thoughts on the matter, but kept on riding the bus.

In 1953, Mrs. Epsie Worthy got on a bus at a transfer point from another bus, and the driver demanded an additional fare. He refused to take the transfer. Rather than pay again, the woman decided that she did not have to go far and would walk the rest of the way. The driver would not be daunted. He wanted another fare, whether she rode or got off, and insisted upon it. Words followed as the woman alighted from the vehicle. She was not quite quick enough, for by the time she was safe on mother earth, the driver was upon her, beating her with his hands. She defended herself, fighting back with all her might. For a few minutes, there was a "free-for-all," as she gave as much as she took. But in the end she was the loser, for when the police were summoned, she was taken to jail and fined fifty-two dollars for disorderly conduct.

Source: Jo Ann Gibson Robinson, *The Montgomery Bus Boycott and the Women Who Started It: The Memoir of Jo Ann Gibson Robinson* (Knoxville: University of Tennessee Press, 1987), 20–22.

The Montgomery Improvement Association (MIA) was developed to coordinate, support and organization the demonstration. **Martin Luther King, Jr.,** the new preacher in town, was elected MIA's president and chosen to give a speech at the first mass meeting at Holt Street Baptist Church. With less than an hour to prepare, King delivered a speech that inspired the crowd to vote unanimously to continue the boycott. This speech also marked the beginning of King's role as leader in the Civil Rights Movement.

Through the efforts and sacrifices of the black community, the Montgomery bus boycott lasted 381 days. Boycotters walked to work, established a large car pool system, and ran extensive fund-raisers to finance the car pool system. Even on the coldest of days, some walked as far as 12 miles a day. Only a month after the boycott began, James H. Bagley, the superintendent of the Montgomery City Bus Lines, expressed frustration with the lack of patronage. The bus system was losing close to $400 daily, as expenses greatly outweighed income. Forced to reduce expenses, Bagley cut schedules, fired drivers, and increased the cost of bus fares. However, the movement needed federal legislation to change **Jim Crow** practices.

On February 1, 1956, NAACP lawyers Fred Gray and Charles Langford filed a lawsuit in the U.S. Circuit Court against Alabama and Montgomery's unconstitutional segregation laws. Gray and Langford filed this suit on behalf of five African American women: Aurelia S. Browder, Susie McDonald, Jeanetta Reese, Claudette Colvin and Mary Louise Smith. Throughout the year, boycott leaders and participants faced much racial violence. Both King's and Nixon's houses were bombed, crosses were burnt on front lawns, and several were arrested for participating in "illegal" boycotts. Through Alabama's state courts, white Montgomery officials successfully made carpooling illegal. Interestingly enough, this state legislation passed the same day the federal court found Alabama's segregation laws unconstitutional.

On December 21, 1956, African Americans boarded the Montgomery city buses and sat where they pleased. This achievement sparked the modern Civil Rrights Movement and heightened racial tensions across the south as more and more blacks demanded freedom. *See also* Streetcars and Boycotts.

Further Readings: Burns, Stewart, ed. *Daybreak of Freedom: Montgomery Bus Boycott.* Chapel Hill: University of North Carolina Press, 1997; Robinson, Jo Ann, with David Garrow. *The Montgomery Bus Boycott and the Women Who Started It: The Memoir of Jo Ann Gibson Robinson.* Knoxville: University of Tennessee Press, 1987; Williams, Donnie, and Wayne Greenhow. *The Thunder of Angels: The Montgomery Bus Boycott and the People Who Broke the Back of Jim Crow.* Chicago: Lawrence Hill Books, 2006.

Emily Hess

Morton, Jelly Roll (1885 or 1890–1941)

Although his claim to be the inventor of **jazz** music has been highly contested over the years, Ferdinand Joseph Lamonthe "Jelly Roll" Morton unquestionably remains an integral player in the creation of the art form during its formative years in the late nineteenth and early twentieth centuries. Morton, a bandleader, composer, and virtuoso pianist, remains a controversial figure in jazz due primarily to his role as one of its early historical subjects in which his recorded recollections of jazz in its earliest days were often subject to bouts of hyperbole, self-adulation, and inconsistent memory. Yet regardless of his revisionist account, Morton remains one of jazz's first icons, developing technique and creating songs that have helped to establish the canon within the art form.

Born in the Fauborg Marigny neighborhood in **Louisiana**, Morton was part of the African- and French-derived Creole community that helped to establish the racially diverse setting of downtown New Orleans at the turn of the twentieth century. New Orleans at the time was rich in its mix of ethnicity, and although racism and segregation unquestionably existed, cultural exchange was inevitable as religion, music, and social rituals converged in the region to create an array of new and revised cultural forms such as jazz that were unique to the world. Creole culture exemplified this hybridity as its people were generally of African and European descent and particularly known for their musical contributions in the New Orleans area. Regarded as one of the city's finest pianists, Morton made his way as a professional player initially in Storyville, a racially diverse but often segregated portion of New Orleans' red light district. Playing in brothels, minstrel shows, and musical theatres, Morton developed his sound and composed regularly to become one of the most recognizable musicians of the period. With compositions such as "Jelly Roll Blues," "Frog-I-More Rag," King Porter Stomp," and "Wolverine Blues," Morton helped to popularize jazz and spread the music from its New Orleans base by touring through Chicago and New York City with his vaudeville act. Morton's technique also helped to fashion the practice of stride piano that incorporated various forms of music, including blues theory within the performance of jazz.

Morton's account of jazz in his 1938 interviews with Alan Lomax and the Library of Congress often did not focus directly on race regardless of Lomax's attempts to inquire about the subject. Morton's account on the subject of race has often been noted as dismissive as history reinforces the idea of jazz's polyracial development, in spite of Morton's personal claim of invention. Segregation, however, was a pervasive way of life for all Americans at the turn of the twentieth century. As a response to **Reconstruction**, laws based upon the premise of racial discrimination were enacted throughout the 1890s that severely restricted the rights of Americans born of African descent. Creoles of Color were also limited in their economic, political, and social opportunities, and Morton inescapably felt the effects of these restrictions. His art form, however, flourished as jazz was uniquely developed in a staunch dichotomy of segregation and cultural diversity, much like the city of New Orleans itself. After several bouts of illness, including injuries left untreated due to a lack of care from segregated hospitals, Morton succumbed to illness and died on July 10, 1941. *See also* Armstrong, Louis; Black Entertainers against Jim Crow; Ellington, Duke.

Further Readings: Lomax, Alan. *Mister Jelly Roll: The Fortunes of Jelly Roll Morton, New Orleans Creole and "Inventor of Jazz."* New York: Pantheon Books, 1993; Wright, Laurie. *Mr. Jelly Lord.* Chigwell: Storyville Publications, 1980.

Kevin Strait

Motley, Constance Baker (1921–1985)

Constance Baker Motley was a lawyer, civil rights activist, politician, and judge. In addition to being a major activist in the movement, she personally broke down many racial and gender barriers during her life.

Early Life

Motley was born in New Haven, Connecticut, on September 14, 1921. She was the ninth of 12 children. Her parents had immigrated to the United States from Nevis in the **Caribbean**. Motley explained that her parents had settled in New Haven because New Englanders traded with the Caribbean during the eighteenth and nineteenth centuries. Her father, Willoughby Alva Baker, was a chef on the Yale University campus, and her mother, Rachel Baker, was a founder of the New Haven Chapter of the National Association for the Advancement of Colored People (NAACP).

Early in her life, she had been exposed to segregation. As a 15-year-old, she was turned away from a beach in Milford, Connecticut, because she was black. She was also denied admission to a roller skating rink. These incidents caused her to become interested in civil rights, and she became the president of the local NAACP Youth Council. She also decided that she wanted to become a lawyer. After graduating from high school in 1939, she worked for a short time as a maid. She then took a job with the New Haven office of the National Youth Administration, a **New Deal**–era government agency that provided part-time jobs to young people between the ages of 16 and 25. Her family's modest means seemed to preclude her from attending college.

A turning point in her life occurred when she was speaking at the Dixwell Community House, an African-American social organization. Her speech, in which she talked about the need for African Americans to be more involved in the organization's operations, was heard by Clarence Blakeslee, the white philanthropist and grandson of abolitionists who had built the Community House. He was so impressed by her speech that he offered to pay for her college education, including her law school tuition. Of Blakeslee, Motley quoted him in her autobiography telling her "I guess if I can send (my grandson) to Harvard, I can send you to Columbia."

Baker entered Fisk University, a black college located in Nashville, Tennessee, in 1941. However, in June 1942 she decided to transfer to New York University's Washington Square College, from which she graduated with a bachelor's degree in economics in 1943. In 1944, she was the first African American woman admitted to the Columbia University Law School, and she graduated with a LLB degree in 1946. She married Joel W. Motley, a real estate broker, in 1946. They had a son, Joel Motley III. She was called to the bar of the State of New York in 1948.

The Civil Rights Movement

In 1945, while still a law student at Columbia, she met **Thurgood Marshall**, who offered her a job with the **NAACP Legal Defense and Education Fund** (LDEF) as a law clerk. Following her graduation from Columbia, she was the LDEF's first female attorney and became an assistant general counsel and later associate general counsel. Many of the early cases she worked on concerned the treatment of African American military personnel during **World War II**, working on appeals of courts-martial. Many of these appeals were based on the premise that African American soldiers were often given more severe sanctions that white soldiers who had been convicted of the same offense. She became the LDEF's chief trial counsel and was also a legal strategist, helping to desegregate Southern schools, buses, and coffee shops.

In 1950, she wrote the original complaint in the case of ***Brown v. Board of Education***, the landmark 1954 **U.S. Supreme Court** case that ended de jure segregation of public schools. During the 1950s, she traveled throughout the South representing plaintiffs in school desegregation cases, including the black children denied entry to Central High School in Little Rock, **Arkansas**. She became the first African American woman to argue a case before the U.S. Supreme Court when, in *Meredith v. Fair* (1962), she successfully argued that **James Meredith** should be allowed to attend the University of **Mississippi**, which had refused to admit African Americans, a court decision that had to be enforced by the use of federal troops. Altogether, she won nine of the 10 cases she argued before the Supreme Court.

She also represented many of the freedom riders jailed during the 1961 effort to force the Kennedy administration to enforce Supreme Court rulings prohibiting the segregation of passengers in interstate transportation. She also successfully argued for the reinstatement of more than 1,000 Birmingham, **Alabama,** school children who had been expelled for demonstrating.

Politics

Baker became interested in politics in the mid-1950s. In 1958, she was appointed to the New York State Advisory Council on Employment and Unemployment Insurance, a post she held until 1964. In February 1964, she won a special election to the New York state senate, serving out the unexpired term of James Watson. Motley, a Democrat, became the first African American woman elected to the New York state senate. She was elected that November. In her brief time in the state senate, she introduced legislation to establish low- and middle-income housing in urban areas. In February 1965, she was chosen by the New York City Council to fill a vacancy as Manhattan borough president, the first woman and the first African American in that position. She was elected to a four-year term in November 1965 with the support of the Democratic, Republican and Liberal parties. As borough president, she worked to decrease racial segregation in Manhattan public schools and for the revitalization of Harlem and East Harlem. In March 1965, she represented New York City on the historic civil rights march from Selma to Montgomery, Alabama.

The Federal Bench

In late 1965, President Lyndon B. Johnson nominated Motley for a seat on the U.S. Court of Appeals for the Second Circuit. However, opposition to her nomination was so intense that on January 26, 1966, Johnson withdrew her nomination and instead nominated her as a federal district court judge for the Southern District of New York; the first African American woman named to the federal bench. She was confirmed by the U.S. Senate on August 30, 1966, despite continuing opposition from Southern senators. She would remain on the bench until her death. In 1982, she became the first African American women to become a chief judge. In 1986, Baker assumed senior status. Among the cases she handled was a 1978 case in which she ruled that the New York Yankees would have to admit a female reporter to the locker rooms at Yankee Stadium and another case that upheld the right of gay protestors to march in front of St. Patrick's Cathedral.

In 1993, she was inducted into the National Women's Hall of Fame, located in Seneca Falls, New York, the site of the first women's rights convention. In 2001, she received the Presidential Citizens Medal, which recognizes American citizens who have performed exemplary deeds of service for the nation, from President Bill Clinton. The NAACP awarded her the organization's highest honor, the Spingarn Medal, in 2003.

Motley died on September 28, 2005 in New York City. *See also* Armed Forces; New England.

Further Readings: Motley, Constance Baker. *Equal Justice under Law: An Autobiography.* New York: Farrar, Straus and Giroux, 1998.

Jeffrey Kraus

Museum of Jim Crow Racist Memorabilia

Inaugurated in 1996, the **Jim Crow** Museum of Racist Memorabilia at Ferris State University, Big Rapids, Michigan, represents the lifelong quest of David Pilgrim to bring attention to the extensive array of memorabilia that demeans the black race through their portrayal "as Coons, Toms, Sambos, Mammies, picaninnies, and other dehumanizing racial caricatures." The collection currently has over 5,000 artifacts ranging from postcards, books, games, signs, photographs, toys, cookie jars, and more. The museum is considered a learning laboratory intended to promote open and honest discourse on racism in American society.

Pilgrim began collecting racist memorabilia as a child in the 1970s while living in Mobile, Alabama. His first acquisition, Pilgrim recalls, was a saltshaker in the shape of a black mammy servant, which he promptly destroyed. He continued to collect items until it reached the current volume. Initially housed in a one-room, 500-square-foot exhibit space in the Starr Building at Ferris State University, the collection moved to a 2,100-square-foot space at the Starr Building in 2008. The collection is organized in six sections to include exhibits titled "Origins of Jim Crow," "Jim Crow and Violence," "Jim Crow and Anti-Black Imagery," "Battling Jim Crow Imagery," "Attacking Jim Crow Segregation," and "Moving Beyond Jim Crow."

The "Origins of Jim Crow" exhibit describes the history of Jim Crow, including the use of blackface performers in minstrel shows to parody black Americans. Examples of these blackface minstrels include Topsy, the black slave girl characterized in *Uncle Tom's Cabin: Life Among the Lowly*

(1852), by Harriett Beecher Stowe, and, of course, Jim Crow, the stage character whose name became synonymous with the practices and laws that marginalized and segregated blacks in American society.

"Jim Crow and Violence" depicts the role of white supremacy and hate groups such as the **Ku Klux Klan** in subjecting black Americans to terrorist acts including mob vigilantism, arson, assault, murder, and other heinous atrocities committed against African Americans. It also illustrates how three-dimensional objects that present blacks as enjoying physical pain attempted to validate violence against African Americans.

"Jim Crow and Anti-Black Imagery" is an extensive collection of caricatures used to promote racism, but the exhibit is in a homelike setting intended to represent the environment in which beliefs and attitudes about race are often molded. "Battling Jim Crow Imagery" tells the story of how African Americans fought against antiblack images; for example, it delineates the efforts in the 1940s and 1950s to get the book *Little Black Sambo* removed from schools and libraries.

"Attacking Jim Crow Segregation" contains representative examples of positive African American images. It includes works by artists who attempted to deconstruct historical negative and racist images of African Americans by creating works that exalt the black race. A civil rights section presents artifacts from anti–Jim Crow initiatives used in the fight against segregation—for example, a sign that reads "I AM A MAN."

"Moving Beyond Jim Crow" features as its focal point a nine-foot-tall mural of persons who died in the civil rights struggle, including **Martin Luther King, Jr.**, James Reeb, and the four little black girls, Denise McNair, Cynthia Wesley, Carole Robertson and Addie Mae Collins, killed in the Sixteenth Street Baptist Church bombing in Birmingham, Alabama, on September 13, 1963. This section also includes examples of contemporary antiracism memorabilia and racist memorabilia like the "Plain Brown Rapper," intended to depict a rap music performer.

While museum organizers recognize the contents of the 5,000-piece exhibit are disturbing and offensive, it is not the intent of the museum to offend museum patrons. Rather, the mission is to educate the public on the extent to which segments of society have denigrated one racial group through creation of derogatory images, propaganda, and laws that promoted and fostered racial segregation in society. Pilgrim comments, "I believe, and know to be true, that objects of intolerance can be used to teach tolerance." *See also* Advertising; Minstrelsy.

Further Readings and Viewing Ethnic Notions, DVD, directed by Marlon T. Riggs, 57 min. California Newsreel, 1987; Henderson, Robin, Leon R. Litwack, and Erskine Peters, *Ethnic Notions: Black Images in the White Mind.* Berkeley, CA: Berkeley Art Center, 1992; Jim Crow Museum. http://www.ferris.edu/news/jimcrow/index.htm (accessed April 11, 2007); Kennedy, Stetson. *Jim Crow Guide: The Way It Was,* 2nd ed. Boca Raton: Florida Atlantic Press, 1990;Woodward, C. Vann. *The Strange Career of Jim Crow,* 3rd ed. New York: Oxford University Press, 1974.

Carol Adams-Means

Myrdal, Gunnar (1898–1987)

A distinguished Swedish economist in his own right on many subjects, Gunnar Myrdal's lasting legacy and enduring contribution to American race relations is his book *An American Dilemma: The Negro Problem and Modern Democracy* (1944).

Myrdal began the long journey of researching this subject when asked by Frederick Keppel, president of the Carnegie Corporation, to travel to the United States in order to study the problem firsthand, especially in the South, where approximately 75 percent of African Americans were living at the time. Keppel and other Carnegie trustees understood that the enormous importance and complexity of the problem required someone akin to Alexis de Tocqueville, the great nineteenth-century French observer of American democracy—someone with proper distance and objectivity, and yet (unlike Tocqueville) someone from a country not tainted with an imperialist past that could cause African Americans to question the validity of the study and its outcomes.

In his capacity as an economics professor at the University of Stockholm, Myrdal had already visited the United States as a Rockefeller Fellow in 1929–1930 and was preparing for a second visit to deliver the Godkin Lectures at Harvard when the invitation was extended to travel through the **Jim Crow** South. The evil he witnessed shocked and rattled him to the core as he began to grapple with the political implications of the problem. Firsthand observation of discriminatory segregation and injustice was a beginning, but by no means an end. Far from a travelogue of a gifted writer's observations, Myrdal assembled a diverse team of scholars to examine the problem from several angles using different methodological perspectives.

The methodological approaches to the research and the diversity within his own research team, combined with his evolving theories of equilibrium and change in economic dynamics to form a multicausal explanation, linking discrimination, education, housing, political empowerment, jobs, health care, belief, and other factors into a complex whole. These interlocking dynamic factors could pull segments of the population downward in what he called a "vicious circle" or, alternatively, be reversed through a "virtuous circle." No single explanation or solution was adequate.

However rigorously Myrdal explored these individual factors and their interrelationships, he believed that a moral dilemma lay beneath them all. Using the (now antiquated) language of his day, he wrote in his introduction to *An American Dilemma*:

> The American Negro problem is a problem in the heart of the American. It is there that the interracial tension has it focus. It is there that the decisive struggle goes on. This is the central viewpoint of this treatise. Though our study includes economic, social, and political race relations, at bottom our problem is the moral dilemma of the American—the conflict between his moral valuations on various levels of consciousness and generality. The "American Dilemma" ... is the ever-raging conflict between, on the one hand, the valuations preserved on the general plane which we shall call the "American Creed," where the American thinks, talks, and acts under the influence of high national and Christian precepts, and, on the other hand, the valuations on specific planes of individual and group

living, where personal and local interests; economic, social, and sexual jealousies; considerations of community prestige and conformity; group prejudice and particular persons or types of people; and all sorts of miscellaneous wants, impulses, and habits dominate his outlook.

In other words, the high ideals embedded in the white majority American beliefs and values did not square with their actions and attitudes towards African Americans, contradicting their own "creed" and ideas about justice and democracy.

Overall, *An American Dilemma* was received favorably by academics, though criticized heavily by those with Marxist leanings. But in the political realm, little happened until 10 years later, when it influenced Chief Justice Earl Warren, who cited it in the ***Brown v. Board of Education*** decision, documenting the detrimental effect of segregated education upon children. The contradiction between American ideals and practice was a theme that civil rights leader **Martin Luther King, Jr.**, picked up on, as is evident in his famous 1963 "I Have a Dream" speech. Myrdal's careful research and recommended reforms received more attention and exerted greater influence on public policy years after the publication of *An American Dilemma* than in his own day.

Further Readings: Clayton, Obie, Jr., ed. *An American Dilemma Revisited: Race Relations in a Changing World.* New York: Russell Sage Foundation, 1996; Jackson, Walter A. *Gunnar Myrdal and America's Conscience: Social Engineering and Racial Liberalism, 1938–1987.* Chapel Hill: University of North Carolina Press, 1990.

Douglas Milford

N

NAACP Legal Defense and Education Fund

The NAACP Legal Defense and Education Fund, Inc., (LDF) was officially chartered in 1940. Yet, the focus of the organization—legally challenging issues of education, voter protection, economic justice, and criminal justice— were central to the NAACP's initial legal campaign, following its founding in 1909. The inception of the LDF and the strategies that were devised are central to understanding how the LDF became the force behind a number of landmark decisions, including *Brown v. Board of Education* (1954) and how it contin- ues to advocate for justice, equality, and fairness.

Beginning in the mid-1920s, the NAACP sought funding from the Garland Fund, a foundation dedicated to radical social reform. Having already sup- ported the NAACP's anti-**lynching** campaign, the Garland Fund began sup- porting legal services offered by the NAACP, including its initial plan to oppose segregation. To begin its challenge on "**separate but equal**," the NAACP published the results of studies that focused on the inequities between white and black schools in **Georgia, Mississippi, North Carolina, South Caro- lina**, and Oklahoma. By 1930, the NAACP litigation campaign's efforts included suits against **residential segregation** and exclusion of blacks. Addi- tionally, the NAACP offered support to cases filed by taxpayers in the Deep South and suits that challenged the inequalities, in particular financial dispar- ities, between white and black schools.

Under **Walter White**'s leadership as executive secretary, and with financial support from the Garland Fund, the NAACP hired Nathan Margold, a former assistant U.S. attorney for the Southern District of New York. Margold was responsible for coordinating the NAACP legal campaign and producing a study on the injustices facing black Americans. When the *Margold Report* was submitted on May 13, 1931, about half focused on school segregation, in part because education was a relatively new area of focus for the NAACP litigation campaign, and the other half discussed residential segregation. The report clearly showed the vast differences between the allocated monies for black and white schools, and the NAACP legal team focused on devising a legal strategy that would confront "separate but equal," as established by *Plessy v. Ferguson* (1896).

Prior to the 1930s, the NAACP legal team had primarily consisted of white attorneys because of the very few black lawyers available and the need for the NAACP to establish credibility in the courts. Yet in the 1930s, the NAACP sought to retain more black lawyers. Black attorneys Charles Hamilton Houston, Louis Redding, and Homer Brown, joined the NAACP legal team helping to expand the group from seven in 1931 to 16 in 1933. In 1934, Houston was hired as special counsel for the NAACP; his credentials for coordinating the NAACP efforts were evident.

Born on September 3, 1895, Houston was the son of William and Mary Hamilton Houston, a general practice lawyer and hairdresser, respectively. Houston attended M Street High School in Washington, DC, the first black high school in the United States. At M Street, Houston was taught by some of the leading black teachers in the country, and his coursework followed a liberal arts curriculum. Following high school, Houston attended Amherst College in Massachusetts, and graduated in 1915 as a newly inducted member of Phi Beta Kappa. After serving in **World War I** and returning home during the tumultuous **Red Summer** of 1919, Houston decided that the best way for him to attack inequalities in the United States was through the law.

In turn, Houston earned his law degree from Harvard University and was the first black elected to the *Harvard Law Review*. In 1924, Houston left the law practice he shared with his father in Washington, DC, to become vice-dean of Howard University Law School. Under Houston's leadership, Howard became known as a leading law school after it received full accreditation. At Howard, Houston trained black men who would become leading civil rights attorneys including Edward P. Lovett, James G. Tyson, Oliver W. Hill, Coyness L. Ennix, and Leslie S. Perry. Houston also helped to craft to new fields of law: civil rights law and public interest law. Outside of Howard, Houston participated in a number of cases involving civil liberties, civil rights, and antidiscrimination activities, including serving as defense attorney for the Scottsboro Nine. Thus in 1934, Houston, considered the "most influential black lawyer in the United States" was the ideal choice to lead the NAACP's legal campaign.

Houston conceived his role as a lawyer as one of a social engineer charged with overturning the ways in which the law had been used to defend and maintain racial discrimination. Trained by Roscoe Pound and Felix Frankfurter at Harvard, Houston also adhered to the philosophy of legal realism. With these principles guiding Houston and those he trained, the NAACP legal campaign launched its attack on segregated education because according to Houston, "discrimination in education is symbolic of all the more drastic discriminations."

Between 1933 and 1950, the NAACP enjoyed considerable success in a revitalized campaign that defeated segregation by challenging the notion of "separate but equal." As the leader of the campaign, Houston stated, "I am primarily the administrator of the campaign, and my ideal of administration is to make the movement self-perpetuating . . . the best administration is self-executing." In developing the movement, Houston recruited his most well-known student, **Thurgood Marshall,** a 1933 graduate of Howard Law School.

Upon graduation, Marshall devoted his energies to both the NAACP legal campaign and to his own private practice in Maryland, his home state. When it became too difficult for Marshall to manage both commitments, Marshall joined the NAACP legal staff in October 1946. Thus with Houston's vision and Marshall's attention to detail, the NAACP legal team move forward with its campaign to attack segregation legally and to help increase the influence of the NAACP in the black community, for the NAACP had begun to feel threatened by the **Communist Party** and the International Labor Defense.

The strategy of the NAACP legal campaign included pursuing higher education cases in state courts seeking mandamus relief, while fighting salary equalization cases in federal court seeking injunctive relief. In 1935, this strategy was first put into action in a case involving Donald Murray, a black graduate of Amherst College and applicant to the University of Maryland Law School, who had been denied admission. After two failed cases involving higher education in North Carolina and Tennessee, the coordination between national and local legal counsels became vitally important to NAACP victories. *Murray v. Maryland* (1935) provided an opportunity whereby national and local knowledge easily merged because of Marshall's familiarity with Maryland.

Together with Marshall, Houston argued against the feasibility of practicing law in Maryland if one was not educated in Maryland and the fact that out-of-state scholarships were instituted only after Murray's case had been filed. Based on these arguments, Judge Eugene O'Dunne ruled that Murray had been denied admission to the state law school because of race, and he ordered the immediate admission of Murray. Three years later in 1938, Murray became the first black graduate of the University of Maryland Law School. In addition to the Murray case, Marshall argued salary equalization cases in Maryland, and by 1941, the state legislature mandated equal salaries.

Together, the Maryland cases and a second higher education case in Missouri began setting precedent for overturning the doctrine of separate but equal. Lloyd Lionel Gaines, a graduate of Lincoln University, applied for admission to the University of Missouri Law School in June 1935, because Lincoln did not have a law school. At first, the Missouri Supreme Court ruled against Gaines, concluding, "Gaines would not be deprived of any constitutional rights as long as the educational opportunities provided by the state [tuition for schools out of state] were 'substantially equal to those furnished to white citizens of the State.'" Two years later, however, in *Missouri ex rel Gaines v. Canada* (1938), the Supreme Court ruled that Missouri's offer of out-of-state tuition to in-state blacks was beside the point. The Court in effect concluded that Missouri did not offer legal education to blacks, and states were required to provide equal educational opportunities. Upon its decision, the Missouri Supreme Court was forced to reconsider its decision. Gaines, however, could not be found, and subsequently the case was dismissed. Despite the dismissal, the case attracted public and scholarly attention and provided a warning to segregated educational institutions.

As more cases formalized, the NAACP legal campaign became a new entity. By 1940, Houston had returned to Washington and was carrying less of the daily responsibilities. Marshall had assumed duties as special counsel to the NAACP and would now also direct the LDF. As the LDF developed, Marshall continued to be assisted by such lawyers as William Henry Hastie and hired additional lawyers including Robert Carter, Jack Greenberg, Constance Baker

Motley, Franklin Williams, Spottswood Robinson Milton Konvitz, Edward Dudley, and Marian Wynn Perry.

The LDF continued its legal attack on separate but equal through the 1940s, with their efforts to set precedent culminating in 1950. Aiding the LDF's efforts was a 1944 publication by Swedish economist and politician **Gunnar Myrdal** entitled *An American Dilemma: The Negro Problem and Modern Democracy*. Myrdal illuminated how the United States' ideals of equality, freedom, and justice had not been reality for black Americans. His findings were evident in the following 1945 statistics: the South spent two to one in favor of whites and four to one on white facilities. White teachers on average earned 30 percent more than black teachers, and transportation for black students attending schools in rural areas was completely ignored. Following the publication of *An American Dilemma,*which raised consciousness about the existence of discrimination, the LDF also began using a sociological argument. Additionally in the 1940s, the LDF won significant cases regarding voting rights, public transportation, and housing.

The **U.S. Supreme Court** in effect abolished the "white primary" with its ruling in *Smith v. Allwright* (1944). The judges stated that denying African Americans the opportunity to vote in the Texas primary election violated the Fifteenth Amendment. In *Morgan v. Virginia* (1946), the Court ruled unconstitutional segregation on interstate transportation. Additionally in *Patton v. Mississippi* (1947), the Court delivered another victory to the LDF by finding unconstitutional all-white juries. The last significant decision in the 1940s occurred when the Court, in *Shelley v. Kraemer* (1948), found that housing covenants designed to keep African Americans out of all-white neighborhoods were unconstitutional, since the covenants denied blacks equal protection under the law. With these victories, increased NAACP membership, and stronger challenges to Jim Crow by black Americans after **World War II**, the LDF moved forward in fully confronting segregated education with two additional higher education suits.

In 1948, George McLaurin, a 68-year-old man, was denied admission to the University of Oklahoma Graduate School of Education. Despite his ordered admission by the court, McLaurin was separated from his white classmates. McLaurin sat in a desk outside of the regular classrooms, studied in a separate section of the library and ate his lunch at a different time than the other students. Because of these conditions, Marshall and McLaurin petitioned the court's decision. By the time the case reached the Supreme Court, McLaurin had been allowed to sit in classes with other students. Yet his desk had been labeled "colored," and his separate designations remained in the library and cafeteria. In *McLaurin v. Oklahoma State Regents for Higher Education* (1950), the Supreme Court ruled that setting students apart by race, as the University of Oklahoma Law School had, immediately labeled one race the superior race and the other the inferior.

In February 1946, Herman Marion Sweatt, a postman, sought a legal education by applying to the University of Texas Law School. After his application was rejected, Sweatt filed a lawsuit against the University of Texas. Following the initial hearing, the state of Texas established a makeshift law school in connection with Prairie View University, a historically black institution, by

NAACP LEGAL DEFENSE AND EDUCATION FUND   559

locating the school in Houston, 40 miles away from Prairie View, renting a few rooms and hiring two black lawyers as instructors. With its acquisition of funds to construct a "real" separate law school, Texas tried to persuade Sweatt to stop his legal actions, but Sweatt and Marshall continued.

Although the district court ruled against Sweatt in 1947, the argument Marshall presented became the center of testimony for the eventual Supreme Court victory in 1950. Marshall attacked separate schools on the grounds that racial separation was scientifically unjustifiable and socially destructive. Earl Harrison, Dean of the University Pennsylvania Law School testified about the environment students enjoyed by attending majority institutions and the psychological detriments of segregation. In his 1949 brief to the Supreme Court, Marshall also used the words of law professors: "By sending Sweatt to a raw, new law school without alumni or prestige, Texas deprives him of economic opportunity which its white students have." For the first time, the LDF argued in *Sweatt v. Painter* (1950) that attending separate but equal institutions was unconstitutional because of the inequality in facilities, resources, prestige, and indirect benefits later utilized by white students. The Supreme Court agreed, for Chief Justice Fred Vinson declared that: "the University of Texas Law School possesses to a far greater degree those qualities which are incapable of objective measurement but which make for greatness in a law school." Subsequently, Sweatt was admitted to the University of Texas Law School. Precedent had now been established for a challenge to segregation in elementary and secondary schools. However, the LDF would have to move forward without Houston, who died on April 22, 1950.

By the fall of 1953, the five collective cases known as *Brown v. Board of Education* (1954) were argued before the Supreme Court by team of LDF lawyers including Marshall, Louis Redding, Robert Carter, James M. Nabrit Jr., Oliver Hill, and Spottswood Robinson. In 1954, *Brown* overturned *Plessy v. Ferguson* and fundamentally challenged the inherent inequalities of "separate but equal." With *Brown* II in effect allowing for the desegregation of public schools to move with "all deliberate speed," the LDF continued to battle the legacy of legal segregation and subsequent resistance to change. LDF lawyers assisted with cases involving the desegregation of public schools, including institutions of higher education, the desegregation of public facilities, and individual rights to **health care**, voting, and equal protection. The LDF also represented such leaders as **Martin Luther King, Jr.**

As the LDF legal team continued to wage legal battles, a major change occurred in 1957, with the LDF becoming independent of the NAACP. Marshall no longer served the NAACP, and he assumed the position of director-counsel. Despite the change, the LDF retained the NAACP name. Also, during the height of the **Civil Rights Movement**, such lawyers as James M. Nabrit III and Marian Wright Edleman joined the LDF. In 1961, Jack Greenberg became director-counsel upon Marshall's appointment by President **John F. Kennedy** to the U.S. Court of Appeals for the Second Circuit. Upon Greenberg's resignation from the LDF, Julius Chambers became director-counsel in 1984. Within 10 years, Elane R. Jones became the first female director-counsel of the LDF, and currently Theodore M. Shaw serves as the fifth director-counsel. Throughout the last few decades, the LDF remains committed to legal cases involving education, voter protection, economic justice, and criminal justice that will advance racial justice and equality.

Further Readings: Greenberg, Jack. *Crusaders in the Courts: How a Dedicated Band of Lawyers Fought for Civil Rights Revolution.* New York: BasicBooks, 1994; Kluger, Richard. *Simple Justice: The History of* Brown v. Board of Education *and Black America's Struggle for Equality.* New York: Vintage Books, 2004; Martin, Waldo E. Brown v. Board of Education: *A Brief History with Documents.* Boston: Bedford/St. Martin's, 1998; Meier, August. "Negro Protest Movements and Organizations." *Journal of Negro Education* 32 (August 1963): 437–50; NAACP Legal Defense and Educational Fund, Inc., Web site. http://www.naacpldf.org/ (accessed May 27, 2008); Tushnet, Mark V. *The NAACP's Legal Strategy against Segregated Education, 1925–1950.* Chapel Hill: University of North Carolina Press, 1987; Ware, Gilbert. "The NAACP-Inc. Fund Alliance: Its Strategy, Power, and Destruction." *Journal of Negro Education* 63 (Summer 1994): 323–35." 'With an Even Hand': *Brown v. Board* at Fifty." Library of Congress exhibition. http://www.loc.gov /exhibits/brown (accessed May 27, 2008).

Michelle A. Purdy

The Nadir of the Negro

The Nadir of the Negro is the era from 1890 to the 1930s. In these years, African Americans lost many of the rights they had won during **Reconstruction**. In the South, whites forced blacks back into noncitizenship, no longer allowed to vote or serve on juries, and cut funding for black schools by as much as two thirds. In the North, organizations ranging from restaurants to organized baseball to the dormitories of Harvard University that had previously admitted African Americans now rejected them.

Historian Rayford Logan, who earned his doctorate from Harvard in 1936 and chaired Howard University's history department in the 1940s and 1950s, established the term in his 1954 book, The *Negro in American Life and Thought: The Nadir.* The same year, **C. Vann Woodward** gave a series of lectures, reprinted later as *The Strange Career of Jim Crow,* telling how African Americans lost citizenship and social rights in the South not right after Reconstruction, but after 1890. Since then, the idea that race relations grew worse around 1890 has become well accepted in American history.

Three events in 1890 signaled the new era. **Mississippi** passed a new constitution, stripping voting rights from African Americans, and although the new law clearly violated the Fourteenth and Fifteenth Amendments, the **federal government** did nothing. The U.S. Senate failed to pass the Federal Elections Bill, which would have helped African Americans (and white Republicans) to vote freely across the South. Worse, after the defeat, when tagged as usual by Democrats as "nigger-lovers," Republicans this time denied the charge and largely abandoned the cause of civil rights. Since the Democrats already labeled themselves "the white man's party," African Americans now found themselves with no political allies. Finally, the Massacre at Wounded Knee, South Dakota, ended the last vestige of Native sovereignty, sending American Indians into their nadir period as well.

What caused the Nadir? The antislavery idealism spawned by the Civil War faded as memories of the war dimmed. By 1890, only one American in three was old enough to have been alive when it ended. Fewer still were old enough to have any memory of the war. Among older Americans, millions had immigrated to the United States long after the war's end and had played no role in it.

Three developments having nothing directly to do with black rights further eroded the position of African Americans. The first was the Indian wars. Although the federal government had guaranteed their land to the Plains Indians "forever," after whites discovered gold in Colorado, Dakota Territory, and elsewhere, they took it anyway. If it was all right to take Indians' land because they were not white, was not it all right to deny rights to African Americans, who were not white either?

Second, immigrants from Europe persisted in voting Democratic, partly because they saw that it was in their interest to differentiate themselves from blacks, still at the bottom of the social hierarchy. Also, Republicans were moving toward Prohibition, hardly a preferred position among Italian, Greek, and Russian newcomers among others. Frustrated politically by the new arrivals from southern and eastern Europe, Senator Henry Cabot Lodge helped found the Immigration Restriction League to keep out "inferior" racial strains. This further sapped Republican commitment to the idea "that all men are created equal."

Third, the ideology of imperialism washed over the United States from Europe. Imperialism both depended upon and in turn reinforced the ideology of white supremacy. The growing clamor to annex Hawai'i included the claim that Americans could govern those brown people better than they could govern themselves. After winning the Spanish-American War, the administration of President William McKinley used the same rationale to defend making war upon our allies, the Filipinos. William Howard Taft, who was made U.S. commissioner over the Philippines in 1900, called the Filipinos "our little brown brothers" and said they would need "fifty or one hundred years" of close supervision "to develop anything resembling Anglo-Saxon political principles and skills." Democrats drew the obvious parallel, "What

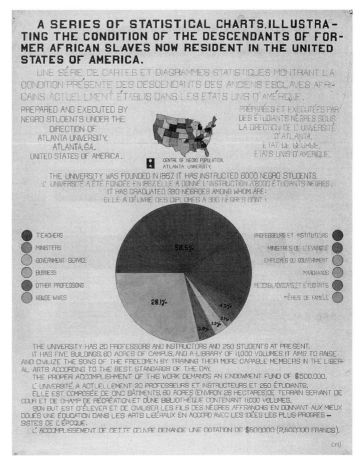

Composed at the height of the nadir of the Negro, this chart demonstrated the economic challenges facing the descendants of slaves, 1900. Courtesy of Library of Congress, LC-DIG-ppmsca-08994.

about our little black brothers in the South?" and Republicans could make no cogent reply.

Seeing that the United States did nothing to stop Mississippi's usurpation of black rights, whites in other Southern states and states as distant as Oklahoma followed suit by 1907. In 1894, Democrats in Congress repealed the remaining federal election statutes, leaving the Fifteenth Amendment lifeless, with no extant laws to enforce it. In 1896, in *Plessy v. Ferguson*, the **U.S. Supreme Court** declared de jure racial segregation legal. Schools were segregated state-wide in Delaware, Maryland, West Virginia, **Kentucky**, Missouri, **Arkansas**, Oklahoma, **Texas**, and Arizona, as well as much of Ohio, Indiana, Illinois, Kansas, New Mexico, and California. The South already had segregated schools, of course.

The new Mississippi constitution required prospective voters to "be able to read any section of the constitution of this State . . . or he shall be able to understand the same when read to him, or give a reasonable interpretation thereof." Other states incorporated similar measures in their new laws. In practice, black would-be voters were required to be able to read a section and interpret it. Local folklore has it that a professor at Tuskegee Institute with a doctorate in political science could not interpret the constitution to the satisfaction of the Macon County, Alabama, registrar, who was a high school dropout. Certainly even jurisdictions like Macon County—84 percent black, and home to two important black institutions, Tuskegee Institute and a large VA hospital—had white voting majorities until the **Civil Rights Movement**.

Not only did these clauses remove African Americans from voting, and hence from juries, they also linked literacy and education as the mechanism. In their wake, every Southern state cut back on black schooling. Their new constitutions commanded racially segregated schools de jure, so it was easy to set up shorter sessions for black schools, require lower qualifications of black teachers, and pay them a fraction of white salaries.

In 1898, Democrats rioted in Wilmington, North Carolina, driving out all Republican officeholders and killing at least 12 African Americans. Astonishingly, the McKinley administration allowed this coup d'etat to stand. Congress became resegregated in 1901 when Congressman George H. White of North Carolina could not win reelection owing to the disfranchisement of black voters. No African American served in Congress again until 1929, and none from the South until 1973. The so-called Progressive Movement was for whites only. In many Northern cities, its "reforms" removed the last local black leaders from city councils in favor of commissioners elected citywide.

Coinciding with the Nadir and helping to justify it was the ideology of social Darwinism—the notion that the fittest rise to the top in society. It provided a potent rationale not only for white supremacy, but also for America's increasing class hierarchy. Its "scientific" handmaidens, eugenics and psychometrics, flourished. Madison Grant, author of the 1916 eugenics tract *The Passing of the Great Race*, helped write the 1924 law that drastically cut immigration to the United States from Asia and southern and eastern Europe. Carl Brigham, concerned that "American intelligence is declining . . . as the racial admixture becomes more and more extensive," developed the Scholastic

Aptitude Test in 1926 to select the brightest students for elite colleges. Popular culture also justified the Nadir. In this era, minstrel shows came to dominate our popular culture. They had begun before the Civil War but flourished after 1890 minstrel shows both caused and reflected the increased racism of the period. As author, politician, and activist James Weldon Johnson put it, minstrel shows "fixed the tradition of the Negro as only an irresponsible, happy-go-lucky, wide-grinning, loud-laughing, shuffling, banjo-playing, singing, dancing sort of being." In small towns across the North, where few blacks existed to correct this impression, these stereotypes provided the bulk of white "knowledge" about what African Americans were like. The first epic motion picture, *The Birth of a Nation*, glorified the **Ku Klux Klan** as the savior of white Southern civilization from the menace of black upstarts during Reconstruction. In 1936, near the end of the Nadir, the Margaret Mitchell novel *Gone with the Wind* sold a million hardbound books in its first month. The book and the resulting film, the highest-grossing movie of all time, further convinced whites that noncitizenship was appropriate for African Americans.

During the Nadir, **lynchings** rose to their height, and not just in the South, although the main "national" database has never included Northern lynchings. Segregation swept through public accommodations, North as well as South. In 1908, touring the North for an article, "The Color Line in the North," Ray Stannard Baker noted the deterioration even in Boston, the old citadel of abolitionism: "A few years ago no hotel or restaurant in Boston refused Negro guests. [N]ow several hotels, restaurants, and especially confectionery stores, will not serve Negroes, even the best of them." Writing of the day-to-day interactions of whites and blacks in the Midwest, Frank Quillen observed in 1913 that race prejudice "is increasing steadily, especially during the last twenty years." In the 1920s, Harvard barred an African American student from the very dormitory where his father had lived decades earlier when attending the university. Whites ousted African Americans from occupations ranging from major league baseball player and Kentucky Derby jockey to postal carrier, mason, firefighter, and carpenter. Even jobs like department store salesclerk and factory worker were closed to African Americans, and not just in Dixie.

Across the North and throughout the Appalachian South and the Ozarks, whites forced African Americans to make a **Great Retreat** from hundreds of communities. These then became all-white **sundown towns** for decades. Communities that had voted Democratic in the 1860s were especially likely to bar African Americans decades later, during the Nadir. Even some previously interracial Republican towns, like Hermann, Missouri, where African Americans had celebrated Emancipation Day in the 1870s, went sundown after 1890.

African Americans thrashed about, trying to cope with their increasingly desperate situation. Early in the Nadir, some left the Deep South for new homes in Kansas and Oklahoma (the Exodus), but Oklahoma entered the Union in 1907 with a constitution modeled after Mississippi's, while Kansas lost its abolitionist edge and developed many sundown towns. **Booker T. Washington** suggested blacks relinquish claims to social equality, concentrating on hard work and education, but this proved difficult because hostile Southern whites often targeted successful black farmers and businessmen.

W.E.B. Du Bois disputed with Washington, but his refusal to condone loss of black rights proved no more workable. Forming black towns like Boley, Oklahoma, and Mound Bayou, Mississippi, gave no relief, because these communities were ultimately under the white thumbs of county and state governments. The **Back to Africa movements** organized by Chief Sam and **Marcus Garvey** also provided no solution.

In this context, the **Great Migration** provided African Americans with environments in which they could vote freely, and hence could bargain for at least some municipal services and other basic rights. However, cities North and South became much more residentially segregated during the Nadir, and many suburbs formed on an all-white basis. Still, African Americans were able to establish small majority-black settlements on Long Island, New York, west of Detroit, south of Chicago, and on the outskirts of other Northern cities.

During the Woodrow Wilson administration, the Nadir intensified. Wilson segregated the navy, which had not been segregated before. He also replaced blacks who held appointed offices with whites. Responding to his leadership, whites rioted against black communities in Chicago, East St. Louis, Omaha, Washington, and other cities in what James Weldon Johnson called the **Red Summer** of 1919. The release of *The Birth of a Nation* led to a rebirth of the Ku Klux Klan, this time as a national organization that displayed astonishing if short-lived clout in Georgia, Indiana, Oklahoma, Oregon, and other states during the 1920s. The Klan prompted the expulsion of African Americans from additional Northern towns and counties. The **Great Depression** of the next decade spurred whites to drive African Americans from additional jobs like elevator operator and railroad fireman.

Anti-Semitism increased as well in the Nadir. Early in the Civil War, people of various religions—including Jews—had founded the the Union League Club to combat the pro-secession sentiment that dominated New York City. When white segregationists removed the widow of an African American soldier from a streetcar, the Union League Club came to her defense. Joseph Seligman, a Jew, leading banker, and friend of Ulysses S. Grant, had been a founder of the club. His son Jesse became a member in 1868. Then, during the 1890s, members refused to admit Jews, as well as Italians, Catholics, and others of "incorrect background." In 1893, after 25 years of membership, 14 of them as a vice president, Jesse Seligman had to resign. Members blackballed his own son Theodore because he was a Jew. During **World War I**, the U.S. Army for the first time considered Jews "a special problem whose loyalty to the U.S. was open to question." Along with other government agencies (and the KKK), the Military Intelligence Department mounted a campaign against Jewish immigrants that helped convince Congress to pass a restrictive immigration bill in 1924.

The Nadir manifested itself in many ways, including treatment of African Americans in Iowa newspapers. During the 1870s, they covered the activities and individual happenings within the African American population. By the 1890s, however, most stories about blacks appeared on the crime page. Even the appointment of an Iowan as ambassador to Liberia, one of the highest posts available to African Americans during the Nadir, drew no notice in the Iowa press.

African American intellectuals despaired of the Nadir. In 1900, African American poet **Paul Laurence Dunbar** wrote "Robert Gould Shaw," a bitter ode to the white colonel who led the 54th Massachusetts Colored Regiment in its charge at Fort Wagner during the Civil War. The poem ended by suggesting that Shaw's "cold endurance of the final pain" had been pointless. Only with the rise of the CIO unions and some important symbolic gestures by First Lady **Eleanor Roosevelt** did the Nadir begin to crack. The Great Migration itself helped end it. Coupled with the Great Retreat, it concentrated African Americans into a few large cities. This enabled blacks to win seats in Northern state legislatures and the U.S. House of Representatives, which in turn prompted white political leaders to moderate their racist rhetoric so as not to alienate urban black voters and political leaders. A second crack in the wall of white supremacy came from the crumbling of imperialism. In a **Cold War** context, America could not afford to offend the nonwhite leaders of newly independent nations in Asia and Africa. Most important of all was the role played by **World War II**. Germany gave white supremacy a bad name. It is always in victors' interests to demonize the vanquished, but Nazism made this task easy. Americans saw in the German death camps the logical result of eugenics and segregation, and it appalled them. As they sought to differentiate ourselves from Hitler's discredited racial policies, the overt racism of the Nadir now made them uneasy. Swedish social scientist **Gunnar Myrdal** called this conflict our "American dilemma" and predicted in 1944, "Equality is slowly winning."

Although the Nadir eased since 1940, it has left the United States with two progeny: sundown towns and warped history. Near the end of the period, in 1935, W.E.B. Du Bois lamented the distorted account of Reconstruction to which it gave rise: "We have got to the place where we cannot use our experiences during and after the Civil War for the uplift and enlightenment of mankind." *See also* Atlanta Compromise.

Further Readings: Baker, Ray Stannard. "The Color Line in the North." *American Magazine* 65 (1908). Reprinted in Otto Olsen, ed., *The Negro Question: From Slavery to Caste, 1863–1910.* New York: Pitman, 1971; Bassett, John Spencer. *A Short History of the United States.* New York: Macmillan, 1923; Bergmann, Leola. "The Negro in Iowa." *Iowa Journal of History and Politics* (1969 [1948]): 44–45; DeVries, James. *Race and Kinship in a Midwestern Town.* Urbana: University of Illinois Press, 1984; Du Bois, W.E.B. *Black Reconstruction.* Cleveland, OH: World Meridian, 1964 (1935), 722; Johnson, James Weldon. *Black Manhattan.* New York: Knopf, 1930; Loewen, James W. *Lies across America.* New York: New Press, 1999; Loewen, James W. *Sundown Towns.* New York: New Press, 2005; Loewen, James W. "Teaching Race Relations through Feature Films." *Teaching Sociology* 19 (January 1991): 82; Logan, Rayford. *The Negro in American Life and Thought: The Nadir.* New York: Dial, 1954; Myrdal, Gunnar. *An American Dilemma.* New York: Harper & Row, 1944; Quillen, Frank. *The Color Line in Ohio.* Ann Arbor, MI: Wahr, 1913; Upchurch, Thomas Adams. *Legislating Racism: The Billion Dollar Congress and the Birth of Jim Crow.* Lexington: University Press of Kentucky, 2004.

James W. Loewen

Nation of Islam

The Nation of Islam (NOI) is a religious black nationalist movement that emerged in the 1930s, just after the "Golden Age" of **Black Nationalism**.

The NOI is one of the few remaining black nationalist movements that has survived from the **Jim Crow** era to the present, and that continues to thrive.

Origins

The Nation of Islam was founded in Detroit in 1930, not by an African American, but by Wallace Dodd, an immigrant from New Zealand. From Dodd's appearance, researchers have speculated that he may have descended from a "mixed" heritage that combined European and either Polynesian or Punjabi ancestry. Dodd's ambiguous racial appearance permitted him to switch his racial identity during his sojourn in the United States, variously claiming to be white, black, or Arab.

During the 1920s, Dodd served a prison sentence in California on a narcotics charge. Upon his release in 1929, Dodd traveled to Chicago and became involved in the Moorish Science Temple (MST), a group that combined new religious teachings with black nationalism. The MST's founder was Timothy Drew (aka Noble Drew Ali, the Prophet). Drew taught that African Americans are descended from "the Moors," and were originally of the Islamic faith. Drew published a book of his teachings that he entitled the *Koran* (not to be confused with the Islamic holy book of the same name). Drew plagiarized most of his *Koran* from previously published esoteric sources. Drew taught that "Moors" (African Americans) were "Asiatics," one of the world's two major races along with Europeans. While Drew's teachings sometimes advocated racial tolerance and equality, he also taught that "Europeans" represent a lower order of humanity who had been banished from Mecca by the Asiatic "Moslems." Thus Drew's theology reversed the logic of Jim Crow–era racism, holding that African Americans are racially superior to white Americans. Drew's religion also espoused black nationalist ideals.

Upon entering the MST, Wallace Dodd took the name "David Ford-el." The group quickly degenerated into internal squabbles. After one of Drew's rivals was stabbed, Drew himself died shortly thereafter, under mysterious circumstances. In the wake of Drew's death, Dodd became a contender for control of the organization. Dodd even claimed to be the reincarnation of "Noble Drew Ali." Because the MST's factional rivalries had devolved into kidnappings, shootouts, and assassinations, Dodd became of interest to Chicago law enforcement, and so he moved to Detroit.

In Detroit, Dodd found work peddling cloth and needles in black neighborhoods. He changed his name to "Wallace Fard," "Wallace Fard Muhammed," "W. D. Muhammed," and similar variations. Taking Timothy Drew as a role model, Fard/Dodd presented himself to residents of the city's black ghetto as a prophet of a new religion that was based on MST. However, Fard's new religion added many elements of his own devising. Fard eventually settled on the name "Nation of Islam" for his organization. While Fard told his followers that he was teaching Islam, his religion bears little resemblance to any orthodox version of Islam, and appears to be mostly of Fard's own invention.

Fard's new religion began to experience conflict with Detroit law enforcement as it had in Chicago. In 1932, one of Fard's followers committed a ritualistic murder. The murderer quoted a passage from a pamphlet Fard had published: "The unbeliever must be stabbed through the heart." He also told police: "Every son of Islam must gain a victory from the devil. Four victories and the son will attain his reward."

Detroit police saw Fard as complicit in the murder. He was not charged, but the police department encouraged him to shut down his religion and to leave town if he wanted to evade charges related to the murder. Fard complied, but snuck back into the city in early 1933 and began preaching again. The police again arrested Fard. In this police interview, Fard described his religion as "strictly a racket," and admitted that he was "getting all the money out of it he could." Fard returned to Chicago. There, Fard was arrested again, for disturbing the peace. Fard then disappeared from the historical record. Fard's common-law wife stated several decades later that Fard had returned to New Zealand. Neither the FBI nor any other researcher has been able to conclusively document Fard's whereabouts after his last arrest in Chicago. After Fard's departure, the NOI broke down in another series of violent internecine struggles. Elijah Poole, better known as Elijah Muhammad, emerged as the NOI's new leader, and retained that position until his death in 1975.

Theology

Elijah Muhammad did not substantially deviate from Fard's religion, but did add a few modifications. Most notably, Muhammad taught that Fard was not just a prophet, but the human incarnation of Allah himself. The NOI's creation myth held that the black race is 78 trillion years old. For most of that time, they were gods enjoying a utopian life. About 6,600 years ago, a deviant black named Yakub, also known as "the big head scientist," created the white race of devils, who would rule over blacks for six millennia. NOI theology thus contains a strong millenarian strain, by prophesizing that white rule is near its end. Fard originally taught that the world would be rid of evil by 1934, but that doctrine has subsequently been modified, with the expected day of reckoning being pushed back several times over the course of NOI's history. Fard taught that when the day comes, planes will be sent to Earth from "The Wheel," a plane made like a wheel. The planes would destroy the Earth, and carry black people away, possibly back to Mars, where people are living already even today. Elijah Muhammad retained this doctrine, as did subsequent NOI preachers such as **Malcolm X** and Louis Farrakhan. Occasionally in later years, the plane was updated to a spaceship.

The primary theme of NOI's millenarian teachings is that black people are destined to regain their status as gods. NOI theology thus explains white malfeasance and black powerlessness in the United States, while also motivating blacks to prepare to seize power from whites. The theology accomplishes this by marrying black racial supremacism with millenarian prophecy.

NOI theology bears a few superficial resemblances to mainstream Islam: separation of the sexes, avoidance of pork, and a vague interest in the Arabic language. However, the core of NOI theology directly contradicts core Islamic beliefs: specifically, the NOI's racial supremacism, its identification of Allah with a specific human being (Fard), its derogation of the Koran, and its belief in a prophet other than Muhammad. NOI theology not only bears little resemblance with mainstream Islam, it probably has more Christian overtones than it does Muslim.

At the core of NOI theology is the argument that black people are gods, and that white people are devils who were created by a demented black scientist. Thus Fard retained Drew's inversion of Jim Crow racial ideology, turning white supremacism on its head. NOI preached overt contempt for the white race.

Growth and Structure

Elijah Muhammad fled Detroit in the wake of the NOI's internal wars over Fard's succession. Muhammad traveled under a variety of aliases to evade the other NOI ministers who challenged his claim to Fard's legacy, and who intended to kill him. Muhammad's own brother had already been killed in the NOI's internecine warfare. NOI members had also engaged in street fights with police in several cities, and so Muhammad was also on the run from disgruntled and vengeful cops. Muhammad wandered from city to city, evangelizing and setting up new "temples." While Muhammad did attract followers in his circumspect travels, they were few in number.

During **World War II**, the **Federal Bureau of Investigation (FBI)** investigated Muhammad's contacts with Japanese agents. A federal court cleared Muhammad of sedition, but imprisoned him on charges of draft evasion. Upon Muhammad's release in 1946, the NOI had fewer than 400 members. But while incarcerated, Muhammad realized that prisoners were a population ripe for conversion. Black prisoners during the Jim Crow era often had strong motivation to be attracted to the NOI's racist, antiwhite teachings. The NOI's prisoner membership began to grow during the postwar period.

Among the new prison converts was Malcolm Little. He had sold drugs, burgled, pimped, been a numbers runner, and worked as a homosexual prostitute. Elijah Muhammad renamed him "Malcolm X." Malcolm was an unusually accomplished orator. He ascended rapidly in the NOI due to his ability to recruit and organize new converts. During the 1950s, NOI grew by leaps and bounds, eventually gaining several hundred thousand members and sympathizers.

Malcolm X was the NOI's major public representative after Muhammad, and his rhetoric was no less incendiary. Malcolm X advocated **lynching** random white people in retaliation for black lynchings. He advocated attacking white men who court black women. He recited all of the "black god/white devil" rhetoric he had learned from Muhammad.

In 1962, Malcolm learned that Muhammad had engaged in many adulterous affairs with his teenaged "secretaries," impregnating a number of them. (FBI surveillance tapes recorded Muhammad seducing his teenage secretaries by bragging about his "divine seed.") Muhammad had even impregnated a member of his own family in an incestuous affair. Furthermore, Muhammad and his family were spending lavish sums on their luxurious lifestyle, using funds appropriated from NOI temples. Malcolm became disaffected with Muhammad's teaching. He publicly criticized Muhammad, and was forced out of NOI in 1964. Malcolm now turned to mainstream Islam, formed his own church, and began to successfully recruit many NOI followers.

For decades, NOI members who publicly disagreed with Elijah Muhammad had often been attacked or killed. When Malcolm went public with his criticism of Muhammad, NOI members turned on him with equal ferocity.

Malcolm told *Ebony* magazine that NOI "got to kill me. They can't afford to let me live . . . I know where the bodies are buried. And if they press me, I'll exhume some."

Louis X (aka Louis Farrakhan) wrote ominously in the NOI newspaper: "Only those who wish to be led to hell, or to their doom, will follow Malcolm. The die is set, and Malcolm shall not escape, especially after such evil, foolish talk about his benefactor. Such a man is worthy of death and would have been met with death if it had not been for Muhammad's confidence in Allah for victory over his enemies." Several attempts were made on the lives of Malcolm X, his wife, and his children. NOI assassins finally succeeded in gunning Malcolm X down while he gave a public address in February 1965.

After Elijah Muhammad died in 1975, his son dismantled much of NOI's business side, abandoned most of the Fard/Muhammad theology, renamed the organization, and began to transform it into a mainstream Islamic church. Several years later, a faction led by Louis Farrakhan splintered off. Farrakhan, whose birth name was Louis Wolcott, eventually announced the restoration of NOI. Farrakhan continues to preach the Fard/Muhammad religion. Farrakhan's NOI still emphasizes the NOI's traditional antiwhite racism. However, under Farrakhan's leadership, NOI rhetoric has become rabidly anti-Semitic. NOI published an anti-Semitic book that blames Jews for oppressions and injuries experienced by American blacks. Farrakhan teaches that Judaism is a "gutter religion," that Jews were responsible for black slavery, and that Jews continue to prey on black people today. Farrakhan began to ally with white supremacist activists when their shared anti-Semitic interests overlapped. Farrakhan and his deputies began to threaten violence against Jews and whites. Catholics and homosexuals are also new NOI targets. NOI rhetoric has become increasingly homophobic.

Violence and Murder

Violence and crime have been endemic to NOI around the country for much of the organization's history. Within the NOI structure, the most feared group is the "Fruit of Islam." This is a paramilitary corps, which functions as bodyguards and enforcers. Furthermore, NOI prison gangs can be found in the correctional facilities in many states.

The Philadelphia NOI has the best documented links to organized crime. In Philadelphia, the NOI developed an extortionist offshoot, who described themselves as the "Black Mafia." This group became notorious for its involvement with a number of spectacularly violent crimes. For example, in 1971, a murderer associated with the Black Mafia was taken in by Elijah Muhammad and made one of Muhammad's personal "Fruit of Islam" bodyguards.

In 1973, an NOI minister from Philadelphia led a gang of assassins to Washington, DC. Their target was a former NOI member who had converted to orthodox Islam, and who had subsequently dared to criticize Elijah Muhammad. The gang invaded the heretic's home, but he was not home. So instead, the assassins murdered everyone who was in the house, including two women and five children. One of the murder victims was a baby only nine days old. Then, the Black Mafia went to Cherry Hill, New Jersey, and murdered a black mayoral candidate with underworld connections, apparently because he had refused to broker a heroin deal for the Philadelphia gang.

The Black Mafia gang routinely kicked back part of its illicit profits to the local NOI temple in Philadelphia. The head of NOI's Temple 12 was Jeremiah Shabazz, also known as "Godfather of the Black Mafia." Local law enforcement overlooked the gang's activities as long as they restricted themselves to extorting black businesses and various other petty, ghetto-based hustles. However, once they transitioned into a large-scale drug trafficking enterprise, a series of arrests followed, in the late 1970s and early 1980s. Since then, the Nation of Islam have constituted one of the largest and most feared prison gangs in the Pennsylvania correctional system. More recently, in 2005, a NOI minister was convicted for racketeering and fraud for his role in misappropriating minority-certified business contracts from the Philadelphia city government.

John Allen Muhammad committed a racist serial murder spree in the Washington, DC, area in 2002. Muhammad and a younger partner killed 10 people in sniper attacks there, and another six or seven in other regions around the country. Muhammad had planned to recruit disaffected black youth all over the United States and Canada, and start up killing sprees in other cities as well. His goal was to spread chaos that would cause society to collapse. While the NOI leadership distanced itself from the killer and his plan, it is clear from trial testimony that Muhammed was motivated by the antiwhite rhetoric and the millenarianism that he had learned within the NOI.

Jim Crow and the Hate That Hate Produced

The violence that follows in the NOI's wake represents the shadow image of Jim Crow. NOI theology teaches an inverted version of Jim Crow racial ideology. The difference is that NOI substitutes black supremacism for white supremacism. NOI's separatist black nationalism is another reflection of Jim Crow. NOI agrees with white supremacists that the races should live separately.

In 1959, CBS produced and aired a television documentary on the NOI entitled "The Hate That Hate Produced." It features an excerpt from a NOI-sponsored play entitled "The Trial," written by Louis Farrakhan. In the play, "the white man" is found guilty of a multitude of sins against African Americans, and is sentenced to death.

Thus, the racial hate engendered by the white supremacism of the Jim Crow era persists into the present. Racial hate is seen in its original, unaltered form in the rhetoric of the KKK and other white supremacist groups. But in the NOI, there is also the hateful legacy of Jim Crow in its mirror image. Just as white supremacism led to extremist violence in the form of lynchings, so does the NOI's racial extremism led to violence.

Further Readings: Beynon, Erdmann Doane. "The Voodoo Cult among Negro Migrants in Detroit." *American Journal of Sociology* 43, no. 6 (May 1938): 894–907; Clegg, Claude Andrew. *An Original Man: The Life and Times of Elijah Muhammad.* New York: St. Martin's Press, 1998; Essien-Udom, E. U. *Black Nationalism: The Search for an Identity.* Chicago: University of Chicago Press, 1995; Evanzz, Karl. *The Messenger: The Rise and Fall of Elijah Muhammad.* New York: Pantheon Books, 1999; Federal Bureau of Investigation,

U.S. "Elijah Muhammad: File 105–24822." http://foia.fbi.gov/muhammad/muhammad1.
pdf (accessed August 2007); Gardell, Mattias. *In the Name of Elijah Muhammad: Louis
Farrakhan and The Nation of Islam.* Durham, NC: Duke University Press, 1996; Griffin,
Sean Patrick. *Philadelphia's "Black Mafia": A Social and Political History.* Dordrecht,
Netherlands: Kluwer Academic, 2003; Griffin, Sean Patrick. *Black Brothers, Inc.: The Vio-
lent Rise and Fall of the Philadelphia Black Mafia.* Lancashire, England: Milo Books, 2005;
Lincoln, C. Eric. *The Black Muslims in America.* 3rd ed. Wm. B. Eerdmans Publishing
Company, 1994; Magida, Arthur J. *Prophet of Rage: A Life of Louis Farrakhan and His
Nation.* Reprint edition. New York: HarperCollins, 1997; McGarvey, Brendan. "Allah
Behind Bars: Even La Cosa Nostra Members Fear the Nation of Islam in Jail." *City Paper,*
November 7–13, 2002; Tsoukalas, Steven. *The Nation of Islam: Understanding the "Black
Muslims."* Phillipsburg, NJ: P & R Publishing, 2001.

Thomas Brown

National Association of Colored Women

In 1896, the National Association of Colored Women (NACW), one of the
first all-black political organizations, was created at one of the lowest points—
the "nadir"—of African American history in response to the birth of Jim
Crow. It was incorporated as the national affiliate for hundreds of clubs dedicated to the social reform activities of its members. The "race women" that
participated in this national club movement were committed to "uplifting
the race" or improving socioeconomic conditions for African Americans. By
the late nineteenth century, critiques of the nation's "Negro Problem"
weighed heavily on the status of African American women, especially as the
burden bearers of the race. They were often considered both the source and
the solution to the many problems African Americans encountered after slavery. Black **disfranchisement**, lynch law/mob rule, "peonage slavery," and discriminatory laws and social customs nullified the civil rights and privileges
African Americans had gained during **Reconstruction**. Consequently, the
1890s was a decade plagued by racial prejudice and violence that severely
affected African Americans. The 1896 landmark *Plessy v. Ferguson* **U.S.
Supreme Court** case, in particular, stipulated the "**separate but equal**" laws
of segregation that would lay firmly the foundation for white supremacy until
the **Civil Rights Movement** of the 1950s and 1960s. In light of the decree for
de jure segregation, African American women galvanized efforts and collected
resources more than ever to overcome obstacles to black survival and racial
progress.

Although they stood in the shadow of icons like Frederick Douglass, **Booker
T. Washington**, and **W.E.B. Du Bois**, black club women nevertheless were
actively involved in the gender and racial politics of the period. They worked
with white women and black men in the suffrage movement and for racial
equality. As a double minority, however, black women of the NACW also
concentrated on gender and racial matters apart from those of the national
club movement among white women. Black women like Fannie Barrier Williams had encountered racism while participating in predominately white
feminist organizations. Sexism was most apparent among black men who
evaluated the roles and responsibilities of black women within the limits of
patriarchy. The NACW then made it possible and necessary for black women

to voice collectively their concerns and secure their autonomy. Within the pages of the *Woman's Era* (and later the *National Association Notes*), the leading publications by and about black women, the NACW campaigned for gender and racial equality.

Another major impetus for NACW activism involved frequent public attacks on African American women in character and body. An infamous letter written in 1895 by a white journalist, for example, ridiculed all black women as prostitutes and thieves. The reputation and image of black women was tarnished by various reports of immorality linked to disease and poverty among the black masses. As during slavery, black women were also vulnerable to sexual violence and harassment with little or no legal protection by the end of the nineteenth century. These are a few justifications for the NACW's call to action to protect black womanhood in particular but to salvage racial pride in general. To address these issues, the first National Conference of Colored Women was held in Boston in July 1895. Led by Josephine St. Pierre Ruffin and other black feminists, the conference had a special agenda to address the needs of black women as wives, mothers, and daughters committed to the race being moral exemplars and civic activists. Their plans mandated a domestic model of racial uplift, making black women responsible for the health care, spiritual welfare, and moral elevation of their families and communities.

A renewed commitment to service and more defined leadership led to the official creation of the NACW following the national conference. Clubs formerly within the National League of Colored Women of Washington, DC, and the National Federation of Afro-American Women were united as a solid governing body and Mary Church Terrell was elected as the first NACW president in 1896. Other members included Margaret Murray Washington (Booker T. Washington's third wife), **Anna Julia Cooper**, Frances Harper, Victoria Earle Matthews, and **Ida B. Wells-Barnett**. Most of the club women were members of the black middle class. They were well-educated professionals distinguished as "New Negroes" who would become race leaders. Their uplift ideology advocated self-reliance *and* defined self-worth in light of Jim Crowism. Like all African Americans, the black elite also experienced discrimination and racial prejudice. When traveling on lecture tours, for instance, Terrell and Wells-Barnett could not always find suitable public accommodations when many hotels, restaurants, and trains catered primarily to white patrons. Inferior rest rooms, seating, and lodging were reserved for blacks only. When faced with such obstacles, club leaders would find black hosts to stay with in the tour cities, hold meetings in black facilities, and, sometimes, travel in Jim Crow cars despite the inconvenience. It has been asserted that some club leaders with fair complexions would, however, pass for white to traverse racial barriers. More formal resolutions were issued by the NACW against segregation, lynchings, and disfranchisement.

Inspired by their motto, "Lifting As We Climb," African American women in the NACW created a legacy of activism and service. They were on a mission to help the massive populations of the black underclass. The NACW members organized to provide adequate day care for children of working black mothers (or in some areas kindergartens), domestic workshops for better household management, shelters for black elderly and/or orphans, and even formed neighborhood patrols to rid the areas most vulnerable to criminal and/or immoral activities. Education was foremost among the objectives of NACW, too. Reading rooms and literary forums were often supported by the NACW and its affiliate clubs. The diverse service work these club women accomplished inspired generations of African Americans as the NACW remained visible within the ranks of black leadership into the twentieth century. *See also* Nadir of the Negro.

Further Readings Giddings, Paula. *When and Where I Enter: The Impact of Black Women on Race and Sex in America.* New York: William Morrow, 1984; Shaw, Stephanie J. "Black Club Women and the Creation of the National Association of Colored Women." *Journal of Women's History* 3, no. 2 (Fall 1991): 1–25; White, Deborah Gray. *"Too Heavy a Load": Black Women in Defense of Themselves, 1894–1994.* New York: W. W. Norton, 1999.

Sherita L. Johnson

National Guard

The National Guard is a hybrid state and federal military force with origins in the late nineteenth century, during the period when **Jim Crow** was established. The National Guard replaced two military institutions—state militia and state-raised wartime volunteers—and inherited the racial practices of those earlier institutions. Due to the state-based organization of the National Guard, the experience of African Americans with the National Guard, whether as members or not, varied greatly from state to state.

During most of the colonial period, American militia forces occasionally contained Christian Native American men as well as free men of African descent. Militia tradition in some colonies considered all adult free men to compose the militia, especially in areas with few slaves. Laws in some colonies made no mention of skin tone or ancestry regarding liability for militia service. True segregation in the militia would not begin until after the end of the War for Independence. However, by the end of the War of 1812, the idea of the general militia obligation declined, and instead quasi-private military companies formed, which often were legitimized by states to provide militia service. Several states, including Louisiana, allowed companies of free blacks to maintain companies, but most slave states did not. After the Civil War, **Reconstruction** state governments in the South created so-called Negro Militia, which included both black and white men, sometimes in the same companies, in order to protect blacks and white Republicans from white supremacist. However with the end of Reconstruction, Southern state governments eliminated blacks from their organized militia, although black units continued to exist in some Northern states

Between the railroad strike of 1877, and passing of the National Defense Act of 1916, these volunteer militia companies evolved into the modern National Guard. By 1914, seven states and the District of Columbia had units of black National Guardsmen. New York and Illinois each had a regiment of black Guardsmen, while most others had separate battalions of blacks. States that allowed for black units normally placed them directly under the state adjutant general, rather than incorporating them into the rest of the state

National Guard structure. Unlike the black units in the regular army, all officers in black National Guard units tended to be black. While each state had its own customs and regulations regarding black National Guardsmen, all were structured so that black officers would never be in charge of white units. Additionally, during peacetime, state authorities were reluctant to mobilize black units for state duties that might involve them in policing white civilians.

The reasons for blacks joining the National Guard were complex, but much of their motivation had to do with respectability. National Guardsmen did not receive pay for training until 1916, and indeed, membership in the National Guard had earlier been a financial burden in many states. Members of the National Guard were overwhelmingly middle class, for enlisted men as well as officers. Thus, membership in the National Guard, which was a state institution, brought with it an overt indication of middle-class respectability. While black people took some pride in black National Guard units in areas where they existed, the National Guard as a whole was an overwhelmingly white organization, and its performance during riots often betrayed the racial prejudices of members and leaders. The most infamous example occurred during the **East St. Louis Riot** of July 1917, when some reports indicated that members of State Guard units, which were militia units raised to replace the National Guard after it entered federal service for **World War I**, participated in the violence inflicted against blacks rather than protected them, but it was not an isolated incident. Blacks, especially in the South and Midwest, where National Guard performed many of the missions that state police were assuming in the Northeast, often saw the National Guard as just another instrument of white oppression.

Overall, the Guard's image during the Civil Rights years was of a pillar of the status quo, and for blacks in the South, the status quo meant Jim Crow. Governor Orval Faubus's attempt to use the **Arkansas** National Guard to prevent integration of Little Rock's Central High School in 1957 was only the most public use of the Guard in this manner. Fortunately, when President Dwight D. Eisenhower federalized the Arkansas National Guard in order to send it home and keep it out of the governor's control, the Guardsmen obeyed the president, and a serious coda to the Civil War was avoided. Likewise, the **Alabama** National Guard's involvement on June 11, 1963, in Governor **George Wallace**'s theatrics at the "school house door" at the University of Alabama again showed that Guardsmen would, if reluctantly, obey federal authority over state. Of course, the fact that the Alabama adjutant general wore an embroidered Confederate battle flag on the breast of his fatigue uniform amply demonstrated where his sympathies were.

During the dramatic uses of the National Guard in the South during the crises over integration and civil rights, blacks were still excluded from serving in the Guard in most Southern states. President **Harry S. Truman**'s **Executive Order 9981**, July 26, 1948, ordering the desegregating the U.S. military, had little immediate impact on the National Guard. The regular army stalled the implementation of the order until the second year of the Korean War, and many states simply ignored it regarding the National Guard. While most Northern, Midwestern, and Western states began integrating their National Guard in the 1950s, the Guard actually became whiter during the 1960s.

The Selective Service Act deferred members of the National Guard from being drafted as individuals into the army, and thus the Guard became a haven for young men seeking to avoid serving in Vietnam. With Guard units filled completely, potential Guardsmen often used family and political connections to get a position. Blacks, with few of either, found Guard units were not in need of their service. *See also* Armed Forces; World War II.

Further Readings: Doubler, Michael D. *I Am The Guard: A History of the Army National Guard, 1636–2000.* Washington, DC: U.S. Government Printing Office, 2001; MacGregor, Morris J. *Integration of the Armed Forces, 1940–1965.* Washington, DC: Center of Military History, 1989.

Barry M. Stentiford

National Socialism

While never a formidable political force in the United States, advocates of National Socialism (Nazism) nonetheless attempted to broaden its racist ideology through astute recruiting efforts, public relations savvy, the repositioning of overt Nazi symbols with a broadened appeal to white unity and by appealing to American religious and patriotic impulses.

In the early 1930s, before Adolf Hitler's rise to power in Germany, a constellation of small Nazi groups arose in the United States composed primarily of German citizens living abroad and disaffected German Americans. Hitler's political ascendance encouraged such organizations and their leaders to redouble their efforts to spread the Nazi vision of ethnic German solidarity and racial purity.

Friends of the New Germany

The most prominent Nazi group at this time, *Friends of the New Germany* (*Bund der Freunde des neuen Deutschlands*), began with support from high-level Nazi leaders Rudolf Hess and Robert Ley. The leader, Heinz Spanknoebel, held the title "Führer of the Nazi Party in the United States." He sought to mobilize Nazi sympathizers in the United States within German American immigrant communities. *Das Neue Deutschland* (The New Germany), a weekly newspaper, was launched to support these efforts. The organization was short-lived. Public outcry over the activity of the *Friends* in New York City and the subsequent violent incidents invited scrutiny by both the German and American governments. German authorities called Spanknoebel home in late 1933 while he was under indictment for failing to register as a foreign government agent. The movement floundered in 1935 when Rudolf Hess ordered all German nationals out of *Friends of the New Germany* (well over half of its 10,000 members) out of concern that it was fueling anti-German sentiment.

German-American Bund

Fritz Kuhn emerged from this disarray as the new American Führer, reforming and unifying the remnants of *Friends of the New Germany* and other like-minded groups into a new organization: the *Amerika-Deutscher*

Volksbund or *German-American Bund*. Having become an American citizen himself in 1933, Kuhn sought to put an American face on the movement. However, he still kept the back door open for German nationals by setting up a *Prospective Citizens League*, accepting them into membership if they filed the initial paperwork for American citizenship and met the standard criteria of accepting Kuhn's leadership and had no black or Jewish ancestors.

The *Bund* attracted primarily urban lower-middle-class people, most of who viewed the organization as a social outlet. A Youth Division was formed, in part, to counteract American anti-German sentiment that developed during **World War I**. It adapted features of the Hitler Youth including lessons on saluting the swastika, learning popular Nazi songs, listening to Hitler's speeches on shortwave radio, and wearing uniforms with Nazi symbols. *Bund* leaders understood the importance of recruiting and indoctrinating youth if the movement was to take root in American soil. Towards this end, a monthly magazine was produced that glorified the German American contribution to American history and the importance of Nordic-German racial identity to its future. American patriotism and strength was linked to racial purity. Anti-Semitic fiction linking Jews to Communism and many other conspiratorial plots were regular features. *Bund* camps were also established. Often first perceived by participants as inexpensive recreation in a socially comfortable German-American setting, leaders used them to openly propagandize for National Socialism.

Bund leaders supported other anti-Semitic organizations that experienced legal trouble and invited them to speak at *Bund* events. They also did not shy away from politics. They understood President **Franklin D. Roosevelt** to be sympathetic to both Jews and Communists (often linked in their minds). One attack advertisement asserted that a Roosevelt victory would result in race mixing, a black republic and a black president. At their 1938 convention, "a socially just, white, Gentile-ruled United States," was at the top of their eight-point program to enliven the movement. Germaness was downplayed while being white and American was emphasized in order broaden the appeal and extend the reach of the movement. Still, Kuhn could not bring himself to eliminate the Nazi salute, though the swastika was thereafter displayed only on special occasions.

As with the *Friends of the New Germany* before them, the *German-American Bund* received close scrutiny from both the American and German governments in the wake of violence surrounding *Bund* rallies and the resulting counterdemonstrations. The German ambassador noted that the *Bund* was not even making inroads into the American-German community, much less America as a whole, and considered it to be a detriment to improving American perceptions of Germany.

In the end, Kuhn was indicted and found guilty of larceny and forgery, sentenced to a two and one-half years, and sent to Sing Sing prison in 1939. The National Committee expelled him from membership. Lacking strong recognized leadership, the organization fell into internal bickering and financial debt from which it did not recover. The executive committee voted to disband the *Bund* the day after the Pearl Harbor attack.

George Lincoln Rockwell and the American Nazi Party

George Lincoln Rockwell picked up the post–**World War II** mantle of leadership for American National Socialism, founding the American Nazi Party in 1959 with the financial backing of Harold Noel Arrowsmith, Jr., who had earlier contributed to the International Association for the Advancement of Ethnology and Eugenics—a group that gathered scientific evidence to support the segregationist position in *Brown v. Board of Education* case.

While Rockwell's primary target was the Jews, he also openly directed his hate speech towards African Americans, whom he wanted to return to Africa or be rounded up into remote relocation centers. Rockwell's strategy to gain power included recruiting and training a small but disciplined group of "stormtroopers," attracting media coverage through hate-speech and the overt use of Nazi symbols in order to bait the Jewish community into emotional overreaction. He would then mobilizing the white population following the race riots he predicted for 1970 and the ensuing economic collapse. Finally, he believed he would be elected president of the United States in 1972 by white people seeking protection from the chaos and the prospects of a Jewish-led Communist takeover.

Drawing on his background as a commercial artist, an advertising man, and the showmanship learned from his vaudeville performer father, Rockwell pulled off several publicity stunts to enrage the African American community, including a "Hate Bus" tour to New Orleans by his stormtroopers to mimic the Freedom Riders, hiring racist singers to perform at "Hate-o-nannies," and portraying himself as the white alternative to **Martin Luther King, Jr.** Even so, he was not beyond working with African Americans who advocated racial separation. Finding common cause with **Nation of Islam** leader Elijah Muhammad, whom he referred to as the "Adolf Hitler of the black man," Rockwell was invited to speak at their 1962 national convention at the Chicago Temple of Islam.

In order to combat this kind of publicity tactic designed to outrage and incite confrontation, drawing media attention, Solomon Andhil Fineberg of the American Jewish Committee worked hard to revive the countertactic of "quarantine," which he created and successfully used in the 1940s against the anti-Semite Gerald L. K. Smith. Originally called "dynamic silence," or the "silent treatment," Fineberg renamed it "quarantine" because it better described the strategy's two critical components: coordinating the major American Jewish community organizations to avoid or minimize public confrontations that draw media attention, and sensitize the news media to American Nazi Party tactics so they understand that lack of news coverage cuts off the publicity necessary for the growth of the movement.

The quarantine was effective and Rockwell increasingly looked abroad to spread his Nazi vision, playing a key role in forming and leading the World Union of National Socialists. One of his last media breakthroughs was his 1966 interview in *Playboy* magazine by Alex Haley who would go on to write *Roots*, a story of Haley's journey to discover his African ancestry. As with the pre–World War II National Socialist organizations, Rockwell came to realize that overt Nazi symbols were abhorrent to many Americans. He sought to broaden the appeal of the organization by denying Holocaust atrocities, by emphasizing "white power" in contradistinction to the "Black Power" movement, and by enfolding white supremacy within the garb of religion. Rockwell realized that the images of the Holocaust were too much to overcome in order to garner popular support. His Holocaust denial propaganda preceded Willis Carto, who is generally credited as the father of American Holocaust denial. While this strategy was designed to decrease the high negative perception of the American Nazi Party among white voters, Rockwell continued to incite racial opposition that he believed would result in publicity and his eventual election as governor of Virginia and later as president of the United States. He was not a factor in the Virginia election. Seizing upon Stokely Carmichael's 1966 "Black Power" slogan, Rockwell countered with a "White Power" campaign to feed the fears of white people. Deviating from Hitler's Nordic-German concept of racial purity, Rockwell created a white/black mythos pitting white people against dark people. This change of strategy is also reflected in renaming the American Nazi Party to the National Socialist White People's Party, consciously mirroring the National Association for the Advancement of Colored People. The final way in which Rockwell tried to make National Socialism more acceptable to whites at large was through the cloak of religion. Correspondence with some of his racist colleagues indicates that while he rejected the teachings of Jesus Christ, he found a Christian veneer useful in reaching the masses. In the racist teachings of the Christian Identity movement, which viewed white Anglos as the literal lost tribes of Israel who needed to wake up to their true identity, Rockwell found a home for Nazis with religious needs and many in Christian Identity churches found a political outlet consistent with their racist beliefs.

Some in his own party and some National Socialists abroad remained purists, considering this sort of "big tent" Nazism as a betrayal of Hitler's ideals. An angry National Socialist Party veteran killed Rockwell on August 25, 1967. The already small and politically ineffective party splintered into additional fragments. *See also* Communist Party; Jews in the South; Ku Klux Klan.

Further Readings: Bell, Leland V. *In Hitler's Shadow: The Anatomy of American Nazism.* Port Washington, NY: Kennikat Press, 1973; Simonelli, Frederick J. *American Fuehrer: George Lincoln Rockwell and the American Nazi Party.* Urbana: University of Illinois Press, 1999; Simonelli, Frederick J. "The World Union of National Socialists and Postwar Transatlantic Nazi Revival." In *Nation and Race: The Developing Euro-American Racist Subculture,* edited by Jeffrey Kaplan and Tore Bjorgo, 34–57. Boston: Northeastern University Press, 1998.

Douglas Milford

Native Americans

Although they were the first Americans, indigenous peoples have faced forms of discrimination similar to that of other nonwhite minority groups in the United States. Since the colonial era, when Europeans debated the essential humanity of Native Americans, tribal groups have experienced racial prejudice, religious persecution, legal discrimination, economic obstacles, and educational barriers that severely hindered their full inclusion in American life. Of racial minorities, however, Indians are unique. They are aboriginal peoples whose tribal governments maintain sovereignty and special political rights within the federal framework. Because of this essential fact, Indian separation and segregation has often been by their own choice. While Indian individuals desired freedom from racial prejudice and discrimination, they often doggedly fought full political and cultural integration into mainstream American society. Native Americans do not always neatly fit the **Jim Crow** experience of other racial minority groups in the United States.

The U.S. Constitution specifically excluded Indian nations from inclusion in the American political system. Classified as foreign nations and "Indians not taxed," the Constitution gave Congress exclusive jurisdiction for dealing with Native American tribes. At the time there were hundreds of tribes, bands, and smaller associations of indigenous groups within what became the borders of the growing nation. Because these units predated the U.S. government, their position in the federal system was extra-constitutional. In light of their semi-foreign status, until 1871, federal officials negotiated approximately 370 treaties with Indian groups, documents that recognized their sovereignty and guaranteed them certain rights. As interpreted by the courts and executive officials, Indians were not citizens so long as they maintained tribal relations. The protections of the Bill of Rights did not apply to them. While many individuals voluntarily abandoned their tribes and assimilated, the majority of Indians prior to the Civil War exhibited little inclination to become U.S. citizens. Major groups such as the Five "Civilized" Tribes of the Southeast stridently fought government efforts to integrate them into the new states of the region; the Cherokees eventually took their case to the **U.S. Supreme Court** to maintain their culture and government. Other tribes, such as the Lakotas and Comanches, fought decades-long wars against the U.S. Army to protect their ancestral homelands. As these examples reveal, U.S. citizenship and political integration was often forced on Native Americans against their will.

Throughout the nineteenth century, American politicians, missionaries, and philanthropists struggled with the so-called "Indian Problem" of having surviving Indian cultures and tribal groups within the borders of the nation. In the landmark Supreme Court decisions *Cherokee Nation v. Georgia* (1831) and *Worcester v. Georgia* (1832), Chief Justice John Marshall determined that the Cherokee and others tribes were "domestic, dependent nations" that retained rights of internal self-government the states could not abridge. Even so, as white settlement proceeded, Indian nations could count on few friends to protect their interests. With the Indian Removal Act of 1830, President Andrew Jackson and Congress mandated the expulsion of Eastern tribes to the newly created Indian Territory (modern Oklahoma) to segregate them from non-Indian society until they eventually assimilated. During the nineteenth century, many politicians such as Thomas Jefferson believed Native Americans, unlike African Americans and **Asian Americans**, would fully amalgamate into American life as equal citizens of the republic. Influenced by the French Enlightenment and Romanticism, American thinkers made the final push for Indian assimilation following the Civil War.

By the late nineteenth century, the vast majority of Indian nations were conquered and safely ensconced on reservations; segregated on generally unproductive lands unwanted by white settlers. During this era, reformers and Western politicians joined forces to solve the "Indian Problem" once and for all. Shortly after the Civil War, the states ratified the Fourteenth Amendment (1868) that granted citizenship to all individuals born or naturalized in the United States and prohibited states from denying civil rights and equal protection under the law to citizens. The Fifteenth Amendment (1870) followed, specifically forbidding states from abridging the right to vote on account of race, color, or previous condition of servitude. While Congress intended these provisions to cover the recently freed slaves, they set the stage for a debate over the rights of Indians under the law. Particularly unsettling was an 1871 congressional law that ended treaty-making with individual tribes, leaving their future status uncertain. In *McKay v. Campbell* (1871) and *Elk v. Wilkins* (1884), the Supreme Court ruled that Indians, as tribal citizens, were not covered by the Fourteenth Amendment and were not citizens of the United States. Although certain treaties provided mechanisms for achieving citizenship, the courts held that absent an all-encompassing federal law, Indians were not citizens and had no avenue for naturalization as did immigrants and African Americans. As a result, Eastern reform groups such as the "Friends of the Indian" endorsed the sweeping **Dawes Severalty Act** of 1887 that provided American citizenship after tribes were dissolved, Indians accepted individual land allotments, and native homesteaders proved their readiness for citizenship during a 25-year waiting period. Related laws such as the Indian Territory Naturalization Act (1890), the Burke Act (1906), and Oklahoma statehood (1907) provided citizenship to Indians in certain areas under certain conditions, whether they wanted it or not.

War service has often provided minorities the opportunity to prove their patriotism and gain rights as citizens. Such was the case with Native Americans when Congress passed the Indian Veterans Citizenship Act of 1919, giving **World War I** veterans full civil rights. White reformers and Indian "Progressives" such as Senator Charles Curtis (Kaw) joined forces to push the Indian Citizenship Act of 1924, finally giving citizenship to all native peoples born in the United States. Congress followed with the **World War II**–era Nationality Act (1940), further clarifying their status. The Indian Civil Rights Act of 1968 extended certain Bill of Rights protections to Indian Americans that did not contravene deeply held tribal beliefs. With these actions, Native Americans were officially incorporated into the body politic.

Even with full citizenship, individuals and state governments found ways to deny civil rights and liberties to Indian citizens. Many Western states, including Arizona, New Mexico, and Utah, denied the vote to tribes under the theories they lived on federal reservations, did not pay state taxes, were incompetent "wards" of the federal government, were illiterate, or were ignorant of local politics. Others such as Minnesota denied the franchise to Indians under the argument they were not civilized. Poll taxes, English-only ballots, lack of polling places near reservations, and gerrymandering were all common tactics employed to deny or negate the Indian vote. As articulated by the Supreme Court in *U.S. v. Sandoval* (1913), the courts believed Indians were "essentially a simple, uninformed and inferior people" incapable of exercising the privileges of citizenship. Not until after World War II, when Native American veterans Miguel Trujillo of New Mexico and Frank Harrison of Arizona with the aid of the U.S. Attorney's office pursued court cases such as *Trujillo v. Garley* (1948) and *Harrison v. Laveen* (1948), did Indians in these states gain the right to vote. When Ute Indian Preston Allen won his case *Allen v. Merrill* (1957), Utah became the last state in the Union to grant the franchise to Native Americans. At the same time, Indians also had to fight to receive state services and federal Social Security benefits routinely granted to others. Subsequent landmark laws such as the **Civil Rights Act of 1964** and the **Voting Rights Act of 1965** provided further protections against discrimination in public accommodations, hiring, and voting.

Native Americans were the only minority group dominated by a federal agency. The **Bureau of Indian Affairs (BIA)** traditionally has exercised broad powers over the lives of indigenous peoples. Until the 1970s, the BIA was a white-dominated, paternalistic agency charged with serving as trustee for Indian lands, steward of tribal resources, and overseer of tribally run programs. Whether enforcing federal laws aimed at destroying Indian cultures or dictating daily life on reservations, government agents traditionally worked against Indian groups managing their own affairs. Until the 1930s-era Indian **New Deal**, BIA officials and federal courts considered Native Americans legal minors; incompetent wards of the **federal government**. Like children, bureaucrats believed indigenous peoples were unable to manage their own affairs, control their lands, purchase alcohol, serve on local juries, or run for public office. Until Indians took up private property, "civilized" ways that included Christianity, and demonstrated individual aptitude for citizenship, they were in a perpetual state of government tutelage and dependency. Much of this liability was racially based, as various federal trust programs centered on presumptions that mixed-blood Indians were more competent and civilized than their full-blood brethren.

As a result of government paternalism, language barriers, and racial prejudice Indian peoples faced serious forms of economic discrimination throughout the United States. Southern groups such as the **Mississippi** Band of Choctaws lost lands to scheming land agents and local court actions, finding themselves forced into **sharecropping** on lands they formerly owned. In the Southwest, Yaquis and Kickapoos were resigned to the life of low-paid, migrant farm work. With the Dawes Act and other allotment-oriented laws, Indians in Oklahoma and elsewhere were dispossessed of two-thirds of their remaining estate while facing an onslaught of economic and political competition from non-Indians. In Midwestern states such as Iowa, Minnesota, and Wisconsin, Indians attempting to work off-reservation often complained that they were the "last hired, first fired," were denied the best skilled jobs at factories, or were passed over for promotions despite their abilities. Ada Deer, the 1970s-era Wisconsin Menominee leader, said it best when she complained her people were engulfed in a sea of racism. As a result, many Native Americans moved to urban centers such as Chicago to escape the prejudice that surrounded the reservation. Although they saw their economic situation improve markedly, many relocated Indians faced subtler forms of discrimination, with government agents ushering them into the lowest economic sector jobs of the city. High rents and discriminatory practices often prevented native families from living in white, middle-class neighborhoods.

Throughout the nation, Indians encountered a host of **Jim Crow** discriminatory laws, customs, and practices. They faced segregation on isolated reservations by federal policy. Non-reservation groups in the South, such as the Jena Choctaws, Tunica Biloxis, and Houmas, self-segregated their people in small, ethnic enclaves apart from larger black and white society. In the American West and Southern states, antimiscegenation statutes such as Virginia's Racial Integrity Act (1924) prohibited interracial marriage between whites and all groups classified as nonwhite. In Western states such as Arizona and Montana, native peoples were treated much the same as African Americans in the Deep South. In Alaska, "**separate but equal**" was the norm. Dry goods stores, hotels, bars, and theaters routinely posted "No Natives Allowed" or "For Natives Only" signs out front. In towns near the Mississippi Band of Choctaws reservation, tribal members were forced to sit in "colored" sections of local movie houses, were denied service in local restaurants, and were prohibited from burial in all-white cemeteries. In many areas of the U.S. racial bias also influenced adoption of Indian children. State and private adoption agencies regularly "placed out" native children to white families under the assumption they were better off with Anglo families than Indian parents. Poorer Native American women often faced forced sterilization. Because of local law enforcement practices and biases, poverty, and other factors, indigenous people experienced higher arrest rates and greater police harassment, and received longer sentences than the Anglo American population. The effects of isolation, poverty, and discrimination have led to disheartening social statistics for Native Americans. A 1970s-era survey found that the majority of **Louisiana** Indians lived below the poverty line. At Pine Ridge Reservation in South Dakota, 1999 statistics revealed a 75 percent unemployment rate, with many residents lacking indoor plumbing, running water, electricity, and telephones. Pine Ridge's disease rates and infant mortality statistics hovered many times over the national average.

For Native Americans, as with other minorities, the most insidious and potentially damaging form of racism centered on the public school system. Unlike African Americans and Hispanics who united to tear down the "separate but equal" doctrine enshrined by the Supreme Court in *Plessy v. Ferguson* (1896), American Indians have had a unique educational experience, with many having qualms about complete school integration. Certain Indian nations such as the Five "Civilized" Tribes maintained a proud tradition of independent, tribally run school systems. For most groups, the BIA controlled the education of Indian students. Whether on off-reservation boarding schools such as Carlisle Industrial School in Pennsylvania or institutions on tribal lands, forced acculturation, detribalization, and basic vocational education were major themes in government-run schools. In most areas of the United States, the government segregated Indian students either based on treaties or reservation boundaries, or because they were classed as uncivilized people in need of training in the arts of modern life. In some areas of the South, however, local officials maintained separate schools based on race. With the

Lumbee Indians of **North Carolina** and the Houmas of Louisiana, a unique three-way educational system developed, with local districts providing separate schools for whites, blacks, and Indians. Native Americans generally resisted any effort to force them to attend schools for African Americans or be classified as black for social or legal purposes. In southeastern Oklahoma after statehood, local whites used education and other incentives to prod mixed-blood Choctaws to identify as "white" in an effort to erase their tribal identity and erode their political power. As a result, Indian mixed-bloods did not face concerted racism, enjoying "white skin color privilege" that included attendance in "Whites Only" schools. In other Southern states such as North Carolina, **Alabama**, and Louisiana, however, local officials repeatedly tried to force Indians into the "black" or "colored" category or denied them schooling altogether. Commonly in states such as California and Nevada, school officers denied local Indians public education claiming they were "wards" or "dependents" of the federal government. In this light, Mississippi Choctaws, Houmas, and others did not have access to a full high school education until the mid-1960s.

In certain regions of the United States, competition with non-Indians has led to widespread conflicts over tribal hunting, fishing, and religious rights guaranteed under treaties. Beginning in the Pacific Northwest during the 1960s, Indian fishermen faced violent and vocal protests when they attempt to exercise their rights to fish in government-protected places. Well into the 1990s, similar standoffs occurred in Wisconsin over spear fishing, with local Chippewas enduring ugly racial epitaphs, shootings, and boat rammings when attempting to fish under various treaties. Perhaps the most significant modern abridgement of indigenous civil rights concerns the First Amendment right of religious freedom. Unlike other minority groups, native peoples have faced government-sponsored programs to eradicate their indigenous spiritual beliefs and practices. While the BIA no longer promotes cultural destruction, issues persist over Indian access to sacred sites, ancient burial grounds, and the return of human remains. The Lakota and other Plains tribes have fought for generations over ownership of Devils Tower, a religious shrine managed by the National Park Service. The Lakota repeatedly have rejected multimillion-dollar cash settlements rather than surrender claims to the sacred Black Hills of South Dakota, most of which is claimed by the National Forest Service. Conflicts also still erupt over Native use of controlled substances such as peyote and environmental laws. In the mid-1980s, for example, federal officials arrested Dwight Dion, a Yankton Sioux, for collecting eagle feathers in violation of the Endangered Species Act. The Supreme Court found that species protection from extinction superseded tribal religious practices.

Native Americans participated in the **Civil Rights Movement** of the 1960s and 1970s, although their aims differed significantly from African Americans and Chicanos. For Indians, the catalyst was the controversial "termination" program of the 1950s and early 1960s, a congressional mandate that sought to end federal supervision over Indian affairs, dissolve tribal entities, and integrate Native Americans as full citizens of the states and the nation. The few tribes subjected to "termination" faced disastrous results. As a result, the National Congress of American Indians and Red Power groups such as the

National Indian Youth Council and the American Indian Movement (AIM) vigorously resisted further termination efforts, instead pushing for greater self-determination, tribal sovereignty, and respect for Indian cultures. These groups stressed equality, but not at the price of complete political and social integration envisioned by other civil rights leaders.

The Indian civil rights movement achieved remarkable gains for native peoples. Tribes like the Houmas and Lumbees won court battles ending school segregation. At the prompting of native leaders, President Richard M. Nixon signed the landmark Indian Self-Determination and Education Assistance Act of 1975, a law that gave tribes greater power to direct local educational, social, and economic programs. The Mississippi Band of Choctaws and Choctaw Nation of Oklahoma have used this act to move toward complete economic independence, with the Oklahoma group funding 80 percent of its tribal programs by 2007. The Indian Child Welfare Act of 1978 placed stringent requirements on non-Indian adoption of native children. The American Indian Religious Freedom Act of the same year paved the way for greater protections of indigenous worship. The 1990 Native American Graves Protection and Repatriation Act resulted in widespread return of sacred funeral remains and objects. Beginning in 1970, when Taos Pueblo regained its sacred Blue Lake from the National Forest Service, the general trend has been for national conservation agencies to allow Indians greater access to their tribal sites. In 2000, the National Park Service went so far as to return part of the Timbisha Shoshones' homeland in Death Valley to the tribe. Because of the work of the Native American Rights Fund and other advocacy groups, Indians routinely exercise both sovereign tribal rights and their individual civil rights. Although discrimination still exists, the legal barriers to Indian citizenship are largely a thing of the past. Working through politics and the courts, Indian nations continue to strive to protect their hard-won rights in modern America. *See also* Apartheid; Japanese Internment; Miscegenation.

Further Readings: McCool, Daniel. *Native Vote: American Indians, the Voting Rights Act, and the Right to Vote.* Cambridge, MA: Harvard University Press, 2007; Prucha, Francis Paul. *The Great Father: The United States Government and the American Indians.* Lincoln: University of Nebraska Press, 1984; Wilkins, David E. *American Indian Politics and the American Political System.* Lanham, MD: Rowman & Littlefield, 2002.

Mark Edwin Miller

Naylor, Gloria (b. 1950)

Author Gloria Naylor was the first child born to Alberta McAlpin and Roosevelt Naylor, a transit worker and telephone operator, on January 25, 1950, in New York City. Shy and quiet, Naylor was a voracious reader. The family moved to Queens in 1963. Naylor followed her mother's lead and became a Jehovah's Witness in 1968. She was deeply attracted to the Witnesses' praise of the power of writing and the written word. During this time period of her life, Naylor noted her lack of exposure to African American literature and other instances within the black American community.

After abandoning the Jehovah's Witnesses, Naylor began a cycle of reinvention and self-assessment. After reading Toni Morrison's *Bluest Eye* in the late

1970s, Naylor decided to pursue her writing seriously. Continuing to work as a switchboard operator, Naylor enrolled in classes at Medgar Evers College and Brookyln College. She completed a BA degree in English in 1979 and enrolled in graduate classes at Yale University in 1981. Her first novel, *Women of Brewster Place*, was released in 1982. A string of other works followed, including *Linden Hills* (1985), *Mama Day* (1988), and, more recently, *1996* (2005).

Through her new understanding of black literature and feminism, Naylor developed characters that analyzed the role of black women in society. *Women of Brewster Place* traces the lives of six women in an inner-city project. Though the city is undefined, Naylor's accounts of the triumphs and the struggles faced as an African American woman allow for those and similar instances to be open to occur anywhere. Naylor retouched on the theme of migration, similar to the **Great Migration** that took place during the **Harlem Renaissance**. The women's search for a place of residency, both in identity and a physical home, give attention to both Naylor's personal experiences moving to Queens and her search for an identity after removing herself from the Jehovah's Witnesses. Also, Naylor joined the pioneering genre of black women's literature, focusing on the issues and concerns special to the plight of the African American woman.

In *Linden Hills*, Naylor slightly changes gears, making observations of the dangers of elitism and its impact on blacks. Though there is little reference to whites, the behavior of blacks living in the lower points of the hill represents the elitism once held strictly by white America. The shameless pursuit of the "American Dream" resulted in the loss of morality and identity of the elitist African Americans in Linden Hills. It is the pursuit of status and the determination to get to the bottom of Linden Hills where the feared and powerful Nedeed mansion was located. Through the stories of characters like the closeted homosexual Winston Alcott, the question of the stretch of social morality and ethics is raised. In order to avoid the scandal of his relationship with another man rocking his career, Winston marries and leaves his lover David. Winston's fear of being socially ostracized dictated his actions and moral center. Similar to "Inferno" in Dante Aligheri's *Divine Comedy*, Naylor intricately creates a social hell in which blacks adapt instead of correct. *See also* Baldwin, James; Homosexuality; Toomer, Jean.

Further Readings: Naylor, Gloria. *Women of Brewster Place*. New York: Viking Press, 1982; Naylor, Gloria. *Linden Hills*. New York: Ticknor & Fields, 1985.

Regina Barnett

Negro League Baseball

Segregation in baseball began in 1858 when the National Association of Baseball Players (NABBP) included in its constitution a clause excluding "persons of color" from playing. After a period of segregation from 1867 to 1871, the rules changed. In 1871, there were no formal rules against blacks in baseball in the newly organized National Association of Professional Baseball Players (NAPBBP). African Americans, including Bud Fowler, Charlie Grant,

George Stovey, and Moses Fleetwood Walker, played on professional integrated teams for a short time. In the 1880s, a "gentleman's agreement" shifted acceptance again, creating a color line in baseball. Owners forced the black players off teams and did not sign new ones.

After the reemergence of segregation in the last two decades of the nineteenth century, African American responded by creating their own teams and leagues. With no professional leagues from the late 1880s to 1920, blacks played on semipro teams. Attempts at organizing leagues proved unsuccessful. In 1886, the League of Colored Baseball included teams in Baltimore, Boston, Cincinnati, Louisville, New York, Philadelphia, Pittsburgh, and Washington, DC. The league lasted for a week, with 13 games played. Other leagues included black teams in their schedule. In 1889, the Penn League included the Cuban Giants and New York Gothams, but lasted only for one season. In 1898, the Acme Colored Giants played for a few months in the Iron and Oil League in Celeron, New York.

After 1898, no other teams of players of color participated in white leagues, and attempts at organizing separate independent leagues began. In 1890, black business owners tried to organize a league with teams in Chicago, Cincinnati, Cleveland, Indianapolis, Kansas City, and Louisville. Finances lacking, the teams never played any games. The International League of Independent Professional Baseball Clubs included teams of Cuban X Giants, Cuban Stars, Havana Stars, and Quaker Giants. In 1907, the league added two white teams, but financial difficulties, again, prevented implementation. Three years later, Chicago lawyer Beauregard Moseley led an effort to create the Negro National Baseball League. At an organizational meeting in December 1910, interested owners elected Moseley president and Felix Payne as secretary/treasurer. This attempt was the most successful in organizing, coming the closest to being a league, but it did not become a reality. Also in 1910, the United States League of Professional Ball Clubs organized, with teams in Baltimore, Brooklyn, Jersey City, New York, Newark, Philadelphia, and Trenton. Owners would include both black and white players. Financial reasons and the fact that this was an outlaw league hindered its development. In 1901, baseball teams had organized to create the National Association of Professional Baseball Leagues (NAPBL). Members of this organizational structure became "organized baseball," those that were not belonging "outlaw." As different teams and leagues attempted to establish themselves, they also had to contend with a formalized structure that discouraged nonmembers. All of the attempts to establish leagues before 1920 and white teams playing against black teams helped establish a foundation for future successes. In the nineteenth century, approximately 70 blacks played on integrated professional teams, with several hundred playing on other kinds of teams.

During the first two decades of the twentieth century, numerous independent black teams, including the long-lasting Baltimore Black Sox (1916–1934), Chicago American Giants (1911–1958), Hilldale Daisies (1910–1930s), Indianapolis ABCs (1902–1940), Homestead Grays (1911–1950), and Leland Giants (1905–1915), successfully kept African Americans playing baseball.

On February 13, 1920, leaders from eight cities met in Kansas City, Missouri, to establish the Negro National League (NNL). Andrew "Rube" Foster organized the business and sports writers. A former player and manager with the Leland Giants and Chicago American Giants, Foster essentially managed all the details of the new league to ensure its success. Born in 1879 in Calvert, Texas, Rube Foster pitched for semipro and independent teams. In 1908, Foster established his own team because he felt the owner of the team he played on did not respect the players. Foster's Chicago American Giants became part of the new Negro League. The National Association of Colored Professional Baseball came into being, with the team owners signing a constitution that placed Foster as president. Teams included the Chicago Giants, Detroit Stars, Indianapolis ABCs, Kansas City Monarchs, and St. Louis Giants. Owners paid an entrance fee and agreed to league rules. Most of the teams did not own, but rented stadiums from white teams. In addition to the regular league teams, other teams could play as associate teams, but the game would not count in league statistics.

In May 1920, the Negro Southern League played after two months of planning, but was not as organized as the NNL. Teams included the Atlanta Black Crackers, Birmingham Giants, Chattanooga Black Lookouts, Jacksonville Red Caps, Montgomery Grey Sox, Nashville Elite Giants, and New Orleans Black Pelicans. In 1921, the league dissolved due to conflicts among the teams. Other leagues including the Continental League (based in Boston), the Negro Western League (based in Kansas, Virginia, and Kentucky), and the Tandy League (based in St. Louis). As the National Negro League continued to develop, teams came into and out of the league. Rube Foster's Chicago American Giants was the only team to compete in all 12 seasons.

In 1923, Ed Bolden of the Hilldale Daisies organized the Eastern Colored League (ECL). To ease the distance in traveling to games and to exert control himself, Bolden's league included teams included the Bacharach Giants, Baltimore Black Sox, Brooklyn Royal Giants, the Eastern Cuban Stars, Hilldale Daisies, and the New York Lincoln Giants. Teams played in the ECL from 1923 to 1928. In 1929, they reorganized as the Negro American League and played for one season.

In the Negro Leagues, contracts with players proved to be an ongoing struggle. Players would move to another team if the owner produced a better offer. Owners of Negro League teams were both white and black. Many team owners held businesses in the community. A handful of them participated in illegal activities. The community loved their local teams, and the team had a central role in the African American community. The community leaders would participate in the games. Games on Sunday would begin after church had ended, and fans would come to the ballpark dressed in their Sunday best.

Baseball teams in the Negro Leagues did not travel by train, but by bus. Play on teams in fluctuating leagues allowed players to play for many teams during the year. With the regular season from April to October, players could continue playing on traveling teams, winter ball teams, or barnstorming against white teams in warmer climates including the West Coast and Latin America. On average, players began their careers when they were 20 and played professionally for about five years. Some players were older or younger, and some played for two or more decades. Segregation made the extensive travel more difficult. Teams might not find hotels that would accept them or restaurants that would feed them. Members of the black community would regularly house the players in their own homes when a team came to town.

Until 1971, the National Baseball Hall of Fame did not consider Negro League players eligible for election. The initial plan was to place them in a separate wing, but, recognizing that it was the segregation of their time and not their ability as a ball player, their achievements are now recognized in the same way as players from organized baseball. Some of the players in the Negro League now in the Baseball Hall of Fame include Satchel Paige, Josh Gibson, Cool Papa Bell, Oscar Charleston, Ray Dandridge, Leon Day, Monte Irvin, Judy Johnson, Buck Leonard, Alex Pompez, Bullet Rogan, and Willie Wells. Each of these players became a member of the Baseball Hall of Fame based on their career in the Negro Leagues.

The decline of the Negro League came with the integration of major and minor league baseball. After **Jackie Robinson** signed a contract with the **Brooklyn Dodgers** in October 1945, played for the minor league Montreal Royals in 1946, and played for the major league Dodgers in 1947, the death knell for Negro Leagues baseball sounded. Fans, players, and owners would choose integration over continued segregation. As more and more players went into major or minor league baseball, fewer top quality players played into the Negro Leagues. One by one, the teams dissolved, and the end of the Negro Leagues is marked in 1960. *See also* Sports.

Further Readings: Heaphy, Leslie A. *The Negro Leagues, 1869–1960.* Jefferson, NC: McFarland, 2003; Holway, John. *The Complete Book of Baseball's Negro Leagues: The Other Half of Baseball History.* Fern Park, FL: Hastings House Publishers, 2001; Lanctot, Neil. *Negro League Baseball: The Rise and Ruin of a Black Institution.* Philadelphia: University of Pennsylvania, 2004; Peterson, Robert. *Only the Ball Was White.* New York: Gramercy, 1999.

Amy Essington

Neighborhood Property Owners Associations

Neighborhood property owners associations were local organizations of home and business owners. Historically, they served to maintain patterns of residential segregation by enforcing racially restrictive covenants, battling blockbusting practices, and terrorizing black families who moved into white neighborhoods. These organizations were also known as neighborhood improvement associations, civic clubs, or homeowner associations.

In the late nineteenth century, neighborhood associations arose to provide services such as street paving for suburban areas that received little attention from city administration. By the early twentieth century, though, the purpose of neighborhood associations began to change. Increasing migration of blacks from rural to urban areas and from the South to the North put pressure on available housing stock. Black residents were increasingly concentrated in particular sections of cities through a combination of government policy, real estate practices, and white resident resistance. Many black citizens resisted this confinement and bravely attempted to move into recently integrated or previously all-white neighborhoods. In response, neighborhood property

Protestors demonstrating against neighborhood integration. Courtesy of Library of Congress, LC-USZ62-116822.

owners associations now also functioned to protect white neighborhoods from black "invasion."

In newly constructed suburbs, property owners associations often formed in order to enforce racially restrictive covenants. Developers attached these covenants to deeds; they prohibited homeowners from selling their property to blacks, and sometimes **Asian Americans**, Jews, and Catholics as well. In the 1920s, the courts had tacitly upheld the use of such covenants because they were private agreements. Restrictive covenants had therefore taken the place of racial zoning, which the **U.S. Supreme Court** had struck down in *Buchanan v. Warley* in 1917.

In existing urban neighborhoods, particularly those bordering black neighborhoods, property owners associations took on a more defensive posture. They formed to combat blockbusting practices, in which real estate agents and speculators would acquire a property, move a black family in, and try to scare the remaining white property owners out of the area. Fleeing white families would often accept low prices in their panic, and the agents turned around and sold to black families at inflated amounts, reaping a huge profit. Property owners banded together to intimidate new black residents and boycott unscrupulous realtors. They held organizing meetings and sometimes introduced their own racially restrictive covenants, going door to door to obtain the necessary signatures.

At the same time, some associations built alliances with local realtors in order to defend the "color line" effectively. Neighborhood residents placed pressure on their neighbors to refrain from selling to minorities. Meanwhile, local real estate boards policed their own by threatening to revoke the license of any realtor who sold property in a white neighborhood to a black person. In other cases, neighborhood property owners associations cooperated with institutions such as local universities or prominent businesses, often procuring key funding for lawsuits.

The U.S. Supreme Court declared racially restrictive covenants unconstitutional in *Shelley v. Kraemer* in 1948. In some communities, they had already become unenforceable anyway, as enough black families managed to move into the neighborhood to render the restrictions hollow. The decline of racial covenants, however, did not pave the way for residential integration. Homeowners increasingly turned to overt acts of resistance. They planted bombs, vandalized property, and attacked their new black neighbors both physically and verbally. Neighborhood property owners associations served organizing and dissemination purposes to draw community support.

Racial prejudice fueled all of these defensive strategies. That racial prejudice, though, was also fundamentally linked to ideas about property ownership. White homeowners resisted black incursion into their neighborhoods primarily because they believed that black neighbors would cause their property values to decline. They believed that a neighborhood containing "undesirable" neighbors would fetch much lower prices on the real estate market. For many of these families, their home represented their single largest investment and demanded protection at all costs. This same logic led neighborhood organizations to wage campaigns against the construction of public housing and nuisance businesses.

The success of the **Civil Rights Movement** and the end of state-sanctioned segregation led neighborhood associations to broaden their agendas. A national neighborhood movement emerged in the late 1960s and early 1970s as residents demanded better city services and resisted urban renewal efforts and freeway construction. While these organizations were less likely to wage explicitly racial campaigns, their actions still had discriminatory effects. Support for neighborhood schools often translated into resistance against school integration. Critics charged that white residents demanded better city services because they felt black neighborhoods had received more than their fair share of government resources through Great Society programs and **Affirmative Action** initiatives. Meanwhile, white residents continued openly to harass new black neighbors late into the twentieth century.

Neighborhood organizations have not disappeared. Homeowners associations have remained particularly prevalent in condominiums and suburban, gated communities, where they try to maintain an air of exclusivity. These associations usually require property owners in a given subdivision to join and pay dues; they then provide services to the community, ranging from security to garbage collection. These associations still employ deed restrictions that serve to limit diversity. Though these restrictions are no longer explicitly racial, they often prescribe minimum purchase prices, maximum occupancy levels, and strict guidelines for property maintenance. By defining a certain lifestyle for community residents, these regulations exclude potential neighbors who do not fit that mold. *See also* Housing Covenants; Segregation, Suburban.

Further Readings: Gotham, Kevin Fox. "Urban Space, Restrictive Covenants and the Origins of Racial Residential Segregation in a US City, 1900–1950." *International Journal of Urban and Regional Research* 24 (2000): 616–33; Hirsch, Arnold. *Making the Second Ghetto: Race and Housing in Chicago 1940–1960.* Chicago: University of Chicago Press, 1998 (originally published in 1983); McKenzie, Evan. *Privatopia: Homeowner Associations and the Rise of Residential Private Government.* New Haven, CT: Yale University Press, 1994.

Alyssa Ribeiro

New Deal

The New Deal was put into place by President **Franklin D. Roosevelt** during the **Great Depression** from 1933 to 1938. New Deal programs created a radical shift in the role of the federal government vis-à-vis the nation's economic sphere in an effort to reform the U.S. economy torn by the Depression. New Deal policies were guided by the "Three Rs": direct relief, economic recovery, and financial reform. However, New Deal initiatives extended well into the 1940s and 1950s, largely to support retuning **World War II** veterans. During the New Deal, under the auspices of Roosevelt and largely controlled by the **Jim Crow** mentality of the South for whom most of the aid was geared toward given the rampant rural poverty of both blacks and whites, the **federal government** transformed into an activist government that sought to advance human well-being and provide economic security to its citizens. The federal government tightened its grip on the nation's economic sector via New Deal programs. Of all the New Deal programs initiated during the course of this activist government's reign, three social initiatives particularly reveal the New Deal government's commitment to alleviating social ills, albeit in a fashion that is largely racist and indeed Jim Crowed (i.e., exclusionary or separate): welfare, work, and war. Aid to Dependent Children (ADC) was the largest social welfare initiative. In regard to the New Deal's influence on labor laws, three laws are worth examining: the National Industrial Recovery Act, the National Labor Relation Act , and the Fair Labor Standards Act of 1938. In regard to war, the Selective Service Readjustment Act was the largest New Deal initiative, and its effects on the country were enormous. However, all of the New Deal initiatives, whether in the North or the South, were implemented in a race-based fashion that at best favored white Americans over African Americans, and at worst was a segregated system that could not escape the all-pervading influence of Jim Crow segregation and exclusion that divided the nation.

Welfare

Aid to Dependent Children passed as one of 11 titles in the 1935 Social Security Act passed in Congress. The federal programs passed under the act, which was designed to provide 30 million Americans with a safety net by virtue of federal government support, in August during Roosevelt's term were Jim Crowed from the beginning. ADC was designed to offer grants to families in which one of the parents, usually the father, was absent. Aid often went to mothers who were divorced, never married, or abandoned, or whose husbands could not work. ADC, and other programs included within the Social Security Act, was funded by both the federal and state governments. However, the programs were governed at that state level, which ultimately made the programs decentralized from the federal government and subject to Jim Crow exclusion and segregation.

Black mothers were largely excluded from receiving such federal and state aid, often in the Jim Crow South where black population was the highest. The racial exclusionary policies of the landmark Social Security Act were employed in terms of labor performed. The act prohibited qualification for aid to those who toiled in the agricultural or domestic service sectors, jobs that were dominated by blacks and Mexicans. Black mothers often had to fight against locally state-controlled bureaucracies that were partially funded by the federal government. In the United States as a whole, 14 percent of children in the program were black. That the relief would be administered at the state level was detrimental to African Americans in the Jim Crow South. Thirty-seven percent of the children in **Louisiana** were African American, but only 26 percent were ADC recipients. Throughout the South, blacks were largely excluded.

Work

During the New Deal era, the National Industrial Recovery Act, the National Labor Relations Act, and the Fair Labor Standard Act were passed to increase working conditions. These three very significant acts gave workers, among other things, the right to bargain collectively with unions, a maximum work week, better working conditions, and a minimum wage. These three acts were generally employed in a discriminatory fashion and ultimately harmed African American workers, both male and female.

The National Industrial Recovery Act (NRA) passed during the famous first 100 days of Roosevelt's administration on June 16, 1933. One of the components of the bill was that it guaranteed workers the right to organize and bargain collectively with unions and other representatives without fear of employer coercion. Further, it put forth "codes of fair competition" that guaranteed a minimum wage and a maximum 40-hour work week. Although the act presented itself and had the potential to help African Americans, it ultimately had devastating consequences on African American workers.

The wage provisions guaranteed by the NRA discriminated and harmed African Americans in a multiplicity of ways. After Southern legislators voiced concern over the consequences that increased wages would have on agricultural profits and easily affordable domestic workers, both industries that African Americans dominated, they agreed not to establish "fair labor codes" for agricultural and domestic labor. Wages in the agricultural and domestic fields remained stable, while wages in other sectors of labor, largely dominated by white workers, increased. The NRA determined the minimum wage in relation to the category of work performed. Consequently, when the NRA minimum wage codes happened to apply to occupations that African Americans dominated, the occupations received a lower classification than similar unskilled "white" occupations, and thus were granted a lower minimum wage. In short, the NRA promoted and practiced separate wage differentials for white and African American workers. In the end, the minimum wage provisions dramatically harmed African American workers; it is estimated to have cost a half a million African Americans their jobs.

The National Industrial Relations Act (NIRA) also attempted to raise wages through collective bargaining. When it came to collective bargaining with unions, blacks faced the same problems they met with wage provisions. The passage of NIRA, under Section 7a, gave racist unions, those that excluded and segregated African Americans in their locals and federations, exclusive bargaining power on behalf of workers in various industries. Before the passage of the NRA, American unions represented a small but significant, 2.25 million members, of whom 50,000 were black. Two months after the passage of the NRA, union membership increased to a little less than four million. Ultimately, the exclusive right to bargain on behalf of workers granted to racist labor unions displaced many African American workers. When African Americans did complain about union discrimination to the National Labor Relations Board, the federal government failed to intrude on their behalf. In response, government officials attempted to pacify African American outrage by pointing out that the act had led to minimum wage laws, the elimination of child labor, and a maximum 40-hour work week, of which some, but by no means a vast majority, African Americans enjoyed.

On May 27, 1935 the Supreme Court declared that the NRA was unconstitutional in *A.L.A. Schecter Poultry Corp. v. United States*. The National Labor Relation Act (NLRA), also known as the Wagner Act of 1935, replaced Section 7a of the NRA. The NLRA guaranteed wage workers the right to organize and bargain collectively with unions, and made illegal "unfair labor practices" used by employers to avoid unionization. Moreover, the act prohibited employer discrimination on the basis of union activity and obliged employers to bargain with these organizations. Additionally, like the NRA's Section 7a, the Wagner Act, through the National Labor Relations Board, made unions the only way to bargain collectively with employers. Union membership rose to eight million by 1941, and by 1948, union membership surged to 14.2 million.

The Wagner Act, however, did not protect black workers. It was implemented in an exclusionary fashion, as it did not contain a clause that protected African American workers, as a result of racist labor unions, particularly the American Federation of Labor (AFL), that successfully lobbyied to keep the clause from protecting African American workers. The Wagner Act also banned company unions, unions that were more racially egalitarian than affiliated unions, and made the hire of strikebreaking workers, usually African American, more difficult. The NLRA, in essence, gave unions governmental validation to exclude black workers from labor agreements.

The minimum wage provisions mandated by the NRA, which were later found unconstitutional by the Supreme Court, were later smuggled in under the Fair Labor Standards Act of 1938 (FLSA). The FLSA guaranteed a minimum wage of 25 cents an hour for the first year of its passage, 30 cents for the second, and 40 cents an hour inside a six-year time period, overtime protections, maximum working hours at 44 hours a week in the first years of its passage, 42 in the second, and 40 hours henceforth, to many wage laborers. The act was designed to advance the cause of white workers. Again, like the New Deal labor laws passed before it, it was implemented in a Jim Crow fashion. Domestic and agricultural workers, an overwhelming majority of which were African or Mexican Americans, were not covered under the act. Further, FLSA cost many Africans Americans their jobs. The disemployment of workers was mostly felt by African American laborers in the South who often performed labor at a rate less than the minimum wage mandated by the government. Two weeks after the passage of the FLSA, it is estimated by the Labor Department that 30,000 to 50,000 workers, predominantly black in the South, had lost their jobs as a result of the minimum wage provisions. For example, the percentage of African Americans in the tobacco industry declined from about 68 percent in 1930 to about 55 percent in 1940.

War

Of all the bills passed during the progressive days of the New Deal, the Selective Service Readjustment Act, also known as the **G.I. Bill**, was implemented in the most discriminatory fashion, and it, more than any other bill, did more to increase the economic gap between African Americans and their white counterparts. The G.I. Bill, passed in 1944, marks the largest social benefit bill ever passed by the federal government in a single initiative. The bill was designed to (re)integrate 16 million returning veterans; it reached 8 of every 10 men born in the 1920s. In a 28-year span from 1944 to 1971, federal spending totaled over $90 billion, and by 1948, a massive 15 percent of the federal budget was geared toward funding the bill. The bill was designed to help returning veterans start a business, buy a home, or attend college. The bill is, no doubt, responsible for the making of the middle class.

The middle class it created was largely white. The G.I. Bill, like the New Deal bills it followed, was written under the patronage of Jim Crow and was prone to practice exclusionary policies that either rejected blacks outright or under funded them dramatically in comparison to their white counterparts. Upon returning from World War II, many black veterans, no doubt, reaped the fruits of the G.I. Bill and attended colleges, started business, and experienced some upward mobility. However, the entrenched racism in the Jim Crow South and throughout America put many obstacles in front of blacks who sought to secure the benefits of the G.I. Bill. The bill was drafted by the openly racist, anti black, anti-Catholic, and anti-Jewish John Rankin of **Mississippi**, and had to pass by Southern members of Congress who insisted that the G.I. Bill be decentralized from the federal government. The G.I. Bill left the administrative responsibilities up to the states. Leaving administrative tasks in the hands of policy makers in Jim Crow South, who feared that blacks would use their new status to dismantle segregation, proved to have negative consequences on African Americans. Locals administering the program at the Mississippi Unemployment Compensation Committee, strongly encouraged blacks not to apply for social benefits. Two years after the G.I. Bill's implementation, the committee had received only 2,600 applications from African Americans, whereas it received 16,000 from white applicants. When black applicants were rewarded funding, they often had to overcome the discrimination of the institutions they wished to attend. Elite universities in the North were reluctant to admit blacks. The University of Pennsylvania, the most racially egalitarian university in 1946, boasted only 40 blacks out of an institutional enrollment of 9,000. Black enrollment in the North and the West never exceeded 5,000 African Americans in the 1940s. As a result, 95 percent of black veterans were forced to attend segregated, all-black colleges. However, because of Jim Crow policies that forced blacks to segregated, all-black institutions, and the failure of Southern states to fund black institutions, black colleges failed to keep up with the demand. Twenty thousand eligible blacks could not find an academic institution to attend in 1947, and as many as 50,000 might have sought admission if there would not have been such widespread Jim Crow policies.

Further Readings: Bernstein, David E. *Only One Place of Redress: African Americans, Labor Regulations, and the Courts from Reconstruction to the New Deal.* Durham, NC: Duke University Press, 2001; "The Depression, The New Deal, and World War II." African American Odyssey, Library of Congress. http://memory.loc.gov/ammem/aaohtml/exhibit/aopart8.html (accessed May 28, 2008); Katznelson, Ira. *When Affirmative Action Was White: An Untold History of Racial Inequality in Twentieth-Century America.* New York: W. W. Norton, 2005; Moreno, Paul. *Black Americans and Organized Labor: A New History.* Baton Rouge: Louisiana State University Press, 2006; Roediger, David. *Working toward Whiteness: How America's Immigrants Became White: The Strange Journey from Ellis Island to the Suburbs.* New York: Basic Books, 2005; Sullivan, Patricia. *Days of Hope: Race and Democracy in the New Deal Era.* Chapel Hill: University of North Carolina Press, 1996; Zieger, Robert H. *For Jobs and Freedom: Race and Labor in America Since 1865.* Lexington: University Press of Kentucky, 2007.

Jack A. Taylor III

New England

New England, a region in the northeast United States comprising of the six states of Connecticut, Maine, Massachusetts, New Hampshire, Rhode Island, and Vermont, had few true **Jim Crow** laws, and saw Jim Crow as a sign of Southern backwardness. Still, customs, homeowners' associations, and prejudice combined to keep blacks segregated or absent in many areas of the region.

Rhode Island, founded by dissidents who disagreed with many aspect of Puritan control over much of the rest of New England, had the largest population of free blacks in New England. This group of free blacks was one of the most literate and perhaps wealthiest black population in the colonies, having their own churches, schools, and other institutions. Paradoxically, Rhode Island also had the largest numbers of slaves in the region during most of the colonial period. While slavery generally played only a small direct role in the New England farm economy, many fortunes of coastal New Englanders were built directly or indirectly on the transatlantic slave trade. However the relatively low numbers of slaves in New England during the colonial era gave New Englanders no long-term attachment to the institution. Slavery was abolished during the Revolutionary era, mainly through the use of the courts. The new state constitutions drafted during or immediately after independence made no provisions for the institution, and enslaved people were able to sue for the freedom. After the Revolution, New Englanders took an ambivalent stance toward **slavery**. Most saw it as a Southern problem and not their concern. Others saw it as a moral wrong, and New England became one of the centers of the abolitionist movement. The region became solidly Republican and backed President Abraham Lincoln throughout the Civil War. Following the Civil War, with the healing of the sectional rift and westward expansion, New England declined in national importance.

The rise of Jim Crow in the South had little initial impact on New England. Most visible signs of Jim Crow—such as separate water fountains—were absent in the region. New Englanders tended to retain a sense of cultural superiority over the South as a whole, and saw the existence of Jim Crow as an indication of Southern violence and backwardness. Blacks remained relatively few in New England, which was absorbing wave after wave of immigrants from the 1840s onward. The Irish formed the first massive wave that challenged the overwhelmingly English ethnic base of New England, and in general, old-stock Protestant New Englanders focused their energies in keeping the Irish down rather than the few blacks. Following the Irish, came waves of French Canadians, Polish, and, especially, Italians, all of whom were overwhelmingly Catholic. With few blacks, each immigrant group tended to occupy much of the social-economic positions blacks held in the South. However, with few true Jim Crow–type laws, immigrant groups usually began voting, and, with fewer physical clues to separate them from other New Englanders, tended to move up the social ladder after a generation or two as newer waves arrived.

The **Great Migration** brought far fewer blacks into New England than it did to the Midwest, West, or the Mid-Atlantic region, but blacks did become more numerous, especially in southern New England. Connecticut, Massachusetts, and Rhode Island all had separate schools for black children in urban areas, where the overwhelming majority of black New Englanders were clustered. The revived **Ku Klux Klan** in the 1920s and 1930s made few inroads into most of New England, although it did tend to find recruits in areas populated by old-stock white Protestants near cities with large immigrant populations. Connecticut had recurring incidents of groups of young white men claiming to be Klan groups, while northwest Rhode Island had a particularly large Klan organization. New England Klan groups were notable for the lack of violent acts perpetrated against Catholic, Jewish, or black persons, although two fires at an African American school in North Scituate, Rhode Island, in 1924 and 1926, were commonly held to have been started by Klansmen. But in general, most incidents of Klan activity that did occur in New England were as often as not directed against growing Roman Catholic power as against blacks.

However, blacks in the region tended to be clustered in certain urban neighborhoods, and thus black children in many New England cities attended what were in all but name segregated schools. The violence that accompanied the court-ordered busing as a means to integrate Boston Public Schools in 1974, served to show complacent New Englanders that racism was not confined to the South, but was alive and well in New England.

Further Readings: Conforti, Joseph A. *Imagining New England: Explorations of Regional Identity from the Pilgrims to the Mid-Twentieth Century.* Chapel Hill: University of North Carolina Press, 2001; Piersen, William D. *Black Yankees: The Development of an Afro-American Subculture in Eighteenth-Century New England.* Amherst: University of Massachusetts Press, 1988.

Barry M. Stentiford

New Negro Movement

The New Negro Movement was a collective political, artistic, and social response to the pressures of **Jim Crow** from the late nineteenth century until the mid-twentieth. It occurred in two phases: first in the post-**Reconstruction** era and, secondly, in the 1920s in its most recognizable form during the **Harlem Renaissance**. In both stages, the movement was led by black intellectuals and artists who were distinguished as "New Negroes" from previous generations of enslaved African Americans. To correspond with the changing times, the concept and figure of a "New Negro" were debated and reconceptualized when social conditions worsen for all African Americans. Black disenfranchisement, "peonage slavery," **lynchings**, race riots, and the creation of **Black Codes** to enforce systematic oppression marked the "**nadir**" of African American history in the last decades of nineteenth and ushered in a new modern age. Ultimately, the New Negro Movement was an opportunity to highlight African Americans' achievements in the arts and letters as possible solutions to the race problem.

New historicists scholars and literary critics trace the development of the movement to the 1890s, when black intellectuals were determined to reconstruct the public image of African Americans. Minstrel characters such as "mammies," "uncles," and "coons" were paraded before American audiences as a popular form of entertainment. These caricaritures of "ole time Negroes" also saturated the consumer market in product advertisements. Such negative stereotypical images of black people were more common to white Americans than the educated, professional class that had emerged since slavery. The conditions of the post-Reconstruction era—the birth of Jim Crow culture—did not halt African Americans' racial progress. The period on the contrary gave birth to the "New Negro," recognized by a difference in physical appearance, behavior, and attitude as a social equal. Such racial representatives were well-educated members of the black middle class. Their individual accomplishments in education, politics, the humanities, and sciences were taken as evidence of racial progress in general. Most importantly, these New Negroes would demand their political rights en masse.

It is more than mere coincidence then that the "nadir" of African American literature corresponds with the birth of Jim Crow. Public debates about the status of African Americans as second-class citizens ignited criticism from writers and poets alike. The corpus of protest literature produced during this first phase of the New Negro Movement address the deterioration of race relations. Crowned the "Poet Laureate of the Race," **Paul Laurence Dunbar** in "Sympathy" and "We Wear the Mask" evokes the pathos and frustration of African Americans. Frances E. W. Harper's political romance novel *Iola Leroy* (1892), Sutton E. Griggs's *Imperium in Imperio* (1899), and Pauline

Hopkins's *Contending Forces* (1900) were among the earliest novels to appear as a sign of a New Negro literary renaissance. This is a period that is also commonly referred to as "Post-Bellum, Pre-Harlem," a phrase coined by the southern black writer Charles W. Chesnutt. His own contributions included short story collections, *The Conjure Woman* (1899) and *The Wife of His Youth and Other Stories of the Color Line* (1899); race problem novels, *The House Behind the Cedars* (1900), *The Marrow of Tradition* (1901), *The Colonel's Dream* (1905); and many political essays and speeches. In *A Voice From the South* (1892), renowned educator **Anna Julia Cooper** also contributed to this debate about race relations. Her text was essential to the development of black feminism as well as the New Negro Movement. **Booker T. Washington's** *Up From Slavery* (1901) and **W.E.B. Du Bois's** *The Souls of Black Folk* (1903) are also key works in the development of a literary tradition created by black writer-activists around the turn of the century.

Altogether, these New Negroes created a body of literature as a testament to the progress of the race. In 1895, Victoria Earle Matthews, noted clubwoman and writer, had issued a call for the collection of such "race literature," which were "all the writings emanating from a distinct class—not necessarily race matter; but a general collection of what has been written by the men and women of that Race: History, Biographies, Scientific Treatises, Sermons, Addresses, Novels, Poems, Books of Travel, miscellaneous essays and the contributions to magazines and newspapers." Matthews, as did many of her contemporaries, firmly believed that, with race literature, African Americans would take their place among the world's greatest civilizations. Poets like George Clinton Rowe and Josephine Delphine Henderson Heard captured the optimism of the age. The assimilationist images of African Americans "rising" to take their place in white society were common in the genteel traditions at the "nadir." While many of these early writers and poets have been dismissed as accomodationists, their collective works testify to the obstacles African Americans overcame as proof of racial survival for future generations.

In response to segregation, two major black political organizations appeared during the first phase of the New Negro Movement. The National Association for the Advancement of Colored People (NAACP) and the National Urban League (NUL) were established in 1909 and 1911, respectively. Du Bois, members of his "Talented Tenth," and liberal white activists worked to make the NAACP the leading advocate for black civil rights. The NUL was created to meet the needs of thousands of African Americans migrating from the South to Northern urban areas. Many black writers would participate in the activities and hold positions in both organizations. James Weldon Johnson's involvement in the NAACP, for instance, would continue well into the second phase of the New Negro Movement. His novel *The Autobiography of an Ex-Colored Man* (1912) is a transitional text, too. Initially published anonymously, the controversial work was later attributed to Johnson in 1927; by then, the author was already considered an architect of the Harlem Renaissance.

The outbreak of race riots after World War I stimulated the literary responses of the "new" Negro Movement of the 1920s. During the **Red Summer** of 1919, over 20 race riots exploded throughout the nation, especially in large cities like Chicago and Washington, DC, with sizable populations of Southern black migrants. After returning from fighting for democracy abroad in Europe, African American soldiers arrived home to join the fight for social equality, too. The militant spirit of this generation, according to Gates, marks the evolution of the New Negro. Within the decade, this modern image and movement would be more political and place greater emphasis on literary aesthetics than the previous phase. Writings by Du Bois, **A. Phillip Randolph,** and Alain Locke signaled the reemergence of the New Negro as an educated, cultured, and, often, radical artist. Like Dunbar before him, Claude McKay became the new poetic voice of the New Negro Movement. His manifesto poem "If We Must Die" (1919) protests racial injustice as inspired by the violence of Red Summer. It introduced audiences to McKay's most important poetry collection, *Harlem Shadows* (1922), and to the black cultural renaissance in Harlem, New York.

For thousands of migrants, Harlem became the Black Mecca. Black Southerners believed it offered a chance to escape the harsh reality of Jim Crow segregation and racism in the South. With its nightclubs, theaters, literary societies, and businesses, the community's social, educational, and economic attractions catered to the black masses that congregated there. An exotic element was added with the arrival of black West Indians. **Marcus Garvey**'s call for Black Nationalism, with his **Universal Negro Improvement Association (UNIA),** appealed especially to thousands of his fellow foreign migrants from throughout the black diaspora. As Locke described it, the "pulse of the Negro World [had] begun to beat in Harlem." White Americans also responded to this "beat" as they flocked to Harlem especially to witness the frenzy of the nightlife. For the black writers and artists, Harlem was a muse and cultural center. **Langston Hughes,** as a key figure of the Harlem Renaissance, helped to usher in this modern era of African American literature and culture that is defined by its creative mix of language and sound, rhythm and soul. He especially used the new American music, **jazz** and **blues,** to create poetry that could mimic the beat of jazz instruments, present the lamentations of a blues singer, or protest injustice, sometimes all in a single poem. Hughes' first poetry collection, *The Weary Blues* (1926), is among the most innovative works of the New Negro Movement. Jean Toomer's *Cane* (1923) and Jessie Redmon Fauset's *There is Confusion* (1924) are also recognized as prolific novels of the new era. This younger generation of New Negro artists also includes poets Countee Cullen, Gwendolyn Bennett, Georgia Douglas Johnson, and Sterling Brown as well as a talented group of other novelists like Nella Larsen, Rudolph Fisher, Wallace Thurman, and Zora Neale Hurston.

Political establishments and generous patrons sponsored most of the literature produced during the 1920s New Negro Movement. Both NAACP and the NUL created awards for emerging writers and poets. Contests were announced in the pages of *The Crisis* and *Opportunity* magazines, the respective publications of the NAACP and the NUL. Banquets well attended by the cultural elite were held in honor of the award winners. Hughes, Fauset, Cullen, and Hurston, among others, were literary stars at these events. Their works attracted the attention of white patrons, whom Hurston nicknamed "Negrotarians." W.E.B. Du Bois and James Weldon Johnson were members of the old guard, or the "Talented Tenth," that formed alliances with these white patrons. By the middle of the movement, however, generational conflicts appeared between the civil rights establishment and members of the "Niggerati," Hurston's label for African American artists themselves. The publication of the infamous journal *Fire!!* (1926), edited by Thurman, led the charge against the older set and their artistic propaganda intentions for the New Negro Movement.

Thurman, Hughes, Hurston, and other younger rebels revolted in their more crude expressions of blackness that repulsed the refined tastes of the political guardians and financial backers of the renaissance. Du Boisian leadership had manipulated the arts and letters of the movement to improve race relations by insisting on aesthetic value as proof of racial progress just as his early contemporaries had envisioned around the turn of the nineteenth century. Hughes and his set were more interested in using their art to promote authentic blackness, images of the common folk, unfiltered for white audiences. As spokesman, Hughes proudly boasted: "We younger Negro artists who create now intend to express our individual dark-skinned selves without fear or shame. If white people are pleased we are glad. If they are not, it doesn't matter. We know we are beautiful. And ugly too. The tom-tom cries and the tom-tom laughs. If colored people are pleased we are glad. If they are not, their displeasure doesn't matter either." The "pure" black soul freely expressing itself was the ultimate goal of the New Negro artist by the end of the movement when the stock market crashed in 1929, leading to the start of the **Great Depression** of the 1930s. *See also* Great Migration.

Further Readings: Bruce, Dickson D. *Black American Writing from the Nadir: The Evolution of a Literary Tradition, 1877–1915.* Baton Rouge: Louisiana State University Press, 1992; Gates, Henry Louis. "The Trope of a New Negro and the Reconstruction of the Image of the Black." *Representations* 24 (Fall 1988): 129–55; Lewis, David Levering, ed. *The Portable Harlem Renaissance Reader.* New York: Penguin Books, 1995; Matthews, Victoria Earle. "The Value of Race Literature" [1895]. *Massachusetts Review* 27 (Summer 1986): 169–91; Wintz, Cary D., ed. *The Emergence of the Harlem Renaissance.* New York: Garland, 1996.

Sherita L. Johnson

Niagara Movement

The Niagara Movement was a short-lived association of mostly college-educated and professional black men in the North who held a series of annual conferences between 1905 and 1909 to call for an end to racial discrimination and to protest racial injustice. The movement, led by **W.E.B. Du Bois** and William Monroe Trotter, carried on its work independent of **Booker T. Washington** and despite his determined opposition. The annual meetings of the association called for full and equal civil rights for black people and rejected Washington's policies of accommodation and compromise. The Niagara Movement is regarded as a forerunner to the National Association for the Advancement of Colored People (NAACP), which was established in 1909.

By 1905, Booker T. Washington had consolidated his position as the leader of the Negro race in the United States with both black and white audiences.

Washington was the founder and president of Tuskegee Institute (today Tuskegee University) and controlled a network of black newspapers, friends, supporters, and improvement associations—such as the Afro-American Council and the National Negro Business League—referred to collectively as the "Tuskegee Machine." His policies relied on the favor of white philanthropists, postponed black claims to civil rights, accepted racial segregation, and rejected protest as an instrument for black advancement. Du Bois and Trotter, among others, were critics of this approach.

Du Bois's classic volume, *The Souls of Black Folk*, published in 1903, included a full chapter entitled "Of Mr. Booker T. Washington and Others" in which he dismissed Washington's approach to racial advancement as deeply flawed and contradictory. Nonetheless, Washington continued to seek Du Bois's cooperation and allegiance, inviting him late in 1903 to join a conference of African American leaders in New York, financed by Andrew Carnegie. There, Du Bois helped form the Committee of Twelve, dominated by Washington loyalists. Finding himself surrounded and outvoted, Du Bois again denounced Washington's policies in print and resigned from the committee in July 1904, parting ways with the Tuskegee Machine.

Du Bois and Trotter, together with Charles E. Bentley, a leading Chicago physician, and Frederick McGhee, a prominent lawyer in St. Paul, Minnesota—all opponents of Washington's accommodationism—agreed to arrange for a meeting of like-minded men in Buffalo, New York. Du Bois circulated a statement of intentions that was signed by some 50 prominent African American men. Twenty-nine of them (and one boy) gathered from July 10–14, 1905, in Fort Erie, Ontario, on the Canadian side of Niagara Falls. Racial barriers at the Buffalo hotel had forced a last-minute change of venue.

Those who gathered at the Niagara meeting represented the elite of the Talented Tenth—lawyers, newspaper owners, physicians, ministers, educators, and businessmen—mostly from the North and Midwest, although six were from the South. (The Far West was not represented.) Du Bois was elected general secretary of the association.

The "Declaration of Principles" issued by the first meeting of the Niagara Movement defined the goals of the group. Using the defiant language of protest, the declaration demanded full civil rights for all black people in the United States. One article states:

> Any discrimination based simply on race or color is barbarous, we care not how hallowed it be by custom, expediency or prejudice. . . . [D]iscriminations based simply and solely on physical peculiarities, place of birth, color of skin, are relics of that unreasoning human savagery of which the world is and ought to be thoroughly ashamed.

Although Booker T. Washington was not mentioned by name, it was made clear that the participants, who were later to be known as the Niagarites, were unanimous in their opposition to his policies. One article of the Declaration reads:

> PROTEST: We refuse to allow the impression to remain that the Negro-American assents to inferiority, is submissive under oppression and apologetic before insults. Through helplessness we may submit, but the voice of protest of

ten million Americans must never cease to assail the ears of their fellows, so long as America is unjust.

There was no question that the Niagara Movement rejected compromise and accommodation in favor of agitation and protest. Again:

Of the above grievances we do not hesitate to complain, and to complain loudly and insistently. To ignore, overlook, or apologize for these wrongs is to prove ourselves unworthy of freedom. Persistent manly agitation is the way to liberty, and toward this goal the Niagara Movement has started and asks the co-operation of all men of all races.

The agent whom Washington had sent to spy on the conclave in Buffalo was foiled by the unexpected change of venue. Afterwards however, with a flurry of letters, his public denunciation of the "Declaration of Principles," orders to black newspapers to ignore the event, and favors of cash to reinforce his opinions, Washington was able to ensure that the Niagara Movement went almost unmentioned in the black press.

The second annual meeting of the Niagara Movement was held in August 1906, at Harper's Ferry, West Virginia, the site of John Brown's famous attempted insurrection. Women were not admitted to the conference, primarily due to the opposition of Trotter. But the assembly voted to allow women to attend the following year. Those who gathered heard reports of racial injustice and rousing speeches calling for Negro rights. Du Bois's "Address to the Country" at the end of the conference summed up: "We claim for ourselves every single right that belongs to a freeborn American, political, civil, and social; and until we get these rights we will never cease to protest and to assail the ears of America." But the movement was almost without financial resources.

By the time of the 1907 meeting in Boston, the Niagara Movement had 34 state chapters, although only one in the South. The Boston conference was the largest ever, attended by some 800 delegates. But neither Du Bois nor Trotter attended the conference in 1908, in Oberlin, Ohio, due to Trotter's personal disputes with Du Bois and with other Niagarites. That year, Trotter broke away to form his own group, the Negro-American Political League.

The last annual meeting was held in August 1909, at Sea Isle City, New Jersey, with members divided and discouraged. Constant opposition from the Tuskegee Machine, financial troubles, and personal disputes had all but destroyed the organization. In 1911, Du Bois sent a circular letter to all members of the Niagara Movement canceling plans for future meetings and disbanding the group. He urged all Niagarites to join the NAACP. Most did.

In terms of concrete political achievements, the Niagara Movement accomplished nothing. However, in the context of Booker T. Washington's near monopoly of power within the black community, his veto over white philanthropy, and his policies of silence in the face of racial injustice, the movement kept alive the tradition of black protest during a conservative era. Fiery sermons on racial equality at the Niagara meetings mostly preached to radical, educated black elites who were already converted. But the movement paved the way for its successor, the NAACP, and for the future **Civil Rights**

Movement, which would carry forward the same cause. *See also* Atlanta Compromise.

Further Readings: Fox, Stephen R. *The Guardian of Boston: William Monroe Trotter.* New York: Antheneum, 1970; Lewis, David Levering. *W.E.B. Du Bois: Biography of a Race, 1868–1919.* New York: Henry Holt and Company, 1993; Niagara's Declaration of Principles, 1905. http://www.yale.edu/glc/archive/1152.htm (accessed May 28, 2008).

Anthony A. Lee

North Carolina

North Carolina had a relatively small slave population before the Civil War, with most slaves confined to the coastal plain. Unlike neighboring **Virginia** and **South Carolina**, much of North Carolina was covered with hills and mountains, and thus poor plantation country. The state was lukewarm about secession. During the **Jim Crow** era, North Carolina followed the practices common in much of the South. Despite the entrenchment of Jim Crow in the state, whites took some pride in what they believed were good race relations, and often contrasted the apparently peaceful nature of race relations in North Carolina with those of other states. The **Civil Rights Movement**, however, drew attention to daily discriminations and humiliations blacks faced, and forced the state to begin to come to terms with its legacy.

The **Republican Party** remained a force in North Carolina longer after the end of **Reconstruction** than it had in most Southern states. In 1898, Democrats rioted in Wilmington, killing a dozen black Republicans and forcing out all Republican officeholders. With this use of overt force and violence, the Democrats were able to destroy the two-party system in North Carolina, and institute Jim Crow without political opposition. With blacks stripped of political power, some towns, such as Spruce Pine, used violence to drive out its entire black population. North Carolina adopted the poll tax specifically to deny African Americans the right to vote without invoking challenges based on the Fifteenth Amendment. However, in 1920, as part of the Progressive reform movement, the state repealed the poll tax, largely because it disenfranchised more whites than blacks.

North Carolina's segregated educational system followed those of most of the South, in that the state rigidly enforced "separation," but paid no heed to "equal." During the 1914–1915 school year, the state spent about $4,000,000 for educating whites, and only about $600,000 on black students. Even given the larger white population of the state, the figure represented a significant lower rate per student for black students. In counties with more black students than white students, more funds went for white schools than black schools. White teachers throughout the state in 1910 earned on average three times more than black teachers.

The presence of the Lumbee Indians in North Carolina led to a three-tier educational system, unlike the two-tier system in most of the Jim Crow South. Native Americans opposed state efforts to classify them as "colored," and did not want their children assigned to the black schools. Part of this came from the stigma of black schools as inferior, but also from cultural and political goals trends of Indians nationwide that were at odds with those of African Americans. Unlike blacks, Indians often resisted attempts to assimilate them, and preferred instead that their children attend schools with other Indians. School districts with tribalized Indian populations created separate schools for blacks, whites, and Indians.

While North Carolina had a medical school for blacks from the Reconstruction era, reforms of medical schools in the early twentieth century closed the school, leaving North Carolina without a source to train black doctors. This was part of a regional trend, until only Howard in Washington and Meharry in Nashville remained as a source of black doctors for much of the South. The result was that black patients either had to see white doctors, or more likely, simply relied on unlicensed folk practitioners, or did without medical care.

Despite the self-image of most white North Carolinians that their state stood separate from most of the South in its race relations, the stirring of the Civil Rights Movement, and the reaction of state officials to challenges to the status quo, exposed the underlying oppression of blacks in the state. In 1946, the **U.S. Supreme Court** ruled in *Morgan v. Virginia* that state laws requiring segregation on buses involved in interstate commerce were unconstitutional. In 1947, a "Journey of Reconciliation" tested whether states were honoring the decision. An interracial group of passengers attempted to travel by bus through the South. In North Carolina, police arrested many of the riders for violating state laws. When the riders refused to pay the fines, they were placed on the state's prison chain gangs.

The town of Greensboro, in the 1950s, saw itself as a paradigm of peaceful race relations, despite the very real presence of Jim Crow segregation. The years since the start of **World War II** had actually seen an increase in segregation in the city. On February 1, 1960, four students from North Carolina Agricultural and Technical College, a black state college in Greensboro, walked into the lunch counter at the local Woolworth's department store and sat down for service. The four young men were Ezell A. Blair, Jr., David Richmond, Joseph McNeil, and Franklin McCain. Under Jim Crow restrictions in force at the time, only white patrons could use the seats, black patrons had to either get their food to go, or eat it while standing. At the time, the Woolworth's lunch counter was one of the nation's largest restaurant chains, and often was responsible for a large percentage of each store's profits. As a national chain, it was more vulnerable to the negative publicity the incident brought. The use of the **sit-in** had been used by the **Congress of Racial Equality** in Chicago in 1942, in St. Louis in 1949, and in Baltimore in 1952, but the Greensboro sit-in caught the attention of the national media. The four students were well dressed and well groomed, polite, and patient. They waited all day, and were not served. The next day they returned, along with about 27 supporters. Within a few days, the number had grown to over a thousand. The movement spread throughout the South, and drew attention to unfairness of many of the daily forms of discrimination most blacks faced. By July, the four were able to sit at the Woolworth's lunch counter and be served.

After the *Brown v. Board of Education* decision in 1954, which ruled segregated schools unconstitutional, states of the South began to desegregate, albeit slowly. In North Carolina, the process more closely followed that of Virginia and the Deep South in opposition and the use of delaying tactics. The eventual integration of public schools, although far from uniformly instituted, resulted in the demotion and displacement of many black teachers. While some of the demotions resulted from the generally lower credentials of many black teachers—itself a legacy of Jim Crow—the dismissal and demotion of many black principals came more from deep-seated white opposition to having a school where white children attended being run by a black person. Additionally, the idea of white teachers having a black principal also caused fear and opposition from whites. Erasing the effects of Jim Crow would take more than court orders—it would take a change in attitudes and, more often, a change of generations.

In much of the South, patterns of residential segregation worked against integration of public schools. If students attended their local neighborhood public school, and the entire neighborhood was all white or all black as a result of generations of **residential segregation**, then school integration was a meaningless concept. Proponents of integration proposed using school buses to ensure some black students attended previously all-white schools, and that some white students attended previously all-black schools. Busing was widely unpopular with white parents but also with some black parents, because it meant long bus rides for their children, and taking them away from their neighborhood school. North Carolina passed a law that prohibited school districts form using busing as a means to integrate schools.

The large school district of Charlotte-Mecklenburg reflected the demographic reality of most of the South, where blacks lived in separate neighborhoods from whites. A series of legal challenges beginning in 1965 led eventually to the U.S. Supreme Court ruling of *Swann v. Charlotte-Mecklenburg Board of Education* (402 U.S. 1) in 1971 that busing was a constitutional and appropriate means of integrating public schools. Busing remained a controversial tactic, but the legality of its use had been settled. As in many other aspects of the long struggle to end Jim Crow, North Carolina provided an unwilling battleground, but its own image of itself as a Southern state spared most of the racial strife of most of the South, made residents uncomfortable with overtly racist politics, and helped bring about the eventual end of Jim Crow. *See also* Greensboro Four.

Further Readings: Crow, Jeffrey, Paul D. Escott, and Flora J. Hatley. *A History of African Americans in North Carolina.* Raleigh: North Carolina Division of Archives and History, 1992; Powell, William S. *North Carolina: A History.* Chapel Hill: University of North Carolina Press, 1988; Ready, Milton. *The Tar Heel State: A History of North Carolina.* Columbia: University of South Carolina Press, 2005.

Barry M. Stentiford

O

One-Drop Rule

The "one-drop rule" is an ideological way of defining blackness as opposed to whiteness based on an individual's ancestral lineage. It assumes that even a miniscule amount of "black blood" (or having only one black ancestor) is enough to classify a mixed-race person "black" despite the dominant racial traits inherited. Terms like "mulatto," "quadroon," and "octoroon" were created to categorize individuals based on the percentage of traceable black ancestry. For example, a mulatto is a person with one black parent and one white parent. The blood equations get more complex with each generation: a quadroon has one black and three white ancestors (or, one-fourth black heritage); an octoroon has one black and seven white ancestors (or, one-eighth black heritage). In each successive generation, a mixed-race person may appear more white than black in complexion.

Historically, the one-drop rule has been used only in America to distinguish between people with a distinct black African heritage and those with a "pure" white European heritage. It reinforced the color line that endorses white supremacy and black inferiority. This was especially the case during **slavery**, when visual perceptions of race and racial differences were based initially on color. Slaves imported from Africa had dark skin and other distinct physical features (e.g., kinky hair, prominent noses, and full lips) unlike their white captors with pale skin, straight hair, and thin noses and lips. These biological traits would become codified cultural markings for racial differences. The common practice of miscegenation, however, made defining race more complicated. The sexual relationships, most often between white men and black female slaves, produced offspring of various complexions. No longer would all black people have specific physical features as visual signifiers of their blackness. Light-complexioned "black" people also undermined the purity of whiteness and its ideological implications; many could "pass" or live as a "white" person easily without detection. By some estimates, from the 1880s throught the 1950s, thousands of mixed-race individuals chose to pass for white rather than live as a black person facing racial prejudice and discrimination in a segregated society.

In the South, early **Jim Crow** legislation authorized the one-drop rule to set precedence for "**separate but equal**" racial segregation. A legal team led by Albion Tourgee chose **Homer Plessy**, a light-skinned shoemaker from New Orleans, to challenge Louisiana's 1890 statute to provide separate accommodations for its black and white passengers. Such restrictions on Southern railways were common, catering more to whites than blacks, with clean and well-kept seating for whites and dirty and second-rate accommodations for black patrons. Plessy deliberately sat in a white section, was arrested only when he identified himself as "colored," and then refused to leave the car. When the case appeared before the **U.S. Supreme Court**, racial classification was a key factor in determining the constitutionality of Louisiana's transit laws. Visual perceptions of race were unreliable in this case when a "black" man who appeared white crosses racial boundaries literally and figuratively. Although others perceived him as "white," Plessy decided not to pass, and the one-drop rule made his blackness visible before a law that was not color-blind. The Supreme Court ruled against the plaintiff in the 1896 ***Plessy v. Ferguson*** case, citing that a mixed-race individual could not be both black and white, but segregation laws could accommodate two races.

Several landmark cases continued to uphold the one-drop rule based on law and custom throughout the twentieth century. Challenges to anti-**miscegenation** laws that forbade interracial marriage usually involved individuals who either passed for white or unknowingly had black ancestry. Fractional equations for defining a black person varied state to state: **Mississippi** and Missouri once had a one-eighth criterion, **Virginia** a one-fourth to one-eighth, and **Louisiana** a one-thirty-second black statute. The latter was contested in 1970 when a blue-eyed, blond woman named Susie Guillory Phipps wanted to change her racial designation from "black" to "white." However, she proved to be the descendent of an eighteenth-century French planter and his slave mistress despite Phipps's unquestionably white appearance.

Scholars argue that race is not a biological classification, but is socially constructed instead. Often individuals are identified in particular communities by a fixed racial identity that may not depend on color but caste. Recent studies suggests that Americans have also depended on more than just sight to "sense race." Understanding the sounds, tastes, touch, and smell of racial characteristics (or a belief in them) may help us to perceive cultural differences (and similarities) that the "one-drop rule" dismisses.

Further Readings Davis, F. James. *Who Is Black? One Nation's Definition*. University Park: Pennsylvania State University Press, 1991; Hollinger, David A. "The One Drop Rule & The One Hate Rule." *Daedalus* 134, no. 1 (Winter 2005): 11–28; Smith, Mark M. *How Race Is Made: Slavery, Segregation, and the Senses*. Chapel Hill: University of North Carolina Press, 2006.

Sherita L. Johnson

Owens, Jesse (1913–1980)

Athlete James Cleveland Owens was born September 12, 1913, in Danville, **Alabama.** His father was a **sharecropper**, and his grandparents were slaves. Owens became a household name during the 1936 Olympic Games in Berlin,

Germany. He won four gold medals, set two world records, and shared a third with his teammates for his performance in track and field. Owens's performance in the Olympic Games was more than rewriting record books. As an African American performing in the capital of Nazi Germany; it served notice that Adolf Hitler's vision of Aryan supremacy was idiocy.

At the age of nine, Owens moved to Cleveland, Ohio. Upon arrival at school, a teacher asked him his name. He replied, "J. C." The teacher interpreted this as "Jesse," and the new moniker stuck. As a teenager, Owens participated in track and field. His performance caught the attention of many universities. Although he earned a spot on the track team at Ohio State University, he was not offered a scholarship and worked evenings as an elevator operator to pay his way through college.

After success at Ohio State, Owens qualified for the U.S. Olympic track and field team, to participate in the 1936 Olympic Games in Berlin. At this time, Germany was governed by the National Socialist (Nazi) Party, which believed the so-called Aryan race was superior to others and should govern the planet. Hitler publicly expressed his desire to use the Olympic Games as an ideological showcase. Because of this, a great amount of pressure was placed upon the United States, and other nations, not to participate. Despite this, the United States sent teams to Berlin. Owens won gold medals in the 100-meter race, 200-meter race, and broad jump. He shared another gold medal with his teammates in the 400-meter relay. His performances set or met individual effort world records in the 100- and 200-meter relays as well as the broad jump. The records stood for over 20 years.

Despite his success, Hitler did not personally congratulate Owens as he did gold medal winners who were white. Years later, when asked about Hitler's snub in Berlin, Owens responded, "I didn't go to Berlin to shake hands with him [Hitler], anyway. All I know is that I'm here now, and Hitler isn't."

After Owens retired from running, he earned a living as a highly paid motivational speaker. His success in public speaking allowed him to found a public relations firm. This firm became a vehicle in which Owens donated his time and money to many charitable organizations, youth sports programs were among his favorites.

In 1976, President Gerald Ford formally recognized Owens's contributions to his country by awarding him with the Presidential Medal of Freedom. In 1979, President Jimmy Carter bestowed to him the Living Legends Award. He lived much of the reminder of his life in Arizona. Owens died March 31, 1980 in Tucson, Arizona. *See also* Great Migration; Sports; World War II.

Further Readings Edmondson, Jacqueline. *Jesse Owens: A Biography*. Westport, CT: Greenwood Press, 2007; Vicchione, Joseph. *The New York Times Book of Sports Legends*. New York: Random House, 1991.

James Newman

P

Parks, Rosa (1913–2005)

Known as the "mother of the civil rights movement," Rosa Louise McCauley Parks is one of the most famous historical figures in American history. By refusing to surrender her seat to a white passenger on a segregated bus, Parks violated one of the many **Jim Crow** laws. Her actions and arrest served as the impetus for the **Montgomery Bus Boycott.**

On February 4, 1913, Rosa was born in Tuskegee, **Alabama**, to James and Leona McCauley. Reared and educated in rural Pine Level, Alabama, Rosa was known as a soft-spoken, intelligent student. She continued her education at Montgomery Industrial School for girls and Alabama State Teacher's College High School. However, due to several illnesses in the family, Rosa postponed graduation to help out at home. In 1932, she married local barber Raymond Parks and received her high school diploma two years later. In Montgomery, the couple worked together in the National Association for the Advancement of Colored People (NAACP). Parks served as the branch secretary and youth leader of the NAACP and worked as a seamstress in a downtown department store.

On December 1, 1955, the 43-year-old Parks boarded the city bus after work. Since all of the seats in the back were taken, Parks sat in the first row of the black section. At the next stop a white male passenger asked for Parks's seat. She refused to move. The bus driver ordered Parks to move and threatened to call the cops. Again, she refused to move and was arrested. Parks never thought she would make history that day; her only desire was "to know once and for all what rights I had as a human being."

Parks became the symbol of hundreds of thousands of African Americans who had suffered as second-class citizens. Her actions served as the spark for the Montgomery bus boycott. The NAACP and Women's Political Council (WPC) had organized long before this incident but had waited for such an event to rally their cause around. Only days after Parks's arrest, the boycott of the Montgomery bus system began.

Shortly after her arrest, Parks lost her job in the department store, and two years later, Parks and her husband moved to Detroit, Michigan. For more than 20 years, Parks worked as an assistant to Michigan's U.S. congressman John

Conyers. In 1987, Parks cofounded the Rosa & Raymond Parks Institute for Self Development, which focuses its efforts on encouraging and leading children to reach their fullest potential.

As an activist, lecturer, and writer, Parks continued to inspire thousands of Americans. In addition to the 43 honorary doctorate degrees, Parks also received the NAACP Springarn Medal, UAW's Social Justice Award, the Martin Luther King, Jr., Non-Violent Peace Prize, the Medal of Freedom, and the Congressional Gold Medal, to name a few. The strong, soft-spoken woman whose courage changed the nation died at the age of 92.

Further Readings: Brinkley, Douglas. *Rosa Parks.* New York: Viking, 2000; Crawford, Vicki L., Jacqueline Anne Rouse, and Barbara Woods, eds. *Women in the Civil Rights Movement: Trailblazers and Torchbearers, 1941–1965.* Brooklyn, NY: Carlson Publishing, 1990; Hine, Darlene Clark, Elsa Barkley Brown, and Rosalyn Terborg-Penn, eds. *Black Women in American: An Historical Encyclopedia.* Brooklyn, NY: Carlson Publishing, 1992; Parks, Rosa, with Gregory Reed. *Rosa Parks: The Faith, the Hope, and the Heart of a Woman Who Changed a Nation.* Grand Rapids, MI: Zondervan, 1994.

Emily Hess

Passing

The common perception of passing is of a light-complexioned African American assuming the identity of a white person. Under the conditions of **Jim Crow**, passing was an opportunity to gain social, political, and economic benefits afforded by white supremacist ideology. This phenomenon occurred regularly during slavery when mulatto slaves wanted to escape or prevent capture once free. In 1848, for instance, William and Ellen Craft devised an elaborate passing scheme when they ran away from a **Georgia** plantation. Ellen was light enough to pass as a white man; she wore the disguise of a sickly gentleman, accompanied by "his" male slave (her husband William) traveling to the North. They figured that it would be more believable for Ellen to appear as a white man rather than face the impropriety of a Southern white woman accompanied by a black man. The Crafts arrived in Philadelphia undetected, and their story was later documented in *Running a Thousand Miles for Freedom* (1860). In places like New Orleans with large populations of free mulattos, many of them could or did easily assimilate into white society throughout the nineteenth century. Such accounts of racial passing were less frequent during the **Reconstruction** era (1863–1877), when more liberal circumstances provided less motivation for passing throughout the South. African Americans, for the first time in American history, enjoyed greater political freedom than ever before. However, Reconstruction ended when Southern states that were readmitted to the Union sought revenge for losing the Civil War and the radical Republican policies that destroyed and made amends for slavery. Segregation was codified and enforced as a systematic form of racial oppression, hence the birth of Jim Crow. Many African Americans who passed for white then did so to avoid the hardships of racial discrimination, prejudice, and often violence. Essentially, they could live as free people in a democratic society. Their choices for education, housing, shopping, employment, transportation, and even entertainment would not be limited by their black racial identity. On the contrary, the chance to acquire equal rights and social privileges then reserved for whites only seemed worth the risk.

Passing required life-altering changes based on the kind and length of the experience. Some individuals might have passed involuntarily if their mixed-race heritage was unknown; they could have been born under such pretenses if their family kept the secret of passing (which they often did). This is the sort of racial tragedy dramatized in fiction, though it occurred often in real life. Others severed ties completely from their black family to live a solitary white life. This separation of family or loss of communal relationships could have been devastating consequences for passing. The disconnection from familiar environments and people could symbolize "passing" as the death of a former life. While investigating race relations in the deep South during the 1930s, sociologists explained this kind of passing as social death and rebirth. When the truth was revealed or while passing, an individual could likely have experienced psychological conflicts about identifying with either race. Those who fully assimilated, however, may not have suffered emotional distress. Some even married "pure" whites to further dilute their bloodline. The fear of producing "black" offspring could then prevent the passer from having any children at all. So having a white complexion alone did not guarantee the passer success.

The discovery of an individual's true identity was a foremost concern when the "**one-drop rule**" was used to define blackness. Having a traceable black ancestry (or any "black blood") was enough to classify a mixed-race person "black" despite the dominant white racial traits inherited. Descriptions of biracial individuals as "near-white" or "white Negroes" suggest racial impurities or an invisible blackness that many whites feared. Black-to-white passers were therefore complicit in their attempts to assimilate under white surveillance, especially in the Jim Crow South. Racial ambiguity threatened segregation and sensitized white Southerners to maintain the status quo. They proclaimed an ability to detect any passers with visible or invisible signs of blackness. If the average African American developed a double consciousness as theorized by **W.E.B. Du Bois** in *The Souls of Black Folk* (1903), passers were even more sensitive to racism. The "peculiar sensation" of "always looking at one's self through the eyes of others" was fundamental to their concealment. Du Bois challenged segregationists' reliance on ocular proof of black inferiority with his American Negro Exhibit at the 1900 Paris Exposition. Many of the photographs on display featured African Americans of questionable racial origins: pale complexions, light eyes, thin noses, and various hair textures. These images of exceptional blacks proved that they could "pass" as model citizens and undermine white peoples' perception of blackness.

Despite close racial scrutiny, the "great age of passing" occurred at the height of Jim Crow during the late nineteenth and early twentieth centuries. Thousands crossed the color line to defy legal segregation, social restrictions, and geographical boundaries. Since the majority of African Americans lived in the South, those wanting to pass would migrate to the North, where they could become "new people" without the burden of race. Or, they could take advantage of the opportunity to live a double life. Alex Manly, a mulatto journalist from North Carolina, fled the South during a race riot in 1898. When he relocated to Philadelphia, he divided his time working as a white man during the day and returned home to his black family in the evening. He eventually decided to live as a black man permanently, though he could not find suitable employment to support his family as such. When passing proved to be a costly venture, other alternatives became attractive options for circumventing the race problem. Some African Americans passed for European immigrants, who would often receive better treatment upon arrival to this country than black people in America. French, Italian, Spanish, and other foreign ethnicities were ideal covers used to explain the variations of colored complexions among African Americans resulting from generations of **miscegenation**. To appear more convincing, passers adopting a foreign ethnicity would even speak in a native tongue when approached by suspicious whites. Mary Church Terrell, a leading civil rights activist and black feminist, would often pass for white inadvertently or on purpose as she traveled through the South on lecture tours during the late nineteenth and early twentieth centuries. Terrell spoke several languages and easily passed for a European native as well as a cultured, white Southern belle when necessary to avoid traveling in filthy Jim Crow railway cars.

Whether passing on a temporary or permanent basis, an individual who passed for white during the Jim Crow era risked their personal safety. There were (or could have been) violent repercussions after discovery. "**Separate but equal**" policies of segregation tried to determine the limits of interracial mixing in public spaces. Yet, the culture of segregation depended on the "myth" of absolute racial differences, and passing violated the metaphorical and legal limits of segregation. Cases of mistaken identity did occur when African Americans with Caucasian features did not appear "black." Such individuals were often treated with dignity and respect by whites who were unaware of the racial stigma that defined the passer's blackness. Charles Chesnutt was a popular light-skinned African American novelist who experienced life on the color line in this way. He withheld his racial identity with the release of early works to avoid racial censure and received critical reviews on the basis of his artistry alone and not his ancestry. When done as a conscious or deliberate act, however, others lived as a spy crossing racial boundaries. These African Americans sat or ate in the "white only" sections of trains, theaters, and restaurants without detection. **Walter White**, for example, was an investigative reporter for the National Association for the Advancement of Colored People (NAACP) during the 1920s. With light skin, blue eyes, and wavy blond hair, the natural disguise White wore to investigate **lynchings** throughout the South protected him. His subversive act of passing could have easily made him a victim of the same crimes that he witnessed and reported on in *The Crisis*. Years earlier as a young boy, White and his father survived the 1906 Atlanta race riots also by passing as white men until they reached the safety of their home.

African American writers have often fictionalized passing narratives to depict Jim Crow race relations. In her 1892 novel *Iola Leroy*, Frances Harper's mulatto protagonist passes as a white woman until her black heritage is revealed after the death of her parents. The novel unfolds as Iola learns to survive as a "black" woman facing racial discrimination and prejudice. She decides not to pass as a white woman because of her familial relations and racial obligations. Both her and her brother devote their lives to "uplifting the race" as they identify with all African Americans in the struggle for civil equality. Their commitment to become race leaders instead of "race traitors" is a decision made by real mulattos like Walter White with his NAACP activism. Charles Chesnutt's novels often depict mixed-race or "tragic mulatto" characters that experience biological and social conflicts due to their "warring blood" or inherited racial traits. Those that do not succumb to a tragic end (death, desertion, exile, etc.) cross the color line and disappear into white society. As art imitates life, Chesnutt's stories explore the options for passing presented to light-skinned African Americans who seek the benefits of the privileged class. In *The Autobiography of an Ex-Colored Man* (1912), James Weldon Johnson examines the racial paradox in America through an anonymous protagonist who passes for both white and black: "I know that I am playing with fire, and I feel the thrill which accompanies that most fascinating pastime; and, back of it all, I think I find a sort of savage and diabolical desire to gather up all the little tragedies of my life, and turn them into a practical joke on society" Using social realism to captivate his readers, Johnson's novel was a successful literary hoax initially since many people believed the autobiography was a truthful account of passing. The republication of the novel with Johnson's authorship finally acknowledged appeared in 1927.

Like Johnson, Nella Larsen, Jessie Redmon Fauset, and George Schuyler were other African American novelists that continued to develop the theme of passing during the **Harlem Renaissance**. Works by Larsen and Fauset are populated by characters with mixed-race ancestries and thus the burden of race. Larsen presents the psychological trauma of mulatto women in her 1929 novel about complex racial, class, and gender identities. Aptly titled *Passing,* the work explores the motivations and consequences of Irene Redfield and Clare Kendry passing as socialites on both sides of the color line. Schuyler's *Black No More* (1931) provides a satirical solution to America's race problem by interrogating the power of whiteness. The plot dramatizes racism when black people are transformed into white people via a commercially successful whitening process invented by a black scientist.

White writers like **William Faulkner** also experimented with the passing theme. He created mulatto characters in works like *Absalom, Absalom* (1936) and *Intruder in the Dust* (1948) that challenged white Southerners' abilities to sense race under segregation. His **Mississippi** settings were ideal to dramatize many white Southerners' racial paranoia. Not only were light-skinned blacks the target of bigots, but liberal whites sympathetic to blacks' civil rights were also labeled "white niggers" like those in Faulkner's fiction.

Reverse passing of "mulattos" with white skin and black behavior made for controversial headlines in twentieth-century divorce cases. The scandalous Rhinelander trial of 1924, as detailed in *Love on Trial: An American Scandal in Black and White* (2002), captured the nation's obsession with racial purity and segregation culture. The marriage of a white New York socialite, Leonard Rhinelander, to a working-class domestic, Alice Jones, was annulled when the husband accused his wife of not being completely white. Jones did have mysterious racial origins, though her family did not try to pass for white. Ultimately, her class status proved more of a moral transgression than the scandalous interracial affair staged for the public. Other examples of white-to-black passers' moral failures were not uncommon in multiracial families. "Pure" white siblings would identify as "black" to keep their family relations with black half-siblings intact. Illegitimate whites would also identify as "black" to avoid the stigma of being born a bastard.

Recently, genealogical research has proven how generations of "white" Americans are actually descendants of light-skinned African Americans who passed for various reasons. Attempts to untangle ancestral roots have resulted in revised historical accounts of slavery, fractured memoirs, and emotional family reunions. Edward Ball, a white descendant of prominent **South Carolina** slaveowners, documents his tedious research into family records in two books, *Slaves in the Family* (1998) and *The Sweet Hell Inside: The Rise of an Elite Black Family in the Segregated South* (2002). In *Life on the Color Line: The True Story of a White Boy Who Discovered He Was Black* (1996), Gregory Howard Williams recalls his coming-of-age during segregation. Shirley Taylor Haizlip likewise reconstructs the difficult past relations of her multiracial family in *The Sweeter the Juice: A Family Memoir in Black and White* (1995); it chronicles the lives of two sisters who were separated for nearly 70 years as each lived in different worlds. The publication of these works and numerous others signals a sort of revival of passing narratives since the demise of Jim Crow.

While the authors present intriguing exposés of passing, first-hand accounts of passing rarely exist because of the fear discovery. Anonymous testimonies were published only when necessary as political propaganda. Many "post-passing" narratives are only now being studied as evidence of the pressures to adapt to racist society; these stories and similar reports about the "past" trend of passing were published in popular black periodicals like *Ebony* and *Jet* during the 1950s. A notable example is John Howard Griffin's **Black Like Me** (1960), his autobiography of becoming a "black" man within the last decade of Jim Crow. Like Walter White, Griffin's mission as a white "spy" was to investigate black life in the Deep South and report his findings to promote racial understanding. His white-to-black passing appealed to American racism by dissecting America's own "white" consciousness. Griffin's timely publication appeared on the cusp of a new era in the history of passing. After all, black-to-white passing at least had become "passé" as the **Civil Rights** and Black Power movements redefined blackness in positive ways. The racial pride anthem "black is beautiful," for instance, proclaimed a new generation of African Americans' acceptance of darker skin complexion and validated black culture in general.

Further Readings: "The Adventures of a Near-White." *Independent* 75 (1913): 373–76; Ginsberg, Elaine K. *Passing and the Fictions of Identity.* Durham, NC: Duke University Press, 1996; Hale, Grace Elizabeth. *Making Whiteness: The Culture of Segregation in the South, 1890–1940.* New York: Vintage, 1998; Sollors, Werner. *Neither Black nor White, Yet Both: Thematic Explorations of Interracial Literature.* Cambridge, MA: Harvard University Press, 1997; Wald, Gayle. *Crossing the Line: Racial Passing in Twentieth-Century U.S. literature and Culture.* Durham, NC: Duke University Press, 2000; Williamson, Joel. *New People: Miscegenation and Mulattoes in the United States.* Baton Rouge: Louisiana State University Press, 1995.

Sherita L. Johnson

Plessy v. Ferguson (1896)

Plessy v. Ferguson was a landmark decision of the **U.S. Supreme Court** in 1896 that upheld the constitutionality of state laws requiring racial segregation in public accommodations (particularly railroad passenger cars) and that established the doctrine of "**separate but equal**" as the constitutional standard for such laws. The Supreme Court held that neither the Thirteenth nor the Fourteenth Amendment to the Constitution could be used to challenge intrastate segregation laws. The decision resulted in a proliferation of laws mandating racial segregation in public spaces throughout the South, providing constitutional justification for hardening the de facto separation of the races established by custom into state law. This decision stood for nearly 60 years until the Court reversed itself, beginning in 1954 with **Brown v. Board of Education** and other cases that followed. The Court specifically outlawed segregation in all public transportation in 1956 in *Gayle v. Browder.*

With the end of the Civil War, Southern states were occupied by Federal troops during the period known as **Reconstruction** (1865–1877). Military occupation could, at first, guarantee that former slaves could fully exercise their voting rights and their civil rights on an equal basis with whites. However, when Reconstruction ended and federal troops were withdrawn, newly won black rights came under attack. Even before the end of Reconstruction, a pattern of racial separation had developed that, while not compelled by statute, pervaded Southern life. By the 1880s, states began to give these patterns the sanction of law.

In 1890 the Louisiana state legislature passed a law that required "equal but separate accommodations for the white and colored races" on all passenger railroads within the state. An exception was provided for nurses attending children of another race. Almost immediately, the black and French-speaking Creole citizens of New Orleans organized to oppose the law. The Citizen's Committee to Test the Constitutionality of the Separate Car Law, known as *Comité des Citoyens*, resolved to establish in court that the law violated the Thirteenth and Fourteenth Amendments to the Constitution. The committee, which included prominent whites in New Orleans, agreed that a 30-year-old shoemaker, **Homer Plessy**, should test the law. Plessy was a French-speaking resident of New Orleans chosen specifically because he was only one-eighth black (an octoroon in the parlance of the time) and, according to his lawyer, "the mixture [was] not discernible." In this way, the committee hoped to expose the arbitrariness of the law.

Clearly, Plessy could have occupied the white car of any train in Louisiana without trouble. But on June 7, 1892, by prearrangement with the railroad company, he sat in a railway car reserved for whites only and refused to leave when asked. The railroad conductor and a private detective hired by the *Comité des Citoyens* then removed him to the police station, where he was booked and released on $500 bond. The railroad company officials seem to have lent some silent support to the committee's court challenge because they were unhappy about the extra expense of providing separate cars for blacks and whites mandated by the law.

Excerpts from *Plessy v. Ferguson,* 1896, pp. 1, 9, 11

That petitioner was a citizen of the United States and a resident of the state of Louisiana, of mixed descent, in the proportion of seven-eighths Caucasian and one-eighth African blood; that the mixture of colored blood was not discernible in him, and that he was entitled to every recognition, right, privilege, and immunity secured to the citizens of the United States of the white race by its constitution and laws; that on June 7, 1892, he engaged and paid for a first-class passage on the East Louisiana Railway, from New Orleans to Covington, in the same state, and thereupon entered a passenger train, and took possession of a vacant seat in a coach where passengers of the white race were accommodated; that such railroad company was incorporated by the laws of Louisiana as a common carrier, and was not authorized to distinguish between citizens according to their race, but, notwithstanding this, petitioner was required by the conductor, under penalty of ejection from said train and imprisonment, to vacate said coach, and occupy another seat, in a coach assigned by said company for persons not of the white race, and for no other reason than that petitioner was of the colored race; that, upon petitioner's refusal to comply with such order, he was, with the aid of a police officer, forcibly ejected from said coach, and hurried off to, and imprisoned in, the parish jail of New Orleans, and there held to answer a charge made by such officer to the effect that he was guilty of having criminally violated an act of the general assembly of the state, approved July 10, 1890, in such case made and provided. . . .

We consider the underlying fallacy of the plaintiff's argument to consist in the assumption that the enforced separation of the two races stamps the colored race with a badge of inferiority. If this be so, it is not by reason of anything found in the act, but solely because the colored race chooses to put that construction upon it. The argument necessarily assumes that if, as has been more than once the case, and is not unlikely to be so again, the colored race should become the dominant power in the state legislature, and should enact a law in precisely similar terms, it would thereby relegate the white race to an inferior position. We imagine that the white race, at least, would not acquiesce in this assumption. The argument also assumes that social prejudices may be overcome by legislation, and that equal rights cannot be secured to the negro except by an enforced commingling of the two races. We cannot accept this proposition. If the two races are to meet upon terms of social equality, it must be the result of natural affinities, a mutual appreciation of each other's merits, and a voluntary consent of individuals. [. . .]

Mr. Justice HARLAN dissenting [excerpt]

In respect of civil rights, common to all citizens, the constitution of the United States does not, I think, permit any public authority to know the race of those entitled to be protected in the enjoyment of such rights. Every true man has pride of race, and under appropriate circumstances, when the rights of others, his equals before the law, are not to be affected, it is his privilege to express such pride and to take such action based upon it as to him seems proper. But I deny that any legislative body or judicial tribunal may have regard to the race of citizens when the civil rights of those citizens are involved. Indeed, such legislation as that here in question is inconsistent not only with that equality of rights which pertains to citizenship, national and state, but with the personal liberty enjoyed by every one within the United States. [. . .]

At Plessy's first trial, the presiding judge was John H. Ferguson, a native of Massachusetts. He had earlier struck down as unconstitutional another Louisiana law that had mandated segregated accommodations for travel between states. This time, however, the law was restricted to travel only within Louisiana. Ferguson ruled that the state could impose such restrictions within its borders without violating the Constitution. The decision was appealed to the Louisiana State Supreme Court, which upheld the ruling. The decision at the state level cited other court decisions that had relied for support on the "natural, legal, and customary differences between the black and white races."

Plessy's case was argued before the U.S. Supreme Court by the white, activist, New York lawyer Albion W. Tourgée, who had protested against racial segregation earlier in newspaper columns. He prepared a case that presented a variety of arguments to the court against the Louisiana law. He argued for a broad interpretation of the Thirteenth Amendment to the Constitution, which had abolished slavery. That amendment, his argument suggested, affirmatively established in law the equality of all citizens. Segregation, therefore, violated the Constitution by perpetuating one of the essential features of slavery.

The case also argued that the Louisiana law deprived Plessy of his right to equal protection of law guaranteed by the Fourteenth Amendment. The purpose of the law was not to promote the public good, but rather to ensure the comfort of whites at the expense of blacks. "The exemption of nurses, "Plessy's lawyer argued, "shows that the real evil lies not in the color of the skin but in the relation the colored person sustains to the white. If he is a dependent it may be endured; if he is not, his presence is insufferable." This could not be called equal protection.

Tourgée also pointed out the arbitrariness of racial classifications, since Plessy had only one-eighth African ancestry and could be taken to be white. Indeed, the definition of who was black and who was white differed from state to state. By granting to railroad conductors (whom the law exempted from civil liability) the power to publicly declare racial designations, the state had deprived Plessy of his reputation (as a white man) without due process of law.

In addition, the arguments for Plessy had to take into account that schools were legally segregated, even in Boston and in Washington, DC, and that **interracial marriage** was forbidden by law in most states (such laws would eventually be found unconstitutional by the Supreme Court in the following century). Those laws might be acceptable, but the matter of seating on railway coaches was different, Plessy's lawyer argued, being much less serious an issue than education or marriage and not affecting future generations. Therefore, the state had no interest in regulating it.

However, the Supreme Court ruled against Plessy on May 18, 1896. The judges voted seven to one to uphold the Louisiana law. Justice Brewer did not participate in the case. Justice Henry Billings Brown, a native of Massachusetts and a resident of Michigan, wrote the majority opinion. Justice **John Marshall Harlan**, a Southerner, wrote a ferocious but solitary dissent.

In the years prior to the *Plessy v. Ferguson* case, this same Court had handed down a number of decisions which limited the scope and effect of constitutional restraints on states rights. These precedents made the Court's 1896 decision almost inevitable. In 1873, the Supreme Court had rejected a broad interpretation of the Thirteenth Amendment in a collection of suits that became known as the *Slaughter-House Cases*. In that decision, the Court held that the sole purpose of the Amendment was to abolish slavery, and perhaps other forms of involuntary servitude. It had nothing to do with equal rights. Furthermore, the decision held that the Fourteenth Amendment was not intended to establish the **federal government** as the "perpetual censor upon all the legislation of the States." That Amendment only forbade state infringement on the rights of United States citizenship, which the court took to be narrow in scope.

In 1876 the Supreme Court had decided (***U.S. v. Cruikshank***) that the Fourteenth Amendment could provide not federal protection against actions committed by private parties, but could only protect against the actions of states. Then, in 1883, the court had held in five cases collected together as the *Civil Rights Cases* that most of the provisions of the federal **Civil Rights Act of 1875** were unconstitutional. The court again ruled that Congress had authority only to prohibit racial discrimination perpetrated by states, not by private citizens. Such precedents made the legal outlook for Plessy's Supreme Court challenge seem bleak indeed. His lawyer deliberately delayed bringing the case to the Court in hopes of finding a more favorable political climate.

Finally, the Supreme Court ruled against Plessy, citing the above precedents. Plessy's appeal to the Thirteenth Amendment was dismissed in favor of a narrow interpretation of the law. The court found, as well, that the Louisiana law did not violate the Fourteenth Amendment to the Constitution. Justice Brown wrote:

> The object of the [Fourteenth] amendment was undoubtedly to enforce the absolute equality of the two races before the law, but in the nature of things it could not have been intended to abolish distinctions based upon color, or to enforce social, as distinguished from political equality, or a commingling of the two races upon terms unsatisfactory to either. Laws permitting, and even requiring, their separation in places where they are liable to be brought into contact do not necessarily imply the inferiority of either race to the other.

The majority opinion noted that the Louisiana law had mandated "equal" accommodations be provided for blacks and whites. Therefore, the separation of the races by law was not an issue of equality, since it was just as illegal for whites to sit in the black areas of railway cars as it was for blacks to sit in the white areas. The court held that the "assumption that the enforced separation of the two races stamps the colored race with the badge of inferiority" was a false one. "If this be so, it is not by reason of anything found in the act, but solely because the colored race chooses to put that construction upon it." The ruling explicitly rejected the idea that racial prejudice could be overcome by legislation and denied that equal rights could only be achieved for blacks by enforcing "commingling" of the races. The Court's majority opinion simply assumed that racial separation was "in the nature of things."

Justice Harlan, who wrote the lone dissent to the majority opinion, was a native of Kentucky and a former slaveowner, although he had fought for the Union in the Civil War and freed his slaves before it ended. Harlan argued forcefully that the Louisiana law was unconstitutional and should be struck down by the courts. He objected that:

> The arbitrary separation of citizens, on the basis of race, while they are on a public highway, is a badge of servitude wholly inconsistent with the civil freedom and the equality before the law established by the Constitution. It cannot be justified upon any legal grounds.

Harlan's dissent specifically accepted a broad interpretation of the Thirteenth Amendment that would exclude laws requiring racial segregation. He states explicitly:

> The Thirteenth Amendment does not permit the withholding or the deprivation of any right necessarily inhering in freedom. It not only struck down the

institution of slavery as previously existing in the United States, but it prevents the imposition of any burdens or disabilities that constitute badges of slavery or servitude. It decreed universal civil freedom in this country.

Harlan's dissent was emphatic. He insisted that the Fourteenth Amendment should bar states from any abridgment, on the basis of race, of civil rights or "personal liberty":

> In respect of civil rights, common to all citizens, the Constitution of the United States does not, I think, permit any public authority to know the race of those entitled to be protected in the enjoyment of such rights. . . . I deny that any legislative body or judicial tribunal may have regard to the race of citizens when the civil rights of those citizens are involved. Indeed, such legislation, as that here in question, is inconsistent not only with that equality of rights which pertains to citizenship, National and State, but with the personal liberty enjoyed by every one within the United States.

Harlan rejected the majority's argument that laws of racial segregation did not discriminate against blacks in language that came close to contempt:

> It was said in argument that the statute of Louisiana does not discriminate against either race, but prescribes a rule applicable alike to white and colored citizens. But this argument does not meet the difficulty. Every one knows that the statute in question had its origin in the purpose, not so much to exclude white persons from railroad cars occupied by blacks, as to exclude colored people from coaches occupied by or assigned to white persons. Railroad corporations of Louisiana did not make discrimination among whites in the matter of accommodation for travellers. The thing to accomplish was, under the guise of giving equal accommodation for whites and blacks, to compel the latter to keep to themselves while travelling in railroad passenger coaches. No one would be so wanting in candor as to assert the contrary.

He went on to say that: "The thin disguise of 'equal' accommodations for passengers in railroad coaches will not mislead any one, nor atone for the wrong this day done."

Harlan insisted that the majority's decision would, in time, "prove to be quite as pernicious as the decision made by [the Supreme Court] in the *Dred Scott* case." At the conclusion of his dissent, he waxed prophetic:

> I am of the opinion that the statute of Louisiana is inconsistent with the personal liberty of citizens, white and black, in that State, and hostile to both the spirit and the letter of the Constitution of the United States. If laws of like character should be enacted in the several States of the Union, the effect would be in the highest degree mischievous. Slavery, as an institution tolerated by law would, it is true, have disappeared from our country, but there would remain a power in the States, by sinister legislation, to interfere with the full enjoyment of the blessings of freedom; to regulate civil rights, common to all citizens, upon the basis of race; and to place in a condition of legal inferiority a large body of American citizens.

Of course, laws "of like character" that enforced racial segregation were eventually enacted in all Southern states, and in some Northern states as well. Such laws relegated African Americans to the status of second-class citizens, excluded from public spaces and vulnerable to public humiliation. Segregated public facilities for blacks were always separate, but very rarely equal to those provided for whites. Nonetheless, the Supreme Court's decision in *Plessy v. Ferguson* protected the constitutionality of such laws and provided them with a legal foundation.

Eventually, the Southern states passed laws that enforced a rigidly segregated society. Every restaurant, every school, every train or public conveyance was segregated by law. Separate facilities for blacks and whites were legislated for hotels, elevators, libraries, colleges and universities, swimming pools, drinking fountains, cemeteries, and prisons. An Oklahoma law segregated telephone booths. Louisiana required separate entryways to circuses for blacks and whites. A **Florida** law demanded that schoolbooks for white schools be stored separately from schoolbooks used in black schools. Such laws rested on the Supreme Court's standard of "separate but equal" established in *Plessy v. Ferguson.*

This standard was finally repudiated by the Supreme Court in 1954, at least with regard to the legal segregation of public schools, in the famous case of **Brown v. Board of Education**. Other cases would follow quickly that found laws of segregation to be unconstitutional in all circumstances. However, the 1896 *Plessy v. Ferguson* decision found its defenders right up until the end. In 1952, William Rehnquist (then a law clerk and later chief justice of the Supreme Court) composed a memo for the Court during early deliberations that led to the *Brown* case. He wrote: "I realize that it is an unpopular and unhumanitarian position, for which I have been excoriated by 'liberal' colleagues but I think *Plessy v. Ferguson* was right and should be reaffirmed." The Supreme Court disagreed unanimously, and *Brown v. Board of Education* marked the beginning of the end of de jure racial segregation in the United States. *See also* Railroads; Streetcars and Boycotts.

Further Readings: Lofgren, Charles A. *The "Plessy" Case: A Legal-Historical Interpretation.* New York: Oxford University Press, 1987; Olsen, Otto H. *The Thin Disguise: "Plessy v. Ferguson."* New York: Humanities Press, 1967; *Plessy v. Ferguson,* 163 U.S. 537 (1896). http://www.law.cornell.edu/supct/html/historics/USSC_CR_0163_0537_ ZS.html (accessed May 28, 2008); Thomas, Brook, ed. *Plessy v. Ferguson: A Brief History with Documents.* Boston: Bedford Books, 1997.

Anthony A. Lee

Plessy, Homer (1862–1925)

Homer Adolph Plessy was an African American artisan, activist, and the plaintiff in the defining **U.S. Supreme Court** case *Plessy v. Ferguson* (1896). Born on March 17, 1863, Plessy grew up in the city of New Orleans. In the pre–Civil War era, his parents, Homer Adolph Plessy and Rosa Debergue, belonged to a sizeable community of free people of color, many of mixed-race descent. These individuals, often known as Creoles (mixed-race people), spoke French, practiced **Catholicism**, could legally own property, and had access to education and other opportunities that slaves did not. Plessy married Louise Bordenave in 1889 and moved to the New Orleans neighborhood of Faubourg Tremé where he worked as a shoemaker, a craft he learned from his family. When he was 30 years old, Plessy challenged the newly passed Louisiana law mandating racial segregation on streetcars and trains. Law enforcement arrested him for sitting in the white section of a streetcar. Plessy appealed his conviction all the way to the Supreme Court, where he lost when the court declared that "**separate but equal**" was constitutional.

Until passage of the 1890 Separate Car Act in Louisiana, streetcars and train stations remained integrated. The new law required that railway companies segregate blacks and whites into separate coaches. A civil rights organization based in New Orleans, Comité des Citoyens (Committee of Citizens), decided to make a test case against the law. Plessy was one of the youngest members of this group of activists and professionals, many of whom came from the free people of color caste. The Comité des Citoyens viewed themselves as full American citizens and believed it was their duty to defend their constitutional rights against prejudice. They chose Plessy to challenge the intrastate law because he was light-skinned. In part, the group hoped that in selecting someone who could pass as white, they might be able to draw attention to the arbitrariness of conductors assigning seats based on race. Ironically, in the brief of *Plessy v. Ferguson*, Plessy was listed as "seven-eighths white," even though he was legally considered black in Louisiana.

On June 7, 1892, Plessy purchased a first class ticket to travel from New Orleans to Covington on the East Louisiana Railroad. When he boarded the train, he sat in the first-class coach, which was designated for whites only. The conductor asked him if he was colored. Plessy replied in the affirmative but refused to move to the "colored car" when ordered to do so. The Comité des Citoyens made arrangements with the conductor to confront Plessy and hired a private detective to arrest him to ensure that he would be taken into custody. The railroad company supported Plessy's challenge to the law because of the financial burden involved with providing separate cars. The East Louisiana Railroad also did not want its conductors to be responsible for making on-the-spot decisions about an individual's racial background. Plessy was tried before Justice John Howard Ferguson of the Orleans Parish Criminal Court and found guilty of violating the Separate Car Act.

Plessy appealed Justice Ferguson's decision to the Louisiana State Supreme Court and eventually the U.S. Supreme Court. One of Plessy's lawyers, Albion Tourgeé, argued that the Separate Car Act had deprived Plessy of his rights to due process and equal protection under the law as outlined by the Thirteenth and Fourteenth Amendments. Tourgeé asserted that Louisiana had imposed a "badge of servitude" on Plessy because the legal definition of a slave was a person with no rights. He reasoned that the Louisiana law made artificial distinctions between blacks and whites simply for the benefit and comfort of the whites. In short, the state had treated Plessy as a second-class citizen. In a seven-to-one decision, the U.S. Supreme Court ruled against Plessy. The Court's majority opinion, delivered on May 18, 1896, stated that the Separate Car Act's distinction between black and white was purely a legal one and did not intrinsically imply the inferiority of any one race. If an African American, such as Plessy, chose to view it as a mark of second-class citizenship, that was essentially a fiction created in the individual's mind. The Court also held that the law was reasonable since it followed the community's standards and traditions designed to keep public order.

As a result of the decision, Plessy appeared once more before the New Orleans court to pay a $25 fine for violation of the law. At the turn of the century, the rise of industrial manufacturing pushed Plessy out of the shoemaking business, and subsequently he worked as a laborer and a life insurance collector. Plessy died in 1925 and is buried in St. Louis Cemetery #1 in New Orleans.

Further Readings: Medly, Keith Weldon. *We as Freemen: Plessy v. Ferguson.* Gretna, LA: Pelican Publishing Company, 2003; St. Augustine Catholic Church of New Orleans. "Famous Parishioner: Homer Plessy." St. Augustine Catholic Church Web site. http://www.staugustinecatholicchurch-neworleans.org/plessy.htm (accessed May 28, 2008); Thomas, Brook, ed. *Plessy v. Ferguson: A Brief History with Documents.* New York: Bedford Books, 1997.

Natalie J. Ring

Poitier, Sidney (b. 1927)

American actor, director, and activist Sidney Poitier was the first African American to win an Academy Award for best actor. He began in theater and moved to film and **television**. Confronted with racism and discrimination, Poitier became active in the **Civil Rights Movement** in the 1960s. He also wrote, directed, and produced films during the latter portion of his career. Poitier became an icon for many African Americans as he garnered popularity and critical success at a time when few African Americans found roles in Hollywood.

Poitier was born while his parents were en route to the United States from the **Caribbean**. His father was of Haitian descent, while his mother was from the Bahamas. He spent his childhood in Miami, Florida, in a segregated section of the city known as Colored Town. By 1920, Miami had one of the highest degrees of **residential segregation** in the United States. Poitier confronted **Jim Crow** laws as a child, including an incident in which police officers stopped him at gunpoint and ordered him to walk back to the African American section of the city, which was several miles away. Hoping to escape the Jim Crow South, he moved to New York City in spring 1943. Upon arriving, Poitier moved from job to job working as a butcher's assistant, drug store clerk, porter, and dishwasher. He joined the U.S. Army later that year and served in the 1267th Medical Detachment at the Veterans Administration Hospital in Northport, Long Island. The army released him the following December.

Poitier's first acting experience was at an apprentice program with the American Negro Theater in 1945. His first role was in a production of *You Can't Take It with You* in 1946. He then accepted a part in the all–African American cast of the Broadway production of the Classical Greek play *Lysistrata*. Poitier moved to California in 1949 and was cast in his first film role in *No Way Out*. The film explicitly portrays racial hatred, and Poitier's role as town doctor Luther Brooks broke many common African American stereotypes. Although the film and Poitier's performance received strong reviews, many Southern theaters banned the film for its racial content. His reputation grew as he garnered further accolades for his performance as a rebellious African American high school student in the 1955 film *Blackboard Jungle.*

By the late 1950s, Poitier found steady work in Hollywood but continued to face hardships as an African American in the predominantly white film industry. He faced strict enforcement of Jim Crow laws while filming in **Louisiana** for *Band of Angels* (1957). While lead actor Clark Gable and the rest of the white cast and crew ate dinner upon their arrival at the airport restaurant, Poitier and the African American cast and crew ate hidden from other patrons behind a makeshift screen in the rear of the building. They were also forced to stay in separate lodging at Southern University, at the time an all–African American college, and to use segregated transportation and bathroom facilities. Poitier continued to receive roles but found these parts to be limited in content, as many of the films were written, directed, and produced solely by whites. He and his friends and fellow actors Paul Robeson and **Harry Belafonte** fought to secure prominent parts for African Americans that were not stereotypical. Poitier received his first Academy Award nomination for best supporting actor for his role as an escaped convict in *The Defiant Ones* (1958). Like his previous films, many Southern theaters refused to run the film despite good reviews due to the close friendship that develops between Poitier's character and a white convict played by Tony Curtis. Many Southern critics also viewed the film as anti-South, pro-integration, and as Communist propaganda.

Poitier balanced his career as both actor and activist at the height of the Civil Rights Movement in the 1960s. In an attempt to help dismantle discrimination and racism in the film industry, Poitier testified before New York Congressman Adam Clayton Powell's Labor Committee about racial discrimination in the entertainment industry in October 1962. He was part of a delegation of actors, including Sammy Davis, Jr., Josephine Baker, and Marlon Brando, to take part in the **March on Washington of 1963**. Poitier went on to make history in 1964 by becoming the first African American to win an Academy Award for best actor for his performance in *Lilies in the Field.*

Later that year he appeared at the White House to congratulate President Lyndon B. Johnson for the signing of the **Civil Rights Act of 1964**. By March 1965, Poitier ranked as one of the busiest Hollywood actors and was the only African American to appear on the list. He starred in *A Patch of Blue* (1965), highlighting an interracial romance that sparked protests throughout the South, including bomb threats made to a theater in Concord, North Carolina.

In 1967, a hotel refused to lodge Poitier while residents protested daily during the filming of *In the Heat of the Night* in Tennessee. The film portrays an African American detective from the North investigating a murder alongside a white police officer in a racist Southern town. White Southern reviewers condemned the film for Poitier's performance as an aggressive African American police officer from the North who physically confronts whites. Later that year, he played actress Katharine Haughton's fiancé in *Look Who's Coming to Dinner.* The interracial romance made the film one of Poitier's most famous and successful productions. However, the film set off protests throughout the United States, including widespread picketing by the **Ku Klux Klan**. Poitier continued to make gains in Hollywood as he made his directorial debut in 1972 with *Buck and the Preacher,* which starred himself and Belafonte.

Poitier continues to make appearances in film and television. In 2000 Poitier received the Screen Actors Guild Life Achievement Award. He also received an honorary Academy Award for Lifetime Achievement in 2002. *See also* Black Hollywood.

Further Readings: Goudsouzian, Aram. *Sidney Poitier: Man, Actor, Icon.* Chapel Hill: University of North Carolina Press, 2004; Poitier, Sidney. *The Measure of a Man: A Spiritual Autobiography.* San Francisco: HarperSanFrancisco, 2000; Public Broadcasting Service. "American Master: Sidney Poitier" American Masters Exhibition, PBS Web site. http://www.pbs.org/wnet/americanmasters/database/poitier_s.html (accessed May 28, 2008).

Frank Cha

Police Brutality

Jim Crow police brutality unleashed upon blacks has roots to the infamous pro-**slavery** patrol systems that developed in such southern states as **Georgia, South Carolina,** and **Louisiana** when African slaves, if found outside the plantation, could be caught, punished, and returned by virtually any white person. Often those patrols were unruly and under the influence of potent alcoholic spirits. With origins dating to the pre–Revolutionary War period, the patrols were essentially an integral part of Southern states' police systems that developed as a way to regulate growing slave populations. As years passed, the patrols—originally consisting of volunteers—became integrated with the local militia and police forces. Simultaneously, such systems developed in Northern states too, including Pennsylvania and New York, and especially if the black population grew or there appeared to be a spike in black crimes against whites. The primarily antiblack patrol system by enforcing "slave codes" or segregation laws became systematic in many U.S. states and has subsequently today influenced the racial-profiling mentality of many police forces throughout America.

White supremacist groups, including the **Ku Klux Klan,** often had intimate ties to such police organizations. Indeed, some law enforcement officers were leaders of local groups terrorizing, beating, and even killing blacks. African Americans learned at very young ages, often due to the brutality that they had witnessed, not to trust the police. The suspicion of police was profound following the Civil War in 1865 and as **Reconstruction** set in, with nervous whites becoming desperate with preserving white power. Whites were particularly concerned with controlling the black labor that was vital for maintaining the huge plantations of the South, often utilizing local police power. In fact, some blacks believed that because of the marauding police following slavery, they were often safer on the plantation during enslavement, since they supposedly had the protection of the so-called master. Although many slave owners were certainly cruel, following slavery, it was very feasible for a black person accused of a crime to receive a severe beating, a very harsh sentence including long-term imprisonment, or even death.

Without overwhelming police enforcement or brutality following Reconstruction, whites would have found it much more difficult to subjugate blacks. By the late nineteenth century, police abuse against blacks and the inequality of the criminal justice system reached a fever pitch. For instance, when one **Alabama** black pleaded self-defense after being attacked by a white conductor, the judge fined the African American accuser $10. And in Hinds County, **Mississippi**, when a black woman was beaten with an ax handle by a white man in 1897 and she sought justice, the justice of the peace responded that he could find nothing against the law. Yet, often, judges did not get to litigate such cases because arresting police officers, or a white mob, would act as the judge, jury, and executioner.

A black man identified as Robert Charles on July 23, 1900, had been waiting with a friend for two women in New Orleans who were scheduled to meet the men after work. As the two men waited outside one of their homes, a police sergeant and two officers approached, and angry words were exchanged. The police attacked Charles as he rose and beat him with a club. Gunfire was exchanged, with Charles wounding an officer and receiving an injury himself. Charles apparently fled and retrieved "his Winchester rapid-firing rifle," as an intense police manhunt ensured, prompting white mobs to attack blacks throughout the city. Charles, however, was eventually cornered and surrounded by at least 1,000 men. The building that he hid in was set afire, and as Charles tried to escape, he was shot, dragged through the street, and shot at repeatedly and then mutilated. Yet, Charles managed to shoot 27 whites, killing seven, including four police officers. At least 12 blacks had been slaughtered and many others injured, according to newspaper reports.

Sometimes, a white mob, occasionally led by political leaders, would take matters into its hands as law enforcement officers did little or nothing to stop the violent orgies, thereby contributing to brutality by default. In 1915 when the Monticello, Georgia, police chief sought to arrest a black man, Daniel Barber, for bootlegging, Barber and his family reportedly resisted. After the family was subdued—including Barber's son and two married daughters—they were sent to jail. However, 200 angry whites stormed the jail and dragged them to the center of the black district. The mob hanged each one of his children as Barber looked on before he too met the same fate. Seventeen years earlier, during the Atlanta race riots of 1898, much of the black community there was destroyed as the local police turned a blind eye while disarming blacks. Many in the state militia, in fact, chose to support the mob.

When 400,000 blacks served in the armed forces during **World War I**, they faced virulent police brutality in Southern cities. When black soldiers were stationed in Houston, Texas, white police attacked and arrested some of the soldiers for refusing to adhere to Jim Crow signs. Detectives also reportedly beat two of the soldiers on a streetcar. Another police assault occurred on August 23 when they beat a soldier who had tried to defend a black woman being attacked by the policemen. A responding black officer, Corporal Charles Baltimore, was also arrested when he tried to intervene, causing about 100 black soldiers to march into town with weapons and take revenge. The resulting shootout between the soldiers, police, and armed civilians left 16 whites dead, including four policemen, and four black soldiers. In a clear indication of how deeply such police brutality would be supported, the U.S. government executed 19 of the soldiers and sentenced 50 to life imprisonment.

Even when blacks tried to escape the wrath of such violence in the South and related police brutality, they had to deal with unbelievable obstacles. For fear of losing valuable labor during the early twentieth century's **Great Migration** of blacks, police often assisted with keeping blacks obligated to the planters and the criminal justice system and tried to stop the circulation of black Northern papers that promoted the North as "the Promised Land."

Following the 1927 flooding in the Mississippi Delta area, thousands of blacks were forced to work by local police and the **National Guard** on levies that were threatened by the flood waters. After the levies broke, taking many black lives, police and the National Guard gathered African Americans to live on the levies in order to stop them from leaving the area due to the fear of cotton planters losing an irreplaceable labor pool. Yet, many of the blacks, who had lived in squalid conditions on the levees for months, were determined to escape North, and traveled to such cities as Philadelphia, New York, Pittsburgh, and Chicago. And when blacks did make it to the so-called land of opportunity in the North, the police reception was often as deleterious as in the South.

The famed black writer **James Baldwin** wrote in his 1962 book, *Nobody Knows My Name,* that about the "only way to police a ghetto is to be oppressive. . . . [Police] represent the force of the white world, and that world's criminal profit and ease, to keep the Black man corralled up here, in his place. The badge, the gun in the holster, and the swinging club make vivid what will happen should his rebellion become overt." Baldwin, who was born and raised in New York City, focused on the police presence in Harlem, where hundreds of thousands of blacks migrated from the South during the 1920s, prompting a legendary arts' movement, the **Harlem Renaissance**. "[The White policeman] moves through Harlem, therefore, like an occupying soldier in a bitterly hostile country, which is precisely what, and where he is, and is the reason he walks in twos and threes."

In East St. Louis, Illinois, in 1917, the police and militia assisted whites with attacking blacks when they became angered over the rising tide of black Southern migrants competing for local jobs. Local newspapers reportedly instigated whites with headlines urging them to make the town "Lilly White." The police began to participate in the slaughter and maiming of the African Americans, according to a special congressional committee report. By the time the violence ended, about 150 had been burned, shot, or hanged, including 40 who were murdered. Small children were found with fractured skulls. Many had been tossed in bonfires lit by the angry white mob. The number of black homeless skyrocketed to 6,000.

As the 1940s approached and the world became engulfed in a second global war, returning black veterans to America faced rampant discrimination from civilian and military police, despite many of their exemplary fighting for American forces. Blacks nationwide were particularly angry about the treatment of the unit primarily manned by African Americans from New York City—the 369th Coast Artillery—in Georgia. New York newspapers described the black soldiers as being housed in a garage and fed substandard meals as their black officers were replaced with whites. The black publications also reported that the soldiers had been harassed and made to obey Jim Cow laws in Savannah as they were beaten by the local police, prompting a demonstration by the NAACP.

However, the brutality and discrimination against blacks by police were not limited to the South. Black labor leader **A. Philip Randolph** fervently pointed out the double standard of blacks risking their lives at war in defense of America, only to return home to racist police that many activists compared with those of Nazis henchmen. Indeed, New York City had proven to be a notable microcosm of the pervasive police brutality against blacks in major Northern metropolitan areas during and following **World War II**. For instance, in May 1942, Wallace Armstrong, reported to be demented, was approached by Officer Harold Reidman near or at the home of Armstrong's mother in Harlem. Armstrong disobeyed orders to not leave the premises and proceeded to walk away with a knife in his hand, only to be confronted by another officer, Patrick Smith, on 128th Street. Although eyewitnesses said Armstrong did not attempt to use his knife, they reported that Smith beat the black man in the head, shooting and killing him as he attempted to escape the blows. Adam Clayton Powell, Jr., pastor of the Abyssinian Baptist Church in Harlem, decided to organize protests as the NYPD vehemently denied wrongdoing. A grand jury, consistent with past rulings in police brutality cases, refused to indict any of the officers.

A major riot erupted in New York in August 1943 after a police officer was accused of shooting and injuring a black 26-year-old military police officer, Robert Bandy. Rumors had circulated that Bandy had actually been killed while trying to protect his mother, prompting more than 3,000 blacks to surround the police station where the officer was being protected. Threatening to reverse the brutal mob **lynching** of blacks in the South and some parts of the North, rioting broke out resulting in six deaths, almost 200 injuries, and 550 arrests.

Lloyd Curtis Jones, a black disabled veteran with ambitions for becoming a musician, was shot three times in the stomach on the evening of August 6, 1947, by a white rookie officer near where Jones had been singing with friends in Central Park close to Columbus Circle. The tragedy occurred after Jones showed the officer identification and began to leave while protesting. Although a brutality case was filed, again there was no subsequent punishment or indictment of the white police officer.

By Memorial Day 1949, as the **Civil Rights Movement** began to ignite throughout the nation, Herman Newton, a black motorist, became involved in a fistfight with another driver, an off-duty policeman named Donald Mullen who was in plain clothes. After Mullen shot at Newton, who fled, Mullen chased him and eventually cornered the black man. Mullen then shot Newton several times, killing him, claiming that Newton had attacked him with a jack-knife. Although there was no subsequent indictment, an all-white Brooklyn jury in a surprising civil-suit verdict awarded a $5,200 judgment, prompting the NAACP to adapt a new strategy in combating police abuse.

Lawsuits and court action through the 1950s and 1960s would be the primary weapons of such civil rights' groups as the NAACP and the **Southern**

Christian Leadership Conference, led by **Martin Luther King, Jr.** In fact, **Thurgood Marshall**, who would become the first black **U.S. Supreme Court** justice, had litigated police brutality cases involving blacks, as well as won landmark segregation cases as an NAACP attorney that included the 1954 *Brown v. Board of Education* case. He had also assisted with a 1956 federal lawsuit related to the segregation of blacks on buses in Montgomery, Alabama, that partially stemmed from the bravery of a black seamstress and civil rights worker, **Rosa Parks**, who refused to give up her seat to a white man leading a city police officer to arrest her.

Civil rights leaders and their attorneys constantly dealt with police-abuse issues and avowed racists such as **"Bull" Connor**, the violent Birmingham, Alabama, police chief who was backed by the **Ku Klux Klan**. Even **Malcolm X**, the celebrated black nationalist with early and very prominent ties to the Black Muslim movement, combated police brutality when he urged blacks in Los Angeles and New York City during the early 1960s not to put up with such law-enforcement unruliness. Some researchers say that there were police ties to the 1968 assassination of King and the 1965 assassination of Malcolm X. If so, then law-enforcement involvement would have been the ultimate expression of police brutality reminiscent of the numerous assassinations of black leaders during Reconstruction.

In 1966, the Black Panther Party for Self Defense was founded by Huey P. Newton and Bobby Seale in Oakland, California, and directly addressed police brutality as the Civil Rights Movement reached a crescendo. The Panthers—whose members sometimes openly carried weapons—had several violent confrontations with police, resulting in their deaths or imprisonment in several major U.S. cities, including Oakland, Philadelphia, New York, and Chicago. *See also* Prisons.

Further Readings: Bouza, Anthony V. *Police Unbound: Corruption, Abuse, and Heroism by the Boys in Blue.* New York: Prometheus Books, 2001; Fry, Gladys-Marie. *Night Riders in Black Folk History.* Chapel Hill: University of North Carolina Press, 1975; Gerdes, Louise I., ed. *Police Brutality.* Farmington Hills, MI: Greenhaven Press, 2004; Johnson, Marilynn S. *Street Justice: A History of Police Violence in New York City.* Boston: Beacon Press, 2003; Litwack, Leon F. *Trouble in Mind: Black Southerners in the Age of Jim Crow.* New York: Alfred A. Knopf, 1998.

Donald Scott

Polite Terms, Epithets, and Labels

One of the more subtle yet pernicious aspects of **Jim Crow** was the constant linguistic attempt by much of white society to humiliate blacks and to rob them of basic dignity and humanity. Labels, both those that were derogatory and those that were at least polite on the surface, were regularly used to reinforce the idea of black inferiority. At the same time, blacks fought back by refusing to accept humiliating labels and designations, insisting on the right to define themselves.

When the first blacks arrived in England's North American colonies, relatively neutral terms such as *African* and sometimes *Guinea* were usually applied to describe them. However, other terms became common early on.

With much of the New World controlled by the Spanish, and much of the slave trade controlled by the Portuguese, Spanish and Portuguese terms for enslaved Africans became widely used in the English-speaking world. Terms such as *negro* and the feminine *negra* soon became common, meaning respectively, a black male, and a black female. The Portuguese term *pequenino,* meaning "little child," morphed into *pickaninny* for black children. When New Orleans and its environs became populated by large numbers of French and Spanish speakers, they reinforced this tendency to use Latin-based words. By the mid-nineteenth century, various terms polite and impolite were used by whites to describe nonwhites. Slave owners usually avoided the term *slave,* preferring the term *servant,* which had a pleasant association with the labor force of European gentry. Terms such as *Sons of Ham* or *Hamites* were also occasionally used, mainly as a biblical justification for the enslavement of people with dark skin. *Black* was an impolite descriptive term, and generally disliked by people of African descent. Throughout the British Empire at the same time, the term "black" was used derisively against a host of indigenous people, such as in India and Australia, and white Americans might have adopted the word as a mildly offensive term from the British.

People of African descent usually described themselves as African, or dark-skinned. The term *Ethiopian* was also occasionally used by educated blacks as well as whites. While the term *Guinea* alluded to the West African origins of most African Americans, this word became a common derogatory term for Italian Americans used by other whites, in essence calling them Africans, or at least not white. By the beginning of the twentieth century, the terms *colored* and *colored people,* which had been in use for a several decades, became the common and most accepted polite term for African Americans, used by blacks and whites. The name of the organization National Association for the Advancement of Colored People reflects its origins in the early twentieth century. *Colored* was in turn replaced by *Negro* as the most common polite term, one generally accepted by blacks and whites. Organizations such as the United Negro College Fund and **Negro League Baseball** reflected their origins in the first half of twentieth century. However, disagreement over whether to capitalize the term remained. Occasionally, the feminine form *Negress* was also used to describe a black woman. The term *nigger,* formed by the slurring of the word *negro* became the most common derogatory term used by whites. While the term was neutral in the seventeenth century, by the mid-nineteenth century it had become insulting. It was used openly and publicly by many elements of white society. Its use became so common that it was often used informally to refer to any persons who were not deemed white,

Roadside sign using vicious racial epithet in the 1940s. Courtesy of Library of Congress, LC-USZ62-120259.

such as Central Americans, Filipinos, and others. However, other impolite terms were also used.

White custom held that black adults were never to be addressed as social equals, thus terms such as "Mr.," Mrs.," and "Miss," were seldom used by white people addressing blacks. In newspapers or even national magazines, blacks were always identified as such, usually with the word *Negro* in front of their person's name. Magazines such as *Time* and *Newsweek* abandoned this practice only in the 1950s. In person, black adults were often addressed by their first name, even in formal situations, or as "Uncle" or "Auntie," which whites saw as terms of affection. Most blacks, however, found the false familiarity offensive. The term *boy* was also common among whites when referring to black men in the second person. The use of *boy* stressed the white concept that adult black males were not men, and *boy* became increasingly offensive to African Americans, leading to the use of *man* by blacks, especially black males, to refer to each other. Other terms used by blacks among themselves, such *brother* and *sister* or *blood*, emphasized an assumed kinship between black Americans. Derogatory terms such as *darkie, coon, spade, spook*, and *tar-baby*, which ranged from mildly to very offensive, took as a given the inferiority of dark skin, whereas terms such as *spear-chucker* and *jungle bunny* reflected a racist debasement of the African homeland of blacks.

Throughout most of the Jim Crow era, the term *niggra* was perhaps the most common epithet used orally by whites in the South to describe African Americans, although its written use was rare. It was so common among whites of all classes in the South that even President Lyndon B. Johnson had trouble dropping it from his vocabulary, even as he was pushing Congress to pass the legislation that would dismantle Jim Crow. This term fell from general use by the 1970s, although its place in spoken English would increasingly be filled with *nigger. Nigger*, or *the N-word*, as it was commonly referred to in print by the early twenty-first century, became increasingly controversial after the end of Jim Crow. Black males used the word themselves, or its derivative *nigga*, originally as a form of defense, as a means of robbing the word of its sting. Its later use has been less intentional and more cultural. The word has largely dropped from open use by middle-class whites, as to be caught using it can seriously hurt a career. Among some segments of the white population, though, continued use of the word is an outward manifestation of the rejection of racial equality. Its use by blacks remains controversial within the black community.

The end of Jim Crow ended the open use of most derogatory terms from polite society. A new stress on dark skin as a positive attribute led to the "Black is Beautiful" slogan. The idea was to break African Americans from seeing their distinctive physical appearance in white terms, and to celebrate their own physical identity. One result of this was the new acceptance of the term *black* to identify people of African descent. Blacks themselves would define what were the polite terms and impolite terms for themselves. Older terms such as *colored* and *Negro* became, if not insults, at least no longer polite. *"People of Color"* also appeared in the 1980s as a polite term, but it did not have wide use, perhaps for its vagueness, or perhaps because it was too close to the term *colored people,* which was no longer generally polite.

Other terms were used with more or less acceptance in the late 1960s and into the 1980s. *Afro-American* became increasingly common in the early 1970s, stressing blacks as an ethnic group and their African origins. However, the term rose and fell with the popularity of a hairstyle, the Afro, which was part of the Black is Beautiful movement in that it celebrated the hair textures of many people of African descent rather than trying to make their hair conform to white standards. By the late 1970s, as the hairstyle began to look dated, the term *Afro-American* began to lose acceptance. It would soon be replaced in the 1980s by *African American,* which would hold place as the most proper term through the end of the century and beyond, although *black* remained in common use and remained a polite term. *See also* Masculinity, Black and White; Racial Customs and Etiquette.

Further Readings: Kennedy, Randall. *Nigger: The Strange Career of a Troublesome Word.* New York: Vintage Books, 2003; Moore, Richard B. *The Name Negro: Its Origin and Evil Use.* Edited with an introduction by W. Burghardt Turner and Joyce Moore Turner. Baltimore: Black Classics Press, 1992.

Max Ford

Poll Taxes

A levy placed on the right to vote, poll taxes were first established in the years following the American Revolution as a substitute for the traditional requirement that only property owners could cast ballots. Initially, the poll tax expanded the number of eligible voters, but was abandoned as states established unrestricted suffrage for most white males. However, when most male citizens were guaranteed the right to vote as a result of the ratification of the Fifteenth Amendment in 1870, the poll tax was resurrected for a more ignoble purpose. Many whites, alarmed at the sight of former slaves voting and holding elective office, were determined to restrict or even eliminate black political influence in the South. Between 1871 and 1902, the states of **Alabama, Arkansas, Florida, Georgia, Louisiana, Mississippi, North Carolina, South Carolina, Texas,** and **Virginia** adopted the poll tax specifically to deny African Americans the right to vote. Georgia was the first state to adopt a poll tax, in 1871. Citizens were required to pay between one and two dollars to their local election commissions several months before a scheduled primary and general election. On Election Day, voters then had to show proof that the tax was paid in order to cast their ballots. If a voter in Alabama, Georgia, Mississippi, and Virginia failed to pay the levy, then his poll tax bill would double for each subsequent election. This cumulative tax erected an additional barrier between economically disadvantaged Southerners and their constitutional rights.

The poll tax was chiefly designed to prevent African Americans from exercising their franchise, but in this regard, it was unsuccessful. It did make it more difficult for citizens to vote and undoubtedly prevented many from casting ballots especially in the states where the levy was cumulative. However it fell far short of its goal of entirely disenfranchising black Southerners. Many were able to pay the tax; for example, in Shelby County, Tennessee, 24,086 African Americans registered to vote in 1931. In addition, the poll tax often disenfranchised more white citizens than black. Largely because it restricted white voting, North Carolina repealed the poll tax in 1920, and Louisiana and Florida followed suit in 1934 and 1937, respectively. Around the same time, reformers in the South began to focus a great deal of attention on the inequities of the poll tax. In November 1938, the Southern Conference for Human Welfare was founded by a group of African American and white reformers to address the economic and political inequality that existed in the American South. The conference's Civil Rights Committee investigated the poll tax, and in 1941, it formed the National Committee to Abolish the Poll Tax. Petitioning Congress to abolish the tax in federal elections, the committee played a large role in convincing several Southern states to abolish the excise. Georgia, the first state to enact a poll tax, repealed the law in 1945. South Carolina abolished the poll tax in 1951, and Tennessee did the same in 1953.

Despite the success of the National Committee to Abolish the Poll Tax, Alabama, Arkansas, Texas, and Virginia refused to abandon the levy. As the **Civil Rights Movement** spread across the South, increased pressure was directed at Congress to abolish the restrictive tax. As a result of this pressure, a constitutional amendment was introduced that would eliminate the use of poll taxes in federal elections. After fierce debate, the amendment passed the House and Senate, and in 1964, the required number of states ratified the Twenty-fourth Amendment to the Constitution. The ability to charge voters to cast ballots in state and local elections came to an end in 1966 when the **U.S. Supreme Court** ruled that Virginia's poll tax violated a citizen's right to equal protection under the law as guaranteed by the Fourteenth Amendment to the Constitution. Although it did not accomplish its primary goal of stripping all African Americans of their right to vote, poll taxes were an important tool in preventing blacks from achieving full equality in the segregated South. *See also* Voting Rights Act of 1965.

Further Readings: Key, V. O. *Southern Politics in State and Nation.* New York: Knopf, 1949; Martin, Waldo E., Jr. and Patricia Sullivan, eds. *Civil Rights in the United States.* New York: Macmillan, 2000; Roller, David C., and Robert W. Twyman, eds. *The Encyclopedia of Southern History.* Baton Rouge: Louisiana State University Press, 1979.

Wayne Dowdy

Preachers

As sources of moral authority, preachers could either advocate or condemn various **Jim Crow** practices and have a wide-reaching influence through the attitudes of their audiences. Among African Americans, preachers were able to challenge Jim Crow more directly because their livelihood depended upon the support of an African American congregation, not on white employers. Among whites, preachers might join the **Ku Klux Klan** or condemn it. Some white preachers actively worked to eliminate Jim Crowism, while others encouraged support. The high level of involvement on the part of preachers allowed opposing arguments to take on religious tones and justifications. Other preachers, however, attempted to avoid racially charged issues as much as possible.

African American Preachers

In the early days of Jim Crow, many African American preachers told their congregations that it was best to submit to the laws and codes to try to avoid conflict. As conditions in the South worsened and economic opportunities in the North opened up, many preachers saw streams of their congregants leaving the South. Preachers in the North did their best to receive and care for this incoming population, although at times, the huge wave of migrants made the task difficult.

Both Northern and Southern African American churches served as not only a spiritual but also a social center for members. Historically, African Americans had been excluded from leadership roles in other social institutions, but the **churches** were an exception. In African American churches, members exerted a level of control and authority that they did not find in other social settings. In many estimations, the church was the nerve center of African American life well into the twentieth century. The space of the church allowed African Americans to develop leadership skills and provided a safe forum for social concerns. In addition to the religious services provided, other groups might be organized within the space of the church. The preacher, as the leader of this spiritual and social center, fulfilled many roles. Preachers might be responsible for providing financial assistance to members, helping them find employment or housing, in addition to serving as a spiritual leader. Due to its central position in the lives of many African Americans, the church was well respected and lent the **Civil Rights Movement** increased credibility.

African American preachers, who were already seen as leaders of the community, were more readily available to take on leadership positions against Jim Crow injustices. Other adult African Americans often worked for a white employer or rented their housing from a white landlord. These adults were discouraged from speaking out against Jim Crow laws and codes because they feared losing their jobs or homes. African American preachers were supported by their congregations, which were made up almost entirely of African Americans. These preachers had greater freedom to challenge Jim Crow, as long as the members of their congregations supported them. In areas where white reactions to such a challenge might be violent, African American preachers were constrained by fear of being attacked. Even in those situations though, African American preachers typically had greater freedom to advocate for civil rights advancements because their livelihood depended on the support of other African Americans, not on a white employer.

One of the most widely known organizations of the Civil Rights Movement was the **Southern Christian Leadership Conference (SCLC)**. Founded in 1957, the SCLC was initially led by African American pastor **Martin Luther King, Jr.** Its ranks were filled disproportionately with African American pastors who wanted to see advancements made against Jim Crow. The executive staff and governing board were comprised almost entirely of primarily Baptist preachers. African American preachers who were SCLC members typically continued to have ties to their congregation, who then provided the grassroots support the SCLC needed to carry out its vision. Organizationally, the SCLC patterned its structure, meetings, and language after the church. They framed the discussion over Jim Crow laws in terms of religious as well as social injustices, adding to their moral legitimacy.

As preachers rose to leadership positions in the battle against Jim Crow, they found language familiar to their religious vocation worked well to motivate others for the civil rights cause. Religious imagery was familiar to African Americans, and preachers used that imagery to encourage a sort of religious fervor towards the push against Jim Crow inequalities. The exodus was a poignant image used during the days of **slavery** and the Underground Railroad to depict enslaved African Americans as a new "chosen" people whom God would redeem. This notion of chosen-ness was invoked long after the legal abolition of slavery. Religious songs were also appropriated or developed by participants of the Civil Rights Movement, further invoking a sense of sacred purpose, religious fervor, and devout commitment. Preachers, who drew on biblical passages, stories, and imagery, lent the movement religious legitimation and fervor.

Some critics accused African American preachers of being "in it" for the money, and some may have been dishonest. Because many African American congregants struggled financially, some resented the monetary pleas of preachers. For those preachers who became involved in politics, it was commonplace to be accused of corruption. While some preachers with large constituencies tried to use the voting power of their congregation to garner alliances and promises from politicians, other preachers entered politics themselves. Whether this was in hopes of improving the plight of their fellow African-Americans or with an eye towards personal benefits can be evaluated on a case-by-case basis, as there were certainly instances of both.

Regardless of political involvement, a preacher's role in cities with an influx of African Americans was widely seen as helping people adjust to life in their new surroundings. Preachers might help congregants find housing, jobs, or financial relief agencies. The church itself sometimes provided financial relief, support networks, child care, and other services. Churches were places for migrants to come into contact with other African Americans who had been living in the cities for a longer period of time. This contact helped newcomers learn the ways of the city and adapt to their new surroundings.

White Preachers

White preachers were also involved in the battle that raged over Jim Crow. Their responses ranged a full spectrum. Many supported Jim Crow laws. Some tried to stay neutral. Other became heavily involved, even serving jail time and risking personal injury for their involvement. Although white preachers did not become involved in a social movement advancing or denouncing Jim Crow laws to the extent that African American preachers became involved in the Civil Rights Movement, they were involved in the moral confrontation.

The Ku Klux Klan was perhaps the closest white preachers came to being leaders of an organized movement advancing Jim Crow laws. A significant number of Klan leaders were drawn from the ranks of white preachers. Just as African American preachers were drawing on biblical passages, their white counterparts advocating for Jim Crowism also mined the Bible for passages supporting slavery or the social subordination of some groups of people to others. Due to the covert nature of the Klan, preachers' involvement in the group was not explicit, although often implicitly recognized by both African Americans and whites. Other white preachers actively resisted identification with the Klan and said Klansmen were unchristian. Klan members did not leave such denunciations unnoticed, and those who openly condemned the Klan risked retaliation.

White pastors who were sympathetic towards the plight of African Americans were often a point of contact between the Civil Rights Movement and whites in the community. These preachers were able to communicate with both African American civil rights leaders, who were often also preachers. The white pastor could then mediate the message of those leaders to his white congregation. Such sympathetic white pastors sometimes engaged in demonstrations against Jim Crow laws with African Americans, sometimes bearing the brunt of violence inflicted by opposing whites.

Impact

Preachers were involved in the struggle over Jim Crow laws, but their positions were not defined simply by their position. African American pastors, while cautious about opposition in some contexts, were largely involved in the fight against Jim Crow and the battle for civil rights. Their impact is immeasurable. Without the freedoms they had from white employers, countless pastor leaders would never have emerged. They strengthened the Civil Rights Movement from all corners. White preachers also had an impact on the fate of Jim Crow laws. Some viscously defended the codes through the Ku Klux Klan or simply through the power of their pulpit to reinforce ideas of white supremacy among their congregants. Other white preachers just as vehemently opposed the laws, although in a less violent manner than their Klansman opponents. These civil rights supporters tried to sway the hearts of their audiences to sympathize with African Americans, and in some cases these pastors joined movement demonstrations. Overall, regardless of their position on Jim Crow laws, pastors had wide-reaching effects on the battle over Jim Crow. *See also* Catholicism.

Further Readings: Chappell, David. *A Stone of Hope: Prophetic Religion and the Death of Jim Crow.* Chapel Hill: University of North Carolina Press, 2004; Fairclough, Adam. *To Redeem the Soul of America: The Southern Christian Leadership Conference & Martin Luther King, Jr.* Athens: University of Georgia Press, 1987; Packard, Jerome M. *American Nightmare: The History of Jim Crow.* New York: St. Martin's Press, 2002; Sernett, Milton C. *Bound for the Promised Land: African American Religion and the Great Migration.* C. Eric Lincoln Series on the Black Experience. Durham, NC: Duke University Press, 1997.

Shawntel Ensminger

Prisons

Southern prisons during the **Jim Crow** era earned the "dubious distinction" of "America's worst prisons." Jim Crow prisons in the South took various, yet equally brutal forms—a traditional penitentiary, a penal farm, a former slave plantation, brickyards, or temporary road camps. The prisons were erected in forests, swamps, mines, brickyards, or levees, and the convicts were housed in tents, log forts, and rolling cages. Jim Crow punishment existed in two phases, during the leasing era, which ran from 1890 to the 1920s, and then in the state control system, from the 1920s to 1965. Distinctive in the penal history of this era, the use of state prisons to control black population are deeply rooted in the South.

Immediately after the Civil War, Southern states turned to the criminal justice system in order to control the newly freed slave population. They also needed a labor force to repair Civil War damages. Although Southern states had built penitentiaries before the Civil War, most of them were so badly damaged during the war that they were unusable. By the early 1900s, blacks comprised anywhere from 85–95 percent of the prison population, although they comprised no more than half of the total population in the South. Black men, women, and children were summarily convicted and delivered by the local sheriffs to a road camp, penal farm, or, less likely, a penitentiary. Moreover, the penitentiary philosophy—to change prisoners and make them productive citizens—did not fit the Southern perception of their prisoners who were still seen as former slaves and not equipped for reformation and change. The terms "slave," "convict," and "Negro," were interchangeable in the white Southerner's perceptions of blacks after the Civil War.

Leasing

On the surface, leasing appeared to address the issues of prisoner security and safety at a minimum cost to the state. Southern states, including **Florida, Texas, Louisiana, Arkansas, Mississippi, Alabama, Georgia,** and Tennessee, turned to a variety of leasing arrangements with private individuals and companies, wherein the state turned over the whole prison operation to a private entrepreneur. **Virginia** never leased its convicts, and the Carolinas did so tentatively and for a short time only. Some states expected the contractor to pay some amount to the state. Others literally gave away complete responsibility for the state prisoners without any monetary or state supervisory expectations; one state even paid the lessee to take the prisoners. Often states signed leases with one individually or organization.

Soon, the leasing of convicts became one of the most exploitative aspects of the prison system during Jim Crow. Prisoners were leased to build railroads, levees, and roads; to work in mines, brickyards, and turpentine camps; and to do agricultural work on former plantations. Conditions under the leasing system were particularly brutal and deadly. Since the lessees did not own the prisoners, they often did not care about their welfare. The life expectancy of convicts in the lease system ranged from 7–10 years. Prisoners died of overwork or of violence from the guards or each other, and an ever-growing population of black convicts allowed for the quick replacement of prisoners.

Leasing came to an end by the 1920s for a variety of reasons. In some states, it was no longer economical. In others, railroad building subsided, and road building was generally designated to local governments. Some states had a penitentiary that they used. As it was purported that many companies who leased prisoners had made millions, other states resumed control hoping such large profits would ensue to the state. Still, the change was not fueled by humanitarian concern for the prisoners. Instead, Southern states switched from leasing to chain gangs and prisons in order to transfer manufactured goods via convict labor to the public sector.

Penal Farm Model

After the 1920s, the two most common forms of punishment systems were the penal farms and the chain gangs. The penal farm is the most notorious type of prison system in the South. More than an agricultural production center, the penal farm followed the plantation model of imprisonment. It incorporated both a structure and philosophy of slave plantations, reinforcing black inferiority and subservience to white planters and prison guards. Though they emphasized economy and agricultural work, the penal farm used isolation and neglect of rehabilitation to break down the mostly black prisoners and inculcate convicts with a sense of worthlessness. The purest form of the plantation model of imprisonment emerged in Arkansas, Louisiana, Mississippi, and Texas. Louisiana and Mississippi eventually established one geographical location for its penal farms, while Arkansas used two and Texas used multiple sites. Angola, Louisiana, is now 18,000 acres, while Parchman, Mississippi, was once 20,000 acres. The two farms in Arkansas, Tucker for white convicts and Cummins for black women and men, were located on 4,500 acres and 16,600 acres, respectively.

Although the type of agricultural work has varied through the years, depending upon the economy, natural disasters, and technological developments, the majority of prisoners at these farms have worked in the fields. To this day, prisoners admitted to Angola must spend their first 90 days in the fields. The geographical isolation of these farms also served multiple functions. Largely kept out of the public eye, isolation of the prison led to the horrific conditions. On occasion, news reports would filter out and reach the national press. Investigating committees would visit and make recommendations, most often to no avail. No fewer than five recommendations, beginning in the 1930s, were made to move the women prisoners out of Angola. They were not moved until 1961, and not removed from Angola's administration until almost a decade later.

The prevailing belief about the limits of rehabilitation helped maintain bad conditions. Neither state nor federal courts interfered with prison business until the late 1960s. Furthermore, agricultural work was believed to be suited to the limited ability of the imprisoned classes, mostly African Americans and Mexican Americans. Such practices had the effect of perpetuating segregation, as black and Mexican American prisoners were then limited to agricultural work once they were released. The emphasis on maximizing product, coupled with the long-held beliefs about black inferiority, precluded the development of a reform movement or rehabilitation of prisoners.

Convict Road Gang

Spurred by the "good road" movement of the 1920s, chain gangs and road gangs emerged all throughout the South. Generally, county criminal justice agencies oversaw the Southern road gangs, also known as chain gangs. For example, the state of Alabama ran the chain gang system. Alabama's road gang was initially all-black, and even when some white prisoners were introduced they were always a minority in both number and proportion of convicts, and they were maintained in separate camps. Conditions were hard and exploitative; discipline was often brutal, but not as deadly as under the lease system. Guards routinely whipped prisoners with a three-inch strap, until Alabama outlawed the practice in 1962. Initially, men were housed in portable wooden barracks and sometimes rolling cages. By the mid-1930s, road camps were standardized with wooden buildings that included dormitories, with showers, a mess hall kitchen, and hot and cold running water.

Gender and Race in Southern Prison Systems

States immediately classified all inmates upon their entrance into the system. They were separated according to age, gender, and dangerousness of offense. These classification systems in the South were consistent with assumptions about race and echoed nineteenth-century notions about gendered divisions of labor. Usually, young black male prisoners were sent to do the most strenuous work tasks on the plantation prisons and road gangs, while white prisoners were sent to do industrial or clerical jobs. Both black and white women worked in gender-specific jobs such as washing and sewing uniforms. When needed, however, black women worked alongside the men in the fields, whereas white women usually did no fieldwork. Initially, Louisiana classified prisoners into four categories, beginning with first-class men (almost entirely black) who were assigned to the most arduous labor, and ending with fourth-class men, who were assigned to the hospital. Almost all white men and women were classified as fourth class, although some white men worked on the plantations and levee camps as clerks. When the crop demanded it, all classes of prisoners labored in fields, particularly during the sugar harvest.

Gendered divisions of labor were also segregated. Black women served as cooks, laundresses, and seamstresses exclusively. They also hoed sugar cane stumps and sorted tobacco leaves in the tobacco barn. During leasing in Alabama, black women worked alongside black men in lumber camps, mining camps, and rock quarries. White women sewed uniforms and bedding, or worked in the canneries. Mississippi employed both black and white women as trustees armed with rifles.

The system of Jim Crow in the prison system rationalized that African Americans and Mexican Americans had limited abilities and could do only physical labor. Since black and Mexican American convicts numbered in the majority of prisoners, Alabama, for example, not only used the bulk of the black male population to create the convict road labor force; they designated the convicts on the road gangs to do the most strenuous maintenance work. Black convicts did the weed cutting, shoulder work on the paved roads, and the most arduous work of all—breaking and crushing rock in the quarries, while the free white laborers working alongside them operated the heavy equipment and the trucks. Although it was in use only from 1883 until 1917, one penitentiary in Texas held only white men, and the inmates worked entirely in factories. The Louisiana penitentiary in Baton Rouge housed mainly white men who made the prisoners' uniforms and sewed flags.

Organization and Security

With a structure similar to an antebellum plantation, Southern prisons in Jim Crow amassed several thousand black workers supervised by a small group of rural lower-class whites, who, in turn, worked directly under the direction of sheriffs and wardens. Convicts worked from sunup to sundown, or as they said, from "can to can't." Plagued by boll weevils, floods, and other natural disasters, many Southern states had not made the anticipated profits since the state took over from the lease system. In a cost savings measure, they turned to the "trusty" convict system. Paid guards were fired and convicts would guard other convicts.

The use of trustees also extended to the living quarters in the prison camp. On the Parchment, Mississippi, prison plantation, prisoners were housed in a number of camps. Each camp had one sergeant, and two assistant sergeants. The sergeant was equivalent to the slave plantation's overseer. He was in charge of the work schedules, disciplining the convicts, and setting the work routine. One assistant sergeant oversaw the fields and functioned as the driver. Called the "rider" in Arkansas, he determined the work quota for the men in the fields. The other assistant sergeant was responsible for the barracks. A number of trusty-shooters watched over the regular convicts, known as gun-men, (rank-men in Arkansas) who worked in the fields. In most circumstances, trusty-shooters and gunmen did not communicate with each other.

Guards and wardens heavily supervised male convicts working in the fields. A typical scenario called for two "high-powers" armed with carbines on horseback and at least three pairs of "shotguns" on foot accompanying the line at different intervals. Usually one pair of guards stood watch some distance from the rear in case of trouble. All these guards were prisoners, or what are commonly called convict-guards. The convict-guards had different ranks and concomitant levels of power, dependent upon the type of prison and work that they supervised. Convict-guards also may have had the ticket to their own release. Occasionally, a convict-guard who shot an escaping prisoner could be rewarded with his freedom. When the federal courts intervened in prison business in the early 1970s, the convict guard or trusty system was declared the worst abuse of power maintained in the Southern prisons.

Treatment and Discipline

Punishment in the penitentiaries, penal farms, and road gangs was brutal and occasionally deadly. Death rates were staggeringly high during leasing. For instance, 216 prisoners died during 1896 in Louisiana, nearly 20 percent of the 1,152 prisoners in the state. Yet in Louisiana State Penitentiary's Biennial Report of the Board of Control for the years 1896–1897, Warden W. H. Reynaud claimed no responsibility for the 1896 death rate but only the 6 percent death rate in 1897, maintaining that he was not appointed warden until August 1896. Since the majority of the prisoners were leased out, his argument that there were no deaths under his watch was correct only in abstract. Prisoners spoke of killings that happened in camps that were almost hidden away. Scandals of prisoners being beaten to death by sadistic whipping bosses emerged in the other Southern states. Although mortality rates generally fell after the states took control of their prisoners, stories continued about cruel treatment, torture, and beatings under state control, sometimes administered by convict guards and sometimes free guards. Although figures are not available for Alabama convict mortality rates, the convicts were susceptible to horrific mining disasters. One of the most famous, the Banner Coal Mine tragedy resulted in 122 convict deaths.

Corporal punishment was the most common penalty for infractions; it was also most often applied without concern for the welfare of the convict. Leather straps known as "Black Annie" in Mississippi and "Old Caesar" in Texas were used for the whippings. Mississippi's "Black Annie" was three feet long and six inches wide. In one year alone, there were 1,547 floggings at Angola, with a total of 23,889 blows. Generally, guards administered whippings on the convict's bare flesh. Men and women alike were required to remove their shirts and/or pull down their pants for the lashings. In order to strike fear or to maintain strict order, guards dispensed punishments in public, requiring convicts to count the number of stripes out loud and in unison.

Prisoners' Resistance

Although they lived under conditions of extreme oppression, Southern prisoners did not always cooperate with the authorities. They used both covert and overt techniques to resist. Whether in penitentiaries, on the plantation prisons or road gangs, prisoners stole, committed arson, faked illness, engaged in sabotage, horribly mutilated themselves, participated in riots and work stoppages, and escaped. Escapes were exceptionally high under the leasing system, as opportunities in the camps and on the farms were greater than inside the penitentiary walls. For instance, from 1872 to 1874, 881 convicts entered the Tennessee prison system. During the same time, 95 escaped. Prisoners, primarily white prisoners, wrote memoirs and some wrote letters to the press revealing the horrible conditions under which they lived and worked. Other prisoners used collective action to start riots.

Although there were few incidents labeled as "riots" in the South, a series of incidents took place that forced authorities to reform conditions. In the "heel-slashing incident" of the early 1950s, 37 white prisoners at Angola, Louisiana, cut their Achilles tendons over two separate occasions to protest work conditions and fears that they would be beaten to death if they went out to the field. In 1935, a group of white Texas prisoners maimed themselves, two by chopping off a lower leg entirely. Self-mutilations became more common over the next decade or more in Texas. The Texas prisoners stated the same reasons that the Louisiana prisoners did—they were afraid of being beaten to death in the fields because they could not make it under the grueling work conditions.

Prisoners also resisted using covert techniques. On the plantation prisons and on the road gangs, convicts used work songs to accompany gang work.

Work songs were used exclusively by African American male prisoners. Although black women sang prison songs, there is no record of them using the songs in the fields as the men did. Prison songs functioned to pass the time, pace the work, and provide safety while doing dangerous tasks and gave the men some control over their daily lives. Convicts could protest by singing things that could not be said in ordinary conversation. They expressed tension, frustration, and anger.

Work songs had a structure, the call-response pattern. The "caller," or work group leader, shouted a phrase and the gang responded. In this manner, the leader slowed down the pace when he noticed that some of the men were having trouble keeping up with the work. All the men had to keep up at the same rate, or they would be beaten. The songs regulated the pace of the teams and the strokes of the axes so that they would not cut each other's limbs. A good work song leader did not necessarily have to have a good voice, but he had to be loud. He also had to know the work and the ability of the men on his gang in order to guide them from sunup to sundown without being injured or beaten.

Gender and Housing

Even as separate women's facilities (reformatories) were being built for women up north, between 1870 and 1930, there were no women's reformatories in the Southern states. In Southern penitentiaries, women could be found anywhere from cells at the end of a male cell block, to a cell block of their own, to a building of their own, which sometimes was located close to the male buildings and sometimes further away. Women remained under the administration of the men's institution well into the 1960s.

During the leasing era and under state control, women were sent to the plantations, mining camps, railroads and road gangs. Sometimes they worked alongside the men. Other times, a small group of female convicts cooked and washed for the leased men. When sharing penal farms with men, the women were particularly vulnerable to physical brutality and sexual assault from prison guards and male convicts. On the plantation prisons, women were housed at a separate camp, situated some distance from the men's camps. However, the security was quite lax, and there was considerable unsupervised interaction between the men and women. Prisoners' memoirs report that men and women met each other in all kinds of secluded places on the prison grounds. At Angola, they met in the sugar cane fields when the cane was tall enough.

Although a married couple was often assigned to supervise the women's camps, the husband often had single unsupervised control over the women. Men supervised women in their work places—the fields, the sewing rooms, and in the canneries. Angola's punishment reports reveal that men administered floggings to the female convicts on their bare backs and breasts. Finally when women worked in the fields alongside men, they were required to answer the call of nature right there in the fields in front of the men.

Further Readings: Ayers, Edward L. *Vengeance & Justice. Crime and Punishment in the 19th-Century American South.* New York: Oxford University Press, 1984; Carleton, Mark T. *Politics and Punishment. The History of the Louisiana State Penal System.* Baton Rouge:

Louisiana State University Press, 1971; Mancini, Matthew. *One Dies, Get Another. Convict Leasing in the American South.* Columbia: University of South Carolina Press, 1996; Oshinsky, David M. *"Worse Than Slavery": Parchman Farm and the Ordeal of Jim Crow Justice.* New York: The Free Press. 1996; Rafter, Nicole Hahn. *Partial Justice: Women, Prisons and Social Control.* New Brunswick, NJ: Transaction Press. 1990.

Marianne Fisher-Giorlando

R

Racial Customs and Etiquette

Racial customs and etiquette predated the period generally designated as the **Jim Crow** era. The forced physical separation of blacks and whites associated with the period began and ended in the North before the Civil War and pervaded the West and Midwest throughout the period of westward expansion in the United States. Jim Crow was legalized in the South by the **U.S. Supreme Court** in *Plessy v. Ferguson* (1896), which declared "**separate but equal**" to be constitutional and permitted the segregation of blacks and whites on **railroads** in **Louisiana**. The ruling provided a legal basis for the development of intricate rules of behavior that applied to all areas of life. Their collective design was to reinforce white supremacy and relegate blacks to second-class citizenship. Such customs varied according to gender, geography, hue, and social climate, and they were more rigidly followed in public situations than in private ones. But they were applied to all known African Americans regardless of their educational or social standing. Given the debilitating, even humiliating, nature of these rules, African Americans sought legal and creative ways to counter their negative social, political, and economic impact. They also made a sustained effort to curb, if not altogether neutralize, the psychological impact of such customs, especially on black children.

Everyday Life

As Jim Crow laws were initiated with systems of transportation, many of the first rules of etiquette emerged in this area and quickly expanded to include other public spaces where blacks and whites encountered each other from day to day. Regardless of social position, identifiably black passengers were forced to ride in Jim Crow cars, which were often unclean and lacked the comforts of those carrying white passengers. When separate accommodations were not possible, as was sometimes the case with city buses, blacks were to sit at the back of the bus. They were also expected to relinquish their seats if whites exceeded the capacity of the section provided for them. In places of business, whites were served first even if black customers were the first to arrive. Black customers were not allowed to try on certain clothing items, particularly shoes, nor could they return such items once purchased because white store

"Members of the Race Find It Hard to Get Waited On," 1916

African American men and women found that race discrimination hindered good service at a prominent Chicago department store, Marshall Fields.

It has been will known that Marshall Field & Co., although considered as the world's greatest department store, had nothing for the Race man nor woman to do since the daughter of the founder of the store fell in love with his coachmen, and after the affair had been discouraged by the father, later gave birth to a child, it is alleged, and since then the family has been against our race. It will well be remembered that the son was supposed to have been shot in the red light district.

Many of their customers have been members of the race, however, but here of late they find it hard to be waited on and that the clerks are indifferent, complaints made to floor walkers have been ignored. The Defender sent two ladies down to investigate. One was so fair that they could not tell that any African blood was in her veins and the other was just the opposite. The first place visited was the main floor and the floorwalker told her that the articles would be found in the basement. Miss A. followed a moment later and asked for the same article and she was directed to the floors above. Getting out of the sight of the informer they both went to the basement. Standing there for several moments the Miss A. was waited upon. No one paid any attention to Miss B.

Finally, a floorwalker named Mr. Simpson, a little, insignificant, bald headed fellow came and asked all those who were standing around, "Are you being waited upon?" with the exception of Miss B. nor asked her what she wanted.

The same two ladies went to the other part of the store. Miss A. was again served, but Miss B. stood there, all the clerks ignoring her. Finally, having orders from this office to see how far a man whom the clerks called Mr. Waller or Wallace; he said he would find her someone to take care of her, but he disappeared and never returned for about thirty minutes. Seeing that she was getting provoked he said, "Have you been standing her all this time?" Miss A. was waiting and timing the affair. Mr. G. was sent to the glove counter; he was ignored. The clerks, going around on the other side, and there engaging in a conversation with other clerks. He went to the floorwalker and was informed that he could not expect the clerks to hurry as it was warm and they were working pretty hard. So noticeable has this state of affairs become that we print the following from a local white journal: Marshall Field's Draw Drastic "Color Line."

The Colored population of Chicago was handed a severe shock this week by an order issued from the management's office at Marshall Field's that this class of trade was to be treated with "indifference" whenever they made their appearance as prospective buyers on the main floor or above and were to be directed to the basement by all sales-persons as the most likely place where they could find the articles they desired to purchase.

Embodied in the same order were the directions to the help in the basement to show Colored patrons "inattention" and treat them in a manner indicative of the fact that their trade was not desired.

It is particularly noteworthy that the order was not put in the form of writing but was carried by a special messenger by word of mouth to each one of the department heads.

Source: Chicago Defender, June 10, 1916.

owners feared that whites would not buy products that had been worn by blacks.

In public hospitals, blacks and whites were cared for in separate wards. Black nurses were permitted to care for white patients, but never the reverse, although white doctors were permitted to treat black patients in the colored sections of segregated hospitals. Racial custom nonetheless dictated that white doctors refrain from showing compassion when treating black patients. Blacks in need of blood transfusions were never to be given blood from whites. The reverse was also true. Black writers of the era, and those who wrote fictional works set during the Jim Crow period, often believed this deleterious act captured the quintessence of racism. Lillian Bertha Horace's *Angie Brown* (1949) opens with the death of the protagonist's child, which occurred because the hospital refused to give blood that had been drawn from whites to a black child. Similarly, Toni Morrison's *Song of Solomon* (1978) opens with a black woman in labor in front of "No Mercy Hospital," the name members of the black community gave the hospital because of its treatment of blacks.

Race and Sex

An elaborate set of customs governed intimate relations between blacks and whites during the Jim Crow era. **Thomas Dixon**'s novel *The Clansman* (1905) and the subsequent movie based on it, ***The Birth of a Nation*** (1915), underscored and reinforced white men's profound fear of interracial mixing, namely between black men and white women, as many white men continued to maintain intimate relationships with black women after the emancipation. Rules on interracial relationships were never applied as strictly to white men as they were to black men during the Jim Crow era.

Black males, regardless of the age, were not to even look at white women, nor were they to touch them. Even an accidental brush was considered to be a serious offense. If a black man saw a white woman approaching on a sidewalk, he was to step off the sidewalk until the woman passed. Black men and boys were beaten, castrated, tarred, feathered, and lynched for purportedly getting out their place with white women. Black men had to stay on constant alert for their safety, especially if a white woman in the vicinity had purportedly been raped. White men, on the other hand, engaged in intimate relations with black women without prosecution or public controversy.

White women who maintained intimate relationships with black men were in danger of social ostracism or disinheritance. When pregnancy resulted, the babies were generally aborted or given up for adoption. Many white women whose affairs with black men were discovered cried rape to protect themselves from disgrace or public censure. Gwendolyn Brooks's "Ballad of Pearl May Lee" (1945) offers one of the most riveting presentations of the peril black men faced when they dared have an affair with white women.

Publicly, white men went to great lengths to protect white female purity, but privately, many continued to have intimate relationships with black women, and they did so without prosecution or public controversy. Such relationships were often explored by black and white fiction writers of the period, with the story usually ending in tragedy. Real life examples also abounded, with one of the most famous cases involving Senator Strom Thurmond, a staunch segregationist, who fathered a daughter, Essie Mae Washington, by a black maid. Given the historic vulnerability of black women to sexual aggression, many black parents from emancipation onwards set out to educate their daughters to preclude their having to "work in a white woman's kitchen," where they were often targets of sexual aggression.

Rural and Urban Areas

In the rural Jim Crow South, racial etiquette was highly articulated and localized. Because most rural black Southerners were farmers, sharecroppers, or tenants, the landlord-tenant relationship shaped most interactions. As a result, segregation, economic exploitation, and oppression were more pronounced in rural areas than in cities.

As the racial composition of towns ranged from predominantly white to predominantly black, variations on the theme existed. In predominantly black towns or predominantly black sections of predominantly white towns, racial etiquette was namely important when occasional white visitors came for various purposes or when blacks ventured outside a given predominantly black enclave. Writer and anthropologist Zora Neale Hurston often gave primacy to such places in her creative writings. Some predominantly white towns were off limits to blacks. Custom, if not the law, precluded blacks' entering them. Sometimes warning signs were posted on the outskirts of towns to discourage black visitors, such as "Niggers, read and run." Even though there were no laws insisting that blacks not enter, custom dictated as much. Blacks learned from experience and by word of mouth which places were off limits.

Boundaries were less rigid in other rural spaces. Country stores, rural roads, and cotton gins were usually not segregated. Certain recreational activities were also not segregated. Young black and white men sometimes drank and gambled together at cockfights, saloons, and card games. At mutual aid events, white landowners and black hired hands frequently worked together as white farm wives and black domestics prepared meals for the laborers. But in such cases, racial etiquette was decidedly pronounced. African Americans had limited access to most small-town retail shops, but some business, such as barbershops that served whites, were out of bounds. Different from cities, most rural towns had few buses, hotels, or restaurants, all of which provided distinct stages for blacks and whites to play their prescribed roles.

Whites in rural and urban areas generally withheld everyday courtesies from blacks. They did not invite blacks to their homes as guests. Black workers and domestics had to go to the back door of whites' houses, although this rule was not universally applied. Visits and courtesy were avoided because they implied equality, a concept contrary to the racial hierarchy that Jim Crow was designed to reinforce. Whites insisted that blacks use titles that showed deference or respect. Black men and women were to address white men and women as "Sir" and "Ma'am" respectively. In less formal situations, black men might also refer to white men of standing as "boss" or "cap'n" without fear of reprisal. Whites, on the other hand, were never to address black men respectfully. Black men regardless of social standing were addressed by their first names or called "boy" "nigger," or "niggra," a polite substitute for the aforementioned derogatory term. Black men were often called by any name a white interlocutor might conjure on a moment's notice, with the name "Jack" being one of the most common substitutes.

White women sometimes permitted their black servants and acquaintances to address them by their first names, but only if they prefaced the name with the title "Miss." Black women, on the other hand, were never addressed respectfully as "Miss" or "Mrs." The term "wench," which dated back to **slavery**, still appeared in some legal documents during the Jim Crow period. Although educated whites sometimes referred to black women collectively as "colored ladies," black women were generally referred to as "auntie," "girl," "gal," or by their first names, which black women generally resented. Texas native Lillian Bertha Horace, an educator and writer, noted in her diary that she felt "hurt, indignant, disgusted" when the greeting in a "long formal letter on definite business" opened "Dear Lilly."

White men were careful not to publicly perform any courteous act that hinted that they treated black women like "ladies," a category reserved for white women. They refrained from such polite habits as addressing black women respectfully as "Miss" or "Mrs.," carrying or lifting heavy packages for black women, helping them into street cars, holding doors open for black women and allowing them to enter ahead first, tipping or removing their hats in the presence of black women, or retrieving on their behalf an item that might have fallen to the floor or ground. The lack of courtesy often approached outright discourtesy.

Educational Institutions

Educational institutions were largely segregated in the Jim Crow South, but black and white educators and administrators still had occasion to interact with each other, particularly during summer certification periods and campus visitations by white supervisors. White officials visiting black schools were often strict, intimidating, and critical as opposed to helpful. Even beyond the South, black students and scholars were not spared the inconveniences of race. In educational institutions in which blacks were admitted, they were often not acknowledged by their professors. Some white professors summarily failed black students, while others never granted black students a grade above "C." The few black scholars who found semipermanent posts at universities outside the South often could not dine in university faculty clubs, nor could they find hotel accommodations when they traveled to professional meetings. Black students, particularly those involved in extracurricular activities such as debate and athletics, faced the same dilemma. Professor Thomas Freeman and members of the Texas Southern University's highly acclaimed debate team had to establish living accommodations with families and religious organizations whenever they had to travel to competitions in the United States. Students, including Barbara Jordan, eventually the first congresswoman in the United States, were coached to maintain their dignity despite the bias they faced.

U.S. Military

Racist customs and etiquette also impacted blacks in the U.S. military, whose unique position as defenders of the nation and its democratic ideals made their sustained encounter with white supremacy particularly unsettling. Black men in uniform instilled pride in African Americans who appreciated the significance of their sacrifice but incited deep resentment in whites committed to white supremacy. One of the most famous photographs of the Jim Crow era captures in still frame the lynched body of an African American soldier in uniform hanging from a noose in the midst of a crowd of jeering, angry whites.

The deep-seated resentment of white civilians was also evident on military bases, where black men were never treated as equals to white soldiers. They were in segregated units, attended separate training schools, and lived in segregated facilities. They were generally limited to service and supply units and were not allowed to command white officers. They also had to bear with the indignities stemming from legalized subjugation. They were often called "nigger" and other derogatory names by their superiors, often mistreated, and generally subject to much harsher reprimand than their white counterparts. The **Houston Riot of 1917** is perhaps the most historic event underscoring the tension that permeated such environments. The riot erupted on August 23, 1917, when black soldiers of the 24th Infantry, then stationed in Houston, **Texas**, armed themselves and challenged the beating of two fellow soldiers by local police. The event resulted in the largest court-martial held in the United States.

Black women in the U.S. military were denied equal treatment as well. They entered the U.S. military first as nurses, with Civil War nurse Susie King Taylor being among the first to record her experiences. During the Spanish American War, most of the 32 black women recruited as nurses were sent to Santiago, Cuba, in July and August 1898, where they rendered service during the worst years of a yellow fever epidemic. Some black nurses were contracted by the surgeon general to serve in the Spanish-American War. Five black graduate nurses joined the army, according to records at the Tuskegee Institute. Black women nurses were also recruited from various hospitals and training centers in Chicago, Illinois; New Orleans, Louisiana; and Washington, DC.

During **World War I**, many black nurses hoped to increase their chances of serving in the Army or Naval Nurse Corps by joining the American Red Cross. Eighteen black Red Cross nurses were offered assignments in Illinois and Ohio not long after the Armistice, but the end of the war precluded the planned assignment of black nurses to other camps. Those who served were limited to caring for German prisoners of war and black soldiers. By August 1919, all were released from duty.

During **World War II**, black women were permitted to join the nurse course, but their number was limited to 56. On June 25, 1941, President **Franklin D. Roosevelt**'s Executive Order 8802 established the Fair Employment Practices Commission, which initiated the eradication of racial discrimination in the U.S. military. In June 1943, Congresswoman Frances Payne of Ohio introduced an amendment to the Nurse Training Bill to eradicate racial bias. Black women's enrollment in the Cadet Nurse Corps quickly mushroomed to 2,000.

In July 1944, the quota for black army nurses was eliminated, and on January 24, 1945, the U.S. Navy opened its doors to black women. Black women were also enlisted in the Women's Army Auxiliary Corps (WAAC), eventually renamed the Women's Army Corps (WAC), which employed 6,520 black women during the war. Black women also joined the Navy WAVES (Women Accepted for Volunteer Emergency Service) and the Coast Guard SPARS (derived from the Coast Guard motto "Semper Paratus," Latin for "Always Ready"). Similar to black men, black women were assigned to segregated living quarters, ate at separate tables, received segregated training, and used separate recreational facilities. They were not allowed to serve white American soldiers until intervention from **Eleanor Roosevelt**.

Impact on Black Children

Racial etiquette and customs impacted the lives of black children as well. They learned the rules governing black and white relations by observation and through conversations with their parents and others. For example, Helen Green, the first black woman admitted into Methodist Hospital of the Dallas School of Professional Nursing, as a child wondered why the white woman whom her mother helped with canning never came to their house, especially given that Green's family had at least more space in their front yard for her and the white woman's little girl to play. She also wondered why the little girl always insisted on naming the games, creating the rules, and changing them for her benefit. Green essentially did not enjoy visits to the white woman's house because she was under constant pressure to be careful. The lessons she and other black children learned directly and indirectly were never easy to receive and were often painfully applied. The often repeated statement "if I don't beat you, the white man will kill you" reflected the rationale some black parents living in Jim Crow cultures used to teach their children respect and even fear of authority, especially given that the ultimate face of authority was white.

Black parents nonetheless found creative ways to insist on a modicum of respect for their children by using titles as first names for their son and daughters, including "King," "Prince," "President," "Princess," "Queen," and "Duke." Others attempted to counter the psychological impact of sustained racism on their daughters by giving them black dolls to help them develop self-respect from their earliest days. Black parents, especially those of aspiring, middle and elite classes, attempted to instill racial pride and "race love" in their children by surrounding them with positive images of blacks, including pictures and Sunday School cards depicting black characters.

Collective Reactions

Many African Americans masked their displeasure with the racial etiquette and customs when in the company of whites. But they expressed their discontent in private, in their personal writings or via the black press. The tenor of such relationships continued to change over time. Black domestics of the early twentieth century, for example, did not demonstrate the same deference to whites in public that their enslaved foremothers had shown, and subsequent generations of blacks found it increasingly difficult to respect the rules. Many even resorted to mocking them, sometimes with deadly results, as in the case of **Emmett Till**. With the help of early black activist scholars, professionals, professional organizations, fraternities, sororities, lodges, clubs, and churches, African Americans and their supporters eventually challenged the legal foundation of Jim Crow, the dismantling of which led to a gradual dissolution of the racial customs and etiquette that legalized discrimination had spawned. *See also* Armed Forces; Humor and Comedic Traditions; Minstrelsy; Polite Terms, Epithets, and Labels.

Further Readings: Brooks, Gwendolyn. *A Street in Bronzeville.* New York: Harper and Row, 1945; Delany, Sarah L., and A. Elizabeth Delany, with Amy Hill Hearth. *Having Our Say: Delany Sisters' First 100 Years.* New York: Dell, 1994; Green, Helen. *East Texas*

Daughter. Fort Worth: Texas Christian University Press, 2003; Franklin, John Hope. *Mirror to America: The Autobiography of John Hope Franklin*. New York: Farrar, Straus and Giroux, 2005; Haynes, Robert V. *A Night of Violence: The Houston Riot of 1917*. Baton Rouge: Louisiana State University Press, 1976; Johnson, Kevin R. "The Legacy of Jim Crow: The Enduring Taboo of Black-White Romance." *Texas Law Review* 84, no. 3 (February 2006): 739–66. http://www.utexas.edu/law/journals/tlr/abstracts/84/84 johnson.pdf (accessed September 2007); Jones, Jacqueline. *Labor of Love, Labor of Sorrow: Black Women, Work and the Family from Slavery to the Present*. New York: Vintage Books, 1995; Kossie-Chernyshev, Karen, ed. *Angie Brown*. Acton, MA: Copley Custom Publishing, 2008; Kossie-Chernyshev, Karen, ed. *Diary of Lillian B. Horace*. New York: Pearson Custom Publishing, 2007; Love, Spencie. *One Blood, The Death and Resurrection of Charles R. Drew*. Chapel Hill: University of North Carolina Press, 1996; McGuire, Phillip, ed. *Taps for a Jim Crow Army: Letters from Black Soldiers in World War II*. Lexington: University of Kentucky Press, 1993; Mitchell, Michele. *Righteous Propagation: African Americans and the Politics of Racial Destiny after Reconstruction*. Chapel Hill: University of North Carolina Press, 2004; Patterson, Tiffany Ruby. *Zora Neale Hurston and a History of Southern Life*. Philadelphia: Temple University Press, 2005; Sheldon, Kathryn S. "Brief History of Black Women in the Military." Women in Military Service for America Foundation Web site, http://womensmemorial.org/Education/ BBH1998.html#2 (accessed September 2007); Walker, Melissa. "Shifting Boundaries: Race Relations in the Rural Jim Crow South." In *African American Life in the Rural South, 1900–1950*, edited by R. Douglas Hurt, 81–107. Columbia: University of Missouri Press, 2003.

Karen Kossie-Chernyshev

Racial Stereotypes

Racial stereotypes of African Americans prevalent in the United States during the Jim Crow era (circa 1877–1954) included gender-specific distorted images of the black man and black woman as well as generalized caricatures of the black child. The predominant **Jim Crow**–era stereotypes of the black adult male fall into two broad categories: a constellation of caricatures that were derived from the buffoonish **slavery**-era Sambo figure and a host of variations on the violent, threatening, and sexually menacing figure known as the Savage. The most prevalent black adult female stereotypes included variations on both the fat, pitch-black, desexualized, matriarchal Mammy, and the mulatto, a light-complexioned, sexual temptress or Jezebel figure. Black children, male and female alike, were caricaturized as pickanninies or undesirable ruffians, ragamuffins, and street urchins.

Black Male Stereotypes

The Sambo caricature, originally created by the slaveowning plantocracy of the antebellum South, characterized the typical slave as happy-go-lucky, childish, docile, lazy, irresponsible, and dependent upon and loyal to his master, and thus justified the institution of slavery. The stereotype suggested that black slaves were content with their lot and that the infantile race benefited from their bondage to paternalistic white masters. The silly-acting Sambo, frequently depicted in cartoon form as a tattered, grinning, watermelon-eating fool, was considered by whites as a lovable if exasperating figure and a sharp contrast to the feared and hated Savage or Brute, a rival stereotype that emerged during **Reconstruction**. While the Sambo represented "happy darkies in their place," the Savage or Brute represented the danger of emancipated African savages running wild and wreaking havoc on white civilization—as depicted in **D. W. Griffith**'s 1915 film *The Birth of a Nation* by a lusting marauding black male, chasing after a pristine white woman considered the epitome of Southern femininity, who prefers leaping from a cliff to her death rather than submitting to the ignominy of interracial rape.

Both the Sambo and the Savage were representations of the purported biological inferiority of blacks. Yet, in fact, they were polar archetypes of the white imagination: the Savage being the repository of white nightmares, fears, and anxieties concerning a black uprising (such as the Nat Turner rebellion), and the Sambo being the embodiment of white dreams and aspirations to transform enslaved Africans into a race of harmless, humble, servile, comedic entertainers. Sambo became the preeminent entertainer on the American stage (although most often depicted by whites in blackface), the "American Jester," differing from traditional medieval court jesters in the fact that he never embodied the principle of sagacity feigning as foolery (the wise man or political satirist playing the part of the fool) but only foolery. In a society made up of immigrants, each ethnic group aspiring to climb the the ladder of the social hierarchy was made the butt of humor and stereotype, a hazing prior to eventual acceptance as an equal first-class American citizens. Irish, Italians, Poles, Jews and other ethnic Americans were all roasted on the national stage before they earned their credentials as white Americans. But as the national jester, the butt of national humor, the perennial outsider and outcast, the perpetual "Other," and permanent second-class citizen in the American ethnoracial hierarchy, the African American stereotype of Sambo, was never outdone or even matched by any of other comedic ethnic stereotypes.

In contrast to the split American stereotypes of the Sambo and the Savage, in Caribbean slave societies, the two polarities were meshed into a single stereotype known as Quashee. According to the stereotype, Quashee frequently would play the fool, giving rise to such **Caribbean** expressions as "Quashee-fool," but from time to time, he exhibited a "dark side" of his personality, a menacing, murderous, rebellious aspect. In the United States, whites, preferring to emphasize their social aspirations for blacks rather than their social apprehensions about them, created dual images rather than a fusion stereotype, highlighting the desired Sambo while downplaying the reprehensible Savage.

The comedic Sambo archetype appeared in a number of variations under several monikers, e.g., "Old Black Joe," "Uncle Ned," "Rastus," "Boy" to cite but a few. Joseph Boskin states that Sambo was the "pre-eminent" caricature, and quips that he was a sort of "first among unequals." Most distorted images of blacks were descendants, relatives or permutations of Sambo. The term "Jim Crow," derived from a phrase in a ditty associated with an early minstrel dance, was one such variant appellation of Sambo. By extension, Jim Crow became an epithet referring to all black people; later the term "Jim Crow laws" became a euphemism for segregation laws enacted against blacks, and eventually the term Jim Crow was used by blacks and whites alike as a synonym for segregation.

Much of the nomenclature and many of the images came from the world of advertising: for example, Uncle Ben, his female counterpart, Aunt Jemima, and the Cream of Wheat Man. Two early caricatures related to the Sambo constellation were the Uncle and the Coon. The Uncle was a plantation-based stereotype of an elder slave. Still considered a buffoon and the butt of jokes, the Uncle was accorded a small measure of veneration in comparison to other slaves, because of his advanced years. The Coon, or Zip Coon, was a stereotype that first emerged in antebellum America in the North where there were concentrated populations of free blacks. Zip Coon's dress was characterized by absurd dandyism and his speech, a ludicrous attempt at erudite exposition, was full of grammatical errors, malapropisms, spoonerisms, and other uproarious mispronunciations. Sambo and Zip Coon were contrasting yet paired images, the first representing, as stated above, happy darkies in their place, and the second representing the utter failure of blacks to adapt to freedom and Western civilization. While decidedly different in their alleged temperaments, both the distorted image of the murderous raping Savage, and that of the foppish, bumbling but innocuous Coon reinforced the notion that people of African descent were unfit for freedom and equality.

It has been argued that the Sambo constellation of stereotypes was omnipresent throughout the American landscape, North and South, from the seventeenth century until its demise in the late twentieth century, but other scholars emphasize that Sambo was initially a figure of regional Southern lore that finally crossed over into mainstream American culture with the publication, in 1898, of Helen Bannerman's illustrated children's book, *The Story of Little Black Sambo*. The publication of Bannerman's book, a scant two years after the historic **Plessy v. Ferguson** "separate but equal" **Supreme Court** decision, and the subsequent profusion of images of Sambo and cognate stereotypes made them central to the cultural milieu of the Jim Crow era. Sambo and other "darky" images such as the Mammy, Uncle, Coon, and Pickanniny, became mascots of the white supremacist South. These caricatures appeared ubiquitously on everyday items, e.g., sugar bowls, saltshakers and other kitchen utensils, postcards, lawn statuettes, and business logos. They were symbols that reinforced white dominance and black subordination during the era of segregation. The offensive practice of publicly displaying such caricatures in the South continued into the late twentieth century, gradually diminishing as a result of black protest. Many African Americans now collect such items as memorabilia of a painful yet never-to-be-forgotten past.

Stereotypes on Stage and Screen

Minstrelsy was another chief format for the widespread dissemination of the Sambo stereotype. Once a means for African American entertainers to eke out a living through song, dance, and comedy, minstrelsy soon became the near-exclusive and very lucrative province of white entertainers performing in blackface (facial makeup prepared from substances such as burnt cork), complete with exaggerated wide red lips, bulging eyes, kinky wool wigs, and dialect. Thereafter, the few employed black minstrels such as the talented actor, Bert Williams, suffered the double indignity of not only being gifted thespians forced to accept such demeaning roles or starve, but of also having to apply blackface, thereby, in effect, impersonating a white impersonator impersonating a black minstrel.

Two distinct popular minstrel characters have been identified: Jim Crow (a synonym for Sambo), the plantation darky, and Zip Coon, the urban dandy. Through the medium of this racial impersonation, whites were able to control and manipulate the image of blacks even more so than through the medium of inanimate caricatures. Ludicrous behavior was posited as the opposite of rational behavior, and the whites impersonating blacks as ludicrous, childish, and dependent creatures fostered an image of black men that was devoid of intelligence, masculinity, dignity, and self-determination. Yet, blackface was also used to disseminate the sexualized and violent stereotype of the Savage. Literary critic and cultural studies scholar Susan Gubar observes that the land-mark films of Hollywood's early history were characterized by whites in blackface impersonating African Americans. The first film classic, *The Birth of a Nation,* and the first talkie, *The Jazz Singer* (1929) employed blackface, though in antithetical ways—as criminal and clown (i.e., Savage and Coon).

In *The Birth of a Nation,* an overtly racist apologia for the **Ku Klux Klan**, whites in blackface depicted African Americans as Savages—sexual predators setting out to defile white womanhood and politically threatening rivals vying with disempowered, defeated Confederates for the rule of the Reconstruction South. The incompetence of these blacks as a

> governing political race, however, is revealed by their stereotypical Coon, rather than Savage, behavior while the state legislature is in session: sleeping with feet propped up on the desks, gnawing on chicken bones, and sneaking sips of whis-key from pocket flasks. A "noble" Klan arises to protect the white American nation from the devastation of this black onslaught, in a film which President Woodrow Wilson characterized as "history written in lightening."

In *The Jazz Singer,* a "liberal" patronizing film, Al Jolson plays a Jewish vaudeville blackface entertainer who struggles with his own ethnic dilemma: whether to assimilate into the gentile world and attain success on stage or remain faithful to family traditions as a cantor (religious singer) in his dying father's synagogue. While sympathetic to the ethnic issues of Jewish Ameri-cans, the film is blatant in its racial insensitivity. The most famous scene of the movie involves Jolson in blackface on bended knee pleading for his Jewish mother's acceptance and declaring love and loyalty to her by singing the song "My Mammy." This scene can be seen to signify that while appearing in blackface, white men feel that they can safely regress to the Oedipal and pre-Oedipal stages of their boyhood. Furthermore, this regression infantilizes and effeminizes the image of black men, distorting them as effectively as the hypermasculinized Savage image in *The Birth of a Nation.*

Five black stereotypical film roles have been identified: Toms, Coons, Mulattos, Mammies, and Bucks. The caricature of Tom first appears in a 1903 12-minute short film inspired by and titled after Harriet Beecher Stowe's novel *Uncle Tom's Cabin.* The typical Tom character as a "Good Negro," despite the fact that they are repeatedly the victims of floggings and terroriz-ing. The Tom figure, or more appropriately Uncle Tom figure, is, of course, the same character as the "Uncle," identified earlier in this article as an elder and revered variant of Sambo. The Pickanniny can be seen as a childhood version of the Coon. In cartoon images and other racial memorabilia objects, black children were often depicted in an unsympathetic manner: disheveled, shamelessly sexualized with nude buttocks or genitalia, and menaced, chased or eaten by wild animals such as alligators.

Hollywood images of the pickanniny were equally denigrating. Topsy, the character in *Uncle Tom's Cabin* was one of the few pickanniny characters in early Hollywood productions with a name. However, by the 1920s and 1930s, in such films as the Our Gang series, a few pickanniny characters who took the role to new heights (or depths) had well-known monikers such as Farina, Stymie, and Buckwheat. As for famous adult Hollywood Coons, there were actors Willie Best, Mantan Moreland (renowned for his famous line "feets don't fail me now"), actor/musician **Louis Armstrong**, and standout Stepin Fetchit, who played a drawling, "lanky, slow-witted simple-minded" character in over two dozen films.

The Celebrated Coons of Radio and Television

The ultimate Coon show may have appeared, however, on **radio** and **television** rather than on the silver screen. *The Adventures of Amos 'n' Andy* began as a "blackface" radio show, i.e., a radio show in which white actors impersonated the roles of blacks with exaggerated ethnic voices, speech patterns and dialect. Freeman Gosden and Charles Correll were the impersonators who originally called their "blackface" show, which debuted in Chicago in 1926, *Sam 'n' Henry* before redubbing it *Amos 'n' Andy* in 1928. The *Amos 'n' Andy* radio show was embraced by blacks and whites alike, who loved the scripts and characters all created and enacted by Gosden and Correll. These characters included Amos, an insecure, earnest, sentimental, and deferential taxicab driver; Andy, a swaggering, bombastic, but slow-witted man; and the wily George Stevens, "the Kingfish" of the Mystic Knights of the Sea Lodge, who was prone to outrageous schemes and equally outrageous infractions of the English language. In the 1940s, Gosden and Cottrell began hiring black actors to perform the roles of secondary and tertiary characters on the radio show; these included Ernestine Wade as the infamous Sapphire, the henpecking wife of the Kingfish, whose role became synonymous with an ugly stereotype—the feisty, hands-on-hip, domineering, loudmouthed, nagging matriarchal black woman—and Amanda Randolph as the even more obnoxious Mama, a hyper version of her daughter Sapphire—the "old battleaxe," as Kingfish dubbed his ever-meddling live-in mother-in-law. In 1951, CBS brought *Amos 'n' Andy* to the television screen with all black actors, including Alvin Childress as Amos, Spencer Williams, Jr., as Andy, and Tim Moore as the star of the show, Kingfish. Other characters included Johnny Lee as Algonquin J. Calhoon, a shyster lawyer, and Horace Stewart (Nick O'Demus) as Lightning, the janitor, a slow-moving, slow-witted, drawling Stepin Fetchit–type character. Although the hilarious sitcom was loved by whites and blacks alike, **Civil Rights Movement** organizations considered Coon stereotypes perpetuated by the show to be both offensive and an obstacle to integration and

assimilation. Seeking to promote dignified media images of Negroes and eradicate undignified ones, the National Association for the Advancement of Colored People (NAACP) spearheaded a lengthy but successful battle (beginning
in 1951 and lasting until 1963) to ban the show, including both prime time
network broadcasts and local station. Another noteworthy television Coon
was Jack Benny's sidekick Rochester, played by Eddie Anderson.

Bucks, Badmen, and Blaxploitation

Another stereotype defined by Bogle is the Buck (the superstud or hypersexualized black male) or more specifically the "Brutal Black Buck" as typified by
the rapacious blackface villain is in the film, *The Birth of a Nation.* In short,
Bogle's Brutal Black Buck is identical with the Brute or Savage, while the
Buck, in general (originally a well-built plantation stud mated with several
female slaves in order to breed muscular workers), became synonymous with
the hypersexualized swaggering action hero, antihero or villain, employing
violence on the behalf of either crime or law enforcement in such black folk-
tale sagas such as Stagolee and in such post–Jim Crow Era blaxploitation films
such as Superfly and Shaft. Thus the Buck or hypersexualized, violent-prone
character appeared not only in the context of white imposed racial stereotypes, but in the context of black folklore, black film, and black literature
(e.g., Bigger Thomas in Richard Wright's *Native Son*) as well. In these black
folk, film, and literary creations, the Buck is known by the term the
"Badman."

King Kong: *An American Nightmare*

Differing from typical renditions of the Savage, King Kong is the Subliminal
Savage, i.e., a symbol of the black man as Savage, which operates on an
unconscious level; the true significance of the story is being communicated just
below the threshold of consciousness. The original 1933 *King Kong* is a thinly
veiled rendition of white America's great nightmare—a slave uprising or black
insurrection. *King Kong* subliminally conveys to its viewers an unspeakable
horror, a black insurrection—a fear as old as the nation itself, the deep-
seated anxiety and nightmare of slave-holding whites in antebellum America.
Anxieties about a massive slave uprising plagued white America's conscience
from colonial times up through the Civil War. It has been noted that the
Southern plantocracy created the image of Sambo to ease their own fears—
i.e., they desperately needed to believe in Sambo so that they could sleep easily
at night. But buried deep in the Southern white psyche was a fear that one
night, while sleeping, their throats would be cut by the people whom they
had enslaved—or worse that they would be awakened to witness that final
moment of horror.

In enslaving and oppressing black people, white Americans slept each night
with an uneasy conscience knowing that they were sitting on top of a racial
volcano that could erupt at any moment. In modern times, the uprising took
on the semblance of a black urban revolt—an inner city insurrection. Bringing
the symbols of the movie to conscious awareness, the message of the film
becomes patently evident. Kong is Nat Turner or the Savage writ large.

Africans have long been derogatorily depicted as apes, and Kong the giant ape depicts millions of Africans, the masses of black people in America. The title of the movie itself suggests the great Mani Kongo or King of the Congo (King of Africa), who has been captured from his homeland and shipped in chains to America. Once he reaches these shores, this great physical specimen is penned in a cage, locked in chains and placed on stage, thereby representing the four roles black men have been relegated to in America—slave (chains), prisoner (cage), entertainer (stage), and athlete (physical prowess). Kong breaks his chains and goes on a rampage through the inner city (riots, insurrections, slave revolts). Having been guilty throughout slavery and segregation of the whole-sale rape of black women, whites have always feared that blacks would retaliate by raping white women. (Hence all of the Jim Crow–era **lynchings** for even "looking too hard" at a white woman.) Fay Wray represents the pure and pristine white womanhood that Kong supposedly lusts after. The climb to the top of the Empire State Building is interesting on many levels, for the architectural monument symbolically embodies at once a phallic symbol and the peak cultural and technological achievement of Western civilization. Hence, Kong is challenging the white man's manhood and his technological and cultural "superiority." Reaching the pinnacle of the building, Kong has reversed societal roles, the black man is on the top and the white man is on the bottom looking up at him. The denouement, which ends the nightmare of the black uprising, is that Kong is shot down—just as **Malcolm X, Martin Luther King, Jr.,** and Nat Turner were "shot down." The threat is eliminated, the nightmare is ended, and white fears are assuaged. The subliminal "lesson" to black America is that any future insurrections will meet with a similar fate.

Black Female Stereotypes

The Mammy and the Mulatto are the classic black female stereotypes. Variations and permutations of these characters, especially the quintessential mammy figure, include caricatures such as Aunt Jemima, Beulah, and Sapphire. The Mammy stood (or rather, bowed and scraped) alongside Sambo as his female equivalent, the predominant stereotype of black womanhood during plantation slavery. Depicted as an obese and unattractive matriarch, the bossy Mammy dressed in tattered clothing and was devoid of sexuality; she was caring, nurturing, and even loving to the children of the slave master whom she raised, yet in contrast, mean and neglectful to her own husband and offspring. In a reversal of the preferred gender roles of white antebellum America (where the white women were expected to be dainty feminine belles placed on a pedestal), black women were depicted as strong and dependable while their black male counterparts were weak, dependent, childlike Sambos. In the context of the pervasive cultural norms of the period (not the nascent women's suffragist philosophy of the period or contemporary feminist perspectives), black women were defeminized or masculinized, while black men were demasculinized or effeminized. In the Jim Crow era, the Mammy was no longer a slave but a domestic, that is, a hired maid or nanny. Although she was now a wage earner, there was little of substance that changed in terms of the stereotype. Several black actresses were associated with the Mammy role on screen and on television, first and foremost of these was Hattie McDaniel, best known for her Oscar-winning role in the 1939 film *Gone with the Wind,* a saga of the old South. McDaniel, Ethel Waters, and Louise Beavers alternately played the title role of an amiable domestic in the 1950s television sitcom *Beulah.* Butterfly McQueen played the role of Prissy, a comedic hysterical servant girl in *Gone with the Wind,* and the role of a neighbor's maid in *Beulah.*

Although depicted as desexualized, the Mammy was actually the victim of repeated rape by white men in both plantation and domestic settings. Impregnated by these forced interracial sexual encounters, she frequently gave birth to light complexioned children. The female offspring of such interracial unions, most especially, were stereotyped as Tragic Mulattos. The Mulatto was considered a tragic figure, because she was often light enough to "pass" for white—yet those "passing" for white were often imperiled by sad or disastrous consequences. In a racist Jim Crow society where black skin designated a lower social caste, passing for white was for many mulattos—quadroons (those with one-quarter black ancestry) and octoroons (those with one-eighth black ancestry)—a great social boon—a means to escape the stigma of blackness and segregation and to achieve upward mobility. Passing, however, was always fraught with painful choices and great difficulties. The stereotypical mulatto was forever plagued by her "dark secret." She experienced both the anguish of having to conceal or even sever ties with her black family and loved ones and the constant threat of some day being discovered or exposed as black. Such exposure inevitably would lead to her being ostracized or banished from white society, deserted and rejected by white friends and lovers.

While the Tragic Mulatto was sometimes portrayed as a sympathetic figure, unwittingly trapped in social circumstances not of her making and exceedingly difficult for her to navigate (e.g., the eponymous character in the 1949 film *Pinky*), a frequent depiction of the Tragic Mulatto in literature and in film was that of the selfish seductress. In Fannie Hurst's novel *Imitation of Life,* which was brought to screen in 1934 and then in a 1959 remake, the mulatto is a selfish seductress who loathes blackness and will resort to any means to capture a white husband and live in the white world. She rejects her self-sacrificing mother (who dies of a broken heart) and her gentlemanly black suitors, in order to marry a white man. Yet her white husband savagely beats her and throws her out on the street when he discovers her secret. Furthermore, the Tragic Mulatto, living on the margins of society, fitting neither into the black world that she rejects or the white world that ultimately rejects her, is often depicted as an emotionally troubled, self-destructive, suicidal personality whose problems make her prone to drug or alcohol abuse. It has been noted that the stereotype of the Tragic Mulatto is not historically accurate, as many mulattos played leadership roles within the black community.

An emphasis on the seductive aspects of the Tragic Mulatto made for another variant of the stereotype—the hypersexualized Jezebel, or Hot Mama. The Jezebel caricature stereotyped the black woman as lewd and promiscuous, a whore with animal-like sexuality. The Jezebel with her hot beastial sexuality was the female counterpart of the hypersexualized male Savage or Brute. In contrast to the desexualized fat black Mammy, the sexually tempting and alluring Jezebel was more often than not depicted as a voluptuous mulatto. Indeed, in the age of Jim Crow, white men who were desirous of interracial sex, often sought out mulattos who were employed in the trade of prostitution or arranged long-term sexual contacts with mulatto concubines. The mulatto Hot Mama stereotype is perpetuated even in the present-day media, where video vixens are virtually all light-skinned women with straight or straightened hair.

Although there is much overlap between the Jezebel or Hot Mama stereotype and the stereotypical Mulatto or light-complexioned woman, the Jezebel stereotype actually transcends skin color. In fact, many of the earliest caricatures of black women's alleged beastial sexuality, have employed dark-complexioned African figures. Saartjie (Sarah) Baartman (1789–1815), the "Hottentot Venus," was a classic example of this. A member of the aboriginal KhoiKhoi or Khoisan (so-called Hottentot) ethnic group of southern Africa, Baartman was exhibited like a carnival attraction in London and Paris, to the delight of Europeans who were fascinated by her physique, which was notably characterized by steatopygia, an enlargement of the buttocks typical of the Khoisan women. Cartoon caricatures of Baartman appeared everywhere, and the distorted image of the oversexualized African woman who was always desirous of sex, provided a justification for the rape of enslaved Africans. Voluptuous naked or scantily dressed savage woman appeared in all sorts of memorabilia during the Jim Crow era. In the 1950s, a very popular set of swizzle sticks for stirring drinks called "Zulu Lulu" depicted the nude African figure, with prominent breasts and buttocks, in various stages of youthful to aging development. The late 1960s and early 1970s witnessed the emergence of the famed cartoonist R. Crumb's underground comix character, Angelfood McSpade (sometimes dubbed as Angelfood McDevilfood), an outrageous satire of the Hottentot Venus/Zulu Lulu–type caricatures that, depending upon the viewer, could easily be misinterpreted as an egregious perpetuation of the stereotype rather than an antiracist parody of the stereotype. It has been noted that the Jezebel stereotype divides into two broad types: a Pathetic Jezebel and an Exotic Jezebel. The Pathetic Jezebel image shades into the Mammy image because it depicts African and African American women with aberrant and unattractive physical, cultural, and social traits (e.g., with exaggerated lips or sagging breasts, uncivilized, inebriated, etc.). Unlike the Mammy image however, the Pathetic Jezebel is always sexualized and depicted as nude or seminude. The Saartjie Baartman/Zulu Lulu/Angelfood McSpade caricatures are examples of the Pathetic Jezebel, while the mulatto Hot Mama is representative of desirous Exotic Jezebel.

It has also been noted that the Jezebel stereotype in all of its variations was historically inaccurate, as most black women were modest, monogamous, and morally virtuous rather than lewd or licentious and were the unwilling victims of white supremacists who forced them into sexual subjugation.

Academia

Sambo made a dramatic appearance in the hallowed halls of academia when the historian Stanley M. Elkins (1959) unleashed a firestorm of scholarly debate and criticism with the publication of a controversial thesis concerning the impact of slavery on the African American personality. Elkins argued that Sambo was a real historical personality type, not a fictive caricature; and that the docile (nonrebellious), infantile Sambo was the most prevalent personality type occurring amongst African American slaves. Furthermore, he asserted that this dysfunctional Sambo personality type was uniquely the product of the oppressive "total institution" or "closed system" of North American slavery, and that the Sambo type did not occur in the relatively "open" (i.e., less oppressive, less restrictive) slave systems of Latin American and the Caribbean, where normal human aspirations for freedom resulted in long-standing traditions of slave revolt. He stressed, however, that a comparable prevalent dysfunctional docile personality type did occur among Jews interred in Nazi concentration camps that were similar in oppressive structure to North American slave plantations. Scholars contended with Elkins on several issues including: a reinterpretation of historical evidence minimizing his crucial distinctions between North American and Latin America slavery, slave docility and rebelliousness (Genovese 1971); the existence of other prevalent African American slave personality types, most notably a rebellious "Nat" [Turner] type (Blassingame 1972); the evidence of a "Quashee" personality type, analogous to Sambo, in the Caribbean slave system (Patterson 1971); the evidence that Sambo was a dissemblance or masquerade, not an internalized personality type (Stampp 1971); and the questionable analogy between North American plantation slavery and Nazi concentration camps (Fredrickson and Lasch 1971). *See also* Advertising; Black Hollywood; *Black Like Me*; Children's Literature; Humor and Comedic Traditions.

Further Readings and Viewings: Barnett, Marguerite Ross. "Distorted Images: Stereotypes of African-Americans in U.S. Popular Art." Exhibition brochure, Muse Community Museum of Brooklyn, July–August 1984; Bogle, Donald. *Toms, Coons, Mulattoes, Mammies and Bucks: An Interpretive History of Blacks in American Films.* 4th ed. New York: Continuum International Press, 2003; Butcher, Deirdre Leake, prod. *The Black Caricature.* Public Broadcasting System (PBS) documentary film, 1996; Eli, Melvin Patrick. *The Adventures of Amos 'n' Andy: A Social History of an American Phenomenon.* New York: The Free Press/Macmillan, 1991; Fredrickson, George and Christopher Lasch. "Resistance to Slavery." In *The Debate over Slavery: Stanley Elkins and His Critics,* edited by Ann Lane, 223–44. Urbana: University of Illinois Press, 1971; Genovese, Eugene. "Rebelliousness and Docility in the Slave: A Critique of the Stanley Elkins Thesis." In *The Debate over Slavery: Stanley Elkins and His Critics,* edited by Ann J. Lane, 43–74. Urbana: University of Illinois Press, 1971; Gibbs, P. J. *Black Collectibles: Sold in America.* Paducah, KY: Collector Books/Schroeder Publishing, 1987; Gubar, Susan. *Racechanges: White Skin, Black Face in American Culture.* New York: Oxford University Press, 1997; Nuruddin, Yusuf. "The Sambo Thesis Revisited: Slavery's Impact upon the African American Personality" *Socialism and Democracy* 17, no. 1 (2003): 291–338; The Jim Crow Museum of Racist Memorabilia. http://www.ferris.edu/jimcrow/menu.htm (accessed May 29, 2008); Riggs, Marlon, prod. *Ethnic Notions.* Public Broadcasting System (PBS) documentary film, 1987; Smith, Jessie Carney, ed. *Images of Blacks in American Culture: A Reference Guide to Information Sources.* Westport, CT: Greenwood Press, 1988; Snead, James. *White Screens, Black Images: Hollywood from the Dark Side.* New York: Routledge, 1994; Strausbaugh, John. *Black Like You: Blackface, Whiteface, Insults & Imitation in American Popular Culture.* New York: Jeremy B. Tarcher/Penguin, 2006.

Yusuf Nuruddin

Radio

Radio is a colorless medium. Even so, the color line was evident from the industry's earliest years. Race was a shifting, contested element, playing a central role in the production and the reception of radio content. Race is relevant in two distinct ways. First, from the earliest radio broadcasts of the 1920s until the civil rights revolution of the 1960s, the color line was a barrier, but a porous one, for African Americans in the production of radio content. As important were the complex ways that race was portrayed in radio. While de jure or de facto was the norm in public, African Americans entered the parlors of white American homes through the radio. Black Americans heard their own American culture portrayed as exotic and alien. And both races listened as **minstrelsy** reemerged with its white construction of black identity.

African Americans on Radio in the 1920s and 1930s

African Americans made appearances on radio from the earliest days of commercial broadcasting. Pianist Earl Hines appeared on pioneering station KDKA in Pittsburgh in 1921. The black vaudeville team of Flournoy Miller and Aubrey Lyles made their radio debut as early as 1922, as did comedian Bert Williams. Black musicians in particular benefited from the new medium. In 1922, the American Society of Composers, Authors and Publishers began demanding royalty payments from radio stations that broadcast recorded music. Over the next few years programmers adapted by broadcasting live performances. Kid Ory's Sunshine Orchestra's live performances at the Plantation Club in Los Angeles were broadcast locally. WHN in New York began broadcasting Duke Ellington's orchestra nightly from the Cotton Club in 1924. Ethel Waters and Fats Waller had regular shows, and dozens of other African Americans appeared across the radio spectrum.

Nevertheless, it was much more difficult for black musicians than white ones to find regular work in radio. **Jazz** and **blues** musicians faced criticism for their "primitive" styles, and much of what passed for jazz music on the radio by the decade of the 1930s were orchestral arrangements by white bandleaders who refused to hire black musicians. The house orchestras of the two major networks were not integrated until the end of the decade. In 1937, trumpeter and actor **Louis Armstrong** headlined a show featuring an all-black cast, but the show was cancelled after a six-week run when confronted with skittish sponsors, and in part because Armstrong refused to read his scripted lines in what the producers of the show intended as Negro dialect.

Fewer black performers appeared on the radio in the medium's second decade. The **Great Depression** fell hard on the black entertainment industry. The Theater Owners' Booking Association (TOBA), the organization that had provided employment for black artists on the vaudeville circuit, collapsed, and with it the opportunity for entertainers to find access to radio audiences. Cutbacks in the production of "race" records meant that fewer black artists were familiar to radio producers or audiences.

The development of radio networks diminished considerably the presence of African Americans on the air. Advertisers, who quickly became the dominant force in radio programming, feared that the association of their products with black consumers would discourage white customers. Advertisers and programmers developed content intended to appeal to Southern affiliates. Sponsor affiliated dance orchestras, such as the Ipana Troubadours and the Lucky Strike Orchestra, replaced pioneer black jazz musicians, and many of the new orchestras would not hire African Americans. White singers covered songs originally recorded by black artists. Radio management was not the only barrier to African Americans. The American Federation of Radio Actors and the Radio Writers Guild was denied to African Americans and refused to accept black members until the 1940s.

Louis Armstrong's troubles highlight a dilemma faced by black performers in the early decades of radio. White listeners made up the great majority of the radio audience, and producers of radio content, who also were white, assumed that African Americans should conform to a familiar stereotype to engage a white audience. With few exceptions, black musicians came from blues, jazz, or gospel traditions. Black actors and comics portrayed only black characters, a peculiar restriction since the radio audience could not see the skin color of the actor. Moreover, the depiction of African Americans on the radio during the 1920s and 1930s conformed to racist stereotypes and to characterizations common to nineteenth-century minstrelsy and, later, vaudeville. As Armstrong discovered, an African American who spoke in too-standard English, who did not conform to the stereotype, might lose access to an audience. Female performers faced similar hurdles. Hattie McDaniel began her career in a family minstrel act as a singer. She moved to Los Angeles in the 1920s to find work in the film industry. Supporting herself working as a maid, she finally found work in radio playing a maid with all the characteristics of the black "mammy" on the *Optimistic Doughnut Hour* on KNX, a role she reprised on the radio show *Show Boat*, and in film in *Gone With the Wind*.

Black male characters were expected to exhibit a narrow range of behavior. Most drew directly from the minstrel characters **Jim Crow** and Zip Coon. A Jim Crow character would satirize the rural African American. He would be slow-witted, ignorant, and servile. Zip Coon was a stereotype of the Northern black dandy. He would be ambitions and vain, but would demonstrate no real understanding of the "white" culture to which he aspired. Both characters spoke in stage "Negro dialect," a drawling mockery of standard English characterized by sustained malapropism. Black male actors would be cast as servants or as unemployed, shirking work for drinking, gambling and womanizing.

The most successful black radio actor was Eddie Anderson, who was cast in the role of Rochester, the chauffeur and valet to Jack Benny on Benny's long-running radio program. Anderson's character spoke in a false-black dialect, worked as a servant to the show's star, and engaged in stereotypical bad behavior. Nevertheless, African American audiences had a wide range of responses to Anderson's portrayal of a member of their race. Particularly in the early years of the series, many black listeners were pleased that at least an African American, rather than a white actor, was cast in the part. Moreover, Anderson's character wielded considerable authority over Benny's. He was indispensable and often wiser than his clueless employer. Anderson himself was impatient with critics of his character and with critics of other stereotypical black characters in radio. He asserted that they were not intended to be representative of a race of people, but were simply singular comic characters. Certainly Anderson's success in radio may have influenced his judgment. Likely he would have seconded Hattie McDaniel's explanation that she would rather play a maid on the radio for $500 a week rather than work as a real maid for $50.

One radio pioneer who resisted the stereotyping and still overcame racial discrimination to pursue a successful and influential career was Jack Cooper. Cooper had begun his career in vaudeville on the TOBA circuit, and had worked for the *Chicago Defender*, the premier African American newspaper in the nation. In 1925 he was hired by radio station WCAP in Washington, DC, to produce comedy sketches in black dialect for a variety show. That would be the last time that Cooper was heard on the radio speaking in "Negro dialect." He soon left that position and returned to Chicago, determined to develop radio content that would appeal to black audiences. Beginning with a modest effort on a low-power station in 1929, Cooper produced *The All-Negro Hour*, a variety show of comedy and music, and featuring many of the prominent black performers in the city. He soon added spirituals to the musical lineup, and then began broadcasting religious services from black churches on Chicago's South Side. In 1932, after a dispute with a pianist who was scheduled to play on *The All-Negro Hour*, Cooper began including recorded music on his broadcasts, an innovation that would lead to the rise of the disc jockey as a cultural icon. Cooper also developed news programs in partnership with the *Chicago Defender*, pioneered in sports broadcasting, and produced public affairs programs with discussions of issues affecting African Americans. This latter effort was particularly significant, since, apart from entertainment programming, most radio stations scrupulously avoided racial issues until the end of the 1930s. Cooper also was the rare pioneer African American radio personality who managed to make a comfortable living in the medium.

Whites in Blackface on the Radio

Even many of the stereotyped characters on the radio did not provide employment opportunities for African Americans. From the early nineteenth century, whites had portrayed African Americans in minstrel shows. The form developed first in the Northern states, drawing on traditions from the British music halls. After the Civil War, **minstrelsy** declined in popularity in the Northern states, but found an unprecedented popularity in the former Confederacy. Revived again with the rise of vaudeville in the 1880s, minstrelsy moved easily into radio. Without the burnt cork makeup of the minstrel show, white performers drew on familiar characters, patter, stylized dialect, and song to create a radio version of a blackface performance. Indeed, white actors played most black roles on radio in the 1920s and 1930s. George Moran and Charlie Mack appeared regularly on *The Eveready Hour* as the Two Black Crows, a vaudeville-style comedy act. Tess Gardella, a white actress, was cast as Aunt Jemima, first as a blackfaced spokeswoman for Quaker Oats pancake flour, then as a featured performer in the Broadway musical *Showboat*. Eventually, she starred in a daily radio broadcast. Marlin Hurt, also white, played the black maid Beulah, first on stage, later appearing regularly on radio in *Showboat, The Fibber McGee and Molly Show,* and finally in her own show. Evidently, radio producers felt that white actors could best portray the white fantasy of a black character.

The most successfully white actors to portray black characters were Freeman Gosden and Charles Correll, creators of the long-running *Amos 'n' Andy* series. Drawing on their experiences in semiprofessional minstrelsy and with the Joe Bren theatrical company of Chicago, Gosden and Correll developed a radio show that drew an unprecedented audience from the earliest days of its broadcast. Executives at WGN in Chicago hired the two to develop a radio serial, a novel idea drawn from the successful comic strip serials in the *Chicago Tribune.* Gosden and Correll decided to play black characters, undoubtedly because of their experience in minstrelsy, but also because, as Freemen Gosden later reported, he believed that blackface was funnier than whiteface. Their earliest incarnations were the characters Sam and Henry, two rural Alabamians who began their radio journey from Birmingham to Chicago on January 12, 1926. The show broadcast for 10 minutes, six nights a week, and consisted solely of Gosden and Correll's scripted dialogue. The show was a hit locally and in other locations where WGN's broadcast could be received. The two men also recorded comic dialogue and songs on the Victor label as Sam and Henry, and these efforts provided them an even wider audience.

Like other blackface radio acts, *Sam and Henry* drew on the conventions of minstrelsy. Freeman Gosden's Sam was a Jim Crow character, sincere, deferential, and naïve. Charles Correll's Henry was the Zip Coon, conniving and ambitious, but in the end as dimwitted and ignorant as his trusting partner. Nevertheless, Sam and Henry were more sympathetic and complex than similar minstrel pairs. The two creators avoided malicious characterizations and racist language. Indeed, they suppressed most racial issues altogether. Like many Southern African Americans in the early twentieth century, the two characters migrate North to find employment in a Northern city; unlike their authentic counterparts, the two black characters confront little in the way of racism and poverty upon their arrival in Chicago.

After their contract with WGN expired in 1928, Gosden and Correll began a national tour, drawing considerable crowds and press. Upon their return to Chicago they accepted an offer from WMAQ, the radio broadcast affiliate of the *Chicago Daily News.* Since WGN owned the rights to *Sam and Henry,* the pair had to develop new names, even if the characters remained constant. After testing a few options, they settled on Amos and Andy, and as those characters Gosden and Correll remained on the air for years, first in Chicago and after 1929 on the national NBC Blue network.

In its early years, *Amos 'n' Andy* was the most popular show on radio. The serial format was in part responsible. Audiences tuned in night after night to hear the narrative unfold. Much of the popularity of the show also was due to the appeal and complexity of Gosden and Correll's creations. While based on the stereotypes from minstrelsy, Amos and Andy were appealing characters. Amos was portrayed as noble and hardworking, and Andy, while certainly more devious than his partner, was a likeable scoundrel. Difficult racial issues were ignored. Indeed, one of the remarkable features of the show was the fact there were no white characters in the series. Nevertheless, the fact that the two characters were part of the **Great Migration** to the Northern cities, gave it an authenticity to which even black audiences were drawn.

That is not to suggest that all African American audience members approved of a show in which white actors portrayed sympathetic, but hardly flattering, black characters. Amos and Andy were sympathetic characters, but the show's humor relied on their malapropism, their gullibility, and their unsuccessful efforts to understand business or politics. In short, the humor depended on the characters' inability to master the culture of their white audience. Gosden and Correll made much of their attention to the authenticity of their creations. Freeman Gosden was a native of Virginia, and had close contact with black Virginians in his childhood. Both creators claimed to have done extensive research in the black communities where the show was set, first in south Chicago and later, when the show moved to network radio, in Harlem. The two made public appearances in the black community, and donated to charities that aided African Americans.

Even so, from the earliest days of the show, there were African Americans who were offended by *Amos 'n' Andy*. Jack Cooper was never a fan of his Chicago rivals, believing that they were inauthentic and degrading. At Howard University, Clarence LeRoy Mitchell criticized Gosden and Correll for leading white audiences to believe that Amos and Andy were typical of the African Americans who had migrated from the Southern states. Bishop W. J. Walls of the African Methodist Episcopal Zion Church was an early critic of the series. Robert Vann, editor of the *Pittsburgh Courier,* criticized the show for its effect on both white and black audiences. In 1931, he began a campaign to have the show removed from the airwaves. The *Courier* announced a campaign to collect a million signatures to petition NBC to abandon the show, and reported in October 1931 that 740,000 had been received. The petition drive was unsuccessful, and opposed by the *Chicago Defender,* the largest black newspaper in the nation, but it set the stage for later critics who saw little value in Gosden and Correll's blackface caricatures.

Race, Radio, and War

With the rise in Europe of fascism, critics of racial stereotyping in American radio found new reasons to press their case. The administration of President **Franklin D. Roosevelt** made effective use of radio from the earliest days of the **New Deal** to explain and promote its economic policies, but race issues were rarely aired. Industry leaders, except for the occasional African American innovator like Jack Cooper, carefully avoided race, except as an element of comedy or musical programming. Beginning in 1938, federal policy makers began tentative steps to address the racial divide in America, and to contrast America's pluralism with the racist regime in Germany.

That year, the Department of the Interior under Harold Ickes produced the first of 26 episodes of *American All, Immigrants All,* broadcast on the CBS network, celebrating the contributions of immigrant and minority Americans.

The series did not recall the struggle of various groups to find a place in America so much as it assured listeners that America was a nation that generously rewarded hard work from anyone regardless of origin, ethnicity, or color. Alain Locke and **W.E.B. Du Bois** served as unpaid consultants on the episode entitled "The Negro." Conflicts with the series' writer and production problems complicated the production, but the result was a more historically accurate portrayal of African Americans than radio listeners ever had heard before. For listeners, one obvious difference would have been the absence of "Negro dialect," even in the dramatic portrayal of antebellum slavery.

For African Americans, an even more significant federally sponsored series was *Freedom's People,* conceived by Ambrose Caliver in the Office of Education in the Interior Department. The first episode aired on the NBC radio network 10 days after the bombing of Pearl Harbor, and continued into the spring of 1942. Advisors to the series included a stellar group of black intellectuals, including Du Bois, Alain Locke, **Mary McLeod Bethune**, Roy Wilkins, Carter Woodson, and Charles Johnson. Paul Robeson appeared in the first episode, and music for the series was provided by such luminaries as W. C. Handy, Joshua White, Noble Sissle. Joe Lewis, Cab Calloway, **Jesse Owens**, Count Basie, Fats Waller, A. Philip Randolph, and **George Washington Carver** made appearances. The series was a critical and popular success, winning rave reviews from professionals and from First Lady **Eleanor Roosevelt**, who helped to secure a promise from her husband to appear on the final broadcast, although it was a promise he failed to keep.

The development of a new consciousness on the part of radio programmers and executives led many African Americans to expect that the medium would be a part of the advancement of civil rights in postwar America. Public affairs shows like *Roundtable* and *America's Town Meeting of the Air* took up, if only hesitantly, issues of race that had been carefully avoided in the prewar years. In New York, WMCA began broadcasting *New World A'Coming* in 1944, a series that examined the challenges faced by African Americans and their expectations for the new era. In 1948, journalist and radio screenwriter Richard Durham began broadcasting *Destination Freedom* on WMAQ in Chicago, a series of biographical sketches of prominent African Americans in history with commentary and analysis that had a clear political intent.

Postwar Radio America

The advancement of a civil rights agenda suffered serious setbacks by the end of the 1940s. The onset of the **Cold War** and the ensuing red scare in America took a toll on black activists in particular. Paul Robeson, who had been both popular and effective as a spokesman for racial issues, was blacklisted and persecuted as a Communist. He was unable to make public appearances for fear of the violence that often erupted. Canada Lee, one of the most successful African Americans in radio and stage, and a childhood friend of Fats Waller, also was blacklisted. Networks scaled back their overtly reformist content for fear of appearing sympathetic to leftist politics and losing sponsors. Nevertheless, overtly racist programming fell out of favor and black radio performers did make quiet advances. In 1951 NBC instituted a code of standards and practices that required that all groups represented on the radio be treated with dignity and respect, a requirement that regularly would be breached in the following decade. The next year the network implemented a policy of "integration without identification," allowing African Americans to appear on the radio without explicit reference to their race, and even clearing the way for black actors to portray white characters.

Meanwhile, the disc jockey format developed by Jack Cooper was gaining in popularity. In Chicago, Cooper's popularity was eclipsed by Arthur Lerner, who appeared after the war on WGES. Benson, a migrant from **Mississippi**, first hosted a religious program, featuring a sermon and gospel music, but after the station management refused to let him sell advertising for a religious broadcast, he transformed his show and himself. As Al "the Ole Swingmaster" Benson, Lerner abandoned Cooper's style of broadcasting in formal standard English and instead employed a black vernacular, adopting current slang terms and stressing his Southern, African American vocal style, and playing records by Chicago jazz and blues musicians. Moving away from the big-band swing music featured on network stations, Al Benson highlighted the emerging rhythm-and-blues music that developed from the synthesis of Southern Delta blues and urban jazz. By the end of the decade he was the most popular radio personality in the city, black or white.

The remarkable success of Al Benson in Chicago influenced African American broadcasters in other cities. The racial pride evident at the end of the war years raised the expectations of black audiences. And while *Amos 'n' Andy* remained on the air in a skeletal form until 1960, the decline of radio minstrelsy opened a space for authentic black voices on the airwaves. Jesse Burke in St. Louis, Ramon Bruce in Philadelphia, Lavada Durst in Austin, and Willie Bryant in New York each developed a stylized patter utilizing rhyme, slang, and rapid-fire delivery that, along with rhythm-and-blues musical format, appealed to a younger audience.

In Memphis, WDIA became the first major station in the nation to develop a full-time format for an African American audience. Struggling in a market in which the national networks were devoting more resources to television, and recognizing the untapped potential of the black consumer market, the white owners of the station began providing incrementally more airtime to programming for the city's black population. In 1948, they hired Nat D. Williams to host *Tan Town Jamboree,* and as "Nat D.," Williams quickly became the station's most valuable asset. Within a year, Williams had persuaded the station owners to complete the transition to an all-black format. The station relied heavily on recorded music, but also broadcast live performances, religious shows, and public affairs programs pitched directly to African Americans. In 1954 the station acquired a 50,000-watt transmitter, and overnight, the station acquired an audience throughout the region.

The decline of the national radio networks, the success of WDIA, and the realization on the part of independent station owners and sponsors that African Americans remained a mostly unexploited market for advertising led to a dramatic increase in the number of stations with programming targeted to a black audience. During the 1950s, hundreds of stations around the nation switched their format to "black appeal," hired black DJs and directed their advertising to black audiences. Despite these developments, ownership of these stations remained overwhelmingly in white hands. Radio provided a platform for African American broadcasters to reach African American audiences, but, except occasionally as local sponsors, the economic benefits remained out of reach.

As R&B music reached a wider audience, black DJs became significant celebrities in their own right. Through the 1950s listeners were entertained and schooled by the likes of Jack Gibson, who eventually left broadcasting to work for Berry Gordy at Motown Records, "Joltin'" Joe Howard, Tommy Smalls, and Jocko Henderson. Henderson, whose *Rocket Ship* show was syndicated in several markets, also worked as a concert promoter, continuing a tradition that still fuels and finances radio production today. With the advent of Top 40 radio and the payola scandals in the late 1950s, the power of radio programming shifted away from the DJs and into the hands of the management of radio stations, but as the civil rights struggle heated up in the 1960s, black DJs were well placed to report events, to contribute to the message, and to provided the soundtrack for the movement. Significantly, when **Martin Luther King, Jr.**, was assassinated in 1968, black DJs around the country acted quickly to get out the news and to discourage violent reaction.

While "urban contemporary" programming occupies a significant fraction of the broadcast spectrum in recent times, the color line is still evident in radio. After a significant increase in the number of black-owned radio stations between the mid-1970s and the mid-1990s, legislative and policy changes began to encourage the corporate consolidation of radio ownership. Jim Crow cannot be heard on the radio, but race is still a contested territory in the medium. *See also* Advertising; Music; Racial Stereotypes; Television.

Further Readings: Barlow, William. *Voice Over: The Making of Black Radio*. Philadelphia: Temple University Press, 1999; Douglas, Susan J. *Listening In: Radio and the American Imagination*. Minneapolis: University of Minnesota Press, 1999; Ely, Melvin Patrick. *The Adventures of Amos 'n' Andy: A Social History of an American Phenomenon*. New York: Free Press, 1991; Hilmes, Michelle. *Radio Voices: American Broadcasting, 1922–1952*. Minneapolis: University of Minnesota Press, 1997; MacDonald, J. Fred. *Don't Touch That Dial! Radio Programming in American Life from 1920–1960*. Chicago: Nelson-Hall, 1979; Savage, Barbara. "Radio and the Political Discourse of Racial Equality." In *Radio Reader: Essays in the Cultural History of Radio*, edited by Michele Hilmes and Jason Loviglio. New York: Routlege, 2002.

William A. Morgan

Railroads

Jim Crow regulations affected both passengers and railroad workers. Separation of the races remains an artifact of American history by the distinction of positioning American blacks as a slave class, establishing slave codes to ensure the continued enslavement of blacks, then by implementing laws to divide and segregate African Americans from other races. As with many other aspects of black life in American society, segregation of African Americans in public conveyances, like the railroads (common carriers), was a practice enforced by laws and culture. Segregation on common carriers like railroads and steamships was frequently challenged in the court system as unconstitutional.

The segregated railway cars to which blacks were assigned became referenced as "Jim Crow" cars. The first documented accounts of segregation on railroads occurred in 1841 and involved black abolitionist David Ruggles of New York. On July 6, 1841, Ruggles was ordered by conductors of the New Bedford and Taunton, Massachusetts, Rail Line to move to a railway car designated for "Negroes." When Ruggles refused, he was forcibly removed from the train. He attempted to sue the rail company, but the case was dismissed. Another incident, September 8, 1841, involved former slave and abolitionist Frederick Douglass as he traveled on the Eastern Railroad. Douglass was ordered by the train conductor to move from the general passenger section to a separate section for blacks. When Douglass refused, several men dragged and seated him in the compartment. Douglass and his companions met similar treatment weeks later on the Eastern Railroad line as he traveled to Newburyport. In other instances, whites who came to the assistance of blacks were also mistreated. Incidents like these and others were reported in the newspapers of the times. Efforts against segregation of blacks on railroads were put in motion by abolitionists of Massachusetts to press for legislative intervention against such treatment. Forms of protest included the boycott of rail lines that used segregated railway cars. Under increased public agitation, pending legislation and pressure from lawmakers, the railroads determined it prudent to abolish its policy of segregated railway cars.

Federal employees using segregated waiting rooms in Washington, DC, 1910s. Courtesy of Library of Congress, LC-USZ62-108282.

Despite the early victory of the Massachusetts abolitionists, segregated railroads sporadically continued in other parts of the country. The resurgence of separate railway cars grew following the Civil War and during the westward expansion of the railroads. **Florida, Mississippi,** and **Texas** were among the first Southern states to enact laws to assign blacks to Jim Crow cars after the war. Regardless of the state, the laws uniformly banished blacks to separate cars. Often these railway cars were connected behind the engine, were unsanitary, and occasionally were not passenger cars at all but were freight cars. Occasionally, the cars were segregated by a partition or curtain. Noted black scholar John Hope Franklin experienced this form of segregation as a youth in Oklahoma when he, his mother and sister were removed from a train for refusing to sit in the "Negro" section.

The **Civil Rights Act of 1875** briefly challenged discriminatory practices in the United States. However, the rights of states to draft laws slowly began to supersede the **federal government,** thus opening the gateways for renewed Jim Crow regulations. In addition, the **U.S. Supreme Court** ruled in 1883 that the 1875 Civil Rights Act was unconstitutional, thus leaving policy decisions about blacks to the states. The ruling undoubtedly facilitated passage of new state laws prohibiting integrated railway cars. Beginning with Tennessee in 1881, other Southern states followed with laws that placed blacks in separate cars from non-black passengers.

One of the most cited legal cases concerning segregated railway cars involved **Homer Plessy,** who challenged an 1890 **Louisiana** law that provided **separate but equal** railway cars for blacks. Plessy, who appeared white, was a member of a civil rights organization based in New Orleans, Comité des Citoyens (Committee of Citizens), which chose Plessy to make a test case against the law. On June 7, 1892, Plessy purchased first-class passage (the white coach) on the East Louisiana Railway for transportation between New Orleans and Covington. Plessy was ordered to leave the first-class section. When Plessy refused to comply, he was removed from the train and jailed. Plessy subsequently filled suit on the basis the Louisiana law was unconstitutional (General Assembly of the State of Louisiana, Acts 1890, No. 111). The U.S. Supreme Court upheld the 1890 law of the General Assembly of the State of Louisiana. thus setting forth the practice of "separate but equal," in the United States. Supreme Court Justice **John M. Harlan** offered a dissenting opinion, "I am of the opinion that the statute of Louisiana is inconsistent with the personal liberty of citizens, white and black, in that State, and hostile to both the spirit and letter of the Constitution of the United States."

Further Readings: Brook Thomas, ed., *Plessy v. Ferguson: A Brief History with Documents.* Boston: Bedford Books, 1997; Otto H. Olsen, *The Thin Disguise: "Plessy v. Ferguson."* New York: Humanities Press, 1967.

Carol Adams-Means

Randolph, A. Philip (1889–1979)

Civil rights leader and union founder A. Philip Randolph was born in Crescent City, **Florida,** the son of the minister of the local African Methodist

Episcopal Church. At an early age, he sought a career as an actor and moved to Harlem in 1911 to pursue that objective. Though he did not achieve success as an actor, he did attend City College of New York, and it was there that he met two fellow students who would shape his future life and career: his wife Lucille Green, and Chandler Owen, a student at Columbia University, and a socialist. Owen and Randolph became social and political friends whose politics dovetailed and made it possible for them, in 1917, to create the *Messenger,* which became one of the first radical Harlem magazines during the first two decades of the twentieth century. The *Messenger* began as the *Hotel Messenger* in 1916; a workers' union paper that pronounced socialism as the only program and ideology that would enable the country to achieve the desirable social change. In 1921, Randolph ran, without success, as the socialist candidate for secretary of state in New York. The *Messenger* would be an important political, cultural, and economic rallying point around which various individuals and groups in Harlem would unite during the 1920s.

The beginning of the 1920s had cultural, political, and economic importance for black Americans in as much as it was the springboard for the **Harlem Renaissance** and the attempt by blacks to move forward while recognizing the importance of the past. The Renaissance represented an internally generated black nationalistic to interpreting the past, contemporary practical policies for the 1920s, and projections for the future. It was an era when nationally, black entrepreneurship was probably at its height, but it was also a period preceding the Stock Market Crash of 1929. Thus, on one side of the social, political, and cultural divide there were those adhering to the policies of **Booker T. Washington**, which sought to explain the possible, and eventual, integration of blacks into the system via capitalism and the free market, through the world of business and entrepreneurship. Randolph represented the other divide: the rejection of capitalism and the free market concepts as unworkable for blacks as well as the nation. There was yet another divide: the National Association for the Advancement of Colored People (NAACP) and its moderate social policies and its goal of racial integration and political moderation.

In 1925, Randolph created the largest black union in the history of the country, the Brotherhood of Sleeping Car Porters. More than 10,000 blacks worked as railroad employees, but lacked union representation. Randolph's plans were violently opposed by the Pullman Company, which launched a vicious attack against Randolph and the Brotherhood and attempted to smear both by calling Randolph a dangerous Communist agitator. They were not able to stop Randolph, and the Brotherhood became an official union within the American Federation of Labor (AFL) in 1935; in 1937, the Brotherhood became the first black union to negotiate a contract with a major national corporation. Randolph kept up a steady attack on labor union leaders in the AFL, and later AFL-CIO, and accused them of failing to challenge and attack the rampart discrimination within labor unions.

On many levels, Randolph was an enigma. Although a socialist, he was not a radical socialist; he was definitely a radical black nationalist, though he was not a separatist, and throughout the 1920s, he denounced **Marcus Garvey** and Garveyism at every opportunity; though he was a radical nationalist, he opposed the use of violence in the struggle. In fact, with respect to violence, he often projected the image of a pacifist. Randolph's nationalist and socialist policies were exemplified in ways other than his editorship of the the the *Messenger*. For example, he was one of the socialist-nationalist leaders attracted to an idea first proposed by the **Communist Party**, the idea of a National Negro Congress. The National Negro Congress (NNC) began in February 1936, and Randolph was its first president. The NCC was proposed as an umbrella congress, a national agency which would include a host of black organizations: unions, religious groups, fraternal groups, and civic groups.

From its very inception, Randolph sensed problems, and he left the congress in August 1936 due to the desire of the Communist Party to control NCC policies and activities. In their own accounts of their involvements in Communist organization, both Richard Wright and later **Harold Cruse** wrote of the demands on them by the party to diminish racial and cultural issues and focus mainly on class matters. As a nationalist, Randolph resisted similar policies by the party, and in doing so, reaffirmed his nonradical socialist orientation. This incident also reaffirmed Randolph's nationalist ties, which meant that he could be a socialist and still maintain nationalist ties to black people.

During **World War II**, Randolph came up with a brilliant idea to force the American government to alter some of its discriminatory policies regarding black citizens. He drew up plans for a massive 100,000, all-black **March on Washington** in July 1941. Disturbed that blacks were being hired only for menial, mainly janitorial work, in defense plants, Randolph wanted the march to protest and to outlaw that practice. The NAACP and other black groups supported Randolph, and President **Franklin D. Roosevelt**, fearing that a March on Washington by 100,000 blacks might be very divisive at a time when the country was at war and needed a display national unity, issued Executive Order 8802, which outlawed discrimination in the defense industries. In addition, Roosevelt established the **Fair Employment Practices Commission**. During this period Randolph was at the helm of groups and organizations challenging the government's unwillingness to fully represent its black citizens. He asserted that this lack of action can be taken as a sign of support for these discriminatory practices. With that in mind, in 1947, Randolph created the League for Nonviolent Civil Disobedience in the **armed forces**. He attacked racial segregation in the military and saw it as a negation of democracy that black men were being sent to fight a war and were living in segregated barracks and ate in separate quarters. As he did with his 1941 March on Washington proposal, Randolph threatened to lead a massive disobedience campaign in which he would urge blacks not to show up if they were drafted. As a result of this threat by Randolph, President **Harry S. Truman** issued an executive order ending segregation in the military. This order also reversed a long-standing policy that prevented blacks from attending the U.S. Military and Naval academies.

Randolph kept up a relentless assault against discrimination in whatever shape or form it appeared. For example, viewing union racial discrimination as an ongoing problem, Randolph continued to attack union officials and their unwillingness to confront unions' exclusionary policies against blacks. The severity of this racial exclusion prompted Randolph and other black AFL-CIO members to form the Negro American Labor Council (NALC) in 1960.

He served as president of NALC from 1960 to 1966. The logic for forming the council was similar to the logic he used in resigning from the National Negro Congress: white leadership had no interest in winning a victory over discrimination; if blacks were ever going to be able to exercise their full political, economic, and cultural freedom, they would have to do so with their own leadership, not with that of whites. This action was taken in 1959 despite his ascendancy to the Executive Council of the AFL-CIO in 1955 and his role as vice president of the AFL-CIO in 1957.

One of the last major national contributions by Randolph was his role in organizing the historic **March on Washington** for Jobs and Freedom on August 28, 1963. Though the march is noted for the fact that it brought together more than 250,000 people and was the site of **Martin Luther King, Jr.**'s famous "I Have a Dream" speech, Randolph was a pivotal member of the planning team, along with King, Whitney Young, James Farmer, **Ralph Abernathy**, and Roy Wilkins. By 1963, he had become one of the elder statesmen of the **Civil Rights Movement** who was widely respected, and many organizations sought his advice on social, political, and economic issues. On September 14, 1964, he was awarded the Presidential Medal of Freedom by President Lyndon B. Johnson, and in 1966, he was the honorary chairman of the White House Conference on Civil Rights. Randolph died in New York City on May 16, 1979, at the age of 90. *See also* Black Nationalism; Du Bois, W.E.B.; New Negro Movement; Railroads.

Further Readings: Blumberg, Rhoda Lois. *Civil Rights: The 1960s Freedom Struggle.* Boston: Twayne, 1984; Carmichael, Stokely. *Black Power.* New York: Vintage Books, 1967; Cruse, Harold. *The Crisis of the Negro Intellectual.* New York: William Morrow, 1967; Franklin, John Hope. *From Slavery to Freedom.* New York: Alfred A. Knopf, 1967; Morris, Aldon. *The Origins of the Civil Rights Movement.* New York: Free Press, 1986; Rustin, Bayard. *Down the Line.* Chicago: Quadrangle Press, 1971.

Rutledge M. Dennis

Reconstruction (1867–1877)

Reconstruction refers to an attempt by the **federal government** to create a new society in the former Confederacy once **slavery** was eliminated as a basic element of society. Reconstruction began during the war, as Union armies came to control large areas of the South, and found their lines filled with "contrabands," as escaped slaves were termed. With the landowners largely absent, Union commanders began settling former slaves on the abandoned estates. By the end of the war in 1865, the federal government required former states of the Confederacy to adopt the Thirteenth Amendment, which abolished slavery, as a condition of readmittance to the Union.

However, the leaders of the states of the former Confederacy, predominantly the owners of large estates who had led the region into secession and war, began to regain political control of the South. States began adopting "**Black Codes**," which reduced freedmen, and even blacks who had never been slaves, to a status similar to slavery. Black Codes tied blacks to white landowners, and made a mockery of the constitutional elimination of slavery.

Democrats in Georgia went so far as to elect Alexander Stephens, former vice president of the Confederacy, to the U.S. Senate. Enraged by a perceived arrogance of Southern Democrats, Republicans in Congress passed the *Reconstruction Acts* in 1867 and 1868, which suspended civil government in the former Confederacy and placed the states of the former Confederacy under military rule.

Part of the impetus for Reconstruction was the Republican need to ensure black men voted, as they would overwhelmingly vote Republican. Republicans controlled Congress, but almost all white Southerners were Democrats. Without the black vote in the South, the Republicans would lose control of Congress. The Radical Republicans in Congress were attempting to use the military to create a biracial society. The army ensured black men could vote, and they overwhelmingly voted Republican. Reconstruction state governments created the so-called Negro Militia, which would allow blacks and white Republicans to protect themselves from violent white supremacist groups. But the Radical Republicans never undertook land redistribution. The idea of breaking up the large estates of Southerners who had made war against the United States had been discussed at length, but never implemented. Thus, blacks had a share of political power as long as the federal troops remained in the South, but they had little eco-

nomic power. The South was overwhelmingly agricultural, and most farmland was owned by white Democrats. Blacks remained economically depended on the former slaveowners. Thus this nascent two-party, biracial, South would last only as long as federal troops ensured black men were able to vote, and Northern patience with Reconstruction had a limited life span. The rise of white terrorist groups such as the White League and the **Ku Klux Klan**, which attempted to use extralegal means to prevent blacks from voting, led Congress to pass the Force Act of 1870 and the Civil Rights Act of 1871, also known as the Ku Klux Klan Act. With this authority, the federal government aggressively countered white supremacist terrorist organizations.

Reconstruction saw the passage of two more amendments to the Constitution, which would form the basis for the legal arguments of the later **Civil Rights Movement**. These were the Fourteenth, in 1868, and the Fifteenth, in 1870. Under the Reconstruction governments that controlled the South, these amendments passed the required amount of states. The Fourteenth Amendment overturned the *Dred Scott v. Sandford* ruling of 1857, which declared that persons of African descent were not citizens. The

Cartoon depicting the redemption of the former Confederate states through race-baiting in 1868. Courtesy of Library of Congress, LC-USZ62-121735.

amendment affirmed that blacks were citizens of their state and of the nation. The Fifteenth Amendment prevented the use of race or previous status as a slave as a factor in denying the right to vote.

In 1875, the **U.S. Supreme Court** ruling of *U.S. v. Cruikshank* curtailed the ability of the federal government to protect blacks in the South. The final end of Reconstruction came in the Compromise of 1877. As part of the Compromise, the federal government withdrew the few remaining troops from the South, in return for the Democratic backing of Rutherford B. Hayes for president. Northerners were tiring of the continued sectional strife, and the end of Reconstruction was popular in the North as well as in the white South. The federal government, powerless after *Cruikshank,* allowed white Democrats to regain control, and deferred to "Southern sensibilities" on race issues. For over half a century, Reconstruction would be interpreted as a tragic time when an overzealous federal government humiliated the South, and put in power a group of ignorant freedmen, corrupt carpetbaggers, and unscrupulous scalawags.

For white Democrats, Reconstruction was interpreted as the world turned upside down. Whites saw the decade of Reconstruction as a time of great suffering across the South, and saw the great tragedy of the South not in the two centuries of African slavery or even in the four years of bloody Civil War, but in the decade in which the federal government ensured black men could vote. Later, the historian William A. Dunning of Columbia University supported this idea of the white South suffering unimaginable horrors under Reconstruction. He gave birth to a field of interpretation, one that found its greatest popular dissemination in the characterization of Reconstruction state governments portrayed in the film *The Birth of a Nation* in 1915. Only beginning in the 1950s would historians begin to reevaluate Reconstruction, seeing it instead as an opportunity lost, a time when better decisions by the federal government could have perhaps prevented the disenfranchisement of blacks and the rise of Jim Crow. *See also U.S. v. Reese.*

Further Readings: Du Bois, W.E.B. *Black Reconstruction in America, 1860–1880.* New York: The Free Press, 1998; Foner, Eric. *Reconstruction: America's Unfinished Revolution, 1863–1877.* New York: Harper and Row Publishers, 1988; Olsen, Otto H., ed. *Reconstruction and Redemption in the South.* Baton Rouge: Louisiana State University Press, 1980; Stampp, Kenneth M. *The Era of Reconstruction, 1865–1877.* New York: Vintage Books, 1967.

Barry M. Stentiford

Red Summer

In the summer of 1919, a series of race riots swept across the country. Triggered by mounting racial tensions, the riots resulted in the deaths and injuries of hundreds of African Americans, mostly at the hands of white mobs. Riots took place in at least 26 and as many as 56 cities, with smaller lynch mobs responsible for many more black deaths. The most infamous riots occurred in Charleston, **South Carolina**; Chicago, Illinois; Longview, **Texas**; Washington, DC; Knoxville, Tennessee; Omaha, Nebraska; and Elaine, **Arkansas**. Although each riot was sparked by an individual incident, the violence was rooted in competition for jobs, housing, and union wages in Northern urban areas. Ongoing labor struggles and fears of radical political organizations also factored into the hostilities in both the North and South. Just as in other forms of interracial aggression, much of the bloodshed was the result of rumors and lack of proper government intervention. Black journalist and civil rights leader James Weldon Johnson dubbed the season of destruction and violence the "Red Summer" of 1919.

The United States experienced massive change during **World War I**. Large numbers of African Americans moved to Northern cities, seeking greater employment opportunities in the booming wartime economy and hoping to leave behind the segregation and discrimination of the **Jim Crow** South. Black workers found factory jobs that had been vacated by laborers who had joined the military effort. White workers often resented the intrusion of black laborers and excluded them from unionization efforts. Employers used the interracial rift and the availability of black workers to hire blacks as strikebreakers. Although black workers did not necessarily want to challenge the unions, they knew that taking jobs as strikebreakers was often the only way to break into a white-unionized industry. Even if their wages were lower than those of unionized workers, black workers were often still earning more money than they did in other occupations.

The influx of black migrants also forced greater competition for housing. African Americans frequently moved into urban neighborhoods that had been dominated by European immigrants. Although it was possible for blacks and other ethnic groups to coexist peacefully, the large numbers of black residents triggered fear in their neighbors. As European immigrants became more commonly accepted as "white," they had greater mobility and could move out of the inner city into less crowded neighborhoods. During World War I, however, there was little new housing available, and existing buildings often had exorbitant rental rates. Contests over living conditions extended to competition for parks, beaches, and other leisure spaces. Housing and living conditions, educational limitations, and job competition all contributed to rising interracial tensions.

In the early twentieth century, African Americans were organizing as a group in new ways. Organizations such as the National Association for the Advancement of Colored People (NAACP) advocated for equal rights and racial integration. The NAACP's official journal, *The Crisis,* shared stories of injustice and lynchings across the country, and the group lobbied extensively for federal antilynching legislation. The vast number of publications such as the *Chicago Defender,* by the black press and intended for black readers, advocated for greater efforts to end racial injustice.

As black workers left the South for greater opportunities in Northern war industries or to serve as soldiers, the dwindling numbers of Southern laborers gained leverage over their employers. Many sharecroppers demanded higher wages and the ability to regulate their own families, purchases, and leisure time. One of the primary fears of white Southerners was "political agitators" who led local blacks to demand new rights. These agitators, especially the NAACP, were blamed for disrupting long-standing racial relations in the South, even though these relationships were typically based on white dominance and the threat of or actual violence against black workers. White elites tried to prevent their workers from listening to such radical ideas and urged black residents to maintain the old racial order. Stirring up long-standing Southern fears of black and white miscegenation, white leaders argued that political agitators were primarily interested in interracial marriage. As a whole, rural white elites feared the rise of black workers, while in urban areas ethnic immigrants and native-born whites feared a loss of status.

As large numbers of soldiers returned from Europe at the beginning of 1919, even greater competition for jobs, housing, and resources ensued. Returning veterans found that black workers had filled many formerly white jobs and had vastly improved their economic circumstances during the war. White veterans wanted to reclaim their jobs and asked the **federal government** to guarantee employment and pensions. The American Legion veterans' organization gained tremendous influence in politics and society.

Having proven their loyalty to the United States through their service, returning black soldiers expected to be able to vote in the South and end discriminatory practices. Leaders throughout the country feared that returning black soldiers had high social aspirations and would disrupt prior patterns of racial segregation and discrimination. More than anything, white leaders feared that black veterans would use their military knowledge to forcefully challenge the status quo. The NAACP and black publications had indeed created a "**New Negro**" who was willing to fight back against injustice. With the rising expectations for racial justice came a rise in black militancy and organization. White-owned newspapers typically interpreted self-defense as black defiance of law and advocated for harsher penalties

Another important factor in the Red Summer of 1919 was the ongoing Red Scare. Many felt that the recent Bolshevik Revolution of 1917 and high numbers of European immigrants left the United States vulnerable to radical forces. Both government and corporate leaders believed that unionization and contentious labor relations between black and white workers and wealthy white capitalists could cause insurrection. More radical labor unions such as the **Industrial Workers of the World (IWW)** were open to interracial unionization, which critics feared would lead to both race and class warfare. Returning white veterans used racial hostilities and the Red Scare to gain tremendous social power and discredit anyone who advocated for racial justice.

Perhaps the most well-known riot of the Red Summer occurred in Chicago on July 27–August 2, 1919. A black youth, Eugene Williams, had accidentally crossed the invisible line separating a black swimming area from a white one at Lake Michigan's 25th Street beach. White swimmers threw rocks at Williams until he drowned, but white police officers refused to arrest the instigators. Black and white mobs attacked each other, and the fighting went on for five days. Unlike other riots, the violence was not restricted to just one section of town, but roamed widely over black and white residential and business districts. At least 38 people died and more than 500 were injured. At least 1,000 African Americans were homeless due to fire and other property damage.

The labor unrest of 1919 revealed itself in the steel strike of September and October. Capitalist employers wanted to break the unions, not just end the

strike. Knowing that the sight of black workers would make the white unionists furious, corporate leaders hired many black strikebreakers, especially in
the area surrounding Chicago. On October 4, black strikebreakers in Gary,
Indiana, crossed the picket lines and were attacked by strikers. Two days of
rioting followed, and federal troops finally restored order. Corporate rhetoric
linked striking workers and black strikebreakers to radical organizations, and
public opinion turned against the workers. Capitalists even blamed middle-
class African Americans for not controlling the lower class. Government officials soon voted to restrict immigration and enforce segregation to minimize
further disorder.

Fear of agitators initiated violence in many cities and minimized the power
of unionization and black collective action in the South. In an effort to keep
local blacks under control, a **white citizens council** in Leggett, Texas, violently
forced the local NAACP president, T. S. Davis, to leave town in August 1919.
The town instituted a curfew for black residents and forbade them to hold
meetings of any kind. Similarly, a mob in Anderson, South Carolina, forced
three NAACP leaders out of town and the branch disbanded. White violence
and intimidation against NAACP branches throughout the South greatly
undermined the organization's power.

One of the largest massacres of African Americans during the Red Summer
took place in the rural delta region of Elaine, Arkansas. There, black sharecroppers and tenant farmers attempted to organize a labor union, the
Progressive Farmers and Household Union, in hopes of securing a fair share
of their cotton crop. The sharecroppers had earned some money during the
wartime rise in wages, which threatened the dominance of white plantation
owners. When planters evicted tenant farmers from their homes in the fall,
the sharecroppers joined the union and held meetings to discuss ways to fight
back. In October, a group of white men fired into a black union meeting in
Hoop Spur and the members returned fire, killing one man and wounding
another.

White residents quickly spread word of an armed "insurrection" by black
workers. The local sheriff deputized men for a posse, and the governor asked
for and received 500 federal troops to quell the supposed rebellion. Along with
the posse and troops, vigilantes covered a 200-mile radius and killed as many
as 200 African American men, women, and children. Some of the victims were
burned alive. Many black people were charged and convicted of crimes in connection with the presumed uprising, including 12 men convicted of murder.
The highest number of post-riot trials followed the **Elaine Massacre**, although
some convictions were later overturned by the U.S. Supreme Court. Violence,
however, continued to operate as the primary social order in the region.

The role of the police and state or federal troops illustrates the vast differences in justice and protection throughout the country. In the **Chicago Race Riot
of 1919**, the police were hampered by a lack of sufficient numbers. African
American residents were wary of the police due to long-time injustices, and
their hostility was confirmed when white policemen did not always stop white
violence against black residents. White police officers focused their attention
on Chicago's Black Belt, leaving other areas of the city vulnerable to even
higher casualty rates. The Chicago riot ended only with the arrival of the state

militia to restore order. However, only the white militia was called out. City leaders feared that black veterans in the state militia would actually lead black citizens to further violence rather than quell the riots.

In some cases, such as Charleston, South Carolina, and Norfolk, **Virginia**, sailors and soldiers initiated the rioting. Animosities between different races and different branches of the military frequently became violent, and innocent bystanders were often caught in the melee. In Elaine, Arkansas, local white officials controlled the police force and the state militia and quickly deputized many local white landowners, with disastrous results for the black residents.

In other locations, such as Omaha, Nebraska, the military was more effective in controlling the violence. General Leonard Wood is particularly noted for his quick imposition of martial law, his clear chain of command, and his better communication with civilian authorities. He censored news released and prevented newspapers from printing questionable or inflammatory rumors. Most importantly, General Wood prevented his federal troops from participating in the violence, as many local or state troopers were more likely to do. In many instances, later investigatory bodies reprimanded the mayor or other leaders for waiting too long to call in military assistance.

Records of arrests and ensuing legal actions demonstrate the ongoing racial discrimination in the country. Police were more likely to arrest black rioters than white ones, and black rioters on trial were more likely to be convicted. In a time of fear, prejudice, and hostility, African Americans suffered greatly at the hands of their neighbors, their employers, and officials sworn to protect them. The call for black resistance was necessary and timely during the Red Summer of 1919. *See also* Great Migration; New Negro Movement.

Further Readings: Arnesen, Eric, ed. *The Black Worker: Race, Labor, and Civil Rights since Emancipation.* Urbana: University of Illinois Press, 2007; Gilje, Paul A. *Rioting in America.* Bloomington: Indiana University Press, 1996; Grimshaw, Allen D. "Actions of Police and the Military in American Race Riots." *Phylon* 24 (1963): 271–89; Schneider, Mark Robert. *African Americans in the Jazz Age: A Decade of Struggle and Promise.* Lanham, MD: Rowman and Littlefield, 2006; Slotkin, Richard. *Lost Battalions: The Great War and the Crisis of American Nationality.* New York: H. Holt & Co., 2005; Tuttle, William M., Jr. *Race Riot: Chicago in the Red Summer of 1919.* New York: Atheneum, 1970; Wormser, Richard. "Red Summer 1919." The Rise and Fall of Jim Crow, Public Broadcasting Service Web site. http://www.pbs.org/wnet/jimcrow/stories_events_red.html (accessed July 2007).

Shannon Smith Bennett

Republican Party

The Republican Party founded in 1854, and in just six years became one of the two major American political parties that have dominated U.S. politics until the present day. The party at its inception contained former Whigs, Free Soil supporters, and Northern Democrats unhappy with their party's stand on the issue of slavery. In essence, the Republican Party maintained the traditional Whig platform of a protective tariff, a national bank, and support for internal improvements, but another major tenet of the new party was opposition to slavery, specifically opposition to the expansion of the institution of slavery into the territories. The Republican opposition to slavery stemmed from several sources; many Republicans opposed slavery on moral grounds, while others sought to preserve the territories to the West as a white man's country. The election of Abraham Lincoln and the outbreak of the Civil War would make the Republican Party's opposition to slavery much more explicit, such that the party platform came to support emancipation and then political and civil rights for African Americans. This transformation was gradual, with Lincoln slowly coming to support immediate emancipation long after many Republican leaders in Congress.

Given that emancipation occurred under a Republican president and the Republican Party's support for political and civil rights for African Americans, the Republican Party gained the loyalty of former slaves for generations to come. Republicans staffed the Reconstruction governments that existed in the South on the conclusion of the Civil War. African Americans from both the North and South held prominent positions in many of these state Reconstruction governments, serving as state legislators and, in some cases, as lieutenant governors and secretaries of state. In addition, under Reconstruction, Southern states elected a number of black Republicans to Congress. African Americans made up a key part of the Republican Party within the South, and support for African American rights was a major tenet of the national Republican Party.

In 1877, the last Reconstruction governments in **Florida**, **South Carolina**, and **Louisiana** fell. In essence, the Republican Party chose to end the Reconstruction project despite the shortcomings of Southern society, due to increasing unpopularity in the North and the high cost of keeping federal troops in the states. With the Democratic Party in firm control of Southern state governments, state legislatures began to curtail the voting and civil rights of African Americans over the course of the 1890s and 1900s, enacting Jim Crow laws that curtailed the spirit of the Fourteenth and Fifteenth Amendments to the Constitution that the Republican Party had worked so hard to enact. The Republican Party did little on the federal level to ensure that the rights of African Americans in the South were protected. Despite this, however, the Republican Party continued to receive overwhelming black support, and African Americans, particularly under Republican president Theodore Roosevelt, received appointments within the federal bureaucracy.

Under William Howard Taft, patronage for blacks was sharply curtailed. Taft gave state's elected representatives a de facto veto over those in federal posts such that Democrats from the South began to bar blacks from federal jobs in their section. In addition, Republicans continued to turn a blind eye to systemic extralegal violence and the violations of black civil rights in the South. In part, this was done in an attempt to gain whites to the Republican Party in the South, though it had little success, as the white South remained staunchly Democratic. Blacks continued to remain in the Republican Party and in some measure, in limited appointments and in expansive rhetoric, the Republican Party continued to support their cause of equality before the law.

Under Democratic president Woodrow Wilson, segregation was instituted in the federal civil service, and upon the election of Republican Warren G. Harding, the practice continued. The Republican Party failed to pass anti-**lynching** legislation despite repeated calls from the black community and prominent Republican leaders. Under Republican presidents Harding, Calvin Coolidge, and Herbert Hoover, the Republican Party consistently failed to meet the demands of the black community as expressed by the National Association for the Advancement of Colored People. This series of presidents, beyond appointments, failed to act on black issues, in part to draw more white Southerners to the party; over time, this destroyed the traditional attachment of African Americans to the Republican Party.

Franklin D. Roosevelt's presidency brought the majority of African Americans firmly into the Democratic Party, where they remained into the twenty-first century. While his presidency failed to address voting and civil rights, **New Deal** programs helped African Americans, providing jobs and economic assistance. In addition, Roosevelt made a concerted effort to win black support personally. Roosevelt convened a panel of black advisors, called the **Black Cabinet**. His wife **Eleanor Roosevelt** in particular actively pushed civil rights issues. Despite the efforts of Eleanor Roosevelt and several other prominent Democratic leaders, President Roosevelt failed to embrace a civil rights agenda. Roosevelt and the Democratic Party were caught in a bind in regard to civil rights. The New Deal programs needed to relieve people hurt by the Great Depression depended on the votes of Southern Democrats who supported Jim Crow laws and segregation. Thus, Roosevelt could not move too far ahead on civil rights lest he endanger support within his own party for his economic agenda. Nonetheless, Roosevelt still garnered black votes, thanks in large part to New Deal programs that provided economic aid to all races. The Republican Party faced no such dilemma in gaining black voters, but their opposition to economic aid during the Depression hurt them with all groups of voters, but African Americans in particular, while Roosevelt's personal charm offensive bore fruit for over three terms.

President Harry S. Truman was the first Democratic president to speak about a civil rights agenda, solidifying the African American drift into the Democratic Party. Truman desegregated the armed services. Still, Truman failed to pass a civil rights act. A number of Northern and Western Republicans recognized that African Americans had started to identify with the Democratic Party, and these Republican leaders were far more active than Truman in calling for a civil rights agenda. Dwight D. Eisenhower enjoyed significant black support and helped to pass the **Civil Rights Acts of 1957 and 1960**. Both acts largely lacked any enforcement provision, but they were the first civil rights acts passed since the era of the Civil War, and the Republican Party overwhelmingly voted them into being while Democrats remained divided. The 1960 act was the product of Republican senator Everett Dirksen of Illinois. Dirksen, as the Republican leader, would also be pivotal in passing the **1964 Civil Rights Act** under President Lyndon B. Johnson, given the opposition of many Southern Democrats to civil rights. The protections given to civil rights under Eisenhower were enacted with Republican votes in combination with Northern Democrats.

In 1954, the Supreme Court in *Brown v. Board of Education* found "**separate but equal**" unconstitutional. Federal courts then started to make rulings that forced school integration. In 1957, Eisenhower, with the support of the Republican Party, used federal troops to enforce such a court decision in Little

Rock, Arkansas, despite the efforts of Governor Orval Faubus and others. Over the course of the 1950s and 1960s, there was an increasingly active **Civil Rights Movement**. The Republican Party found itself in an odd position. In the first stages of the movement, there were few Republican officeholders in the South invested in the current system. Yet at the same time, there were white voters who might be brought into the party with the decline of segregation, given the divisions inherent in the Democratic Party. Despite this division within the party, the **John F. Kennedy** administration spoke a great deal about civil rights legislation, and under President Johnson, such legislation was passed, most notably the **Voting Rights Act of 1965** that barred literacy tests, **poll taxes,** and other methods Southern states had used to get around the Fifteenth Amendment to the Constitution. In addition, the act had the enforcement provisions necessary to ensure that the **federal government** could intervene to monitor the process. Johnson is often quoted as saying shortly after signing the act that he had just lost the South for the Democratic Party, which was largely true, as increasingly from that point the South turned Republican, a trend that had already begun to occur in presidential elections, but that would come to define elections to state legislatures and the U.S. Senate and House of Representatives.

The Republican Party first introduced political and civil rights for African Americans under President Abraham Lincoln and the Radical Republicans in Congress. Over the course of the nineteenth century, however, in an attempt to garner more white votes and create a stronger party in the South, Republicans often soft-pedaled the protection of those rights. It was not until the presidency of Franklin D. Roosevelt that blacks began to become a major constituency of the Democratic Party. Even so, the Republican Party during the 1950s and 1960s often had a better overall record on combating Jim Crow laws in the South, whereas Democrats remained deeply divided, often having the loudest supporters for the Jim Crow system and its loudest detractors. Nonetheless, the Republicans benefited from the ultimate break by Johnson with that Southern Democratic Party support for segregation, as the white South became largely Republican while African Americans became staunch Democratic Party voters.

Further Readings: Burk, Robert Frederick. *The Eisenhower Administration and Black Civil Rights.* Knoxville: University of Tennessee Press, 1984; Foner, Eric. *Free Soil, Free Labor, Free Men: The Ideology of the Republican Party before the Civil War.* New York: Oxford University Press, 1970; Gould, Lewis L. *Grand Old Party: A History of the Republicans.* New York: Random House, 2003; Jensen, Richard J. *Grass Roots Politics: Parties, Issues, and Voters, 1854–1983.* Westport, CT: Greenwood Press, 1983; Sherman, Richard B. *The Republican Party and Black America: From McKinley to Hoover, 1896–1933.* Charlottesville: University Press of Virginia, 1973; Weiss, Nancy J. *Farewell to the Party of Lincoln: Black Politics in the Age of FDR.* Princeton, NJ: Princeton University Press, 1983.

Michael Beauchamp

Resistance

Jim Crow segregation (1880s–1965) replaced slavery as the dominant pattern of race relations in post–Civil War America. Emerging gradually after the defeat of Radical **Reconstruction** governments, Jim Crow segregation had fully matured by the turn of the nineteenth century. A result of the defeat of Radical Reconstruction governments throughout the South, Southern "Redeemers" developed state constitutions that either repealed or circumvented Reconstruction Acts and amendments that had guaranteed black civil rights. Moreover, the withdrawal of federal troops, the decline of Radical Republican politics in the South, and the **federal government**'s disregard for safeguarding black civil rights exacerbated and hastened Jim Crow's development.

Similar to the institution of **slavery** in the United States, Jim Crow segregation enforced a hierarchical and systemic racial-class system of oppression aimed at maintaining white supremacy and black social, economic, legal, and political degradation. It was predicated upon African American exclusion or unequal access to voting, juries, education, housing, public accommodations, recreation facilities, etc. In addition, white Southerners adopted economic arrangements that stymied or obliterated black economic development such as **sharecropping**. White Southerners believed Jim Crow segregation was necessary because African Americans were incapable of self-government and that black political and economic equality would invariably result in social equality between blacks and whites, which white Southerners singlemindedly equated with **miscegenation** or interracial sex. Intent on preserving these sociocultural roles, rigid social, political, and economic boundaries had to be maintained in order to insure white racial domination.

White Southerners accomplished segregation by excluding or limiting black civil and political rights through laws, custom, and violence. While laws and court decisions defined the contours of Southern race relations, racial etiquette informed everyday social relations between whites and blacks. A system of racial etiquette was necessary because it made intangible Jim Crow laws and court decisions "real" and provided a reflexive structure and mechanism by which whites could readily monitor racial boundaries and impose white domination. For example, African American suffered daily indignities such as being relegated to entering through back doors, sitting in the back of buses or "nigger pews" in theaters, and drinking at "nigger" labeled water fountains to name a few. Moreover, white Southerners routinely lynched African Americans who violated racial etiquette or challenged segregation. While a minority of African Americans accepted life "behind the veil," others vigorously challenged the "cultural logic" and institutional arrangements that bolstered white supremacy.

During the era of Jim Crow, African Americans persistently resisted segregated education, protested **disenfranchisement**, and challenged white employers' exploitative labor practices. During slavery, mass illiteracy had symbolized black social and intellectual deprivation. African American slaves and subsequent generations believed education was critical to personal independence and civic participation, and thus in the post–Civil War era, African Americans enthusiastically sought "book learning." Yet, their desire for education often constituted a "dream deferred" during Jim Crow.

Jim Crow educational facilities were separate and highly unequal, which stymied (but did not curtail) black educational progress. White secondary schools were dramatically better funded than comparable black schools. Typical of the segregated educational system in Southern states, **North Carolina** public school expenditures totaled approximately $6 million during 1914 and 1915. White public schools received roughly $4 million for education expenses, whereas black schools received only $600,000. Even in majority black counties with larger black student populations, African American schools were allotted less funding than white schools. In seven black majority counties in **Virginia**, the African American student population totaled 13,000 students, while the white student population totaled 6,000. Over time, disparities in public expenditures for black and white education expanded. **South Carolina** blacks received 29 percent of total education expenditures in 1900. They received a paltry 12 percent in 1915. Moreover, African Americans were prohibited from riding school buses, which forced them to walk miles to school. They attended school in dilapidated buildings and received obsolete supplies and books. In plantation regions, African American youth attended school irregularly because the plantation regime was labor intensive and required whole families, including children, to work in the fields. Black parents reluctantly withheld black children from schools in order to plant and harvest crops. These students averaged four to five months of schooling, whereas white children averaged seven to eight months.

In addition to unequal facilities and supplies, black secondary teachers were paid significantly less than their white counterparts. In North Carolina, white teachers earned three times more than black teachers between 1905 and 1915. During the same period, white teachers' salaries increased by as much as 100 percent, whereas black teacher salaries increased by less than half and, in many cases, remained stagnant. Black teachers often protested school districts that refused to provide them equal pay and comparable books and supplies that white teachers enjoyed. In 1919, black teachers successfully campaigned to replace white teachers in all-black schools in Charleston, South Carolina. Historically, white teachers had monopolized teaching positions at all-black schools in urban areas and thus restricted black teachers' access to employment opportunities. Black communities desired black teachers because they believed they were better suited to teach black pupils and represented greater community control and employment opportunities for blacks excluded from white schools.

In response to segregated education, African Americans developed separate black educational institutions and sued local and state governments on the basis that separate educational facilities for blacks and whites were unequal. Between the years 1870 and 1915, African Americans developed dozens of normal schools, federal land grant colleges, and private colleges that were funded primarily by white philanthropic and missionary societies. The Tuskegee and Hampton institutes were the most notable and well-funded black educational institutions developed during this period because their socially and politically conservative educational agenda attracted support and financing from racist white Southerners as well as Northern industrial businessmen. The Tuskegee and Hampton institutes emphasized teacher training and industrial education, and sought to inculcate the desirability and dignity of manual labor, political accommodation to Jim Crow, economic thrift, and moral asceticism. **Booker T. Washington**, known as the "Wizard of Tuskegee," exemplified the philosophical and practical objective of industrial education when he famously advised black Southerners to "cast down your buckets where you are." In contrast to the Tuskegee-Hampton model, other lesser known black schools such as Clark University (presently Clark Atlanta University), Shaw University, Meharry Medical College, and Tougaloo College emphasized liberal arts training and encouraged black students to acquire middle-class culture and professions such as teaching, medicine, law, and business. These private black colleges sought to instill a "racial uplift" ethos that emphasized political agitation and black self-help. Even as black educational institutions differed in curriculum and political philosophy, black higher education institutions provided a quality education for blacks excluded from white institutions; but more importantly, these institutions imbued black students with a social conscience to serve the race and become the next generation of black leaders that would further the struggle against racial **discrimination** and oppression.

While African Americans developed separate educational institutions, the National Association for the Advancement of Colored People (NAACP) began to challenge the constitutionality of segregated schools in state and federal courts. In 1896, the **U.S. Supreme Court** ruled in *Plessy v. Ferguson* that the Constitution did not prohibit separate educational facilities for blacks and whites provided that they were equal. By the early 1930s, NAACP lawyers believed they could easily disprove the "**separate but equal**" doctrine by demonstrating black schools and facilities' deplorable financing and conditions in the South and could force Southern governments to equally fund a dual system. In theory, the NAACP hoped that an equally funded dual-school system would erode Southern governments' desire and financial ability to maintain separate schools for black and white students. In 1938, the NAACP legal strategy materialized in the *Gaines v. Canada* case. The Supreme Court upheld the NAACP's claim that the University of Missouri had unfairly denied Lloyd Gaines admission to law school and argued that Missouri was legally obligated to provide a "substantially equal" education for both blacks and whites. In response to the Supreme Court decision, the University of Missouri and other Southern public universities developed law schools and graduate programs for African Americans. Eventually, the NAACP's legal strategy won other key legal victories, including the landmark 1954 *Brown v. Board of Education* decision that repealed the 1896 *Plessy v. Ferguson* decision and sparked the school **desegregation** movement throughout the United States.

"Jim Crow" Southern governments and constitutions had a chilling effect on black voter registration, voting patterns, and black officeholding throughout the South. During Radical Reconstruction, in some places, as much as 97 percent of eligible black voters were registered voters, and consequently, blacks were able to elect black police chiefs, mayors, state congressmen, and senators. During Jim Crow, white Southerners systematically eliminated black voting blocs through poll taxes, literacy tests, and understanding clauses. If these measures failed, whites resorted to fraud, intimidation, and violence. The 1890 **Mississippi** state convention and constitution's sole purpose was to eliminate blacks from political life. Gradually, other Southern states followed suit. As a result, Southern black voter registration declined precipitously. Between 1890 and 1892, black voter registration plummeted from 190,000 to 8,000 registered black voters in Mississippi. In all black counties in Mississippi, the effect of disenfranchisement was even more dramatic. Washington County, Mississippi, contained 9,103 eligible black voters; however, only 103 black voters (less than 1 percent of eligible voters) were registered in 1892. Black Mississippians elected one black congressman, two black U.S. senators, two black state secretaries, and one lieutenant governor during Reconstruction; yet, with the onset of Jim Crow policies, black officeholding ceased to be a factor in political life.

Despite the many tactics and strategies aimed to prevent black voting, African Americans refused to accept disenfranchisement. African American households saved meager earnings to pay exorbitant **poll taxes**. Even though women were prohibited from voting, black women viewed their spouse's vote as a familial vote. African Americans organized study groups to prepare for citizenship tests, which were used to deny potential black voters who could afford to pay poll taxes or meet other tedious requirements to vote. African Americans persistently challenged disenfranchisement by continually seeking to register to vote. On January 1, 1919, African Americans in Jacksonville, **Florida**, initiated and led a statewide voter registration campaign. In the wake of women's suffrage, Jacksonville blacks decided to test the legitimacy of the Nineteenth Amendment. As the movement grew larger, Florida blacks believed they could revitalize the Florida Republican Party and defeat white Democratic control of Florida politics. The Florida voter registration movement was rooted in preexisting black organizational and institutional networks. Women's clubs, fraternal orders, labor unions, and churches all enlisted members in voter registration campaign. Members of the Knights of Pythias took an oath to pay poll taxes and register to vote. In Florida, potential voters were required to pay two years' payment of poll taxes in order to register. Fraternal lodges and women clubs donated poll tax fees to African Americans who could not afford to pay. Institutional networks and their movement leaders and recruiters organized "citizenship meetings" to provide voter education seminars and recruit new organizers and workers for the voter registration campaign. By November 1920, 7,000 black women (over half the female population) and 1,000 black men had been registered in Jacksonville as along with hundreds of other blacks in counties throughout Florida. In response to black voter registration, the **Ku Klux Klan** organized chapters in areas where blacks organized voter registration leagues and systematically used threats, intimidation, and violence to keep blacks from voting. During the presidential election of 1920, election workers harassed blacks patiently waiting in line to vote, purged hundreds of blacks from voter lists, and refused to allow blacks to use voting booths. In the election's aftermath, Congress organized hearings and investigated the Florida election, but ignored the blatant violations of black voting rights. The Florida voter registration campaign ultimately failed to destroy white Democratic control in Florida or gain election reform; however, the institutional and organization networks that facilitated the voter registration campaign provided a basis upon which African Americans in

African American man protesting segregation in a movie theater in Nashville, Tennessee, 1961. Courtesy of Library of Congress, LC-USZ62-110971.

Florida continued to protest against disenfranchisement, economic exploitation, and **lynching**.

In addition to segregation and disenfranchisement, black Southerners were restricted to menial and agricultural labor. By the dawn of Jim Crow, at least 80 percent of blacks were either sharecroppers or tenant farmers. Sharecropping was premised upon landowners providing land, supplies, housing, and a small cash advance in exchange for a sharecropper's labor. Sharecroppers and landowners generally agreed to split the proceeds of cotton sales evenly minus the cash advance. In many cases, though, plantation owners denied black sharecroppers their portion of cotton profits by inflating the amount of money originally borrowed prior to the cotton harvest. The recurring cycle of inflated debt bogged down efforts of black sharecroppers to purchase their own farm and gain economic independence.

During a brief period during **World War I**, when cotton prices skyrocketed, black sharecroppers enjoyed relatively higher wages and slightly better work conditions. When cotton prices dramatically declined in the immediate post–World War I period, Mississippi and Arkansas Delta planters sought to reassert pre–World War I wage levels and work conditions. In response, black sharecroppers and tenant farmers in Elaine, Arkansas, organized the Progressive Farmers and Household Union of America (PFHUA) and planned to sue plantation owners for lost wages in 1919. Black farmers demanded better working conditions and higher wages comparable to those attained during World War I. In order to galvanize black agricultural workers, PFHUA held meetings to recruit and educate workers on the cotton market and formed armed posses to protect meeting halls from anticipated attacks. Plantation owners in Elaine mounted an extensive and organized campaign of violence against farm workers because they believed workers posed a grave threat to white racial domination and, ultimately, their economic interests. In order to squelch the nascent labor movement, planters arrested dozens of blacks, assassinated prominent labor leaders, and murdered countless sharecroppers. Some newspaper reports even suggested that bombs were dropped on Elaine's black community. Estimates of blacks killed in the Elaine massacre ranged from a few dozen to 856 persons. Despite the disparities in the estimates, Elaine planters destroyed black organized protest to the sharecropping regime, which further entrenched their power within the South's cotton-based economy.

During the era of Jim Crow, African American resisted segregated education, protested disenfranchisement, and challenged white employers' exploitative labor practices because these institutional arrangements denied African Americans' social, political, and economic equality. Black resistance relied upon informal and formal networks (such as churches, fraternal orders, and women's clubs), which provided the resources and organization necessary to challenge Jim Crow. Antiblack representations, segregated public accommodations, and lynching denigrated black humanity and compelled a response whereby blacks either had to fight back or surrender to annihilation. African American resistance hardly provided clear-cut victories, and in some instances, it retarded hard-won victories already achieved. Despite the success or failure of black protest to Jim Crow, African Americans' desire for freedom and equality never wavered and, in many ways, black perseverance during Jim Crow provided a foundation for future assaults during the **Civil Rights Movement**. *See also* Elaine Massacre; Nadir of the Negro.

Further Readings: Anderson, James. *The Education of Blacks in the South, 1860–1935.* Chapel Hill: University of North Carolina Press, 1988; Chafe, William, et al. *Remembering Jim Crow: African American Tell about Life in the Segregated South.* New York: New Press, 2001; Harlan, Louis R. *Separate and Unequal: Public Schools Campaigns and the Racism in the Southern Seaboard States 1901–1915.* Chapel Hill: University of North Carolina Press, 1958; McMillen, Neil R. *Dark Journey: Black Mississippians in the Age of Jim Crow.* Urbana: University of Illinois Press, 1990; Ortiz, Paul. *Emancipation Betrayed: The Hidden History of Black Organizing and White Violence in Florida from Reconstruction to the Bloody Election of 1920.* Berkeley: University of California Press, 2005; Woodruff, Nan. *American Congo: The African American Freedom Struggle in the Delta.* Cambridge, MA: Harvard University Press, 2003.

Karlos K. Hill

Rhythm and Blues

Rhythm and Blues (R&B) is a term used to describe or designate certain types of music associated with the African American community. R&B has had a number of different meanings over the years: it was used by *Billboard* magazine as a broad category to track the sale of music produced and consumed by African Americans from the 1940s on; it also referred to a specific genre of African American music that fused blues sensibilities with danceable rhythms and beats, peaking in popularity from the late 1940s through the early 1960s; and, finally, in contemporary times, it refers to modern interpretations of soul music. The postwar genre of R&B had the most relevance to

Common stereotypes of African Americans were printed on sheet music in the nineteenth century, 1847. Courtesy of Library of Congress, LC-USZ62-37348.

the African American struggle against **Jim Crow**. This specific incarnation of R&B, with its driving backbeats, its instrumental virtuosity, and its positive energy, led to the creation of **rock and roll**, played a pivotal role in moving black culture into mainstream America, and channeled black aspirations for integration.

R&B in the 1940s developed out of three traditions in black music: jump **blues**, a dance-friendly style of blues that came out of African American urban areas; **gospel music**, which had its origins in all-black Christian churches; and the performances of the blues shouters, who lamented lost loves in powerful (and often racy) lyrics. Featuring smaller lineups than the big bands of the swing era, R&B groups often included four to eight members, with a lead vocalist and lead instrumentalist, a rhythm section, and a percussion section. R&B was another manifestation of the **Great Migration**, the decades-long movement of blacks out of the rural South and into Southern cities and Northern metropolises such as Chicago and Detroit. Featuring a more modern sound than traditional acoustic blues, R&B made use of the electric guitar and the electric bass to provide a soundtrack to blacks celebrating their improving economic standing in urban America. A number of musicians helped create R&B's distinctive sound and performance style, including Muddy Waters, who gradually shifted from a rural, rustic sound featuring slow and stilted tempos to a polished, urban style that emphasized dance-friendly backbeats. While male performers such as Waters, Big Joe Turner, and Billy Ward and the Dominoes, were central to R&B's development, black women also made major contributions to the genre. Ruth Brown and LaVern Baker, for example, each had numerous R&B hits, and both achieved some crossover success on the pop market, helping the genre overcome the racial divide.

Two significant changes in the music industry helped black R&B artists gain a wider audience for their music in the postwar period. The first major change involved **radio**. Although radio stations had previously ignored most music played by and for African Americans, that trend changed in the late 1940s and early 1950s. As national broadcast networks began to invest more resources in the burgeoning medium of television, radio networks scrambled to fill available airtime. As a result, programmers increasingly turned to music outside the mainstream, including black music such as R&B. These stations quickly became popular, as black audiences, eager to hear African American music, tuned in. Gradually, stations such as WDIA in Memphis, Tennessee, became exclusively devoted to black music, and R&B musicians had increased opportunities for their songs to reach a wider black audience. In the process, these stations also attracted white listeners, who appreciated the musical inventiveness they heard from black musicians.

The other major change in the music industry involved record labels. As the economy boomed in the postwar period and the cost of recording technology dropped, new "independent" labels formed, such as Chess Records and Atlantic Records. Because the major labels such as Capitol, Decca, and RCA had locked up most of the major pop stars, these independent labels turned to alternative forms of music, hoping to find market niches that had escaped the majors' attention. R&B proved to be one such opportunity, and independent label owners were delighted to see the demand for the music among black (and select white) audiences. As sales for R&B records boomed, independent labels sought out more black performers to record, hoping to cash in on the genre's popularity. Major labels followed suit, unwilling to let independents earn all of the profits. Legendary R&B musicians such as T-Bone Walker, who signed with Capitol, and Arthur Crudup, who signed with RCA, produced records directed at the black market for these major labels. While most black-oriented radio stations and record labels (including both the independents and the majors) were controlled by white owners and managers, black musicians nonetheless had more opportunities to produce their music for a consumer audience. In the process, they also reached across the color line, introducing whites to aspects of black culture of which they had been previously unaware.

Because of its increasing popularity with white audiences, R&B played a pivotal role in the development of rock and roll. White musicians and performers such as Elvis Presley, Bill Haley and His Comets, and Jerry Lee Lewis borrowed heavily from the songs and sounds of R&B as they launched their careers in the mid-1950s. Indeed, Presley's "Hound Dog" was originally by Big Mama Thornton, Haley's "Shake, Rattle, and Roll" was by Big Joe Turner, and Lewis's "Great Balls of Fire" was by Otis Blackwell—all R&B performers and composers. Although rock and roll performers often changed R&B songs, adding elements of country and speeding up the tempo, they were clearly indebted to black artists, and many felt that white rock and rollers appropriated—and outright stole—from R&B pioneers. The term "rock and roll," a slang expression for sexual intercourse, masked the black origins of the music—R&B—for some listeners. However, rock and roll's increasing popularity also led to demand for R&B versions of songs, and for R&B performers. Thus, Chuck Berry, "Little Richard" Penniman, and other black performers became stars with black and white audiences across the country, playing in front of integrated crowds and achieving success on both the R&B and pop charts. As more R&B songs crossed over to the pop charts, black artists had increased opportunities for financial success as musicians.

Although R&B certainly opened up opportunities for black musicians, and had some positive effects on integration, there were some negative impacts of R&B's popularity as well. Many R&B songs featured sexually explicit lyrics (usually masked by creative double entendres) that came out of the blues tradition. Expressing delight in the pursuit of sexual pleasure, and animosity at members of the opposite sex who did not come through in providing that pleasure, these songs were clearly tongue-in-cheek, part of a broader trend in

African American culture that emphasized witty verbal sparring. However, while black listeners understood these songs to be one small slice of African American life, many white listeners took the themes of these songs to be representative of black culture at large, and thus used this material to bolster stereotypes of African Americans as lustful, violent, and incapable of controlling their emotions and sexual appetites. Indeed, many nervous whites lamented rock and roll's popularity among white teens precisely because they feared that their youth were being exposed to the hedonism supposedly inherent to the African American community. White fans' appreciation of black musicians did not necessarily mean that white audiences would be more receptive to black calls for civil rights; fraternities at white Southern schools such as the University of Virginia, for example, welcomed black bands to perform but wholeheartedly supported segregationist efforts well into the 1960s.

As R&B evolved in the 1950s and early 1960s, two offshoots of the genre provide insight into the hopes of black performers and many in the black community at large. The first innovation was "doo wop," which developed from urban a cappella groups. Usually featuring four members, doo wop groups often featured teenagers who hailed from specific local communities. Instead of featuring the bawdy lyrics and raucous rhythms of earlier R&B performers, these young musicians instead sang about romantic love and youthful heartbreak. Groups such as Frankie Lymon and the Teenagers rose to the top of the charts with songs like "Why do fools fall in love," and were embraced by black and white audiences alike for their smooth vocals, their polished image, and their nonthreatening personas. Following the lead of popular groups such as the Platters, these doo wop artists actively courted an integrated audience, optimistic that the changes taking place in civil rights in the 1950s, such as the **U.S. Supreme Court** decision in ***Brown v. Board of Education***, portended a more equitable future for black Americans.

Black pop artists of the late 1950s and early 1960s followed a similar trajectory. Smooth male balladeers, such as Sam Cooke, and "girl groups," such as the Shirelles and the Supremes, courted an integrated youth audience by singing pop music tinged with R&B sounds and styles. Berry Gordy's founding of Motown Records in 1959 reflected similar aims. A black-owned and largely black-run organization, Motown reached out to a wide audience in its early years by creating a distinct R&B sound that was radio-friendly. By dressing his artists in glamorous attire, Gordy assured nervous whites that these performers were no threat to conventions of middle-class respectability. And by having his in-house songwriters focus on romantic love instead of sexual pleasure, these artists avoided radio censorship. Hopeful that the end of Jim Crow segregation was drawing near, and optimistic that integration would solve most of the black community's problems, these groups also tended to eschew overt political themes in their songs (although never ignoring the political, economic, and social realities of blacks' lives entirely). Singing pop standards and courting an integrated audience, these groups—male balladeers, the "girl groups," and the Motown acts of the early to mid-1960s—represented the apex of black hopes for integration.

By the mid-1960s, however, many of those hopes for integration were dashed, as the **Civil Rights Act of 1964** and the **Voting Rights Act of 1965** improved conditions for African Americans but largely failed to address the ongoing economic inequalities that ravaged the country. As the civil rights movement shifted to an emphasis on "black power" and black solidarity, these changes were reflected in African American music: R&B gave way first to soul music, which featured a greater emphasis on the black gospel tradition, and then to funk, which employed heavily syncopated rhythms and Afrocentric attire. Although the term R&B would continue to be employed in various contexts through to the present day, the trend-setting genre of the 1940s, 1950s, and early 1960s would largely be relegated to the bin of "oldies" music. However, it had a lasting impact on popular music and social movements, playing a pivotal role in the development of rock and roll, soul, funk, and present-day hip hop, and providing an outlet for African Americans to express their hopes for black equality and uplift. *See also* Black Entertainers against Jim Crow; Country Music; Racial Stereotypes.

Further Readings: Altschuler, Glenn C. *All Shook Up: How Rock 'n' Roll Changed America.* New York: Oxford University Press, 2003; George, Nelson. *The Death of Rhythm & Blues.* New York: Pantheon Books, 1988; Guralnick, Peter. *Sweet Soul Music: Rhythm and Blues and the Southern Dream of Freedom.* New York: Harper and Row, 1986; Ward, Brian. *Just My Soul Responding: Rhythm and Blues, Black Consciousness, and Race Relations.* Berkeley: University of California Press, 1998.

Gregory Kaliss

Rice, Thomas D. (1808–1860)

Thomas D. Rice was a white performer and playwright who used African American vernacular speech, song, and dance to become one of the most popular entertainers of his time. Although his most famous character—known as **Jim Crow**—later became synonymous with American racism and discrimination, there is no evidence that Rice himself was racist.

Rice was born on Manhattan's lower east side, near the bustling commercial district of the East River docks. His father may have been John Rice, a ship's rigger, and his mother may have been Eleanor Rice. Most likely the family was poor, Protestant, and of English ancestry. After some schooling, Rice apprenticed in his teens with a woodcarver named Dodge, but somehow soon found his way to the stage. By 1827, he was an itinerant actor, appearing not only as a stock player in several New York theaters, but also performing on frontier stages in the Ohio River valley and the coastal South.

The actual genesis of the Jim Crow character has become lost to legend. Several sources describe how Rice happened to encounter an elderly black stableman working in one of the river towns where Rice was performing. The man—with a crooked leg and deformed shoulder, according to some accounts—was singing about Jim Crow, and punctuating each stanza with a little jump. A more likely explanation is that Rice had observed and absorbed African American traditional song and dance over many years: first while growing up in a racially integrated Manhattan neighborhood, and later while touring the Southern slave states. African folktales of trickster birds, such as crows and buzzards, may also have influenced the vernacular traditions observed by Rice.

Whatever its origins, Rice had made the Jim Crow character his signature act by 1830—dressed in rags and torn shoes, his face and hands blackened, impersonating a very nimble and irreverently witty African American field hand who sang, "Turn about and wheel about, and do just so. And every time I turn about I jump Jim Crow." There had been other blackface performers before Rice, and there were many more afterwards. But it was "Daddy Rice" who became so indelibly associated with a single character and routine.

During the years of his peak popularity, from roughly 1832 to 1844, Rice often encountered sold-out houses, with audiences demanding numerous encores. He not only performed in more than 100 plays, but also created plays of his own, providing himself slight variants on the Jim Crow persona—as Cuff in *Oh, Hush!* (1833), Ginger Blue in *Virginia Mummy* (1835), and Bone Squash in *Bone Squash Diavolo* (1835). Moreover, Rice wrote and starred in *Otello* (1844), transforming Shakespeare's tragedy into a musical in which Othello and Desdemona live happily ever after; he also played the title character in *Uncle Tom's Cabin,* starting in 1854. On one of his stage tours in England, Rice married Charlotte B. Gladstone in 1837. She died in 1847, and none of their children survived infancy. As early as 1840, Rice suffered from a type of paralysis, which began to limit his speech and movements, and eventually led to his death.

Although several studies have pointed to the hostility and racism underlying much blackface **minstrelsy** in the late nineteenth and early twentieth centuries, more recent scholarship—particularly by W. T. Lhamon, Jr.—regards Rice as a daring interracial rebel who mocked the discriminatory stereotypes of African Americans and championed the working class by ridiculing the authority figures of the day, all of whom were white. In Rice's songs and plays, poor blacks align themselves with poor whites to express solidarity of the underclass that would subsequently find more lasting expression in the work of Karl Marx, Elvis Presley, and others. *See also* Humor and Comedic Traditions.

Further Readings: Lhamon, W. T., Jr. *Jump Jim Crow: Lost Plays, Lyrics, and Street Prose of the First Atlantic Popular Culture.* Cambridge, MA: Harvard University Press, 2003; Lhamon, W. T., Jr. *Raising Cain: Blackface Performance from Jim Crow to Hip Hop.* Cambridge, MA: Harvard University Press, 1998; Lott, Eric. *Love and Theft: Blackface Minstrelsy and the American Working Class.* New York: Oxford University Press, 1993.

James I. Deutsch

Robinson, Jackie (1919–1972)

Jackie Robinson was an African American athlete, activist, and businessman, most famous for his Hall of Fame pioneering career in Major League Baseball. Born in 1919 in Cairo, **Georgia**, Robinson moved with his mother and four older siblings to Pasadena, California, in 1920, where he grew up in a majority white neighborhood. Although involved in minor acts of vandalism and confrontations with the police as a youth, Robinson moderated his behavior under the influence of Karl Downs, a young black minister in the area. Excelling in a variety of sports in high school, Robinson chose to attend Pasadena Junior College (PJC) to be close to home and his beloved mother, Mallie. At PJC, Robinson set national marks in the broad jump and led the football team to an undefeated season in his sophomore year, earning acclaim in nearly every area newspaper for his brilliant open-field running as the team's quarterback. In February 1939, Robinson enrolled at the University of California at Los Angeles (UCLA), where he became the first athlete in the school's history to letter in four sports: baseball, track, football, and basketball. He earned the most acclaim for his performance on the football field, where, as a junior, he teamed with two other black starters, Kenny Washington and Woody Strode, to lead UCLA to a 6–0–4 record, only narrowly missing the school's first-ever invitation to the Rose Bowl.

After leaving UCLA in February 1941 to earn money to support his mother, Robinson briefly played professional football in Hawai'i before being drafted into the military in March 1943. Sent to Fort Riley, Kansas, for basic training, Robinson earned high marks in a variety of tests, thanks to his intelligence and physical aptitude, but was consistently passed over for admission into Officer Candidate School because of his race. Robinson's friendship with famed heavyweight boxer Joe Louis, also stationed at Fort Riley, helped gain him entrance into the school, where he earned the rank of second lieutenant. After being transferred to Camp Hood, **Texas**, Robinson faced court-martial charges after refusing to move to the back of a military bus when ordered to do so by the bus driver. Asserting his rights as an officer and an American citizen, Robinson was arrested. Eventually acquitted, Robinson was granted an honorable discharge because of an ongoing ankle ailment in November 1944. Robinson then played one year of baseball for the Kansas City Monarchs, a **Negro League Baseball** team.

Robinson's performance for the Monarchs attracted the attention of Branch Rickey, the president of the **Brooklyn Dodgers**, a Major League Baseball team. Although there were no formal rules against black players in the major leagues, an unwritten "gentleman's agreement" had kept African Americans out of the sport since the late nineteenth century. Robinson's athletic ability and strong character made him the ideal candidate to integrate Major League Baseball, and Rickey signed him to play that role in August 1945. The decision was announced publicly in October of that year. In 1946, Robinson played for the Dodgers' top minor league affiliate, the Montreal Royals. Although encountering bitter racism from fans, opposing players, and even some teammates and coaches, Robinson excelled and helped lead his team to a league championship. He also married his long-time girlfriend, Rachel Isum, at the conclusion of the 1946 season. The following spring, Robinson trained with the Dodgers and earned a starting spot on the team for the 1947 season.

On April 15, 1947, Robinson became the first African American player to participate in Major League Baseball in the modern era when he took the field with the Brooklyn Dodgers at the age of 28. Robinson faced racist taunting from opposing players and fans, and players often attempted to injure him by throwing pitches directly at him and deliberately "spiking" him with their cleats. African American fans turned out in droves to support him, and some white fans, particularly youths, were also enthusiastic admirers. Robinson initially received little support from his teammates, but an early series against the Philadelphia Phillies, managed by virulent racist Ben Chapman, helped unite the Dodgers. As Robinson withstood a torrent of racial abuse from the Phillies players without responding (a strategy of nonconfrontation he and Rickey had agreed upon), his teammates rallied to his support. In another key incident from that season, team shortstop Pee Wee Reese, a Southerner and one of the Dodgers' best players, silenced a hostile Boston crowd by putting his arm around Robinson and chatting with him on the field. In his nine-year career, Robinson won numerous accolades, including the National League Rookie of the Year in 1947, the National League Most Valuable Player in 1949, and a World Series championship in 1955. Following Robinson's debut, other clubs began to sign African American baseball players, and many consider Robinson's successful turn in baseball, "the national pastime," a pivotal event in the broader struggle for African American civil rights. He was awarded the Spingarn Medal in 1956 by the National Association for the Advancement of Colored People (NAACP) for his contributions to civil rights as a baseball player, the first athlete ever to receive the award.

After retiring from baseball in 1956, Robinson became a vice president for "Chock Full o' Nuts," a popular brand of coffee. He also became active in the NAACP, campaigning as a fund raiser and supporting a variety of civil rights causes across the country. Although beloved by the black community on the whole, Robinson generated controversy in later years by campaigning for Richard Nixon in the 1960 presidential election, a decision he later regretted. He remained a supporter of the Republican Party until 1964, when the nomination of Barry Goldwater over friend Nelson Rockefeller led him to leave the party. He also resigned from the board of the NAACP in 1967 because he thought that long-time executive director Roy Wilkins had become too autocratic and was not open to new ideas and young leaders. In his last years, as he struggled with diabetes, Robinson bitterly complained in his autobiography *I Never Had It Made* about the lack of black managers in baseball and the ongoing racial inequalities that persisted across the country. One of his last major public appearances was for Major League Baseball's celebration of the 25th anniversary of his first game. He appealed to baseball owners to hire black managers and executives, but did not live to see it happen. He died in October 1972 from complications of diabetes, and was buried in Cypress Hill Cemetery in Brooklyn, New York. Posthumously, he was awarded the nation's highest civilian award, the Medal of Freedom, in 1984. Major League Baseball also retired his number, 42, in 1997, to honor the 50th anniversary of his debut with the Dodgers. *See also* Sports.

Further Readings: "Baseball and Jackie Robinson." The Library of Congress American Memory Web site http://memory.loc.gov/ammem/collections/robinson/ (accessed May 29, 2008); Robinson, Jack, with Alfred Duckett. *I Never Had It Made.* New York: G. P. Putnam's Sons. 1972; Rampersad, Arnold. *Jackie Robinson: A Biography.* New York: Alfred A. Knopf. 1997; Tygiel, Jules. *Baseball's Great Experiment: Jackie Robinson and His Legacy.* New York: Oxford University Press. 1983.

Gregory Kaliss

Rock and Roll

Rock and roll is a musical genre that first emerged in the 1950s. Heavily influenced by African American music, particularly **rhythm and blues** (R&B),

rock and roll galvanized the nation's emerging teen culture with its pulsating beats, ecstatic vocals, and risqué lyrics. Spread predominantly through black **radio** stations in its early years, rock and roll became wildly popular across the color line, and many saw it, either fearfully or hopefully, as a powerful integrationist force. Generating anxiety among the elders of both races, rock and roll stirred up controversy and helped push black culture into the mainstream.

The term "rock and roll" was first used to describe this musical genre in 1951 by famed white disc jockey Alan Freed. Although originally a euphemism for sexual intercourse, Freed's term became widely accepted as the genre's name. The new moniker was accepted in part because it had none of the racial connotations of R&B, a term coined by the music industry to refer to popular African American music in general, but one that had come to define a genre in its own right. Rock and roll was closely aligned with R&B, and three musical traditions that shaped R&B in the 1940s and 1950s—jump **blues, gospel music,** and blues shouters' performances—deeply influenced rock and roll's evolution as well. However, many casual fans were unaware of the influence black music had on rock and roll, and some have claimed that the genre's change of name served to slight the importance of African American musicians. This was one of many criticisms of uncredited appropriation of music styles, songs, and performance elements by white musicians. Although it is quite clear that rock and roll leaned heavily on R&B, the genre also changed as it was performed by white musicians. "Rockabilly," one subgenre of rock and roll, fused R&B with white country instrumentation and vocal styles, for example. Other white musicians, such as rock and roll pioneers Bill Haley and His Comets, sped up the tempo of R&B songs such as "Shake, Rattle, and Roll," replacing their sensuousness with a frenetic pace that appealed to young, high-energy audiences.

Rock and roll's increasing popularity owed a good deal to the changing character of radio in the late 1940s and early 1950s. The same factors that propelled R&B's increased accessibility to white audiences—national broadcast networks' decisions to invest more resources in the burgeoning medium of television, which left radio networks scrambling to fill available airtime—similarly impacted rock and roll's fortunes. As programmers increasingly turned to music outside the mainstream, up-and-coming rock and roll artists (black and white) found more opportunities to have their music reach a wider audience. Freed played a key role in this development, as his radio show for Cleveland radio station WJW (called the "Moondog Rock 'n' Roll Party") showed that the genre could attract numerous listeners, particularly teenagers. Freed then moved to New York in 1954, generating even more interest in rock and roll with radio station WINS. Even as the music reached a wider audience through radio, controversy over rock and roll's racial politics continued to dog the genre—with many white parents concerned by the fact that white teens were listening to black musicians and attending concerts with mixed-race audiences. These anxieties only increased as the music made its way into films such as 1955's *Blackboard Jungle.*

Elvis Presley's ascension to stardom as a rock and roll musician marked a particularly important moment in the genre's history, expanding rock and roll's appeal to a wide audience but also illustrating the complicated racial terrain that stars navigated. Presley, originally from Tupelo, Mississippi, was a 19-year-old truck driver, movie usher, and part-time musician, when he recorded his first record with Sam Philips at Sun Records Studio in Memphis. His first local hit was a cover of the blues song "That's All Right," originally performed in 1946 by black musician Arthur Crudup. As the record received more airtime, it became increasingly popular with black and white audiences, who admired Presley's vocals and the fusion of country and R&B styles. After releasing a number of songs in 1954 and 1955, and gaining in popularity across the South, Presley became a national sensation in January, 1956, when he released "Heartbreak Hotel." While many or Presley's early hits were covers of black artists' R&B songs, such as "Tutti Frutti" and "Hound Dog," he earned considerably more airtime and wealth than black performers, in part because of his race. Appropriating black songs and some elements of black performance styles, Presley was more palatable to mainstream audiences than black R&B performers, a fact that black artists lamented then and in later years. As Presley launched his career, however, he acknowledged his indebtedness to black artists, especially Crudup, and his covers of R&B songs also led to greater wealth and exposure for black songwriters. Unlike other unscrupulous white artists, who simply copied black songs' instrumentation and performance style, Presley also significantly changed the music when he covered the material, adding a high, tremulous vibrato to his vocals and using different instrumentation. As he rose to stardom, nervous parents lamented his hip-shaking dance moves and worried about the racial origins of his songs, but teen audiences—both black and white, initially—could not get enough, suggesting that rock and roll could reach across the color line to the nation's diverse population of youth.

Rock and roll's impact on integration remains a contested issue, although a number of examples suggest both the possibilities and the limitations of the genre to effect lasting change. On the one hand, many rock and roll shows in the 1950s were attended by interracial audiences, and while violence sometimes broke out, most attributed the behavior to the music and not to racial tensions. Indeed, performers reported that black and white teens on occasion pulled down barriers meant to segregate them at rock and roll shows in the South, and black stars delighted in their popularity with white youth culture. The black press, in general, trumpeted rock and roll's popularity, pointing to African American musicians' cultural contributions and praising the color-blind nature of the record-buying public. Spotlighting the successes of black stars such as Antoine "Fats" Domino and Chuck Berry, many in the black press saw rock and roll as proof that the color line could be permanently erased and that equality could be achieved. There were signs of this potential everywhere: the nationally popular television show "American Bandstand," which featured teens dancing to the latest rock and roll hits of the day, integrated in 1957, for example. Although the show did not depict interracial couples—black teens danced with other black teens alone—the image of both black and white teens dancing to rock and roll must have had symbolic resonance for many across the country.

However, there were significant limits to rock and roll's integrationist potential. In 1957, the same year "Bandstand" integrated, Freed's rival show *Rock 'n Roll Dance Party* was cancelled in part because of widespread outrage when black teen performer Frankie Lymon spontaneously danced with a white teen girl as the show was ending. The **Ku Klux Klan** also targeted rock and roll concerts and radio shows for violent protests because of the music's popularity across the color line. Releasing broadsides that indicated that rock and roll's interracial popularity would lead to **miscegenation**, Klan leaders played on long-held stereotypes of black male sexual predators. On the business side, white covers of black artists' songs also received disproportionately more air-play than black originals, revealing that ongoing inequalities persisted even in the supposedly color-blind realm of popular music. As a result, inferior white performers such as Pat Boone, who cultivated a lily-white image, out-sold black stars such as Little Richard, and many lamented that black perform-ing artists were not being given a fair opportunity to succeed in the music business. Chuck Berry, for example, was bilked out of royalty rights by white record executives, a common experience for black artists. African American leaders worried, too, that rock and roll's association with black culture would lead whites to equate blackness with the genre's supposedly negative traits, such as lewdness, wild behavior, and juvenile delinquency. For African Amer-icans hoping to break into the expanding middle class, Rock and Roll seemed dangerous because of its association with "low" culture and its eschewal of middle-class conventions of behavior and deportment. Finally, white fan appreciation of black musicians did not necessarily mean that white audiences would be more receptive to black calls for civil rights; fraternities at white Southern schools, for example, wholeheartedly supported segregationist efforts well into the 1960s, even as they welcomed black bands to perform.

Women performers also found restrictions on their ability to participate in the burgeoning genre. While black women such as Ruth Brown and LaVern Baker were major R&B stars who had considerable success in the early years of rock and roll, very few women participated in the latter half of the 1950s. White women were especially absent from rock and roll groups, a reflection of the dominant gender ideologies of the time, which expected women to be submissive and chaste. Because rock and roll concerts demanded that perform-ers cut loose on stage, it was considered inappropriate for women to partici-pate. Black women initially had greater freedom to take part in rock and roll's excessive energy and celebration, but only because they were often ignored by mainstream cultural ideals of womanhood. However, as the **Civil Rights Movement** gained momentum in the late 1950s and aspirations for integration ran high in the black community, black women performers also became less conspicuous in R&B and rock and roll. "Girl groups" such as the Shirelles and the Supremes became more popular, with their stars dressing in elegant attire and singing hyperfeminine, smooth pop hits.

Three key African American performers of the 1950s, Domino, Berry, and "Little Richard" Penniman, highlight some of the avenues open to black male rock and roll artists as well as the color line's continuing importance. All three became major stars among both black and white audiences (all coincidentally releasing their first rock and roll hit songs in 1955), and cashed in on their success: Domino's "Ain't That a Shame" launched him to stardom with interracial audiences, Richard scored with "Tutti Frutti," and Berry first made it into the mainstream with "Maybellene." Each continued to produce major hit songs in the ensuing years, and headlined well-attended concerts across the country, showing the possibilities for black recording stars to reach a nationwide, biracial audience.

However, each of these three stars also faced certain limitations in their music and performances that showed the ongoing power of Jim Crow. When writing songs, each was careful to avoid explicitly addressing issues of racial injustice in their music. Although certain songs such as Berry's "Brown-Eyed Handsome Man" hinted at racial oppression, none targeted racism explicitly. Apparently fearful that they would be shunned by the industry and the general public, these recording artists shied away from the political, social, and legal issues being raised by the ongoing Civil Rights Movement. These artists also strategically managed their public images. Domino's portly physique, jolly demeanor, and dutiful black wife, for example, allayed any fears that nervous whites may have had of him as a sexual predator; similarly, Richard's over-the-top hairstyle, outrageous makeup, and closeted, though apparent, **homosexuality** made him a nonthreatening figure as well. Aware of long-standing white fears of black men, these artists carefully crafted images that enabled them to succeed in mainstream America, still cautious of the Jim Crow line even as they achieved remarkable success. Berry even changed the protagonist of his 1958 hit song "Johnny B. Goode," from a "colored boy" to a "country boy," so that he would not alienate any white fans.

As rock and roll evolved into the genre of "rock" in the 1960s, issues of race continued to take center stage. When the Beatles and the Rolling Stones kicked off the so-called British Invasion in the early 1960s, both groups enthusiastically credited black R&B performers as their major influences, drawing more attention to rock and roll's history of racial crossing-over. Ironically, however, bemused British musicians often found that they had to educate white American fans who were unaware of the debt rock and roll owed to black performers of the 1940s and early 1950s. Meanwhile, as rock evolved in the 1960s, black musicians drifted away from the genre, devoting more energy and attention to music styles that seemed to fit better the changing climate of the late Civil Rights Movement, such as soul and funk, before eventually turning to hip hop in the 1980s. While some black performers continued to play rock music, such as the legendary guitarist Jimi Hendrix, on the whole, the genre gradually came to be dominated by white artists and white fans. The tenuous interracial coalition that had propelled rock and roll to the top of the charts in the mid to late 1950s largely dissolved. Its cultural legacies, however, in the form of crossover artists, the various subgenres that formed in its wake, and the visible signs of an integrated America, remained resonant for years to come. *See also* Black Entertainers against Jim Crow; Racial Stereotypes.

Further Readings: Altschuler, Glenn C. *All Shook Up: How Rock 'n Roll Changed America.* New York: Oxford University Press, 2003; Bertrand, Michael T. *Race, Rock, and Elvis.* Urbana: University of Illinois Press, 2000; "Chuck Berry." Rock and Roll Hall of Fame and Museum Web site http://www.Rockhall.com/exhibitfeatured/chuck-berry/ (accessed May 29, 2008); Szatmary, David P. *Rockin' in Time: A Social History of Rock-*

and-Roll. Upper Saddle River, NJ: Pearson/Prentice Hall, 2007; Ward, Brian. *Just My Soul Responding: Rhythm and Blues, Black Consciousness, and Race Relations.* Berkeley: University of California Press, 1998.

Gregory Kaliss

Roosevelt, Eleanor (1884–1962)

Eleanor Roosevelt, wife of **Franklin D. Roosevelt** (FDR), and First Lady during the **Great Depression** and **World War II**, was the most prominent white American to work actively toward elimination of the country's **Jim Crow** laws.

The niece of President Theodore Roosevelt, Roosevelt was born into a wealthy family in New York City in 1884. Both her parents died during her childhood, but she grew up in a privileged household and attended a distinguished boarding school in England. FDR, a distant cousin, was part of her socially prominent circle of friends. They were engaged in 1903 and married in 1905. The couple had six children, including a son who died in infancy.

Roosevelt first acted on her concern for social activism in work with poor immigrant families at a settlement house in New York's Lower East Side during the early years of the twentieth century. When FDR was stricken with polio in 1921, she cared for him devotedly and encouraged him to remain in politics. At the same time, she herself continued to work for social service agencies for the benefit of the underprivileged. When FDR was elected president in 1932, Roosevelt transformed the role of first lady, traveling the country, lecturing, holding press conferences, and writing a daily syndicated newspaper column titled, "My Day." By the time she began to speak on behalf of African Americans during the Great Depression, Roosevelt was already well experienced in conducting herself in the public eye and speaking out, in a moderate tone, on issues of justice and democracy.

From the start of her husband's presidency in 1933, Roosevelt was in the planning and implementation of progressive **New Deal** programs designed to help poor Americans. This work led her to counter Jim Crow laws. "There must be equality before the law," she wrote, "equality of education, equal opportunity to obtain a job according to one's ability and training and equality of participation in self government." But her egalitarian beliefs ran counter to the Southern social mores. An indication of the resentment Roosevelt engendered was the rumor that spread across the South of "Eleanor Clubs," which were said to have been organized among black domestics to agitate for better pay and working conditions. No evidence was ever found to substantiate the existence of any such clubs.

Eleanor Roosevelt worked with New Deal administrators to mitigate the effects of Jim Crow. In 1935, for example, she pushed **Works Progress Administration** officials to enact equitable policies in the administration of relief funds to black Southerners. She was also effective in involving black leaders in New Deal initiatives. For example, she brought to prominence **Mary McLeod Bethune**, who would become the most prominent African American in the New Deal, and the first black woman to hold an influential position in the U.S. government. Through Eleanor Roosevelt, Bethune would become a powerful influence in White House policies throughout the national crisis of the Great Depression.

Eleanor and Franklin Roosevelt worked together, in a sense, to weaken Jim Crow. FDR though he could not himself directly attack long-standing Southern social traditions without losing necessary political support from white, Southern Democrats, but Eleanor Roosevelt felt compelled to be more outspoken on behalf of racial justice.

Her approach to Jim Crow was seen most famously in her appearance at the 1938 Southern Conference on Human Welfare (SCHW), held in Birmingham, **Alabama**. The high-water mark of Southern liberalism during the Great Depression, the conference brought together 1,200 black and white Southerners, labor leaders, the poor, and the dispossessed, along with political and business leaders, newspaper editors, and academics. The conference called for equal salaries for black and white teachers and endorsed federal antilynching laws.

Unexpectedly, the SCHW was forced to confront racism directly. Conference organizers had not planned to address the issue of segregation, but Birmingham's police chief decided to enforce an ordinance requiring segregation in the city's municipal auditorium. To avoid arrest, conference participants decided to arrange their seating with blacks on one side of the hall's central aisle and whites on the other.

Eleanor Roosevelt arrived late and quickly took a seat with the black participants. When a policeman informed her that she would have to move, the first lady moved her chair to the middle of the aisle. Asked later about her actions, Roosevelt avoided making any inflammatory remarks. "In the section of the country where I come from, it is a procedure that is not followed," she explained. "But I would not presume to tell the people of Alabama what they should do." Typical of her approach to questions of Jim Crow, Eleanor Roosevelt allowed the symbolism of her action to carry the weight of her beliefs. Conference organizers responded by vowing never again to conduct a segregated meeting.

By the time of the SCHW's 1942 meeting, Eleanor Roosevelt felt emboldened enough to claim the conference's work "is really as important as the war ... because making the South a real part of the United States, and progressive in its racial and labor attitudes, is the finest work any one could do at the present time."

Eleanor Roosevelt actively supported a variety of initiatives aimed at ameliorating the injustice experienced by African Americans, including a controversial federal antilynching bill and the abolition of poll taxes. She famously resigned from the Daughters of the American Revolution when the organization refused to allow black opera singer Marian Anderson to perform in Constitution Hall in the spring of 1939. Eleanor Roosevelt's resignation was front-page news in hundreds of papers, and it turned the incident into a national event. The result was the scheduling of a groundbreaking concert in which Anderson sang to a live, nationwide radio audience from the steps of the **Lincoln Memorial**.

After her husband's death in 1945, Roosevelt became even more vocal in her opposition to Jim Crow. She joined the Board of Directors of the National

Association for the Advancement of Colored People, in which capacity she lobbied the Truman administration to introduce low-income, federally financed housing. President Harry S. Truman's subsequent decision to integrate the military was instrumental in Roosevelt's decision to endorse his candidacy for the presidency in 1948.

During the 1950s, Roosevelt worked with **Martin Luther King, Jr.,** and **Rosa Parks** to raise money for the **Montgomery Bus Boycott** and supported the Southern Conference Education Fund's work in desegregating hospitals. She warmly endorsed the **U.S. Supreme Court**'s landmark 1954 decision in ***Brown v. Board of Education*** that called for the desegregation of nation's public schools. In her public addresses, she took aim at the hypocrisy of segregationists' simultaneous criticism of Communism and support for Jim Crow. During the **Civil Rights Movement,** Eleanor Roosevelt was a staunch defender of nonviolent civil disobedience. Indeed, in her elder years, before her death in 1962, Roosevelt called for a new "social revolution" to defeat the forces of segregation.

Further Readings: Egerton, John. *Speak Now Against the Day: The Generation Before the Civil Rights Movement in the South.* New York: Alfred A. Knopf, 1994; "Eleanor Roosevelt and Civil Rights." Eleanor Roosevelt National Historic Site Web site. http://www.nps.gov/archive/elro/teach-er-vk/lesson-plans/notes-er-and-civil-rights.htm (accessed May 29, 2008); Freidel, Frank. *FDR and the South.* Baton Rouge: Louisiana State University Press, 1965; Sitkoff, Harvard. *A New Deal for Blacks: The Emergence of Civil Rights as a National Issue.* New York: Oxford University Press, 1978; Sullivan, Patricia. *Days of Hope: Race and Democracy in the New Deal Era.* Chapel Hill: University of North Carolina Press, 1996.

Louis Mazzari

Roosevelt, Franklin D. (1882–1945)

Franklin Delano Roosevelt, who served as U.S. president from 1933 until his death in 1945, did more for racial justice in the United States than had any chief executive had since Abraham Lincoln. The **Civil Rights Movement** of the 1950s and 1960s had its beginning in the efforts of black and white Americans working under the auspices of the Roosevelt administration to ameliorate the most injurious effects of **Jim Crow.** Indeed, Roosevelt and his **New Deal** policies were responsible for the great majority of black Americans to shift their allegiance to the **Democratic Party** from their traditional base, the **Republican Party** of Lincoln.

Elected to lift the nation out of the **Great Depression,** Roosevelt's initial primary focus was resurrecting the American economy, and to do so, he needed the cooperation of the Southern Democrats in Congress. So he did not directly challenge Jim Crow, leaving the states to determine their own laws concerning race. Instead, he relied on liberals in his administration to push the South and the country toward equality and integration. In a sense, Roosevelt traded acquiescence to the South, in terms of segregation, for support for his liberalizing economic policies. In spite of his refusal to actively work toward ending Jim Crow, Roosevelt's administration was the nation's first to promote equality both in the workplace and on Main Street.

Roosevelt's focus on economic restructuring necessarily ate away at the underpinnings of Jim Crow. The New Deal's extensive programs in support of Americans' general welfare, in the areas of health, education, and housing, as well as workplace and agricultural reforms, meant the institution of greater federal planning. Inevitably, Southern states' control of their own racial policies was undermined by federal regulations that had the effect of standardizing even social policies across the nation. Federal efforts to strengthen American society in general worked to enervate local efforts to maintain white supremacy. New Deal programs themselves and the way they touched more blacks, from the use of birth certificates to the introduction of agricultural extension agencies, brought the **federal government** closer to the average African American and made the idea of political participation more likely.

Roosevelt's belief in the activism of the progressives he had attracted to his administration allowed him to avoid speaking directly to the inequalities of race and class in America. For example, FDR depended on the guidance of social scientists he brought to Washington—many of them from the University of North Carolina at Chapel Hill—to plumb the fallacies beneath the South's racial myths, and to turn new knowledge into practical service. Socialist leader Norman Thomas remembered a meeting with the president, in which Roosevelt refused to back Thomas's call for strong union legislation. "I know the South," Roosevelt told him, "and there is arising a new generation of leaders in the South and we've got to be patient."

Roosevelt hired for the upper echelons of New Deal agencies more than a hundred African Americans. He appointed the first black federal judge and the first black general officer in the U.S. Army. The New Deal disturbed the social, as well as economic, relations that Southern society had developed over decades. Important among the possibilities created by the New Deal was the destruction of Jim Crow laws.

Typical of Roosevelt's approach to **racism** and Jim Crow was his executive order integrating defense production, signed on June 25, 1941, as Europe was embroiled in **World War II** and the United States prepared for the possibility of entry into the conflict. Black leaders saw an opportunity to secure work in defense plants and to integrate the armed forces. **A. Philip Randolph,** president of the Brotherhood of Sleeping Car Porters, the nation's first black labor union, formulated the idea for a **march on Washington** to demonstrate African Americans' desire for their share of defense work, and the nation's black newspapers overwhelmingly supported the concept.

Roosevelt's response was characteristic. He invited Randolph and **Walter White,** head of the National Association for the Advancement of Colored People, to the White House and promised fairer treatment in the workplace. Randolph wanted what Roosevelt did not want to give him—a piece of legislation that conservatives could hold against him. With war imminent, the president did not intend to alter the makeup of the military, but he was willing to legislate against job discrimination once he was assured that it would not diminish war production. Randolph called off the march a week before black Americans were set to converge on Washington.

The order promulgated the rationale that the nation needed all the help it could get, "in the firm belief that the democratic way of life within the Nation can be defended successfully only with the help and support of all groups within its borders." Typically, Roosevelt couched this effort on behalf of black Americans in language that claimed no special prerogatives for minorities, but spoke instead to national security and the general welfare of all Americans. Innocuous as it seemed, the executive order set a precedent against discrimination in hiring that would be cited time and again in the coming years of the Civil Rights Movement.

If Roosevelt thought he could not push to abolish Jim Crow laws, he was happy to be tugged along by the tide created by black leaders, including Randolph, White, and **Mary McLeod Bethune**, president of the National Association of Colored Women, as well as white civil rights leaders, including—most prominently—**Eleanor Roosevelt**, his wife.

Eleanor Roosevelt knew her husband's true feelings about civil rights. She wrote about a conversation with FDR and Walter White. "You go ahead," the president told White. "You do everything you can do. Whatever you can get done is okay with me, but I just can't do it." Afterwards, she asked, "Well, what about me? Do you mind if I say what I think?" Roosevelt answered, "No, certainly not. You can say anything you want. I can always say, 'Well, that is my wife; I can't do anything about her.'"

The initial steps taken by Roosevelt toward racial equality created an enormous influence on the subsequent generation of Democratic politicians. Among the most ardent, young New Dealers came the sentiment that Roosevelt "was just like a daddy to me always." A died-in-the-wool Texan, Lyndon B. Johnson, would knowingly sacrifice the white Southern vote to the Republicans for generations by sponsoring the most important civil rights legislation since **Reconstruction**, legislation that finally killed legal Jim Crow. "I don't know that I'd have ever come to Congress if it hadn't been for him," Johnson claimed. "But I do know I got my first great desire for public office because of him—and so did thousands of young men all over the country."

Further Readings: Egerton, John. *Speak Now against the Day: The Generation before the Civil Rights Movement in the South.* New York: Alfred A. Knopf, 1994; Freidel, Frank. *FDR and the South.* Baton Rouge: Louisiana State University Press, 1965; Sitkoff, Harvard. *A New Deal for Blacks: The Emergence of Civil Rights as a National Issue.* New York: Oxford University Press, 1978; Sullivan, Patricia. *Days of Hope: Race and Democracy in the New Deal Era.* Chapel Hill: University of North Carolina Press, 1996; Woodward, C. Vann. *The Strange Career of Jim Crow.* New York: Oxford University Press, 1955.

Louis Mazzari

Rosewood (1923)

In 1922, Rosewood was a small, close-knit, and predominantly African American town of roughly 120 residents, located in the pinewoods of Levy County, west central **Florida**, close to the Gulf of Mexico. The Rosewood community consisted of 20 to 30 families, the black-owned Goins and Brothers' Naval stores company, a one-room school, at least two churches, a Masonic lodge and a railroad depot connected to the Seaboard Air Line. However, by February 1923, this small world of Rosewood had been destroyed, razed to the ground in the wake of a brutal racial assault on the town and its black residents.

The larger backdrop for the events that unfolded at Rosewood was the widespread white racism and vicious mob violence directed against African Americans across the United States during the opening decades of the twentieth century. This era witnessed campaigns of terror orchestrated by the resurgent, or second, **Ku Klux Klan**; race riots in New Orleans (1900), Atlanta (1906), Springfield (1908), East St. Louis and Houston (1917), and Chicago (1919); as well as thousands of **lynchings**. The racial ideology of the period found popular expression in the motion picture *The Birth of a Nation* (1915), with its crude stereotypes of blackness, heroic portrait of the Ku Klux Klan, and profound fear and vilification of black male sexuality.

Similarly, racial tensions were rising in Florida, with large Klan demonstrations and frequent lynchings in the early 1920s. The violence in Rosewood itself began on New Year's Day 1923. Frances Taylor, a 22-year-old white housewife, in the nearby town of Sumner, alleged that a black man had entered her home, physically assaulted, and robbed her. As reporters and historians of the riot have discovered, Rosewood's black community recounted a very different version of events. According to Sarah Carrier, who did laundry for Taylor, and Carrier's granddaughter, Philomenia Goins, they had witnessed a white man visiting Fannie Taylor, who then left shortly before she made her allegations. African American residents believed that Taylor had been conducting a romance with the mysterious stranger and that they had quarreled. Taylor then attempted to protect herself, blaming a black man for the evidence of her lover's physical abuse.

In response to Taylor's allegations, the white community assumed there had been a sexual assault, and a group of Sumner's male residents formed a posse to search for the assailant. A black convict named Jesse Hunter, who had recently escaped from a chain-gang road construction crew, became the focus of the lynch mob's hunt. In pursuing Hunter, the white mob came across Rosewood's Aaron Carrier (who may have assisted in the flight of Taylor's white lover) and brutally beat him. Next, the mob followed the trail to Sam Carter's home and accused him of aiding the attacker in escaping. The mob then shot and killed Sam Carter after torturing him.

Three days later, on Thursday, January 4, word reached Sumner that Taylor's assailant was being sheltered by Sylvester Carrier in Rosewood. A group of white gunmen went to the town and opened fire on the Carrier home. However, the mob met fierce resistance and two whites were shot and killed by Sylvester Carrier as they tried to storm the house. The posse retreated, but continued to lay siege throughout the early hours of Friday morning. Reinforced by Klansmen from Gainesville, the white mob started to burn down the town, shooting any remaining black residents they discovered as they cleared the area.

While Rosewood's racial troubles were blamed on black lawlessness in the Florida press, Northern and African American newspapers called for anti-lynching reforms and condemned Florida, and the South in general, for the persistence of racial violence. Thereafter, the racial cleansing of Rosewood was almost forgotten until investigative journalist Gary Moore published an article on the town's fate in the *St. Petersburg Times* in July 1982. This was followed the year later by a CBS *60 Minutes* report. In 1994, following a detailed investigation by an academic research team, the Florida legislature awarded over $2 million to survivors and descendants of former residents whose homes were destroyed in the attack on Rosewood. African American director John Singleton's cinematic rendition, *Rosewood,* was released in 1997, while in 2004 the state of Florida erected a historical marker at the site of the former town. *See also* Red Summer.

Further Readings: D'Orso, Michael. *Like Judgment Day: The Ruin and Redemption of a Town Called Rosewood.* New York: G. P. Putnam's Sons, 1996; Tuttle, William M. *Race Riot: Chicago in the Red Summer of 1919.* New York: Atheneum, 1970.

Stephen C. Kenny

Rustin, Bayard (1912–1987)

Bayard Taylor Rustin was an organizer and activist for racial equality around the world. As one of the earliest American proponents of nonviolent direct action, he brought groundbreaking protest strategies out of the pacifist movement to leaders in the Civil Rights Movement. Rustin worked behind the scenes for many organizations, and leaders including **A. Phillip Randolph** and **Martin Luther King, Jr.**, considered Rustin's gifts as a strategist and theorist integral to their campaigns. As an openly gay African American man, Rustin personally faced a good deal of discrimination, even within the progressive organizations with which he worked. Of Rustin's many achievements, he is perhaps best known for serving as the chief organizer for the 1963 **March on Washington** for Jobs and Freedom. Throughout his life, Rustin sought to illuminate connections between racial discrimination and economic inequality and to reveal the power of nonviolence as a tool for social change.

Born on March 17, 1912, Rustin was raised by his grandparents Julia and Janifer Rustin in West Chester, Pennsylvania. Julia Rustin, raised her grandson as a Quaker and taught him about nonviolence and about respecting all people as part of a human family. Julia Rustin also helped charter West Chester's National Association for the Advancement of Colored People (NAACP) chapter. The Rustin household served as a guest house for African American leaders denied service at local hotels, including **W.E.B. Du Bois** and James Weldon Johnson. West Chester remained segregated during Rustin's youth, but the town's small size necessitated the integration of West Chester High School. Rustin excelled athletically, academically, and socially in high school, but began to feel the sting of racism more clearly as he got older. Rustin cultivated friendships with students of many different backgrounds, but found that they could not interact freely outside of school or on school trips.

Rustin spent time at Wilberforce University in Ohio and Cheney State Teachers College in Pennsylvania from 1932 to 1936. He joined the Society of Friends (Quaker) in 1937 and soon moved to New York City. Living in Harlem in 1937, Rustin embraced a locally thriving gay community that allowed him a good deal of personal growth, even within a larger African American culture that urged extreme discretion in matters of sexual identity.

Rustin joined the Young Communist League (YCL) at City College of New York in 1938, drawn by the **Communist Party** of America's commitment to peace and civil rights. Rustin left the YCL in June 1941, and began working with influential African American labor leader A. Philip Randolph. Randolph made Rustin a youth director for a planned "March on Washington for Negro Americans." When President **Franklin D. Roosevelt** integrated the defense industry to avoid the demonstration, Randolph cancelled the march. Rustin bitterly disagreed with Randolph's decision, but their work in 1941 began a long partnership between the two leaders.

In 1941 Rustin also began working with A. J. Muste at the pacifist Fellowship of Reconciliation (FOR). As a youth secretary with the FOR, Rustin traveled throughout the South teaching about nonviolent direct action, or using techniques of peaceful protest in an organized way to agitate for social change. Rustin's work slowed in 1943, however, when the **federal government** sent him to prison for resisting the draft as a conscientious objector. In the Ashland, Kentucky, prison where he was held, Rustin led protests against Jim Crow eating areas within the facility. Upon his release in March 1947, Rustin returned to the FOR and worked with Muste, **James Farmer**, and George Houser in the affiliated **Congress of Racial Equality (CORE)**.

Farmer, Houser, and Rustin planned the Journey of Reconciliation through the upper South to test the **U.S. Supreme Court** decision in *Morgan v. Virginia* (1946), which prohibited segregation on interstate transportation. The CORE plan called for interracial duos of men to travel from Washington, DC, on public buses and nonviolently resist orders to abide by Jim Crow seating

Bayard Rustin and others protest segregation in Ford's Theater in Baltimore, 1948. Courtesy of Library of Congress, LC-USZ62-131559.

Bayard Rustin, "We Challenged Jim Crow"

Rustin wrote about the earliest Freedom Rides through the upper South at the end of the 1940s.

From Winston-Salem to Statesville the group traveled by Greyhound. [Wallace] Nelson ["freelance lecturer"] was seated with [Ernest] Bromley ["Methodist minister from North Carolina"] in the second seat in the front. Nothing was said. At Statesville, the group transferred to the Trailways, with Nelson still in front. In a small town about ten mile from Statesville, the driver approached Nelson and told him he would have to move to the rear. When Nelson said he was an interstate passenger, the driver said that the bus was not interstate. When Nelson explained that his ticket was interstate, the driver returned to his seat and drove on. The rest of the trip to Asheville was through mountainous country, and the bus stopped at many small towns. A soldier asked the driver why Nelson was not forced to move. The driver explained that there was a Supreme Court decision and that he could do nothing about it. He said, "If you want to do something about this, don't blame this man [Nelson]; kill those bastards up in Washington." The soldiers explained to a rather larger, vociferous man why Nelson was allowed to sit up front. The large man commented, "I wish I was the bus driver." Near Asheville the bus became very crowded, and there were women standing up. Two women spoke to the bus driver, asking him why Nelson was not moved. In each case the driver explained that the Supreme Court decision was responsible. Several white women took seats in the Jim Crow section in the rear.

Source: From *Down the Line: The Collected Writings of Bayard Rustin* (Chicago: Quadrangle Books, 1971).

arrangements on a moral and legal basis. Authorities in Chapel Hill, North Carolina, arrested Rustin and sentenced him to 30 days on a chain gang. While the journey was only marginally successful, it marked a turning point in Rustin's work, and inspired the Freedom Rides attempted by CORE and the **Student Nonviolent Coordinating Committee (SNCC)** in 1961. Throughout the 1950s, Rustin worked closely under Muste and Randolph and spoke around the world. However, in January 1953, California police arrested and prosecuted Rustin for sodomy (coded as "lewd conduct"), a charge that Rustin denied. Muste then distanced himself from his protégé because of the negative publicity the arrest could bring in the intolerant political climate of the 1950s.

Rustin denied the charges and found his feet quickly as executive secretary for the War Resisters League (WRL). On a short leave of absence in 1956, Rustin traveled South to offer counsel to the new leader of the **Montgomery Bus Boycott**, Martin Luther King, Jr. Rustin became one of King's closest advisors and strengthened King's commitment to nonviolence in all aspects of his life and work. From New York, Rustin continued to speak with King about effective organizing techniques, and about the need for a permanent organization to build on the success of Montgomery. At meetings in Atlanta and New Orleans, Rustin worked with Stanley Levinson and Ella Baker to draft the original documents that would form the **Southern Christian Leadership Conference (SCLC)** in 1957; stressing voter education and the use of nonviolent mass protest to force integration. Rustin remained in the SCLC for several years and helped coordinate plans to stage protests at the Democratic National Convention in 1960. Harlem Congressman Adam Clayton Powell, Jr., upset at being excluded from planning, jealously threatened to publicize rumors centering on Rustin's sexuality. King flinched at the potential damage the threat held, and accepted Rustin's resignation from the SCLC. Distraught over yet another ousting from the inner circle of movement leadership, Rustin turned to international peace activism in Europe and Africa in the early 1960s.

Rustin's return to the national Civil Rights Movement came again at Randolph's insistence in 1963. Randolph asked Rustin to plan a march in Washington, DC, to decry the still unrealized promise of freedom for black Americans. Randolph and Rustin sought the involvement of a broad coalition of progressive groups, including the SCLC, the NAACP, the Urban League, CORE, SNCC, and various labor unions. Randolph countered NAACP head Roy Wilkins's objections to Rustin's involvement by agreeing to head a committee to organize the march, and immediately naming Rustin as his deputy. Thus, Rustin controlled of all aspects of the march, delegating responsibility and orchestrating among the sponsor organization. In roughly two months, Rustin planned the "March on Washington for Jobs and Freedom" that took place on August 28, 1963. The march brought hundreds of thousands of people into the capital to peacefully protest continued segregation around the country and to plead for economic equality. Rustin deftly coordinated between leaders of all involved movement groups, metropolitan and police authorities, transportation and sanitation services, thousands of volunteers, celebrities and speakers, and with the U.S. government. The March on Washington proved a success, and has been judged by many to be a high point in the national Civil Rights Movement, anchored by King's "I Have A Dream" speech. National publicity as well as face-to-face meetings between the civil rights leaders, President **John F. Kennedy**, and members of Congress helped garner support for the legislation that would eventually become the **Civil Rights Act of 1964** and the **Voting Rights Act of 1965** which invalidated Jim Crow practices around the U.S. After the march, Rustin appeared with Randolph on the cover of *Life* magazine.

Rustin found himself disappointed at the inability of civil rights groups to build upon the success and consensus of the March on Washington. As factionalism grew between and within groups like SNCC and the SCLC, Rustin also found himself becoming more distant from their leadership. Rustin served as an advisor during SNCC's **Mississippi** "Freedom Summer" in 1964, working to help plan the mass voter registration campaign, and training volunteers in nonviolence at the request of **James Lawson**. His work with SNCC to fight Jim Crow in Mississippi that summer was among his last operations with SNCC. Once the young radical, Rustin came to view participation in the political process, as opposed to direct action, as the next step in achieving racial equality. His influential essay, "From Protest to Politics: The Future of the Civil Rights Movement" (*Commentary*, February 1965) evinced the widening gap between Rustin and militancy and racial separatism gaining popularity among young activists. In March 1965, Rustin announced the creation of the A. Phillip Randolph Institute (APRI). As head of the organization, Rustin worked to strengthen relationships between civil rights groups and labor unions in order to build coalitions that would affect social and economic equality. Rustin viewed the oppression of racial minorities and systemic poverty as closely intertwined, and saw solving both problems as a necessary and achievable goal.

Rustin continued to work for peace and civil rights throughout the 1960s, leading youth marches for integrated schools in New York and mobilizing for King's Poor People's Campaign in 1968. Rustin remained active internationally through the 1970s, speaking against the Vietnam War and bringing attention to the struggles of refugees in Southeast Asia. In the 1980s, Rustin began to speak out more publicly for gay rights, pointing out the continuities between oppression based on sexuality and race. Bayard Rustin died in August 1987 at the age of 75. *See also* Homosexuality.

Further Readings: Anderson, Jervis. *Bayard Rustin: Troubles I've Seen.* New York: HarperCollins, 1997; D'Emilio, John. *Lost Prophet: The Life and Times of Bayard Rustin.* New York: The Free Press, 2003; Levine, Daniel. *Bayard Rustin and the Civil Rights Movement.* New Brunswick, NJ: Rutgers University Press, 2000; Rustin, Bayard, Devon W. Carbado, and Donald Weise, eds. *Time on Two Crosses: The Collected Writings of Bayard Rustin.* San Francisco: Cleis Press, 2003.

Brian Piper

S

Segregation, Residential

Residential segregation is a spatial isolation based on race rather than income, education, or other factors. While there has not been official, de jure residential segregation in the United States, housing separation by race has been a common, de facto practice justified by cultural, economic, and political policies. Residential segregation becomes cyclical when housing placement influences access to education, job opportunities, or prejudicial cultural practices that reduce the ability to change one's housing circumstances. Poverty, unemployment, and crime are often the results of residential segregation practices.

Racial difference was inscribed in the United States through the institution of slavery, which dictated that one's "place" in society was determined by one's appearance or ethnic background. Prior to the Civil War, some African Americans were not enslaved and lived freely throughout the country, but most experienced some level of discrimination in housing and business practices. Enslaved African Americans in the South typically lived in close proximity to white people, but spatial intimacy was offset by the restrictions of **slavery**. With emancipation and the end of the Civil War, previously enslaved black people had the opportunity to move or work in other places. While many African Americans moved to cities or other areas to seek work, others could not afford to leave and had to take low-paying jobs as domestic servants or sharecroppers. The desire for mobility and equality was undermined by the reality of poverty and discrimination. In time, **Jim Crow** laws marked racial difference when the system of slavery no longer fulfilled that role.

In the late nineteenth and early twentieth centuries, immigrants from Europe and other areas often lived in the same neighborhoods as African Americans. During **World War I**, large numbers of black people left the South and moved into Northern cities as part of the **Great Migration**. Black workers sought greater job opportunities in the booming wartime industrial economy, while they simultaneously hoped for freedom from Jim Crow laws and discrimination in the South. Like other immigrant groups, blacks from the South tended to settle in areas near family and friends, often with lower housing costs and less quality housing. Even as they lived near people most like themselves, European immigrants and African American migrants mixed somewhat freely on the streets and in business practices.

As more African Americans competed for jobs and housing with immigrants and native-born Americans, many of whom were becoming commonly recognized as "white," tensions rose in the workplace and in overcrowded neighborhoods. As their wealth and education grew, white immigrants moved out of small urban neighborhoods and into outlying areas with higher-quality housing and better schools. Black tenants, however, were more limited in their housing options. Since few working-class people owned their own homes, landlords could restrict their clientele and many practiced racial discrimination in housing. Assuming that the presence of black tenants would decrease their property values, some landlords even signed restrictive covenants, in which property owners vowed not to sell or rent homes to African Americans, with other landowners to ensure that their buildings would remain white. Middle-class blacks who owned their homes and businesses tended to cluster in particular neighborhoods, such as Chicago's "Black Belt," where they had more freedom to control their own real estate and business practices. This clustering was not necessarily by choice, as local zoning and cultural restrictions limited black opportunities to expand into other neighborhoods. Such segregation resulted in a lack of understanding between groups that often led to riots, economic hardship, and reduced interracial unionization.

Residential segregation reached its height following **World War II**. More African Americans moved to Northern and Western cities during the Second Great Migration. Returning veterans took advantage of the **G.I. Bill** by attending universities and buying houses in larger numbers than ever before. Government policies and social practices emphasized consumption as an important form of citizenship, and homeownership was a key element of this practice. People who had previously rented an apartment in the city desired to purchase a home in the suburbs. Using war-industry knowledge of prefabricated materials and supply chain management, new housing developments such as **Levittowns** made owning a home affordable. However, private contractors assumed that they were building exclusively white communities and enacted policies to preserve their profit margins, including both official and unofficial covenants. Although the **U.S. Supreme Court** declared in *Shelley v. Kraemer* (1948) that it was unconstitutional for the state to enforce racially based restrictive covenants, voluntary agreements between homeowners continued to impact the composition of suburban neighborhoods. As white renters moved to the suburbs, they were replaced by black residents until many inner-city neighborhoods were almost completely populated by African Americans.

Government practices often supported and perpetuated postwar residential segregation. Local zoning practices in new suburbs typically restricted multi-family housing, thereby limiting residents to those of certain economic classes. Long-standing federal programs to subsidize home repairs and new construction became even more focused on fostering white homeownership. Through tax incentives, selective credit programs, public/private collaborations, and mortgage subsidies, the Federal Housing Administration (FHA) worked with mortgage lenders and banks to address the housing shortage. By insuring private mortgage companies against loss, the government expanded the pool of mortgages available to private homeowners, thus making homeownership feasible for many first-time buyers. Government agencies and other lenders also shifted to long-term, amortized mortgages to accommodate those with smaller incomes, thus freeing other money for further consumption. In the postwar era, the Veterans Administration's (VA) mortgage benefits were primarily reserved for white veterans. Although the FHA removed explicit language of racial categorization from its policies in the late 1940s, discrimination continued in practice well into the 1960s, especially because integrated neighborhoods continued to be considered risky financial investments.

Historians typically refer to the exodus of white urban residents to the predominantly white suburbs as "white flight." As African Americans continued to move into cities and take vacant tenant positions, white residents became alarmed at the possibility of losing their majority status. Close quarters also fostered the fear of racial mixing, a long-standing dread since the days of slavery and especially post-Reconstruction Jim Crow laws. As African Americans demanded more space, white residents answered by escaping to the suburbs.

Although racial fears explain some of the reasons for white flight, economic factors played perhaps a larger role in the residential shift. White property owners believed that the presence of minority groups would undermine their property values. Many sociological and economic studies demonstrated that such assumptions were unfounded, but white people continued to fear for their investments. By claiming that they were protecting property values rather than discriminating by race, white citizens justified residential segregation in culturally acceptable economic terms.

The arrival of black families in exclusively white neighborhoods was often met with fear and intimidation. Some white occupants resorted to throwing rocks or even burning crosses on lawns, but more often, they exerted political pressure to influence government policies against integration. One of the most common types of intimidation occurred when white residents pressured their neighbors not to sell their houses to black buyers. Although they did not always sign official racial covenants, white sellers often refused to participate in an exchange with black buyers. Some groups even went door-to-door throughout their communities to extract promises from their neighbors not to participate in realtor blockbusting. They typically phrased their concerns in economic rather than racial terms, but the results still amounted to housing discrimination. Such intimidation also caused black home buyers to reconsider moving into predominantly white neighborhoods, thus continuing the cycle of segregation.

Real estate agents played an integral role in maintaining residential segregation. Many realtors refused to assist black families in finding homes in white neighborhoods. When they did help black clients, real estate agents often steered them into predominantly black neighborhoods. The agents claimed that they were protecting the investments of other homeowners by not introducing elements that may reduce property values. Real estate agents often utilized the practice of "blockbusting" to increase profits. If a black family moved into a white neighborhood, agents encouraged white homeowners to sell quickly before their property values declined. The agents then turned around and sold the home to black buyers at exorbitant prices. Both buyers and sellers suffered from this practice, but real estate agents made tremendous profits by feeding off the fears of white residents.

Another practice that supported residential segregation was that of redlining. Mortgage lenders sought stable communities with minor turnover and little threat of mortgage defaults. They assumed that this ideal place was a white neighborhood. Lenders often designated black neighborhoods as high risk and drew a red line around them on a map. The refusal to invest in these areas severely limited the opportunities for African Americans to purchase their own homes. When black buyers were able to obtain loans, they often carried a higher interest rate or shorter payment schedule, making them a greater financial burden than most mortgages for white people. Over time, the lack of investment in black neighborhoods led to a decrease in property values and a general decline in the physical structures of the area. Deteriorating circumstances then made such black neighborhoods prime candidates for urban renewal projects.

At the same time government agencies subsidized white homeownership, they also implemented policies that further segregated public housing. Fearing that too many white residents would move to the suburbs, some urban politicians used new urban renewal legislation to clear existing black neighborhoods. By taking down old apartment buildings and replacing them with new ones, landowners increased their property values and the corresponding rents. New buildings were usually too expensive for the former residents to occupy, so the tenants were forced to leave the vicinity or apply for public housing. Federally funded housing projects contained black tenants in a regulated space with few opportunities for economic or educational advancement. Urban renewal programs frequently undermined vibrant communities and replaced them with institutionalized housing that led to greater rates of poverty and crime. Today, gentrification projects bring new investments to revitalize urban cores, but often drive up housing costs and force lower-income tenants out to continue the cycle of residential segregation.

The government was not always blind to unjust practices, and both government and social organizations sought housing reform. The Fair Housing Act of 1968 was enacted to protect minority groups against discrimination in public and private housing. The act affected all levels of government, from local to federal, and established a system for people to file complaints if they experienced discriminatory practices. Although critics have long-debated the effectiveness of the act, it was one step in civil rights legislation toward the possibility of a more integrated society.

The results of residential segregation are widespread. Predominantly white and predominantly black communities frequently differ in the allocation of resources, their access to consumer goods, the availability of quality housing, and access to upwardly mobile jobs. Income discrepancies result in widely varying tax bases, which in turn impact education, law enforcement, and future investment. Poverty is often concentrated in urban cores and leads to higher rates of crime. Over time, inequalities become more difficult to overcome. As racial difference is mapped onto urban space, the inner city becomes synonymous with crime and poverty, while the suburbs are viewed as a refuge. Residential segregation negates many possibilities for cross-group cooperation and promotes fear and lack of understanding. *See also* Segregation, Suburban.

Further Readings: Cohen, Lizabeth. *A Consumers' Republic: The Politics of Mass Consumption in Postwar America.* New York: Vintage Books, 2004; Freund, David M. P. *Colored Property: State Policy and White Racial Politics in Suburban America.* Chicago: University of Chicago Press, 2007; Kruse, Kevin M., and Thomas J. Sugrue, eds. *The New Suburban History.* Chicago: University of Chicago Press, 2006; Massey, Douglas S., and Nancy A. Denton. *American Apartheid: Segregation and the Making of the Underclass.* Cambridge, MA: Harvard University Press, 1998; Sugrue, Thomas J. *The Origins of the Urban Crisis: Race and Inequality in Postwar Detroit.* 2nd ed. Princeton, NJ: Princeton University Press, 2005.

Shannon Smith Bennett

Segregation, Rural

Rural Southern race relations built upon traditions forged under **slavery**. Masters and slaves occupied positions in a clear hierarchy, but generally not in a segregated one. They shared the space of the plantation, where whites insisted upon close physical proximity to their African American laborers in order to direct their work and prevent their escape. After emancipation, this centralized pattern of residence was altered, as black wage laborers and tenants scattered their cabins a distance from the homes of their landlords. Yet, while this dispersal opened some space between black and white homes, it did not establish a regionwide pattern of residential segregation. Instead, rural residential segregation, or its absence, came to be shaped by the particular racial demography of each rural community.

In subregions where one race made up an overwhelming majority, de facto residential segregation resulted, and little social interaction or cultural exchange took place between the races. For example, in places like the **Georgia** and **South Carolina** coast, large parts of the Mississippi Delta, and in some communities in the Cotton Belt, most residents lived, prayed, and worked in a completely segregated, all-black world. In *Souls of Black Folk* (1903), **W.E.B. Du Bois** described just such a setting. On a tour of a southwest Georgia county, he traveled 10 miles past decaying antebellum mansions and saw "no white face" but only a vast and impoverished "black peasantry." Similarly the poor, sandy-soil regions, the hillcountry, and the mountainous regions of **Appalachia**, the Cumberlands, and the Ozarks never contained many African Americans. In many counties in these sections, whites drove out the few black residents in the late nineteenth and early twentieth centuries, creating **sundown towns** and counties. Generally, this seems to have been an action by white tenants who resented competition with black sharecroppers. But as the census manuscripts attest, in many parts of the South, black and white farmers frequently lived on neighboring farms, whether as tenants, yeomen, or planters. Because much of the rural South remained a highly local, walking and wagon culture until **World War II**, a high level of interracial interaction was possible, and sometimes nearly unavoidable in such communities.

The history of segregation's origins is still debated. The historian **C. Vann Woodward** argued that it arose in late nineteenth-century legislation, beginning in trains and train stations, and then spreading and systematizing to cover most imaginable points of social contact between blacks and whites. Other critics responded by arguing that late nineteenth-century, legally mandated segregation merely encoded preexisting de facto segregation; or more frequently, the complete exclusion of African Americans from a wide range of privately owned restaurants, motels, and other establishments. All agree that by 1920, the South was legally segregated by a confining thicket of regulations. But most historians of the field have followed Woodward's lead in telling the story essentially from an urban and legal perspective. Meanwhile, the majority of Southerners lived in rural communities until the 1950s, and their interaction across the race lines has left little evidence and attracted the attention of few historians. For the most part, their distinctive story can be explored directly only through oral history, the classic sociological studies of the early twentieth century, and rural autobiographies.

Whatever the exact origin of the practice of segregation, its elaboration into a methodical separation of space into black and white zones was a child of the Progressive movement, when expert planners sought to employ systematic solutions to the nation's problems. Historians have argued that urban elite and middle-class whites systematized segregation as a means of maintaining white supremacy in an anonymous, tumultuous social setting. Urban African Americans were achieving upward mobility and gaining new purchasing power in stores, restaurants, and trains, thereby taking for themselves the symbols of middle-class respectability that had previously been badges of white privilege. Segregation offered a "modern," uniform, scientifically approved means by which urban whites could reestablish clear marks of their superiority. In a white Progressive culture preoccupied with "racial purity" and hygiene, and that identified interracial social and sexual mixing with uncleanliness, segregation opened "sanitary" space between black and white bodies without relying on the disruptive power of private white violence for its ordinary enforcement. According to Southern Progressives, the day-to-day violence needed to defend white supremacy could be supplied by urban police forces, which were formally trained to employ legal force.

In contrast, rural elite and middle-class whites at the turn of the twentieth century had less need of new methods of distinguishing their status from that of their African American neighbors. Generally, rural African Americans did not have access to the symbols of middle-class attainment. Most dressed in overalls or simple dresses and worked in the fields of white landlords. Additionally, rural people were sewn into a culture of personalism, in which each individual, and the particulars of his economic status, was well known to all others in the community. Familiarity, proximity, and black economic dependency provided rural whites with powerful tools by which to remind black neighbors of their "place," and to punish any who strayed from it. The well-dressed and apparently independent black stranger who caused such discomfort to urban whites was a rarity in the countryside. Rural whites also maintained unambiguous white supremacy through an elaborate and humiliating system of racialized social etiquette by which black and white people daily used word and gesture to demonstrate their understanding of their relative place in the social order.

In rural spaces, interracial interaction—not racial segregation—actually was the primary means of symbolizing white supremacy. And in the end, violence stood as the instrument in reserve, to threaten or make object lessons of African Americans who too directly challenged the status quo. Usually, white-on-black violence took the form of one-on-one, ostensibly legal murder; but ultimately, individual white violence was backed up by the terrifying power of the mob and the noose. As white farmers were already armed with all of these powerful sanctions, social segregation appeared as a superfluous urban innovation, ill-fitted to the actual conditions of much of the rural south. Segregation, after all, is impossible without spaces and institutions to segregate. The rural South had few restaurants, motels, libraries, parks, theaters, swimming pools, train stations, and stadiums. These existed overwhelmingly in the county seats, although towns and villages might have a restaurant or train station, frequently housed in a country store. The only segregateable spaces commonly appearing in the countryside were schools and churches, which will be examined below.

As rural white supremacy winked at all manner of white-on-black crime, in reality, African Americans had no rights that a white person was legally bound to recognize. In general, white Southerners were free to act as they wished, and demonstrated the full range of possible responses, including pathological violence, contemptuous nonrecognition, paternalistic condescension, and neighborly decency. Yet, although expression ranged widely, white supremacy remained a constant. Even the most neighborly relationships were marked by signs of the racial hierarchy. For example, blacks used "Mr." or "Ms." when addressing whites, while whites invariably called blacks by their first names.

The intimacy encouraged by the nonsegregation of most rural residential space and by the culture of personalism posed a series of problems for rural African Americans. For them, physical proximity made it easier for planters to exploit and attempt to direct their labor. It put them at more direct risk to daily insults and casual violence from whites generally. And it exposed black women, particularly those who worked in white homes as domestic servants, to the threat of sexual abuse and rape.

Without the power to demand the legal rights of citizenship, some rural African Americans sought a degree of protection from white patrons. Paternalistic white elites often were willing to consider a few individual African Americans as "exceptions" worthy of extra benefits. Sometimes they would assist a longtime tenant to landowning status, or help a black neighbor obtain government benefits. They could shield their tenants or other black individuals from mob violence and sometimes from legal action as well. Planters controlled law enforcement in their counties, and sometimes made their plantations off-limits to sheriffs and deputies, all the while retaining the right to intervene in their tenants' personal lives themselves, including the use of personal violence. These benefits of patronage were privileges. They could be abrogated at any time and thus gave white elites control—which is what they wanted after all. Ultimately, this system respected not black civil rights, but the right of the white elite to protect their favorites.

Other African Americans sought to lessen the humiliations of the Jim Crow system by withdrawing where possible from contacts with whites. The black sociologist Charles Johnson believed that this was the most common type of response of African Americans in this era. In some places, particularly in Oklahoma, African Americans built all-black towns in the decades after the Civil War. In the 1920s, **Marcus Garvey** tapped this separatist impulse and cultivated it through black nationalist ideology. Recent scholarship shows that the **Universal Negro Improvement Association** had more chapters in the rural South than it did in any other region of the United States. Particularly in counties with heavy black majorities, rural African Americans turned to Garvey's message of racial pride, economic development, self-defense, and racial separation from whites.

Some rural white individuals also tried to isolate themselves from interracial contacts. Particularly if they lived in a mostly white community, it was possible to withdraw into a more racially homogenous world. Yet, in the countryside, unlike the city, this choice was frequently not supported by community pressure or economic self-interest, much less by legal barriers. Early in the twentieth century, one white movement proposed a more thoroughgoing, intentional segregation of rural space. In 1913 at the height of the movement to codify residential segregation in the urban south, Clarence Poe, the editor of the widely read *Progressive Farmer,* began a two-year campaign to extend systematic **residential segregation** across the countryside. Rural whites unequivocally rejected this urban solution. The idea of farming without black laborers close at hand seemed unworkable to most white landlords.

Necessity reinforced the Southern tradition of neighborliness. When a man was incapacitated, neighbors plowed his field; when a woman was unable to work, nearby families would bring plates of food and help manage the household. This was not merely a practical application of Sunday school lessons. Everyone knew that illness and injury could befall anyone. Next year, perhaps you would need neighborly assistance. Oral histories attest that neighborly assistance crossed the race lines in both directions. Other forms of premodern, noninstitutional community aid also were sought and given without respect to color. Families of poor women about to give birth would seek out the nearest midwife, regardless of color. So too, when someone fell ill with ailments beyond the skills of their family, someone would run for the nearest herb specialist or root doctor. If illness was leading to death, the neighbors would increase their support, allowing the stricken family to sleep by taking turns sitting up first with the dying person, and then for a couple of days with the body in deathwatches.

Necessity of a sort also promoted another aspect of the rural South's interracial culture. In part because of the diffuse scattering of families, rural children played with any other children who were nearby. Rural Southern autobiographies attest to the frequency of interracial play among children in many regions of the South. But as they approached adolescence and the threshold of their public adult identities, they became subject to adult rules regarding interracial relationships, particularly those governing relationships between black men and white women.

In rural counties during the **Jim Crow** period, there were few professionally organized entertainments, and aside from churches, the few spaces set aside for leisure were usually concentrated in the county seats. These social activities—the theater, restaurants, the circus, and the county fair—were systematically segregated. Social activity in farm country tended to be informal, and so was not subject to strict segregation. As a result, depending on the particularities of their local culture, rural individuals were often free to socialize interracially. Most entertainment centered on the famous Southern propensity for talk, which happened everywhere across race lines: fields, roads, country stores, and ginhouses. Entertainment was also found at fishing holes, which were shared or used on a first-come, first-served basis, and on hunting expeditions, which were sometimes interracial affairs. In many parts of the rural South, sporting events drew black and white people together. While athletic contests in towns were invariably segregated, outside of town, farm boys frequently did not have enough local talent to field a team, much less a league. As a result, black and white baseball players faced each other on segregated or blended teams in isolated pastures, sometimes with an audience standing in the bushes. Sometimes high school baseball or football teams set up informal games where local bragging rights could be settled. Other social activities were less pastoral. Across the South, men gathered to gamble or drink moonshine at campfires by the railroad tracks and isolated cabins in the woods. Although gambling sites tended to be predominately white or black, the players cared mostly about the color of one's money; and the moonshining profession was famously interracial.

When people live close to each other, sexual relations will occur. While interracial sexual activity had fallen well off its peak in the colonial era, Jim Crow plantation belt counties still witnessed a wide range of relationships, almost entirely between black women and white men: rape, prostitution, casual sex, concubinage, and long-term common-law marriage. How these relationships were dealt with depended entirely on the culture of race relations in a local community. Sometimes offending couples were driven from the county; sometimes they were left in peace.

Schools and churches were the central institutions in the rural South. The schools were absolutely segregated, and memoirs sometimes note bursts of interracial violence between racially segregated groups of children on their way to school. Yet during most of the era of Jim Crow, most rural people attended them for only a few years. Churches, on the other hand, drew attendees throughout their lives. Under slavery, many planters required their slaves to attend services in white churches. After emancipation, most African Americans left these churches, and brought out into the open the secretive, all-black "brush arbor" churches that they had also been attending. This religious migration established the mostly segregated sacred spaces that persist to the present. Yet, when examined closely, the story is more complex than it appears at first glance. A small number of black farmers continued to attend white churches, in part because as African Americans had few citizenship rights, one of their best means of obtaining legal protection in the rural South lay in cultivating the patronage of an influential white person, such as a pastor. Yet, by the twentieth century, few African Americans regularly attended white churches, although some continued to make irregular visits. Some rural whites also visited black churches during the early decades of the twentieth century, drawn by the music or the oratorical gifts of a minister. Usually, the visitors would sit on a separate bench, frequently at the back of white churches and the front of black churches. Then, in the 1920s, this tradition of interracial church visitation contracted. Visitors continued to come, but only during revival services or other special events. In the years following **World War II**, this tradition attenuated further, and only funerals would draw rural people from across the race lines and into interracial space.

A person's class powerfully shaped the context of his interaction with others across the race lines. Black farm owners usually found a white patron to assist them in difficulties, but they could otherwise retreat somewhat from the humiliations of Jim Crow on their own land. Black tenants on the other hand regularly dealt with their landlord or his agent. Similarly, white planters normally had many contacts with long-term black dependents: domestics, tenants, and wage laborers. These white elites could act as they wished toward them. They could murder recalcitrant laborers without fear of punishment, or they could maintain close relationships under the rhetorical cloak of paternalism. Poor whites did not share these privileges. Sometimes eager to validate their superior racial status, sometimes willing to extend neighborly mutual aid or exchange hospitality, they seemed an unpredictable mystery to African Americans.

What has been described is neither integration nor segregation, both of which imply intentionality. Rather, race relations in the rural South were marked by premodern haphazardness. These traditions never entirely died out, but they attenuated throughout the first half of the twentieth century, and did so most steeply as the rural South depopulated and the **sharecropping** system of labor collapsed around World War II. In these years, federal programs and war munitions factories quickly replaced what was left of the tattered garments of paternalism. As rural neighbors moved to different parts of town, their opportunities for interaction declined, even as black opportunities for economic advancement and escape from Jim Crow's humiliations increased. Meanwhile, out-migration opened space between the homes of rural neighbors; paved roads, television, and bureaucratic systematization intervened; and much that had given shape to the distinctively intertwined lives of black and white farmers unraveled. *See also* Great Retreat; Housing Covenants; Police Brutality; Racial Customs and Etiquette.

Further Readings: Cell, John W. *The Highest Stage of White Supremacy.* Cambridge: Cambridge University Press, 1982; Chafe, William H., ed. *Remembering Jim Crow.* New York: New Press, 2001; De Jong, Greta. *A Different Day.* Chapel Hill: University of North Carolina Press, 2002; Gilmore, Glenda Elizabeth. *Gender and Jim Crow.* Chapel Hill: University of North Carolina Press, 1996; Hale, Grace Elizabeth. *Making Whiteness.* New York: Pantheon Books, 1998; Kirby, Jack Temple. *Rural Worlds Lost.* Baton Rouge: Louisiana State University Press, 1987; Litwack, Leon F. *Trouble in Mind.* New York: Knopf, 1998; Rolinson, Mary G. *Grassroots Garveyism.* Chapel Hill: University of North Carolina Press, 2007; Rosengarten, Theodore, comp. *All God's Dangers: The Life of Nate Shaw.* New York: Knopf, 1974; Schultz, Mark. *The Rural Face of White Supremacy.* Urbana: University of Illinois Press, 2005; Williamson, Joel. *The Crucible of Race.* New York: Oxford University Press, 1984.

Mark Schultz

Segregation, Suburban

Though suburbs are often imagined as primarily white and middle class, they in fact have a long history of racial and class diversity. However, that diversity has often existed within the boundaries of **residential segregation**. Over the first several decades of the twentieth century, residential patterns became increasingly segregated as suburbanization occurred. Suburban segregation was fostered and maintained through a combination of transportation availability, restrictive covenants, zoning, real estate practices, federal policies, and white community resistance. It became the norm in not only the South, but the rest of the nation as well. Though explicitly racial restrictions declined starting around 1950, suburban segregation persisted throughout the rest of the century through indirect mechanisms.

Up through the late nineteenth century, the lack of affordable transportation meant that cities remained relatively small and manageable for pedestrians. For this reason, wealthy citizens with access to carriages were the first to build residences far outside the city. When railroads established routes feeding into cities, upper- and upper-middle-class residents began to build homes in communities located along the radiating spokes of rail lines. These homeowners required support staff in order to attain the contemporary ideals of domestic comfort. Thus, the working class and racial minorities followed them out of the city. Domestic help, though, no longer automatically lived under the same roof as their employer. At each rail station outside the city, a pattern of roughly concentric development appeared. Wealthier suburbanites with carriages built their estates farther away from the train station. Domestic workers, still limited to foot travel, constructed dwellings within walking distance of the rail line. For those residents remaining in the city, it was not uncommon for whites and blacks to live in the same neighborhoods.

With the advent of affordable transportation in the form of streetcars and then automobiles, suburban areas became more accessible. Beginning in the early twentieth century, community builders and developers began to employ restrictive covenants and subdivision regulations to limit who could live where. Restrictive covenants had remained relatively rare in the late nineteenth century, but by the 1910s, they had gained popularity and were the rule in 1920s housing developments. These covenants were agreements attached to property deeds, which placed prohibitions on the use or sale of the property. Developers originally employed the covenants to protect subdivisions from nuisance businesses such as slaughterhouses and maintain a level of uniformity in the neighborhood. Soon they also prohibited sale of property to nonwhites and became a primarily mechanism of maintaining residential segregation. In 1926, the **U.S. Supreme Court** upheld their constitutionality in *Corrigan v. Buckley* because they were private contracts. Neighborhood property owners associations often formed to enforce the covenants. While these agreements were usually set for an initial term of approximately 20 years, they renewed automatically unless a majority of property owners voted to remove the covenants. That renewal mechanism meant that in reality, these covenants persisted indefinitely.

Though the Supreme Court eventually declared restrictive covenants unconstitutional in 1948s *Shelley v. Kraemer*, the Federal Housing Administration did not begin to heed the ruling until 1950, and still largely ignored it for years thereafter. During political campaigns in the 1950s and 1960s, many candidates faced accusations of owning property covered by racially restrictive covenants. The more general use of restrictive covenants endured throughout the twentieth century. By placing limits on purchase price, occupancy, and setting strict maintenance requirements, developers and homeowners associations continued to pursue an air of exclusivity by excluding portions of the general population.

Even in their heyday, though, restrictive covenants only applied to subdivisions, were difficult to enforce fully, and could not control what happened with adjacent property. Therefore, covenants worked in tandem with zoning, which soon became another popular exclusionary mechanism. Baltimore enacted racial zoning in 1910, and other cities followed suit until the practice was declared unconstitutional in *Buchanan v. Warley* in 1917. After that, zoning typically did not use any explicitly racial classifications, but that did not curb its discriminatory effects. Rather, municipal zoning set out what areas of land could be used for which purpose. Zoning decisions had a discriminatory impact because class overlapped so heavily with race. For example, white residents were much more likely to possess the resources to afford a single-family detached dwelling. Black residents, particularly the black working class, were more likely to reside in row housing or multiunit properties such as apartment complexes. Thus, when a municipality zoned an outlying area as single-family detached residential, it served to exclude many blacks and other racial minorities. The rise of comprehensive land-use planning increased local government control over the contours of growth, and the distribution of municipal services reinforced racial and class lines. In Atlanta, for example, the city manipulated the paving of new streets and closed or disrupted old ones to separate white and black neighborhoods and traffic. Proponents of residential segregation often argued that it would reduce conflict by preventing recurrent confrontations over housing.

Real estate practices reinforced racially restrictive covenants and zoning. Real estate had become more professionalized and consolidated in the early twentieth century; a small minority of powerful real estate agents set standards for the rest of the field. Up through 1950, the Code of Ethics of the National Association of Real Estate Boards prohibited agents from changing the existing character of a neighborhood and disrupting its stability. That included introducing any racial minorities into an all-white neighborhood. Meanwhile, some independent agents practiced "blockbusting" tactics. Blockbusters would introduce one or more black families into a white neighborhood, scare the remaining white homeowners away, and buy up their properties at a discount. They would then turn around and sell the homes to black residents at inflated prices, reaping a large profit. These tactics accelerated racial turnover in outlying neighborhoods and hindered stable integration.

Beginning with the **Great Depression** and the resulting **New Deal**, federal policies began to influence suburban segregation as well. The Home Owners

Loan Corporation (HOLC), established in 1933, set the precedent for long-term mortgages with low monthly payments and created a formalized appraisal system. This appraisal system rated black neighborhoods unfavorably, while giving the highest ratings to white, homogenous, outlying neighborhoods. Private lenders across the country soon adapted the HOLC system. Because they had such unfavorable ratings, it was difficult to obtain a loan to buy property in older, black, or integrated neighborhoods. At the same time, the Federal Housing Administration endorsed racially restrictive covenants as a means to maintain the racial and social homogeneity of suburban areas. Urban renewal projects controlled the expansion of black populations by destroying existing housing stock, often replacing it with more expensive units or changing the land use altogether. The federal government left planning for public housing projects at the local level, thereby allowing patterns of residential segregation to persist. Local control of federal funding for highways produced similar results. City officials sometimes planned highways to serve as racial boundaries or remove black populations from the area.

The two World Wars and increasing mechanization of the Southern cotton industry released a **Great Migration** of Southern blacks, first from the rural South to Southern cities, and then to the urban North and West. Black migrants moved in search of better opportunities, but often found formidable resistance to their residential dispersal in their new hometowns.

These considerable barriers, though, did not prevent blacks from moving to suburbs. The first wave to do so was predominantly working class and looked to the suburbs for some measure of economic independence in the early twentieth century. They sometimes built their own houses, tended gardens, rented rooms, and raised small livestock to help make ends meet. Others lived near employment in industrial suburbs. By the 1940s and 1950s, black migration to the suburb was more heavily middle class, as families drew upon their economic resources to leave the crowded city and claim their own piece of domestic tranquility. Some black suburbanites found the experience isolating. They had distanced themselves from the black working class, but white suburbanites did not accept them as equals. As a result, black leaders built a strong community within the bounds of segregation, where black churches and businesses remained central. By the 1960s and 1970s, blacks were moving to the suburbs in unprecedented numbers, and over one-third of the black population would live there by the end of the century.

Other black families moved into already integrated outlying neighborhoods, deemed relatively safe in comparison to all-white areas. Some went through a third party when purchasing property to limit confrontations with inhospitable whites. Black families that settled in previously all-white neighborhoods often faced dire circumstances. White neighbors harassed them at all hours, damaged their property, and, in the worst cases, inflicted bodily injury. Local law enforcement often refused to provide protection. Many of these families relied on friends, family, or occasionally groups of sympathetic, liberal-minded whites to stand vigil over their homes and loved ones. While some stuck it out, others eventually made the decision to leave and seek safer accommodations for their families.

Fair and open housing policies sought to overcome barriers to residential integration by prohibiting discrimination in the sale and rental of housing. In the decade following the 1954 ***Brown v. Board of Education*** decision, fair housing made headway at the local and state level. Fair housing laws had been enacted in 22 states by 1968, though none of those were in the South. In 1962, President **John F. Kennedy** signed an executive order that curbed discrimination in federally associated housing and loans; a federal fair housing law finally passed in 1968. These laws are difficult to enforce because aggrieved parties must report individual cases of discrimination. They are also unpopular because much of the population views housing as a private realm that should not be subject to government interference. A property rights movement began to emerge in the mid-1960s, culminating in voters' rejection of California's fair housing law. The Nixon administration soon declared that the federal government would not force subsidized low-income housing upon suburbs; subsequent administrations emulated this nonintervention policy. State policies have not necessarily been effective, either. In the 1975 and 1983 *Mount Laurel* decisions in New Jersey, the state supreme court struck a blow against exclusionary zoning, declaring that suburban communities had to provide their "fair share" of low-income housing. Politics influenced enforcement, though, and suburbs were allowed to participate in a regional credit system where they could pay other areas to build up to half their share of low-income housing.

Though the legal space for housing discrimination shrank over the course of the twentieth century, residential segregation persists, with pervasive consequences. Suburban segregation has impacted the demographic profile of both outlying and city schools. Because predominantly white suburbs often draw upon a larger tax base, their public schools are better funded than their inner-city counterparts. White suburbs were also largely successful in preventing mass transit from extending into their communities, choosing instead to rely on automobiles and freeways. Their lack of accessibility has further served to limit residential diversity. Many black suburbanites still live in predominantly black neighborhoods. In addition, residents remaining in central cities are often isolated from job opportunities on the booming suburban fringe. The result has been enduring disparities along racial lines. *See also* Federal Government; Housing Covenants; Neighborhood Property Owners Associations.

Further Readings: Bayor, Ronald H. *Race and the Shaping of Twentieth Century Atlanta.* Chapel Hill: University of North Carolina Press, 1996; Delaney, David. *Race, Place, and the Law 1836–1948.* Austin: University of Texas Press, 1998; Fogelson, Robert M. *Bourgeois Nightmares: Suburbia, 1870–1930.* New Haven, CT: Yale University Press, 2005; Lamb, Charles M. *Housing Segregation in Suburban America Since 1960.* New York: Cambridge University Press, 2005; Meyer, Stephen Grant. *As Long as They Don't Move Next Door: Segregation and Racial Conflict in American Neighborhoods.* Lanham, MD: Rowman and Littlefield, 2000; Plotkin, Wendy. "Racial and Religious Restrictive Covenants in the U.S. and Canada." http://www.public.asu.edu/~wplotkin/DeedsWeb/index.html (accessed June 1, 2008); Sugrue, Thomas J. *The Origins of the Urban Crisis: Race and Inequality in Postwar Detroit.* Princeton, NJ: Princeton University Press, 1996; Wiese, Andrew. *Places of Their Own: African American Suburbanization in the Twentieth Century.* Chicago: University of Chicago Press, 2004.

Alyssa Ribeiro

Separate but Equal

"Separate but equal" refers to the creation of a system in which states were allowed to provide separate facilities and accommodations for blacks and whites. These separate facilities and accommodation help to give birth to Jim Crow segregation through the country. The legal precedence for separate but equal laws and policies were established in the cases of *Roberts v. the City of Boston* (1848) and **Plessy v. Ferguson** (1896). Each ruling confirmed the states' right to segregate blacks and whites as long as both groups received equal treatment and services.

Although laws required that separate, "equal" facilities be maintained, the states were largely unmonitored and left to their own implementation and devices. As a result, many African Americans, especially those located in the Southern region of the country, were exposed to grossly unequal facilities and accommodations. Separate schools for African Americans were poorly funded. The students were not provided with the necessary tools needed for learning that white students were given. Hospitals, water fountains, public restrooms, and other accommodations provided for African Americans were substandard.

Many activist groups, such as the National Association for the Advancement of Colored People (NAACP), sought recourse through the courts, but the **U.S. Supreme Court** refused to entertain the cases or intervene until the 1954 case of **Brown v. Board of Education.**

FOR THE SUNNY SOUTH.
AN AIRSHIP WITH A "JIM CROW" TRAILER.

Segregation in public transportation, 1913. Courtesy of Library of Congress, LC-SZC2-058.

The *Brown* case provided the NAACP with the opportunity to challenge the legality of separate but equal policies in the public school system. The NAACP's dream team of attorneys, led by **Thurgood Marshall**, who would later become a U.S. Supreme Court justice, argued that segregated public schools were unequal and psychologically damaging to African American children. They reminded the Court that the Fourteenth Amendment gave the federal government the power to prohibit racially discriminatory state actions such as those that existed in the public school system. In a surprising ruling, the Supreme Court ruled in favor of plaintiffs, outlawing segregated public education facilities for African American and white students, overturning *Plessy*'s separate but equal doctrine. Chief Justice Earl Warren handed down the verdict noting that:

> Segregation of white and colored children in public schools has a detrimental effect upon the colored children. The impact is greater when it has the sanction of the law, for the policy of separating the races is usually interpreted as denoting the inferiority of the Negro group ... Any language in contrary to this finding is rejected. We conclude that in the field of public education the doctrine of "separate but equal" has no place. Separate educational facilities are inherently unequal.

The Court ruling enraged many Southern whites. They turned to scare and intimidation tactics to prevent the Court's ruling from being enforced. In **Arkansas**, Governor Orville Faubus vowed to maintain the state's separate school system. He respected the Court's ruling only after President Dwight D. Eisenhower sent in federal troops to enforce it.

In **Mississippi**, Governor Ross Barnett attempted to block African American student James Meredith's entrance into the all-white University of Mississippi, even after a U.S. Supreme Court ruling granting him entrance was handed down. President **John F. Kennedy** federalized the **National Guard** to enforce the Court's ruling. Before the ruling was enforced, a riot ensued and two people were killed.

The Brown ruling also laid the foundation for the challenging of separate but equal policies in other areas. In *Bolling v. Sharpe*, separate but equal polices were outlawed at the federal level of government. In *Loving v. Virginia*, the Court deemed all race-based legal restrictions on marriage in the United States unconstitutional. *See also* Desegregation; Discrimination.

Further Readings: Harris, John. "Education, Society, and the *Brown* Decision: Historical Principles Versus Legal Mandates." *Journal of Black Studies* 13 (1982): 141–54; "Separate Is Not Equal: *Brown v. the Board of Education*." Smithsonian National Museum of American History Web site. http://americanhistory.si.edu/brown/history/5-decision/courts-decision.html (accessed July 2007).

Barbara A. Patrick

Sharecropping

Sharecropping, an agricultural labor system, emerged in the Southern United States after the Civil War destroyed the slave labor economy. After emancipation, former slaves suddenly needed to support themselves, and cash-poor planters required cheap labor to raise and harvest crops. Since planters had little capital and freed slaves had no land, equipment, or farm animals, many entered into labor agreements whereby planters furnished land and equipment and former slaves worked the fields. They split the harvest, and the Freedmen's Bureau, established in 1865 to protect the interests of former slaves, initially considered these agreements beneficial. Sharecroppers were provided between 25 and 40 acres to grow their own food and sell what was left over after they provided the planter with his half of the harvest.

Sharecroppers paid for the rental of tools, wagons, animals, and shelter with additional liens on their crop. Provisions like coffee, sugar, flour, cornmeal, and even clothing were available to them through "furnishing merchants" who also accepted liens. After renting and purchasing everything he needed, a sharecropper could find himself down to 25 percent or less of the proceeds of his harvest. Plantations, as in slave days, were closed communities, and sharecroppers were required not only to purchase their supplies and provisions from the landlord's furnishing merchant, but to market their crop through him. All debts were settled at harvest time. A few bad seasons could doom a cropper to a life of revolving debt and credit, and by 1869, the Freedmen's Bureau could no longer advocate for him. President Andrew Johnson not only disbanded the Bureau, but also returned most of the confiscated land to Southern planters. This dashed all hope of land redistribution that the Freedmen's Bureau had advocated for the former slaves.

Sharecropping was part of a three-tier system that included tenant farming, share renting, and sharecropping. In a tenant farming arrangement, the landlord provided land, a cabin, and fuel, for which the tenant paid a fixed rental rate per acre. Most tenant farmers were poor whites who had lost their land, but still had tools and farm animals. In share renting, the landlord provided the same things, and the share renter pledged to pay him one-quarter to one-third of his crop. Most share renters were also white. In sharecropping, however, the landlord provided *everything* and the cropper divided the harvest with him—less the cost of supplies and provisions purchased from the furnishing merchant. By law, tenant farmers and share renters owned the crops they produced and therefore could sell them wherever they chose. The sharecropper, however, had to sell through the plantation's furnishing merchant.

Since furnishing merchants controlled the commissaries and kept all the accounts, the sharecropping system was fertile ground for abuse. If a cropper challenged the landlord's figures, he and his family could be evicted from the plantation. Sharecropper families often worked 10-hour days and were closely supervised by overseers. Women labored in the fields as well as in the home and child labor was shamelessly exploited. Despite the U.S. Congress passing legislation in 1867 outlawing debt servitude, croppers who owed their landlords money were not permitted to leave the plantation until they worked it off. If they escaped, they were often tracked down and returned by local law enforcement officers. Many of the restrictions imposed on sharecroppers were simply extensions of the slave system.

Organizing sharecroppers into alliances to demand reform was difficult because croppers were spread out over many plantations, and landlords threatened to evict them for even associating with organizers. The Colored

Farmers Alliance, an early attempt, was established in Leflore County, **Mississippi**, in 1888 by Oliver Cromwell to win the right to trade with stores and cooperatives outside the plantations. Black organizing terrified white planters, who tended to equate it with slave insurrection. In 1889, Cromwell was ordered to leave Leflore County. He refused, and when a group calling themselves the "Three Thousand Armed Men," organized to protect him, the governor sent in the state militia. Cromwell escaped, but 25 Alliance men were killed, and Leflore County's Colored Farmers Alliance was disbanded. By 1890, however, chapters were operating in Norfolk, Charleston, New Orleans, Mobile, and Houston.

In 1919, a group of black **World War I** veterans under the leadership of Ike Shaw and C. H. Smith organized the Farmers and Laborers Household Union of America in Phillips County, **Arkansas**. They drafted a legally binding contract with plantation owners to provide croppers with a written guarantee of their percentage of the harvest as well as a written statement of account at the end of each season. The planters refused to negotiate, but despite their almost constant intimidation, with assistance from allies in law enforcement and the **Ku Klux Klan**, union membership increased. On September 30, 1919, a sheriff, his deputy, and a black trustee broke up a Farmers and Laborers union meeting at a church in Hoop Spur, Arkansas. In the ensuing struggle, one of the officers was killed and the other wounded. A posse returned the following morning to arrest the union leaders but the armed membership surrounded and protected them. Advised that a race war was imminent, the governor sent in 500 state militia troops who burned the church, killed 29 blacks, and arrested hundreds. The idea of black sharecroppers controlling their own destinies was so terrifying to white planters that they were willing to commit massacres in order to destroy the organizers and intimidate croppers into submission.

In the spring of 1931, black sharecroppers and tenant farmers in Tallapoosa County, **Alabama**, organized the Croppers and Farm Workers Union under the leadership of Ralph and Tommy Gray and Mack Coad, a black steelworker from Birmingham who organized industrial workers for the **Communist Party**. During the 1930s the Communist Party succeeded in creating bargaining units of black and white industrial workers in Birmingham and Memphis, and black sharecropper alliances in rural Alabama and Georgia. The Croppers and Farm Workers Union recruited 800 members in just two months, and in July 1931, at a meeting held in a local church, they voted to support cotton pickers in their demand for a one dollar a day wage. (They were earning 50 cents.) Local sheriff Kyle Young and his deputy Jack Thompson, who had been tipped off about the meeting by a cropper who wanted to earn extra points with his landlord, broke up the gathering, killing Ralph Gray, wounding five union members, and arresting dozens more. After Young was wounded, the church was burned to the ground. Once again, the effort to unionize ended in violence and death

Tommy Gray, his daughter Eula, and black communist Al Murphy, reorganized as the Share Croppers Union. By the summer of 1932, they had reclaimed 600 members. The Croppers Union revived the demand for a one-dollar-a-day cotton picker wage, and demanded payment for the cropper's share of the harvest in cash instead of merchant script, credit, or supplies. They also sought freedom to buy what they needed at any store they chose; and the right to sell their crops to whomever they chose. These demands, structured as they were to defeat the planters' monopoly, posed a threat not only to white supremacy but to the planters' cheap labor supply and planters became determined to destroy this union as they had the Croppers and Farm Workers.

In December 1932, Sheriff Cliff Elder went to the Reeltown, Alabama, farm of black Tallapoosa County organizer Clifford James (one of the few black landowners in the county), to impound his two mules and a cow as payment for a six-dollar-debt he owed a white grocer. Without his stock, James could not farm, and he refused to surrender the animals. A dozen armed members of the Croppers Union stood with him. Elder left, but later returned with an armed posse. The subsequent shootout left the sheriff and several deputies wounded, Clifford James dead, and many croppers injured. Thirty-two were arrested, and five were later convicted of assault with a deadly weapon. A search of the James home uncovered a Share Croppers Union membership list, and vigilantes terrorized everyone on it. Many were beaten and jailed and hundreds subsequently left the county. Despite the ongoing violence, however, the union continued to grow. By June 1933 nearly 2,000 members were operating in 73 locales across the Deep South.

During the last decade of the nineteenth century and into the early years of the twentieth century, a sharecropper could net $333 in a good year, a share renter $398, and a tenant farmer as much as $478. The outbreak of World War I, however, disrupted the world cotton market, and prices fell precipitously. They remained depressed throughout most of the 1920s. The end of that decade brought droughts, dust storms, boll weevil infestations, and eventually the **Great Depression**. Bankrupted Southern planters lost their land at twice the national average as the price of cotton fell from 20 cents a bale (500 pounds) in 1927, to less than five cents in 1932. Many croppers found themselves not only unemployed, but also homeless. In 1933, in response to Southern planters' pleas for federal assistance, the administration of President **Franklin D. Roosevelt** established the Agricultural Adjustment Administration (AAA). Planters who agreed to reduce their crop by 30 percent were guaranteed rental payments and the promise of an additional subsidy if their harvests did not cover their costs. It was an attempt to revive the agricultural economy by limiting supplies of cotton, corn, and soybeans and hoping that consumer demand would increase market prices. These federal agreements stipulated that tenant farmers and sharecroppers were to receive a percentage of the payments. Most never did. The **New Deal**'s agricultural policies changed the lives of sharecroppers and tenant farmers forever. After cotton production was drastically reduced, planters no longer needed as many tenants and croppers were turned off the plantations. The cities, plagued by a concurrent industrial depression, could not absorb them and without income or shelter, many starved. Others became radicalized.

As mass evictions from the plantations began, the Share Croppers Union in Tallapoosa County, Alabama (which remained a black Communist organization), grew to almost 8,000. At the same time, a socialist-supported interracial alliance, the **Southern Tenant Farmers' Union** (STFU), was organized on the

Fairview Cotton Plantation near Tyronza, Arkansas, on July 11, 1934. Eleven white and seven black men met at a local schoolhouse and vowed to stop the evictions on the Fairview Plantation and to demand their fair share of AAA money. Founding members included white socialists H. L. Mitchell and Ward Rodgers and black cropper Ike Shaw, who had survived the 1919 Hoop Spur, Arkansas, massacre. Despite its name, the STFU consisted largely of black and white sharecroppers and day laborers. Interracial organizing was rare, since the sharecropping system by its very nature drove poor whites and blacks into competition. Animosity was not unusual, since black sharecropper labor was cheaper, and when times were hard, the landlord accepted fewer tenants. Plantation owners encouraged racial divisiveness because it kept agricultural workers with similar grievances against them divided. New Deal politics, however, had convinced the croppers and tenants that they shared a common misery and that there was strength in numbers. In Arkansas a large percentage of the evicted sharecroppers were white.

Late in 1934, the STFU sent a delegation to Washington, DC, to meet with Secretary of Agriculture Henry Wallace to demand that planters stop evicting tenants and croppers and pay them their share of the rental and parity subsidies. The Roosevelt administration subsequently created the Resettlement Administration and charged it with assisting destitute landless farmers. When this agency proved bureaucratic and unresponsive, the STFU took matters into its own hands. In August 1935, just before picking season, they threatened to strike. Ultimately they won a 75-cent wage increase without resorting to the strike and grew so rapidly that by 1936, there were over 25,000 members in the South. That year the Farm Security Administration (FSA) replaced the Resettlement Administration. This agency's Tenant Purchase Program bought failed plantations and offered them for sale at low interest rates to croppers and tenants. Most sharecroppers were not in a financial position to buy land, however. Housing projects were also acquired for dispossessed farm workers, but since the program was mandated federally but administered locally, the housing projects were often segregated, and white croppers and tenants ultimately received the largest share of assistance.

Another factor that mitigated against reform was disenfranchisement. Croppers, especially black croppers, did not vote. Some were illiterate, some were too intimidated by their planters to register, and others could not afford to pay the poll tax, a common barrier in the Deep South. Poll taxes compounded every year after age 21 and were required to be paid in full before a citizen could vote. Lack of political clout cut croppers off from the help those liberal Southern politicians who might have extended them under the umbrella of New Deal reform.

By 1936, the Alabama Share Croppers Union had chapters in **Louisiana** and Mississippi and counted 12,000 members. It made several overtures to the STFU, whose membership was spread over Arkansas, Mississippi, Tennessee, and Missouri, to merge, but the socialist STFU leadership was not interested in joining forces with Communists. Traditional Southern racial attitudes had also infiltrated the movement by that time. Although the STFU had been established as a biracial organization, its black membership grew more quickly and ultimately constituted a majority. White croppers and tenants began to drop out and form their own splinter unions. This pleased planters, who feared the threat that interracial organizing posed to their cheap labor supply and to the entire segregated system.

By 1939, the South finally began to recover from the devastation of the Great Depression, and New Deal assistance was no longer either needed or welcome. While Franklin Roosevelt had baled planters out with his Agricultural Adjustment Administration policies, they had no intention of allowing New Deal liberals and the activist first lady **Eleanor Roosevelt** to encourage union organizing or farm worker reform. The region reverted to its traditional distrust of "big government" and its determination to maintain white supremacy.

Despite strikes, protests, the support of many New Deal liberals, and winning some minor reforms, small wage increases, and benefits, the STFU and the SCU were not able to solve the fundamental problems of sharecroppers. Ultimately croppers and tenants were needed less and less, as machinery designed to plant, pick, and harvest cotton became affordable. By 1937, the Share Croppers Union had liquidated and transferred its membership to the Agricultural Workers' Union, an affiliate of the American Federation of Labor. That same year, the Southern Tenant Farmers' Union affiliated with the Congress of Industrial Organization's (CIO) agricultural workers. Two years later, however, it withdrew, and tried to establish itself once again as an independent union. But by that time, membership had fallen drastically, as thousands of sharecroppers left the South. In the end, it was not the reformers or the activists, or even the croppers themselves who ended the system that had locked them into virtual slavery, but economics. It was tractors, mechanical cotton pickers, and the shift in efficiency from tenancy to seasonal wage earners that changed the course of sharecropping. *See also* Agricultural Adjustment Act; Colored Farmers Alliance.

Further Readings: Beecher, John. "The Share Croppers' Union in Alabama." *Social Forces* 13 (October 1934); Biegert, M. Langley. "Legacy of Resistance: Uncovering the History of Collective Action by Black Agricultural Workers in Central East Arkansas from the 1860s to the 1930s." *Journal of Social History* (Fall 1998); Clark, Thomas D. "The Furnishing and Supply System in Southern Agriculture Since 1865." *Journal of Southern History* 12 (February 1946): 28–33; Kelley, Robin D. G. *Hammer and Hoe: Alabama Communists during the Great Depression.* Chapel Hill: University of North Carolina Press, 1990; McMillen, Neil R. *Dark Journey: Black Mississippians in the Age of Jim Crow.* Urbana: University of Illinois Press, 1989; Raper, Arthur F., and Ira De A. Reid. *Sharecroppers All.* Chapel Hill: University of North Carolina Press, 1941; Rosengarten, Theodore, comp. *All God's Dangers. The Life of Nate Shaw.* New York: Vintage Books, 1984.

Mary Stanton

Shelley v. Kraemer (1948)

In 1948, the **U.S. Supreme Court** decided the case of *Shelley v. Kraemer,* 334 U.S. 1 (1948), in which the Court unanimously ruled that it was unconstitutional to enforce private agreements between neighbors that purported to forbid the sale of property to racial minorities. This case is significant not only because it promoted the rights of African Americans to purchase property freely and discouraged the ghettoizing of American neighborhoods, but also because it added momentum to the **Civil Rights Movement** and the Supreme Court's trend of interpreting the Constitution to expand minority rights.

In 1945, the Shelley family, who were African American, bought a house in St. Louis, Missouri. When the Shelleys purchased the home, they were unaware that a prior owner had agreed along with neighbors to execute a restrictive covenant (a legal obligation written into a property's deed) that purported to prevent the sale of the home to "people of the Negro or Mongolian Race." Upon learning that the Shelleys had been sold the home in violation of the restrictive covenant, a neighbor sued the Shelleys in an attempt to prevent them from moving in. The Missouri trial court ruled in the Shelleys' favor. However, when the case was appealed by the neighbors, the Supreme Court of Missouri reversed the trial court's decision and ruled that the restrictive covenant was enforceable and that the Shelleys could not take possession of the property they had purchased. The Shelleys, with the support of civil rights organizations, appealed the Missouri Supreme Court decision to the U.S. Supreme Court.

Represented by a legal team that included National Association for the Advancement of Colored People (NAACP) counsel **Thurgood Marshall**, the Shelleys' attorneys argued to the U.S. Supreme Court that discriminatory restrictive covenants should be unenforceable under the U.S. Constitution. The Court agreed, deciding that the equal protection clause of the Constitution's Fourteenth Amendment prevented the government from using its power to enforce a private agreement that violated the constitutional requirement of the government treating the races with equality. In reaching this decision, the Court reasoned that discriminatory restrictive covenants are not themselves unconstitutional because they are merely a contract between private citizens that does not involve the government's endorsement or participation. However, a person seeking to *enforce* a discriminatory restrictive covenant would require the involvement of the courts and other government agencies to put the restriction into effect. Because the Fourteenth Amendment bans government actors from using their power to enforce unequal treatment based on one's race, the restrictive covenant in the *Shelley* case could not be enforced because doing so would require government involvement to impose it. Therefore, the Court ruled that the covenant was unenforceable and the Shelley family was entitled to live in the home they had purchased.

The *Shelley* case is a milestone in legal and civil rights history. Narrowly read, it had the effect of preventing racist landowners from refusing to allow property sales to minorities. The destruction of discriminatory restrictive covenants had the effect of promoting the rights of African Americans to freely buy, sell and enjoy home ownership. More broadly, the success of *Shelley* encouraged the growth of the Civil Rights Movement by signaling that the Supreme Court was inclined to promote civil rights and also served as an impetus for federal, state and local legislatures to implement laws that clearly defined the illegality of housing discrimination. *See also* Housing Covenants; Levittowns; Segregation, Residential.

Further Readings: Rosen, Mark. "Was *Shelley v. Kraemer* Incorrectly Decided?" *California Law Review* 95 (2007): 451–512.

Gabriel H. Teninbaum

Sit-ins

Sit-ins were a tactic used frequently as a means of nonviolent direct action against **racial segregation**. In 1960, prompted by a sit-in in Greensboro, **North Carolina**, a national sit-in movement developed, usually involving students. Between 1960 and 1964, sit-ins were one of the key tactics of the **Civil Rights Movement**. The sit-ins established many of the philosophical positions and tactics that would underscore the movement. Many activists who would go on to play leading roles in the Civil Rights Movement were first involved in sit-ins.

During the 1940s and 1950s, sit-ins were used sporadically as a tactic by organized labor and early civil rights organizations. Both the Fellowship of Reconciliation (FOR) and the **Congress of Racial Equality (CORE)** supported the use of sit-ins as a tactic during the 1940s. In Marshall, Texas, a sustained challenge to Jim Crow during the late 1940s and early 1950s saw the use of several sit-ins, which were supported by FOR and CORE. Sit-ins were used in several locations throughout the 1950s to challenge segregation. In July 1958, sit-ins helped desegregate Dockum Drugs in Wichita, Kansas, and one month later, sit-ins were held at the Katz Drug Store in Oklahoma City. Various other sit-ins took place in border states during the last years of the 1950s, often helping to achieve integration of the establishment targeted. Despite the success of these sit-ins, the tactic failed to grow into the mass movement it would become in the 1960s.

The sit-in movement was sparked by a sit-in in Greensboro, North Carolina. On February 1, 1960, four students at North Carolina Agricultural and Technical College staged a sit-in at the lunch counter of the F. W. Woolworth's department store in Greensboro. The sit-in was not a spontaneous event: the four protestors—Ezell Blair, Jr., Joseph McNeill, David Richmond and Franklin McClain—had all been members of National Association for the Advancement of Colored People (NAACP) college or youth groups (although the sit-in was not conducted under the auspices of the NAACP), and had spent many hours discussing ways in which they could participate in the integration movement. They had also been exposed to the burgeoning Civil Rights Movement: Greensboro had been visited by both **Martin Luther King, Jr.,** and the African American students involved in the Little Rock, **Arkansas**, desegregation case. The group intended to use the sit-in to illustrate the hypocrisy of allowing African Americans to shop in the store, but preventing them from using the lunch counter. Woolworth's was chosen specifically because it was a national chain and was vulnerable to pressure from outside the South. Having made purchases in the store, the four sat at the lunch counter and asked for service. When they were refused, they remained at the lunch counter until the store closed.

Unlike earlier sit-ins, the Greensboro protest prompted an almost instant movement. While previous sit-ins had been part of local protests and had not necessarily made connections with other local movements, news of the Greensboro sit-in spread quickly through a network of young activists, often connected to black colleges, black churches, and local civil rights groups in the South. The four protestors themselves contacted Floyd McKissick, an

NAACP Youth Council leader, on the evening of the first sit-in. McKissick, along with the Reverend Douglas Moore, who was the **Southern Christian Leadership Conference**'s (SCLC) North Carolina representative, soon arrived in Greensboro, where they helped to organize the sit-ins. Both men had protest experience: Moore in particular had been involved in direct action in Durham, North Carolina, including a sit-in in a segregated ice cream parlor. The presence of older, more experienced activists like McKissick and Moore helped to maintain the momentum created by the first sit-in and to coordinate the enthusiasm of the growing numbers of student protestors eager to participate.

The next day, the group returned to Woolworth's and again requested service at the lunch counter; once again, they were refused service. However, the group had been joined by 19 other students; by the third day of the protest, over 80 students took part in the sit-in. Over the course of the week, under the guidance of McKissick and Moore, increasing numbers of students from a variety of colleges (including some white colleges) joined the Woolworth's sit-in, and began sit-ins in different stores in downtown Greensboro. By the end of the first week of sit-ins, over 400 students were participating in sit-ins in Greensboro. By this point, white mobs were gathering to harass the protestors, and store managers, who until then had attempted to accommodate the protests, were threatening legal action. When the manager of Woolworth's closed the store at lunchtime, claiming a bomb threat had been received, the protestors decided to halt the sit-ins to allow negotiations to take place. When the store opened on Monday, the lunch counter remained closed.

The Greensboro sit-ins quickly inspired similar protests elsewhere. Moore and McKissick made use of the their connections to activists in other states and were pivotal in helping the sit-in movement to spread other North Carolina cities and into other states. Within days of the first Greensboro sit-in, other protests had taken place in Durham and Raleigh, as well as other communities in North Carolina. Central to the quick spread of sit-ins was the network of civil rights activists that was spread throughout the South. Fred Shuttlesworth of the SCLC witnessed a sit-in in High Point, North Carolina, and was impressed not only by the tactic, but also by the way in which the protestors conducted themselves. Such was his enthusiasm for sit-ins that he urged King to get involved. Sit-ins moved quickly from upper South states like North Carolina, and within a week of the first Greensboro sit-in, sit-ins had taken place in Rock Hill, **South Carolina**, under the auspices of an SCLC minister.

Of all the locations to which sit-ins spread, it was in Nashville, Tennessee, that the movement developed what would come to be its identifying characteristics. Nashville was fertile ground for sit-ins. A cadre of student activists, many of whom, such as Diane Nash and John Lewis, were students at Fisk University, had been searching for a way in which to challenge segregation. Many of these students had been attending nonviolent workshops run by **James Lawson**, a divinity student at Vanderbilt University, who had been urged to relocate to the South from Ohio by Martin Luther King, Jr. Lawson was planning to instigate several protests against segregation in downtown department stores. The Greensboro sit-ins presented themselves as the ideal way in which to do this.

Lawson organized a meeting to discuss the use of sit-ins in Nashville, at which over 500 volunteers, as well as the 75 students who had attended the nonviolent workshops, were in attendance. The volunteer's enthusiasm for sit-ins was so overwhelming that, in spite of his reservations, Lawson—who was at least a decade older than most of the students—agreed to begin sit-ins the following day. The meeting closed after Lawson had instructed the volunteers how to behave during the protests. Lawson's greater experience and links to the burgeoning Civil Rights Movement were crucial to establishing the Nashville sit-in movement, articulating its underlying philosophy of nonviolence and organizing it so that pressure could be persistently applied to segregation. However, the enthusiasm and devotion to the cause of the student volunteers drove the movement and provided a constant stream of protestors to participate. The day after the meeting, over 500 neatly dressed protestors entered stores in downtown Nashville to politely ask for service.

For two weeks, daily sit-ins were held in downtown Nashville. As in many cities in which sit-ins were held, the authorities did not react immediately, hoping that the protests would peter out; indeed, the presence of so many students led authorities, as well as the media, to assume that sit-ins would be a short-term movement. As it became clear that the protests were organized, disciplined, and persistent, store owners became increasingly concerned that sales would be lost. The chief of police announced that, at the request of store owners, trespassing and disorderly conduct arrests would be made. This was a development for which many in the Nashville movement had prepared themselves, but it was a particular source of anxiety of the organizers of the movement, who would in effect be advocating that the protestors staged sit-ins in the knowledge that they were likely to be arrested. Sit-in protestors in Raleigh, North Carolina, had already been arrested, and few in Nashville were deterred by this possibility. Indeed, being arrested and jailed would quickly become a mark of honor for protestors; the tactic of "jail, not bail" would soon spread to other forms of direct action.

In response to the Nashville chief of police's announcement, John Lewis committed to paper a code of conduct, by which protestors should abide. These underscored the tenets by which the movement had thus far been conducted and included reminders not to strike back if struck or abused, to be friendly and courteous at all at times, and to remember love and nonviolence. On February 27, as they took up seats at the lunch counters of chosen downtown stores, protestors were attacked by hostile whites; police arrested 77 protestors and five whites. Sixteen of the protestors, including Lewis and Diane Nash, declared that they would not accept bail, but would instead serve a jail sentence. Nash told the judge that in refusing bail, they were rejecting the practices that had led to their arrest. On hearing Nash's speech, the majority of the other protestors decided spontaneously also to refuse bail.

The jailing of the protestors sparked outrage in Nashville, but also brought the sit-ins to national attention. As the protestors were sentenced to workhouse detail, support was received from people such as Ralph Bunche, **Harry Belafonte**, and **Eleanor Roosevelt**. Further controversy was created when James Lawson was expelled from Vanderbilt's divinity school. If this was designed to distance Vanderbilt from the sit-ins, it backfired: the story made the front page of the *New York Times,* and Lawson was reinstated. In response to growing external criticism, the mayor of Nashville offered a compromise: in return for the ending of protests in the downtown, the jailed protestors would be freed, and a biracial committee to consider the desegregation of downtown would be established. Unbowed by her imprisonment, Diane Nash quickly led a protest at the lunch counter of the Greyhound bus terminal, which was not included in the compromise deal. Unexpectedly, the protestors were served, and segregation at the bus terminal ended suddenly.

The arrest of the Nashville protestors revealed a growing gap between their outlook and that of the wider black community in Nashville, as well as many older activists in the movement. The NAACP's **Thurgood Marshall** believed the students had made their point through the sit-ins and their arrests. He argued that such protests should now be abandoned and integration pursued through the courts. John Lewis roundly dismissed this approach and identified a fundamental philosophical difference between the protestors and older activists. To Lewis, the sit-ins had created a mass movement that was confronting Jim Crow; the strength of the sit-in movement was the energy and spontaneity of the large numbers of protestors who were willing to risk abuse, violence, and imprisonment to challenge segregation. This difference would find its expression in the formation of the **Student Nonviolent Coordinating Committee (SNCC)** at a conference at Shaw University, Raleigh, in April 1960, which brought together many of the young activists involved in the sit-in movement. While King hoped that the activists would use their enthusiasm and power for the SCLC, those attending the conference resisted this, and SNCC remained independent of other organizations.

By the point at which SNCC was formed, the sit-in movement had spread to other states. Between February and April, sit-ins were held in over 70 locations, and had reached **Georgia**, West Virginia, **Texas** and Arkansas. As well as capturing the zeal of so many activists who were eager to challenge Jim Crow, sit-ins proved to be a successful method of ending segregation. In Greensboro, the persistence and organization of the sit-in movement offset authorities' hopes that the summer would see a dip in sit-in activity; locals and high school students had been mobilized to carry on the protests when student numbers declined during nonterm time. The pressure brought by continued sit-ins forced the authorities to negotiate. In particular, the economic effects on businesses helped sit-ins to achieve their aims. The combined effects of the sit-ins, the loss of African American business through attendant boycotts, and the loss of business from whites who were discouraged from entering stores because of the protests, meant that Woolworth's lost $200,000 in Greensboro in 1960. By the end of July, lunch counters in downtown Greensboro had been integrated.

Other success occurred elsewhere: in Nashville, the city finally conceded in the face of the unstinting pressure of the sit-ins, and downtown lunch counters were integrated in early May. In Durham, downtown businesses began to desegregate as a direct result of sit-ins, while in Virginia, two drugstore chains planned to end the segregation of lunch counters. The **federal government** also stepped in, and U.S. Attorney General William Rogers negotiated with the owners of chain stores in the South to end segregation. Trailways announced that it would desegregate restaurants in bus terminals throughout the South. Although these victories were achieved relatively rapidly, they came as a result of the tenacity and vigor of the protestors, whose refusal to bow to white intimidation and the more moderate approaches of older activists helped to underline the value of sit-ins.

Indeed, the early burst of the sit-in movement helped to frame the Civil Rights Movement that was coalescing under the leadership of King. As well as sit-ins, other forms of direct action, often involving young activists, became keystones of the movement. Many young African Americans were inspired to action by seeing news coverage of sit-ins, and activists like Bob Moses and Cleveland Sellers would later credit the sit-ins as their introduction to the Civil Rights Movement, and for many more, sit-ins were their first active involvement. By the end of 1960, over 70,000 students had participated in sit-ins or direct action inspired by the sit-ins, and more than 3,600 protestors had been arrested. Sit-ins became perhaps the most identifiable tactic of the Civil Rights Movement and were used consistently in the first half of the 1960s.

While the Greensboro sit-ins and the protests they prompted elsewhere helped to erode some of Jim Crow's unassailability, segregation continued to exist in many forms. As the Civil Rights Movement developed, sit-ins were held throughout the South, including those cities in which segregation had already been partly overcome. Organized sit-ins, such as that which sought to integrate the Toddle Inn restaurant chain in Atlanta, Georgia, continued to be a vital source of protest. During the winter of 1962–1963, a boycott of downtown Jackson, Mississippi, was accompanied by sit-ins. The reaction of white mobs, which shouted abuse at protestors, doused them in food, and dragged them from stools, brought to national attention the extent to which whites in that state were resisting integration. Such sit-ins continued to follow the model established by the Greensboro and Nashville movements, and nonviolence remained the underlying philosophy. Other, less prolonged, forms of sit-ins were also employed. During marches and demonstrations, protestors would often spontaneously stage a sit-in, frequently when faced with **police brutality**, while variants such as pray-ins at segregated churches, or in the face of violence, and wade-ins at segregated beaches were also used.

After the passage of the **Civil Rights Act of 1964** and the **Voting Rights Act of 1965**, sit-ins became less relevant as the goals of the movement shifted. Indeed, in some states, such as Mississippi, sit-ins were a relatively minor tactic, often limited to urban areas. With the passage of legislation outlawing segregation, the frequency of sit-ins declined. Although sit-ins were still used from time to time, as the focus of the movement turned from segregation to voter registration and broader economic goals, new tactics took their place. The emergence of Black Power also undermined the value of sit-ins, as the validity of nonviolence as a tactic and philosophy was increasingly questioned. *See also* Gandhi, Mahatma.

Further Readings: Branch, Taylor. *Parting the Waters: America in the King Years, 1954–63.* New York: Simon and Schuster, 1988; Carson, Clayborne. *In Struggle: SNCC and the Black Awakening of the 1960s.* Cambridge, MA: Harvard University Press, 1981; Chafe, William H. *Civilities and Civil Rights: Greensboro, North Carolina, and the Black*

Struggle for Freedom. New York: Oxford University Press, 1980; Lewis, John, with Michael D'Orso. *Walking with the Wind: A Memoir of the Movement.* New York: Simon and Schuster, 1998; Moody, Anne. *Coming of Age in Mississippi.* New York: Bantam Doubleday, 1968.

Simon T. Cuthbert-Kerr

Slavery

Slavery in the American context was a system of labor and social control whereby the enslaved people did not own the fruits of their labor, nor did they own their person. Slaves were chattel property, to be used as the owner saw fit. While the English enslaved some of the Indians as war captives during the first decades of settlement, African slaves were available through the Atlantic slave trade, and by the beginning of the eighteenth century, most slaves in the English colonies were Africans. The institution of slavery set race relations between blacks and whites in the United States in a pattern that would long outlast slavery. While the legacy of slavery did not lead directly to **Jim Crow**, in that race relations under Jim Crow were in many important ways quite different than during slavery, slavery did establish a strong cultural acceptance of white supremacy and black inferiority, which would later find expression in Jim Crow laws.

Slavery existed in some form in most of the colonies, although in general, the North and upland farms in the South had far fewer slaves. While the popular image of the Old South is of the large plantation with dozens or even hundreds of slaves, most slaves lived on much smaller farms, with three slaves or fewer. Slave owners in the South as a group were a relatively small percentage of whites, but they held most of the economic and political power. The area that later became the United States took in a relatively small percentage of enslaved Africans, perhaps 4 or 5 percent of the total number who made the Middle Passage. Most enslaved Africans ended up in the **Caribbean** or in Brazil. The United States banned the importation of slaves in the early nineteenth century, thus slave owners had a vested interest in ensuring the reproduction of the slaves. In the United States, slave status was inherited through the mother; thus, any children of a slave woman became the property of her master, regardless of the status of the father. While slave owners often encouraged the formation of families, in that they tended to make a slave less likely to run away, and provided the next generation of slaves, such marriages had no legal standing. The death of owners often meant the forced breakup of slave families.

In the years after the Revolution, Northern states abolished slavery either through immediate emancipation, such as in southern **New England**, or gradual emancipation, such as in New York, Pennsylvania, and New Jersey. The nation became increasingly divided on the slave issue. Southerners tended to desire the expansion of slavery into the Western territories, while Northerners tended to oppose the expansion of slavery. The slave states were seriously outnumbered in the House of Representatives, so they fought to keep a balance of free and slave states in the Senate to maintain the ability to block legislation deemed hostile to slavery. Southerners also pressed for a federal fugitive slave law, one that the **federal government** would enforce, to allow slave owners to retrieve slaves who had escaped to the North.

Despite the relative powerlessness of the slaves, white Southerners in areas with large slave populations lived in almost constant fear of slave revolts. Slave owners tended to justify the institution, claiming that their "servants" were happy, and almost like family. This contrasted sharply with the large slave patrols and militias maintained in slave areas, and the savage reprisals for even the slightest hint of an uprising. Lurid stories of slave uprisings, especially from the Caribbean, were passed around, increasing the fear slave-owners felt. Such stories, which usually included white families having their throats slashed while they slept, indicate that despite their public pronouncements, slaveowners knew that their human property yearned to be free. Slavery set the pattern for whites that blacks should be feared, controlled, and kept subservient.

The existence of African slavery in the United States gave rise to a class of free blacks, often of mixed ancestry, who formed a middle group between free whites and enslaved blacks. In slave areas, they were sometimes looked at with suspicion by whites, as a people likely to lead a slave revolt; but in practice, such people often owed much of their status to the continuation of slavery. The free man, no matter what his skin color, was always the social superior of the slave. Communities of free blacks and mulattoes thrived in some areas of the South, such as Charleston, South Carolina, and around New Orleans. Some even became slave owners themselves. With the ending of slavery in 1865 and the rise of Jim Crow, such communities lost much of their separate identity, and those who could not "pass" in to white society were forced by laws and custom into black society.

While slavery was deeply entrenched in the law, customs, and economy of the South in the early nineteenth century, its maintenance rested on violence or the threat of violence. Slaves were at the mercy of their owners. Punishments for running away, disobedience, or a host of other infractions ranged from humiliation to whippings to mutilations. Slave patrols ensured that slaves had only the freedom of movement granted to them by owners. Slave women were vulnerable to sexual exploitation by owners or other white males, with no legal recourse. Slave owners had little or no liability for the abuse or even killing of their slaves. The question of whether a slave could testify in court, or even initiate legal action, remained in flux in many states. While slaves in Connecticut and Massachusetts sued for their freedom during the Revolutionary era based on the new state constitutions that made no provisions for slavery, as the nineteenth century progressed, slaves had fewer and fewer legal rights.

The **U.S. Supreme Court** ruling in *Dred Scott v. Sandford* in 1857 marked the final act of stripping slaves, and even free blacks, of any civil rights. The ruling went far beyond the initial question of whether a slave became free when his master took him to free territory. The Court ruled that Congress had no authority to outlaw slavery in any territories, that no person of African descent could ever be a citizen, regardless of their status, and that slaves had no standing to bring suit in court. The ruling, which fulfilled most desires of the slaveowners, created unease among even moderates in the North that the slave owners had too much power in the nation.

As with later Jim Crow, slavery stripped enslaved people of human rights, legal rights, and basic dignity. It did not, however, create a segregated society. In general, slaves were not able to use public entertainments, but slave labor existed with white foremen, overseers, and others who interacted regularly with the black labor force. In an age without public transportation or automobiles, blacks and whites often lived in close proximity. The culture of slavery in the American South created the impression that keeping blacks powerless was the normal order of things, a situation Jim Crow would later reimpose after the end of **Reconstruction** in 1877. *See also* Sharecropping.

Further Readings: Genovese, Eugene D. *Roll, Jordan, Roll: The World the Slaves Made.* New York: Vintage Books, 1976; Morgan, Edmund. *American Slavery American Freedom.* New York: W. W. Norton, 1975; Winthrop, Jordan, *White over Black: American Attitudes Toward the Negro, 1550–1812.* New York: W. W. Norton, 1977.

Barry M. Stentiford

Smith, Bessie (1892/1894–1937)

Bessie Smith deserved her title of "Empress of the **Blues**," recording over 180 songs and selling over a million recordings. In the late 1920s, she was the highest-paid black performer in the country. Her songs, including at least 30 she wrote herself, expressed the realities of life for working-class African Americans, especially black women. Known for her rounded sound and emotional delivery, she sang about heartbreak, jealousy, prison, homelessness, eviction, unemployment, poverty, alcohol, sex, suicide, murder, as well as independent women, adultery, and spousal abuse, all which reflected her rough-and-tumble lifestyle and tough upbringing. Her music and style transcended segregation, inspiring both black and white performers, such as Billie Holiday, Mahalia Jackson, and Janis Joplin, for decades after her death.

Despite her popularity, many aspects of her life remain unclear and overshadowed by myth, including the year of her birth and the events surrounding her tragic death. According to census records, she was born Elizabeth Smith in July 1892, in Chattanooga, Tennessee, to William and Laura Owen Smith. Later in life, she claimed April 15, 1894, as the date of her birth, the date recognized by her family. Her father, a farm laborer and onetime minister, died when she was a small child. Her mother worked as a washerwoman and maid to provide for Bessie and her seven older siblings, but segregation provided few opportunities for advancement or decent pay. Everyone in the family contributed to the family income, including Bessie, who sang and danced with her older brother on street corners for tips.

Her road to a professional singing career began at age eight, when she won a dollar in a talent contest. Within a year, she began singing regularly at Ivory Theatre for eight dollars a week. Around the same time, her mother died, forcing her and her younger siblings to move in with Bessie's oldest sister, Viola. Unhappy with home life, she soon joined the Rabbit Foot Minstrel Show, which starred the legendary blues singer Gertrude "Ma" Rainey. She toured the South as a child singer and learned the business from Rainey. Within a few years, she joined Milton Starr's Theatre Owner's Booking Agency, known as TOBA but frequently referred to by black entertainers as "Tough on Black Artists" because of the poor pay. In 1919, she created her own show, the Liberty Belles, at the "91" Theatre in Atlanta. Although her popularity grew in the South, her auditions for white record companies between 1920 and 1922 in the North failed because they thought her style was too rough and uncouth, illustrating a regional and racist bias.

In 1923, Smith married Jack Gee, a Philadelphia police officer. That same year, she recorded "Gulf Coast Blues" for Okeh Records, the "race music" branch of Columbia Records, which sold 750,000 copies. She continued to record throughout the 1920s with notable musicians, including Fletcher Henderson, Eddie Cantor, and Clarence Williams, and became the highest paid black entertainer in the country. The songs she is best known for are "St. Louis Blues," recorded with **Louis Armstrong** in 1925, and "Back Water Blues," recorded in 1927.

By 1929, alcoholism affected her performances and popularity. In addition, the **Great Depression** hurt record sales and lessened the appeal of blues music in general. Poor again, Smith took jobs where she could, but eventually returned to the stage. On the verge of a comeback, she died on September 26, 1937, from injuries suffered in a car accident outside Clarksville, Mississippi. Although rumored that she bled to death because a white hospital denied her care, eyewitness accounts claim a white doctor attended to her at the scene, after which she was taken to an African American hospital, where she never regained consciousness. Over 7,000 people attended her funeral at Mount Lawn Cemetery in Philadelphia, Pennsylvania, where she was buried in an unmarked grave. Musicians and local members of the NAACP paid for a headstone in 1970, which reads "The Greatest Blues Singer in the World Will Never Stop Singing." She was inducted into the **Rock and Roll** Hall of Fame in 1989. *See also* Harlem Renaissance.

Further Readings: Abertson, Chris. *Bessie.* Rev. and exp. ed. New Haven, CT: Yale University Press, 2003; Davis, Angela Y. *Blues Legacies and Black Feminism: Gertrude "Ma" Rainey, Bessie Smith, and Billie Holiday.* New York: Pantheon Books, 1998.

Katherine Kuehler Walters

South Carolina

With South Carolina as the primary architect of the Confederacy that was formed to preserve **slavery** in America and the first state in 1860 to attempt to leave the Union—severely fracturing the American republic to ignite the Civil War—the state later became an epicenter of **Jim Crow** violence. The brutality, discrimination, and segregation against blacks following post–Civil War **Reconstruction** accelerated in the mid-1870s through the zenith of the **Civil Rights Movement** during the 1960s.

Even at the dawn of the twenty-first century, the National Association for the Advancement of Colored People (NAACP) urged that potential visitors boycott South Carolina because officials refused to remove the Confederate flag flying above the statehouse in Columbia. And although the state's large black population over the years had largely overcome Jim Crow hatred and implemented progressive changes, Greenville County on January 16, 2006, was the last county in America officially to adopt a paid holiday for black civil rights leader **Martin Luther King, Jr.**'s birthday. Ironically, King's associate, Jesse L. Jackson, was born in Greenville in 1941, when the segregation and hate of Jim Crow were still routine.

During and since the Jim Crow days of the early 1900s, King and other black activists, including **Ida B. Wells-Barnett**, William Pickens of the NAACP, and **Fannie Lou Hamer**, had protested in South Carolina, where King's mentor Benjamin Mays was born in 1894 and who once called South Carolina the epitome of racist America. In fact, Mays, who became an educator, clergyman and president of Morehouse College in Atlanta, where King attended as an undergraduate during the mid-1940s, noted that his parents were born into slavery and lived as tenant farmers who experienced the very worst of Jim Crow discrimination.

South Carolina's white power structure had for centuries been very cognizant and wary of black empowerment ever since slavery was introduced there by Spanish explorers in 1526. Countless slave revolts throughout the state's history as the black population exponentially grew would prompt white authorities to form extremely repressive laws to control enslaved Africans with roots to such West African countries as Angola, the Congo, Senegal, Benin, Guinea, and the Gambia. Many such blacks, early on, were imported to the Americas, including South Carolina coastal areas and islands, for their rice-growing skills as practiced in West Africa.

Slave "patrols," which some historians argue developed into the Reconstruction-era **Ku Klux Klan**, were also instituted to control blacks in South Carolina by 1636 via an act that allowed any white to "apprehend, properly chastise, and send home" slaves found to be outside their master's plantation. Similar acts were passed in 1704 and 1721, and by 1860, such patrols had been combined with "military force" and the local militia. The patrol system thus evolved systems of control designed to institutionalize effective social and economic control of the black population.

There were more blacks than whites in South Carolina, something that white settlers watched closely for fear of uprisings. As a result of repeated slave escapes and those rebellions, or attempted insurrections, many "**black codes**" or laws were passed in South Carolina as early as 1712 that became a model for many slaveholding colonies, as South Carolina's whites became increasingly concerned about their burgeoning black population. That year, whites learned of a plot for enslaved Africans to destroy Charleston, and to escape with the help of the Yemassee Indians to St. Augustine, Florida. Many blacks, as a result, were hanged and others burned alive. Future rebellions, often led by Angolans, were as well dealt with severely, including a 1739 revolt of 60 to 100 enslaved blacks led by a slave called Jemmy, said to be an Angolan. Although about 40 whites and 20 blacks were killed in the ensuing battle, the revolt was not successful, resulting in many of the black survivors being decapitated, with their heads placed on top of fence posts as a warning to others. The Negro Act of 1740, a harsh measure that resulted from this revolt, became the basis of the slave code in South Carolina.

Such laws became the forerunner of Jim Crow practices starting in the late 1860s and following the Reconstruction period after the Civil War. Before then, though, in 1820 when South Carolina's black slaves skyrocketed to almost 60,000 with whites numbering only about 20,000, ex-slave Denmark Vesey organized a rebellion, with the help of several Angolans including Jack Purcell or "Gullah Jack," that would have likely wiped out most of the white power structure in and around Charleston. Although Vesey, whose African name was Telemaque, was hanged on July 2, 1822, he is credited with organizing the largest potential slave revolution in American history, utterly terrifying whites. About 35 of Vesey's alleged conspirators were also hanged or executed. Again, very restrictive laws curtailing free and enslaved blacks' travel, congregating, and otherwise communicating were instituted as a precursor for future Jim Crow initiatives.

Blacks in South Carolina, though, continued to push back on white dominance, even during the Civil War. Robert Smalls (1839–1915) became a hero to the Union in 1862 when he commandeered a Confederate steamer near Beaufort, South Carolina, where he had been born a slave. After the war, Smalls returned to South Carolina, purchased his master's home and served in the state's house of representatives, its senate, and then the U.S. House of Representatives for five terms, before becoming the collector of customs for the Port of Beaufort.

The ultimate influx of Union troops during the Civil War in South Carolina, including many of the 180,000 black soldiers who joined the fight to save the Union and wipe out slavery in the South, led to the establishment of black institutions in South Carolina after that great struggle. They included Penn Center School on St. Helena Island off the coast between Charleston and Savannah, Georgia, with the help of black educator Charlotte Forten of Philadelphia, where Martin Luther King, Jr., later held strategy sessions during the 1960s Civil Rights Movement.

Furthermore, the African Methodist Episcopal Church grew to 44,000 members by the end of Reconstruction, with 12 AME ministers serving the South Carolina legislature. With blacks clearly outnumbering whites by 1868 and becoming members of Lincoln's Republican Party, about 68,000 out of 84,000 voted to change South Carolina's constitution. To most whites' consternation, African Americans ascended to such positions as county commissioners, tax assessors, constables and judges.

Whites were particularly suspicious of black preachers, including Charleston native Daniel Payne (1811–1893), a bishop in the African Methodist Episcopal Church that had been founded in 1794 by the ex-slave Richard Allen in Philadelphia. Although Payne started a school for African Americans that closed in 1834 because South Carolina would not permit the education of slaves, he founded the first African American–controlled college in America, Wilberforce University of Ohio in 1865, as the Jim Crow era began to spawn. White South Carolinians ultimately realized that such theologians completely countered historical pro-slavery, preaching that blacks were inferior and meant to serve Caucasians. Indeed, black ministers were not immune to the rampant violence during the Jim Crow era, including Payne whose activism endangered him in South Carolina many times.

In 1870, as federal soldiers withdrew from South Carolina, many blacks and their ministers faced great hostility and even death, such as the AME's Wade Perrin, who was assassinated that year. David Wyatt Aiken, who owned a plantation with about 40 slaves before the war, was said to be a primary instigator of such tragedies, declaring in the summer of 1868 that "before the white man should be ruled by niggers, they would kill the last one of them." Aiken County in South Carolina today is named for Aiken's politician cousin, William. David Wyatt Aiken was also implicated in the homicide of B. F. Randolph, a black Methodist preacher and member of the state legislature, who was fatally shot by three men at a train station in Hodges Depot, South Carolina.

In Abbeville County, where the Confederacy was conceived and the first meetings to plot a rebellion against the federal government were held, one federal army officer in 1868 amassed a huge record of incidents where blacks were killed or otherwise assaulted, with homes being burned down, by whites. Black codes were reinstituted and metamorphosed into the rampant Jim Crow discrimination that would shape the bitter timbre of racial hatred well into the twentieth century in a state where many native whites still viewed South Carolina as separate from the Union.

Born August 1, 1894, in Ninety-Six, the future mentor of Martin Luther King, Jr., Benjamin Mays, witnessed the impact of those black codes that also restricted black voting rights, as well as the brutality of Jim Crow in Greenwood County during the Phoenix Riot of 1898. That is when several African Americans were lynched over blacks' fight for enfranchisement—an empowerment that racist whites consistently fought to stomp out. One of Mays's earliest memories during that period was watching his father, Hezekiah Mays, kowtowing or sinking to his knees and touching his head to the ground in front of a white mob to avoid certain death.

Such early episodes helped Mays to become a prolific student, graduating valedictorian of his 1914 class at South Carolina State College in Orangeburg, where in 1968, four black students would be massacred by city police during a civil rights demonstration. Meanwhile, by the mid-1930s Mays completed his doctorate at the University of Chicago in theology, becoming a highly esteemed educator, preacher and president of Morehouse where he began to counsel a young student named Martin Luther King, Jr. during the 1940s. Mays, via the strong Christian principles of his mother, Louvenia, and inspired to fight the Jim Crow hatred that he had experienced in South Carolina, convinced King that Christian activism through nonviolence was an excellent way to fight racism. Some sources indicate that he also helped to introduce King to the concepts of **Mahatma Gandhi**, who utilized pacifism to knock down the pillars of racism in South Africa and India.

As the 1900s approached, South Carolina's blacks continued to face virulent racism and violence from such groups as the Ku Klux Klan with memberships soaring due to anger over losing the Civil War and black advancements. Such whites sought to punish blacks and keep them subjugated, making South Carolina's blacks some of the most prevalent passengers of the early 1900s

Great Migration to Northern cities. African Americans were still hampered from voting and accessing public and private facilities, as well as relegated to primarily menial and sharecropping or tenant-farming jobs in South Carolina and other Southern states.

Indeed, the sharecropping system of the late 1800s and well into the 1900s forced South Carolina's blacks to work the very plantations on which they had been enslaved, as Benjamin Mays' parents had, but usually at very substandard wages that often kept them indebted to unscrupulous white landowners who rented land at unfair prices. Daring to speak out or challenge South Carolina's stupendously racist social norms often meant an agonizing death.

Yet, such brave anti-lynching warriors as Ida B. Wells-Barnett, born July 16, 1862, in Holly Springs, **Mississippi**, dared to speak out against such injustices throughout the country and in South Carolina. After participating in a 1913 women's suffrage demonstration in Washington, DC, she spoke to President William McKinley about the escalating violence against blacks in South Carolina. She wanted it stopped immediately.

William Pickens, Sr., born in Anderson County, South Carolina on January 15, 1881, was destined to become the first field secretary for the NAACP and traveled to the deepest reaches of the South, including his home state, to combat Jim Crow during the early 1900s. Credited with recruiting an unparalleled number of members and organizing chapters throughout the United States, Pickens earned degrees ranging to a doctorate from Talledega College in

African American school with teachers and students, perhaps in South Carolina, 1910s. Courtesy of Library of Congress, LC-DIG-ppmsca-13304.

Alabama, Yale University, Fisk University, Selma University and even a law degree from Wiley University in Marshall, Texas.

National and local news articles of the countless victims of lynching in South Carolina attest to that state's notorious Jim Crow reputation, as revealed in Ralph Ginzburg's "100 Years of **Lynchings**." For instance, the *Washington Times* reported on February 18, 1900, that a 19-year-old black teen was lynched in Aiken County after a "crowd of 250 tracked the negro fifty miles across Aiken, Edgefield, and Greenwood counties." The young man, "without hesitation," and apparently petrified, had been ordered to climb a tree and jump from a limb after a rope was tied to it and his neck. When the rope broke, he was "hoisted up and then shot to pieces."

White mobs were particularly vicious if a black man was accused of being intimate with a white woman. One black man was killed and another hurt in 1922 near Florence, South Carolina, because the deceased was suspected of having a relationship with a white woman. "The wounded negro was driving a buggy into which the other man had leaped in an attempt to elude the mob. ... Letters from the white woman were found in the pocket of the dead man after the lynching," according to a January 14, 1922 report in the *Memphis Commercial Appeal*. The white woman realized she too was in trouble for fraternizing with an African American man.

Such abhorrence over interracial relationships certainly reached the highest governmental levels in South Carolina, as indicated by Governor Cole Blease's 1911 statement: "Whenever the Constitution comes between me and the virtue of white women of South Carolina I say 'to hell with the Constitution!'" Indeed, such beliefs reflected the firm attitudes of many white South Carolinians following Reconstruction that their state would never succumb to federal efforts to elevate blacks and absolutely not permit white women and black men to have relationships. Many whites, in fact, viewed the state as separate from the Union, despite losing the Civil War. They realized that the North's military victory, at that point, was simply temporary, and such racist institutions as the Ku Klux Klan and other groups would soon take control. If a black man had been accused of rape, the consequences were often unspeakably horrible, including burning at the stake and dismemberment, especially of the sexual organs that were among body parts often handed out as souvenirs following rallies that were usually attended by thousands of whites.

Although the number of lynching incidents in South Carolina, as well as other states, cannot be pinpointed because countless blacks were killed secretly or without their identities known, it is likely that the figure totals to thousands in South Carolina. Furthermore, the segregation of blacks at public facilities, as well as the hampering of voting rights and economic empowerment, was routine practice in a state that conceptualized and actualized the Confederacy in order to preserve slavery and Jim Crow hatred.

Strom Thurmond, who became the longest serving and oldest U.S. senator before his death in 2003 at age 100, was a former South Carolina governor who became a symbol of racial segregation nationwide, despite his later authenticated sexual relationship with a black worker with whom he fathered a child. During Thurmond's 1948 Democratic bid for president, he said, "that there's not enough troops in the Army to force the Southern people to break down segregation and admit the nigger race into our theatres, into our swimming pools, into our homes and into our churches." In 1957, in opposition to the Civil Rights Act, the senator filibustered for a record-setting 24 hours and 18 minutes.

News reports in 2007 also indicate that Thurmond's ancestors owned a slave whose family line developed into the black activist Al Sharpton's family, crystallizing the legacy of South Carolina's pro-slavery and Confederate reality that some observers insist still exists to some degree today.

Although the Confederate flag was removed from the top of the South Carolina statehouse due to pressure from the NAACP and placed on a pole at the street level in July 2000, the divisive symbol of white supremacy and pro-slavery fervor still flies in front of the building.

Further Readings: Documenting the American South. http://docsouth.unc.edu/church/hamilton/hamilton.html (accessed July 22, 2007); Fry, Gladys-Marie. *Night Riders in Black Folk History.* Chapel Hill: University of North Carolina Press, 1975.Jim Crow Heroes in South Carolina. http://www.jimcrowhistory.org/scripts/jimcrow/heroes.cgi?state=South%20Carolina (accessed July 29, 2007); Litwack, Leon F. *Trouble in Mind: Black Southerners in the Age of Jim Crow.* New York: Alfred A. Knopf, 1998; *Negro Plot: An Account of the Late Intended Insurrection among a Portion of the Blacks of the City of Charleston, South Carolina.* Boston: Printed and published by J. W. Ingraham, 1822; Rowland, Lawrence S., et al., *The History of Beaufort County, South Carolina.* Volume 1, 1514–1861. Columbia: University of South Carolina Press, 1996.

Donald Scott

Southern Christian Leadership Conference (SCLC)

Founded as a tight coalition of spiritual leaders, the Southern Christian Leadership Conference (SCLC) emerged in the late 1950s as the leading Christian civil rights organization. It championed nonviolence, voting rights, anti-poverty, and social justice in its campaign to abolish **Jim Crow. Martin Luther King, Jr., Ralph Abernathy, Joseph Lowery,** and Fred Shuttlesworth, all ordained ministers leading prominent congregations in **Alabama** and **Georgia,** were the original executive body of the SCLC. From its birth in 1957 to the present, the SCLC has maintained a political agenda aimed first at dismantling institutionalized racism, then addressing the emotional and economic wounds caused by Jim Crow in American communities.

The **Montgomery Bus Boycott** of 1955–1956 provided the greatest influence on the formation of the SCLC. The Montgomery Improvement Association (MIA) invited Martin Luther King, Jr., to provide spiritual leadership for the boycott volunteers and participants. In Montgomery, King befriended Ralph Abernathy and other politically active members of the black church. The success of the boycott and the desegregation of Montgomery's bus lines motivated King, Abernathy, Lowery, Shuttlesworth, and C. K. Steele to form a faith-based organization in January 1957. The ministers settled on the name, Southern Christian Leadership Conference, as a representation of the organization's membership, congregations, churches, civic confederations, and associations of groups for social justice. The SCLC preferred not to have individuals as members; instead, it practiced collective action with nonviolent resistance as its principle philosophy.

In the first half of the **Civil Rights Movement**, the SCLC emphasized desegregation of public accommodations and voting rights. In 1961, the SCLC sheltered more than 1,000 supporters of the Freedom Rides in its churches. It led voting registration campaigns in Alabama and **Mississippi** in 1962. In 1963, SCLC triumphed over segregation in the nation's most segregated city, Birmingham, Alabama. The city remained a bastion of segregation, despite the *Brown v. Board of Education* decision and the growing popularity of desegregation movements across the nation. In Birmingham, segregation was absolute and complete in every part of life, including in schools, restaurants, city parks, cemeteries, and department store dressing rooms. Although blacks were about 40 percent of the population, fewer than 12 percent of blacks had registered to vote.

The SCLC embarked on a slightly different strategy from that of Montgomery—boycotting department stores and leading protest marches through downtown Birmingham. The SCLC asked for black children to join the marches and to risk jail to protest segregation. The children endured disturbing violence, in the form of attacking police dogs and high-pressure fire hoses. National outcry at the photographs and television images of children and young adults under attack had cemented public opinion against the city of Birmingham. The SCLC demanded and received an end to racist hiring practices and segregation, inaugurated by a biracial committee overseeing desegregation. The organization had similar success three years later in protesting segregation in Selma, Alabama, in 1965.

The SCLC's successful organization of Birmingham's desegregation however, did not quell violent reactions to the group or its supporters. A few days after the announcement of a peaceful conclusion to the marches, more than 1,000 Klansmen burned crosses in a city park. Then bombs exploded in the Birmingham home of Alfred Daniel King, Martin Luther King's brother. In Jackson, Mississippi, a Klansman murdered civil rights leader **Medgar Evers** in his driveway in June. In September 1963, a bomb left at the Birmingham Baptists Church killed four black girls. All of the events had the effect of attracting even more support to the Civil Rights Movement, particularly among Northern whites, who were eager to facilitate the Black Revolution underway. Progressive white Americans, too, faced considerable violence. For instance, in March 1965, Viola Luizzo, a white housewife from Detroit, was shot and killed by a Klansman in a passing car as she drove civil rights volunteers to voting registration drives in Alabama.

The SCLC reached its organizational highpoint with the August 1963 **March on Washington** for Jobs and Freedom. The march benefited from a broad base of support, including the AFL-CIO, the National Council of Churches, and the National Conference of Catholics for Interracial Justice. The appeal of King and the persuasiveness of the SCLC urged Americans to overcome their racial fears and insecurities; nonviolent protest spoke to the peaceful, political goal of full inclusion and equal rights for African Americans. With **A. Philip Randolph** and **Bayard Rustin** as the primary organizers, the March on Washington drew between 200,000 and 250,000 participants

A bomb demolished the Gaston Motel in Birmingham, Alabama, during the meeting of the SCLC in 1963. Courtesy of Library of Congress, LC-U9-9771-17.

to Washington, DC, on August 28, 1963. From its success, the SCLC was catapulted to the position as the primary civil rights organization. It brought moral pressure on President **John F. Kennedy**, and then President **Lyndon B. Johnson** to sign the **Civil Rights Act of 1964** and **Voting Rights Act of 1965**.

Widespread and deeply rooted poverty in the 1960s, coupled with intransigent resistance to civil rights activism, challenged the SCLC to take on antipoverty as its next concern. The SCLC also recognized the opportunity to move beyond the notion of Jim Crow as a Southern issue. Job discrimination, unequal school funding, restrictive housing covenants, and police brutality had long troubled race relations in northern cities and states. In 1966, at the invitation of the Chicago Freedom Movement, the SCLC set up an office in Chicago, for the purpose of challenging the city to reform its housing practices. Mayor Richard Daley and the Chicago Police Department, aware of the SCLC's strategy of provoking confrontation that risked embarrassing national exposure, pledged their protection of marchers in peaceful demonstrations within the city's limit. The organization held fast to its principles of nonviolence, but its demonstrations were met with vitriolic riots in the all-white suburbs of Chicago. The Chicago campaign ended with a summit agreement between Daley and civil rights organizations to address the issue of housing segregation. Yet, failing to achieve a Birmingham-style reversal of segregation, the SCLC retreated to reexamine its tactics.

After the disappointment in Chicago, the SCLC regrouped and began planning another high profile march, the Poor People's Campaign. Like the goals of the 1963 March on Washington, the Poor People's Campaign's guiding mission was to create awareness of poverty and its debilitating effects on Americans across the country. In 1967, the SCLC announced its plan to bring thousands of poor, unemployed, and working Americans to Washington, DC, to demand federal programs promoting antipoverty and economic security. As the final preparations for the Poor People's Campaign were well under way, by the beginning of spring 1968, King embarked on a new direction in Memphis. Joined by Jesse Jackson and Ralph Abernathy in early April 1968, King lent the SCLC's support of the striking sanitation workers. The striking workers sought higher wages and better working conditions, demands that exemplified the new path of the SCLC. King's assassination on April 4, 1968, profoundly wounded the organization. In the short term, public sympathy and political sensitivity afforded to the SCLC immense support for the Poor People's Campaign. In the long term, the loss of a charismatic leader hurled the SCLC into a prolonged state of confusion. After six weeks of daily protest marches and continuous calls for an Economic Bill of Rights, the police dismantled "Resurrection City," the Poor People's Campaign's tent city, and evicted its 2,000 residents. The country turned its attention away from the civil rights struggle, instead focusing on the Vietnam War. The SCLC never regained its pre-1968 stature.

Without tangible goals, in the 1970s the organization drifted. In late 1971, Jesse Jackson left the organization after a falling-out with Ralph Abernathy, King's successor as president. Jackson founded Operation PUSH (People United to Save Humanity), developed a high profile for his fiery rhetoric and quickly organized protest marches. Furthermore, the SCLC could no longer attract or inspire student activists. The forceful and aggressive philosophies of **Malcolm X** and the Black Power movement drew a younger, more militant generation of leaders away from the principles of nonviolence. A divisive battle between older religious leaders and Vietnam-era student protesters brought the SCLC to the brink of collapse in the mid-1970s. Abernathy resigned as president, and Joseph Lowery, a founding member, replaced him in 1977.

Currently, the SCLC, led by Charles Steele, maintains its commitment to voting rights, conflict resolution, and social justice. Though the organization possesses less political and religious clout in its current incarnation, the SCLC retains its place of authority in the history of the Civil Rights Movement. *See also* Ku Klux Klan.

Further Readings: Branch, Taylor. *At Canaan's Edge: America During the King Years, 1965–1968.* New York: Simon and Schuster, 2006; Branch, Taylor. *Parting the Waters: America During the King Years, 1954–1963.* New York: Simon and Schuster, 1988; Fairclough, Adam. *To Redeem the Soul of America: The Southern Christian Leadership Conference and Martin Luther King, Jr.* Athens: University of Georgia Press, 1987; Garrow, David. *Bearing the Cross: Martin Luther King and the Southern Christian Leadership Conference.* New York: Vintage, 1986; Peake, Thomas. *Keeping the Dream Alive: A History of the Southern Christian Leadership Conference from King to the 1980s.* New York: Peter Lang, 1987.

Nikki Brown

Southern Tenant Farmers' Union

The Southern Tenant Farmers' Union (STFU) was a biracial labor union founded in Tyronza, **Arkansas**, in 1934. By 1938, the organization claimed

35,000 members, the majority of whom resided in eastern Arkansas. The STFU sought to organize the South's poorest and most vulnerable agricultural workers and managed to attract a great deal of publicity to the plight of the impoverished sharecropper. However, they were fundamentally unable to extract major concessions from Southern landowners or to halt the mechanization of agriculture, which made the South less dependent on the efforts of individual laborers.

Despite the fact that the land they farmed contained some of the richest cotton-producing soil in the United States, Arkansas tenant farmers and sharecroppers were hard-pressed to eke out more than a subsistence livelihood each year. Planters frequently kept these agricultural workers in financial subservience through unscrupulous record keeping and outright intimidation as well as by charging exorbitant interest rates on the annual loans necessary to keep the croppers afloat in a cash-poor economy.

The financial situation of this class of agricultural laborers, precarious in the best of times, only worsened with the beginning of the **Great Depression**. However, even before the rumblings on Wall Street impacted life in the cotton fields, Arkansas was hit with a series of natural disasters, beginning with the Mississippi River flood of 1927, followed by a series of tornadoes in the spring of 1929, and the drought of 1930–1931. These natural disasters, coupled with the chaos in the nation's financial sector, left the agricultural economy in turmoil.

In May 1933, Congress passed the **Agricultural Adjustment Act**, which was designed to address the agricultural crisis through an elaborate scheme of crop reduction and government subsidies. In order to reduce agricultural surpluses and thereby increase prices, the **federal government** paid landowners to take a portion of their acreage out of production. In addition, the government gave planters "parity payments" to subsidize the market price of cotton. In theory, owners were to spread acreage reductions across their plantations, thereby reducing each tenant's plot slightly. Planters were also supposed to share federal monies with their sharecroppers. However, more often than not, landowners neglected to equitably distribute this **New Deal** bounty. Furthermore, many chose to concentrate crop reductions, to eliminate some plots altogether, and then to evict the unneeded laborers.

Neither the federal government nor the Agricultural Adjustment Administration officials were willing to intervene in the planter/tenant relationship on behalf of the dispossessed croppers. Abandoned by the federal government and at the mercy of the local landowners, a group of Arkansas tenant farmers gathered in Tyronza, Arkansas to establish the STFU. Inspired by a recent visit of socialist leader Norman Thomas, and under the leadership of H. L. Mitchell and Clay East—white, local businessmen and members of the Socialist Party—a group of disgruntled sharecroppers met at a schoolhouse on a large plantation to discuss the possibility of unionization and collective bargaining with local planters. After quickly agreeing upon the premise of the union, the first item on the agenda was to determine whether two separate segregated unions should be formed or one integrated one.

According to Mitchell, the dilemma was settled on the basis of two eloquent speeches favoring biracial class solidarity. Burt Williams, a white cropper, favored integration saying, "You know my pappy rode with the KKK, we drove the Republican officeholders out of Crittendon County some forty years ago. That time has passed, and we have to forget all that stuff." Ike Shaw, an African American who had been involved in an attempt to unionize that turned into race-based massacre in Elaine, Arkansas, in 1919, concurred, saying, "As long as we stand together black and white . . . nothing can tear [the union] down."

Shaw was right to the extent that the union was tenacious. Despite planter reprisals, STFU members continued to meet and to agitate for wage increases for day laborers and an equitable distribution of New Deal funds throughout the 1930s. The STFU managed to win some small wage increases after a cotton picker's strike in 1935. However, a similar strike in 1936 met with disastrous results when Governor Junius Marion Futrell called out the **National Guard**, which forced the strikers to disperse at gunpoint.

Ultimately, the STFU did very little to directly ameliorate the economic conditions of the state's croppers. Their efforts were met with violent reprisals by the local population of landowners and their allies. However, the STFU did manage to bring the plight of the sharecropper to the attention of the national media. For example, on June 16, 1936, a group of white land owners beat two white STFU supporters, social worker Willie Sue Blagden and Presbyterian minister Claude Williams. The sensational incident of the whipping of a Southern white woman sparked something of a media frenzy, and pictures of Blagden's bruised thighs were published from coast to coast. Due in large part to negative publicity, Governor Futrell appointed a commission to study the problems inherent in farm tenancy, and violent intimidation began to abate.

However, the STFU was plagued by internal as well as external problems. Although the leadership of the organization was integrated, many locals remained segregated, and racial tensions flared from time to time. In addition, arguments arose over whether or not the union should join the Congress of Industrial Organizations (CIO), and rumors abounded about alleged Communist infiltration in the STFU. These disputes led many of the group's most ardent followers to abandon the organization.

Although both the federal and the state governments were eventually pressured into conducting investigations of farm tenancy in Arkansas, these studies did not result in tangible reforms of the kind envisioned by the STFU. AAA monies allowed planters to begin to mechanize cotton production, and the organization of agricultural laborers in Arkansas quickly became a moot point. It was not until 1972 that Arkansas cotton was 100 percent machine-harvested; however, the need for farm workers steadily decreased after 1940, and former sharecroppers began leaving the state in large numbers. The STFU never formally disbanded, but in 1944, Mitchell migrated westward to organize migrant laborers in California and to found the organization that was to succeed the STFU, the National Farm Labor Union.

The STFU's most enduring legacy was that it modeled a nearly unprecedented degree of interracial cooperation, which was not to be seen on as grand a scale again until the advent of the modern **Civil Rights Movement** of the 1950s and 1960s.

Further Readings: Conrad, David Eugene. *The Forgotten Farmers: The Story of Share-croppers in the New Deal.* Westport, CT: Greenwood Press, 1965; Kirby, Jack Temple. *Rural Worlds Lost: The American South, 1920–1960.* Baton Rouge: Louisiana State University Press, 1987; Wolters, Raymond. *Negroes and the Great Depression.* Westport, CT: Greenwood Press, 1970.

Jennifer Jensen Wallach

Sports

Sports provided a key terrain for contesting the boundaries imposed by **Jim Crow** segregation. Although whites in the South and North consistently tried to deny African Americans the right to participate in a variety of amateur and professional sports activities, black people fought for their rights on playing fields and courts. Eventually, the supposed "level playing field" of athletics led to some opportunities, for black men in particular, to participate in integrated competition and reap some of the benefits, including professional prize money, college scholarships, Olympic glory, and a sense of personal dignity and worth. However, Southern whites were dogged opponents of integrated sports competition, and some sports, such as professional baseball, acceded to Jim Crow customs for decades. As a result, black institutions, such as **Negro League baseball**, developed and provided an alternate playing field on which African Americans could participate with their peers. While integrated sports competition helped break down Jim Crow barriers to some degree, many believe that sports have also perpetuated stereotypes of African Americans, as some white observers have attributed black athletic success to animalistic traits supposedly inherent to the black race.

In the years following the Civil War, African Americans had some opportunities to participate in integrated sports competition and were often very successful. Horse racing, for example, was dominated by black jockeys in the late nineteenth century: 14 of the 15 jockeys racing in the first Kentucky Derby, in May 1875, were African American. Even more remarkably, of the first 28 Derbys, 15 were won by black riders. Isaac Murphy, an African American from Kentucky, was perhaps the best jockey of all time, winning numerous races and earning significant prize money. The first jockey to win the Kentucky Derby three times, Murphy died of pneumonia at age 35 in 1896. Some early professional baseball leagues also permitted black players in the 1870s and 1880s, although these opportunities were rare and players sometimes passed as Latino or Indian in order to play. College **football** also became more popular in this time period, and scattered black players earned considerable acclaim at majority white universities in the East and Midwest. William Henry Lewis, for example, was an All-American at Harvard in 1892 before going on to a successful career as a lawyer and federal assistant attorney general under President William Howard Taft. Frederick Douglass "Fritz" Pollard also earned national acclaim at Brown University from 1916 to 1917, and Paul Robeson starred at Rutgers College from 1915 to 1919. The success of these pioneers inspired many in the black community, particularly those in the black press, who believed that athletic achievement would prove blacks' capacities in other areas of life, and would open up new opportunities for the

African American community on the whole. All of these players, however, were subject to racial abuse and taunting from opposing fans, players, and coaches (and often even from members of their own teams), suggesting the limitations sports had for effecting change. Indeed, on the whole, "big-time" college football remained largely segregated, and Jim Crow customs eventually forced black jockeys out of horse racing as the sport became more popular with the general public in the 1920s.

One sport that did provide opportunities for African Americans was professional boxing. Although the sport was illegal in many states, it nonetheless became increasingly popular in the years leading up to the turn of the twentieth century as Boston heavyweight boxer John L. Sullivan, an Irish-American, became a cult hero to the working class in the 1880s. Sullivan, however, steadfastly refused to fight black boxers, including Australian heavyweight champion Peter Jackson. Although black boxers in less prestigious weight classes had some opportunities to fight white boxers for championships (Joe Gans earned the lightweight title in 1902, for example), the heavyweight division remained off-limits to black participation because of its prestige. Finally, in 1908, African American boxer **Jack Johnson** defeated Australian Tommy Burns for the heavyweight title. Outraged whites—stunned that a black man held the title of heavyweight champion of the world—called boxer James Jeffries out of retirement to restore the championship to the white race. When Johnson defeated Jeffries on July 4, 1910, riots broke out across the country as whites violently assaulted African Americans celebrating Johnson's triumph. Johnson's victory was particularly unsettling to many whites because of his personal life; marrying white women, driving expensive cars, and wearing extravagant clothes, Johnson seemed a direct affront to notions of white male supremacy. For many blacks, on the other hand, Johnson's triumph was so inspiring precisely because it challenged long-held beliefs in white male superiority. In the months after the bout, film footage of the fight was banned in many states, a sign of the symbolic importance accorded to Johnson's triumph. Federal authorities eventually convicted Johnson of violating the Mann Act in 1913, a dubious case that was settled by an all-white jury, and Johnson fled the country. He finally lost the championship to white heavyweight Jess Willard in 1915. Because Willard refused to take on black challengers, the championship then remained in the hands of white boxers for more than 20 years.

Baseball, by far the most popular spectator sport in America in the first half of the twentieth century, was strictly a segregated affair as it reached its ascendant popularity. Although scattered blacks had played professionally in the nineteenth century, an unwritten rule against black participation became well established in the two major professional organizations that would eventually unite to form Major League Baseball (MLB)—the National League by the late 1880s, and the American League from its inception in 1901. Because MLB proved particularly intractable in permitting black players to participate in the game, denying blacks access to the money and prestige earned by white players, African Americans established their own barnstorming teams and eventually a variety of "negro leagues."

The first black professional baseball team was the Cuban Giants, established in 1885 in Babylon, New York, and a number of teams followed suit in the ensuing years, including the Kansas City Monarchs and the Homestead (Pennsylvania) Grays. Black professional leagues also sprung up across the country, although they seldom lasted for long and were dogged by financial difficulties. Finally, in 1920, Andrew "Rube" Foster established the Negro National League, with eight teams: Chicago American Giants, Chicago Giants, Cuban Stars, Dayton Marcos, Detroit Stars, Indianapolis ABCs, Kansas City Monarchs and St. Louis Giants. This league was the dominant black league until it folded after the 1931 season because of the **Great Depression**. A second Negro National League debuted in 1933, however, and lasted until 1949. Two other leagues, the Negro Southern League and the Negro American League, were also successful and long-lasting. These leagues provided opportunities for black professional baseball players to earn a living, although their pay was never as high as their white counterparts and their traveling accommodations were never as appealing. Still, the Negro Leagues were very popular for urban African Americans in particular, who eagerly supported their hometown teams. Countless star athletes earned acclaim by playing on these teams, including legendary players such as Josh Gibson and Satchel Paige.

As the various Negro Leagues found firmer footing in the 1920s, other sports gradually opened their doors to more integrated competition. The 1930s, in particular, showed significant signs of progress. In boxing, heavyweight Joe Louis became the first African American since Johnson to hold the heavyweight boxing crown, a title he held for 12 years, when he defeated James Braddock in 1937. Louis also earned national acclaim for his defeat of German boxer Max Schmeling in 1938, a bout many saw as a contest between American democracy and Nazi fascism. Louis's popularity with both white and black fans suggests the transcendent capability of sports, but also its limits in effecting change. While Louis was certainly popular with many white fans across the country, discrimination continued unabated in most aspects of life, and Louis was careful to avoid any behavior that would have linked him to Johnson. Meanwhile, black Olympic athletes also inspired national pride in the 1930s. Although there had been African American Olympians (and medalists) since the 1904 games, **Jesse Owens**'s dominating performance in the 1936 Olympics in Berlin was the most nationally celebrated. Winning four gold medals at the games, the most ever won by an American track athlete, Owens visibly challenged German leader Adolf Hitler's assertions of Aryan supremacy, and Owens was celebrated as a national hero. However, advertisers also shunned Owens for endorsement opportunities because of his race when he returned to the States, and he struggled to earn a living once he concluded his amateur career. In the realm of college sports, the 1930s also saw some significant changes as more black athletes gained positions on teams in the North and West (although still in relatively small numbers), and integrated competition slowly started to take place between Southern and Northern schools. The University of North Carolina, for example, traveled north to square off against New York University and its black star Ed Williams in 1936, although games played in the South continued to require black athletes to sit out.

Perhaps the most important single event in the integration of sports in the United States occurred when **Jackie Robinson** took the field for the MLB **Brooklyn Dodgers** on April 15, 1947. Robinson, signed by Dodgers president Branch Rickey, was the perfect candidate to integrate baseball because of his athletic ability and strong character. Facing racist taunting from opposing players and fans, with players often attempting to injure him by throwing pitches directly at him and deliberately "spiking" him with their cleats, Robinson held his emotions in check, fearful that an outburst might set back the process of integration. His strong play earned him the National League Rookie of the Year Award in 1947 and inspired tens of thousands of black fans to come out to games to see him play. In his nine-year career, Robinson won numerous accolades, including the National League Rookie of the Year in 1947, the National League Most Valuable Player in 1949, and a World Series championship in 1955. Following Robinson's debut, other clubs began to sign African American baseball players: Larry Doby was the second black player in MLB history when he joined the Cleveland Indians midway through the 1947 season. Many consider Robinson's successful turn in baseball, "the national pastime," a pivotal event in the broader struggle for African American civil rights. Robinson's success in MLB, however, also sounded the death knell for the Negro Leagues. With the best black players leaving for the higher salaries and better accommodations of MLB, the black-run Negro Leagues could no longer complete, although the Negro American League held out until 1961. Integration of MLB teams was also painfully slow: the Philadelphia Phillies were the last National League team to integrate, in 1957; and the Boston Red Sox were the last American League team to integrate, in 1959. And it was not until 1975 that the first black manager was hired, when Frank Robinson became player-manager for the Cleveland Indians.

Jackie Robinson's debut inspired integration in a wide range of sports. The National Football League (NFL) welcomed its first black players in 1946, soon after the announcement of Robinson's signing with the Dodgers organization; that year, the Los Angeles Rams signed Kenny Washington and Woody Strode, both former teammates of Robinson at UCLA. The National Basketball Association (NBA), meanwhile, saw three black players debut for the 1949–1950 season: Chuck Cooper of the Boston Celtics, Earl Lloyd of the Washington Capitals, and Nat "Sweetwater" Clifton of the New York Knicks. In the same era, colleges and universities across the country also began opening up their teams to black athletic participation, although many schools in the South opposed integration into the early 1970s. Black college stars such as Bill Russell, who won back-to-back NCAA national championships in basketball with the University of San Francisco in 1955 and 1956, and Jim Brown, who earned All-American honors in football and lacrosse at Syracuse University in 1957, symbolized the growing presence of black athletes in big-time college athletics. In the South, black schools such as Tennessee A&I and Florida A&M built their own athletic powerhouses and competed in their own all-black conferences. Black coach John McLendon also led Tennessee A&I to the National Association of Intercollegiate Athletics (NAIA) championship in men's basketball in 1957 (the NAIA was a national organization of small colleges and universities and included both black and white schools).

Women athletes also generated publicity: **Althea Gibson**'s stunning success in tennis in the late 1950s earned her the Female Athlete of the Year award from the Associated Press in 1957 and 1958, and Wilma Rudolph earned that same award in 1960 for winning three gold medals in that year's Olympics. Many African Americans took pride in these wide-ranging accomplishments and continued to see sports as an entry point into mainstream American culture. Most hoped that black athletic achievement would contribute to a lessening in bigotry and would continue to erode the walls of Jim Crow segregation.

Black fans' hopes for sports were met in some ways and dashed in others. Although black athletes continued to break through the walls of discrimination in a variety of sports in the second half of the twentieth century, prejudice continued to infiltrate athletics. Teams in nearly every sport were reluctant to hire black managers and executives, even as black players began to dominate rosters. High-profile positions, such as the quarterback in football and starting pitcher in baseball, were often reserved for white players. Many black activists and leaders also lamented the decline in black institutions' athletic programs, such as the professional Negro Leagues and **historically black colleges and universities**. Reports of exploitation of black college athletes at previously all-white schools also troubled leaders and activists, as some worried (and continue to worry) that African American student-athletes were not being prepared for a life outside of athletics. Black athletes who took public stands against government policies—such as outspoken heavyweight boxer **Muhammad Ali**, who refused induction into the military, and Olympic sprinters Tommie Smith and John Carlos, who raised their fists in a "black power" salute on the medal stand at the 1968 Summer Olympics—were often criticized scathingly in the white press.

It is unclear how much of an impact sports have had on broader conceptions of race and on bigotry. Although many white fans cheer for black athletes, some ascribe black success to supposedly inherited biological factors and continue to believe in stereotypes of intellectual inferiority. While, undoubtedly, sports helped to break down the walls of Jim Crow segregation, and have inspired some to abandon prejudiced beliefs, it is as yet unclear if sports have won the victory for black equality that many black leaders had hoped for. *See also* Basketball; Racial Stereotypes.

Further Readings: "Baseball and Jackie Robinson." The Library of Congress American Memory Web site http://memory.loc.gov/ammem/collections/robinson/ (accessed May 28, 2008); George, Nelson. *Elevating the Game: Black Men and Basketball.* Lincoln: University of Nebraska Press, 1992; Gorn, Elliott and Goldstein, Warren. *A Brief History of American Sports.* New York: Hill and Wang, 1993; Grundy, Pamela. *Learning to Win: Sports, Education, and Social Change in Twentieth-Century North Carolina.* Chapel Hill: University of North Carolina Press, 2001; Miller, Patrick B. ed. *Sporting World of the Modern South.* Urbana: University of Illinois Press, 2002; Sammons, Jeffrey. *Beyond the Ring: The Role of Boxing in American Society.* Urbana: University of Illinois, 1988; Tygiel, Jules. *Baseball's Great Experiment: Jackie Robinson and His Legacy.* New York: Oxford University Press, 1983; Ward, Geoffrey C. *Unforgivable Blackness: The Rise and Fall of Jack Johnson.* New York: Knopf, 2004; Wiggins, David K. *Glory Bound: Black Athletes in a White America.* Syracuse, NY: Syracuse University Press, 1997.

Gregory Kaliss

Streetcars and Boycotts

Streetcar boycotts in the early 1900s and bus boycotts in the 1950s were significant acts of consumer protest by urban blacks. The boycotters wanted equal access to city services, and this meant overturning the **Jim Crow** laws of the time, laws that insisted that blacks go to the "back of the bus" or trolley. The streetcar boycotts failed to overturn the Jim Crow laws, but the bus boycotts did lead to changes in local laws in Baton Rouge and may have been helpful in influencing the 1956 federal court ruling that found bus segregation to be illegal.

The Streetcar Boycotts

These boycotts by black consumers occurred in more than 25 Southern cities from 1900 to 1906. The boycotts took place at a time of increasing hostility on the part of Southern whites and indifference on the part of Northern whites, a dual circumstance that may have encouraged acceptance of subservience as the prevailing attitude of Southern blacks.

The boycotts were initiated in response to Jim Crow streetcar laws enacted as part of the wave of segregation legislation passed in Southern states at the turn of the century. The streetcar companies generally opposed Jim Crow laws. The companies were concerned about the expense and difficulty of enforcing the laws. They also feared a loss of black customers, not a small consideration since blacks often constituted a majority of local riders.

Although technically, the new segregation laws represented an abridgment of the consumer right to choose in that blacks were required to sit in the back of the streetcar, symbolically they represented much more—unjust acts whose effect upon blacks was that of humiliation and degradation. Many blacks responded to the boycotts called in their cities by refusing to ride on the streetcars. Moreover, all of the states of the old Confederacy were affected with the connection between the segregation laws and the boycotts being apparent to its black urban residents. Some of the boycotts lasted for several weeks, while others extended for much longer periods, with one in Augusta, **Georgia**, continuing for three years. But the boycotts were unable to reverse the legal tide of segregation in the South. As the only protest mechanism realistically available to blacks, however, the boycott tactic continued to be pursued even though failure was inevitable.

Bus Boycotts

About 50 years later, Southern blacks once again vented their frustrations relating to the problems they experienced with urban public transportation, only this time, buses rather than streetcars had become the focus. The bus boycotts were of historic importance. The **Civil Rights Movement** of the 1950s with its direct action component was an outgrowth of the bus boycott campaigns. These campaigns brought major disruptions to such state capitals as Baton Rouge and Montgomery.

Looking first at Baton Rouge, in June 1953, the city's black community initiated a boycott against the Jim Crow bus system. The boycott was led by T. J. Jemison, pastor of one of Baton Rouge's largest black churches. As a church leader, Jemison had close ties to the black people of Baton Rouge and to the city's black clergymen and these two linkages gave the boycott its strength.

To finance the boycott, money was raised at nightly mass meetings in the churches and it was used to pay for a "free car lift" and an internal "police force." The free car lift consisted of private cars that transported the boycotting workforce just as the buses had done prior to the boycott. The internal police department was used to patrol the black community and to provide bodyguards for the boycott leaders.

The boycott was completely effective, and a *New York Times* report found about 90 percent compliance. The boycotters had two primary demands—that blacks be permitted to fill bus seats on a first-come, first-served basis, and that no seats be reserved for whites. Within a few days of the boycott's inception, local white officials offered a compromise that largely accepted the first-come, first-served demand. The compromise was accepted at a mass meeting attended by 8,000 local blacks. The boycott, which ended officially on June 25, 1953, was a major victory against segregated busing.

The Montgomery boycott was perhaps the best-known protest action and most influential consumer boycott in American history. It marked the beginning of the Civil Rights Movement and introduced to the world the man who would become the movement's leader, the Reverend **Martin Luther King, Jr.** The Montgomery bus boycott was triggered on Thursday, December 1, 1955, by the arrest of a black woman, **Rosa Parks**, for refusing to yield her seat on a city bus to a white man. Her action, a violation of local segregation laws, came two years after the successful Baton Rouge bus boycott.

On the night of Parks' arrest, local black leader Jo Ann Robinson, after conferring with colleagues, decided to organize a bus boycott of Montgomery for the following Monday, December 5. With two trusted aides, she distributed to local blacks a message urging them to join the boycott. The one-day boycott was a dramatic success in that fewer than 10 percent of Montgomery's blacks rode the city buses. Since most of the passengers who normally rode were black, the boycott engendered a substantial loss in bus revenues.

By Monday afternoon, local black leaders were well aware of the success of the boycott and looked for someone to lead its continuation. They had been favorably impressed with King, a newcomer to Montgomery. A local organization called the Montgomery Improvement Association (MIA) was formed to continue the boycott, and King was selected as its leader. By that Monday evening, his oratorical powers were made clear to an audience of six thousand blacks whom he addressed at a local church.

The response to King's words bordered on pandemonium. The audience apparently felt they had found a boycott leader to confront the white power structure of Montgomery. The bus boycott continued for 382 days, from December 5, 1955, to December 21, 1956, a period far longer than its leaders could have foreseen.

The yearlong boycott was impressively executed. Not only did black riders stay off the buses on December 5, but they continued to stay away for the duration of the boycott. Their abstinence from the city buses was made possible by the creation of an alternative transportation system by the MIA. The system, which started as a crude voluntary effort, soon became far more sophisticated and reliable as the MIA secured funds from a variety of sources to establish an effective transportation service.

However, the success of the boycott campaign did not come easily, with serious signs of strain emerging in Montgomery after the first few weeks of the campaign's success. Matters intensified in late January when King's house was bombed. Moreover, just a month later a grand jury returned indictments for 90 of the leaders and supporters of the MIA, charging them with conspiring to carry out an illegal boycott.

The boycotters were defended by the National Association for the Advancement of Colored People (NAACP), which took the case to federal court. Several months later, the federal court in Montgomery declared on June 5, 1956, that bus segregation was illegal. The court's 2-to-1 decision was upheld by the **U.S. Supreme Court** on November 13, and a month later, Montgomery officials were notified of the ruling by federal marshals. The next day, December 21, 1956, the boycott ended and blacks resumed riding the buses.

These changes to the bus desegregation laws that came in the mid-1950s did not occur in a social vacuum. The strategies used by King were influenced by those employed by Theodore J. Jemison in the successful bus boycott campaign he led in Baton Rouge just a few years earlier. The decisions rendered by the Montgomery federal court and the U.S. Supreme Court reflected the successful court battles waged by attorneys for the NAACP, battles led by its respected special counsel, **Thurgood Marshall**, the man who would become the first black member of the Supreme Court. Moreover, the court decisions may also have been influenced by the national attention given to the yearlong Montgomery bus boycott campaign and the effect its eloquent and brave leader had on the American people. *See also* Montgomery Bus Boycott.

Further Readings: Friedman, Monroe. *Consumer Boycotts: Effecting Change through the Marketplace and the Media.* New York: Routledge, 1999; Meier, August, and Elliott Rudwick. "The Boycott Movement against Jim Crow Streetcars in the South, 1900–1906." *Journal of American History* 55 (March 1969): 756–75; Morris, Aldon D. *The Origins of the Civil Rights Movement.* New York: Free Press, 1984.

Monroe Friedman

Student Nonviolent Coordinating Committee (SNCC)

The Student Nonviolent Coordinating Committee (SNCC) was a civil rights organization that operated during the 1960s. It was known for its radicalism and for rejecting the perceived conservatism of other organizations. SNCC's high point was its work in **Mississippi**, where it sought to establish long-term movements within black communities. SNCC later espoused Black Power, but disagreements over philosophy and direction ended SNCC's effectiveness as a civil rights organization by 1966.

SNCC emerged from the burgeoning student movement that had been engaged in **sit-ins** since the late 1950s. Many of those involved in its founding had been involved with the Nashville Student Movement. SNCC was created at a conference of young activists held at Shaw University, Raleigh, **North Carolina. Martin Luther King, Jr.**, who spoke at the conference, hoped that the activists would join the SCLC, but instead, urged by the SCLC's Ella

Baker, who would be an important early influence on SNCC, a separate organization was created, which would cooperate with all other civil rights organizations, but which would have formal affiliation with none (for a time, SNCC shared the SCLC's Atlanta office, but the separation between the two organizations was clear).

From its foundation, SNCC stood apart from other civil rights organizations. Many of those attending the conference at Shaw University were critical of the tactics that the National Association for the Advancement of Colored People (NAACP) and SCLC tended to deploy, and were keen to adopt a more radical approach that addressed a wider range of issues. In particular, SNCC rejected the model of charismatic leadership that other civil rights organizations followed, and emphasized the autonomy of local communities and movements, arguing that this was required to sustain local activism. At the Shaw University conference **James Lawson**, who had earlier been involved with the SCLC, set out much of what would become SNCC's early philosophical standpoint. Rooted in the tenets of Christianity and **Ghandi**an nonviolence, Lawson made clear the moral and spiritual dimension that would underpin SNCC's direction. Along with Diane Nash, Marion Barry (SNCC's first chairman), and John Lewis, Lawson was part of the Nashville movement that would dominate SNCC's early period.

SNCC's participation in the Freedom Rides helped establish it as an important civil rights organization. The **Congress of Racial Equality (CORE)** had undertaken the Freedom Rides to test compliance with the desegregation of interstate travel facilities. Following attacks on freedom riders in Alabama in May 1961, SNCC, CORE, and the SCLC joined forces to continue the project. The Kennedy administration sought to defuse the situation and called for a cooling-off period, but the Freedom Rides continued, and hundreds of riders were arrested in Jackson, Mississippi, over the next three months. Rather than accept bail, freedom riders chose to serve their sentence, the first true example of SNCC's "jail, not bail" philosophy.

The Freedom Rides positioned SNCC as a more radical organization than the likes of the SCLC and NAACP. Loudly critical of white America's hypocrisy in allowing **Jim Crow** to go unchallenged in the South while advocating freedom and liberty across the world, SNCC emerged as a credible challenger to the civil rights orthodoxy represented by King. SNCC's founding spiritual and philosophical roots were soon obscured by a viewpoint founded both on the experiences of the Freedom Rides and independence from other civil rights organizations. The Freedom Rides emphasized the value of using direct action to forcefully demand the end of segregation, and SNCC's refusal to compromise with perceived moderates became a central part of SNCC's philosophy. For many SNCC staffers, the Freedom Rides, and subsequent imprisonment, was a seasoning process that helped to demarcate the line between the conservative tactics of the established civil rights leadership and their own urgency and vigor.

Although SNCC's early orientation was toward direct action and confrontation, another early strand became arguably more important. In the summer of 1960, Bob Moses, who had originally travelled to Atlanta to work with the SCLC, travelled to Mississippi at the suggestion of Ella Baker. In

Mississippi, he met with Amzie Moore, an NAACP activist in the Delta town of Cleveland, who suggested to Moses that SNCC should send volunteers into the state to assist with voter registration. Moses took up this idea enthusiastically, and it would become a fundamental part of SNCC's ideology.

While Moses was enthused by the idea of working directly with black communities, others in SNCC reacted with greater scepticism. SNCC was marked by its tolerance of different intellectual and philosophical positions, but when voter registration was first mooted, activists who were intent on pursuing an active course of direct action were particularly scornful. This was partly a reaction to the Kennedy administration's efforts to deflect SNCC's radicalism onto activities considered to be less controversial. After the Freedom Rides, President Kennedy encouraged SNCC to focus its attention on voter registration in the South. Some SNCC activists argued, with justification, that Kennedy was merely trying to divert their activities from more high-profile, and arguably more effective, direct action in order to reduce the pressure on his administration to tackle the inevitable clashes and controversy that would attend direct action, as had been the case with the Freedom Rides.

While there was some truth in this charge, some SNCC staff agreed with Moses about the value of voter registration. The debate over whether to pursue direct action or voter registration marked the first real threat to SNCC's stability, as supporters of direct action threatened to leave the organization if voter registration were pursued. The intervention and continued influence of Ella Baker helped avoid a split, and SNCC essentially formed two wings a this point, one to engage in direct action, the other to work on voter registration. These two wings were held together by James Forman as executive secretary, but tensions over the direction and philosophical position of SNCC would continue to cause debate and instability.

Despite the discussions over whether SNCC should engage in voter registration, its work with black communities in Mississippi was arguably SNCC's most enduring contribution to the **Civil Rights Movement**. The establishment of a voter registration project in McComb, under the guidance of Bob Moses, in the summer of 1961 marked the start of a significant, long-term approach to challenging Jim Crow in Mississippi. In undertaking such a project, SNCC embarked on a path that no other civil rights organization had traveled. Direct action to that point had tended to be coordinated and led by the urban middle class, and often relied on short-term confrontation. In undertaking voter registration activity, SNCC engaged directly with the most disenfranchised communities in Mississippi. Recognizing the political impotence of such communities, and the reasons for that impotence, SNCC endeavoured to work with communities to help develop the tools required to register to vote, to make effective use of the vote, and to bring about long-term change.

SNNC's activity in McComb set the template for future voter registration activity in Mississippi. While attempting to engage with all sectors of the black community, SNCC was particularly keen to establish itself among young people who could both participate with SNCC and lead future activism. SNCC's efforts led to an almost immediate rise in the number of blacks trying to register to vote, but also to increased intimidation and violence, including the murder of Herbert Lee, a black farmer. This violence ended SNCC's McComb activities, but the lessons learned would be put to use during the summer project of 1964. Part of SNCC's direct action wing was also active in McComb, and several protestors were jailed for their part in sit-ins. The McComb sit-ins, especially the involvement and jailing of local black youths, eroded the trust of the black community, and direct action of this sort never became a central part of SNCC's later activity in Mississippi.

SNCC's activities and its refusal to follow the lead of other civil rights organizations helped it gain an increasingly extreme reputation. This reputation was underlined by SNCC's participation in the **March on Washington** in August 1963. The March attracted the most prominent civil rights leaders and was seen widely as an opportunity to support Kennedy's proposed civil rights legislation and bring the civil rights cause to national attention. SNCC participated, and had been part of the delegation that President Kennedy had attempted to persuade to abandon the march, but many of its staff were unenthused and declined to take part. SNCC chairman John Lewis intended to use his speech to criticize fiercely the **federal government** for failing to protect blacks from **police brutality**. Before the march, a cadre of civil rights leaders met with Lewis to convince him to tone down the speech, but he insisted on castigating the government for its part in perpetuating the injustices of Mississippi. Most evocatively, Lewis called for a revolution to sweep the nation and to bring freedom to blacks. Lewis's speech crystallised SNCC's radical reputation, and marked the distance between SNCC and other civil rights organizations.

SNCC stepped up its voter registration activity in Mississippi, and ahead of the general election of November 1963, it organized a Freedom Vote, which would allow black Mississippians to register and vote in a symbolic election that followed exactly the state procedure. More than 80,000 blacks participated, and SNCC argued that this illustrated the frustrated demand for black electoral participation in Mississippi. Much of the registration work of the Freedom Vote was conducted by white volunteers from Northern universities. This tactic had a dual purpose of focusing attention on Mississippi and reducing incidents of violence against civil rights workers.

The success of the Freedom Vote persuaded SNCC to embark on a larger, Mississippi-wide project, the Mississippi Summer Project (also known as Freedom Summer) during 1964. Although Freedom Summer operated officially under the auspices of the Council of Federated Organizations (COFO), an umbrella group of civil rights organizations that included CORE and the NAACP, as well as various Mississippi groups, SNCC was at the forefront of the project and was responsible for much of its strategic and philosophical direction as well as for providing the majority of volunteers. As with the Freedom Vote, SNCC again decided to use white students as volunteers, although this was the subject of considerable discussion within SNCC. While some thought that such volunteers would help gain publicity for Freedom Summer, others believed that the presence of whites undermined black self-reliance and placed too much emphasis on white leadership.

These discussions reflected wider concerns within SNCC about the role of whites in the Civil Rights Movement. As the number of whites working with SNCC grew (in 1964, around 20 percent of SNCC's staff was white), some

black activists feared that they would begin to dominate, even if uncon-
sciously, and reduce the role of blacks within SNCC, as well as alienating the
black Mississippians who were to be the focus of Freedom Summer. As a compromise, the Southern Students Organizing Committee (SSOC) was formed
and was initially considered a white counterpart to SNCC. SSOC's relationship with SNCC was never clear, and it gradually became more closely aligned
to Students for a Democratic Society. Despite the formation of SSOC, many
Freedom Summer volunteers were white (indeed, SNCC's efforts to recruit
black volunteers had been relatively unsuccessful, and whites accounted for
the majority of volunteers). Some within SNCC were troubled by the suggestion that white volunteers should be prevented from assisting in challenging
Jim Crow. The place of whites within the organization was a philosophical
disagreement that would continue to trouble SNCC.

During orientation sessions, the gap between the experience and philosophical outlook of SNCC staff and summer project volunteers was clear to see. On
several occasions, SNCC veterans clashed with volunteers. Experienced SNCC
staff had well-formed intellectual positions about the purpose and aims of
Freedom Summer, and many of them had firsthand experience of the extent
to which Jim Crow was entrenched in Mississippi; few volunteers shared these
experiences or such highly developed philosophical ideologies. Moreover, the
volunteers were nervous, and SNCC staff was anxious about sending them
into Mississippi. This resulted in several, often robust, debates about the
meaning of Freedom Summer. Throughout the course of the summer project,
differences in tactics and purpose would be a continued source of tension
between SNCC staff and volunteers.

The main purpose of Freedom Summer was voter registration, but the
project used a range of techniques and strategies to engage black Mississippians and help them to develop the skills and confidence to challenge Jim
Crow. SNCC viewed Freedom Summer as an opportunity for the mass mobilization of black communities throughout Mississippi. Increasingly critical of
the approach of organizations like the SCLC and the NAACP, SNCC hoped
to use Freedom Summer to help develop local leadership within black communities. Rejecting the concept of imposed leadership from above, SNCC's
intention was for black communities to set their own agendas that could
bloom into self-reliant, long-term initiatives.

A guiding principle for the summer project, one that Bob Moses had particularly influenced, was that black communities should make decisions for
themselves. In order to help them develop the skills and knowledge to do so,
freedom schools were an important part of Freedom Summer. Freedom
schools were an attempt to counter the traditionally poor education offered
to black children in Mississippi, but they also served to develop leadership
within black communities. Eschewing traditional pedagogical approaches,
freedom schools emphasized the experience and knowledge of the students
and encouraged debate and challenge, placing the onus on students rather than
teachers to set and define learning aims. As well as providing standard school
subjects, freedom schools also held lessons on African American history and
the philosophies and purposes of the Civil Rights Movement. Students were

encouraged to explore and discuss notions of democracy and to question the validity of Jim Crow.

Freedom schools were a central function of SNCC's summer project strategy. Claiming that Mississippi institutions were fundamentally closed to black people, SNCC argued that it was necessary not to open them, but to create new institutions; education was such an institution. SNCC expected to reach around 1,000 11th- and 12th-grade children during Freedom Summer, but in fact, around 2,500 people of all ages attended. In encouraging students to express themselves and to understand and challenge the ideology of white supremacy, freedom schools did much to challenge the tenets of Jim Crow, as well as developing local leadership.

Freedom Summer also saw the creation of the Mississippi Freedom Democratic Party (MFDP), established to challenge the seating of the Mississippi delegation at the Democratic national convention in August 1964. The MFDP would serve to illustrate the extent to which black people were excluded from Mississippi politics, and MFDP delegates were selected using the same method used by the state **Democratic Party**. SNCC hoped that grass roots activists would dominate, but other interests within COFO ensured that around half of the delegates represented the black middle class. Although several northern Democratic Party delegates had pledged their support for the MFDP, it failed to receive the votes required to be seated.

The MFDP was offered a compromise that would see some of the delegates seated as nonvoting special guests, but SNCC argued that any such compromises must be rejected. Against the advice of more moderate supporters such as Martin Luther King and **Bayard Rustin**, as well as some MFDP delegates who were aligned more closely with the NAACP, the MFDP delegation chose to reject the compromise. Led by SNCC activists, delegates engaged in direct action protests, including a sit-in on the conference floor. These protests led to the offer of a second compromise, which was again rejected by MFDP delegates. The MFDP brought together local activists from across Mississippi, notably **Fannie Lou Hamer**, and would continue to be a hub for activism for several years.

Following Freedom Summer, SNCC underwent a period of self-analysis as it sought to decide its future direction and purpose. Since 1960, SNCC had become increasingly separate from other civil rights organizations, as well as from earlier liberal supporters. SNCC's increasing radicalism and its criticism of organizations like the NAACP and SCLC, as well its failure to distance itself from accusations that it had links with Communism, distanced it from the civil rights mainstream. In the analysis of Freedom Summer, while SNCC had achieved some success, the failure of many projects was clear. As the summer project came to an end, many projects were abandoned or left understaffed as volunteers returned home. The links that Freedom Summer had helped create between SNCC and black communities were strained, and organizations that SNCC had helped to create, such as the MFDP, became increasingly autonomous; rather than address this, SNCC turned inwards, as it tried to decide on its future. This marked the decline of SNCC's influence as a civil rights organization.

The tensions that had long existed within SNCC were brought into sharp focus after Freedom Summer. Many felt that the failure of so many Freedom Summer projects confirmed a need for greater control and bureaucracy, while others continued to resist this argument. SNCC's efforts in Mississippi had negative effects on its activities in **Alabama**, **Georgia**, and **Arkansas**, which had been denied resources and attention because of Freedom Summer. Disagreements about the role of whites continued, and SNCC increasingly developed projects that were staffed only by black activists, before eventually expelling whites from the organization in 1966.

After the disappointment of the Democratic National Convention in 1964, SNCC had become increasingly disillusioned with mainstream politics, but after Freedom Summer, the organization struggled to find a defining purpose, and it became less effective and less influential. While it achieved some success in Georgia, where Julian Bond was elected to the state House of Representatives (although the House refused to seat him because of his public criticism of the Vietnam War, a decision that the Supreme Court overturned in 1966), and in Alabama, where Stokely Carmichael helped to found the Lowndes County Freedom Organization, SNCC lacked direction, and continued to drift further from the civil rights mainstream.

In 1966, Carmichael replaced John Lewis as chairman, dismissing the more moderate tactics of other civil rights organizations and espousing the doctrine of Black Power. In urging African Americans to unite and define their own goals, Black Power had links to SNCC's tactics during Freedom Summer, and Carmichael argued that SNCC had never fought to integrate, but to challenge white supremacy. By this point, however, SNCC had little support from other civil rights organizations and the Black Power position essentially ended SNCC's involvement in the civil rights movement. In 1967 H. Rap Brown replaced Carmichael as chairman, but, troubled by lack of funds and a declining membership, SNCC had essentially ceased to function by this point.

Further Readings: Branch, Taylor. *Parting the Waters: America in the King Years, 1954–63.* New York: Simon and Schuster, 1988; Branch, Taylor. *Pillar of Fire: America in the King Years, 1963–65.* New York: Simon and Schuster, 1998; Carson, Clayborne. *In Struggle: SNCC and the Black Awakening of the 1960s.* Cambridge, MA: Harvard University Press, 1981; Dittmer, John. *Local People: The Struggle for Civil Rights in Mississippi.* Urbana: University of Illinois Press, 1995; Lewis, John, with Michael D'Orso. *Walking with the Wind: A Memoir of the Movement.* New York: Simon and Schuster, 1998; Mills, Kay. *This Little Light of Mine: The Life of Fannie Lou Hamer.* New York: Dutton Signet, 1994; Zinn, Howard. *SNCC: The New Abolitionists.* New York: Beacon Press, 1965.

Simon T. Cuthbert-Kerr

Sundown Towns

A sundown town is any organized jurisdiction that for decades kept African Americans or other groups from living in it and was thus "all-white" on purpose. They are so named because some marked their city limits with signs typically reading, "Nigger, Don't Let The Sun Go Down On You In ___."

These towns were not, in fact, all white. "Sundown suburbs" excepted and, to a degree, accepted black live-in servants in white households. Moreover, some communities that took pains to define themselves as sundown towns nevertheless allowed one or even two exceptional black households within their otherwise all-white populations. When Pana, for example, in central Illinois, drove out its African Americans in 1899, killing five in the process, residents did not expel the black barber and his family. With an exclusively white clientele, hence friends in the white community, no one complained about him. Pana did post sundown signs at its corporate limits, signs that remained up at least until 1960, and permitted no other African Americans to move in, so it became a sundown town. Other sundown towns have let in more temporary intruders: flood refugees, soldiers during wartime, college students, and visiting interracial athletic teams and their fans. Most sundown towns and suburbs outside the West—and some in that region—allowed **Asian Americans** and Mexican Americans as residents. Thus, "all-white" towns may include nonblack minorities and even a tiny number of African Americans.

Sundown towns range from hamlets like Deland, Illinois, population 500, to large cities like Appleton, Wisconsin, with 57,000 residents in 1970. Sundown suburbs could be even larger, such as Glendale, a suburb of Los Angeles, with more than 60,000; Levittown, on Long Island, more than 80,000; and Warren, a Detroit suburb with 180,000. Entire counties went sundown, usually when their county seats did.

These towns and practices date back to the **Great Retreat** that whites forced African Americans to make between 1890 and 1940. This period is becoming known as the "nadir of race relations," when **lynchings** peaked, white owners expelled black baseball players from the major (and minor) leagues, and unions drove African Americans from such occupations as railroad fireman

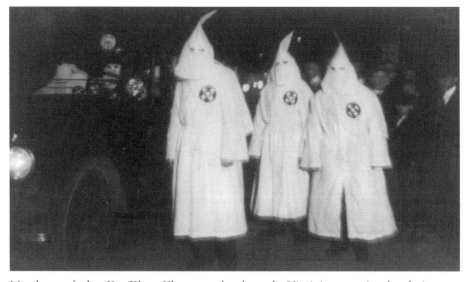

Members of the Ku Klux Klan parade through Virginia counties bordering on Washington, DC. The Klan and other paramilitary terrorist groups played a significant role in driving African Americans and other people of color out of town by nightfall. Courtesy of Library of Congress, LC-USZ62-96308.

and meat cutter. In those years, thousands of towns across the United States expelled their black populations or took steps to forbid African Americans from living in them. Independent sundown towns were soon joined by "sundown suburbs," mostly between 1900 and 1968. Many suburbs kept out not only African Americans but also Jews.

Towns that had no African American residents passed ordinances, or thought they did, forbidding blacks from remaining after dark. In California, for example, the **Civilian Conservation Corps** in the 1930s tried to locate a company of African American workers in a large park that bordered Burbank and Glendale. Both cities refused, each citing an old ordinance that prohibited African Americans within their city limits after sundown. Some towns believed their ordinances remained in effect long after the 1954 ***Brown v. Board of Education*** decision and the **Civil Rights Act of 1964**. The city council of New Market, Iowa, for example, suspended its sundown ordinance for one night in the mid-1980s to allow an interracial band to play at a town festival, but it went back into effect the next day. Other towns never claimed to have passed an ordinance but nevertheless kept out African Americans by city action, such as cutting off water and sewage or having police call hourly all night with reports of threats.

Sundown towns have also maintained themselves all-white by a variety of less formal measures, public and private. As far back as the 1920s, police officers routinely followed, stopped, and harassed black motorists in sundown towns. Suburbs used zoning and eminent domain to keep out black would-be residents and to take their property if they did manage to acquire it. Some towns required all residential areas to be covered by restrictive covenants—clauses in deeds that stated, like this example from Brea, California, "[N]o part of said premises shall ever be sold, conveyed, transferred, leased or rented to any person of African, Chinese or Japanese descent." After a **U.S. Supreme Court** 1948 decision in ***Shelley v. Kraemer*** rendered such covenants hard to enforce, some suburbs relied on neighborhood associations among homeowners, allowing them to decide arbitrarily what constituted an acceptable buyer. Always, lurking under the surface, was the threat of violence, such as assaulting African American children as they tried to go to school, or milder white misbehavior, such as refusing to sell groceries or gasoline to black newcomers.

The **Civil Rights Movement** left sundown towns largely untouched. Indeed, some locales in the border states forced out their black populations in response to *Brown v. Board of Education*. Sheridan, Arkansas, for example, compelled its African Americans to move to neighboring Malvern in 1954, after the school board's initial decision to comply with *Brown* prompted a firestorm of protest. Having no black populations, these towns and counties then had no African Americans to test their public accommodations. For 15 years after the 1964 Civil Rights Act, motels and restaurants in some sundown towns continued to exclude African Americans, thus having an adverse impact on black travelers who had to avoid them or endure humiliating and even dangerous conditions.

At their peak, just before 1970, the United States had perhaps 10,000 sundown towns. Illinois alone probably had at least 500, a clear majority of all incorporated places. In several other northern states—Oregon and Indiana, for example—more than half of all incorporated communities probably excluded African Americans. Whole subregions—the Ozarks, the Cumberland, a band of counties on both sides of the Iowa-Missouri border, most of the suburbs of Los Angeles—went sundown—not every town, but enough to warrant the generalization. However, except for some suburbs that became all white mostly after 1930, sundown towns were rare in the traditional South. There, whites were appalled by the practice, not wanting their maids to leave.

The practice of exclusion was usually quite open. Hundreds of towns posted signs. The Academy Award–winning movie of 1947, *Gentleman's Agreement,* was about the method by which Darien, Connecticut, one of the most prestigious suburbs of New York City, kept out Jews, and that publicity hardly ended the practice. In the 1960s, some residents of Edina, Minnesota, the most prestigious suburb of Minneapolis, boasted that their community had, as they put it, "Not one Negro and not one Jew." Residents of Anna, Illinois, still apply the acronym "Ain't No Niggers Allowed" to their town.

Even though proud to be all white, elite sundown suburbs have usually tried to avoid being known for it. This is the "paradox of exclusivity." Residents of towns such as Darien, Connecticut, for instance, want Darien to be known as an "exclusive" community of the social, moneyed elite rather than as an "excluding" community, especially on racial or religious grounds. So long as elite sundown suburbs like Darien, Kenilworth (near Chicago), Edina, or La Jolla (a community within San Diego) appear to be "accidentally" all white, they avoid this difficulty.

Until 1968, new all-white suburbs were forming much more rapidly than old sundown towns and suburbs were caving in. That year, Title VIII of the Civil Rights Act, along with the *Jones v. Mayer* Supreme Court decision barring discrimination in the rental and sale of property, caused the **federal government** to change sides and oppose sundown towns. Since then, citywide residential prohibitions against Jews, Asian American, **Native Americans,** and **Hispanics/Latinos** have disappeared. Even vis-a-vis African Americans, many towns and suburbs—certainly more than half—relaxed their exclusionary policies in the 1980s, 1990s, and 2000s. Hotels and restaurants, even in towns that continue to exclude black residents, are generally open. However, many towns still make it uncomfortable or unwise for African Americans to live in them. *See also* Housing Covenants; Segregation, Residential; Segregation, Rural.

Further Readings: Blocker, Jack S. *A Little More Freedom: African Americans Enter the Urban Midwest, 1860–1930.* Columbus: Ohio State University Press, 2008; Jaspin, Elliot. *Buried in the Bitter Waters.* New York: Basic Books, 2007; Loewen, James W. *Sundown Towns.* New York: New Press, 2005; Newman, Dorothy K., et al. *Protest, Politics, and Prosperity.* New York: Pantheon, 1978, 144; Pfaelzer, Jean. *Driven Out.* New York: Random House, 2007; Pickens, William. "Arkansas—A Study in Suppression." In *These "Colored" United States: African American Essays from the 1920s,* edited by Tom Lutz and Susanna Ashton, 34–35. New Brunswick, NJ: Rutgers University Press, 1996.

James W. Loewen

T

Talmadge, Eugene (1884–1946)

Eugene Talmadge was a dominant figure in **Georgia** government for 20 years (1926–1946), and for a decade after his death, the Talmadge faction that organized around him ran Georgia. Talmadge was one of the state's and the nation's most ardent supporters of **Jim Crow**. Two essential elements of the Talmadge political agenda was to keep African Americans out of the political system and to keep the poor whites and poor African Americans so desperate that they would work for starvation wages. V. O. Key (109) called Talmadge "Georgia's demagogue."

Talmadge ran for statewide office in every **Democratic Party** primary from 1926 to 1946 except one. He won seven elections and lost three. He was elected commissioner of agriculture for three two-year terms, served as governor for three two-year terms, lost two races for the U.S. Senate and one for governor. He won the election for governor in 1948 but died before he was inaugurated. He lost elections for the U.S. Senate in 1936 and 1938 and governor in 1942.

The state Democratic Party was so dominant that nomination in its primary was in effect election in the general election. Eugene Talmadge's influence was so strong that Talmadge and anti-Talmadge factions wrestled for state elected offices.

Georgia's "county unit system," conceived in 1876 and enacted as the Neill Primary Act of 1917, allocated electoral power on the basis of county population, This winner-take-all election system gave the smallest 121 counties two votes each, the next 30 largest counties four votes, and the eight largest counties six votes. Three of the smallest counties could nullify the vote of one of the largest counties. The county unit system helped Talmadge. In his last campaign for governor, for example, he came in second in the popular vote with 44 percent, but won because the county unit system awarded him 59 percent of the county units.

The Georgia Democratic Party platform was nostalgia for the Lost Cause, brutal racism, and pretense that it represented the poor whites. In fact, Talmadge was supported by big business, especially the railroads, the oil companies, the powerful law firms, the Georgia Power Company, and Coca-Cola

Company for his ability to keep government small, oppose taxes, and leave business alone.

Talmadge often bragged that the African American boys called him "mean Lugene." Talmadge said that he liked the "nigger" well enough in his place, and his place was at the back door, with his hat in his hand and saying, "Yes, Sir." Talmadge confessed to having flogged at least one African American. On his death bed, he told his Baptist preacher that the black race was created inferior by God. He said the white race was on top, the yellow race next, then the brown and red races, and at the very bottom, the blacks who were created to be servants to all other races.

Talmadge acted aggressively to enforce Jim Crow. His response to two federal court orders decided in 1946 illustrates his attitudes. In *Morgan v. Virginia*, the **U.S. Supreme Court** ruled that racial segregation on busses engaged in interstate commerce was unconstitutional. Talmadge pledged that there would be no more interstate bus travel in Georgia, only intrastate. Passengers would have to get off the bus before entering Georgia and buy a ticket good only for transit through Georgia. When they had crossed Georgia, they would get off and buy a ticket to the other state.

On March 8, 1946, the federal district court ruled in *Albright v. Texas* that political parties could no longer exclude African American voters. Admitting African Americans, about a third of the state's population would begin the end of total control of state government by Talmadge and other white supremacists. Talmadge announced plans to call a special session of the state legislature to overturn all the state's election laws. His plan was thwarted in part because eliminating all election laws would also eliminate the county unit system. Instead, he ran for governor on a platform of white supremacy.

Talmadge's 1946 inflammatory campaign speeches were credited with inspiring two notorious racial incidents. On May 9, the **Ku Klux Klan** held a giant cross-burning and membership recruiting rally at Stone Mountain. The national press reported that his inflammatory campaign tirades against African American inspirited white men to brutally murder four African Americans, two men and two women, in Monroe County. Talmadge received substantial support from the Klan. The hooded KKK held rallies at many rural county courthouses to intimidate any African Americans who tried to vote. Talmadge also received support from Nazi sympathizers such as the Brown Shirts. He said he believed a Julius Caesar was born in every century, and that he was the nineteenth century's Caesar. Talmadge opposed most of the **New Deal** relief programs. He opposed slum clearance, child labor laws, old age pensions, the **Civilian Conservation Corps**, the **Works Progress Administration**, and essentially all other New Deal initiatives. He said that the way to handle a relief program was like Mussolini—to line up poor people and use the troops and make them work. He opposed many New Deal programs also because they paid white and African Americans the same wages, a move that Talmadge feared would undermine Jim Crow.

Although he had promised union organizers that he would never use troops to break up a strike, in September 1934, he sent 4,000 armed Georgia **National Guard** soldiers to arrest thousands of striking workers and put them in temporary enclosure made with barbed wire. The militia broke the strike and brutally beat a man to death as his family watched.

Talmadge's world view was rooted in Georgia before the Civil War. Talmadge's New Jersey–born great grandfather, Tom, first arrived in Georgia while serving under General Andrew Jackson in the campaign to chase **Native Americans** deep into Florida. Tom returned to make his fortune growing cotton on wilderness land in Monroe County, Georgia, near Forsyth.

Tom Talmadge prospered in a time when most Georgians experienced extreme economic deprivation. So did his only son, Aaron, born in 1858, and his grandson, Thomas Remalgus (T. R.) Talmadge. T. R. was educated in the best available schools and the University of Georgia. T. R.'s son, graduated from the University of Georgia in 1904 with a Phi Beta Kappa, and from the law school in 1907. Eugene Talmadge's early heroes were Napoleon and the Populist Party politician Tom Watson. He bragged that he had read Adolf Hitler's manifesto, *Mein Kampf,* seven times, and was reading it again when he died.

Talmadge was a dictatorial public official. He did not recognize any court's authority to control his behavior, even when it held him in contempt. He used the Georgia National Guard to take over government offices. He declared martial law, fired state employees at will, sent safecrackers to blast open safes containing the state's money, and spent money that had not been appropriated by the legislature. Talmadge fired the dean of education at the University of Georgia who was rumored to be promoting racial integration in teacher training. His political interference cost all the state's white colleges their accreditation by the Southern Accrediting Commission on Institutions of Higher Learning.

Eugene Talmadge had two personas. He tried to be a simple hick farmer; his family had great wealth from farming and business. Both personas were resolute in his defense of Jim Crow. *See also* National Socialism; White Primary.

Further Readings Anderson, William. *The Wild Man from Sugar Creek: The Political Career of Eugene Talmadge.* Baton Rouge: Louisiana State University Press, 1975; Bass, Jack, and Walter De Vries. *The Transformation of Southern Politics: Social Change and Political Consequence Since 1945.* New York: New American Library, 1976; Henderson, Harold Paulk. The Georgia Encyclopedia. 2004. http://www.georgiaencyclopedia.org/nge/Article.jsp?id=h-1393 (accessed June 1, 2008); Key, V. O. Jr., with Alexander Heard. *Southern Politics in State and Nation.* New York: A. A. Knopf, 1949; Talmadge. Herman. Speaking on behalf of Eugene Talmadge. Georgia State University Government Documentation project, GSU APR 1992.3; Talmadge, Herman, with Mark Royden Winchell. *Talmadge: A Political Legacy, a Politician's Life.* Atlanta, GA: Peachtree Publishers, 1987; Watkins, Thayer. "Eugene Talmadge of Georgia." http://www.applet-magic.com/talmadge.htm (accessed June 1, 2008).

Joan C. Browning

Television

Television was formally introduced to the American public at the New York World's Fair on Sunday, April 30, 1939. The concept and experimental television began in the late 1800s and the early 1920s. Beyond the experimental laboratories of Radio Corporation of America (RCA), Vladimir Zwordykin,

Allen B. DuMont and Philo T. Farnsworth, came the media networks, principally the National Broadcasting Company (NBC) Red and Blue networks, the Columbia Broadcasting System (CBS), and the DuMont Television Network. NBC, CBS, and DuMont were joined by the American Broadcasting Company (ABC) to round- out the early television networks. The major networks, established during the "golden era" of radio, also became the early commercial television broadcasters. Regardless of the progressive technological innovation, the technology exceeded the social development of the country as the content of television programming simply emulated the content of previous entertainment forms and information media when it came to the representation of black Americans, often as caricature stereotypes.

Before television, there was radio, film, theater, and printed literature, including novels, pamphlets, paperbacks, newspapers, broadsides and leaflets. These media collectively recorded events of American society; some content reflected the social conditions of the day inclusive of the racial climate in America. Once television became a viable form of communication, its early programming also mirrored the content of its media predecessors.

Early television programming was also a combination of news, soap operas, sporting events, serial dramas, variety acts, game shows, and comedies. The content of these programs invariably drew upon historical stereotypes and contemporary ideologies about race, more specifically about the black race. Some examples of these programs included *The Beulah Show (The New Beulah Show)* and **Amos 'n' Andy**. Both programs garnered tremendous popularity on radio and then television; at one point, the program attracted 40 million listeners. However, their popularity was met with criticism from organizations like the National Association for the Advancement of Colored People (NAACP) because of the negative stereotypes like mammies, coons, angry black bucks, tragic mulattoes, and "Uncle Toms."

Beulah was a domestic servant/housekeeper, stout with a dark complexion, jovial, boisterous, calculating, and a mother earth who was steadfastly loyal to her white employers, the Henderson family. Beulah was a comic strip as well as a radio and television program. In the comic strip, Beulah was typically drawn as a mammy-life figure. Her rotund physique was inked in black with two, wide, white orbs for eyes and thick, white lips. She was attired in head-bandana and servants uniform with apron. She often kept her employers in check by offering witty retorts. Beulah was an early radio spinoff program, since the character was first heard on a radio program titled *Hometown Incorporated*. Marlin Hurt, a white male, initially played the roll of Beulah and used a stereotyped thick, mimicked Southern, black dialect for the character's voice.

The Beulah character was featured on several radio programs, including *That's Life, Fibber McGee and Molly,* and *The Marlin Hurt and The Beulah Show*. After Hurt's death in 1946, Hattie McDaniel played the Beulah character on radio until 1953. McDaniel was the first African American to receive an Academy Award in 1939 for Best Supporting Actress for her performance, as Mammy, in the movie *Gone with the Wind*.

The television version of *The Beulah Show* was a 30-minute situation comedy that aired weeknights on the ABC network beginning in 1950. *Beulah* was one of the first weekly television programs to feature an African American in a leading role. Two actors, Ethel Waters, from 1950 to 1952, and Louise Beavers, 1952 to 1953, also played Beulah on television. The show also featured black actors Dooley Wilson, Ernest Whitman, Butterfly McQueen, and Ruby Dandridge during its run from 1950 to 1953.

Another radio and television program that was immensely popular, but was based on stereotypes of African Americans was *Amos 'n' Andy*. Former minstrel performers Freeman Gosden and Charles J. Correll, two white male actors skilled in mimicking their interpretation of Southern "black" dialect complete with mispronounced words, developed *Amos 'n' Andy* based on characters they performed in a minstrel stage act. Previously, Gosden and Correll had created the characters of Sam and Henry, two hapless Southern blacks who migrate north to Chicago. The program aired on WGN, the *Chicago Tribune* radio station in 1927. The two left WGN and joined the *Chicago Daily News* station WMAQ, where they resumed their broadcast careers with the creation of *Amos 'n' Andy* in 1928 which became one of the most popular radio programs of the time. That popularity transferred to the CBS television program under the same title, but with minor storyline changes from 1951 to 1953. However, the idea of two white actors in blackface did not translate well for commercial television and a search began for black actors to play the parts. Such was the popularity of this program that two American presidents, Presidents Harry S. Truman and Dwight D. Eisenhower made recommendations on where and how the producers might find suitable black actors for the roles. Eventually, two black actors were selected to play the lead characters, Tim Moore as George "Kingfish" Stevens and Spencer Williams as Andy, Andrew Hogg Brown. Alvin Childress played the other title character, Amos Jones, a philosophical, Aesop-like taxi driver who often added a moralistic value-lesson to the program when the Kingfish's schemes went awry. The characters on *Amos 'n' Andy* resided in a segregated black world, in Harlem, where its characters rarely made contact with the white community.

The black stereotypes portrayed in *Beulah* and *Amos 'n' Andy* reflected the social and historic cultural perceptions about blacks as interpreted by white-dominated American electronic media. The developers of *Amos 'n' Andy* were also opportunistic in their subject matter, first by capitalizing on media audience perceptions about blacks as a race, then perpetuating these perceptions by using minstrel show and racist stereotypes. These characters were plucked from a significant social event of the time, the **Great Migration** of Southern blacks who moved north to seek better employment opportunities and relief from segregation and discrimination in the South only to encounter a new form of racism in the North.

The NAACP complained in a 1951 lawsuit filed against CBS that *Amos 'n' Andy* portrayed blacks in the most derogatory manner and only served to affirm society's prejudices against African Americans. Rising protests about the perceived negative depiction of African Americans led to its eventual network cancellation of the program. However, *Amos 'n' Andy* continues to live on in cyberspace on Web sites and catalogs where the programs may be heard and/or purchased.

Several other television situation comedies featured blacks in supporting or recurring roles. *The Jack Benny Show* included Eddie "Rochester" Anderson as Benny's personal valet; Willie Best (Stepin Fetchit, Sleep and Eat) was Charlie, an elevator operator, on *My Little Margie*, and Best also appeared on *Trouble with Father* (1950–1955) as Willie, the handyman. Lillian Randolph played Louise the family housekeeper on *Make Room for Daddy* (1953–1957) and *The Danny Thomas Show* (1957–1964). Randolph also served as housekeeper Birdie Lee Scoggins, on the *Great Gildersleeve* in the 1940s and 1950s. The dawn of television, despite all its technological innovations and business opportunity, missed the opportunity to rectify past media mistakes; instead, it simply fostered mass audience prejudices in the new media environment of television.

Variety Shows

Other television program offerings like variety shows presented opportunities for black entertainers who were already familiar to the public for their stage show performances as singers, dancers and musicians. Bill "Bojangles" Robinson frequently appeared on variety shows like the *Texaco Star Theater* (1948–1956) hosted by Milton Berle on CBS. Popular crooners Billy Daniels and Nat "King" Cole were logical choices as black hosts for variety shows. In a history-making event, they were offered variety shows of their own. A third program, *Sugar Hill Times,* also had a short television run. Other variety shows were hosted by African Americans Bob Howard (CBS, 1948–1950) and pianist Hazel Scott.

Major network variety and talent shows like *Talk of the Town, The Ed Sullivan Show, Tonight, The Steve Allen Show, Texaco Star Theater, Ted Mack Original Amateur Hour, The Mitch Miller Show/Sing along with Mitch, The Lawrence Welk Show,* and others, made it possible for black talent to enter American homes in a most unobtrusive way—on the small screen.

Prime-Time TV

The 1960s was also an era of war, espionage, and civil unrest, and weekly television reflected the period by creating programs that symbolically paralleled the time. Prime-time television also began to feature racially mixed casts in which blacks did not play a subservient role or as background humor. Black actors began appearing as social equals and professionals in the 1960s. Several actors had recurring prime-time television roles in racially mixed casts on programs including *Hogan's Heroes* (CBS), set against the backdrop of World War II, and featured a cast of international prisoners of war held at Stalag 13, a German prison camp; *I Spy* (NBC), a weekly show in which American secret agents Robert Culp and Bill Cosby, foiled sinister plots against the government; *Mission Impossible* (CBS), another group of elite, clandestine, counterespionage agents; *Ironside* (NBC), a detective program; and *Star Trek* (NBC), which not only included a multiethnic cast, but an intergalactic cast as well.

Network television ushered in a modern era of black lead characters with the debut of *Julia* in 1968. Diahann Carroll starred in the lead role as Julia, a

Selected Weekly Programs from the 1940s to the 1960s That Featured an African American Lead Actor or Actor(s) in a Recurring Role

Amos 'n' Andy (CBS, 1951–1953): Spenser Williams as Andrew Hogg Brown, Tim Moore as George "Kingfish" Stevens, and Alvin Childress as Amos Jones.

Edge of Night (1967): Al Freeman, Jr., as assistant district attorney Ben Lee. (He also appeared on *One Life to Live* beginning in 1972 as police captain Ed Hall. Hall became the romantic interest and husband of Carla [Clara] Grey/Carla Bonari)

Julia (NBC, 1968–1971): Diahann Carroll as Julia, a nurse and widowed single mother.

Room 222 (ABC, 1969–1974): Denise Nichols as guidance counselor, Liz McIntyre; Lloyd Haynes as history teacher Pete Dixon.

Hogan's Heroes (CBS, 1965–1971): Ivan Dixon as Staff Sgt. James "Kinch" Kinchloe.

Ironside (NBC, 1967–1975): Don Mitchell played Mark Singer, Ironside's personal aide and occasional bodyguard.

I Spy (NBC, 1965–1968): Bill Cosby as secret agent Alexander Scott and co-starred show director, Robert Culp as Kelly Robinson his partner agent.

Mannix (CBS, 1967–1975): Gail Fisher as Peggy Fisher, a police officer's widow.

Mission Impossible (CBS, 1966–1973): Greg Morris as Barney Collier.

Mod Squad (ABC, 1968–1973): Clarence Williams III as Linc Hayes, an undercover crime fighter.

One Life to Live (ABC, 1968–present): Ellen Holly as Carla (Clara) Greyand Carla Bonari, who began as a secretary.

Star Trek (NBC, 1966–1969): Nichelle Nichols as communication officer Lieutenant Uhura.

The Beulah Show (ABC, 1950–1952): Ethel Waters played Beulah from 1950 to 1951, and Louise Beavers played the role from 1952 to 1953. Butterfly McQueen and Ruby Dandridge were Oriole, the maid next door, in the 1950 to 1952 season and 1952 to 1953 seasons, respectively.

The Bill Cosby Show (NBC, 1969–1971): Bill Cosby as Chet Kincaid, a physical education teacher, and Hilly Hicks as Eddie Tucker.

The Leslie Uggams Show (CBS, 1969): Leslie Uggams, host.

Twilight Zone (1960): "The Big Tall Wish" included Ivan Dixon and Bolie Jackson.

---

nurse and widowed, single mother. Marc Copage played Julia's young son, Corey. Julia and Corey lived in a modern, racially integrated apartment complex. She was everything her black female television predecessors were not. Julia was articulate, sophisticated, svelte, attractive, fashionable, and a professional. Other than *Amos 'n' Andy*, television audiences rarely saw a black professional on prime-time television. Julia occasionally had male suitors, alternately played by Fred Williamson and Paul Winfield. Programs like those described here belie what is not here, major employment opportunity for black actors, performers, and media professionals. Many television casts then as today rarely had a single black performer in the cast or as television extras in the background.

Network Evening News

America's nightly news was delivered by the voice of credible authority and usually that voice was a white, male voice. Prime-time network television news remained segregated longer than the nightly sitcoms and dramas. The road toward black news anchors began with black network reporters.

Newspaper journalist Mal Goode of the *Pittsburgh Courier* became the first black network television news reporter when he joined ABC News in 1962.

Network News and the Civil Rights Movement

Despite the dearth of black news personnel on network television, the networks could not ignore the rising national tension associated with the modern **Civil Rights Movement** and the fight against racial segregation. **Rosa Parks's** arrest in 1955 for refusing to enter a bus from the rear launched the Montgomery, Alabama bus boycott and unraveled the "**separate but equal**" doctrine, it led to a **U.S. Supreme Court** decision that segregation on public buses was unconstitutional. Civil rights marches, **sit-ins** and restaurant counter demonstrations, attacks and murders of Freedom Riders, school desegregation, the **March on Washington of 1963**, the Sixteenth Street Baptist Church bombing in 1963, Bloody Sunday in Selma, Alabama, in 1965, the assassinations of **Medgar Evers** in **Mississippi** in 1962, and **Martin Luther King, Jr.** in Memphis, Tennessee, in 1968, were monumental events that could not be dismissed by the news media. News coverage of the efforts of the Civil Rights Movement and activist groups ushered in a new era for American blacks.

In 1957, journalist Edward R. Murrow devoted an episode of his program, *See It Now* (CBS), to school desegregation. The episode titled, "Clinton and the Law: A Study in Desegregation," illuminated violence in school desegregation. Another episode, in 1959, titled, "The Lost Class of '59," addressed school closings to avoid desegregation in Norfolk, Virginia. J. Fred MacDonald considers ABC's five-part series, *Crucial Summer* (1963), and NBC's *The American Revolution of '63* as two major network contributions to bringing national attention to the civil rights struggle.

Children's Television

Children's programs like the *Mickey Mouse Club, Howdy Doody, Captain Kangaroo,* and *Romper Room* never featured African Americans in the early days of commercial television. *Sesame Street,* a project of the Children's Television Workshop (Sesame Workshop) first aired on the Public Broadcasting Corporation (PBS) network in America in 1969; it became the first multiracial children's educational television program.

Soap Operas

Named "soap operas" because their advertising sponsors were often soap manufacturers, soap operas became a popular hit in early commercial radio. Like other media entertainment, soap operas migrated to the new television medium as well. African Americans began to appear on television soap operas in the 1950s. While some roles continued to employ black actors as servants, daytime television began a shift from portraying blacks in menial, background roles by introducing blacks in other occupations. *Edge of Night* (CBS, 1956–1975; ABC, 1975–1984) introduced Al Freeman, Jr., as assistant district attorney Ben Lee. While *One Life to Live* (ABC) preserved the role of black family servant played by Lillian Hayman as Sadie Gray. The program also introduced the character Clara "Carla" Grey, performed by Ellen Holly, a "tragic mulatto" and erstwhile daughter of Sadie. Grey passed for white as Carla Bonari by day, and lived as black (Clara Grey) by night. Carla was an actor, then a secretary, and at one point in the serial, developed a white male love interest who was not initially aware that Carla was black. The plotline advanced to the pending marriage between Carla and Dr. James Craig (Robert Milli), but the wedding was called off and the storyline advanced to black male love interests, including actors Peter DeAnda and Al Freeman, Jr. Carla eventually married and divorced detective Ed Hall (Freeman). Before she left the show, Holly had additional romantic liaisons. Her character as a tragic mulatto was ideally suited to the melodramatic television soap genre. Despite the introduction of these characters, soap operas were slow to develop characters and story lines around black characters. The network received frequent complaints about Holly's interracial relationships.

Audiences and Advertising

The longevity of commercial television programs is often tied to audience viewership and advertising. A household sampling process called ratings determines television viewership. Ratings are designed to measure the number of households tuning in to a program, but ratings are not the only determinants that affect the life of a program. Program scheduling, the time slot in which a program airs, can also affect its ability to attract an audience, and program distribution is another factor. In which communities will the program air? Advertising also affects the success of a television program since advertising dollars help defray the expense of producing a television program and generates profits for the networks. African American television programs were impacted by all these factors. *The Nat King Cole Show, The Leslie Uggams Show,* and *The Billy Daniels Show* all suffered from budget, ratings, and external pressure leading to their demise. Even programs with strong followings like the *Ed Sullivan Show* were occasionally criticized for featuring black talent. J. Fred MacDonald writes that Southern NBC affiliate television stations refused to air the cultural and well-sponsored *NBC Opera Theater* in 1955 and 1957 because famed opera singer Leontyne Price performed lead roles during the broadcast. Politicians and viewing audiences also pressured networks to limit programming in which black interacted with whites as their social equals.

Television Ownership

The road to black television ownership was also difficult, and in the twenty-first century, ownership continues to have a minimal showing. *See also* Black Hollywood.

Further Readings: Bogle, Donald. *Toms, Coons, Mulattoes, Mammies, and Bucks: An Interpretive History of Blacks in American Film.* 4th ed. New York: Garland, 2001; MacDonald, J. Fred. *Blacks and White TV: African Americans in Television since 1948.* 2nd ed. Chicago: Nelson-Hall, 1992; McLeod, Elizabeth. *The Original Amos 'n' Andy: Freeman Gosden, Charles Correll, and the 1928–1943 Radio Serial.* Jefferson, NC: McFarland, 2005.

Carol Adams-Means

Texas

The institution of **slavery** in the United States is generally seen as an institution confined to the South, but Texas, which is more Southwestern than Southern, was a slave state from its earliest beginnings. From the early days of Spanish colonialism until the Civil War, slavery was an essential part of the development of Texas. The state legislature passed **Black Codes** after the Civil War to restrict the rights of blacks and drive them back to the farms and into semi-slavery as victims of peonage. The use of terror to bolster the political, legal, economic, and social systems that regulated black behavior and racial etiquette that was developed during slavery was reestablished in **Jim Crow** form after **Reconstruction**. Immediately after the Civil War, during the period from 1865 to 1868, white Texans committed hundreds of acts of violence and murder against blacks. The racial groundwork laid into the social fabric of society by slavery created the narratives for the creation and facilitation of Jim Crow institutions after the Civil War. Although slavery was abolished in 1865, a form of peonage lasted well into the twentieth century and left a legacy that endures in social problems today.

When slavery was abolished, Robert E. Lee, the former commander of Confederate forces, influenced segregated models that were to be established. Lee established a relationship with the Episcopalians and James Steptoe Johnston, a former Confederate soldier, to develop the idea of "Negro **education**" projects in Texas. One such Jim Crow institution was St. Phillip's College in San Antonio, which sought to keep African Americans in low-paying and servile jobs. Education in Jim Crow institutions consisted of learning how to sew, cook, and wait on white people's needs. This model would be adopted throughout Texas, as whites sought forms of cheap labor, attempted to limit competition with whites for jobs, and sought ways to keep African Americans segregated and in a servile status. The influence of Robert E. Lee helped to give birth to **Booker T. Washington**'s social formula that surrendered to white racism and forged the eventual Jim Crow that governed the South after Reconstruction.

During Reconstruction, former Confederates attempted direct sabotage of the progressive ideas of the period. Texan John Salmon "Rip" Ford, a former commander of the Rio Grande Military District, led a band of ex-Confederates who worked to undermine Reconstruction and the granting of civil rights to African Americans, Ford was also the editor of an Austin newspaper that routinely attacked blacks and Mexican Americans is the most racist language and stereotypes. In Corpus Christi, during the 1870s, many Mexicans were beaten and hanged for supporting the federal cause and the rights of black people. In San Antonio, racist vigilante forces attempted to destroy Mexican support for blacks and in later years redefined racial models that labeled Mexicans "white" in an attempt to divide and conquer the coalitions between blacks and Mexicans that had been established over many years.

By the 1880s, the constitutional rights guaranteed to African Americans by the Reconstruction amendments had undergone severe setbacks as a result of the removal of Union troops and state elections that removed Radical Republicans from office. Segregation or **separate but equal** status for African

Americans gradually became the norm and codified in the law. Even before the **U.S. Supreme Court** decision of *Plessy v. Ferguson* (1896), Texas was well on its way in maintaining separation of the "races." Jim Crow laws were numerous in Texas and included about 27 statues and policy changes that were passed in the state.

In many east Texas towns, blacks were systematically removed or forced to leave. Many went to Mexico. The 1877 withdraw of federal troops created the "exodusters," a mass movement to escape the terror of Southern racism. Though this movement peaked in 1879, later attempts eyed Mexico as a refuge for African Americans. The father of poet **Langston Hughes** was one such advocate of going to Mexico to escape the injustices of Jim Crow in the 1890s. In fact, during this same period, William Ellis, an African American from Victoria, Texas, envisioned a mass exodus to Mexico of African Americans who were being denigrated by Jim Crow laws.

Blacks were forced to pay for their own segregation, when in 1866, a law required that all taxes paid by blacks must be allocated to maintaining segregation in public schools throughout the state. Texas managed to enact only one antisegregation law during Reconstruction in 1871, barring separation of the races on public carriers, but this was invalidated in 1891 by the 22nd Texas Legislature when it passed segregation statutes that became known as the Jim Crow law. In 1876, with Reconstruction defeated, voting laws required electors to pay a **poll tax**, which was used to prevent African Americans from voting, and a state statue was passed in 1879 that barred interracial marriage. Racial tensions were increased as a result of the separation of the races. After the killing of a black soldier, a riot of black troops occurred at Fort Concho in 1881 near San Angelo, Texas. In the skirmish they destroyed property and wounded a white man.

Other racial riots took place in Texas involving Mexican Americans as well. The Rio Grande City Riot of 1888 occurred after the arrest and killing of a local Mexican American. The killing was justified by a claim that he was attempting to escape, a typical charge used by Southern racists. The incident served as combustible material, and widespread anger against the sheriff increased because he was implicated in the racist lynching of several other Mexicans. In 1899, the Laredo Smallpox Riot was initiated among Mexican American residents who protested being forcefully removed from their homes by Texas Rangers who were responding to reports of a smallpox outbreak. Texas Rangers were often sent in to subdue mobs and often sided with the whites. White racists in border towns often used health issues to remove Mexicans from Texas, and when the Texas Rangers were called in, hundreds rioted. That same year, troops of the Texas Volunteer Guard were dispatched to Orange to suppress a mob organized to drive blacks out of Orange County. The mob was bent on removing all blacks from the area after a black man, accused of rape, was removed from the jail by a mob of between from 300 to 500 men. The black man was lynched and at least 100 shots were fired into his body.

Between 1900 and 1920, the killing of Mexicans and African Americans on the Texas-Mexico border was a frequent event. Some of these killings were the result of a plan by a group of Mexicans to free African Americans from discrimination and help the black community establish six states of their own after Mexico recovered the lands that were taken by Texas slavers to set up the independent Republic of Texas. This plan was called the "Plan of San Diego." When word of this proposal reached the Texas Rangers, they went on a murderous hunt to find the individuals who were planning this insurrection. The revolutionaries managed to destroy a train at Brownsville on October 18, 1915, and carried out numerable raids across the state. When some of these revolutionaries were captured, they were tortured to death or just shot on sight. Many of these revolutionaries were socialists and harbingers of the 1917 Russian Revolution.

During the turbulent years of the prelude to the Mexican Revolt, and the eventual revolution against Porfilio Diaz, 1900–1920, whites in Slocum, Longview, and Waco, Texas, went on rampages and riots in which blacks were burned out and hanged. In Slocum in 1908, approximately 20 African Americans were murdered by a mob of whites. Jesse Washington was burned alive at the stake in 1916 in Waco by a mob of 15,000 to 20,000 whites. In Longview, it was reported that blacks armed themselves and ambushed a train carrying a white racist killer, who they killed. In this period, Jim Crow laws increased as the Mexican Revolution exacerbated the level of terror against African Americans.

After years and years of laws and social rules that produced hate-filled narratives, there were bound to be racial explosions. The Brownsville Raid of August 1906, an alleged attack by soldiers from companies of the black 25th U.S. Infantry, resulted in the largest summary dismissals of troops in the history of the U.S. Army. When these soldiers arrived in Brownsville, they were immediately confronted with racial discrimination at business establishments and reported physical mistreatment. An alleged attack on a white woman, a standard charge in the South and in Texas, infuriated many white residents. When shooting broke out and claimed the life of a white resident and the wounding of a police officer, unsupportable claims were made that the black troops were responsible.

By 1909, the Texas legislature passed further Jim Crow laws that provided separate waiting areas for white and black passengers. Many Jim Crow laws were in part a reaction to the victory of Texas-born boxing champion **Jack Johnson** over white opponents. White anger grew across the nation and calls for a "great white hope" echoed across the racial landscape after the defeat of white boxer James J. Jeffries in 1910. In the aftermath of the Johnson victory, racial hatred increased against African Americans and riots broke out across the nation. In 1914, the Texas legislature went so far as to pass laws preventing African American railway porters from sleeping on bedding intended for whites. On a consistent basis, these Jim Crow laws were passed creating a hateful atmosphere in Texas that would soon lead to more violence. In the wake of Jack Johnson's relationships with white women, a state code was approved in 1915 providing imprisonment in the penitentiary from two to five years for interracial marriage.

The **Houston Riot of 1917** was started by about 150 black troops of the 24th U.S. Infantry from Camp Logan shortly after the United States entered **World War I**. Black troops were mindful of the tasks that white supremacy had set for them in fighting Indians and Mexicans while being denied human dignity. The riot, touched off by the arrest of an African American woman in the Fourth Ward of Houston and the beating of a black military policeman by a white Houston police officer, was the culmination of white racial hatred against armed black men. Local white police officers and residents routinely harassed blacks. Many whites were killed in the fighting, and the African American soldiers were court-martialed at Fort Sam Houston in San Antonio. Most of the black men were found guilty. Nineteen African American soldiers were hanged on the Salado Creek, while 63 were given life sentences. Not a single white civilian was brought to trial.

Blacks were being excluded from every aspect of public life including use of the public libraries. In 1919, a state statute ordered that blacks use separate libraries. Vagrancy laws were used to force blacks into slave like conditions by arresting them and forcing them to work off fines on farms. The use of vagrancy laws against blacks and Mexicans to farm out free labor (peonage) was still in use in 1926 and extended well beyond that. Against this backdrop the Longview Race Riot of 1919 occurred, during the "**Red Summer**." It was also the time of the first "Red Scare," a time in which the **federal government** began attacking real and imagined "communist" enemies and violating civil liberties.

In Longview, whites needed only to feel threatened by perceived acts of black independence for violence to erupt. In this case, racial tensions were exacerbated because two prominent African American leaders had recommended that black growers bypass established white brokers and sell cotton directly to markets in Galveston, Texas. Governor William P. Hobby ordered Texas Rangers to Longview, and eventually placed some 250 Guardsmen in the town after violence increased. The Democrats increased racial tensions by disenfranchising African Americans in 1922. A voting law was passed preventing blacks from voting in the **Democratic Party** primary elections in Texas. By 1925, state statutes codified segregation, made **miscegenation** a felony, and, within about 10 years, went on to create segregated health care facilities. Between 1943 and 1958, segregation was extended to city buses, parks, swimming pools, and other public facilities

Violence sometimes broke out because of competition over jobs between blacks and whites. In Brenham, rioting broke out over the hiring of a black employee by a railway company. The **Beaumont, Texas, Race Riot** of 1943 had its roots in the tensions of competition for jobs between blacks and whites and Jim Crow. In 1941, and after the United States entered **World War II**, Beaumont became a magnet for people seeking work when employment opportunities in the shipyards and war factories were announced. Consequently, large numbers of workers raced to the town, but housing facilities were not plentiful enough to enforce Jim Crow laws. Whites were forced into quarter in proximity to blacks. In the shipyards and factories, blacks began to have access to jobs that were normally reserved for whites. When Jim Crow laws could not be enforced, little excuse was needed for a major eruption of violence. A white mob, outraged at the alleged assault of a white woman by a black, terrorized black residents resulting in two deaths and one hundred homes being destroyed.

Violence in Texas as elsewhere was fueled by the racial structure created by Jim Crow. Even after the **Civil Rights Movement** pressured for the passage of the **Civil Rights Act of 1964**, which invalidated Jim Crow laws, the legacy of Jim Crow remained. With the passage of the **Voting Rights Act of 1965**, Jim Crow laws were eliminated in voting, but the violence continued. In 1967, a riot at Texas Southern University in Houston resulted in the death of one police officer and the wounding of several others. The cause of the riot was the arrest of a student, but the incident was related to general racial tensions created from years of Jim Crowism in Houston. Many social scientists believe **police brutality** has become one of the racial debris of the Jim Crow legacy. The legacy of Jim Crow extended rioting to San Antonio when in April 1969, members of **Student Nonviolent Coordinating Committee (SNCC)** organized a mass demonstration against police brutality that resulted in property damage and the arrest of individuals from a unique group of SNCC Black Panther members. *See also* Hispanics/Latinos; Louisiana.

Further Readings: Barr, Alwyn. *Black Texans: A History of African Americans in Texas, 1528–1995.* Norman: University of Oklahoma Press, 1996; De Leon, Arnoldo. *They Called Them Greasers: Anglo Attitudes toward Mexicans in Texas, 1821–1900.* Austin: University of Texas Press, 1983; Gomez, Laura E. *Manifest Destinies: The Making of the Mexican American Race.* New York: New York University Press, 2007.

Mario Marcel Salas

Thurmond, Strom (1902–2003)

James Strom Thurmond, known only as "Strom" to his constituents, was the longest-serving U.S. senator in American history. Born in Edgefield, **South Carolina,** he attended Clemson University and was admitted to the bar. He served in a variety of elected posts in South Carolina, including state senator, county superintendent of education, and a judgeship. In 1946, he became governor.

Protesting **Harry S. Truman**'s civil rights policy, Thurmond and Fielding L. Wright ran as "States' Rights Democrats," or **Dixiecrats**, in the 1948 election, breaking with the mainstream **Democratic Party**. According to biographers Jack Bass and Marilyn W. Thompson, their candidacy, which earned the electoral votes of **Louisiana, Mississippi, Alabama**, and South Carolina, "shook the foundations of the Democratic 'solid South' " (2003, 2). Their platform was solidly anti-integration, and their motto was "Segregation Forever!" After their defeat, Thurmond did not disappear from public life. In 1954, he won as a write-in candidate for the Senate, where he filibustered against the **Civil Rights Act of 1957**. By 1964, he had aligned himself with the **Republican Party**, which had gained credibility in the segregationist South by nominating Barry Goldwater, who had advocated against civil rights measures, including the abolition of the **poll tax**.

After the civil rights victories of the 1960s, Thurmond's legacy was revised to include the legend that he had renounced the politics of the 1948 presidential election, during which he proclaimed that "there's not enough troops in the army to force the Southern people to break down segregation and admit the nigra [*sic*] race into our theaters, into our swimming pools, into our homes, and into our churches." South Carolinians and other supporters avidly claimed that Thurmond had mended his ways, but as late as 1980, he recalled his presidential run fondly as a "battle of federal power versus state power." In 1988, he assured the *Washington Post* that he ran for president to "protect the rights of the states and the rights of the people." By 1991, he had changed his rhetoric, arguing that he now supported voting rights because African Americans had "come up" from the servant class to the mainstream of American life.

In 2002, Thurmond passed his centenary birthday, and was feted by Trent Lott, who claimed that had the "rest of the country" followed Mississippi's lead in voting Dixiecrat, "we wouldn't have had all these problems over the years." Responding to the controversy that followed, Lott resigned from the Senate leadership. Six months after Thurmond's death in June 2003, Essie Mae Washington-Williams, the daughter of Thurmond family maid Carrie Butler, acknowledged that Thurmond was her father. Washington-Williams was conceived when her mother was 16 and Thurmond was a 22-year-old Clemson undergraduate. In an interview with Dan Rather, Washington-Williams was restrained on the question of her mother's sexual consent, saying only that "she didn't go into any detail" about Thurmond's advances. Soon after her public declaration, Thurmond's family acknowledged her lineage, but was less accommodating to Al Sharpton, who revealed in 2007 that his great-grandfather Coleman Sharpton, was owned by their cousin Julia Thurmond. Thurmond cousin Doris Strom Costner urged Sharpton to be proud of their family connection because "he's in a mighty good family." Though his legacy is ambiguous, public memory in his native state tells a surer story: Thurmond's statue stands near that of white supremacist Pitchfork **Ben Tillman** on the South Carolina statehouse grounds.

Further Readings: Bass, Jack, and Marilyn W. Thompson. *Ol' Strom: An Unauthorized Biography of Strom Thurmond.* Columbia: University of South Carolina Press, 2003; "Essie Mae on Strom Thurmond: Part I of Dan Rather's Interview with Biracial Daughter." CBS News Web site, December 17, 2003. http://www.cbsnews.com/stories/2003/12/17/60II/main589107.shtml (accessed June 1, 2008); "Lott Apologizes for Thurmond Comment." CNN Web site, December 10, 2002. http://archives.cnn.com/2002/ALLPOLITICS/12/09/lott.comment/ (accessed June 1, 2008); Noah, Timothy. "The Legend of Strom's Remorse." *Slate,* December 16, 2002. http://www.slate.com/id/2075453/ (accessed June 1, 2008); "Sharpton's Ancestor was Owned By Thurmond's." *Washington Post* Web site, February 26, 2007. http://www.washingtonpost.com/wp-dyn/content/article/2007/02/25/AR2007022501518.html?nav=rss_politics (accessed June 1, 2008); Washington, Essie Mae. *Dear Senator: A Memoir by the Daughter of Strom Thurmond.* New York: Harper Perennial, 2006.

Jennie Lightweis-Goff

Till, Emmett (1941–1955) and Mamie Till Mobley (1921–2003)

In the summer of 1955, while visiting Money, **Mississippi,** 14-year-old Chicago native Emmett Till breached **Jim Crow** etiquette and spoke to a white woman. His punishment was murder. This horrific event revealed that Jim Crow laws and **white supremacy** were alive and well in the South. With great courage, Emmett's mother, Mamie Till Mobley, turned her personal tragedy into a catalyst for the **Civil Rights Movement**. Emmett Till's death alerted the nation of the thriving persecution of African Americans under Jim Crow laws.

The son of Mamie and Louis Till, Emmett was born on the south side of Chicago in 1941. Although Till struggled with a bout of polio at age five, leaving him with a slight stutter, he became a confident child known for his pranks and outgoing personality. In the summer of 1955, Till went to Mississippi to visit relatives and stay with his uncle, Mose Wright. As a Mississippi native, Mobley warned her son of the ways of the South before he boarded the train. While Till had been exposed to segregation in the North, he was unaware of how far white supremacists would go to preserve their Southern way of life.

During his stay in Money, Mississippi, Till and his cousin, Curtis Jones, visited Bryant's Grocery and Meat Market on a Wednesday evening. While Jones started a checkers game with an older man outside the store, Till went inside and bought some gum. As Till left the store he said "bye, baby" to white cashier Carolyn Bryant, the store owner's wife. The man playing checkers with Jones told the boys they should leave before Bryant got her pistol. The scared boys left quickly in Wright's 1941 Ford, and Till begged Jones not to mention the market incident to his uncle. Days passed without incident until Carolyn's husband Roy returned to Money after being away on a trucking job.

Late that Saturday night, Roy Bryant, along with his brother-in-law J. W. Milam, drove to Wright's cabin. Bryant and Milam greeted 64-year-old Wright with a flashlight and a gun. Bryant wanted the boy who talked to his wife. Wright pleaded with the two men asking them not to take the boy. He told them Till was just 14 and from the North; he did not know how to treat white folks. Bryant and Milam pulled Till out of his bed at gunpoint, dragged him into their car, and drove off. The men threatened Wright's life if he mentioned anything of the incident.

The next morning, Curtis Jones called the sheriff to report Till missing. Three days later, a boy fishing in the Tallahatchie River discovered Till's body. His body was so disfigured by the beating that Mose Wright could identify his nephew only by the initialed ring he wore; it was his father's. Before being shot in the head, Till was brutally beaten. His forehead was shattered on one side, an eye was gouged out, and a 75-pound cotton-gin fan was tied around Till's neck with barbed wire. After finding the body, Jones called Till's mother in Chicago.

After the casket arrived in Chicago, the mortician told Mamie Till Mobley that he signed an order for the sheriff of Money that promised Till's casket would not be opened. Mobley opened the casket herself. After seeing her only child's body mutilated beyond recognition, Mobley wanted everyone to see what happened to her 14-year-old son in the Jim Crow South. On September 3, thousands of people came to the open casket ceremony at Rainer Funeral Home. A picture of Till's lynched corpse also appeared in *Jet,* a weekly black magazine, for the whole nation to see.

Less than two weeks after Till's burial, Bryant and Milam were tried for the murder of Emmett Till in Sumner, Mississippi. Although four African Americans, including Mose Wright, were brave enough to testify against Bryant and Milam in the segregated courthouse, the all-male, all-white jury deliberated a little over an hour before returning with not-guilty verdicts for both defendants. That same year, Bryant and Milam sold their confessional story of killing Emmett Till to white journalist William Bradford Huie, for $4,000. Their story appeared in *Look* magazine on January 24, 1956. *See also* Lynching; Racial Customs and Etiquette.

Further Readings: Hudson-Weems, Clenora. *Emmett Till: The Sacrificial Lamb of the Civil Rights Movement*. Troy, MI: Bedford Publishers, 1994; Till-Mobley, Mamie, with Christopher Benson. *Death of Innocence: The Story of the Hate Crime That Changed America*. New York: Random House, 2003; Whitfield, Stephen J. *A Death in the Delta: The Story of Emmett Till*. Baltimore: Johns Hopkins University Press, 1991.

Emily Hess

Tillman, Ben (1847–1918)

In appearance, words and deeds, Benjamin Ryan Tillman figured prominently as a grand cyclops of **Jim Crow** segregation. His career as a planter, terrorist, and politician was defined by a fearsome devotion to the era's racial project of white male supremacy.

Tillman was born near the town of Trenton, in the cotton plantation district of Edgefield, **South Carolina**. Owning over 2,500 acres and nearly 50 slaves, his family was among the wealthiest 10 percent of slaveholders in the area. The world of this slaveholding planter elite, thinly disguised by the self-comforting rhetoric of paternalism, was one in which white males sought to maintain control of the enslaved through a system of threats and the application of physical punishment. Losing an eye to illness at the age of 16, Tillman was prevented from defending slavery's racial dominion by serving in the Confederate army. However, by the time of **Reconstruction**, Tillman had recovered his health and exercised his desire to restore white male mastery by joining a paramilitary rifle-club movement, which sought to topple the Palmetto state's black-majority Republican government. In this period, Tillman participated in the Hamburg Massacre of July 1876, in which five members of a black Republican militia defending an armory in the small-town were coldly executed by white rifle-club members wearing improvised red shirt uniforms. During the state's gubernatorial election that same year, these "Red Shirts" used tactics of violence and intimidation towards black voters to help carry the former Confederate general and **Ku Klux Klan** leader Wade Hampton III to power.

During the late 1870s, Tillman enjoyed economic success as a planter, but after experiencing droughts and crop failures in the early 1880s, he took up the cause of agricultural reform and began to articulate serious political ambitions. Despite the comforts and privileges of his upbringing and lifestyle, Tillman aligned himself with the common farmers of South Carolina and railed against the elitism of the Bourbon political aristocracy, the so-called Redeemers of white rule who he claimed were failing to address the state's crisis in agriculture. Tillman's Farmer's Association movement demanded a variety of reforms, the most substantial of which was the call for a farmer's college. Elected governor of **South Carolina** in 1890, Tillman eventually oversaw the founding of Clemson College for white males and Winthrop College for white women, but repeatedly frustrated efforts to improve black educational opportunities.

In 1895 Tillman played a leading role in the South Carolina constitutional convention that established key elements of Jim Crow legislation: the various **poll tax**, literacy, education, and understanding requirements that conspired to disenfranchise black men in the state for long decades to come. That same year Tillman was elected to the U.S. Senate, in which he served until his death in 1918. Here he earned a reputation as an ill-mannered and volatile orator, as well as his nickname "Pitchfork Ben," following a speech he made on the Senate floor in 1896 in which he threatened to "poke" President Grover Cleveland "with a pitchfork." In an infamous address to the Senate in March 1900, Tillman peddled an undiluted racist poison that endorsed white mob violence: "We of the South have never believed [the black man] to be the equal to the white man and we will not submit to his gratifying his lust on our wives and daughters without **lynching** him."

Bearing the deeply misleading legend—"friend and leader of the common people"—a Tillman monument was erected on the statehouse grounds of Columbia, South Carolina, in 1940. Standing alongside the relocated **Confederate flag** and on the same complex as a monument to Wade Hampton III and a statue of the **Dixiecrat Strom Thurmond**, Tillman's bronze figures as a central pillar in the state's pantheon of white Jim Crow rule.

Further Readings: Edgar, Walter. *South Carolina: A History.* Columbia: University of South Carolina Press, 1998; Kantrowitz, Stephen. *Ben Tillman and the Reconstruction of White Supremacy.* Chapel Hill: University of North Carolina Press, 2000; Simpkins, Francis Butler. *Pitchfork Ben Tillman: South Carolinian.* Baton Rouge: Louisiana State University Press, 1944.

Stephen C. Kenny

Toomer, Jean (1894–1967)

Jean Toomer was an African American author, born Nathan Pinchback Toomer to parents Nathan Toomer, a planter, and Nina Pinchback on December 26, 1894. Toomer's mother was the daughter of Pinckney Benton Stewart Pinchback, former governor of Louisiana, the first black governor in the nation. Because of his light complexion, Toomer could easily pass for white, a common practice during an earlier period of his life. After Nathan Toomer abandoned Toomer and his mother, they moved to Washington, DC, to live with Nina's parents. Pinckney Pinchback, began to refer to young Nathan as Eugene Pinchback Toomer, although his name was never legally changed. Toomer grew up in a racially integrated neighborhood but attended segregated schools. Nina remarried and Toomer lived briefly in New York. Upon his mother's death, Toomer returned to Washington, graduating in 1914 from the all-black Dunbar High School. After graduation, Toomer studied a wide range of disciplines, including literature, philosophy, and agriculture.

During his stint in Sparta, Georgia, Toomer's racial consciousness was roused. As the superintendent of Sparta's Industrial and Agricultural Institute,

Toomer became inspired by both his racial heritage and surroundings in the rural South. The product of Toomer's combined influences was the collection *Cane,* released in 1923. Though similar in format to American writer Sherwood Anderson's *Winesburg, Ohio* (1919), *Cane* focused on the racial tensions and social structure of the segregated South and its transcendence into Northern society. Toomer's usage of natural imagery reflected the romanticized relationship between African Americans and primitivism in the South. "Blood-burning Moon," a short story about a **lynching**, used the figures of the moon and cane fields to demonstrate the invisible but understood boundaries between blacks and whites. The character Bob Stone, a white man, desired to see Louisa, a black woman who is the love interest of Tom Burwell, a feared black man. In order to avoid being seen, Tom and Louisa meet in cane fields, which though easy to navigate through, were sharp and painful. The moon was described as red and full, was believed in Southern tradition to be the cause of hysteria and madness. The color red symbolized blood and death. It was during the blood red moon the main characters were both murdered— Bob Stone by Tom Burwell, and Tom by a white lynch mob.

The second half of *Cane* takes place in the urbanity of Washington, DC, and Chicago. "Bona and Paul," a story about an unknowingly interracial couple's date in Chicago, ends with a dramatic explanation between a black doorman and Paul, a "**passing**" black man. After conversing with the doorman, Paul realizes Bona has disappeared. A reason behind Bona's disappearance was her realization of Paul's race because of his urgency to talk to the African American doorman. Bona's epiphany sheds light on the looming existence of racial separation, even in the urban North. Toomer's division of *Cane* invokes the reader to think about the role of race in society and identity, regardless of geographic location. *See also* Baldwin, James; Ellison, Ralph; Faulkner, William; Louisiana.

Further Readings: O'Daniel, Therman B. *Jean Toomer: A Critical Evaluation.* Washington, DC: Howard University Press, 1988; Toomer, Jean. *Cane.* New York: Boni and Liveright, 1923.

Regina Barnett

Truman, Harry S.

Harry S. Truman, 33rd president of the United States, was the first chief executive in the twentieth century to take substantive action in support of political and social equality for African Americans. In September 1946, a delegation of African American leaders, including National Association for the Advancement of Colored People (NAACP) executive director **Walter White**, met with Truman in the White House to discuss the rise of racial violence then occurring across the American South. The president was particularly shocked by the brutal attack upon an African American soldier in **South Carolina**.

Honorably discharged from the army in February 1946, Sergeant Isaac Woodard was traveling by bus through South Carolina when, during an unscheduled stop, he asked the white driver if he could use the restroom. The driver refused permission and cursed Woodard, who responded in kind. When the bus arrived in Batesburg, the driver informed police chief Lynwood Lanier Shull that Woodard had been unruly during the trip. Boarding the bus, the police chief arrested Woodard for disturbing the peace. When he protested that he had done nothing wrong, Shull savagely beat the discharged sergeant, blinding him in both eyes. The president, deeply troubled by this brutal act, vowed to take action. Under Truman's direction, the Justice Department prosecuted Schull for violating Woodard's civil rights, but an all-white jury found him not guilty. The beating of Sergeant Woodard and the acquittal of his assailant had a profound effect on President Truman. From that point on, he was determined to end legalized discrimination and racial violence from American life.

In December 1946, one month after Schull's acquittal, Truman issued an executive order creating the President's Committee on Civil Rights to investigate civil rights abuses and propose federal statutes that would prevent them in the future. As the committee began its work, Truman continued to call for an end to racial discrimination. On June 29, 1947, the president spoke at the annual meeting of the NAACP, the first chief executive to ever do so. Standing on the steps of the **Lincoln Memorial**, Truman committed the **federal government** to ensuring equal rights for African Americans. Four months later, the president was given the tools to make his commitment real when his civil rights committee presented him with its 178-page report on October 29, 1947. Entitled *To Secure These Rights,* the report not only catalogued egregious abuses of civil rights, but also recommended federal action to protect the constitutional liberties of all Americans.

Despite the considerable political risks, Truman sent a special message to Congress on February 2, 1948, proposing a set of laws designed to secure full equality for African Americans. The president's ambitious program included the creation of a civil rights commission and a Justice Department civil rights division to investigate and prosecute violations of civil liberties, establishment of a federal commission to prevent discrimination in the workplace and ensure fair employment practices, antilynching legislation, outlawing segregation in facilities servicing interstate transportation, and further protection for the right to vote.

As might be expected, Truman's message ignited a political firestorm in the American South. Bitterly opposed to his proposals, white southern Democrats attempted to deny Truman their party's presidential nomination. When that failed, they formed the States Rights or **Dixiecrat** Party, and nominated **Strom Thurmond** of South Carolina for president. Although 82 percent of the American people were reportedly opposed to the presidents' civil rights program, Truman defeated Thurmond and Republican Thomas E. Dewey in the November election. The Dixiecrats were unable to prevent Truman's election, but their allies in Congress did successfully block Truman's civil rights measures from becoming law. In the face of congressional inaction and the hatred of Southern reactionaries, the president remained unbowed. On July 26, 1948, Truman issued two executive orders that weakened the bonds of legalized segregation. Executive Order 9980 required all federal departments to insure equal employment opportunities for all applicants regardless of race, color, religion or national origin and established a Fair Employment Board to oversee compliance. The second one, **Executive Order 9981**, was even more radical.

For decades, one of the most segregated institutions in the country was the U.S. military. Denied opportunities to advance, most black servicemen were prevented from service in combat units and were allowed only to engage in menial activities. In the Marines, for example, blacks could only enlist as kitchen personnel while in the army, only one African American in 70 was a commissioned officer. Appalled by this, Truman ordered military commanders to integrate the armed forces. High-ranking military leaders, most notably army chief of staff General Omar Bradley, bitterly denounced the plan, but again Truman refused to back down. Before the end of his presidency in January 1953, Truman also appointed African American lawyer William Hastie to the U.S. Court of Appeals and integrated federal housing programs.

Truman was the first American chief executive to commit the power of the federal government to the elimination of legalized segregation. Although conservatives in Congress blocked

"Teach me one o' them 'race predujices,' Uncle Louie. Every kid on th' streets got one but me."

Cartoon from *New York Star*, November 26, 1948. President Harry S. Truman banned discrimination and segregation in the armed forces, which had the effect of reducing social segregation in civilian life after World War II. Courtesy of Library of Congress, LC-USZ62-86571.

most of his civil rights program, Truman courageously ignored Southern reactionaries such as the Dixiecrats and integrated both the armed forces and federal bureaucracy. At the same time, in calling attention to the discriminatory nature of Jim Crow segregation through the creation of the Presidential Committee on Civil Rights and his address to the NAACP, Truman laid bare the plight of African Americans and emboldened their struggle to achieve social and political equality. *See also* Civil Rights Movement; Desegregation.

Further Readings: Gardner, Michael R. *Harry Truman and Civil Rights: Moral Courage and Political Risks.* Carbondale: Southern Illinois University Press, 2002; *To Secure These Rights: the Report of the Presidents Committee on Civil Rights.* http://www.trumanlibrary.org/civilrights/srights1.htm (accessed May 31, 2007); "Harry S. Truman." In *Civil Rights in the United States*, edited by Waldo E. Martin, Jr., and Patricia Sullivan, 2 vols. New York: Macmillan Reference USA, 2000; "President's Committee on Civil Rights." In *Civil Rights in the United States*, edited by Waldo E. Martin, Jr., and Patricia Sullivan, 2 vols. New York: Macmillan Reference USA, 2000.

Wayne Dowdy

Tulsa Riot of 1921

The Tulsa riot of May 31 and June 1, 1921, was the last of the terrible **World War I**–era riots. Like many of the other riots, from East St. Louis in 1917 to the riots of the summer of 1919 in such places as Chicago; Elaine, Arkansas; Omaha, Nebraska; and Washington, DC, it involved an attack on an African American community. Like those other riots, the causes were both long-standing conflicts between the expectations of the white community and the increasing prosperity and self-confidence of the African American community in the wake of the war. As the strictures of **Jim Crow** broke down and the African American communities developed and acted on the grand idea of equality, they grew more confident. The communities organized to protect themselves against violence and to protect against the violence and segregation of Jim Crow.

Those long-standing sentiments of the idea of equality (what Oklahoma native **Ralph Ellison** labeled in his novel *Invisible Man* "the great constitutional dream book") were particularly strong in the Tulsa African American community. In September 1920, following a **lynching** of a young black man in Oklahoma City, the *Tulsa Star,* Tulsa's leading African American newspaper, criticized the Oklahoma City community for not doing more to prevent the lynching. The *Tulsa Star* boldly stated that Oklahoma City residents had the legal right, indeed, duty to take action to protect against lynchings. They had the right to take life if necessary to uphold the law.

Leaders of Tulsa's African American section, Greenwood, frequently met in the Williams' Dreamland Theater to discuss the great ideas of the renaissance, particularly how to respond to violence and threatened lynchings. Those people read and discussed the vehicles of the renaissance, including the National Association for the Advancement of Colored People's (NAACP) *The Crisis.* Moreover, many of those leaders were veterans of the World War. **W.E.B. Du Bois**'s May 1919 editorial in *The Crisis,* "Returning Soldiers," captures well the sentiments of those African American veterans. "We return. We return from fighting. We return fighting. Make way for Democracy! We saved it in France, and by the Great Jehovah, we will save it in the United States of America, or know the reason why."

Those long-running ideas of equality clashed with Jim Crow in late May 1921. The riot was set off when the sensationalist *Tulsa Tribune* reported on May 31, 1921, that a young African American man, Dick Rowland, had attempted to attack a young white woman, Mary Paige, the day before. That led a mob to collect at the Tulsa courthouse on the evening of May 31. At the same time, African American men met in Greenwood to talk about how to protect Rowland. They decided to make a trip to the courthouse and offer to help protect Rowland. When several dozen African American veterans appeared at the courthouse around 10:00 PM, a police officer tried to disarm them; gunfire ensued, and the riot was on. Throughout the evening, the local units of the Oklahoma **National Guard** and the police department worked to devise a plan to disarm and arrest everyone in Greenwood. The police department hastily deputized hundreds of white men and those who did not have guns were issued them by the police department. Meanwhile, throughout the night, there was fighting across the railroad tracks that separate white Tulsa from the Greenwood section.

At about daybreak on June 1, the police, their deputies, and the local units of the National Guard crossed the railroad tracks in Greenwood. Amid some-times fierce fighting, the police, deputies, and National Guard methodically moved through Greenwood. Thousands of Greenwood residents were arrested and taken into custody, then held in what newspapers referred to as "concentration camps" around the city. Others who did not go willingly were shot. As the residents of buildings in Greenwood were taken into custody, they were looted, then burned. The Oklahoma Supreme Court acknowledged in a lawsuit in 1926 that some of the people doing the burning wore deputy police badges.

At one point on the morning of June 1, airplanes appeared overhead. Some claimed that the planes were shooting at Greenwood residents and dropping incendiaries on Greenwood. The city claimed the planes were used only for gathering intelligence about the riot. It is difficult to establish the ways that planes were used, but no one disputes they were in the air.

By about 10:00 AM on June 1, much of Greenwood was on fire or was already burned. By noon, units of the Oklahoma National Guard based in Oklahoma City had begun to restore order. Their commander, General Charles F. Barrett, later recalled that when his troops arrived, they found "[t]wenty-five thousand whites, armed to the teeth, [ravaging] the city in utter and ruthless defiance of every concept of law and righteousness." Barrett commented about the special deputies that were "the most dangerous part of the mob."

Even as the riot itself died out, the process of restoring order remained. Thousands of Greenwood residents were held in the concentration camps around the city until a white employer vouched for them. But even once they were released from the camps, they had little place to go, for dozens of blocks of Greenwood were destroyed. Thousands of people were left homeless and for months they lived in tents provided by the Red Cross. Others left Tulsa for good, sometimes walking along the railroad tracks, headed for cities like Chicago, St. Louis, Kansas City, even Los Angeles. Leaders of the Greenwood renaissance were particularly fearful that they would be prosecuted for inciting riot. A. J. Smitherman, editor of the *Tulsa Star*, fled to Boston, where he continued to work in the newspaper business. During the Christmas holiday of 1921, he published a poem that retold the story of the riot. It included this description of the start of the riot:

> So they marched against the mobbists
> Gathered now about the jail,
> While the sheriff stood there pleading,
> Law and order to prevail.
> Thus responding to their duty,
> Like true soldiers that they were,
> Black men face the lawless white men
> Under duty's urgent spur. . . .

However, the final stanza told of the importance of the riot for the lessons it taught the white community—that Greenwood residents would act to uphold the law:

Though they fought the sacrificial
Fight. with banners flying high,
Yet the thing of more importance
Is the way they fought—and why!

The process of recovering was long, and city leaders were in little mood to assist Greenwood residents. While the Red Cross provided assistance and some leaders of Tulsa pledged to make good the damage, Tulsa's mayor responded with a plan to relocate Greenwood further away from downtown Tulsa and to require expensive fireproof materials in rebuilding. Some Greenwood residents attempted to sue the city and their insurance companies, which frequently denied coverage on insurance policies citing "riot exclusion" clauses. The lawsuits were uniformly unsuccessful. So the Greenwood residents who stayed rebuilt using their own resources.

As the years passed, the riot receded from memory. Two events helped change that. In 1982, historian Scott Ellsworth published a book on it, *Death in a Promised Land;* more than a decade and a half later, in the late 1990s, State Representative Don Ross introduced a bill in the Oklahoma legislature that established a commission on the riot. The commission's report, issued in 2001, presented the most comprehensive picture of the riot available; it also led to major controversy around the issue of whether the legislature should pay "reparations" to riot victims.

The legislature issued an apology in 2001, but offered nothing in terms of payments to survivors of the riot. In response, in 2003, lawyers led by Harvard Law School Professor Charles Ogletree filed a lawsuit against the city and state, alleging that they were liable for much of the damage during the riot. The city and state responded that the lawsuit was being filed too late. In 2004, the U.S. District Court in Tulsa dismissed the lawsuit, and the U.S. Court of Appeals upheld the dismissal. The Supreme Court refused to hear the case. Thus ended the riot victims' long-running battle to obtain relief through the courts. There are still nearly 100 survivors, and Charles Ogletree continues to press their case for compensation. In April 2007, U.S. Congressman John Conyers introduced a bill in the House of Representatives that would allow the lawsuit to go forward. More than 85 years after the riot, the victims await justice. *See also* Chicago Race Riot of 1919; Elaine Massacre; Houston Riot of 1917; Red Summer; Rosewood; Wilmington Race Riot.

Further Readings: Brophy, Alfred L. *Reconstructing the Dreamland: The Tulsa Riot of 1921.* New York: Oxford University Press, 2002; Ellsworth, Scott. *Death in a Promised Land: The Tulsa Riot of 1921.* Baton Rouge: Louisiana State University Press, 1982; Oklahoma Commission to Study the Tulsa Race Riot of 1921. "Tulsa Race Riot: A Report by the Oklahoma Commission to Study the Tulsa Race Riot of 1921." Oklahoma City: The Commission, 2001.

Alfred L. Brophy

Tuskegee Syphilis Experiment

Beginning during the **Depression** years of **Jim Crow** segregation in 1932, just before Adolf Hitler came to power in Germany, the Tuskegee syphilis experiment remains one of the most shocking episodes in the troubled history of human experimentation. Sponsored by the U.S. Public Health Service (PHS), the Tuskegee experiment ran for a full 40 years before the disturbing details of the nontherapeutic and unethical medical trial were disclosed to the American public by Jean Heller of the Associated Press in a story published by the *Washington Star* on July 25, 1972.

Jim Crow–era economic deprivations, racial divisions, and white racial prejudices provide an essential framework for understanding what happened to the victims of the Tuskegee study and why the experiment was allowed to continue for so long. The South's post-**Reconstruction** regime of legally sanctioned and violently enforced racial **apartheid** trapped many rural African Americans in a vicious cycle of debt peonage, illiteracy, fear and ill health. Adding insult to injury, white Americans also invented and circulated a number of negative stereotypes of blackness. One of the most common post–Civil War misrepresentations of African American men was that of the "brute" or "black beast." This distorted caricature portrayed black men as primitive, savage, and, in particular, as an uncontrollable sexual threat to white women. White physicians and social scientists echoed and amplified the core ideology of Jim Crow, discovering allegedly high incidences of anatomical irregularities, constitutional weaknesses, and venereal diseases among the black population—with syphilis rates among African American males becoming a chief preoccupation of white public health officials.

The Tuskegee experiment had its immediate origins in a 1929 Julius Rosenwald Foundation–funded PHS study designed to determine the prevalence, and implement methods for control, of syphilis among rural black males in six counties spread across five Southern states. This privately financed health plan initiative was discontinued in the fall of 1930, but not before researchers had identified Macon County, **Alabama**, as the study's area of greatest need. Tragically, as few of the syphilis sufferers discovered in Macon County had ever received any treatment, they were later targeted (by then–assistant surgeon general Taliaferro Clark) as an "unparalled opportunity" to develop a new research project, examining "the effect of untreated syphilis on the human economy." In total, 400 men, already infected with syphilis, and a further 200 serving as uninfected controls, were selected for the experiment, centered at Tuskegee Institute's John A. Andrew Memorial Hospital. In addition to prominent white physicians and public health officials, several black medical professionals played key parts in the research. Perhaps the most notable African American involvement came from public health nurse Eunice Rivers, who acted as a trusted liaison between the men in the study and the PHS doctors. There has been much debate as to nurse Rivers's knowledge of and complicity in the experiment. By way of understanding her position, historian Susan Reverby explains that the complex world of Tuskegee's race, class, gender, and professional politics created peculiar pressures that sometimes forced individuals like Rivers into contradictory and compromising roles.

The men were recruited via a number of coercive and deceptive incentives—such as the offer of "special free treatment" (including painful diagnostic procedures, such as spinal puncture), free transport to and from hospital, free hot lunches, and free burial insurance (but only after permission for an autopsy had been granted). None of the subjects enrolled in the study were ever provided with appropriate or adequate treatment; indeed, they were discouraged and even actively prevented from seeking treatment outside the program and were also denied the most effective antibiotic therapy against the disease—penicillin—when it eventually became widely available in the 1940s. Nor were the men properly or fully informed that they were human guinea pigs participating in a medical research experiment. Instead they were told that they were being treated for "bad blood," a vernacular term used to describe several illnesses in the rural black community (including syphilis, anemia, and fatigue). This was a group of very vulnerable patients, with few alternatives, who were victims of a long-term cruel combination of racial discrimination and medical callousness.

Racism and exploitation have deep roots in American medicine, especially in the Southern states. For example, in neighboring Montgomery County, Alabama, during the era of antebellum **slavery**, Dr. James Marion Sims performed a variety of medical experiments on slave men, women, and infants. Between 1844 and 1849, Sims developed a method of repairing injuries suffered during childbirth and later gained international fame as the "father of American gynecology." However, Sims owed the perfection of his surgery to the role of enslaved women, upon whom he conducted repeated operations (without anesthesia). In the same era, Southern medical schools demonstrated what has been termed "postmortem racism," encouraging the use of black cadavers (many obtained without permission and stolen from graveyards) in anatomical training and the use of black body parts in medical museums. This long history of medical abuse and differential treatment created a legacy of mistrust and fear towards white physicians in the African American community, often resulting in an understandable reluctance to participate in clinical trials.

The 1972 media exposé led to the termination of the study. However, by this stage, a number of the men had died and many family members had been infected. The most positive outcome of the tragedy was the crucial role it played in making Americans rethink the ethics of human experimentation. It gave impetus to the National Research Act of 1974, making written informed consent of human subjects a fundamental condition of participation in medical research trials. Furthermore, in July 1973, Macon County civil-rights attorney Fred Gray filed a $1.8 billion class-action lawsuit, which resulted in an out-of-court settlement a year later for $10 million to be divided among the study's living participants and heirs of the deceased.

On May 16, 1997, in the presence of eight survivors of the study, family representatives of the deceased, political activists, and historians, President William J. Clinton issued a formal federal apology for the Tuskegee Syphilis Experiment. As a commitment to long-term efforts heal the wounds inflicted by the study, the Clinton administration also supported the building of a National Center for Bioethics in Research and Health Care at Tuskegee University, which opened in 1998. The study also left a cultural legacy, becoming the subject of poems, documentaries, a play and HBO award-winning movie, *Miss Evers's Boys*. *See also* Folk Medicine; Health Care.

Further Readings: Brandt, Allan M. "Racism and Research: The Case of the Tuskegee Syphilis Study." In *Sickness and Health in America,* edited by Judith Walzer Leavitt and Ronald L. Numbers. Madison: University of Wisconsin Press, 1997; Hornblum, Allen M. *Acres of Skin: Human Experiments at Holmesberg Prison.* London: Routledge, 1998; Jones, James H. *Bad Blood: The Tuskegee Syphilis Experiment.* New York: Free Press, 1981, revised 1992; Reverby, Susan M. ed. *Tuskegee's Truths: Rethinking the Tuskegee Syphilis Study.* Chapel Hill: University of North Carolina Press, 2000.

Stephen C. Kenny

U

U.S. Supreme Court

Over the years, the U.S. Supreme Court has played a pivotal role in African Americans' fight against racial segregation. However, this role has been tenuous, at best. The previous statement is based on the fact that prior to *Brown v. Board of Education*, 347 U.S. 483 (1954), the Court's interpretation of the Fourteenth Amendment and other congressional enactments promoted the interest of white segregationists rather than that of blacks seeking judicial remedies in order to combat racial segregation and **Jim Crow** laws.

Beginning as early as 1857 in *Dred Scott v. Sandford*, 60 U.S. (19 How.) 393, the Court invalidated state efforts to grant freedom to slaves and citizenship to freed slaves. The Court's reasoning, or lack thereof, in *Dred Scott* relegated blacks to the status of property and validated the continuation of slavery in America. The Court concluded as follows:

> The question is simply this: Can a negro, whose ancestors were imported into this country, and sold as slaves, become a member of the political community formed and brought into existence by the Constitution of the United States, and as such become—entitled to all the rights, and privileges, and immunities, guaranteed by that instrument to the citizen? . . . We think they are not, and that they are not included, and were not intended to be included, under the word "citizens" in the Constitution, and can therefore claim none of the rights and privileges which that instrument provides for and secures to citizens of the United States. On the contrary, they were at that time considered as a subordinate and inferior class of beings, who had been subjugated by the dominant race, and, whether emancipated or not, yet remained subject to their authority, and had no rights or privileges but such as those who held the power and the Government might choose to grant them. . . . [Colonial laws] show that a perpetual and impassable barrier was intended to be erected between the white race and the one which they had reduced to slavery, and governed as subjects with absolute and despotic power, and which they then looked upon as so far below them in the scale of created beings, that intermarriages between white persons and negroes or mulattoes were regarded as unnatural and immoral, and punished as crimes, not only in the parties, but in the person who joined them in marriage.

The *Dred Scott* ruling remained the law of the land until passage of the Civil War Amendments—Thirteenth (1865), Fourteenth (1868), and Fifteenth (1870) Amendments of the U.S. Constitution. The Thirteenth Amendment abolished slavery; the Fourteenth Amendment granted U.S. and state citizenship, equal protection, and due process of laws "to all persons born or naturalized in the United States, and subject to the jurisdiction thereof"; and the Fifteenth Amendment provided the right to vote to all male citizens.

Despite the passage of the Thirteenth, Fourteenth, and Fifteenth Amendments; the Court continued to render decisions in opposition to the interest of blacks. For example, even though the *Slaughterhouse Cases*, 83 U.S. (16 Wall.) 36 (1873), involved the legality of a Louisiana law regulating the slaughtering of animals, the Supreme Court's ruling in these cases focused primarily on providing a judicial interpretation of what constituted citizenship under the Fourteenth Amendment. The Court reasoned as follows:

> The first section of the fourteenth article, to which our attention is more specifically invited, opens with a definition of citizenship—not only citizenship of the United States, but citizenship of the States. No such definition was previously found in the Constitution, nor had any attempt been made to define it by act of Congress.... The first observation we have to make on this clause is, ... [t]hat its main purpose was to establish the citizenship of the negro can admit of no doubt.... The next observation is more important in view of the arguments of counsel in the present case. It is that the distinction between citizenship of the United States and citizenship of the State is clearly recognized and established. Not only may a man be a citizen of the United States without being a citizen of a State, but an important element is necessary to convert the former into the latter. He must reside within the State to make him a citizen of it, but it is only necessary that he should be born or naturalized in the United States to be a citizen of the Union.... Having shown that the privileges and immunities relied on in the argument are those which belong to citizens of the States as such, and that they are left to the State governments for security and protection, and not by this article placed under the special care of the Federal government.

The 1878 case of *Hall v. DeCuir*, 95 U.S. 485, exemplifies even more the Court's role in providing credence to racial segregation in America. In *Hall*, the Court declared a Louisiana law ending racial segregation in interstate travel unconstitutional. The Court stated that the Louisiana legislature had engaged in an activity—regulation of interstate commerce—reserved to Congress.

An additional example of the Court's stance may be found in the *Civil Rights Cases—United States v. Stanley, United States v. Ryan, United States v. Nichols, United States v. Singleton, Robinson & Wife v. Memphis and Charleston Railroad Company*, 109 U.S. 3 (1883)—in which the Court ruled that the **Civil Rights Act of 1875** did not prevent racial discrimination by private individuals or businesses. The statutory intent of this act was to prohibit private persons from violating the right of "all persons within the jurisdiction of the United States ... to the full and equal enjoyment of the accommodations, advantages, facilities, and privileges of inns, public conveyances on land or water, theaters, and other places of public amusement; subject only to the conditions and limitations established by law, and applicable alike to citizens of every race and color, regardless of any previous condition of servitude."

In the *Civil Rights Cases,* the Court stated that "[t]he first section of the Fourteenth Amendment (which is the one relied on), after declaring who shall be citizens of the United States, and of the several States, is prohibitory in its character, and prohibitory upon the states . . . It is State action of a particular character that is prohibited. Individual invasion of individual rights is not the subject-matter of the amendment. . . . It does not authorize Congress to create a code of municipal law for the regulation of private rights; but to provide modes of redress against the operation of State laws, and the action of State officers executive or judicial, when these are subversive of the fundamental rights specified in the amendment."

As a reactionary response to the Court's posture on racial segregation, many Southern states passed Jim Crow laws during the 1880s and 1890s. The purpose of these laws was to erect a wall of separation between black and whites. Jim Crow laws required racial segregation in public places, inclusive of public schools, transportation, restaurants, hotels, parks, swimming publics, and other public facilities.

The constitutionality of Jim Crow laws was tested in **Plessy v. Ferguson,** 163 U.S. 537 (1896). In this case, Homer Plessy challenged the constitutionality of an 1890 Louisiana law requiring all railway companies to separate black and whites passengers. Unlike *Hall, Plessy* did not involve the issue of interstate travel. However, the Supreme Court once again issued a ruling that served as yet another obstacle for blacks attempting to secure equal rights and racial justice in America. In *Plessy,* the Court stated as follows:

> A statute which implies merely a legal distinction between the white and colored races—a distinction which is founded in the color of the two races, and which must always exist so long as white men are distinguished from the other races by color—has no tendency to destroy the legal equality of the two races, or reestablish a state of involuntary servitude. . . . Laws permitting, and even requiring, their separation in places where they are liable to be brought into contact do not necessarily imply the inferiority of either race to the other, and have been generally, if not universally, recognized as within the competency of the state legislatures in the exercise of their police power. . . . [E]very exercise of the police power must be reasonable, and extend only to such laws as are enacted in good faith for the promotion for the public good, and not for the annoyance or oppression of a particular class. . . . The argument also assumes that social prejudice may be overcome by legislation, and that equal rights cannot be secured to the negro except by an enforced commingling of the two races. We cannot accept this proposition. . . . Legislation is powerless to eradicate racial instincts or to abolish distinctions based upon physical differences, and the attempt to do so can only result in accentuating the difficulties of the present situation. If the civil and political rights of both races be equal one cannot be inferior to the other civilly or politically. If one race be inferior to the other socially, the Constitution of the United States cannot put them upon the same plane.

Not until 1954, in *Brown v. Board of Education,* did the Court finally interpret the Fourteenth Amendment and applicable congressional enactments as protecting the rights of Black. In *Brown,* the Court overturned its *Plessy* ruling and finally provided a judicial avenue for black and other integrationists in their fight against the racial segregation of both public and private facilities. *See also Brown v. Board of Education,* Legal Groundwork for; Federal Government; Marshall, Thurgood; *Shelley v. Kraemer; U.S. v. Cruikshank; U.S. v. Reese*

Further Readings: Dahl, Robert A. "Decision-making in a Democracy: The Supreme Court as a National Policy-maker." *Journal of Public Law* 6 (1957); Davis, Abraham L., and Barbara L. Graham. *The Supreme Court, Race, and Civil Rights.* Thousand Oaks, CA: SAGE Publications, 1995; Higginbotham, A. Leon. *In the Matter of Color: Race and the American Legal Process.* New York: Oxford University Press, 1978; Klarman, Michael. *From Jim Crow to Civil Rights: The Supreme Court and the Struggle for Racial Equality.* New York: Oxford University Press, 2006; Lee, Francis G. *Equal Protection: Rights and Liberties under the Law.* Santa Barbara, CA: ABC-CLIO Publishers, 2003.

Olethia Davis

U.S. v. Cruikshank (1875)

U.S. v. Cruikshank (92 U.S. 542) was a **U.S. Supreme Court** case involving a conspiracy to deny the voting rights of a large group of black men in **Louisiana**. The Supreme Court, in its ruling, set forth the principle that although the **federal government** was supreme over state governments, it could not "grant nor secure rights to citizens" not expressed nor implied under its protection, and that "[s]overeignty, for the protection of the rights of life and personal liberty within the respective States, rests alone with the states." The ruling became a cornerstone in the abrogation of any federal responsibility in ensuring that state governments respect the civil rights of African Americans. In deciding *Cruikshank,* the Court opted for a narrow interpretation of the Fourteenth Amendment to the Constitution and refused to expand federal jurisdiction, even though the outcome clearly denied justice.

The case began with an incident on Easter Sunday, April 13, 1873, during **Reconstruction,** when a mob of white Democrats attacked and killed about 280 black Republicans in Colfax, Louisiana, during a contested local election. The blacks had sought protection inside the courthouse, which was guarded by a small contingent of so-called Negro Militia. The white mob also purported to be a militia, but it acted under its own authority, and contained many members of the White League and the **Ku Klux Klan**. After the attack, federal officials arrested and tried three white men for leading the mob. The three were convicted under the federal *Enforcement Act of 1870,* which made it a crime to interfere with any citizen's constitutional rights, in this case the right to vote. The defendants then appealed their convictions. Eventually the case worked its way to the U.S. Supreme Court.

The Supreme Court at the time was anxious to reassert its authority, particularly over matters pertaining to the South, where the legislative branch of government had exercised almost unlimited authority since the end of the Civil War. The Court's ruling in the case was unanimously in favor of the accused. Because the original indictment against the three white men did not allege that their actions were based upon race, their interference with the victims' right to vote was not a federal crime. The Court ruled that the Bill of Rights applied only to the relationship between citizens and the federal government, not the relationship between citizens and their state government. The First Amendment right to assembly "was not intended to limit the powers of the State governments in respect to their own citizens" and that the Second Amendment "has no other effect than to restrict the powers of the national government."

The ruling set forth that the Due Process and Equal Protection clauses of the Fourteenth Amendment protected citizens only from government action, not from the actions of other citizens. Thus, the federal government had no authority to protect blacks, or in theory, any citizen who attempted to vote, from mobs. Such protections would have to come from the state governments. With Southern state governments increasingly in the hands of Redeemers— white Democrats who firmly believed in white superiority and the exclusion of blacks from all aspects of the political process—such protection would not be forthcoming.

The *Cruikshank* ruling seriously hampered federal efforts at Reconstruction. The ruling sent a message to blacks and whites across the South that the federal government would do nothing to ensure the safety of blacks attempting to vote. Instead, ensuring the safety of voters was a state responsibility, and the states ignored that responsibility. More than any other court ruling, *U.S. v. Cruikshank* nullified the Fifteenth Amendment to the Constitution, and eliminated blacks from voting booths across the South. With Southern state governments under the control of white Democrats who were committed to white supremacy, and the federal government abdicating any responsibility to ensure the rights of black men to vote, the adoption of Jim Crow legislation was all but inevitable. Not until the passing of the **Civil Rights Acts of 1957** and **1964** would the federal government again take a direct role in ensuring that blacks were able to exercise their right to vote. *See also Plessy v. Ferguson.*

Further Readings: Goldman, Robert M. *Reconstruction and Black Suffrage: Losing the Vote in Reese and Cruikshank.* Lawrence: University Press of Kansas, 2001; Kahn, Ronald, and Ken I. Kersch. *The Supreme Court And American Political Development.* Lawrence: University Press of Kansas, 2006; Kersch, Ken I. *Constructing Civil Liberties: Discontinuities in the Development of American Constitutional Law.* New York: Cambridge University Press, 2004.

Barry M. Stentiford

U.S. v. Reese (1876)

In *U.S. v. Reese* (92 U.S. 214), the **U.S. Supreme Court** ruled, with two dissentions, that the Fifteenth Amendment the Constitution did not guarantee the right of citizens to vote, but instead only prevented states and the **federal government** from using race, color, or previous condition of servitude specifically as a reason for denying the vote. The case was the first test of the meaning of the Fifteenth Amendment, and in its ruling, the Court interpreted the amendment in the narrowest terms possible.

The case began when two inspectors of a municipal election in Kentucky refused to register the vote of a black man, William Garner, in a local election.

Excerpt from *U.S. v. Reese* (1875), pp. 3–6

The Fifteenth Amendment does not confer the right of suffrage upon any one. It prevents the States, or the United States, however, from giving preference, in this particular, to one citizen of the United States over another on account of race, color, or previous condition of servitude. Before its adoption, this could be done. It was as much within the power of a State to exclude citizens of the United States from voting on account of race, &c., as it was on account of age, property, or education. Now it is not. If citizens of one race having certain qualifications are permitted by law to vote, those of another having the same qualifications must be. Previous to this amendment, there was no constitutional guaranty against this discrimination: now there is. It follows that the amendment has invested the citizens of the United States with a new constitutional right which is within the protecting power of Congress. That right is exemption from discrimination in the exercise of the elective franchise on account of race, color, or previous condition of servitude. This, under the express provisions of the second section of the amendment, Congress may enforce by "appropriate legislation."

It remains now to consider whether a statute, so general as this in its provisions, can be made available for the punishment of those who may be guilty of unlawful discrimination against citizens of the United States, while exercising the elective franchise, on account of their race, &c.

It would certainly be dangerous if the legislature could set a net large enough to catch all possible offenders, and leave it to the courts to step inside and say who could be rightfully detained, and who should be set at large. This would, to some extent, substitute the judicial for the legislative department of the government. The courts enforce the legislative will when ascertained, if within the constitutional grant of power. Within its legitimate sphere, Congress is supreme, and beyond the control of the courts; but if it steps outside of its constitutional limitations, and attempts that which is beyond its reach, the courts are authorized to, and when called upon in due course of legal proceedings, must, annul its encroachments upon the reserved power of the States and the people.

To limit this statute in the manner now asked for would be be make a new law, not to enforce an old one. This is no part of our duty.

We must, therefore, decide that Congress has not as yet provided by 'appropriate legislation' for the punishment of the offence charged in the indictment; and that the Circuit Court properly sustained the demurrers, and gave judgment for the defendants. . . .

MR. JUSTICE CLIFFORD and MR. JUSTICE HUNT dissenting.

MR. JUSTICE CLIFFORD [excerpt]:

I concur that the indictment is bad, but for reasons widely different from those assigned by the court.

States, as well as the United States, are prohibited by the Fifteenth Amendment of the Constitution from denying or abridging the right of citizens of the United States to vote on account of race, color, or previous condition of servitude; and power is vested in Congress, by the second article of that amendment, to enforce that prohibition "by appropriate legislation."

Since the adoption of that amendment, Congress has legislated upon the subject; and, by the first section of the Enforcement Act, it is provided that citizens of the United States, without distinction of race, color, or previous condition of servitude, shall, if otherwise qualified to vote in state, territorial, or municipal elections, be entitled and allowed to vote at all such elections, any constitution, law, custom, usage, or regulation of any State or Territory, or by or under its authority, to the contrary notwithstanding.

Beyond doubt, that section forbids all discrimination between white citizens and citizens of color in respect to their right to vote; but the section does not provide that the person or officer making such discrimination shall be guilty of any offence, nor does it prescribe that the person or officer guilty of making such discrimination shall be subject to any fine, penalty, or punishment whatever.

The election officials were indicted in federal court under Sections 2 and 3 of the Enforcement Act of 1870. Section 2 required that administrative preliminaries to elections be conducted without regard to race, color, or previous condition of servitude, while Section 3 forbade wrongful refusal to register votes where a prerequisite step "required as aforesaid" had been omitted. The ruling held that Section 3 was unenforceable because it did not specifically use the terms "race," "color," or "previous condition of servitude." The Fifteenth Amendment stated that the right to vote would "not be denied or abridged by the United States or any State," but made no mention about protecting that right from individuals who denied others the right to vote. The Court ruled that the Enforcement Act was still valid at the federal level, but had no authority as far as state or local elections.

The ruling held that all the Fifteenth Amendment did was prevent exclusion from voting specifically on racial grounds. The result of the decision was that states were free to develop literacy tests, grandfather clauses, **poll taxes**, and other means to disenfranchise blacks as long as they did not specifically list race as a reason for denying the vote. The *Reese* decision, along with *U.S. v. Cruikshank*, effectively ended any remaining chance that **Reconstruction** would result in a biracial society, or at least one where blacks would be able to participate in the political process. Following *Reese*, Mississippi led the South in developing a host of requirements for voting, which while they did not specifically mention skin color, had the intended result of disenfranchising most blacks and very few whites.*See also* Mississippi Plan; *Plessy v. Ferguson*.

Further Readings: Goldman, Robert M. *Reconstruction and Black Suffrage: Losing the Vote in Reese and Cruikshank*. Lawrence: University Press of Kansas, 2001; Kahn, Ronald, and Ken I. Kersch. *The Supreme Court and American Political Development*. Lawrence: University Press of Kansas, 2006; Kersch, Ken I. *Constructing Civil Liberties: Discontinuities in the Development of American Constitutional Law*. New York: Cambridge University Press, 2004.

Barry M. Stentiford

Universal Negro Improvement Association (UNIA)

The Universal Negro Improvement Association was founded and led by **Marcus Garvey**, a Pan-African nationalist, and it became the largest black organization in American history, with millions of followers and tens of thousand of members across the United States. The UNIA enabled Garvey to become one of the most important black leaders of the 1920s. Indeed, one cannot understand the significance of the UNIA without understanding Garvey. Garvey's passion and charisma, along with his message that blacks should help themselves, unite with one another, and reject integration, caused many other black leaders, such as **W.E.B. Du Bois**, to revile Garvey, while Garvey's supporters admired him and worked tirelessly for the UNIA.

Marcus Garvey was born on August 17, 1887, in St Ann's Bay, Jamaica, a British colony at that time. He worked as an apprentice printer and witnessed the terrible living and working conditions on the island as well as the nature of colonial rule and racism. In 1911, he moved to England, where he met African intellectuals and read widely about African history and culture. This motivated Garvey to work for the advancement of all people of African descent, in Africa and the Americas. When he returned to Jamaica in 1914, he founded the Universal Negro Improvement and Conservation Association and African Communities League. Garvey admired the work of **Booker T. Washington**, particularly Washington's focus on building up the wealth and skills of the black community, and therefore he hoped to develop a trade school along the lines of Tuskegee. However, he found limited opportunities in Jamaica.

With problems mounting in Jamaica, Garvey left for the United States in 1916, as part of an influx of Caribbean immigrants to urban areas, in particular New York City. Garvey decided to tour the United States to speak on black pride and how to restore black greatness—on this tour, he became an amazing orator that captivated all who listened. His message found a receptive audience in black communities facing economic dislocation, racism, segregation and disfranchisement at the height of **Jim Crow**. He organized the first U.S. branch of the UNIA in 1917, and began to publish the *Negro World,* which articulated his **Black Nationalist** ideas and informed readers about the activities of the UNIA. Garvey set up his UNIA headquarters in Harlem, New York City, the home to a new and emerging black disaffected and urban working class.

From his office in New York, Garvey pushed for a back-to-Africa movement, and an Africa free from European colonial rule; a cause he passionately pursued all his life. As a result, he became the most popular black leader in the United States, and the UNIA mushroomed in size, with scores of local chapters throughout the nation. The pageantry and titles of the UNIA also attracted followers in droves. For example, the African Legionaries and Black Cross Nurses in splendid garb marched through the streets on Harlem in a show of black pride—the like of which had never been seen before. But the UNIA was more than just image; it had a real message and agenda. The UNIA focused on the goals of economic advancement and the uniting of all people of African descent. The UNIA funded many black businesses and provided loans and insurances to developing a community. The UNIA certainly invested their money in their mission. For example, evidence survives of dozens of UNIA-funded grocery stores, restaurants, laundries, printing presses, factories, and the like. These businesses served as symbols of black progress but also provided jobs, incomes, and opportunities. The center of UNIA activity was in Harlem, but in cities across the United States, the UNIA owned similar facilities. Thus the UNIA uplifted many African Americans, men and women, and it gave African Americans the belief in their own abilities, and this led to self-help.

UNIA was so successful in part because of Garvey, but there was more to it than that. Timing was a major contributor to the success of the UNIA. The prophet of self-help for African Americans, Booker T. Washington, had died in 1915 and the recently formed National Association for the Advancement of Colored People (NAACP) and the Urban League could not fill the void at that time. The UNIA preached self-help and provided a practical agenda for everyday black men and women to succeed. In addition, after **World War I**, African Americans wanted a new type of country and better conditions; millions had recently moved North in the **Great Migration**, and they needed a leader and an organization that represented them and their aspirations. The UNIA would provide this and much more.

Scholars have debated who joined the UNIA in the United States. From the evidence, it is clear that the membership fell into two categories. There was a cadre of leaders with experience and a history of organizing. Perhaps the most famous was Thomas Fortune, an editor, activist, and ally of Booker T. Washington. Other black leaders from the intelligentsia also became leaders, such as Henrietta Vinton Davies. In addition, many black religious leaders also joined and held prominent positions in the UNIA. Not surprisingly, perhaps, a vast number of local leaders were from the **Caribbean**. The rank and file of the UNIA is also fascinating. All the members (and leaders) were black; there were no white members (as in the case of the NAACP). Most were Americans, and it seems that most were determined to improve their lives. In fact, many were small businessmen, hard-working laborers, and young people who wanted to do well and had determination and belief in self-help and black power. One scholar successfully argues that many of the members or followers of the UNIA were first-generation, Southern-born African Americans living in the urban North. Men and women joined in huge numbers. It is true that the UNIA was rather masculine and somewhat sexist, though for its time, this was not that unusual. However, many women held local leadership positions and played key roles in campaigns, organizing, and recruitment. Women joined in large numbers and worked hard to make the UNIA a success.

In the past, historians have suggested that the UNIA was more dominant in the North than the South of the United States. However, a recent study of black political struggle plausibly argues that in fact the majority the UNIA was located in the South in rural areas and small towns. Over half of the local UNIA divisions were in the South, with **Louisiana** having the most divisions in the South. Although major cities such as New Orleans, Atlanta, and Raleigh had significant UNIA activity, the small towns of the South witnessed the most activity. The UNIA's *The Negro World* was widely circulated in the South and local organizers became radicalized. Many of the organizers and followers of the UNIA in the South would become activists in the modern **Civil Rights Movement** of the 1950s and 1960s.

Garvey was a charismatic leader, but a poor businessman. Although the UNIA provided thousands of jobs to poor blacks and set up many businesses (black owned and operated) several of the UNIA's ambitious programs failed. For example, in 1919, Garvey purchased three ships and developed the Black Star Steamship Line, selling stock to African Americans, as a symbol of black power. The line failed due to high costs and mismanagement. In the early 1920s, Garvey sought to work with the Liberian government to settle African Americans there, but this also ultimately failed. Garvey also hoped to get the League of Nations to grant the UNIA possession of the former German colony of Tangaruka. This failed too, not least because the European colonial powers could not allow an independent black nation in Africa. As a result the Pan-Africanist agenda of the UNIA did not succeed in a material sense. Through it all, however, Garvey's adherence to **Black Nationalism,** Pan-Africanism and pro-working class aspirations, made him a hero to his followers.

The UNIA's relationship with other black organizations at the time was very tense. Garvey and other leaders of the UNIA dismissed the work of the NAACP as too narrow and controlled by whites, and Garvey believed that integration was a fool's errand. Indeed, the UNIA did not build alliances with other black organizations and black leaders. The philosophy and political approach of the UNIA was too different to the NAACP and the Urban League, for example. W.E.B. Du Bois despised Garvey and opposed the UNIA (though late in his life, Du Bois adopted many of the tenants of Black Nationalism). **A. Philip Randolph,** a key black leader in Harlem, saw Garvey as a fool. Garvey and the UNIA responded in kind, and the divisions within the black leadership did not help the plight of everyday African Americans, but it does illustrate the gamut of opinion on how to solve the problems of Jim Crow, racism, and political powerlessness.

As Garvey's power and prestige increased and the number of the UNIA's adherents swelled, the U.S. government worried about Garvey's influence and the radicalism of the UNIA as it empowered a restless black urban population, along with disgruntled black intellectuals. Thus, the **federal government** sought to discredit Garvey and smash the UNIA. A young J. Edgar Hoover masterminded the campaign to destroy Garvey and the UNIA. Garvey was arrested on mail fraud charges and was convicted and sentenced to five years in jail in 1925. Without their magnetic leader, the UNIA declined rapidly into a shell of its former self. For example, the businesses owned by the UNIA closed, and much of its property was sold. There was no leader to take over from Garvey; he *was* the UNIA. Although President Calvin Coolidge commuted Garvey's sentence in 1927, he was deported back to Jamaica (he was never a U.S. citizen). He left a hero to many African Americans. In Jamaica, Garvey tried to continue the work of the UNIA, but the old magic was lost. In 1935, he left for Great Britain, where he died in 1940 a broken man.

In his lifetime, Garvey worked tirelessly for the equal rights of people of African descent, and he dismissed the idea of integration. He saw the struggle for equality in the United States as only part of the problem facing people of color. The UNIA made a huge difference in the lives of African Americans, particularly the poor. The UNIA empowered blacks, helped the poor with various social programs, and rejected racism and integration. The UNIA was radical with a far-reaching and transformative agenda. In Pan-Africanism, Garvey and the UNIA hoped to unite a mass world movement to liberate Africans from European and white control. In this endeavor, the UNIA failed. However, the legacy of the UNIA and Garvey is crucial. He provided hope and inspiration to a more militant group of younger blacks. In the 1960s, he became an icon to **Malcolm X,** the black power movement, and the independence movements in the Caribbean and Africa.

Further Readings: Burkett, Randall. *Gareyism as a Religious Movement: The Institutionalization of a Black Civil Religion.* Metuchen, NJ: Scarecrow Press, 1978; Cronon, E.

David. *Black Moses: The Story of Marcus Garvey and the Universal Negro Improvement Association.* Madison: University of Wisconsin Press, 1955; Garvey, Marcus. *Philosophy and Opinions of Marcus Garvey.* New York: Atheneum, 1969; Hahn, Steven. *A Nation Under Our Feet: Black Political Struggles in the Rural South from Slavery to the Great Migration.* Cambridge, MA: Harvard University Press, 2003; Stein, Judith. *The World of Marcus Garvey: Race and Class in a Modern Society.* Baton Rouge: Louisiana State University Press, 1991.

James M. Beeby

V

Van Der Zee, James (1886–1983)

James Augustus Joseph Van Der Zee was a noted Harlem photographer who was "discovered" through New York City's 1967 Metropolitan Museum of Art exhibition, *Harlem on My Mind: Cultural Capital of Black America, 1908–1968*. His artistic and sometimes romanticized images are noted for the dignity and pride emanating from the sitters, whether the rich and famous or the average Harlem resident. Plus, the photographs have historic significance. Although self-taught and regularly conversing with only one other photographer, Van Der Zee's creatively posed images seemed to capture the essence of the subject. He amassed probably the most important collection of African American photographs of the early twentieth century.

Born in Lenox, Massachusetts, to parents who were maid and butler to ex-president Ulysses S. Grant and his wife when they lived in New York City, Van Der Zee and his brothers also assisted their father when he became a sexton in Lenox. While a teenager, he bought his first camera and began to practice photography, already demonstrating his artistic skills. Those early photos from Massachusetts, **Virginia**, and New York also display his understanding on the use of light.

After moving to New York in 1907, Van Der Zee worked as a waiter and violinist; he later played with Fletcher Henderson's Orchestra and became first violinist in the John Wannamaker Orchestra. In 1907, he married Kate Brown, but the marriage ended in divorce after eight years because she wanted him to end his involvement in photography and obtain a more secure position for them and their child. "The Picture Takin' Man" opened his first studio in Harlem, Guarantee Photos on West 135th Street in 1915, with Gaynella Greenlee Katz, a telephone operator whom he married the following year. For over 50 years with her support, he captured thousands of images of the Harlem community, mostly at the G.G.G. studio on Lenox Avenue to which he moved in 1942.

Besides photographing the likes of boxer **Jack Johnson**, Bill "Bojangles" Robinson, Paul Robeson, Adam Clayton Powell, Sr., Florence Mills, and Countee Cullen, he also took pictures ranging from tasteful nudes to community groups such as the Black Jews of Harlem. He was also **Marcus Garvey**'s personal photographer, thoroughly documenting his famous 1924 convention, for instance. Another aspect of his business was photographing the dead at funeral parlors or churches, a common practice at the time so that the family could send the images to relatives in various parts of the country. Toni Morrison's novel *Jazz* (1992) was influenced by one of the images that she saw in *The Harlem Book of the Dead.*

Van Der Zee painted his own backdrops to enhance his images. He also used a double-printing technique, combining two photographs to show what a person might be dreaming or thinking. The technique was not new to photography, but was one that he discovered independently. Some of his photographs exhibit humor, such as a seemingly formal portrait of a woman sitting in a rocking chair ("Undeclared War"). However, when one notices the time on the clock and the old flat irons and dishes by the side of the chair, the implication is that she is waiting for her husband to come and the items are to throw at him, if need be. Other effects that Van Der Zee used in his photographs included adding smoke to cigarettes, touching up wrinkles and hairlines, and doing whatever he could to enhance his sitters. His goal was to add dignity and beauty to the clients in an era in which blacks were still fighting for basic human rights.

It was the *Harlem on My Mind* exhibit that brought national fame to Van Der Zee. By the late 1960s, Van Der Zee stopped photographing but in 1980, he began working again. Gaynella died in 1976, and in 1978, he married Donna Mussendon, who coaxed him out of retirement. At age 86 and still using the heavy 8 x 10 and 5 x 7 view cameras and later confined to a wheelchair, he photographed notables such as Bill Cosby, **Muhammad Ali**, and Cicely Tyson. The style of the images reflected that of his earlier works and he also used some of the same props. James Van Der Zee died in Washington, DC, following the receipt of his third honorary doctorate from Howard University. He was 96 years old.

Both the National Portrait Gallery in Washington, DC, and the Howard Greenberg Gallery in New York hung an individual exhibition of Van Der Zee's works, titled *Retrospective,* in 1994. Among his acknowledgments are honorary doctorates from Seton Hall University (1976), Haverford College (1980), and Howard University (1983). Other professional awards include the American Society of Magazine Photographers Award (1969), Life Fellowship at the Metropolitan Museum of Art (1979), the first Pierre Toussaint Award (1978), the International Black Photographers Award (1979), and the Living Legend Award (1979). The U.S. Postal Service honored him with a postage stamp.

Further Readings and Viewings: Bey, Dewoud, and Colin Westerbek, eds. *James Van Der Zee: The Studio.* Chicago: The Art Institute of Chicago, 2004; De Cock, Liliane, and Reginald McGhee. *James Van Der Zee.* Dobbs Ferry, NY: Morgan and Morgan, 1973; Haskins, James. *James Van Der Zee: The Picture Takin' Man.* New York: Dodd Mead and Company, 1979. Reprint, Trenton, NJ: Africa World Press, 1991; McGhee, Reginald, comp. *The World of James Van Der Zee: A Visual Record of Black Americans.* New York: Grove Press, 1969; Schoener, Allon, ed. *Harlem on My Mind: Cultural Capital of Black America, 1900–1968.* New York: Dell, 1979. Reprint, New Press, 2007; *Uncommon Images: The Harlem of James Van Der Zee.* Motion picture, directed by Evelyn Barron, Filmakers Library. 22 min. 1977; Van Der Zee, James, Owen Dodson, and Camille Billops.

The Harlem Book of the Dead. Dobbs Ferry, NY: Morgan and Morgan, 1978; Van Der Zee, James. *James Van Der Zee, Photographer: A Traveling Exhibition of Photographs by James Van Der Zee.* New York: James Van Der Zee Institute, 1972; Willis-Braithwaite, Deborah, Rodger C. Birt, and James Van Der Zee. *Van Der Zee: Photographer, 1886–1983.* New York: Harry N. Abrams, 1998.

George H. Junne, Jr.

Veterans Groups

Veterans groups are voluntary fraternal organizations whose members shared a common experience of serving in the U.S. **armed forces,** usually, but not always, during wartime. Until the latter half of the twentieth century, most veterans' groups were segregated, although in some areas outside of the South where blacks were relatively few, black veterans were often allowed to join, either officially or unofficially. In areas with larger black populations, black veterans formed their own groups, although such black groups were usually chapters of larger white-dominated organizations.

During the **Jim Crow** era, the very existence of the black veteran had often been denied, in that the image of the American soldier during wartime shown in movies and books was of a white man. Black participation was usually mildly celebrated during wartime, but forgotten and denied after the fighting ended. As serving in the military has historically been tied to the concept of the citizen, and thus the obligation to serve was often linked to the right to vote, the denial or denigration of black military service was a cornerstone in upholding Jim Crow. In general, veterans groups followed the practice of the U.S. military in that they allowed blacks to join, but segregated them into separate chapters or posts, reserving all state and national leadership positions to white men. Only when the military itself began integrating, albeit slowly, did veterans organizations begin integrating.

American military veterans have formed formal and informal groups since colonial times, but the latter half of the nineteenth century saw the rise of large politically active groups of veterans groups, notably the Grand Army of the Republic (GAR), composed of Union veterans from the Civil War. The GAR remained a conservative political voice in the North until age thinned its ranks into oblivion around the end of **World War I.** As the Union army was by the last year of the Civil War almost 10 percent black, and the Union navy in general had black sailors as part of the crews on warships, the potential for black membership in the GAR was high. However, many blacks who served in Union forces in the Civil War came from the South, and many returned to the South following the war, where GAR chapters did not exist. Additionally, in some areas, white veterans did not allow blacks to join the local GAR post. The very low membership of black veterans in the GAR worked against the development of separate GAR chapters for black members. Some chapters, particularly in areas that had been strongholds of abolitionist sentiment before and during the war, occasionally had one or two black members.

Conversely, Confederate veterans groups by the turn of the century increasingly sought to publicize black participation in the Confederate armies, in order to support the post-**Reconstruction** reinterpretation that slavery had played a minuscule part in causing the war. Some Confederate veterans groups thus maintained an ambivalent stance toward black Confederate veterans, publicizing their existence to the North to refute Northern claims that the South fought to defend slavery, yet at the same time Southern whites denied that blacks had earned the right to exercise their political rights through their service in the Civil War. However, as black participation in the Confederate armies had been minuscule, the black veterans who did exist were more of a novelty to most of the South.

The mass participation in the military during the wars of the twentieth century led to a new flowering of veterans organizations. Prior to World War I, veterans organizations were normally for veterans of a particular war. However, the twentieth century saw the creation of large veterans organizations, reflecting the mass involvement in war that characterized much of the century. The new veterans organizations created in the twentieth century varied in requirements for membership. The American Legion was the broadest, accepting veterans from any branch of the military, regardless of whether the veteran served in war or peace, or if the veteran had volunteered for military service or been drafted. The Veterans of Foreign Wars (VFW) was more selective, requiring members to have served in combat. Black chapters of these larger organizations began within a few years of their formation. The American Legion began granting charters to black posts in the 1920s. Part of the justification for granting charters to black posts came from the self-images of the American Legion, that it spoke for all veterans and was thus the main voice to lobby Congress regarding veterans' issues. Since all veterans, black or white, benefitted from the activities of the American Legion, then black veterans should share part of the financial burden of supporting the Legion's efforts through their dues.

Veterans organizations played several roles in society. Foremost, they gave veterans an opportunity to gather with others who had shared a similar life experience. At the same, their collective voice gave veterans more power in society than they had since the decades after the Civil War. However, veterans organizations tended to follow the Jim Crow practices that existed in the military, and thus most major veterans organizations such as the American Legion and the VFW had separate chapters for black veterans. Only during the 1960s and 1970s would individual chapters drop the color bar. *See also* World War II.

Further Readings: Edgerton, Robert B., *Hidden Heroism: Black Soldiers in America's Wars* Boulder, CO: Westview Press, 2001; Mason, Herbert Malloy, Jr. *VFW: Our First Century*. Lenexa, KS: Addax Publishing Group, 1999; Rumer, Thomas. *The American Legion: An Official History, 1919–1989*. New York: M. Evans and Co., 1990; Severo, Richard, and Lewis Milfords. *The Wages of War: When America's Soldiers Came Home: From Valley Forge to Vietnam*. New York: Simon & Schuster, 1989.

Barry M. Stentiford

Virginia

During the **Jim Crow** era, the Commonwealth of Virginia, an Upper South state, had some of the strictest laws in the nation that kept nonwhites subordinated to whites. Additionally, Virginia led the nation in its anti**misce-genation** laws and in its zealous pioneering efforts at eugenics. The state was also the scene of some of the key events in the **Civil Rights Movement**, which led to the disestablishment of Jim Crow.

Virginia had been the birthplace of black **slavery** in the United States, and as a colony and into the federal period, Virginia slave owners made much of their wealth exporting surplus slaves for an expanding national market. Laws from the 1830s required emancipated blacks to leave the state within one year of graining their freedom. The Virginia slave code went beyond that of most slave states, forbidding conversion to Christianity as grounds for granting freedom to slaves. Slaveowners had no legal liability for causing the death of their slaves, either by accident or intentionally. Fearing that literacy in part tended to lead to slave rebellions, the act of teaching a slave to read became a crime.

Following the Civil War and **Reconstruction**, Virginia followed the **Mississippi Plan** to deprive blacks of the right to vote, mainly using poll taxes and property qualifications, which also tended to disenfranchise poor whites. Virginia also used understanding tests, in which an election official would ask the potential registrant to explain a given passage in the Constitution. Usually, the responses of blacks were judged to be insufficient to allow the black person to register to vote.

Virginia's real pioneering efforts were in eugenics, the pseudoscience of improving the population by preventing those deemed "less fit" from reproducing. Its Racial Integrity Act of 1924 required that each child born in the state be assigned to a racial category, and its defining racial characteristics described. The act also specifically outlawed marriages between white and nonwhite persons. Virginia's law went further in this respect than similar laws in other states, in that Virginia made the state of marriage itself a crime if it was between a white and a nonwhite person. Thus, an interracial couple legally married in New York could be arrested if they came to Virginia. Most states with similar laws simply refused to issue marriage licenses to couples of different "races." Virginia also in 1924 passed the Sterilization Act, allowing the state to sterilize anyone deemed "unfit." The law fell hardest on poor uneducated whites and nonwhites who were institutionalized. Virginia's eugenics policies were upheld by the **U.S. Supreme Court** in 1924 in the *Buck v. Bell* ruling, which held that the state had a vested interest in preventing those found mentally deficient from reproducing. Virginia's eugenics program would later be the model for similar programs created by the Nazi Party in Germany in the 1930s.

The linkage of Virginia's antimiscegenation law and its sterilization law stemmed from the work of Professors Arthur Estabrook and Ivan McDougle, who published a deeply flawed 1924 study of a mixed population near Lynchburg of what they termed the "WIN" tribe, which stood for "White, Indian, and Negro." According to Estabrook and McDougle, throughout history, whenever white populations lived for long periods with blacks, the result was the "mongrelization" of the whites, and the decline of society. The heavily biased study concluded that mixed-race persons inherited the "worst" traits of each parent stock, and thus allowing mixed-race people to be created was to be prevented using the full power of the state. Virginia had little interest in preventing the interbreeding of various nonwhite peoples, and state laws specifically applied only to preventing white and nonwhite mixing.

Despite this fear of racial mixing, and Virginia's strict racial classification laws, where the "**one-drop rule**" prevailed, as opposed to the one-eighth rule that was more common in the South, a notable exception was enshrined in Virginia law. Most of the so-called First Families of Virginia claimed descent from the Powhatan Pocahontas from her marriage to John Rolfe. To accommodate these families, many of whom were prominent politically or economically, the law declared that persons who were one-sixteenth or less of Indian descent, and otherwise white, were to be considered 100 percent white under Virginia law.

In the years after **World War II**, Virginia's Jim Crow laws came under increasing pressure from several sources. The massive expansion of the **federal government** under the New Deal and especially during the war had led to enormous growth in the northeast part of the state, directly across the Potomac from Washington. Many of the state's new residents were from outside the south and far less inclined to support overt discrimination. Additionally, the State Department put specific pressure on Maryland and Virginia to abolish racial discrimination, at least in the areas around Washington, as they created international difficulties for the United States in trying to bring newly emerging African nations into alliances with the United States and a rejection of the Soviet bloc. However, Virginia politicians, backed by politicians throughout the South, proved unsympathetic to State Department difficulties, and took no immediate actions to lessen at least the more obvious signs of Jim Crow.

Virginia's strict enforcement of Jim Crow led to two important legal challenges that would lead to great victories in abolishing the entire system. In a case that began when a black Virginia woman traveling to Maryland was arrested in 1944 for refusing to get to the back of a Greyhound bus, the U.S. Supreme Court ruled in *Irene Morgan v. Commonwealth of Virginia* (1946), that racial segregation of bus passengers in interstate travel was unlawful. In 1960, the Court extended the ruling in *Boynton v. Virginia*, which outlawed segregated waiting rooms and other facilities for passengers at bus terminals serving bus lines involved in interstate travel.

Other Jim Crow laws in Virginia would provide fodder for other legal challenges to legalized discrimination. The 1954 **Brown v. Board of Education** case was based in part on the earlier *Davis v. Prince Edwards County School Board, Virginia* case, which was filed by National Association for the Advancement of Colored People (NAACP) attorneys. The Davis case began in 1951 out of student protest against the disparities between spending on white and black public school in Virginia.

Following the *Brown* decision, Governor Thomas B. Stanley announced that Virginia would resist integration of its public schools. He then formed the all-white **Gray Commission**, ostensibly to study the impact of the *Brown* decision, but in reality to attempt to avoid implementing it. Its chairman and namesake, **Garland Gray**, was a staunch segregationist. Five years after *Brown*, few school districts were integrated. Some Virginia counties closed their public schools rather than integrate. This tactic was ruled unconstitutional in the 1964 U.S. Supreme Court ruling of *Griffin v. School Board of Prince Edward County, Virginia.*

A legal challenge to Virginia's strict anti-interracial marriage law ended with the nullification of all such state laws nationwide. The 1967 U.S. Supreme Court ruling in *Loving v. Virginia* held that all state laws banning interracial marriages were unconstitutional. In the ruling, Chief Justice Warren noted "the fact that Virginia prohibits only interracial marriages involving white persons demonstrates that the racial classifications . . . [were] measures designed to maintain White Supremacy." Thus the very extreme nature of Virginia's law helped abolish all such laws nationwide. *See also* Cold War.

Further Readings: Heinemann, Ronald L. *Old Dominion, New Commonwealth: A History of Virginia, 1607–2007.* Charlottesville: University of Virginia Press, 2007; Smith, J. Douglas. *Managing White Supremacy: Race, Politics, and Citizenship in Jim Crow Virginia.* Columbia: University of South Carolina Press, 2001; Wallenstein, Peter. *Cradle of America: Four Centuries of Virginia History.* Lawrence: University Press of Kansas, 2007.

Barry M. Stentiford

Vocational Education

Vocational education, also known as industrial education or curriculum, has, for hundreds of years, provided black Americans with technical and ideological training to replicate and accept their low-wage and servant-class status. Courses in schools at every educational level throughout the nation trained the sons and daughters of slavery as manual laborers, janitors, chauffeurs, laundresses, servants, cooks, maids, porters and bellmen. To "civilize" and control, rather than allow for upward mobility, schools, in both the North and South, before and after the Civil War, subjected blacks to vocational education. Institutionalized by **Booker T. Washington** and like-minded white philanthropists, vocational education became the predominant method of educating blacks through the civil rights period in America with a legacy that continues into present-day segregated schools.

Schools employing vocational education trained blacks for "Negro jobs," those that working-class whites eschewed to move up the socioeconomic ladder. Manual labor, rather than scholarship, defined educational excellence as administrators self-consciously and intentionally provided blacks with very different educational courses than those experienced by whites in America's newly developing public education system. This curriculum has resulted in generations of blacks trained to constitute a docile industrial caste of semi- and low-skilled workers.

Throughout the South, in all forms of education, from elementary and secondary to college, the primary form of education that most blacks received was vocational education. Promoted by General Samuel Chapman Armstrong, founder of Hampton Institute, Booker T. Washington, his mentee, carried on the tradition at Tuskegee Institute. Perceived as the black community's spokesman and voice of authority on educational issues, Washington preached to educational experts nationally to ensure that the burgeoning education being made available to blacks would be vocational.

Guiding this philosophy was Washington's 1895 proclamation, known as the **Atlanta Compromise**. In this highly-publicized speech at the World's Fair, Washington advised the sons and daughters of slaves to be as separate as the fingers on the hand and to cast down ones buckets where they stood to "dignify and glorify common labor." Washington believed that blacks should be trained to excel in the jobs to which they were allotted by whites prior to moving up the social, political, and economic ladder. In these low-skill jobs reminiscent of slavery, Washington advised African Americans to be patient, thrifty, and industrious so that whites would see their diligence and allow them to move up. Industrial education, according to Washington, would promote blacks' achievement within a strict **Jim Crow** system rather than challenge a system which forbid blacks from many occupations, particularly the professions. As such, vocational curriculum promoted the values of Jim Crow laws and perpetuated black citizens' second-class status by training them not only to fulfill but also to accept and validate their menial roles within society.

Elementary and Secondary Education

In the post-**Reconstruction** South through the Civil Rights era, most black children received only the most rudimentary education. School boards and local governments refused to fund public education for black children, instead using blacks' taxes to build schools for white children. Many black parents worked hard to educate their children by contributing funds from their minimal incomes to build schools and hire teachers, but their efforts were often thwarted by the **Ku Klux Klan** and other vigilantes by destroying schools and scaring away teachers. While many children and parents believed in the transformative value of education for social and economic improvement, few children attended school for longer than three or four months a year (so that they could aid their parents in sharecropping) or for more than four years. The schools they attended were often located miles away from home, with no transportation besides their poorly shoed feet, in one-room, drafty buildings with dozens of other children of all ages, and a teacher often with little more education than the oldest in the room. As a result, blacks in the South were disastrously uneducated compared with their Northern counterparts, both black and white.

Two historical forces combined to generate thousands of schools in the South for those who clearly needed them, but which also institutionalized vocational education throughout the land. First, nearly abandoned by the defunct Freedmen's Bureau, Southern blacks were desperate for education. Second, a generation of wealth built through America's industrial revolution that saw the rise in a variety of industries, from oil and steel to retail and railroads, found largely Northern white men with philanthropic ideologies seeking worthwhile causes. Believing in the need of training blacks for their own industries and enterprises (though at the lowest level) while simultaneously using their finances for a philanthropic cause, many Northern white philanthropists were attracted to possibilities of building schools and financing teachers, provided that they subscribed to their philosophies.

After Reconstruction, philanthropists stepped into the void created by the Freedman's Bureau's departure and changed the educational landscape for Southern blacks. Many of these men viewed black education as misguided missionary work and set out to train millions of black youth to fulfill their role as menial laborers in the growing industrial economy. The largest donor to these schools was Julius Rosenwald (founder of Sears) who served on the Board of Directors of Tuskegee. Consulting with Washington, Rosenwald donated funds to build nearly 5,000 schools. Although providing schools to many children who otherwise would have been without education, the ideology employed in many of these schools largely replicated the racial hierarchy by ensuring that students attending them would be unable to pursue higher education. Indeed, many philanthropists forbid headmasters from employing a liberal arts curriculum in common schools.

In these schools, vocational education taught black students to be productive and obedient servants, rather than productive citizens. Children learned basic writing and math skills with limited vocabularies. Insufficient desks, pencils, papers, and books were supplemented with a wide variety of tools, such as cooking utensils, gardening tools, and cleaning supplies, necessary for children preparing to enter the servant class. A notable absence in the curriculum of the larger schools is the lack of required academic core curriculum. Many floor plans find not a single room devoted to academic endeavors, but sufficient space for barbering, janitoring, hairdressing, laundries, and rooms for learning how to be a maid. For many children attending these schools, the highest profession to which they could aspire was teaching nonacademic curriculum in the same low-quality schools to which they were subject.

Both children and their parents critiqued this curricular emphasis given their desire to improve their opportunities through education. Students, in particular, sought education that would transcend their parents' daily lives of oppression through menial jobs and transform them into students prepared for higher education and white-collar professions. Therefore, parents counseled their children against enrollment in industrial courses, especially avoiding majoring in this curriculum, and instead encouraged them to take "elective" academic courses.

Although designed for widespread Southern implementation, local black leaders, teachers, and a small number of progressive whites believing in the value of academic education for the black community subverted the emphasis on vocational education. **W.E.B. Du Bois** was a particularly vocal critic of vocational education who recognized the insidious effects that this curriculum would have on generations of black youth and their potential to develop their intellects to the best of their abilities, move out of the segregated caste system in which they were embedded, and integrate into America's social and economic community. Though often required to submit reports to the funding sources, teachers and black leaders nevertheless worked hard to instill their schools with a liberal arts curriculum, hire teachers well-trained for this curriculum, and produce students who could compete with their white counterparts. Particularly in large cities with large populations of black students, educators created academically rigorous learning environments for their students that nurtured both their minds and their spirits by instilling in them a knowledge of black history and culture. These schools, though they received considerably less funding than those of whites, succeeded in fostering a sense of community, as teachers nurtured African American children and provided them with safe spaces to learn, express their ideas, and develop the tools necessary to survive in a white world.

Vocational education was not just reserved for blacks in Southern schools. In Northern schools, as in the South, black students in segregated schools and in segregated classes within integrated schools were trained to be servants, washerwomen, cooks, bellhops and elevator operators in white-owned homes and businesses. In cities such as Newark, Philadelphia, Boston and New York City, African American children received separate and inferior education similar to that of their Southern counterparts. Interestingly, this vocational training in the North was similar to that received by racialized European immigrants in many urban centers as well. In larger cities, boys and girls often attended sex-segregated junior and senior high schools were young women were taught to cook, sew, and clean while boys were taught to polish shoes, work an elevator, and the most efficient ways to carry luggage. For example, in New York City during the 1950s, the Board of Education assigned white children to academic high schools where they learned subjects necessary for a college entrance diploma, but sent blacks to vocational high schools where they learned to be servants and earned a high school certificate. This was little more than an attendance certificate and did not meet college admission requirements, thereby producing the same underclass of workers prepared only for the lowest-skilled jobs in urban areas.

Therefore, in both the rural South and urban North, blacks attended segregated, underfunded, and academically lacking schools for nearly 80 years prior to efforts to change schools and their curriculum through integration following the landmark 1954 *Brown v. Board of Education* decision. As schools for Southern white students improved, those for blacks remained in the same impoverished conditions as they had been in the years immediately following slavery. Drafty and rundown, these schools served only to reproduce the social hierarchy in the South by failing to upgrade curriculum during and after the World Wars and continuing to employ industrial education or teach students only the most basic skills. The differences between black and white students widened as high schools were built for white students in areas far from where the (mostly rural) black population lived.

College Level Vocational Education

At the college level, black education, with few exceptions (such as Morehouse, Howard, and Fisk) was similarly abysmal to that found in lower grades. Many colleges could not support or maintain sufficient professors, laboratory equipment, or libraries to provide students with an academically rigorous curriculum beyond the high school level. To improve their colleges financially, administrators collaborated with white philanthropists or state governments dedicated to blacks' political disenfranchisement and economic subordination. Colleges, particularly those including the words, "agricultural," "technical," and "mechanical" were often the only ones available to blacks. Indeed, many were developed by states required to provide black students with "**separate but equal**" education due to lawsuits challenging the lack of higher education for blacks and their unwillingness to desegregate more prestigious state schools due to the ruling racial ideology of the era.

Blacks attending these colleges learned rudimentary math and reading skills while engaging in trades to pay for their tuition, oftentimes constructing the very buildings in which they were to live and learn. Particularly problematic was that many trades students learned were outdated and of no practical use to these young students. For example, in some schools, black men learned how to make bricks by hand and then bake them out in the sun. However, mechanized brickmaking had already been invented as a more efficient way to make uniformly sized bricks, thereby making this training irrelevant. Others plowed fields with horses and oxen even as tractors and mechanized plows became commonplace. Teachers at these schools were also required to construct school buildings and work in the fields to provide role models of a hard work ethic and the value of hard labor for students.

Students were not taught the most technically skilled careers, such as training that would prepare them to become plumbers, electricians, or printers. Instead, they were trained to be apprentices. For example, in carpentry classes, rather than learning to build an entire house, students learned to make window sashes and frames but little else. These were intentional efforts by the schools to ensure that blacks were not trained to compete with whites for high-skill jobs and to maintain and justify a segregated labor force given the differences in skills. These efforts worked, as many graduates of Hampton in the late 1800s could be found working as porters and waiters.

Many attending schools such as Hampton protested the mediocre commitment to academic subjects and simultaneous exaltations to perform hard labor throughout much of the school year. Those in academic courses found themselves simply reviewing what they had learned in grade school, particularly those in the program of study to become teachers in Southern schools. Students demanded practical and technical training as to all, rather than just the most basic aspects, of the trades to ensure their ability to compete and acquire for jobs in local labor markets. *See also* Black Codes; Education; Historically Black Colleges and Universities.

Further Readings: Anderson, James D. *The Education of Blacks in the South, 1860–1935.* Chapel Hill: University of North Carolina Press, 1988; Kozol, Jonathan. *Shame of the Nation: The Restoration of Apartheid Schooling in America.* New York: Three Rivers Press, 2006; Tyack, David. *The One Best System: A History of American Urban Education.* Cambridge, MA: Harvard University Press, 1974; Watkins, William H. *The White Architects of Black Education: Ideology and Power in America, 1865–1954.* New York: Teachers College Press, 2001.

Melissa F. Weiner

Voting Rights Act of 1965

The Voting Rights Act of 1965 was passed on August 6, 1965, under the administration of President Lyndon B. Johnson. Its overall purpose was to outlaw the many discriminatory voting practices that were in put in place in Southern states following Reconstruction.

The act was passed in an attempt to uphold the intention of another edict ratified 95 years earlier: the Fifteenth Amendment to the U.S. Constitution. The amendment, adopted in 1870, was the first legislative action taken against "discrimination on the basis of race, color, or previous condition of slavery." As the attempted **Reconstruction** ended in failure, Southern states began to find ways to keep blacks from voting by using means that were not stated in the Fifteenth Amendment. State officials did this through violence, intimidation, and enacting **Jim Crow** laws that included literacy tests, poll taxes, and grandfather clauses that gave otherwise disqualified voters whose grandfathers voted the right to vote. The effect of putting racially motivated restrictions on the voting process ultimately prevented blacks from gaining any political and economic power.

In 1954, state-sponsored segregation in public schools was ruled unconstitutional in the *Brown v. Board of Education* case. The Civil Rights Act of 1964 and the Voting Rights Act eventually overruled any Jim Crow laws that were still in existence. Despite the fact that the Fifteenth Amendment was used to clarify and solidify voting rights, many Southern blacks and other minorities were still denied voting rights through the 1960s. By the mid-1960s, the rights of African Americans and other minorities in the United States was a matter of great importance within the American political system. Each month went by with more demonstrations, more rallies, and more violence towards them. The tipping point was an incident in Selma **Alabama**, when peaceful protestors were meaninglessly attacked by state troopers. President Johnson immediately began pressuring Congress more to generate civil rights legislation. Some of his goals were met when, in 1965, the Voting Rights Bill was passed.

Congress resolved that the antidiscrimination laws of the day were not strong enough to hold up against state officials who were reluctant to enforce the Fifteenth Amendment. This spurred legislative hearings that discovered how ineffective much of the legislation had been. Taking one discriminatory practice at a time made no difference—as soon as one biased practice was prohibited, a new tactic, which was not mentioned in any legislation, was instantly adopted.

The National Voting Rights Act of 1965 banned the idea that in order to be considered an eligible voter in the United States, one must first pass a literacy test. This also required for the federal registration of voters in regions that had less than 50 percent of eligible voters registered.

The act also gave the Department of Justice power to act on any unlawful voting practices. It now had jurisdiction over the registration process, changes in voting laws, and any "devices" that could be used to limit voting. The Voting Rights Act had an immediate impact on the empowerment of the African American population throughout the country by doing away with many of the restrictions that state laws had enacted. In 1966, the **U.S. Supreme Court** upheld the constitutionality of the Voting Rights Act, stating that "after enduring nearly a century of systematic resistance to the Fifteenth Amendment, Congress might do well to shift the advantage of time and inertia from the perpetrators of evil to its victims."

Excerpts from the Voting Rights Act of 1965, pp. 1, 3

Be it enacted by the Senate and House of Representatives of the United States of America in Congress assembled, That this Act shall be known as the "Voting Rights Act of 1965."

SEC. 2. No voting qualification or prerequisite to voting, or standard, practice, or procedure shall be imposed or applied by any State or political subdivision to deny or abridge the right of any citizen of the United States to vote on account of race or color.

SEC. 4. (a) To assure that the right of citizens of the United States to vote is not denied or abridged on account of race or color, no citizen shall be denied the right to vote in any Federal, State, or local election because of his failure to comply with any test or device in any State with respect to which the determinations have been made under subsection (b) or in any political subdivision with respect to which such determinations have been made as a separate unit, unless the United States District Court for the District of Columbia in an action for a declaratory judgment brought by such State or subdivision against the United States has determined that no such test or device has been used during the five years preceding the filing of the action for the purpose or with the effect of denying or abridging the right to vote on account of race or color: Provided, That no such declaratory judgment shall issue with respect to any plaintiff for a period of five years after the entry of a final judgment of any court of the United States, other than the denial of a declaratory judgment under this section, whether entered prior to or after the enactment of this Act, determining that denials or abridgments of the right to vote on account of race or color through the use of such tests or devices have occurred anywhere in the territory of such plaintiff. An action pursuant to this subsection shall be heard and determined by a court of three judges in accordance with the provisions of section 2284 of title 28 of the United States Code and any appeal shall lie to the Supreme Court. The court shall retain jurisdiction of any action pursuant to this subsection for five years after judgment and shall reopen the action upon motion of the Attorney General alleging that a test or device has been used for the purpose or with the effect of denying or abridging the right to vote on account of race or color.

If the Attorney General determines that he has no reason to believe that any such test or device has been used during the five years preceding the filing of the action for the purpose or with the effect of denying or abridging the right to vote on account of race or color, he shall consent to the entry of such judgment.

(b) The provisions of subsection (a) shall apply in any State or in any political subdivision of a state which (1) the Attorney General determines maintained on November 1, 1964, any test or device, and with respect to which (2) the Director of the Census determines that less than 50 percentum of the persons of voting age residing therein were registered on November 1, 1964, or that less than 50 percentum of such persons voted in the presidential election of November 1964.

A determination or certification of the Attorney General or of the Director of the Census under this section or under section 6 or section 13 shall not be reviewable in any court and shall be effective upon publication in the Federal Register.

(c) The phrase "test or device" shall mean any requirement that a person as a prerequisite for voting or registration for voting (1) demonstrate the ability to read, write, understand, or interpret any matter, (2) demonstrate any educational achievement or his knowledge of any particular subject, (3) possess good moral character, or (4) prove his qualifications by the voucher of registered voters or members of any other class.

Three months after the passing of the Voting Rights Act of 1965, nearly 8,000 African Americans had registered to vote in Dallas County, Alabama. Only months earlier, violence was used against peaceful demonstrators wanting nothing more than to be treated equally. In **Mississippi,** African American voter registration skyrocketed from 6.7 percent of the population prior to the enactment of the Voting Rights Act to 59.8 percent by 1967. The Voting Rights Act of 1965 also resulted in a huge increase of African American elected officials. According to the Joint Center for Political and Economic Studies, fewer than 1,500 blacks held elective office in 1970, compared to the current estimate of 9,000. Section Five of the act was interpreted very loosely by the Supreme Court until 1970, when Congress eventually decided that the Supreme Court's interpretations were too broad and hearings on the matter were held. The hearing testimonies were filled with examples of discriminatory practices. The testimonies made clear that on the local level, "gerrymandering, annexations, adoption of at-large elections, and other structural changes" were all loopholed through the national legislation. Furthermore, recognition of the same kinds of discrimination against other ethnic minority groups materialized in the hearings. Regardless, Congress ultimately validated the Supreme Court's position by extending the bill for 12 years.

The *White v. Regester* decision (412 U.S. 755 [1973]), shaped law through the 1970s against many unfair gerrymandered redistricting plans. It determined that some multimember districts were unconstitutionally being used to restrict the power of minority votes. Even in the twenty-first century, restrictions on ballet access and minority vote intensity remain as serious obstacles to voting rights. Such policies as last-minute location changes of heavily minority polling places, discouragement of non-English-speaking citizens from voting, the use of extremely confusing registration requirements, racially centered campaigning, and intimidation and violence all are discouragements and hindrances for many African Americans to be a part of the voting process.

The Voting Rights Act of 1965 undoubtedly empowered African Americans and other minority groups with the right to vote. It is also directly responsible for giving members of those communities a say in shaping the social and economic problems that have plagued them for so long, through local, state, and county elected officials. The Voting Rights Act of 1965 remains as a pivotal piece of American legislation and the fight for equality among races. It is a frontier peace of legislature in maintaining ideals of quality, fairness, and tolerance.

Certain provisions of the Voting Rights Act were set to expire in 2007. Congress responded and the Fannie Lou, Rosa Parks, and Coretta Scott King Voting Rights Act Reauthorization was signed for a 25-year extension by President George W. Bush on July 27, 2006. *See also* Civil Rights Act of 1964.

Further Readings: The Avalon Project. "Voting Rights Act of 1965. August 6, 1965." http://www.yale.edu/lawweb/avalon/statutes/voting_rights_1965.htm (accessed May 8, 2007); U.S. Department of Justice. "The Voting Rights Act of 1965." http://www.usdoj.gov/crt/voting/intro/intro_b.htm (accessed June 15, 2007).

Arthur Holst

W

Walker, Madam C. J. (1867–1919)

Madam Charles Joseph Walker was an African American beauty culture entrepreneur who came to prominence by successfully marketing her own brand of hair-care and **cosmetics** products designed and marketed specifically for black female consumers. Alongside the leading African American political figures of the early twentieth-century, **Booker T. Washington, W.E.B. Du Bois** and **Marcus Garvey**, Walker worked to encourage black pride and economic independence during an era of extreme white racial discrimination and limited opportunities for blacks. On her death, Madam Walker was the wealthiest African American woman in the United States, perhaps even the country's first black female millionaire.

Born during the turbulent aftermath of the Civil War, she was christened Sarah by her formerly enslaved parents, Owen and Minerva Breedlove. Her early years were ones of hardship, sorrow and struggle, growing up on a cotton plantation in the tiny village of Delta, **Louisiana** (directly across the Mississippi River from Vicksburg). The harsh and febrile environment of Delta orphaned Sarah at the age of six, when both her parents died in a yellow fever outbreak. She and her older sister Louvenia initially survived this calamity by working in the cotton fields, later moving to Vicksburg to work as domestic servants. Sarah was married to Moses McWilliams when she was 14 years old, had a daughter (A'Lelia) at age 19, and became a widow at age 20. Her second marriage to John Davis took place in 1894 and ended in 1903, at which point Sarah traveled to St. Louis where she labored as a laundrywoman and domestic, saving money to educate her daughter, as well as becoming involved with several charities and the African Methodist Episcopal Church.

Sarah began to experience hair loss in her mid-twenties, perhaps a physical symptom of her life's many tests and challenges. In response, she sought a relief by carrying out trials with assorted home remedies and popular medicines, such as ''Poro,'' a patented treatment marketed by another pioneering black female entrepreneur, Annie Turbo Malone. Evidently, Sarah experienced positive benefits from these hair and scalp treatments, as it was during this period that she also started to sell such products door-to-door as an agent for Malone. Following a move to Denver, Colorado, in 1905, she met and married Charles Joseph Walker. Charles Walker was a newspaper owner with a flair for marketing and with his help, and adopted initials, Sarah launched the Madam C. J. Walker Manufacturing Company.

To promote her brand of beauty products, such as Madam Walker's Wonderful Hair Grower, she and her husband embarked on an exhausting door-to-door sales drive throughout the country, giving demonstrations, and training sales agents. In 1910, Madam Walker moved her business headquarters to Indianapolis—then the country's largest manufacturing base and a key node in the national railroad network—and expanded the company's reach internationally to the **Caribbean**. Such was the success of the Walker Company, that by 1919 it was reported to have employed over 3,000 workers at the factory, with another 20,000 sales agents spread across the nation. Opening a Pittsburgh-based beauty training school in 1908, the Lelia College for Walker Hair Culturists, Walker helped create new economic opportunities for black women, at a time when, for many, **domestic work** or **sharecropping** was often the only alternative. Madam Walker's influence could also be felt in numerous black colleges throughout the South, where she had gained permission to install beauty parlors and promote the Walker system of hair preparation.

Madam Walker's business career was not without controversy. African American leaders, such as Washington and Garvey, were deeply opposed to the cosmetics industry on the grounds that its hair-straightening and skin-lightening products demeaned black people and promoted white standards of beauty. However, in marked contrast to the explicitly racist language and imagery seen in the advertisements of many white-owned cosmetics manufacturers, the Walker Company's marketing campaigns were highly effective in circulating positive images of black femininity and in fostering racial pride. As well as being a generous supporter of black colleges and charities, Madam Walker encouraged political activism in her employees. Following the **East St. Louis Riot of 1917**, she joined the campaign to have **lynching** made a federal crime and appeared as the keynote speaker at numerous National Association for the Advancement of Colored People (NAACP) fund-raisers on behalf of the antilynching effort.

Madam Walker died at the age of 52. Her daughter A'Lelia, who became a central figure in the **Harlem Renaissance**, succeeded her as president of the C. J. Walker Manufacturing Company. *See also* Cosmetics; Women.

Further Readings: Bundles, Alecia. *On Her Own Ground: The Life and Times of Madam C. J. Walker.* New York: Scribner, 2001; Lasky, Kathryn. *Vision of Beauty: The Story of Sarah Breedlove Walker.* Cambridge, MA: Candlewick Press, 2000; Peiss, Kathy. *Hope in a Jar: The Making of America's Beauty Culture.* New York: Metropolitan Books, 1998.

Stephen C. Kenny

Wallace, George (1919–1998)

George Corley Wallace was an **Alabama** governor who fought desegregation efforts during the 1960s. Wallace was born in Clio, Alabama, on August 25, 1919. As a child, Wallace expressed a great desire to involve himself in politics, seeing it as a way to help him, and others, out of poverty. After receiving an undergraduate degree from the University of Alabama, he enrolled in law school. Shortly after graduation, he was called to serve his country in the Army Air Corps during the Second World War. Almost immediately upon his return from the Pacific theater, he began a long career of public service. He served as a circuit judge, and later, he served in the Alabama House of Representatives. Wallace initially took a progressive stand on issues of civil rights and integration in particular. This changed dramatically after he lost a gubernatorial election in 1958 to a candidate who took a stronger stand against integration. Wallace blamed his loss on his moderate stand on civil rights issues.

Wallace first gained national attention when he physically stood in the doorway of the building where students at the University of Alabama registered for classes. His intention was to fulfill a campaign promise to physically prevent African American students from registering for classes at an all-white school. While the stand was largely symbolic and completely ineffective in preventing his goal of preserving segregation, this scene was displayed to a national audience by way of network television. This event propelled his political career that would span two decades as an elected official.

During this time in office, he campaigned against the expansion of integration. He regularly spoke against integration and used his position as governor to slow the progress of integration and impede the spread of civil rights for African Americans. He served as Alabama governor for four terms, 1963 to 1967, 1971 to 1975, 1975 to 1979, and 1983 to 1987. He was a presidential candidate for the **Democratic Party** in 1964, 1972, and 1976. He also ran as an independent in 1968. During Wallace's first term as governor, an Alabama governor could not succeed himself. After a failed attempt to eliminate this restriction, he convinced his wife, Lurleen, to run for governor. She succeeded and was governor from 1967 until her death in May 1968. Having his wife in office enabled him to continue to influence Alabama's state government and provided a base of support for his campaign for president through his American Independent Party. Although he won the electoral votes of several Southern states, he came up short in his presidential bid. After his reelection to the Alabama governorship in 1970, he began his third attempt to run for the presidency. This time, he ran for president as a Democrat. After a respectable showing in early primaries, he was shot by a gunman while campaigning at a shopping mall in Maryland. One of the bullets lodged near his spinal cord and left him paralyzed from the waist down. This injury effectively ended his presidential campaign and any future hopes of becoming president. After an easy reelection as Alabama's governor in 1974, he attempted his fourth and final run for the presidency. After weak showings in early primaries, he withdrew from the race. He mounted his final gubernatorial campaign in 1982. Once again, he was successful. He decided not to run for reelection in 1986, citing complications from injuries stemming from the gunshot wounds, which took a toll on his health.

After his retirement from public service, Wallace spent a great amount of time apologizing for his actions and words that caused so much harm to so many people. He visited with many of the leaders of the civil rights era and other elected African Americans for the purpose of asking their forgiveness.

Many of his former adversaries publicly forgave Wallace for his actions and stated he had a changed heart. Wallace died of heart failure on September 13, 1998. *See also* Folsom, James; National Guard.

Further Readings: Carter, Dan T. *The Politics of Rage.* New York: Simon and Schuster, 1995; Lesher, Stephan. *George Wallace: American Populist.* Reading, MA: Addison-Wesley Publishing Company, 1994; McMillen, Neil R. *The Citizens' Council: Organized Resistance to the Second Reconstruction, 1954–64.* Urbana: University of Illinois Press. 1971; Rohler, Lloyd. *George Wallace: Conservative Populist.* Westport, CT: Greenwood Press, 2004.

James Newman

Waller, Fats (1904–1943)

Thomas Wright "Fats" Waller, one of the giants of twentieth-century **jazz** piano, was born in New York City on May 21, 1904. Shortly after his birth, his family moved to Harlem. His father was an assistant pastor at Adam Clayton Powell, Jr.'s Abyssinian Baptist Church; his mother was an organist and singer. Waller developed his skills first on the organ at the church, and later on a piano that his family purchased. He left DeWitt Clinton high school before graduating, finding work as an organist at the Lincoln Theater and spending his late nights playing at "rent parties" in Harlem at which aspiring pianists would compete for the audience's favor. When he was 16, he met pianist and composer James P. Johnson, who remained a friend and mentor for the rest of his life. Waller played in local clubs and made his first recording on Okeh Records, a label that specialized in "race records" in 1922, backing **blues** artist Sara Martin. Waller recorded a number of sides for Okeh, both as an accompanist and as a featured artist. He also quickly made a name for himself as a composer. In 1923, he first sold a composition, *Wildcat Blues,* to Clarence Williams, a promoter and publisher who specialized in race music. That same year he landed his first gig on the radio, broadcasting from the Fox Terminal Theater in Newark, New Jersey.

In 1926, Waller began recording on the Victor label. His early musical efforts drew the attention of musicians and jazz audiences, but he was not paid well for his efforts. Black musicians made less than their white counterparts in both studio and live performances. White publishers routinely exploited black composers, although like many of his peers, Waller would sell a composition more than once in an effort to make more money from it. With lyricist Andy Razaf, with whom he collaborated for most of his career, Waller had his first great success composing the songs for the all-black show *Connie's Hot Chocolates,* which opened in New York's Hudson Theater in the summer of 1929 and ran for over 200 performances before going on the road. Among the Waller compositions featured was "Ain't Misbehavin'." In the 1930s, Waller moved to California and performed regularly in the New Cotton Club in Los Angeles. He appeared in two films in 1935, and continued a hectic touring and recording schedule.

Despite his celebrity, Waller still faced discrimination, particularly outside of his native Harlem. He and his fellow musicians were refused accommodations, particularly in Southern and Western states. During a 1943 tour, he and his manager were refused service in the dining room of a hotel in Omaha, Nebraska, just before Waller was scheduled to play a benefit concert for servicemen in that city. Even in New York City, Waller experienced the risks of crossing the color line. In 1938, two white women approached Waller and his brother Edward as they were getting into a cab, hoping to get Waller's autograph. Their white male escorts, annoyed by the attention paid to the black men, began beating the women. In the altercation that ensued, Edward Waller was shot and seriously wounded by one of the men.

Fats Waller died in the last days of his 1943 tour, after he boarded a train in Los Angeles to return to New York. Despite his early death at age 39, he left behind a remarkable body of work, both as a virtuoso musician and as a prolific and popular composer. *See also* Cinema.

Further Readings: Kirkeby, Ed. *Ain't Misbehavin': The Story of Fats Waller.* New York: Dodd, Mead, and Company, 1966; Shipton, Alyn. *Fats Waller: The Cheerful Little Earful.* New York: Continuum, 2002; Waller, Maurice, and Anthony Calabrese. *Fats Waller.* New York: Schirmer, 1977.

James Ivy

Waring, J. Waties (1880–1968)

Julius Waties Waring was a federal judge appointed to the Eastern District of **South Carolina** on January 26, 1942. Nominated by U.S. Senator Ellison DuRant ("Cotton Ed") Smith, a white supremacist, Waring was the son of a Confederate war veteran, and for most of his long life he moved in the exclusive circles of the Charleston Club, the St. Cecilia Society, and the Charleston Light Dragoons.

Waring graduated with honors from the College of Charleston in 1900, and passed the bar two years later. In 1913, he married socialite Annie Gammell, and they had one daughter, Anne. In 1920, he established the Waring & Brockinton law firm, became active in South Carolina's white **Democratic Party** politics, and in 1931 was appointed city attorney for Mayor Burnett Maybank's administration. Maybank later became governor (1939–1941) and ultimately a U.S. senator (1941–1954). By 1938, Waring had advanced in the Democratic Party to Charleston's point man for Cotton Ed Smith's senatorial campaign.

During his first two years on the federal bench, Waring functioned as a traditional and rather unremarkable jurist, but in 1945, he began to question Southern mores. That year, Viola Duvall filed a class action suit on behalf of Charleston's black teachers who earned substantially less than the city's white teachers. National Association for the Advancement of Colored People (NAACP) attorney **Thurgood Marshall** presented the case, and Waring ruled that if black teachers could offer educational credentials comparable to white teachers, they were entitled to receive comparable pay.

In 1946, Waring divorced his wife of 32 years and married Elizabeth Avery Mills Hoffman, a Northern divorcee and outspoken critic of segregation. When the judge subsequently demanded that black men and women be addressed as Mr., Miss, or Mrs. in his court, abolished segregated jury seating, and appointed a black bailiff, many of his old friends blamed Elizabeth Waring for turning him against the Southern Way of life. He insisted, however, that "when you're practicing law you're representing a particular interest [but] ...when you're on the bench you're not interested in who wins the case. You're interested in seeing the case handled justly and right."

Gradually, the Warings became almost completely ostracized by Charleston's white society, and the judge was no longer welcome at St. Cecelia Society Balls or in the private clubs that he had frequented for over 40 years. Former friends insisted that they had abandoned him because of his scandalous divorce rather than for his new ideas about racial justice.

In the summer of 1946, Waring presided in a suit brought against a white South Carolina police officer by black army veteran Isaac Woodward. After his discharge from the army at Fort Benning, Georgia, Woodward had boarded a bus for **North Carolina**. At the first rest stop, he and the driver argued about how much time the soldier had taken. The police were called and Woodward was charged with drunk and disorderly conduct. When he denied being drunk, the arresting officer beat him so severely that both his corneas were destroyed and he was permanently blinded. The officer's defense was that he believed Woodward had tried to take his gun. Since there were no witnesses, the jury refused to convict. Waring described both the U.S. attorney's defense of Woodward and the jury's verdict as "disgraceful."

That October, George Elmore, black manager of the Waverly Five and Dime in Columbia, South Carolina, was denied a ballot for the Democratic primary at Richland County's Ward Ninth precinct. Again, the NAACP brought suit, this time to challenge the constitutionality of the **white primary**. As the Democratic Party was the only party in the state, voting in the primary was more important than voting in the general election, since whoever won the primary won the election. Denying blacks access to the primary effectively denied them voting rights. Thurgood Marshall argued *Elmore v. Rice* before Judge Waring on February 21, 1947, and on July 12, Waring ruled that South Carolina's Democratic Party could not legally exclude qualified blacks from voting in primary elections, a decision that was upheld on appeal by the **U.S. Supreme Court**. When Democratic Party officials attempted to evade his ruling by requiring that all registered voters swear allegiance to separation of the races, Waring threatened to hold the county chairs in contempt and either fine or imprison them. They backed down, and the votes of 35,000 South Carolina blacks counted that year. Waring became one of the most hated men in the white South. Several attempts were made to impeach him, since federal judgeships are lifetime appointments, but he was never removed.

Waties and Elizabeth Waring scandalized their neighbors by entertaining blacks in their Charleston home, and she outraged the community when, in a 1949 presentation at the city's black YWCA, she referred to segregationists as "sick, confused and decadent people." Her address was widely reported in the national press. Both Warings believed that Southern white moderates were more destructive to the cause of black civil rights than virulent segregationists, since moderates maintained that segregation and reform could coexist. Waring knew that was impossible. Southern moderates, and even those who considered themselves liberals, subscribed to what he called "the false god of gradualism." Waring knew that voluntary **desegregation** was a Southern pipe dream, and he became a strong advocate of federal intervention to abolish legal segregation.

Early in 1950, Joseph Armstrong DeLaine, black principal of Silver School in Summerton, South Carolina, sued the Clarendon County School District to provide bus transportation for black pupils as it did for whites. Once again, Thurgood Marshall presented the case before Judge Waring, who assured the NAACP attorney that he was wasting the **NAACP Legal Defense Fund**'s time and money in suing to force school districts to fund dual education systems. Waring suggested that Marshall withdraw the suit and refile a class action challenging the constitutionality of segregated schools. Marshall took his advice and, on May 28, 1951, argued *Briggs v. Elliott* before a panel of three federal judges, including George Bell Timmerman, a segregationist; John Parker, a moderate; and Waring. As expected, the NAACP lost the decision, but in a scathing dissent, Waring declared that the 1896 *Plessy v. Ferguson* decision that established the principle of "**separate but equal**" accommodations based on race was unconstitutional. Anticipating the Warren Court's historic 1954 decision, Waring argued that separate educational facilities were inherently unequal. Appealed all the way to the U.S. Supreme Court, *Briggs v. Elliott* became one of the four cases heard in **Brown v. Board of Education**, and although the Warren Court never cited his dissent, *Briggs* is perhaps Judge Waring's greatest contribution to American judicial history.

Waring retired in 1952 and he and his wife moved to New York City, where they were active in a variety of civil rights organizations. To the end of his life, the judge supported the use of aggressive federal intervention to break the back of racial segregation. He died on January 20, 1968, and Elizabeth Waring died a few months later. Both are buried in Charleston's Magnolia Cemetery.

Further Readings: Brown, Cynthia Stokes. *Refusing Racism: White Allies in the Struggle for Civil Rights.* New York: Teachers College Press, 2002; Southern, David W. "Beyond Jim Crow Liberalism, Judge Waring's Fight against Segregation in South Carolina 1942–52." *Journal of Negro History* 66 (Autumn 1981): 209–27; Yarbrough, Tinsley E. *A Passion for Justice: J. Waties Waring and Civil Rights.* New York: Oxford University Press, 1987.

Mary Stanton

Washington, Booker T. (1858–1915)

African American leader Booker Taliaferro Washington was born into slavery in a slave cabin on a **Virginia** tobacco plantation to a white father who he did not know and a slave mother who could not read or write. His mother taught him lessons in thrift and virtue. These lessons, in addition to the slave code of ethics, in which it was acceptable to steal from those who enslaved you, would prove useful to Washington throughout his life. After the Emancipation Proclamation was signed, he and his family moved to West Virginia. As a young man, he learned of Hampton Institute and, on October 1, 1872, began his journey to Hampton, Virginia. He completed this journey, by foot and by railroad. Part of Washington's entrance requirements to Hampton Institute included sweeping the auditorium. He cleaned the auditorium more than once, which is a testament to Washington's diligence, hard work, and personal development.

While Washington had his challengers, he also served as an inspiration to many around the world. His approach has been criticized and dismissed for more overt displays of racial protest and petition for social change. Washington was called "the great accommodator" by **W.E.B. Du Bois** and has even been called an "Uncle Tom" for being too compromising with whites and for going so far as telling jokes in black dialect to white audiences. Washington's accommodating stance and compromise with whites can be understood within the context of the **Jim Crow** South, his Tuskegee project, and his demands for blacks' individual and economic development.

Washington wanted blacks to be self-sufficient but to understand the collective struggle. He pushed for advancement despite oppression and was very devoted and committed to his efforts, despite the overt and more covert obstacles that he faced. Washington believed that both blacks and whites were responsible for making blacks productive and valuable to America's industrial growth. This great compromise was achieved through soliciting the support of whites while urging blacks not to agitate whites or challenge the status quo in demand of civil rights. Washington also called for blacks to forego social parity with whites in favor of greater economic development, and he felt it was possible to be segregated from whites but for there to still be economic ties to whites. He accomplished this by gaining middle- and upper-class whites' economic support for Tuskegee Institute.

Washington wanted to change black America from all angles and did not believe that blacks would forever be second-class citizens. He believed that there were contexts in which blacks would be advanced and have educational and economic opportunities. Washington, therefore, asked blacks to reflect on the accomplishments since the Emancipation Proclamation and how much more can be accomplished if blacks work together and form an economic base for self-sufficiency. This self-sufficiency would also make blacks and whites economically interdependent, rather than blacks being solely dependent on whites, and allow blacks to be prepared for their full citizenship rights and integration in American society.

With integration and assimilation in American society, Washington pushed for blacks to advance but not to isolate themselves socially by servicing blacks only or only supporting businesses because they were black-owned. Washington's challenge to blacks was to maintain an individual will through which the collective will can be mobilized and realized. Individual will included skill attainment, higher education when attainable, sobriety, and devoutness.

Washington was greatly inspired by abolitionist Frederick Douglass because Douglass was also born into slavery and learned and understood the virtues of being self-made and focusing on individual development. Douglass argued that blacks failed to attain a skill base and this failure is the foundation for the "Negro problem." Douglass, therefore, was an advocate of blacks learning a trade so that they can gain parity with whites and have greater opportunities. In agreement with this sentiment, Washington thought that earning a dollar

Booker T. Washington on African American Citizenship

On December 20, 1901, Booker T. Washington appealed to a predominantly white audience at the Outlook Club in Montclair, New Jersey, to focus on the economic security of African Americans, not deportation.

Booker T. Washington addressed the Outlook Club here to-night, and pleased a big audience, who applauded heartily his remarks. His subject was "The Citizenship of the American Negro."

Among other things he said, that there were over 9,000,000 colored people in the United States, and that the way to solve the negro problem is not by deporting the negroes.

"When 600 started for Liberia some time ago some people thought the question had been solved, but 600 black babies were born the next day. Deportation won't work.

"You can't set apart land for the Negroes and wall them in. One wall would not keep the Negroes in, and five walls would not keep the white men out. You can't absorb them, for the minute you get 1 percent of black blood in a white man, he becomes a negro. Nor are there any signs or indications of decay in the race."

The speaker said that with the different colored persons included in our new possessions, altogether over 18,000,000, he thought that the white man had a big problem before him. The speaker recommended as one solution of the problem that the white man make the negro more useful, and help him to secure an education. The negro candidly responds to stimulating influences. The speaker compared two parts of Alabama, one where instruction had been given the negroes and another where dense ignorance prevailed—and showed that intelligence and education had brought in their track land ownership, prosperity, and higher morality.

"The material or industrial betterment of a people," he said, "always improves their morality. Dependence upon law alone will not accomplish everything. Through sympathy, active help, and financial assistance the white people can do much for the negro. The problem will not [go] down till settled in justice and righteousness."

Source: "Citizenship of the Negro: B. T. Washington Tells Montclair People that Education and Kindness Will Solve the Problem," *New York Times,* December 21, 1901.

through a trade was worth more than the opportunity to spend a dollar in white establishments. Industrial education was deemed a necessity by Washington, whereas higher education was an option, not a priority. Washington knew that the majority of blacks would not have access to higher education, although Washington's own children did.

Washington and Douglass both believed that the South was the best place for blacks, that blacks should not move to the North, and that blacks should accumulate wealth in order to be more self-sufficient and have greater opportunities. Both Washington and Douglass also compared the potential for the development and advancement of blacks with the realized development and advancement of Jews. The Jews were admired for their pride, their unity, and their success upon assimilation, despite obstacles. Instead of complaining, blacks should have individual motivation and advancement so that they can advance as a people and actually contribute to society. The importance of learning a trade and the belief that blacks were to blame for the "Negro problem" was deemed simplistic in its logic by the critics of both Douglass and Washington because economic development was not *the* solution to the "Negro problem."

Washington and Douglass differed in that Washington placed greater emphasis on the individual accountability, self-sufficiency, and self-reliance components of Douglass's message whereas Douglass's overall message was more militant. In his militancy, Douglass maintained an assimilation stance without mocking blacks and making jokes about black dialect in front of white audiences. Douglass was often critical of whites' acts of oppression and partially attributed the conditions of blacks to this oppression. Unlike Washington, Douglass did not make jokes about blacks in front of whites or appear to go too far in his attempts at assimilating. Washington criticized this militancy because it had generally lost its effectiveness. Political and social agitation did not have a substantial grounding in economic development. However, Douglass did not live in the South and, despite the obstacles that Northern blacks faced, could afford to take a more militant approach.

Washington and Du Bois are often presented as adversaries with contrasting and conflicting views; however, they shared the ultimate objective, but differed mostly in strategy. Washington was similar to Du Bois in that he was committed to social change and social action and used various institutions to bring about such change, including Tuskegee Institute and the National Negro Business League. He did not openly discuss all of his affiliations and strategies for change but rather covertly fought for change. Washington knew that change was a process.

Among Du Bois's criticisms of Washington was that his advice was sought by presidents, politicians, philanthropists, and scholars, and that he was made into the Negro representative. Washington's appointment as as the Negro representative was seen as a contradiction to the funding and support whites provided to Washington's Tuskegee Institute. This creates the image that Washington's interests and efforts are not purely in the interests of Negroes but are, instead, greatly influenced by whites. Whites supported Tuskegee and upheld him as the only valued black leader as long as he advocated segregation. Washington solicited this support of middle- and upper-class whites to back Tuskegee financially and to keep lower-class whites from interfering with Washington's efforts.

To understand Washington's stance, he must be placed within the context of the Jim Crow South, just as to understand Du Bois's and Douglass's approaches, they must be placed in the more Northern contexts in which they lived. Northern blacks faced inequality but in a different type of an environment, and were more educated, economically independent, and critical. Washington's approach of entrepreneurship and thriftiness appealed to Northern blacks. However Northern blacks did not support Washington's belief that there can and should be protest without the appearance of protest and that fights for civil and political rights should be abandoned in favor of individual and economic development. He felt as though Du Bois and others were showing whites "their hands" rather than focusing on silent protest that would result in the development and true advancement of the Negro. Tuskegee Institute was one example of slow change and long-term investment for a larger goal. In the Jim Crow South, revolt and overt protest would have resulted in Washington being lynched and the struggle being lost.

Washington's efforts had been overshadowed and largely overlooked while Du Bois's and his counterparts' efforts of desegregation and social justice were advanced. Washington's platform appealed to blacks' needs and urged blacks to forego their more immediate wants. As a result of the increased unpopularity of Washington's approach in favor of the approach of Du Bois and his counterparts, there continued to be a shortage of black entrepreneurs and blacks' consumerism and dependency on whites increased with **desegregation** and an increase in voting and civil rights. Therefore, the efforts of Du Bois and his counterparts were successful in the short term, but blacks failed to become more self-sufficient as Washington envisioned. Washington's message is not completely lost because he continues to serve as a motivation and challenge to black entrepreneurs and blacks who are concerned with individual and collective moral and economic development. *See also* Albany Civil Rights Movement; Atlanta Compromise; Carver, George Washington.

Further Readings: Adegbalola, Gaye Todd. "Interviews: Garvey, Du Bois, and Booker T." *Black Books Bulletin* 3 (Spring 1975); Brock, Randall E. "Cast Down Your Buckets Where You Are." *Crisis* 99 (1992): 2; Burns, Haywood. 1970. *Afro American Studies: An Interdisciplinary Journal* 1, no. 1 (May 1970); Champion, Danny. "Booker T. Washington versus W.E.B. Du Bois: A Study in Rhetorical Contrasts." In *Oratory in the New South*, edited by Waldo W. Braden. Baton Rouge: Louisiana State University Press, 1979; Cunnigen, Donald, Rutledge M. Dennis, and Myrtle Gonza Glascoe, eds. *Research in Race and Ethnic Relations*. Vol. 13, *The Racial Politics of Booker T. Washington,* 105–31. Oxford: JAI Press, 2006; Flynn, John P. "Booker T. Washington: Uncle Tom or Wooden House." *Journal of Negro History* 54 (July 1969); Hancock, Gordon B. "Booker T. Washington: His Defense and Vindication." *Negro Digest* 13, no. 7 (May 1964); Harlan, Louis R. "Booker T. Washington in Biographical Perspective." *American Historical Review* 75 (1970): 1581–99; Washington, Booker T. *Up from Slavery*. Garden City, NY: Doubleday, 1900.

Rutledge M. Dennis

Watson, Thomas E. (1856–1922)

Thomas E. Watson was a **Georgia** attorney, publisher, and politician who served as a Democrat in the Georgia State House of Representatives (1882–1883), a Populist in the U.S. House of Representatives (1890–1892), and a Democrat in the U.S. Senate (1920–1922). The Populist Party convention nominated him as its vice presidential candidate in 1896 to run with William Jennings Bryan and as its presidential candidate in 1904 and 1908. Watson also ran unsuccessfully to keep his seat in Congress in 1892 and 1894. Although Watson served no more than a total of five years in public office, he exerted a tremendous influence on Southern and national politics with his flamboyant political oratory and his support for other candidates. Watson is best known for his controversial political career and sudden about-face. In the early years he advocated a more egalitarian creed and championed the political and economic rights of poor white and black farmers. In the later years he gained notoriety for his virulent antiblack, anti-Semitic, and anti-Catholic views.

Watson was born in McDuffie County, Georgia, to a slaveholding family and spent most his childhood on his grandfather's plantation. After attending Mercer University, Watson practiced law but maintained a strong connection to agrarian life. He entered politics at the age of 23 in support of the small farmers who had revolted against the state's leading industrial capitalists. In the 1880s, Watson supported the economic platform of the National Farmers'

Alliance, and in the 1890s, he became a prominent leader in the Populist Party. Both the Alliance and the Populist Party challenged the entrenched power of the **Democratic Party** in the South. Aggrieved farmers called for such reforms as the dissolution of corporate monopolies, government regulation of railroads, a graduated income tax, the establishment of cooperative buying plans, and relief from high-interest credit. Watson discovered that the key to political success lay in soliciting not just the votes of white farmers but also the votes of African Americans. Both the Democrats and the Populists recognized that if the white vote splintered, then the black vote could decide an election. The two parties battled with each other for the political loyalties of black voters and engaged in a variety of tactics, including persuasion, fraud, bribery, and violence.

Poor white and black farmers in the South often struggled with the same economic difficulties, and Populists tried to draw attention to the farmers' common grievances and enemies. In Watson's early career, he labored to build a new political alliance that united the races economically. He pointed out how racial antagonism had been used by white elites to oppress the farming class. When Watson campaigned for his seat in the Georgia Assembly in 1882, he received a substantial number of black votes. In the 1890s, he denounced laws that limited black suffrage and called for the right of African American men to cast a ballot without coercion or fear of intimidation. The Populist leader also spoke out against **lynching** and, at one point, provided refuge to a black minister who was an ardent party member being sought by a mob. Many of Watson's contemporaries considered him to be somewhat radical in his stance. Yet there were limits to biracial cooperation. Watson never promoted the right of African Americans to hold public office. He made it very clear that he did not want "social equality" of the races. For most white Southerners, this phrase conjured up images of intermarriage between the races, blacks socializing with whites, equal access to public accommodations, and interracial schools. Whether Watson genuinely believed in a limited kind of equality or acted out of political expediency is still debated.

After failing a second time to regain his seat in Congress in 1894, Watson retreated from public life and politics for eight years. When he reentered the political fray, he had changed his mind about the merits of black suffrage. In 1906, Watson supported the Democratic candidacy for governorship of Hoke Smith, who championed black disfranchisement and was a vocal advocate of white supremacy. Watson and Smith argued that black political equality would undoubtedly lead to "social equality." During the course of the campaign, white newspapers inflamed racial tensions by detailing alleged sexual assaults on white women by black men and other supposed black criminal atrocities. These lurid reports provoked a riot in which whites attacked and killed dozens of blacks as well as destroyed many black-owned businesses. Shortly after, Smith won the election in an overwhelming victory. Two years later the Georgia legislature rewrote the state constitution to severely curtail, if not abolish, black suffrage.

Watson's alliance with Smith marked the beginning of a significant shift in the tenor of his political rhetoric. He unleashed a fury of vitriolic attacks on Catholics, Jews, and African Americans and earned a reputation as one of the South's most notorious orators. The year Smith won the election, Watson founded a newspaper, the *Jeffersonian,* and a magazine, *Watson's Jeffersonian Magazine,* which he used as mouthpieces for racial and religious bigotry. He warned about black domination, the sexual threats priests posed to white Protestant women, and the danger of the Jewish aristocracy. Watson's frenzied tirades were so outrageous that he provoked the U.S. Post Office to ban the *Jeffersonian* from the mail and the U.S. Justice Department to try him for obscenity. The former Populist leader continued to rail against industrial capitalists and the oppression of the farming class, but his racial and religious obsessions occupied most of his attention from 1910 onward. Watson's reactionary political style was emblematic of a new breed of politicians known as demagogues, who appealed to the prejudices and baser emotions of the people. Until the last day of his life, Watson persisted in lashing out at his perceived enemies. He died in 1922 of a cerebral hemorrhage following a lengthy struggle with illness.

Further Readings: Crowe, Charles. "Tom Watson, Populists, and Blacks Reconsidered." *Journal of Negro History* 55 (April 1970): 99–116; Fingerhut, Eugene R. "Tom Watson, Blacks, and Southern Reform." *Georgia Historical Quarterly* 60 (Winter 1976): 324–43; Historic Home of Thomas E. Watson. Hickory Hill. Watson-Brown Foundation. http://www.hickory-hill.org/index.html (accessed June 1, 2008); Shaw, Barton. *The Wool Hat Boys: Georgia's Populist Party.* Baton Rouge: Louisiana State University Press, 1984; Woodward, C. Vann. *Tom Watson: Agrarian Rebel.* New York: Oxford University Press, 1938.

Natalie J. Ring

Wells-Barnett, Ida B. (1862–1931)

Ida Bell Wells-Barnett fought a battle against slavery's legacy of racism and segregation. She was born enslaved on July 16, 1862, in Holly Springs, **Mississippi**. Under the institution of slavery, her father, James Wells, had learned carpentry, thereby acquiring a higher social status than other enslaved persons. Ida Wells gained an education in schools operated by the Freedmen's Bureau, an organization set up after the Civil War. For a short while, she attended Shaw University, called Rust College until 1890, until her frequent clashes with the president, W. W. Hooper, led to her expulsion. In 1878, a yellow fever epidemic killed over 200 whites and about half as many blacks in Holly Springs, including Wells's parents and her baby sister. Because she was visiting her grandmother, she escaped the deadly virus. She learned of her parents' deaths and her siblings' whereabouts by letter and traveled back to her home after doctors reported safe conditions. Determined to keep the family together, Wells secured a job as a public school teacher at the age of 16. In 1881, she and her brother George and sister Annie joined their aunt in Memphis, where Wells soon began teaching in the city schools.

In September 1883, Wells directly attacked **Jim Crow** segregation by refusing to leave the first-class railroad car to sit in the smoky car reserved for blacks. Whites in the South were unaccustomed to the well-dressed and articulate African Americans more visible as access to education and transportation networks improved. Although middle-class blacks were an affront to social customs and Southern norms, many adopted respectability to counter racism. Wells, like other blacks who challenged segregation on streetcars and railroads, reasoned that she paid the price to sit in the nicer car and should be treated as such. Her defiance led the railroad conductor to use physical force to remove her from the car. She fought back, biting the conductor and clinging to her seat, but was no match for the other passengers who helped carry her to the second car. Wells filed suit after this incident and another and won cash settlements for both. The Tennessee Supreme Court eventually overturned the rulings but was not able to quiet Wells or end her activism. The incidents and others actually proved to be a major catalyst in her decision to pursue a career in journalism.

Wells's first articles dealt with her proceedings with the railroad company. She soon adopted the pseudonym, Iola, for her essays, and by the end of 1885, her work commonly appeared in newspaper columns. Wells often used her words to defend black women's virtue from the popular attacks in white and even black writings. Female writers faced resistance from some black men who felt threatened by sharing the literary field with females. The stereotypes surrounding black womanhood, especially the images of the Jezebel and Mammy, proliferated throughout the Jim Crow era. Many white-authored histories portrayed black women as Jezebels, the exact opposite of the ideal woman of the Victorian age. Mammy represented the antithesis of the libidinous Jezebel. Whites portrayed Mammy, who usually served in domestic capacities or as a caregiver to white children, as a woman without sexual desires. Wells wrote to attack the many institutions that became conduits for perpetuating these controlling images of black women. Many times, black men criticized Wells for ignoring society's definition of the proper roles for women.

Along with her teaching, in 1889, Wells became a co-owner of, and a writer for, the *Free Speech and Headlight,* a newspaper founded in Memphis by Taylor Nightingale and J. L. Fleming. Wells used the *Free Speech* as a mouthpiece for the unequal justice meted out to blacks and whites. Her classroom teaching ended in 1891, when the Memphis school board fired her for her criticism of the school system printed in the *Free Speech.* Since her salary as editor paid little, Wells worked to increase the circulation of the newspaper to make ends meet. These experiences mark the beginning of a lifelong crusade to inform the whole society about discrimination in general and **lynching** in particular.

After Wells reported the brutal murders of her associates and prominent members of the Memphis black community, Thomas Moss, Calvin McDowell, and Lee Stewart, antilynching became her main cause. The investigation of the brutal murders did not lead to any arrests since local law officials often cooperated with lynch mobs, the pinnacle of white terrorism in the United States. Understood later as motivated by the economic competition the African American businessmen represented, Wells used her reports on the lynching to encourage blacks to leave Memphis. She also chastised the white press that sensationalized the murders and demonized the upstanding black men. On May 21, 1892, the *Free Speech* published a piece by Wells that proclaimed the falsity of the often-echoed charges of rape that drove mobs to action. She hinted at some white women's willful participation in sexual liaisons with black men, angering whites in Memphis who destroyed her printing press and threatened her life. Wells fled Memphis for Chicago where she joined the staff of the *Age,* a black newspaper edited by T. Thomas Fortune.

In Chicago, Wells worked to correct the conception that mob members were mostly poor or ignorant whites. She also revealed that charges of criminality leveled at the victims of lynch mobs often resulted from racism rather than attempted or actual offenses. At first, Wells, like many whites, believed the charges of rape leveled at lynching's victims until she learned of its falsity firsthand. White men claimed the protection of white womanhood as a major validation for lynching. Like the Jezebel myth, the stereotype of the black male rapist emerged as evidence of the need for the separation of blacks and whites that defined Jim Crow. Wells worked to correct these assumptions on black personalities to end the deadly consequences these negative caricatures often elicited.

Wells was an example of the "new" African American woman in the context of Women's Rights and the Black Clubwomen's Movement of the late nineteenth century. A network of black women supported her crusade from the start. Like larger society, these clubs also reflected racial separation. In the fall of 1892, African American women in New York, Philadelphia, and Boston organized a well-attended reception where Wells delivered an emotional address about the Moss, McDowell, and Stewart lynchings and her exile from Holly Springs. The event drew support from the black press and an audience of over 200 people who provided the finances needed for Wells to publish *Southern Horrors,* her first pamphlet on lynching.

Ida B. Wells' antilynching campaign pamphlets *Southern Horrors* (1892), *A Red Record* (1892), and *Mob Rule in New Orleans* (1900) reflected a massive increase in violence toward black people after emancipation. In *Southern Horrors,* Wells argued that whites lynched blacks in response to the franchise, since access to the vote represented another privilege many whites in the South reserved for themselves. As such, Wells's essays protested the disenfranchisement of African Americans even though her gender barred her own participation in electoral politics. She then implicated the press that played an integral role in perpetuating the myth of the uncontrolled lust of black men. She also chided those men and women who refused to speak out against lynching. Wells declared that white men shamelessly murdered black men to protect white economic interest rather than white women.

In *A Red Record,* Wells recorded reported lynchings and their supposed causes. The plethora of descriptions of lynchings, all from white-authored sources, proved the compliancy of state police departments and elected officials. Wells played on whites' religious sensibilities by referring to the mobs as Christians. She also laid bare the issues she held with Women's Christian Temperance Union president Frances Willard, who defended the mobs in the name of white women. She finished her second pamphlet by calling for readers to be proactive in spreading the word on lynching. It ended by encouraging readers to support the 1894 Blair Bill that called for investigations into mob violence. Wells's final pamphlet chronicled the life and death of Robert Charles, whose actions in self-defense set off a mob of whites in New Orleans who then indiscriminately targeted the whole black community. The white press presented Charles as a murderer, but in actuality, his crime was working alongside Henry McNeil Turner in garnering support for emigration to **Liberia**. This detailed case of unbridled white violence disproved the black beast theory as justification for lynching, and reiterated that perpetrators remained unpunished. Like Wells's other writings, it used religious references and the gendered rhetoric of manhood to plead her case.

Following in the footsteps of the abolitionist Frederick Douglass, Wells carried her message to Europe to gain support for her campaign against lynching in 1893. Many foreign leaders considered America a symbol of freedom and democracy. Wells sought to provide a more nuanced vision of the nation that included the nature of Jim Crow legislation and the extent whites took to keep the races socially separate. She worked to inform other countries about the second-class status afforded African Americans in hopes that these countries would pressure leaders in the United States to protect the black civil rights. She returned to England a year later to conduct a second tour and further articulate her disgust of the U.S. government for seeming to ignore the continued humiliation and discrimination practiced on the basis of race.

In many ways, Wells was the antithesis of the theoretical model of true womanhood, though she did adhere to some prescribed gender roles. In 1895, she married Ferdinand Barnett, a lawyer and owner of the *Chicago Conservator.* After the marriage, she became editor of the *Conservator* and continued to use print media to wage a battle against Jim Crow. As a wife and mother of four children, Wells-Barnett's national influence declined, but not her zeal for antilynching and reform. Before her renown as the major voice of the antilynching campaign, Wells joined with other black leaders to dismantle segregation and discrimination. She held memberships in the National Afro-American League and the Southern Afro-American Press Association, and she became the National Colored Press Association's first female officer. She was also a member of the **National Association of Colored Women** and the National Association for the Advancement of Colored People and supported suffrage for women. Her writings called for organization and concrete strategies to fight segregation and discrimination. Although Congress never passed the Blair Bill or any other form of antilynching legislation, Wells-Barnett's efforts did lead to a decrease in instances of lynching in the United States.

Further Readings: Duster, Alfreda M. ed. *Crusade for Justice: The Autobiography of Ida B. Wells.* Chicago: University of Chicago Press, 1970; McMurry, Linda O. *To Keep the Waters Troubled: The Life of Ida B. Wells.* New York: Oxford University Press, 1998; Royster, Jacqueline Jones. *Southern Horrors and Other Writings: The Anti-Lynching Campaign of Ida B. Wells, 1892–1900.* Boston: Bedford Books, 1997; Schechter, Patricia. *Ida B. Wells-Barnett and American Reform, 1880–1930.* Chapel Hill: University of North Carolina Press, 2001.

Christina L. Davis

White Citizens Council

White citizens councils were established to thwart the spread of civil rights in the South by means of economic retribution against citizens who supported civil rights workers or their cause. Membership consisted primarily of wealthy white business owners and elected officials. Most White Citizens Councils were first established following the **U.S. Supreme Court** decision of May 17, 1954, in the case of *Brown v. Board of Education*, when the Court reversed the 1896 ruling in *Plessy v. Ferguson*, declaring that racial segregation in schools was unconstitutional. The first White Citizens Council was formed in Greenwood, Mississippi, shortly before the *Brown v. Board of Education* ruling.

The councils were created to counteract the activities of the National Association of for the Advancement of Colored People (NAACP) and prevent the advancement of integration. Their formation met with varying degrees of success. Councils in **Mississippi** tended to possess more members than those in other states. The Deep South states of **Alabama, Georgia, Louisiana,** and **South Carolina** typically had more councils with more members than in other Southern states such as Tennessee, **Arkansas,** and **North Carolina**.

Often referred to as "the white collar Klan," this organization sought to use its economic and political clout to deter and punish an individual's involvement in the NAACP and advancing civil rights. Typically, their activities would involve firing a person, denying a loan, or boycotting the person's business if that person was believed to be involved in supporting integration. Some

---

"Ask Yourself This Important Question," 1963

The advertisement asks white people to donate to their local Alabama White Citizens Council.

ASK YOURSELF THIS IMPORTANT QUESTION:

What have I personally done to Maintain Segregation?

If the answer disturbs your, probe deeper and decide what you are willing to do to preserve racial harmony in Selma and Dallas County.

Is it worth four dollars to prevent a "Birmingham" here? That's what it costs to be a member of your Citizens Council, whose efforts are not thwarted by courts which give sit-in demonstrators legal immunity, prevent school boards from expelling students who participate in mob activities and would place federal referees at the board of voter registrars.

Law enforcement can be called only after these things occur, but your Citizens Council prevents them from happening.

Why else did only 350 Negroes attend a so-called mass voter registration meeting that outside agitators worked 60 days to organize in Selma?

Gov. Wallace told a state meeting of the council three weeks ago: "You are doing a wonderful job, but your should speak with the united voice of 100,000 person. Go back home and get more members."

It is worth four dollars to prevent sit-ins, mob marches and wholesale Negro voter registration efforts in Selma?

If so, prove your dedication by joining and supporting the work of the Dallas County Citizens Council today. Six dollars will make both you and your wife members of an organization which has given Selma nine years of Racial Harmony since "Black Monday."

Source: *Selma Times Journal,* June 9, 1963.

groups sought to gain public support through advertising. Groups would often purchase advertising space in local newspapers to present their thoughts on integration and recruit members.

Some elected officials and other white community leaders openly favored laws that would maintain the status quo in the state's segregation practices. These individuals were often members of White Councils, or worked closely with them. A good example of this is the relationship Alabama governor **George Wallace** enjoyed with White Citizens Councils in his state. These groups would often support his candidacy through votes and monetary contributions. Mississippi's governor during the 1960s, Ross Barnett, also possessed close political ties with these organizations. Despite the strong ties with particular governors in the Deep South, White Citizens Councils were largely ineffective in other parts of the country.

The demise of White Citizens Councils came quickly in many parts of the South, but slowly in the Deep South. The last organized councils existed in Mississippi into the 1970s. Many of their official records were destroyed or sealed by state and local judges. In the later part of the twentieth century, most of the sealed records became available for viewing by the public. It provided a glimpse into the activities and meticulous records some White Citizens Councils kept on the activities of civil rights workers of the time. *See also* Ku Klux Klan.

Further Readings: McMillen, Neil R. *The Citizens' Council: Organized Resistance to the Second Reconstruction, 1954–1964.* Urbana: University of Illinois Press, 1971.

James Newman

White Primary

The white primary effectively disenfranchised African Americans by barring their political participation in the nomination of political candidates. Southern Democrats used it to establish a one-party political system by unifying its members behind one candidate and lessening the divisive effect of internal factionalism. In regions that had a black majority, it was used most effectively in combination with the **poll tax**, the literacy and the grandfather clause.

The direct primary, or the direct election of a party's candidate, grew in popularity as a reform measure during the Gilded Age based on the idea that choosing a candidate based on party members' opinion was more democratic than through nomination conventions ruled by party leaders. Local parties throughout the country used it sporadically as early as the 1870s, but by the 1890s it had become more common on in local contests. The first statewide primary in the South, albeit unofficial, occurred in **Louisiana** in 1892, when a bitter fight within the Democrats threatened to split the party and allow a Republican-Populist coalition candidate a chance at victory. To prevent this outcome, which Democrats threatened would mean a return to the **Reconstruction** days of "negro-rule," both sides agreed to deciding the candidate through a preelection primary and to uphold that decision in the general election for the sake of white supremacy. Essentially, they restricted the electorate to include only white Democrats and made the inner-party contest the more important election, eliminating the effectiveness of third parties on the state level. In the South, since most African Americans voted Republican, the Democratic primary did not need to restrict access to the election by race.

Mississippi installed the first official white primary by law. By 1915, all states of the former Confederacy had joined Mississippi in its institution. Yet, motivations for having a white primary varied from state to state, as did the combination of **disenfranchisement** laws, so each state had different rules governing the primary. Some Democrats wanted to undermine the Populist Party's efforts at the polls and bring them eventually back into the party of white supremacy. Other Democrats demanded a purification of the vote because of failed attempts to pass prohibition legislation. By the time states instituted primary elections by law, most Southerners assumed the Democratic primary to be for whites only. As a result, some states, such as **Texas**, did not specifically deny access by race but gave that power to local election officials until circumstances forced a change.

Legal efforts to dismantle the white primary began in 1919 on the grassroots level by black businessmen in Texas after white women gained the right to vote. With a diverse racial and ethnic population, which included many recent immigrants from Europe and Mexico, Texas did not have alternative disenfranchisement laws, such as the literacy clause and the grandfather clause, but relied on the poll tax and the primary, which it restricted to the Democratic Party through a substantial minimum party membership requirement. In 1923, due to a contested election and civil rights cases, Texas changed its ambiguous 1905 law to explicitly restrict primary elections to whites only.

Quickly, the National Association for the Advancement of Colored People (NAACP) joined the grassroots movement, led by black attorney R. D. Evans, to combat the white primary in the courts in *Love v. Griffith,* which failed in the **U.S. Supreme Court** in 1924. After removing local counsel and amassing a white legal team from the Northeast, the NAACP continued their fight after Lawrence Nixon, a black physician in El Paso, was denied the right to vote in a local primary in 1924. In *Nixon v. Herndon,* the U.S. Supreme Court struck down the Texas white primary law for violating the Fourteenth Amendment. In response, the Texas legislature adapted the election law to restore the white primary by declaring rules for party membership to a private power of state party committees, a private entity. Nixon and the NAACP tested the changed law in *Nixon v. Condon* and, again, won in a 1932 U.S. Supreme Court decision. The Texas legislature, however, continued to adapt its law to maintain white control over elections. When the Democratic Party of Texas passed a resolution to limit its membership to whites only, Richard Grovey of Houston, Texas, challenged the law without the aid of the NAACP in *Grovey v. Townsend* in 1935. In a setback decision, the U.S. Supreme Court found in favor of the Democratic Party by recognizing the right of political parties to decide their own members. The NAACP and black Texans reached a final victory over the white primary in the 1944 U.S. Supreme Court decision of *Smith v. Allwright. See also* New Negro Movement.

Further Readings: Hine, Darlene Clark. *Black Victory: The Rise and Fall of the White Primary in Texas.* New Edition. Columbia: University of Missouri Press, 2003; Kousser,

J. Morgan. *The Shaping of Southern Politics: Suffrage Restriction and the Establishment of the One-Party South, 1880–1910.* New Haven, CT: Yale University Press, 1974; Walters, Katherine Kuehler. "The Great War in Waco, Texas: African Americans, Race Relations, and the White Primary, 1916–1922." Master's thesis, Southwest Texas State University, 2000.

Katherine Kuehler Walters

White, Walter (1893–1955)

Antilynching activist and field secretary to the National Association for the Advancement of Colored People, Walter Francis White was often described as a voluntary black man whose ability to pass as white offered him a measure of privilege to investigate lynchings, riots, and racial clearances in the South. Yet, that privilege was also a burden for White. His autobiography, *A Man Called White,* begins with the self-justifying words: "I am a Negro. My skin is white, my eyes are blue, my hair is blond. The traits of my race are nowhere visible upon me" (3). Despite that accident of physiogonomy and the "magic in a white skin [and] tragedy, loneliness, and exile in a black skin," White insisted upon maintaining black identity (3). The decision emerged when his family was threatened by a lynch mob during the 1906 Atlanta race riots. Witnessing the cruelty of the mob, White decided not to "tak[e] advantage of the way of escape that was open to" him because he did not want to "be one of the race which had forced the decision" upon African Americans (5).

From the **Harlem Renaissance** to the mid-century, White was famous as an editor and activist, as well as an advisor on civil rights to Presidents **Franklin D. Roosevelt** and **Harry S. Truman**. Both Roosevelt's establishment of the Fair Employment Practices Commission and Truman's federal order for the desegregation of the **armed forces** are products of White's counsel and lobbying. His closeness to both administrations afforded him a pragmatic, voting-based perspective on African American activism and power. In the year leading up to the narrowly won presidential election of 1948 between Democrat Truman, Republican Thomas Dewey, and **Dixiecrat Strom Thurmond**, White argued for the necessity of African Americans in electoral coalitions in his essay "Will the Negro Elect the Next President?" This pragmatism, as well as his continued advocacy of the franchise as the route to change and support for American governmental power, was a countervailing force against the international activism of figures like **W.E.B. Du Bois** and Paul Robeson in the changing political climate of the 1950s and 1960s.

Since the renewed interest in **lynching** triggered by the exhibition *Without Sanctuary: Lynching Photography in America* in 2000, White's seminal work *Rope and Faggot: A Biography of Judge Lynch* (1929) was reprinted by the University of Notre Dame Press in 2002. Rather than simply a firsthand account of his lynching investigations in the 1920s and 1930s, the book is, in White's words, "the first attempt to analyze the causative factors of lynchings" (98). Bringing to bear his travels in the South, including his near-lynching upon being discovered as an African American in Elaine, Arkansas, the book suggests that lynching was an economic phenomenon that consolidated whiteness along lines of both caste and class. *See also* Costigan-Wagner Anti-Lynching Bill; Ku Klux Klan.

Further Readings: Apel, Dora. *Imagery of Lynching: Black Men, White Women, and the Mob.* New Brunswick, NJ: Rutgers University Press, 2004; Dray, Phillip. *At the Hands of Persons Unknown: The Lynching of Black America.* New York: Modern Library, 2003; Goldsby, Jacqueline. *A Spectacular Secret: Lynching in American Life and Literature.* Chicago: University of Chicago Press, 2006; White, Walter. *A Man Called White.* Athens: University of Georgia Press, 1995; White, Walter. *Rope and Faggot: A Biography of Judge Lynch.* South Bend, IN: University of Notre Dame Press, 2002.

Jennie Lightweis-Goff

Williams v. Mississippi

Williams v. Mississippi, 170 U.S. 213 (1898), limited the power of Constitutional amendments and affected **Reconstruction** in the South. In *Williams,* the **U.S. Supreme Court** unanimously ruled that disenfranchisement clauses, literacy tests, and the grandfather clause used in **Mississippi** did not discriminate against African Americans by violation of the Fifteenth Amendment. The Fifteenth Amendment in 1870 made it unconstitutional to affect the right to vote because of race or previous condition of servitude. As a result of the ruling in *Williams,* many other Southern states adopted qualifications for black voters and effectively limited the numbers of eligible black voters and potential jurors.

In *Williams v. Mississippi,* an all-white jury indicted Henry Williams, an African American man from Mississippi, for murder in 1898. He was sentenced by another all-white jury to be hanged, but Williams challenged the indictment and trial. He argued that he did not receive a fair trial because blacks were excluded from serving on the jury, which constituted a violation of the equal protection clause of the Fourteenth Amendment. Since only qualified voters could be eligible for jury duty and Mississippi had literacy and **poll tax** qualifications for voting, the number of registered black voters was severely limited.

The low number of qualified black voters was in large part due to the implementation of the **Mississippi Plan** by the Mississippi Democrats in 1890. The plan included laws to prevent blacks from voting without disenfranchising poor whites and making explicit reference to race. One law included high literacy and property requirements for African American voters. Another law, the poll tax regulation, enforced an annual tax that a person had to pay in order to vote. Legislators also used a "grandfather clause" to secure the votes of poor whites, since this rule exempted anyone from these tests who had voted or whose grandfathers had voted before 1867. If an African American met all of the requirements to vote, then an "understanding" clause blocked his eligibility. This clause allowed registrars to ask potential voters any questions about the state constitution before registering to vote.

Even though African American voters faced several prerequisites to vote in Mississippi, the Supreme Court decided on April 25, 1898, that the possibility of discrimination did not invalidate the Mississippi provisions. It stated that Williams had not proved that the administration of Mississippi suffrage provisions was discriminatory because these mechanisms did not directly mention race and there was no evidence that these provisions were given in a discriminatory manner to exclude voters based on race. Hence, literary tests, poll taxes, and other voting requirements tests did not violate the Fifteenth Amendment, provided they were applied to all applicants. The *Williams* decision provided a legal basis for blocking Africans Americans from voting and serving on juries and ensuring white political supremacy in the South. The ruling also essentially marked the lack of protection of African Americans' civil rights by the federal judiciary. The **Civil Rights Act of 1964** and the **Voting Rights Act of 1965** later superseded *Williams*, since they prohibited exclusionary tests and devices in states and areas of disproportionate minority voters.

Further Readings: Ayers, Edward L. *The Promise of the New South: Life after Reconstruction.* New York: Oxford University Press, 1992; McMillen, Neil R. *Dark Journey: Black Mississippians in the Age of Jim Crow.* Urbana: University of Illinois Press, 1990.

Dorsia Smith

Williams, Bert (1874–1922)

A century ago, the most famous African American, aside from **Booker T. Washington,** was entertainer Egbert Austin "Bert" Williams. Born on November 12, 1874, in Nassau, Williams immigrated with his family at the age of two years, living first in New York City. The family returned to the Bahamas, but again migrated to the United States, living in Florida and in San Pedro, California. The family's finances made it impossible for Williams to pursue a college degree, so he began his career as an entertainer with Martin and Selig's Mastodon Minstrels in 1893. He was joined in the company by George Walker, with whom he would form a successful partnership that would last for over a decade. Beginning in 1896, the two, billed as "The Two Real Coons" found considerable success in vaudeville and in all-black musical reviews.

As minstrel performers, Walker and Williams were remarkable not just as black men in blackface. They also managed to undermine the stereotype "coon" characters as they worked within the conventions of minstrelsy. Despite their reliance on black stage dialect and stereotyped behaviors, the performers often played characters who were as clever and ambitions as the men behind the burnt cork masks.

In 1903, the pair starred in *In Dohomey,* the first all-black musical produced on Broadway. The show toured in England and played for a birthday celebration for the Prince of Wales. The "Cakewalk," a dance featured in the show, became a sensation on both sides of the Atlantic. Other successes followed, but Walker's failing health forced his retirement in 1909. In 1910, Williams joined Flo Ziegfield's *Follies* as the company's first black headliner, a move that outraged many of the show's white cast members. He returned to the *Follies* regularly through 1919. He also appeared in a number of Biograph shorts and recorded dozens of disks for Columbia Records.

Williams called the character he reprised on stage and in recordings the "Jonah Man," a hard-luck everyman whose misfortune provides the occasion for an audience's laughter. His signature song, "Nobody," exemplified the gentle humor and pathos of that character. And while Williams retained the blackface makeup and the speech of the minstrel coon, his dignified stage persona, subtle humor, and precise execution defied the stereotype. Many of his comic monologues obliquely challenged the racial order.

Offstage, Williams found less humor in Jim Crow America. A great celebrity, he still was refused lodging and service while on tour. He confided to his colleague and friend Eddie Cantor that having to ride the service elevator at the back of a hotel would not be so bad had he not still recalled the applause from the evening's show. His frequent European tours provided a contrast to the burdensome limitations of American life. Williams died on March 4, 1922, a few days after collapsing during a show in Detroit.

Williams insisted that there was nothing "disgraceful in being a colored man" but that he "often found it inconvenient—in America." Throughout his career, he artfully made clear that distinction. *See also* Minstrelsy.

Further Readings: Chude-Sokei, Louis. *The Last "Darky": Bert Williams, Black-on-Black Minstrelsy, and the African Diaspora.* Durham, NC: Duke University Press, 2006; Debus, Allen G. "Bert Williams on Stage: Ziegfeld and Beyond." Liner notes to *Bert Williams: The Middle Years, 1910–1918.* Archeophone Records, 2002–5; Debus, Allen G., and Richard Martin. Liner notes to *Bert Williams: The Early Years, 1901–1909.* Archeophone Records, 2004; Forbes, Camille F. " 'Dancing with 'Racial Feet': Bert Williams and the Performance of Blackness." *Theatre Journal* 56 (2004): 603–25; Martin, Richard, and Meagan Hennessey. Liner notes to *Bert Williams: His Final Releases, 1919–1922.* Archeophone Records, 2001–4; Smith, Eric Ledell. *Bert Williams: A Biography of the Pioneer Black Comedian.* Jefferson, NC: McFarland, 1992; Williams, Bert. "The Comic Side of Trouble." *American Magazine* 85 (January 1918): 33–35.

James Ivy

Wilmington Race Riot (1898)

Scholars have referred to the events that occurred on November 10, 1898, in Wilmington, North Carolina as a "race riot," a "coup," and a "massacre." The appellation matters less than the fact that racial conflict that occurred marked a turning point in the history of race relations in the city, the state, the South, and the nation. The racial violence unleashed upon the city's African American population drove the interracial board of aldermen from power and effectively silenced the state's most successful black business class. The display of force two days after Democratic electoral success set the stage for the introduction of Jim Crow laws that had already taken effect in the Deep South. The lack of federal action on behalf of the city's black citizens and its interracial government reiterated the **U.S. Supreme Court** decision in ***Plessy v. Ferguson*** (1896): the promise of **Reconstruction** had been broken, and Southern blacks were now at the mercy of lynch mobs and legislators.

In the years before the riot, Wilmington's black population had established an unprecedented level of economic stability and political influence. African Americans held elected and appointed offices, including seats on the board of aldermen and the federal collector of customs. African Americans performed essential services for whites and blacks; restaurants, barber shops, and shoe stores were predominantly black-owned businesses. Many of the city's artisans were also black. The city's port industry relied heavily upon black labor. The black community's economic success contributed to its infrastructure, including two black schools, two black fire departments, and several black fraternal organizations. In addition, Wilmington featured the black-owned *Daily Record* that claimed to be the only black daily newspaper in America. Black Wilmingtonians achieved significant influence when the Republican Party formed a coalition with Populists to seize power from Democrats. The Populists compelled the state's farmers to place class interests above racism, and the coalition seized the legislature in 1894. The subsequent 1896 electoral victory of the "Fusion" Party extended the coalition's power to the governor's mansion. The Fusionists eliminated manipulation of local elections by Democrats and permitted the formation of an interracial city government in Wilmington in 1897. However, Democrats did not idly watch their enemies dismantle the white supremacist infrastructure. The 1898 electoral season proved to be a heated contest that determined the state's racial policy for more than a half-century. Wilmington was at the center of that contest.

Furnifold M. Simmons, the chairman of the state's **Democratic Party**, orchestrated the campaign against Fusion rule. He focused upon black officeholding and the perceived threat to white womanhood that Fusion rule represented. Simmons manipulated the fears of the state's agricultural classes to restore Democratic rule. In order to concoct the type of rape scare that white Southerners employed to justify lynch mobs' torture and execution of more than a thousand blacks across the South, Simmons developed a multifaceted propaganda campaign. Raleigh *News and Observer* editor Josephus Daniels circulated reports of black criminality and disrespect, particularly when the white victim was a woman. Sidewalk incidents between the races symbolized the larger struggle between blacks' demands for equality and whites' expectations of subservience. In a short period of time, Democratic newspapers had manufactured a statewide rape scare; the defeat of the Fusion ticket in November was the only solution. Simmons also organized speaking tours across the state, designed to inflame the emotions of whites through fiery oratory. **South Carolina** Senator "Pitchfork" **Ben Tillman** was the greatest attraction, and he helped usher in the third component of Simmons's campaign strategy: the Red Shirts. The Red Shirts were responsible for South Carolina's redemption during Reconstruction, and **North Carolinians** organized their own mounted band of defenders of the race. The armed Red Shirts participated in parades and attended rallies as a display of force. In addition, whites organized White Government Unions, in which membership was compulsory and racial solidarity was preserved.

Wilmington's Democratic press reprinted Georgian Rebecca Latimer Felton's impassioned plea for the protection of white womanhood in August 1898 as a call to arms to all white men. Felton demanded that white men "lynch a thousand times a week if necessary" to rid the South of the black beast rapist and rescue white women. Alexander Manly, the editor of the *Daily Record,* published a response to Felton's comments. He challenged the belief popular among whites that sex between a white woman and a black

man was always rape. On the contrary, Manly argued that many of these
affairs were consensual. He chastised white men for their failure to protect
their women, who chose black companions as a result. Manly's claim that
white women willingly bedded with black men attracted the outrage of white
North Carolinians, who perceived the claim as a slander against the purity of
white womanhood. The editorial was reprinted frequently and prominently
on the pages of Wilmington's Democratic newspapers.

The election, held on November 8, 1898, brought the results Simmons
expected—a statewide Democratic victory. Predictions of polling-place violence proved incorrect, although electoral fraud was rampant. However,
Wilmington's city government, which was decided in off-year elections,
remained in Fusion hands. In a series of secret meetings, Wilmington's leading
white businessmen developed a plot to seize power from the interracial
government. Their plot began to unfold the day after the election, when the
city's white men gathered at Thalian Hall to discuss the city's Negro Problem.
The rally produced the White Declaration of Independence, which declared an
end to interracial cooperation in Wilmington and demanded Manly's expulsion. Former Confederate officer Alfred Moore Waddell, a popular campaign
speaker, assumed a leading role. He presented the document to the leaders of
the black community, who had little choice but to accept the restoration of
white supremacy in the city. Their acceptance letter did not reach Waddell in
time as a result of an unfortunate turn of events, and on the morning of
November 10, a white mob gathered, prepared to carry out the declaration's
tenets. City and state Democratic leaders may not have intended to unleash
hell in Wilmington, but the party's campaign rhetoric enflamed racial tensions
and drove many white men to their breaking points by instilling in them the
fear of the imminent assault upon their wives and daughters.

Waddell led the mob to Manly's office. Members of the mob searched the
office, although Manly had already fled Wilmington. During their examination of the building, someone started a fire and the building burned beyond
repair. Rumors of bloody racial clashes circulated, and tensions boiled over
into gun battles across town. The city's black population was at a disadvantage; the conspirators had blocked their attempt to arm themselves ahead of
certain violence. In response to the chaos in Wilmington, Fusion governor
Daniel Russell ordered the Wilmington Light Infantry to restore order. Russell
was unaware that the infantry's commander, Walker Taylor, was one of the
conspirators; the state militia entered the conflict on the side of the white
mobs. The riot transformed into a coup as the conspirators' plot further developed. The city's board of aldermen was convened at city hall, where they were
instructed to resign one-by-one, and the Democratic leaders instructed remaining members to appoint new members. This element of the plot revealed the
conspirators' savvy: the reconstitution of the board of aldermen followed the
letter of the law. Skirmishes continued throughout the day, but the conflict
came to an end by nightfall. The death toll remains unknown; estimates range
from a few blacks to more than 100. Actual numbers are difficult to pinpoint
because many blacks simply left the city. Some hid in the surrounding swamps
after fighting broke out; others boarded trains bound for the North, leaving
behind the dead dream of Wilmington. In addition to those who voluntarily

fled, the city's new leadership banished leading members of the Fusion Party and the black community, effectively crushing any potential opposition to the new order. City officials, residents, and outside observers appealed to President William McKinley for assistance, but his action did not extend beyond a short-lived investigation into the events of November 10. Federal inaction preserved and validated the riot and coup that restored white supremacy in Wilmington.

In 1899, the state legislature instructed railroad companies to observe the principle upheld by the *Plessy v. Ferguson* ruling. In 1900, North Carolina voters ratified a suffrage amendment that followed the **Louisiana** model, including a literacy test, **poll tax**, and grandfather clause. Public facilities such as hospitals and libraries set aside black sections. The delegation of blacks to separate facilities informed them that their race was inescapable; despite black Wilmingtonians' economic success, their class did not matter in the eyes of their white counterparts. Although the state's Democratic leadership, particularly paternalistic Governor Charles B. Aycock, offered minimal state funding to programs for blacks, these resources required black submission to white authority.

The events of 1898 provided a model for whites to employ in order to suppress African Americans. Georgia gubernatorial hopeful Hoke Smith borrowed heavily from Simmons's campaign strategy in order to win the Democratic nomination. Memories of the riot served as a warning to those who intended to challenge the order established by revolution of 1898. For example, the governor reminded black activists in Wilmington that whites had once punished black advances with brute force, a thinly veiled warning that they would meet a similar fate if they continued to challenge Jim Crow. Memories of the riot continued to inspire fear within the African American community and suspicion of the city's white leaders. In this climate, Jim Crow continued to thrive on the events on November 10, 1898. *See also* Beaumont, Texas, Race Riot; Detroit Race Riot of 1943; Tulsa Race Riot.

Further Readings: Cecelski, David C., and Timothy B. Tyson, eds. *Democracy Betrayed: The Wilmington Race Riot of 1898 and Its Legacy.* Chapel Hill: University of North Carolina Press, 1998; Prather, H. Leon. *We Have Taken a City: Wilmington Racial Massacre and Coup of 1898.* Cranbury, NJ: Associated University Presses, 1984; Umfleet, LeRae. "1898 Wilmington Race Riot Report." Research Branch, Office of Archives and History, North Carolina Department of Cultural Resources. http://www.ah.dcr.state.nc.us/1898~wrrc (accessed June 12, 2008).

J. Vincent Lowery

Wisdom, John M. (1905–1999)

John Minor Wisdom served on the U.S. Court of Appeals for the Fifth Circuit for nearly 42 years. Wisdom was born on May 17, 1905 to a white, wealthy, and conservative New Orleans family. He graduated college from Washington and Lee University. After attending Harvard for one year of graduate study in literature, Wisdom pursued a law degree at Tulane University in New Orleans. Upon graduating first in his class, he began what became a successful law practice with former classmate Saul Stone.

In the early 1950s, Wisdom greatly helped to revitalize the **Republican Party** of **Louisiana**. Because of Wisdom's commitment to the Republican Party and Dwight D. Eisenhower's subsequent victory in Louisiana during his Presidential election, Eisenhower appointed Wisdom to the Fifth Circuit Court of Appeals in 1957. As a member of the Fifth Circuit, Wisdom considered himself as one of the four liberal judges, a group comprised of Richard Rives, John Brown, and Elbert Tuttle. Together, this group advanced civil rights.

For example in *United States v. Louisiana* (1964), Wisdom opposed Louisiana's use of citizenship tests that called for citizens, in particular black citizens, to interpret part of the Constitution. As in other Southern states, "interpretation" tests were used to disenfranchise potential black voters but rarely potential white voters. Often writing opinions for the Court, Wisdom wrote the following in *United States v. Louisiana* (1964): "The new test, or any other procedure more demanding than those previously applied to the white applicants, will have the effect of perpetuating the differences created by discriminatory practices of the past." Wisdom's decision was upheld by the passing of the **Voting Rights Act of 1965**.

Wisdom was also a leader in enforcing school desegregation. On June 25, 1962, Wisdom, joined by Judge John Robert Brown, announced the court's decision in *Meredith v. Fair* (1962) by ordering the admission of **James Meredith**, a black American, to the University of **Mississippi**. Another important case regarding school desegregation was *United States v. Jefferson County Board of Education* (1966), which involved the public schools in Birmingham, **Alabama**. Citing the failure of courts to implement ***Brown v. Board of Education*** (1954), Wisdom asserted that districts would need to take "affirmative action to reorganize their school systems by integrating the students, faculties, facilities, and activities." Furthermore, Wisdom acknowledged the legitimacy of race-conscious action:

> The Constitution is both color blind and color conscious. To avoid conflict with the equal protection clause, a classification that denies a benefit, causes harm, or imposes a burden must be based on race. In that sense, the Constitution is color blind. But the Constitution is color conscious to prevent discrimination being perpetuated and to undo the effects of past discrimination.

In addition to these cases, Wisdom authored opinions involving the **Ku Klux Klan**, products liability, insurance, and the relationship among taxes and oil and gas operations. Looking back on his career, Wisdom believed that total desegregation should have been ordered in the 1954 *Brown* decision, for *Brown* II allowed Southern states to move with "all deliberate speed" in desegregating schools. Never retiring from the Fifth Circuit, Wisdom died on May 15, 1999. Through his actions and words, John Minor Wisdom influenced the ways in which civil rights were implemented throughout the South and consequently the nation. *See also* U.S. Supreme Court.

Further Readings: Barnett, Robert B. "John Minor Wisdom: 'O Rare.'" *Yale Law Journal* 109 (April 2000): 1261–65; Barrow, Deborah J., and Thomas G. Walker. *A Court Divided: The Fifth Circuit Court of Appeals and the Politics of Judicial Reform.* New Haven, CT: Yale University Press, 1988; Couch, Harvey C. *A History of the Fifth Circuit, 1891–1981.* Washington, DC: U.S. Government Printing Office, 1984; Garrow, David J.

"Visionaries of the Law: John Minor Wisdom and Frank M. Johnson, Jr." *Yale Law Journal* 109 (April 2000): 1219–36; "John Minor Wisdom, 1905–1999." *Journal of Blacks in Higher Education* 24 (Summer 1999): 32; Marshall, Burke. "In Remembrance of Judges Frank M. Johnson, Jr. and John Minor Wisdom." *Yale Law Journal* 109 (April 2000): 1207–18.

Michelle A. Purdy

Women

Long before **Booker T. Washington**'s Atlanta Exposition Address in 1895 or the founding of the National Association for the Advancement of Colored People (NAACP) in 1909, African American women created clubs and organizations devoted to rescuing and protecting women from the worst abuses of **Jim Crow**. False impressions of African American women's impropriety, indolence, and immorality were widespread in American political and popular culture since the 1890s. The specious rationale of white chastity and nonwhite promiscuity became symbols of racial antagonism, as well as catalysts of intolerance generating terrible violence. Yet, Jim Crow also had the consequence of marginalizing African American women by race, gender, and class. The narrative of African American women in the twentieth century often demonstrates their difficult navigation of Jim Crow, often by relying heavily on some aspects of their identity over others. However, African American women's politics and culture have maintained their strong challenge to negative stereotypes, lack of visibility, racism, and sexism by promoting a variety of positive images and taking control of their own representation.

Rise and Peak of the Club Movement, 1890–1920

Respectability emerged as an important element in the early twentieth-century history of African American woman. The popular stereotypes of African American women characterized them as sexually and morally indiscriminate, lazy, and difficult to control. African American women organized to combat the insults. In 1893, middle-class black women of Boston formed the New Era Club and published a monthly magazine called the *Woman's Era* that featured articles on fashion, healthy, and family life. In 1895, the president of the New Era Club, Josephine St. Pierre Ruffin, issued a nationwide call to black women to form a national organization representing black women. The women were compelled to organize after journalist James W. Jacks wrote an open letter to the nation's largest newspapers claiming that black women were "prostitutes, thieves, and liars."

Ruffin drew together 104 women in Boston in order to confer on issues facing African American women in particular. The group in Boston created the National Federation of Afro-American Women in 1895. A year later this group merged with another national group, the Colored Women's League of Washington DC, and in 1896, the **National Association of Colored Women (NACW)** was formed. The NACW elected Mary Church Terrell as its first president, and adopted the self-help phrase "Lifting as We Climb" as its motto. The NACW stressed the moral, mental, and material advancement of

African American women. It was also the largest black organization in the United States until 1920. In 1914, the NACW had 50,000 members in 1,000 clubs nationwide. During this same period, the NAACP had 6,000 members and 50 local branches.

However, most African American women in the early twentieth century were not middle class or college-educated like the women of the NACW. African American women, 95 percent of whom lived in the South prior to **World War II**, were domestic servants and farmers. A small fraction of black women worked as businesswomen, teachers, and nurses. For instance, **Madame C. J. Walker** became a millionaire selling cosmetic products, while Maggie Lena Walker (no relation) presided over the highly prosperous St. Luke's Penny Savings Bank. Between 1880 and 1914, 97 percent of married white women were homemakers, and at the same time, 46 percent of all married black women worked outside the home. One-

Advice for parents who want to raise respectable African American daughters, from *Golden Thoughts on Chastity and Procreation,* by John William Gibson, 1903. Courtesy of the Library of Congress, LC-DIG-ppmsca-02926.

fourth of all black women had no children and made no plans to have children. Education and literacy were keys issues in black families and black communities. Education led the way out of poverty and disenfranchisement for all African Americans. For example, during the school year, few black children worked. They were kept out of the workforce as many months as possible during the school year.

Black women played a pivotal role in the spiritual and social welfare activities of the church, which served as an instrument of political liberation during Jim Crow. The two main denominations among African American communities were the African Methodist Episcopal (AME) Church and the Baptists. African American women, particularly the Women's Convention of the National Baptist convention, concentrated their efforts on programs of moral, spiritual, and emotional support with social welfare and private charity. The AME church operated 25 schools around the country for blacks, and the

Baptist church oversaw nearly 14 colleges and universities for blacks. From the church, women followed a path into the profession of teaching, one of the most respectable vocations for African American women.

Suffrage Movement, World War I, and the 1920s

Black clubwomen advocated for women's voting rights on a national scale, arguing that when African American women won the right to vote, Jim Crow and the disenfranchisement of African American men would be reevaluated, then dismantled. Elite black women also claimed they had a special duty to educate working-class women about their political rights. The woman suffrage movement drew African American women to the cause from across the country. **Ida B. Wells-Barnett** worked for the suffrage movement in Illinois, and Mary Church Terrell lobbied for suffrage in Washington, DC.

Woman suffrage became the most hotly debated political issue in the country between 1910 and 1920. The movement also suffered from the divisions caused by fears of racial mixture and black political power. A deep rift between white suffragists and black suffragists emerged by 1915 over African American women's voting rights. The woman suffrage movement also threatened to overturn the racial etiquette of the day, since disenfranchisement laws had stripped black men of their political power. White Southern men generally were opposed to granting any black person, man or woman, the right to vote. Facing white opposition in the South, white suffragists opted to ask black women to distance themselves from the suffrage movement. For the sake of political expedience, white suffragists said they could not afford black women's support. Conservative white suffragists campaigned for literacy tests and understanding clauses, in order to limit the number of black voters.

At the same time that the suffrage movement gathered strength, **World War I** also influenced the lives and labor of African American women. Racial segregation in the military during World War I presented a difficult challenge to African Americans who chose to serve the country. Black women, for their part, did their best to maintain the home, family, and community during the war. One primary concern was dealing with the food rations, as well as looking out for working black women who found short-term jobs in factories. Black women's club work filled in the gaps left by the war, by leading literacy training, domestic science courses, and food conservation classes. Black women also got together to make comfort kits for black soldiers, which held scarves or mittens, cigarettes, a Bible or other reading material, and a pen and paper. African American women also formed recreation clubs for black soldiers or sent soldiers these comfort kits through the mail.

World War I also ignited a mass relocation of African Americans, known as the **Great Migration**. Demographical studies estimate that between 1910 and 1920, some 500,000 blacks moved from Southern states to the Northern cities. African American women moved from rural areas to urban areas in Southern states, and then from Southern states to Northern states. The Great Migration presented unprecedented opportunities to working-class black women, particularly Southern domestic workers, to earn higher wages and gain autonomy over the work they did. Creating a more pleasant work environment and maintaining agency over one's labor were objectives that resounded among Southern black domestics. They found nontraditional employment in areas outside of the South, though African American newspapers initially focused on the movement of black working men migrating to the North. Black women's wartime employment also cultivated greater interest in **labor unions**, which African American labor experts predicted would lead to job security and economic advancement.

In the postwar period, growing populations of African Americans in Northern cities took greater interest in mass political and artistic movements, such as **Marcus Garvey**'s movement and the **Harlem Renaissance**. Women were active members of the Garvey movement of the 1920s, particularly Garvey's wife, Amy Jacques Garvey. She was chiefly responsible for publishing a collection of Garvey's papers, lectures, and addresses in the *Philosophy and Opinions of Marcus Garvey*. African American women wrote some of the most important novels of the Harlem Renaissance—Zora Neale Hurston and *Their Eyes Were Watching God*; Nella Larsen and *Passing*; Jessie Fausett and *There Is Confusion*. African American women also engaged in sharp political debates about the artistic and political purposes of African American literature. Zora Neale Hurston was joined by her friends, **Langston Hughes** and Wallace Thurman, in arguing that literature must remain true to its subjects and present all aspects of African American life, including the seedy or embarrassing sides.

The Great Depression and World War II

The **Great Depression** devastated the middle-class America and brought an abrupt end to the Harlem Renaissance, but most blacks only saw a slight change in their economic status. The majority of black farmers were at the mercy of an agricultural system that exploited their labor. One of the key problems of the Depression was the collapse of crop prices, especially corn, wheat, and cotton. Many black families of the South, who were sharecroppers or tenant farmers, found themselves nearly pushed off the farm and into very hard times. In the North, blacks lost jobs that they had held all through the 1920s. Blacks in the North often worked in low-paying jobs such as garbage collection, domestic services, cooks, and janitors. As desperation set in, whites in the North and South competed for these jobs and pressured employers to hire only whites.

The effects of the Great Depression were deeply felt among African American women and domestic work. In the 1920s, black women workers concentrated on domestic service and laundry work. At the peak of the Depression, many middle-class families and even upper-class families could no longer afford domestic service. With the large numbers of impoverished women coming into the cities, white families with women found that they could pay almost nothing and still employ desperate women. In 1935, two black women, Marvel Cooke and Ella Baker, published an exposé of the exploitation of women laborers and they called it "The Bronx Slave Market." Cooke and Baker described how in the Bronx, black women gathered on street corners and waited for affluent white women to select them for one day's labor. The women received wages as low as 15 to 25 cents per hour, for two or three hours a day.

The outbreak of World War II propelled the second wave of the Great Migration. More than 300,000 African American men abandoned **sharecropping** and took jobs in the defense industry. Between 1940 and 1944, the percentage of black women workers in the industrial workforce increased from 6.8 percent to 18 percent, and nearly 400,000 African American women labored in factories and defense plants. Domestic service witnessed a transformation in wages and working conditions. Good-paying industrial and defense labor jobs allowed more American families to earn significantly more money, which in turn allowed them to hire domestic workers. The demand for domestic workers reached such heights that domestic workers actually set their own wages.

In terms of military service, African Americans contributed to the war effort chiefly as members of the National Association of Colored Graduate Nurses. The nurses were stationed in England, Scotland, and parts of Europe. African American women also served in the Women's Army Auxiliary Corps, since the army and navy granted admission to black women as nurses in January 1945.

Civil Rights Movement

African American women played crucial roles in the **Civil Rights Movement** of the 1950s and 1960s. Gender segregation within the Civil Rights Movement stifled much of women's work. It was a bitter pill for many black woman activists to swallow. Yet, African American women participated on every level of the movement. They completed the necessary, unglamorous clerical and logistical work: they typed memos, ran the offices, connected outsiders to neighborhoods, wrote legal briefs, wrote affidavits, wrote speeches, ran neighborhood organizations, participated in **sit-ins**, and registered voters.

African American women also achieved a number of firsts in the Civil Rights Movement. **Autherine Lucy** and Vivian Malone Jones were the first African Americans to desegregate and graduate from the University of Alabama. Pauli Murray became the first African American to receive a law degree from Yale University in 1965. Ada Lois Sipuel broke the color barrier at the University of Oklahoma Law School in 1949. Dorothy Counts was joined by three other students in 1957 who desegregated Harding High School in Charlotte, North Carolina. Mamie Till Mobley provided the emotional foundation of the Civil Rights Movement by allowing the country to see the battered, murdered body of her son, **Emmett Till,** who was lynched in 1955. **Rosa Parks** was a long-time member of the NAACP, whose arrest ignited the **Montgomery Bus Boycott. Constance Baker Motley** was a coleader in the **NAACP Legal Defense Fund.** Ella Baker encouraged students to follow nonviolent resistance as a discipline and to form the **Student Nonviolent Coordinating Committee. Fannie Lou Hamer,** an outspoken activist, led the Mississippi Freedom Democratic Party. Indeed, the success of the Civil Rights Movement depended heavily on the work of women, both ordinary citizens and prominent leaders.

By the mid-1960s, the growing issue of sexism in the Civil Rights Movement led African American women to approach other protest organizations. The formation of the National Organization for Women (NOW) in 1966 came about during a brainstorming session and included the prominent voices of Pauli Murray and Aileen Hernandez. African American women found that political questions relating to gender—equal pay, equal opportunity, maternity leave, child care, welfare for mothers—had remained unresolved. NOW promised to put those issues on the forefront. NOW also made popular the act of "consciousness raising" and the notion of the "personal is political."

However, NOW had trouble appealing to women of color. An early claim that white women were oppressed like slaves offended African American women; similar missteps with other women of color appeared to indicate that the race remained a divisive factor even among groups facing gender oppression. As a result, African American women did not join mainstream women's rights organizations in large numbers. The competing oppressions of race, gender, and class divided African American women's loyalties, as it had during the suffrage movement.

African American women continued to address the lingering effects of Jim Crow, primarily by forming organizations to define themselves and their consciousnesses. The 1970s witnessed a tremendous growth in black women's organizations, including the National Black Women's Feminist Organization and the Combahee River Collective. Bolstered by a new generation of activists, African American women have carried on the steady work of maintaining the political agenda of the Civil Rights Movement and challenging the movement to embrace a wider vision of civic equality for all Americans. *See also* Domestic Work; Nadir of the Negro.

Further Readings: Brown, Nikki. *Private Politics and Public Voices: African American Women's Activism from World War I to the New Deal.* Bloomington: Indiana University Press, 2007; Collier-Thomas, Bettye, and V. P. Franklin. *Sisters in the Struggle: African American Women in the Civil Rights–Black Power Movement.* New York: New York University Press, 2001; Crawford, Vicki L., Jacqueline Anne Rouse, and Barbara Woods. *Women in the Civil Rights Movement: Trailblazers and Torchbearers, 1941–1965.* Bloomington: Indiana University Press, 1993; Gilmore, Glenda Elizabeth. *Gender and Jim Crow: Women and the Politics of White Supremacy in North Carolina, 1896–1920.* Chapel Hill: University of North Carolina Press, 1996; Hine, Darlene Clark. *A Shining Thread of Hope: The History of Black Women in America.* New York: Broadway Books, 1998; Jones, Jacqueline. *Labor of Love, Labor of Sorrow: Black Women, Work, and Family from Slavery to the Present.* New York: Basic Books, 1985.

Nikki Brown

Woodward, C. Vann (1908–1999)

C. (Comer) Vann Woodward was an eminent American historian whose scholarship focused primarily on the South and Southern race relations. He was the author of the revisionist (and now classic) book, *The Strange Career of Jim Crow* (1955), which opened a new field of the study of racial segregation in the United States.

Born in Vanndale, **Arkansas**, on November 13, 1908, he received a PhB from Emory University in 1930, an MA from Columbia University in 1932, and a PhD from the University of North Carolina in 1937. He subsequently taught history at the University of Florida (1937–1939), the University of

Virginia (1939–1940), Scripps College (1940–1943), Johns Hopkins University (1946–1961), and Yale University (1961–1977). He was professor emeritus at Yale from 1977 to 1999.

Woodward's book *Origins of the New South, 1877–1913* (1951) won the Bancroft Prize and established him as one of the leading historians of the American South. He received the Pulitzer Prize in 1982 for *Mary Chesnut's Civil War* (1981), his edited edition of a Confederate woman's Civil War diaries. He married Glenn Boyd MacLeod in 1937, and they had one son.

Woodward was active in the **Civil Rights Movement** during the 1950s and remained politically active until the end of his life. The National Association for the Advancement of Colored People in 1953 asked him, along with John Hope Franklin, to assist in preparing the legal brief for the **Brown v. Board of Education** case before the **U.S. Supreme Court**. Two years later, he published his controversial and best-selling *The Strange Career of Jim Crow*. The book was to become so influential that **Martin Luther King, Jr.**, would refer to it as "the historical Bible of the civil rights movement."

Strange Career was based on a series of lectures Woodward had delivered at the University of Virginia. The book overturned the conventional historical approach to the Southern system of legal segregation, which up to that time had been assumed by historians to have developed immediately after **Reconstruction** (1867–1877), and was understood to have returned the South to a system of racial separation that had functioned under **slavery**. The history of race relations in the South was more complicated than that, Woodward argued, with rigid legal segregation not being solidified into law until the 1890s. Under slavery, he insisted, Southerners had lived unsegregated lives, with whites maintaining dominance over blacks by other means. Between the end of the Civil War and the turn of the century, a variety of racial accommodations characterized the South, involving varying degrees of tolerance, experimentation, and integration. Racial segregation in the legal form that was overturned by the Supreme Court in 1954 was a product of the New South and not the Old South, according to Woodward.

Woodward characterized the rise of a legal system of segregated churches, schools, jobs, waiting rooms, and public places as developing in the 1890s. It represented a sharp break, an aberration in his view, in the history of the South—which had previously been characterized by unequal, but never spatially separated, relations between the races. Segregation, he argued, had emerged primarily as a tool of wealthy, white Southern elites, who used it to combat the threat of white and black Populism, in a kind of divide-and-conquer stratagem. Woodward's book was primarily responsible for establishing the term "Jim Crow" as a shorthand term for the whole system of legal segregation, disenfranchisement, **lynching**, and violence against blacks that marked the South in the twentieth century.

Woodward's thesis has had strong critics as well as supporters. The critics have suggested that Woodward seriously underestimated the racial segregation that existed in Southern cities, and in the North as well, before the 1890s. They point to continuities with slavery times, rather than discontinuities. Woodward responded often to his critics, revising *Strange Career* in

1957, 1966, and 1974. After his retirement, he published *Thinking Back: The Perils of Writing History*, a memoir of his career as an historian.

Woodward's conclusions have been considerably modified by recent scholarship. Nonetheless, his *Strange Career* remains still the only full-length study of the history of racial segregation across the South. Whatever its shortcomings, Woodward's book was the first to recognize that Jim Crow was not a natural, unchanging phenomenon, but a series of man-made institutions with a checkered history that could be studied.

Further Readings: Roper, John Herbert. *C. Vann Woodward, Southerner*. Athens: University of Georgia Press, 1987; Roper, John Herbert, ed. *C. Vann Woodward: A Southern Historian and His Critics*. Athens: University of Georgia Press, 1997; Woodward, C. Vann. *The Strange Career of Jim Crow*. New York: Oxford University Press, 1955.

Anthony A. Lee

Works Progress Administration

On May 6, 1935, President **Franklin D. Roosevelt** issued Executive Order 7034, which created the Works Progress Administration (WPA). Authorized by the Emergency Relief Appropriation Act, the WPA was established to alleviate unemployment caused by the **Great Depression**. Between 1935 and 1943, the WPA employed 8.5 million Americans in the completion of 1.5 million publicly financed projects, which ranged from the building of bridges and schools to the writing of travel guidebooks, the painting of murals in public buildings, and the production of theatrical performances.

The **federal government** expressly forbade discrimination in the hiring of workers for WPA projects, but unemployed African Americans soon found that this directive was ignored by relief administrators in the South. In most instances, it was more difficult for African Americans to qualify for WPA jobs, and they were paid less than their white co-workers. This was especially true in Atlanta, where white workers were paid $32.66 per month while their black counterparts received a mere $19.29. In addition, blacks were restricted to manual and unskilled positions regardless of education, experience, or ability. Only 100 African Americans out of 4,000 WPA workers in St. Louis worked in white-collar positions. In Memphis, administrators removed blacks from the relief rolls in order to force them to pick cotton on nearby farms. On the whole, fewer African Americans were able to qualify for relief work, with only 350,000 employed annually. As a result of these restrictive measures, only 11 African American supervisors were in the whole of the Southern states five years after the program began.

Many Southern whites, in spite of their success in restricting African Americans from fully benefiting from the WPA, deeply resented the fact that black WPA workers labored outside their traditional work roles, and did all they could to discourage participation. For example, armed guards monitored the labor of female construction workers in Jackson, **Mississippi**. White Southern Democrats also opposed the program because it was perceived to strengthen the power of the federal government over that of the states. Nor were they sanguine in 1936 when President Roosevelt received 76 percent of black votes, which resulted in African Americans becoming a powerful voting bloc within the **Democratic Party**. Consequently, the WPA was frequently used as a weapon by conservative Democrats to castigate Roosevelt's **New Deal** reforms.

Arguably, the Works Progress Administration was the most efficient public works program in the history of American government. It averaged a payroll of $2,112,000 per month between the years 1935 and 1941, which provided significant assistance to destitute Americans. For African Americans in particular, the WPA provided much needed employment despite the fact that it condoned segregation and discrimination. At its height, the WPA was the greatest source of income for African Americans living in the Southern United States, while a quarter of a million black citizens were taught to read as a result of their involvement in the program. Perhaps more importantly, in giving African Americans employment outside of agriculture and domestic service, the Works Progress Administration strengthened their resolve in the struggle to dismantle legalized segregation.

Further Readings: Biles, Roger. *Memphis in the Great Depression.* Knoxville: University of Tennessee Press, 1986; Biles, Roger. *A New Deal for the American People.* DeKalb: Northern Illinois University Press, 1991; Cobb, James C., and Michael V. Namorato, eds. *The New Deal and the South.* Jackson: University Press of Mississippi, 1984.

Wayne Dowdy

World War I

World War I involved the United States directly for only about a year and a half. The war occurred during one of the worst periods of oppression of black people in the United States since the end of **slavery**. Yet, the war also began to unleash forces that would, in the long run, begin the dismantling of **Jim Crow**. About 400,000 black men, and some black women, served in the American military during the war, which subjected them to both the military's version of Jim Crow, while at the same time exposing many of them to a world beyond Jim Crow in Europe. Additionally, the economic mobilization of the war years brought new economic possibilities, and began the **Great Migration** of blacks from the rural South to the urban South, and eventually to the urban North. However, in the two years following the end of the war, blacks were victims of the worst racial violence since **Reconstruction**.

Jim Crow was justified in part by the idea that black men were naturally cowards, or that they would not fight for the United States. Most history of black participation in previous wars had been largely purged from historical memory. Men who would not fight were not fit to vote. Thus, many in the military and government, especially Southern whites, were hesitant over the idea of using blacks in combat. While most racists had little problem with using blacks in the military in support or transportation units, the idea of arming blacks and training them to kill Germans threatened to undermine the whole Jim Crow system. Black leaders put pressure on the **federal government** to allow black men to serve in the infantry, hoping that a strong showing of black men defending the United States would give a moral argument for allowing black men to vote. Under pressure from blacks and their white liberal allies, the government adopted a policy whereby Selective Service was instructed to induct blacks as well as whites, and for the army to create new infantry regiments and even divisions of black men.

When the United States declared war on the Central Powers in April 1917, the regular army contained two infantry and two cavalry regiments of African Americans, for a total of almost 10,000 black men. This number included an influx of 4,000 men who joined during a recruiting drive in 1916. Of these four black regiments, three remained in the United States throughout the war, while one served in the Philippines. The National Guard contained another 10,000 black men, almost all of whom were from Northern states. However most black men who served in the military during the First World War, like their white counterparts, entered the military through Selective Service. Thirty-four percent of black registrants were later drafted, compared to 24 percent for whites. A total of 13 percent of draftees were black, although blacks constituted only around 10 percent of the total population. However, in the spring and early summer of 1917, whites were actively sought for voluntary enlistment into the military, whereas most blacks were denied enlistment, so that the eventual wartime army roughly reflected the ratio of blacks to whites in the nation. **W.E.B. Du Bois**, among other black intellectuals, urged blacks to support the war effort fully, believing that black opposition would be used to justify further oppression, whereas faithful support of the nation during wartime would bring recognition of the rights of blacks as Americans. In September 1917, Emmett J. Scott, former secretary to **Booker T. Washington**, was appointed special assistant to the U.S. secretary of war. Scott's mission was to assure that Selective Service did not discriminate.

With the war coming at the height of the Progressive Era, the army attempted to use "scientific" intelligence testing to place drafted men into the most suitable position. Two professors, Walter D. Scott, and Robert Yerkes, developed a series of questions that they believed measured innate intelligence, but actually tested familiarity with upper middle-class white culture. With 90 percent of blacks from the rural South illiterate, their knowledge of, for example, characters in the works of Charles Dickens was limited. According to the tests, almost half of all white and 89 percent of black draftees rated as "morons." While white supremacists tried to use the tests as "proof" that blacks were inferior to whites, the tests also showed that, on average, black Northerners outscored rural white Southerners. Such reports angered white Southerners, and the army disregarded the tests.

African American soldiers following Lincoln to patriotic service, 1918. Courtesy of Library of Congress, LC-USZC4-2426.

Excerpt from "Negro Troops in France," 1919

Robert Russa Moton (1867–1940) was an African American author and educator. He was appointed principal of Tuskegee Institute in 1915, following the death of Booker T. Washington, and served in that position until he retired in 1935. This letter written by Moton, who visited France after the war, urged black soldiers to rise above Jim Crow upon their return to the United States.

A letter that I saw written by a lady overseas to another lady in the United States, stated that the writer had been told by the Colonel of a certain unit, whose guest she was, that he would not feel it safe for her to walk, even with him, through this camp of Negro soldiers.

Another letter from a high official in a very important position with the overseas Negro troops, written unofficially to a very prominent official on this side, stated, that, in the 92nd Division alone, there had been at least thirty cases of the unmentionable crime.

Another rumor, equally malignant and damaging, was to the effect that the fighting units commanded by Negro officers had been a failure. On other words, "the whispering gallery," which was most active in France on phases of life overseas, said that the 92nd Division, in which Negroes in American took special pride, and with good reason, had failed utterly; that, wherever they had been engaged, the Negro officers had gone to pieces; and that in some cases the men had to pull themselves together after their officer had shown the "white feather" [shown cowardice].

Moton's remarks to black soldiers later in his trip:

The record you have made in this warm, of faithfulness, bravery, and loyalty, has deepened my faith in you as men and as soldiers, as well as in my race and country. You have suffered hardships and many privations. You have been called upon to make many sacrifices. Your record has sent a thrill of joy and satisfaction to the hearts of millions of white and black Americans, rich and poor, high and low. Black mothers and wives, sweethearts, fathers, and friends have rejoiced with you and with our country in your record.

You will go back to America as heroes, as you really are. You will go back as you have carried yourselves over here—in a straightforward, manly, and modest way. If I were you, I would find a job as soon as possible, and get to work. To those who have not already done so, I would suggest that you get hold of a piece of land and home as soon as possible, and marry and settle down. Save your money, and put it into something tangible. I hope no one will do anything in peace to spoil the magnificent record of your troops have made in the war.

Source: *Southern Workman*, May 5, 1919, 219–24.

Most blacks who served in the military during the war served in the army. The Marine Corps admitted no blacks, while the navy took in about 1 percent. Of 400,000 blacks who served in the war, some 42,000 served in combat, a ratio slightly lower than for whites. Before the war, the black regular army regiments were stationed in the West or at overseas posts, as with most white regiments. However, the needs of the rapid mobilization for the war made necessary the construction of large mobilization and training camps, the majority of which were in the South, where land was cheaper and the warmer climate would allow more training over the winter of 1917–1918. Many blacks in the army assumed that their status as soldiers of the United States would protect them from Jim Crow, and for many Northern blacks, their time at training camps in the South would be their first experience with Jim Crow.

However, the army was sensitive to the opposition it faced from Southern political leaders over the very idea of arming and training black men, and bringing large numbers of them together. Southern political leaders often protested to the federal government when they found a black unit was to be stationed nearby. Among Southern whites, the use of black men by the federal government during the Civil War and Reconstruction was seen as an act of barbarity. The army feared the backlash from any incident that might occur. As a result, the army imposed strict Jim Crow–style regulations over its black soldiers, and in general sought to ship black units to Europe quickly, often before they had been properly trained or equipped. However much the army attempted to mollify Southern whites by keeping the black soldiers under tight control, incidents were bound to occur.

The worst incident came on August 23, 1917, at Camp Logan, near Houston, Texas, involving soldiers from the 24th Infantry regiment, one of the four black regular army regiments. Many members of the 24th were relatively new soldiers, and the regiment had only recently been transferred to the South, where it was providing protection for a new training facility while it was under construction. However, the 24th, as with many regular regiments, had recently lost many of its long-term noncommissioned officers who had been assigned to the newly forming regiments in the national army. Additionally, many of the soldiers in the 24th had little firsthand experience with Jim Crow, and assumed their status as soldiers of the United States would shield them. Instead, the soldiers found themselves constantly harassed by civilians and police. When one of their own was arrested by local police, about 100 soldiers from two battalions used their army weapons in an attempt to free him. In the resulting melee, 16 white people died, including five policemen, and about a dozen others wounded. In the aftermath, the army tried by courts-martial 155 men in all. Nineteen of the men were hanged by the army, with no advanced public notice. The incident shocked blacks, who saw it as a **lynching**. Throughout the South, white communities interpreted the violence in Houston as an example of what happens when Northern blacks come to the South, and whites in the South became even more vigilant in ensuring Northern blacks respect the color line. The secretary of war, Newton D. Baker, a liberal, told President Woodrow Wilson that Jim Crow was the cause of the problems with the black units.

Racial violence between white civilians and black soldiers, such as in Houston, was used to justify keeping black soldiers in labor battalions and not issuing them weapons. As labor units, the African Americans performed superbly. One regiment, working as stevedores at a French port, was expected to unload 6,000 tons a month, based on French estimates. In September 1918 alone, they unloaded 800,000 tons. But many blacks, both soldiers and civilians, resented their serving only as laborers and clamored for black combat units. The army relented and reluctantly agreed to create more infantry units. Since segregation was the rule of the day in the army, black units were not comingled with white units. Instead, the army took the various black National Guard regiments and battalions and mixed them with newly formed regiments of black draftees, to create two new divisions, the 92nd and the 93rd.

Blacks also wanted to see black officers, not just black enlisted men. The army had, at the start of the war, very few black officers. Indeed almost all of the officers in the four black regular army regiments were white, although almost all of the officers in the black National Guard units were black. The highest ranking black officer at the start of the war was Lieutenant Colonel

Charles A. Young, a West Point graduate who served with the 10th Cavalry in Arizona. The army received complaints from Southern congressmen when white Southern junior officers were assigned to the 10th, which would mean serving under Colonel Young. Despite a flawless record, including combat in Cuba and Mexico, Young was forcibly retired, extensively on medical grounds, but in reality to placate Southern congressmen. Colonel Young appealed his retirement, but was not returned to active service until just before the war ended. Southern congressmen insisted that in no situation would white men be commanded by a black man. They dropped their opposition to the army creating a black Officers Candidate School only when the Army assured them that black officers would never command white troops. At Fort Des Moines in Iowa, some 639 black men received commissions—106 as captains and the rest as lieutenants—out of 1,250 candidates. Almost all of these black officers were then assigned to the new black infantry regiments in the national army. However, even as officers, these men soon found that the qrmy treated them as inferiors and subjected them to the same Jim Crow as enlisted black soldiers.

Prejudice against black soldiers within the army created the self-fulfilling prophecy of failure of black soldiers in battle. The most notorious example was the 92nd Division. The division suffered from poor training, lack of equipment, no artillery, and uneven officer quality. While some of the officers, especially the lower-ranking officers, were black, most officers, including all the higher-ranking officers, were white. Many of the white officers assigned to black units were either the castoffs from other divisions or self-identified racists in the belief that they "knew how to handle blacks." Thrown into battle on unfamiliar terrain two days after arrival in the Argonne, two battalions from the 368th Regiment failed in combat, while others performed well. The failure of some elements of the 92nd was projected to the entire division, and then to all black soldiers. The failure of the 92nd was cited as "proof" that blacks were naturally unfit for combat. As a result, most black combat soldiers had their weapons taken away and were employed in manual labor, especially as stevedores. This stigma would last through **World War II**.

In sharp contrast to the experience of the 92nd Division was that of the 93rd. The 93rd Division was "loaned" to the French Army, in part to ward off pressure from the French to take control of the entire American Expeditionary Force. While the French army was segregated by colonial or metropolitan origins of each regiment, it was not technically segregated on the color line. More importantly, the French had no stereotype of Africans or blacks being cowards or unfit to serve as soldiers. The French separated the four regiments of the 93rd and attached them to French divisions. Black American officers were shocked to find that French officers treated them as equals, as brother officers, something that never occurred in the U.S. Army. With French equipment, proper training, and capable leadership, the African American regiments performed well, earning 550 French decorations, including 180 of the Croix de Guerre, while suffering 35 percent casualties. They held their front for 191 days without losing territory, while capturing many Germans. The French government was so pleased with the performance of the black American soldiers that it heaped honors and praise on the fighting ability of the black Americans, which in turned led to the U.S. government requesting that the French cease its high praise, lest the black Americans come home demanding that they be treated as equals.

The worst period of violence against blacks came in the two years after the war, when postwar economic readjustment put many strains on American society. While labor violence erupted in Washington State and Oregon, and in Boston, the police strike took the occupation of the city by the State Guard to restore order, the worst violence in the nation was racial. Mississippi had the worst violence since the end of Reconstruction. Some whites bemoaned that they would have to lynch thousands of black men in order to restore the status quo as it had been before the war. Whites feared black men who had fought Germans—a white people—in Europe, and who had been "spoiled by French whores," would forget their place in America. While black Americans would celebrate units such as the 369th Regiment, the "Harlem Hellfighters," which saw heroic service with the French army, white America soon forgot all about black service and loyalty during the war, and instead subjected blacks to increased racism and savage violence, lest blacks think the war might change race relations in the nation. The experience would be a bitter lesson for black Americans. *See also* Armed Forces; National Guard; Red Summer; Veterans Groups.

Further Readings: Buckley, Gail L. *American Patriots: The Story of Blacks in the Military from the Revolution to Dessert Storm.* New York: Random House, 2002; Donaldson, Gary A. *The History of African-Americans in the Military.* Malabar, FL: Krieger Publishing Company, 1991; Edgerton, Robert B. *Hidden Heroism: Black Soldiers in America's Wars.* Boulder, CO: Westview Press, 2001.

Barry M. Stentiford

World War II

World War II was a pivotal event in history as it marked the emergence of modern America. The country came out of the war as a world economic and military power. Thousands of war veterans moved to the middle class thanks to housing and education loans through the federal **G.I. Bill** (officially known as the Serviceman's Readjustment Act). The role of government changed as did the place of African Americans and women in society. During the war, factories increased production to provide war goods to the armed services. The creation of this defense industry allowed African Americans and women to attain better-paying factory jobs that were never open to them before. After working in factories during the war, American women began to permanently move out of the home and into the workforce, changing gender and family dynamics. Many African American workers left the rural South to take advantage of job opportunities in the cities of the North and West. New types of jobs were open to black women, as many moved out of domestic positions and into the service sector. Most African Americans were eager to contribute to the war effort. Many black men, in an attempt to show their patriotism joined the armed forces. Segregation in the military and the treatment of blacks as second-class citizens at home angered many blacks and prompted them to advocate for equality in America as the country was fighting for freedom and against Fascism in Europe.

Migration

During the war, the nation's factories increased production to make goods for the war, providing much needed jobs in the wake of the **Great Depression**. Since many white men had gone to war, women and African Americans took their places in factories. The availability of better-paying factory jobs attracted rural blacks to industrial centers all over the country. African Americans living in rural areas of the South migrated to Southern cities, which were industrializing for war production. Hundreds of thousands of Southern blacks who wanted to escape violence and **Jim Crow** chose to leave the South completely, migrating to cities in the North and West. This migration, often referred to as the Second **Great Migration**, caused various effects in the places from which migrants left and those to which they traveled. Many blacks found better-paying positions during the war in factories producing goods for the military. This notwithstanding they also faced discrimination in their new homes. Moreover, overcrowding of black communities and subsequent expansion of black residence into other communities, competition over war industry employment, unequal access to skilled employment, and race antagonisms were all effects of the World War II migration.

Blacks moved en masse to cities in the West such as Oakland and Los Angeles, where huge shipyards and new aerospace industries were located. African Americans also moved to cities with heavy industry—for example, steel and automobile factories, which could be easily converted to produce war goods. The black populations of Detroit and Chicago skyrocketed during the war. Black migrants also continued to settle in New York City even though the city's factories converted to wartime production much later than other cities because of the lack of heavy industry.

The influx of blacks in Northern and Western cities caused changes to the population of these cities, which often led to racial tension and competition over jobs and resources. As more and more blacks moved into Western cities in areas where they had never lived, African American faced increased discrimination from white residents. In these new areas of black settlement like Los Angeles and Richmond, California, black residence was restricted to declining neighborhoods.

In Detroit and Chicago, cities with a large black population, more and more blacks moved there, settling in the existing black neighborhoods and straining the community resources available. Because the number of blacks skyrocketed in these cities and the areas where they could reside did not, the migration resulted in overcrowding of black neighborhoods, higher mortality rates, and increased crime. The standard of living in many of these urban black communities declined.

Black Labor

Though the industries of the North and West attracted Southern blacks, there were factors pushing them to leave the South. Technological innovations displaced agricultural black laborers in the South, prompting many to look for employment in urban factories. The mechanical cotton picker made the share-cropper system obsolete. Mechanization of farming through the adoption of tractors, harvesters, and sprayers made the need for black farm workers decline. Therefore, World War II provided industrial opportunities for blacks looking to leave a Southern economy that had less and less of a place for them. As the migration continued, the black community in Southern rural areas was gradually erased.

Many black migrants were not initially able to take advantage of the labor shortages in the early years of the war, especially in construction, heavy indus-try, and the aircraft industry. Employers hired white workers, ending white unemployment, while blacks remained without jobs, without training, and deprived of income because of reductions in Depression-era federal relief pro-grams. Many companies, especially aviation factories that produced planes for the military, refused to employ black workers, a policy supported by the trade unions representing white workers. The United States Employment Service (USES), a federal agency, continued to fill "white only" requests from factory employers. The Employment Service's general policy was to operate according to the pattern of the local community; therefore, if industries in a community did not hire black workers, their office would not, either. The policy of the USES reinforced discriminatory hiring practices of employers. For these rea-sons, during the early war years, African Americans often had trouble finding any position other than custodian in war industries.

In the South, where much defense industry was located, the National Youth Administration could not enroll blacks in training programs. There were no technical schools for blacks in the South, and because of Jim Crow laws, blacks could not enroll in white schools to learn these skills. In their efforts to exert greater control in government worker recruitment, Southern gover-nors increasingly relied on closed shop agreements with trade unions of the American Federation of Labor (AFL). This collusion between local govern-ments and the AFL would restrict who received the expanding employment benefits, a fact that had large implications for African Americans since they were often excluded from AFL membership. Southern employers preferred to use white women instead of blacks to fill labor vacancies in order to preserve the racial configuration and power relations of Southern society. In this way, federal mobilization agencies became the battleground over labor control in the South.

In 1943, circumstances in the labor market changed that prompted factories nationwide to open their doors to black workers. Increased demands for war production and a manpower shortage forced factories to hire black workers. With labor shortages becoming more acute each day and the government considering plans for manpower allocation, employers began to relax the bars to hiring, and unions found it more difficult to maintain restrictive policies. African Americans began to find skilled and semiskilled positions in the nation's factories, earning more money than they had before. Black women in particular moved out of domestic jobs and into jobs in factories and service industries.

Social Effects of the Migration

In the South, employment of blacks in factories unsettled race relations. Whites in the rural South who were anxious about **miscegenation** openly resented wage increases for African Americans. These advances made Negroes too independent in their eyes, which was a dangerous development because it would foster African Americans' quest for social equality. Many blacks received war jobs, and some even managed to obtain skilled positions in plants. In general, however, the most menial and work-intensive jobs were given to black workers. White workers largely rose in status and income, but black workers entering the labor market took over the worst positions. Moreover, the traditional labor system of the South was being disrupted. To ensure adequate and efficient war production, the War Manpower Commission recruited Southern black workers to move to the Midwest and West Coast. This further undermined the low-wage labor system of Southern industries and large-scale agriculture.

The migration affected social and racial patterns in Northern and Western cities also. In Western cities, where few blacks had lived before the war, the migration had enormous employment and social effects. The massive wartime influx of black migrants to Los Angeles and San Francisco changed the racial and regional composition of the population. The arrival of unskilled migrants who would work for less pay prompted a restructuring of production methods from craftsmanship to mass production. In response, unions tightened their control on membership, excluding black workers. The Brotherhood of Boilermakers, the AFL craft union for shipyard workers, was the most vocal opponent of the new labor process.

In reaction to black migration white residents often placed more stringent social controls on African Americans. Between 1940 and 1945, over 340,000 black people migrated to California to take advantage of employment opportunities in the new war industries. After the passage of Executive Order 8802 banning race discrimination in defense industries, black workers accelerated their movement into the state. As black newcomers flooded the cities, whites abandoned them, confining African Americans to isolated neighborhoods. Increased racial segregation, changing economic and social relations, forging of bonds between black old-timers and newcomers, and expansion of the black industrial workforce were all results of the migration. Municipalities from Los Angeles to San Francisco responded to the influx of black migrants by establishing more stringent social, political, and economic restrictions on all black residents, newcomers and longtime residents alike. Local newspapers and police departments began to characterize crime in racial terms, giving a distorted picture of black criminal activity and stigmatizing the entire community.

The new migration also had political effects. The influx of new black working class voters and the corporatist nature of municipal politics during the war enabled a coalition of labor, blacks, and other progressive groups to mount an attack on conservative rule. Under the leadership of a united labor movement, this coalition grew to become major contenders in postwar urban politics, especially in Oakland.

Variations of the patterns and processes in California were at work in Detroit, Chicago, and New York City as well. Centers of production provided blacks with greater economic and social opportunities, and facilitated the rise of the black middle. However, due in part to migration, the cities' blacks faced pervasive discrimination and competition from whites, which caused blacks to have to endure inferior employment opportunities, substandard housing, inadequate health facilities, inferior education, and problems with drugs, crime, and insecurity. The migration of blacks to urban areas during World War II indelibly affected the social, political, and economic landscape of American cities.

Blacks in the Military

African Americans had been treated as second-class citizens for more than a century in the United States. Many blacks believed that white Americans would more likely see blacks in this country as full citizens if they proved their love for and dedication to the country. As in **World War I**, black men volunteered as soldiers fighting to defend the nation and its democratic principles in an effort to demonstrate their bravery and their status as American citizens. Most black soldiers, however, were never accepted as equals. When blacks enlisted in the military, many were placed in segregated combat units, training schools, and camp facilities. Moreover many black soldiers, though trained, never saw actual combat. Instead they made up the service and supply units, often acting as porters and messmen, the same positions to which many black men had been relegated as civilians.

African American organizations like the National Association for the Advancement of Colored People (NAACP), the National Urban League (NUL), and the Brotherhood of Sleeping Car Porters (BSCP) pressured the government to end segregation in the armed forces. Walter White, executive secretary of the NAACP, and **A. Philip Randolph**, president of the BSCP, met with President **Franklin D. Roosevelt** and other military officials to express their views. These leaders advocated for integration of the military and asked the **federal government** to denounce discriminatory practices, goals that were not fully reached until President **Harry S. Truman**'s executive order in 1948.

Black soldiers were also targets of racial violence in American cities. Mobs of whites attacked black soldiers, many of whom were in uniform. During the war, incidents of racial violence increased as they had in previous American wars. Racial violence took place involving white and black soldiers in several American cities including Alexandria, **Louisiana** (1942); Florence, **South Carolina** (1942); Phoenix, Arizona (1942); Flagstaff, Arizona (1943); and Valleg, California (1943). Violence broke out between black soldiers and white soldiers, police, and civilians in these incidents.

The Riots of 1943

The challenges to equality that African Americans faced during the war exploded in 1943. More than 240 racial incidents occurred in 47 different towns and cities during that year. Full-scale race riots broke out in Detroit, Harlem, and Los Angeles, and numerous lynchings occurred in a number of different states. Tensions between whites and blacks in many cities were exacerbated by migration, overcrowding in defense centers, competition for jobs, and conflict over housing. These tensions erupted in violence and in some cases escalated to race riots.

The **Detroit Race Riot of 1943** was the most infamous and destructive race riot that year. A dispute between black youths and whites over access to the Belle Isle amusement park started the riot. The violence moved to the black section of the city, and African Americans began to stone white-owned stores and cars driven by whites. Many blacks rioted out of frustration about limited economic opportunities, police brutality, substandard housing, segregation, and inadequate recreational facilities. White rioters were acting out racial prejudice, and many were angry about having to compete with blacks for jobs, housing, and recreational facilities. The two days of racial violence ended with nine whites and 25 blacks dead. Nearly 700 people were injured. The riot resulted in nearly $2 million worth of property stolen or damaged before state and federal troops regained order.

Similar dynamics set off a riot in Harlem less than two months later. The frustration blacks felt at employers' continued refusals to employ them in higher-paying war industries contributed to an explosion of discontent in the summer of 1943. On the night of August 2, a riot began in response to a white police officer shooting an off-duty black soldier. The police charged the soldier with interfering in the arrest of a black woman in the lobby of a Harlem hotel. False rumors circulated accusing the officer of having killed the soldier who was trying to defend his mother. In response to the rumors, black rioters broke store windows, looted, damaged property, and attacked policemen. By the morning of August 3, five persons had been killed, 400 injured, and hundreds of stores had been looted. Property damage was estimated at $5 million. Many African American leaders believed this burst of violent action was an outgrowth of the lack of economic opportunities for New York City's African Americans.

The underlying causes of the racial violence in Detroit and New York City illustrate how African Americans felt in other centers of defense production during the war. Police violence and competition over limited resources and jobs contributed to a rash of racial conflicts between whites and blacks during the war. Though violence was one manifestation of black frustration, black leaders and black organizations sought other methods to alleviate some of the problems blacks in cities faced.

1940s Jim Crow and the Beginning of Civil Rights Activism

Increasingly, scholars have identified World War II as a catalyst for black activism and a more militant African American consciousness. African Americans linked the issues of victory over Fascism abroad with victory over racism at home and began a campaign for racial equality. The **Double V Campaign** was the term used for the myriad of activities undertaken by black leaders and organizations to achieve full citizenship for African Americans. "Double V," a term initially used in a newspaper article appearing in the *Pittsburgh Courier,* stood for "Victory at Home and Abroad."

Black workers used the mobilization process and federal programs to gain economic and social mobility. Labor activism was especially important to African Americans because legislation was passed in 1941 prohibiting discriminatory hiring practices in war industries. During the war African American demands for civil rights were focused on the workplace. Black workers and activists, following in the footsteps of A. Philip Randolph, emerged as leaders in local and national struggles for black rights. African Americans used the need for factory workers and fair employment to force the federal government into acting for the equality of black workers. Southern black activists in trade unions and civic organizations, local offices of the NUL and NAACP, and other locally based grassroots groups comprised a national effort to get African Americans jobs in war projects.

World War II spelled the end of Jim Crow, 1944. Courtesy of Library of Congress, LC-USZ62-86142.

Black organizations took action to resist discrimination in 1941. In April Lester Granger, Executive Secretary of the NUL, Walter White, leader of the NAACP, Channing Tobias of the YMCA, **Mary McLeod Bethune** of the National Youth Administration and A. Philip Randolph of the Brotherhood of Sleeping Car Porters asked President Roosevelt to forbid discrimination in the **armed forces** and defense industries. Secretary of War Henry Stimson and Secretary of the Navy Frank Knox refused to desegregate the armed forces, and Roosevelt did not insist. Afraid of angering employers and Southern Democrats, the president merely issued a statement condemning discrimination. The black delegation felt that this was not enough and proposed a march on Washington, DC, at a meeting in Chicago. Randolph agreed to lead the **March on Washington Movement** and publicly announced plans for such a march to demand an executive order to end racial discrimination in defense industries.

This outpouring of black discontent and the threat of a mass protest forced the federal government to relent. On June 25, 1941, the pressure from the March on Washington Movement pushed President Roosevelt to issue an executive order banning discriminatory hiring practices in industries with government war contracts. Not only did Executive Order 8802 prohibit discrimination in hiring practices, but also prohibited government training programs from discriminating against black workers as well. Finally, the executive order established the **Fair Employment Practices Commission** in the Office of Production Management. The committee was to receive and investigate complaints of discrimination in violation of the executive order, and take appropriate steps to redress grievances which it found to be valid.

The March on Washington Movement was the beginning of a newer, more militant, outright demand for civil rights; a demand spurred by economic hardships. Black organizations pressured government agencies to enforce fair employment legislation. In 1945, a breakthrough in fair employment legislation came in New York with the passage of the Ives-Quinn Law, which outlawed discriminatory hiring practices in the state. Black newspapers continuously ran stories on discrimination against black soldiers and workers, informing black readers of the prejudice and rallying support for the activities of black organizations to alleviate these problems. There is also evidence that black servicemen after fighting in the war refused to accept prewar racial practices. Black veterans, many of whom had lived in the South, were more likely to reenlist, and twice as likely to relocate to a different region after the war.

Legacy

Many historians believe that World War II was a catalyst for processes that ended in the ghettoization of urban black communities. Moreover, many use the end of the war as the marker of the beginning of urban decline. They argue that racism prevented blacks from moving into the middle class, and restrictive covenants, redlining, and denial of federal housing loans kept blacks out of the growing suburbs. Consequently, many African Americans were trapped in decaying cities. Moreover, racist implementation of the federal G.I. Bill also gave unfair economic advantage to white war veterans who could use government loans for housing to buy homes in the suburbs and tuition loans to go to college. Using the G.I. Bill, white veterans and their families entered the middle class, while black veterans were not afforded those opportunities. Some link the more militant protests it engendered to the beginning of the **Civil Rights Movement.**

No matter the arguments about the long-term effects of the war, the Second World War was very significant for African Americans. The availability of factory jobs to African Americans, which prompted migration, changed the face of American cities. Black men and women were able to find better-paying jobs in factories, and black women moved out of domestic occupations and into clerical and service positions after the war. For the first time, the majority of blacks no longer resided in rural Southern areas. In fact, after the 1940s, the African American population was no longer concentrated in the South, but spread more evenly throughout the country. World War II created not only modern America, but modern black America as it was known for the rest of the twentieth century. *See also* Zoot Suit Riots.

Further Readings: Blum, John M. *V Was for Victory: Politics and American Culture during World War II.* San Diego, CA: Harcourt Brace Jovanovich, 1976; Capeci, Dominic J., Jr., and Martha Wilkerson. *Layered Violence: The Detroit Rioters of 1943.* Jackson: University of Mississippi, 1991; Chamberlain, Charles D. *Victory at Home: Manpower and Race in the American South during World War II.* Athens: University of Georgia Press, 2003; Dalfiume, Richard M. "The 'Forgotten Years' of the Negro Revolution." *Journal of American History* 55, no. 1 (June 1968): 90–106; Johnson, Marilynn S. *The Second Gold Rush: Oakland and the East Bay during World War II.* Berkeley: University of California Press, 1993; Lemann, Nicholas. *The Promised Land: The Great Black Migration and How It Changed America.* New York: Albert A. Knopf, 1991; Lynch, Hollis R. *The Black Urban Condition: A Documentary History, 1866–1971.* New York: Crowell, 1973; McGuire, Phillip. "Desegregation of the Armed Forces: Black Leadership Protest and World War II." *Journal of Negro History* 68, no. 2. (Spring 1983): 147–58; Polenberg, Richard. *War and Society: The United States, 1941–1945.* Philadelphia: J. B. Lippincott Company, 1972; Wynn, Neil. *The Afro-American and the Second World War.* New York:

Holmes and Meier, 1976; Wynn, Neil. "The 'Good War': The Second World War and Post-war American Society." *Journal of Contemporary History* 31, no. 3 (July 1996): 463–82.

Carla J. DuBose

World's Columbian Exposition

The World's Columbian Exposition, held in the city of Chicago, commemorated the 400-year anniversary of Christopher Columbus' "discovery" of America in 1492. Between May and October 1893, more than 20 million visitors visited the World's Fair and explored its many attractions. The fairgrounds—designed by the landscape architect Frederick Law Olmsted—boasted of 400 newly constructed buildings on a 700-acre site, located seven miles south of the Chicago Loop.

The buildings housed cutting-edge examples of new technologies, as well as the achievements of modern farming, mining, and transportation. Visitors saw refrigerated railcars that could carry fresh grapefruit from Florida to other parts of the United States, and watched clocks and listened to alarms that were timed by wire signals sent from Washington, DC. They gaped at a giant cannon made by the German Krupp company, and a huge telescope that would be donated to the University of Chicago. In addition, visitors heard lectures on social, cultural, and historical issues. For example, the historian Frederick Jackson Turner read a paper, "The Significance of the Frontier in American History," which raised the question of how the recent "closing" of the Western frontier would shape the future of American democracy, while Jane Addams of Chicago's Hull House spoke on domestic labor and factory work. On a lighter note, fairgoers could gaze at a large map of the United States—made entirely out of pickles. The World's Columbian Exposition, however, was not only meant to entertain; organizers wanted to promote a new vision of Gilded Age society, in which art, industry, and technology fostered cultural cohesion and social stability, in which capital and labor coexisted in harmony (but with capital in command), and in which "civilization," embodied in a hegemonic white manhood, presided over a hierarchy of subordinate races and genders.

The exposition displayed a controversial version of American civilization. Between the 1860s and 1890s, there were wide-ranging challenges from below, as African Americans, industrial workers, and women struggled against the class, race, and gender boundaries that had long defined American society. For instance, black Americans demanded and fought for the abolition of **slavery** and inclusion into the United States as full citizens. However, white Southern resistance and Northern ambivalence led to the collapse of **Reconstruction** during the 1870s, paving the way for new systems of white dominance in the 1880s and 1890s: a vicious **lynching** culture, ongoing economic exploitation, disfranchisement, and segregation. In 1893, African Americans were still struggling to achieve their citizenship rights as guaranteed under the Thirteenth, Fourteenth, and Fifteenth Amendments. In industry, cyclical recessions and frequent strikes underlined the persistence of serious class divisions in American society. The Panic of 1873 caused massive unemployment, and working-class discontent led to violent confrontations between employers and labor in 1877 (the year of the Great Railroad Strike), 1884–1886 (the "Great Upheaval" that concluded with the Haymarket bombing), and 1892 (the year of the Homestead steel strike in Pennsylvania,). The political assertiveness of immigrant workers and foreign radicals alarmed many native-born white Americans, who believed their society stood on the brink of collapse. Amid this unrest, social reform causes allowed middle-class women to cultivate new roles in public life, challenging the idea that only men could participate in economic affairs or political activities. The activities of the Women's Christian Temperance Union (WCTU), the settlement house movement, and the National Woman Suffrage Association (NWSA) pointed to the prominence of women in political matters. In response to the various social groups who questioned their authority, well-to-do white men hoped the World's Columbian Exposition would quell dissent by presenting to the public the social and cultural dividends of industry, technology, and white male supremacy: improved personal convenience, economic opportunity, enhanced communications, and national prestige.

The physical arrangement of the exposition's grounds and exhibits pointed to the organizers' social and cultural agendas. The buildings and exhibits of the "Court of Honor" (known as "White City") provided the architectural and technological centerpieces of the fair. Evoking the earlier empires of Ancient Greece and Rome, organizers constructed nine neoclassical buildings, each made of iron skeletons and skins of gleaming white plaster: "Administration," "Agriculture," "Electricity," "Horticulture," "Fisheries," "Machinery Hall," "Manufactures and Liberal Arts," "Mines and Mining," and "Transportation." According to exhibitors and organizers, the technological achievements of the Industrial Revolution and the grandeur of Western architecture exemplified modern "civilization"—a powerful response to workers, radicals, and unionists who accused industrialists of unrestrained greed. Machinery Hall featured 17 acres of mechanical wonders, offering visitors extensive proof of American civilization's technological accomplishments. Organizers encoded civilization as synonymous with white manhood, as the main exhibition buildings only featured white males' inventions. The Court of Honor excluded African American contributions outright, while relegating white women's cultural achievements to a separate site on the fairgrounds. The fair's commissioners, composed solely of white men, relegated persons of color to the Midway Plaisance—a tangential section of the fair where visitors could contrast the whiteness of the Court of Honor with caricatures of Egyptian, American Indian, central and southern African, and Persian villages. The titanic whiteness of the Court of Honor starkly contrasted with tiny villages of scantily clad black women and men (in "skirts") who urged visitors to enjoy a glimpse of primitive society.

That the World's Columbian Exposition reproduced and justified racial, class, and gender inequalities was not lost on black observers. Because the organizers promoted a segregated event by excluding African Americans from the planning committees and the exhibition halls, the antilynching activist and author **Ida B. Wells-Barnett** called on black Americans to voice their protest by boycotting the fair. White organizers attempted to suppress African

Americans' complaints of discrimination by creating a separate, one-day program known as "Colored American Day." Frederick Douglass, the former
slave and lifelong activist on behalf of black civil rights, described the segregated White City as "a whited sepulcher." He also condemned the undignified
association of American black men and women with the backward African vil-
lagers on the Midway Plaisance.

Both Douglass and Wells-Barnett contributed to a widely read pamphlet,
*The Reason Why the Colored American Is Not in the World's Columbian
Exposition,* which challenged the fair's racial segregation, tokenism, and
offensive stereotypes by arguing that African Americans, rather than whites,
were the more civilized race. Confronted with white racism and discrimination both inside and outside the fairgrounds, African Americans questioned
whites' claims to high civilization. Were segregation, discrimination, and
"race hate" the benchmarks of a civilized, forward-thinking people? As Douglass argued, black men and women's many advancements in the handful of
years since emancipation proved that African Americans were the better exemplar of progress and civilization; and, he continued, it was African American
labor that built so much of America's vaunted civilization.

The white male organizers of the exhibition segregated women's cultural
achievements in a separate building, the diminutive Woman's Building
(designed by architect Sophia Hayden). Situated away from the Court of
Honor and near the Midway Plaisance, women existed—literally—in the
space between civilization and savagery. While the Board of Lady Managers
at the fair tried to show that women, like men, had made many contributions
to modern civilization, the Woman's Building exhibits focused on domesticity,
motherhood, the arts, reform, religion, and beauty as pillars of civilized white
womanhood. White male organizers insisted that women's activities were not
central to American civilization; rather, they were secondary in importance to
men's innovations and endeavors. Despite the exclusion of women from White
City, white women's partial recognition and actual separation from the Midway's racialized backwardness showed they still enjoyed a more privileged status than African Americans. Organizers thought of white women as closer to
civilization than blacks.

After the World's Columbian Exposition concluded in the autumn of 1893,
fires swept through the site and burned many of the buildings. While the exposition was over, and much of the fairgrounds were in ashes, the values articulated during the event continued to impact American culture and society. In
1894, for instance, the use of federal troops to put down the Pullman Strike
in the Chicago area showed capital's continued commitment to the suppression of challenges from below; and two years later, in 1896, the Supreme
Court's **Plessy v. Ferguson** decision formally affirmed the practice of racial
segregation in the American South. Organizers hoped the exposition would
authenticate the greatness of American civilization, but the fair both mirrored
and intensified patterns of injustice and prejudice. *See also*Masculinity, Black
and White; Jim Crow; Nadir of the Negro; Racial Stereotypes.

Further Readings: Bederman, Gail. *Manliness and Civilization: A Cultural History of
Gender and Race in the United States, 1880–1917.* Chicago: University of Chicago Press,
1995; Brands, H. W. *The Reckless Decade: America in the 1890s.* Chicago: University of

Chicago Press, 1995; Reed, Christopher Robert. *"All the World Is Here!" The Black Presence at White City.* Bloomington: Indiana University Press, 2000; Trachtenberg, Alan. *The Incorporation of America: Culture and Society in the Gilded Age.* New York: Hill and Wang, 1982.

Gregory Wood

Wright, J. Skelly (1911–1988)

As a U.S. attorney, a Federal District Court judge, and a judge in the U.S. Court of Appeals, James Skelly Wright was one of the principal architects in the demolition of **Jim Crow** in **Louisiana** public schools between 1950 and 1962. Early in his career, Wright earned a reputation for judicial activism for the cause of social justice, a status that remained intact until his death. His rulings also authorized desegregation in higher education, city offices, and public facilities in Louisiana long before other states of the Deep South yielded to the directives of the ***Brown v. Board of Education*** decision of 1954.

A native of New Orleans, Wright was born in 1911 to a working class family. He was educated in the New Orleans city school district, then entered Loyola University of New Orleans on an academic scholarship. After completing a degree in Philosophy, Wright immediately entered Loyola University Law School in the early years of the **Great Depression**. When finding gainful employment as an attorney in the midst of the Depression proved impossible, Wright returned to Loyola to teach history and practice law in 1934. He was appointed to assistant U.S. attorney for New Orleans in 1936 and served until the early 1940s, when he joined the Coast Guard during **World War II**. His politically liberal approaches to the law as assistant U.S. attorney caught the attention of President **Harry S. Truman**, who appointed Wright as the U.S. attorney for New Orleans in 1948.

Wright was promoted again to the Federal District Court of the eastern Louisiana district in 1950. At the time, he was the youngest federal judge in the country. The three-judge district court was assigned the National Association for the Advancement of Colored People (NAACP) suit against Louisiana State University (LSU) in Baton Rouge in 1950. Shortly after World War II, the **NAACP Legal Defense Fund** had launched new and inventive attacks against Jim Crow, arguing that segregated colleges and professional schools for blacks were still inherently unequal, given that white students had access to greater resources, better-trained faculty, and more space. The civil rights organization had successfully argued on behalf of Herman Sweatt for his admittance to the University of Texas Law School in the Supreme Court case of *Sweatt v. Painter* in 1948.

Applying the same tactic at LSU, Roy Wilson was the lead plaintiff in a lawsuit challenging the **"separate but equal"** statutes commonly manipulated to disguise inadequate university education for African Americans. The three judge panel found that LSU must admit African Americans to its law school, despite the proximity and availability of the historically black Southern University in Baton Rouge. It was Wright's first integration order, and it led to the desegregation of the professional and graduate schools at LSU in 1950, followed by the undergraduate schools in 1953.

After the *Brown* decision, the state of Louisiana devised other tactics to evade the segregation order. For instance, Louisiana maintained that segregation was so widespread and long-standing that it could not possibly desegregate in the time specified by *Brown* II, nor would the state be able to undo decades of division that made racial segregation a fixture in Louisiana culture. Recognizing that the state's intention to defy Supreme Court and the *Brown* decision, Wright concluded that "the magnitude of the problem may not nullify the principle. And that principle is that we are, all of us, freeborn Americans, with a right to make our way unfettered by sanctions imposed by man because of the work of God." In *Bush v. Orleans Parish School Board* (1961), Wright wrote the opinion for the unanimous decision to throw out Louisiana's attempt at "interposition," or the state's rejection of the *Brown* decision. In Wright's opinion, Louisiana had no protection against desegregation, nor did the state rest on a solid foundation to defy the Supreme Court. Louisiana was ordered to abandon its tactics preventing the desegregation of its public schools.

One of Wright's most noted rulings concerned Tulane University and the issue of racial segregation in admission standards at private universities. In 1962, two African American students, Barbara Guillory and Pearlie Elloie, sued Tulane for illegally using race as a factor in denying them admission. Wright ruled that Tulane must desegregate and admit the two students, despite Tulane's claim that as a private university, it was not bound by the regulations for public institutions and it was not funded by public monies or resources. Wright argued in *Guillory v. Administrators of the Tulane University of Louisiana* (1962) that "Reason and authority strongly suggest that the Constitution never sanctions racial discrimination in our schools and colleges, no matter how 'private' they may claim to be." Wright's decision was overturned on appeal; however, Tulane admitted Guillory and Elloie in the 1964–1965 academic year. The Tulane decision was the last in a long line of Wright's controversial rulings while living in New Orleans. After political pressure from Louisiana's senators prevented an appointment to the Fifth Circuit Court of Appeals or the Supreme Court, Wright was promoted to the U.S. Court of Appeals for the District of Columbia in 1962. He relocated from his home in New Orleans to Washington, DC.

Wright's career flourished in Washington. He ruled on the publication of the Pentagon Papers in 1971, which triggered the political scandal, and he maintained his socially progressive positions on cases regarding race, poverty, and labor unions. He retired from the bench in 1986 and died of prostate cancer in 1988.

Further Readings: Baker, Liva. *The Second Battle of New Orleans: The Hundred-Year Struggle to Integrate the Schools.* New York: HarperCollins, 1996; Cartledge, Connie. "J. Skelly Wright: A Registry of His Papers in the Library of Congress," Manuscript Division, Library of Congress. http://hdl.loc.gov/loc.mss/eadmss.ms003076 (accessed June 4, 2008); Fairclough, Adam. *Race and Democracy: The Civil Rights Struggle in Louisiana, 1915 to 1972.* Athens: University of Georgia Press, 1995; Woodward, C. Vann. *The Strange Career of Jim Crow.* New York: Oxford University Press, 2002.

Nikki Brown

Z

Zoot Suit Riots (June 1943)

The Zoot Suit Riots were race riots targeting mainly Mexican Americans that took place over a series of weeks primarily in East Los Angeles during the month of June 1943. U.S. servicemen on leave, primarily white Southerners, went into minority communities in search of "zoot suiters" to attack violently.

The "zoot suiter" was portrayed in the media as an unpatriotic, juvenile delinquent. The zoot suit style actually evolved much earlier out of African American jazz clubs in **Harlem**, New York, in the 1930s. By the **World War II** era, some teenagers in the Mexican American community adopted this fashion, characterized by the colorful broad-shouldered, narrow-waisted suit with tapered pants. Since there was fabric rationing in place to help the war effort, these young people in baggy clothing were viewed as possibly having fascist sympathies. The mainstream media viewed youth in this subculture as not doing their patriotic duty, even though most of the clothing was bought secondhand in thrift stores. By most estimates, less than 10 percent of Mexican Americans were members of the jitterbug scene.

Mexican Americans continued to experience de jure segregation during this period. They were regularly denied equal access to public facilities such as restaurants, theaters, swimming pools, housing, and schools. The increased demand for workers during wartime did open up some job opportunities that had previously been closed because of race, such as in the defense industry. Majority opinion often begrudged these small economic gains by minorities, with a general view that such progress would cause minorities to forget their proper place in society. Tensions increased when white servicemen on leave carousing would enter into minority, segregated communities, often with the goal of teaching proper respect to uppity minorities. One particular target was the zoot suiter, perhaps because of the negative media accounts. The intimidation included both verbal threats and physical violence. The Mexican American youth did not take these threats lightly and often fought back. Rumors spread between both groups that each was sexually victimizing each other's women and many skirmishes took place before the outbreak of the actual riot. It was this atmosphere of superpatriotism, racism, and economic and sexual competition that set the stage for the race riots.

The incident that created the spark for the riot occurred on May 30, 1943. Approximately, 12 servicemen on leave saw some Mexican American women walking on the opposite side of the street and decided to turn around and follow them. Some young men in zoot suits intercepted them. One of the sailors grabbed the arm of one of the civilians and a fight ensued. The servicemen received the worst of it. After they returned to base they planned to retaliate. On June 3, about 50 sailors roamed around looking for zoot suiters to attack. They found only a few young boys, whom they stripped of their clothing and beat up. It was then decided to go into the Mexican American communities of East Los Angeles and Boyle Heights, where there had not been any previous clashes, and attack any Mexican Americans they could find. The Los Angeles police did not step in and stop the rampaging servicemen; instead, they arrested the civilians who had been assaulted. The riots also spread into African American and Filipino communities.

The riots were not quelled until the Mexican ambassador complained to the State Department. There were also fears that the riots might be used as Axis propaganda by the State Department and they ordered the military to control their men. On June 7, the military made Los Angeles off-limits to all military personnel and on June 8, the city banned the wearing of the zoot suit, with violators given a 30-day jail sentence. The clashes subsided, and the governor ordered an investigation of the riots. The committee found that the principal cause of the violence was racism. *See also* Hispanics/Latinos; World War II.

Further Readings: Pagán, Eduardo Obregón. *Murder at the Sleepy Lagoon: Zoot Suits, Race and Riots in Wartime L.A.* Chapel Hill: University of North Carolina Press, 2003; Mazon, Mauricio. *The Zoot Suit Riots.* Austin: University of Texas Press, 1988.

Julieanna Frost

SELECTED BIBLIOGRAPHY

Books

Anderson, James. *The Education of Blacks in the South, 1860–1931.* Chapel Hill: University of North Carolina Press, 1988.

Ayers, Edward. *The Promise of the New South: Life after Reconstruction.* New York: Oxford University Press, 1992.

Barbeau, Arthur, and Florette Henri. *Black American Troops in World War I.* Philadelphia: Temple University Press, 1974.

Bay, Mia. *The White Image in the Black Mind: African American Ideas about White People, 1830–1925.* New York: Oxford University Press, 2000.

Bogle, Donald. *Toms, Coons, Mulattoes, Mammies, and Bucks: An Interpretative History of Blacks in American Films.* New York: Viking Press, 1973.

Branch, Taylor. *Parting the Waters: America in the King Years, 1954–1963.* New York: Simon and Schuster, 1988.

———. *Pillar of Fire: America in the King Years, 1963–1965.* New York: Simon and Schuster, 1998.

Brown, Nikki. *Private Politics and Public Voices: African American Women's Activism from World War I to the New Deal.* Bloomington: Indiana University Press, 2007.

Carson, Clayborne. *In Struggle: SNCC and the Black Awakening of the 1960s.* Cambridge, MA: Harvard University Press, 1981.

Clark-Lewis, Elizabeth. *Living In, Living Out: African American Domestics in Washington, D.C., 1910–1940.* Washington, DC: Smithsonian Institution Press, 1994.

Collier-Thomas, Bettye, and V. P. Franklin, eds. *Sisters in the Struggle: African American Women in the Civil Rights—Black Power Movement.* New York: New York University Press, 2001.

Cooper, Anna Julia. *A Voice from the South.* New York: Oxford University Press, 1988.

Crawford, Vickie, Jacqueline Rouse, and Barbara Woods, eds. *Women in the Civil Rights Movement: Trailblazers and Torchbearers.* Brooklyn, NY: Carlson Publishing, 1990.

Cruz, Bárbara C., and Michael J. Berson. "The American Melting Pot? Miscegenation Laws in the United States." *OAH Magazine of History* 15, no. 4 (Summer 2001). Organization of American Historians Web site, http://www.oah.org/pubs/magazine/family/cruz-berson.html (accessed July 21, 2008).

Dray, Philip. *At the Hands of Persons Unknown: The Lynching of Black America.* New York: Modern Library, 2003.

Du Bois, W.E.B. *The Souls of Black Folk.* New York: Library of America, 1903.

Egerton, John. *Speak Now against the Day: The Generation before the Civil Rights Movement in the South.* New York: Alfred A. Knopf, 1994.

Floyd, Samuel A. *The Power of Black Music: Interpreting Its History from Africa to the United States.* New York: Oxford University Press, 1995.

Franklin, John Hope, and August Meier. *Black Leaders of the Twentieth Century.* Urbana: University of Illinois Press, 1982.

Frederickson, George. *The Black Image in the White Mind: The Debate on Afro-American Character and Destiny, 1817–1914*. New York: Harper and Row, 1971.

Gibson, Jo Ann Robinson. *The Montgomery Bus Boycott and the Women Who Started It*. Knoxville: University of Tennessee Press, 1987.

Gilmore, Glenda Elizabeth. *Gender and Jim Crow: Women and the Politics of White Supremacy in North Carolina, 1896–1920*. Chapel Hill: University of North Carolina Press, 1996.

Hahn, Steven. *A Nation under Our Feet: Black Political Struggles in the Rural South from Slavery to the Great Migration*. Cambridge, MA: Harvard University Press, 2003.

Hall, Jacquelyn Dowd Hall. *Revolt Against Chivalry: Jessie Daniel Ames and the Women's Campaign against Lynching*. New York: Columbia University Press, 1993.

Hampton, Henry, and Steve Fayer, eds. *The Voices of Freedom: An Oral History of the Civil Rights Movement from the 1950s through the 1980s*. New York: Bantam Books, 1990.

Harlan, Louis T. *Booker T. Washington: The Making of a Black Leader, 1856–1901*. New York: Oxford University Press, 1972.

———. *Booker T. Washington: The Wizard of Tuskegee, 1901–1915*. New York: Oxford University Press, 1983.

Hine, Darlene Clark, Elsa Barkley Brown, and Rosalyn Terborg-Penn, eds. *Black Women in America: An Historical Encyclopedia*. Brooklyn, NY: Carlson Publishing, 1993.

Hunter, Tera. *To 'Joy My Freedom: Southern Black Women's Lives and Labors after the Civil War*. Cambridge, MA: Harvard University Press, 1997.

Jones, Jacqueline. *Labor of Love, Labor of Sorrow: Black Women, Work, and the Family from Slavery to the Present*. New York: Basic Books, 1995.

Kellogg, Charles. *NAACP: A History of the National Association for the Advancement of Colored People*. Baltimore: Johns Hopkins University Press, 1967.

Kelly, Robin D. G. *Hammer and Hoe: Alabama Communists during the Great Depression*. Chapel Hill: University of North Carolina Press, 1990.

Lewis, David Levering. *W.E.B. Du Bois: Biography of a Race, 1868–1919*. New York: Henry Holt and Co., 1993.

———. *W.E.B. Du Bois: The Fight for Equality and the American Century, 1919–1963*. New York: Henry Holt and Co., 2001.

———. *When Harlem Was in Vogue*. New York: Alfred A. Knopf, 1981.

Litwack, Leon. *Been in the Storm So Long: The Aftermath of Slavery*. New York: Vintage, 1980.

———. *Trouble in Mind: Black Southerners in the Age of Jim Crow*. New York: Knopf, 1998.

Lomax, Alan. *Mr. Jelly Roll: The Fortunes of Jelly Roll Morton, New Orleans Creole and "Inventor of Jazz."* New York: Grove Press, 1950.

McMillen, Neil. *Dark Journey: Black Mississippians in the Age of Jim Crow*. Urbana: University of Illinois Press, 1989.

Marable, Manning. *Race, Reform, and Rebellion: The Second Reconstruction in Black America, 1945–1982*. Jackson: University Press of Mississippi, 1984.

Marks, Carole. *Farewell—We're Good and Gone: The Great Black Migration*. Bloomington: Indiana University Press, 1989.

Moody, Ann. *Coming of Age in Mississippi*. New York: Dell Press, 1968.

Patterson, James. *Brown v. Board of Education: A Civil Rights Milestone and Its Troubled Legacy*. New York: Oxford University Press, 2000.

Payne, Charles. *I've Got the Light of Freedom: The Organizing Tradition and the Mississippi Freedom Struggle*. Berkeley: University of California Press, 1995.

Rabinowitz, Howard. *Race Relations in the Urban South: 1865–1890*. New York: Oxford University Press, 1978.

Stovall, Tyler. *Paris Noir: African Americans in the City of Light*. New York: Houghton Mifflin, 1998.

Sullivan, Patricia. *Days of Hope: Race and Democracy in the New Deal Era*. Chapel Hill: University of North Carolina Press, 1978.

Washington, Booker T. *Up from Slavery: An Autobiography*. New York: Doubleday, 1902.

Watkins, Mel. *On the Real Side: A History of African American Comedy*. New York: Lawrence Hill Books, 1999.

Woodward, C. Vann. *The Strange Career of Jim Crow*. New York: Oxford University Press, 1957.

X, Malcolm. *The Autobiography of Malcolm X*. With the assistance of Alex Haley. New York: Ballantine Books, 1973.

Web Sites

Cutler/Glaeser/Vigdor Segregation Data. http://trinity.aas.duke.edu/~jvigdor/segregation/index.html (accessed July 21, 2008).

The Fight for Desegregation. http://library.thinkquest.org/J0112391/the_fight_for_desegregation.htm (accessed July 21, 2008).

Library of Congress. "From Jim Crow to Linda Brown: A Retrospective of the African-American Experience from 1897 to 1953." http://memory.loc.gov/learn/lessons/97/crow/crowhome.html (accessed July 21, 2008).

"*Plessy v. Ferguson* (1896)." Landmark Cases, Supreme Court, http://www.landmarkcases.org/plessy/home.html (accessed July 21, 2008).

Public Broadcasting Service. "The Rise and Fall of Jim Crow." http://www.pbs.org/wnet/jimcrow/ (accessed July 21, 2008).

Remember Segregation. Interactive Web site, http://www.remembersegregation.org/ (accessed July 21, 2008).

INDEX

A. Philip Randolph Institute, 708–9

AAA. *See* Agricultural Adjustment Administration

Abernathy, Ralph David, 1–4, 327, 500, 672, 746, 749; M. L. King and, 2–4, 21, 328, 482

abolitionists, 225, 226, 596, 737. *See also* slavery

Absalom, Absalom! (Faulkner), 292–93, 613

accomodationism, 56–57, 133, 362, 416, 598, 828; Niagara movement and, 601–2

Acheson, Dean, 164

Adams, Henry, 431

Adams, Herbert Baxter, 237

Adams, John Henry, Jr., 43

Adams, Numa Pompilius Garfield, 307

Addams, Jane, 869

advertising, 4–10, 597; African Americans in, 4–8; notable black icons in, 8–10, 652; radio, 666; television, 777

affirmative action, 10–11, 229, 590, 847

AFL-CIO, 670, 672, 747. *See also* American Federation of Labor; Congress of Industrial Organizations

African Blood Brotherhood (ABB), 12–13, 177

African Community Leagues, 320

African culture, 472–73. *See also* culture

African diplomats, 300; U.S. racism and, 167–68

African heritage, 306; black nationalism and, 94; Ethiopia, 269–73. *See also* Back to Africa Movement; Liberia

African Methodist Episcopal (AME) church, 38–39, 135, 136, 225, 343, 821; Du Bois and, 250, 252; women in, 849

African Muslims, 398. *See also* Nation of Islam

Afro-Cubans, 122–23

Afro hairstyle, 195, 631

Age (newspaper), 835

Agricultural Adjustment Act, 13–14, 244, 337, 750

Agricultural Adjustment Administration (AAA), 13–14, 728, 750, 751

agricultural labor, 537, 538, 864; Black Codes and, 78–83, 84; in Haiti, 356; on penal farms, 637. *See also* cotton economy; sharecropping; tenant farmers

Ahmadiyyah movement, 398–99, 493–94

Aid to Dependent Children (ADC), 591–92

Aiken, David Wyatt, 743

Air Force, U.S., 35; Tuskegee Airmen, 154, 247

A.L.A. Schechter Poultry Corp. v. United States (1935), 593

Alabama, 2, 15–21, 231, 261, 264, 468, 625; antimiscegenation law in, 534; black disenfranchisement in, 562; Council on Human Relations (1954–1961), 18–21;

Dixiecrats in, 234, 236, 782; Folsom as governor of, 15–16, 307–8; Freedom Riders in, 289–90; Lowndes County Freedom Organization, 765; poll tax in, 631, 632; prisons in, 636, 638, 640; resistance to desegregation in, 482; Scottsboro Boys case in, 178, 268, 414; Selma-Montgomery march (1965), 16–17, 169, 470; sharecropper unions in, 727–29; vagrancy laws in, 81; voter registration campaign in, 747; White Citizens Council in, 837, 838. *See also* Birmingham, Alabama; Montgomery Bus Boycott (1955–1956); University of Alabama; Wallace, George

Alabama State College, 1, 19

Albany (Georgia), 323; Civil Rights Movement in, 21–23, 186, 297, 327–28

Albany State College, 22

Albright v. Texas, 770

Alexander, Alger "Texas," 99

Alexander v. Holmes County (1969), 541

Ali, Muhammad, 23–24, 139, 756

Alien Land Law (1901), 401

Allen, Richard, 135, 225, 252, 742

Allen v. Merrill (1957), 581

All-Negro Hour (radio program), 662

Almond, Lindsey, 335

Education (1899), 202–4; gradual formulas for, 215–17, 218–19, 827; of military, 35, 140, 144, 155, 164, 179, 247, 680; Nashville Plan, 216; racist opponents of, 214, 215; sit-in movement and, 184; SRC and, 18–19; in Washington, DC, 101–2, 165–66. *See also Brown v. Board of Education;* school desegregation

Detroit, 862, 864; Nation of Islam in, 566; race riot (1943), 219–22, 866

Dewey, Thomas E., 234, 788, 840

DeWitt, John, 402–3, 404

direct action. *See* nonviolent direct action

Dirksen, Everett, 680

discrimination, 222–29, 507, 671, 788; in Chicago stores, 644; in Chicago world's fair (1893), 870–71; Civil War and, 226–27; in defense industry, 67, 155, 220, 279, 286–87, 497, 499, 863, 864, 866–67; in employment, 229; labor union, 455, 593, 670, 863; in Latin America, 458; Native Americans and, 582; poverty and, 710; racism and, 222; Supreme Court and, 227; Waller and, 824–25; white superiority and, 224–25, 226, 228

disenfranchisement, 229–33, 465–66, 684–86, 729, 802; in Florida, 685–86; in Georgia, 832; Mississippi Plan, 211, 480, 536, 542–45, 684, 811, 841–42; in Texas, 781; white primary and, 839; women's suffrage and, 850. *See also* voting rights

Dixiecrats, 182, 212, 233–34, 284, 496; Thurmond, 234, 236, 343–44, 788, 840; Truman and, 782, 788, 789. *See also* Wallace, George

Dixon, Thomas, Jr., 74, 76, 237–40; *The Clansman,* 238, 351, 444, 524, 533

Doby, Larry, 755

Doctrine of Interposition, 335

Dodd, Wallace, 566

domestic work, 5, 240–45, 649, 699, 720, 852; Great Depression and, 851; Great Migration and, 242–44, 340, 850; professionalization of, 242, 245; on television, 772–73. *See also* mammy figure

Dominican Republic, 121–22

Domino, Antoine "Fats," 696, 697–98

Don't Buy Where You Can't Work Campaign, 246

Dorsey, Thomas, 330

Double V campaign (WWII), 35, 146, 247–49, 251, 282, 381, 515, 866

Douglas, Aaron, 44

Douglas, Paul, 167

Douglas, Robert L., 62

Douglass, Frederick, 60, 95, 282, 668, 836, 871; B. T. Washington and, 828–30; Exodusters and, 431

Dred Scott v. Sandford (1857), 464, 673, 738, 796–97

Drew, Timothy (Noble Drew Ali), 493, 566

Du Bois, W.E.B., 133, 188, 238, 249–53, 599, 840; *An Appeal to the World,* 164; Atlanta compromise and, 57, 544; Atlanta Conferences (1897) and, 324; B. T. Washington and, 199, 250, 251, 564, 828, 830–31; on blacks in unions, 453; on crisis in Ethiopia, 271–72; criticism of vocational education, 815; editorials in *The Crisis,* 362, 790; Garvey and, 60, 322, 474, 802, 805; Locke and, 665; NAACP and, 144, 153, 250; Niagara Movement and, 600, 602; quote from, 565; Rustin and, 705; *Souls of Black Folk,* 199, 251, 323, 324, 598, 601, 611, 714; Talented Tenth and, 57, 199, 250, 341, 598, 599; World War I and, 247, 857

Dudley, Edward, 164, 558

Dunbar, Paul Lawrence, 253–54, 392, 565, 597, 599

Duncanson, Robert S., 41

Dunning, William A., 674

Durham, Richard, 665

Dyer, Leonidas C., 255–56, 469

Dyer Anti-Lynching Bill, 177, 197, 255–56, 469

East, Clay, 750

Eastland, James O., 149, 167, 358

East St. Louis riot (1917), 194, 255, 257–58, 574, 626, 704

Eaton, Hubert, 329

Ebbinghaus, Herman, 396

Ebony (magazine), 423, 424

Eckford, Elizabeth, 476, 479

Economic Bill of Rights, 749

economic pressure, 365. *See also* Great Depression; poverty

economic recovery, 337–38

Edelman, Marian Wright, 559

Edmondson, William, 46

education, 258–64, 573, 682–84; for blacks in Georgia, 323–24; for blacks in Texas, 778; Civil Rights Act of 1964 and, 263–64; elementary and secondary, 814–16; freedom schools, 159, 185, 763–64; G.I. Bill and, 315–16; literacy and, 562; Native Americans and, 582–83; race relations, 18–19; vocational, 215, 238, 378, 683–84, 813–17. *See also* black teachers; *Brown v. Board of Education;* school desegregation

Educational Amendments of 1972, 263

Edwards, Paul K., 6

Eisenhower, Dwight D., 38, 65, 144, 167, 680, 773, 847; desegregation of military and, 284; Little Rock crisis and, 145, 157, 166, 212, 261, 300–301, 477–78, 574, 680–81; school desegregation and, 165–66, 725

Elaine (Arkansas) Massacre (1919), 264–67, 677, 678, 686–87, 751, 840

Elkins, Stanley M., 658–59

Elk v. Williams (1884), 580

Ellington, Duke, 91, 267–68, 409, 660

League of Nations, 272
Lee, Canada, 665
Lee, Harper, 141–42
Lee, Herbert, murder of, 762
Lee, Robert E., 778
Lee-Smith, Hughie, 45, 47
legislation, 462–70; Native
    American rights and, 584; slave
    codes, 223, 526, 827. *See also*
    antimiscegenation laws; Black
    Codes; Civil Rights Acts;
    Voting Rights Act
Lehman brothers, 413
Lenin, Vladimir I., 176–77
The Leopard's Spots (Dixon),
    237–38, 351, 444
Lerner, Arthur, 666
"Letter from Birmingham Jail"
    (King), 147, 158, 440, 500
Levison, Stanley, 179, 707
Levittown, housing covenants in,
    385–86, 471, 711
Lewis, Edmonia, 42
Lewis, John, 160, 297, 436, 454,
    760, 762, 765; sit-in movement
    and, 733, 734, 735
Lewis, William Henry, 752
Lhamon, W. T., Jr., 692
Liberia, 164, 300, 431, 472–75,
    564; African American
    colonists in, 59, 472, 804, 836
Liberty Halls, 322
Liebowitz, Samuel, 414
Light in August (Faulkner), 291,
    292
Lincoln, Abraham, 229, 282,
    432, 475, 596, 681;
    assassination of, 75;
    Emancipation Proclamation
    and, 226, 343, 463, 499, 679;
    Radical Republicans and, 229,
    526, 681
Lincoln, C. Eric, 494
Lincoln Memorial, 475–76, 501,
    700
Lincoln University, 378
Linden Hills (Naylor), 585
Linnaeus, Carl, 528
literacy, 856. *See also* education
literacy tests, 231, 323, 344, 818,
    838; labor unions and, 452;
    Mississippi and, 227, 358, 542,
    684, 841, 842; in North
    Carolina, 846; Voting Rights

Act and, 681; white primary
    and, 838
literature, 851; black poets, 253–
    54, 597, 599, 791–92;
    children's, 128–34, 652;
    Faulkner, 291–94, 535, 613;
    Federal Writers Project, 268,
    302–3; G. Naylor, 584–85;
    New Negro movement, 597–
    98, 599; of passing, 612–13.
    See also specific writers
Little, Earl, 342, 492
Little, Malcolm. *See* Malcolm X
Little Richard, 689, 697–98
Little Rock Nine (1957), 31–32,
    38, 217, 261–62, 476–79, 732;
    C. B. Motley and, 550; *Cooper
    v. Aaron* and, 186–88, 262; D.
    L. Bates and, 31, 64, 65, 477;
    Eisenhower and, 145, 157,
    166, 212, 261, 300–301, 477–
    78, 574, 680–81. *See also*
    Faubus, Orval
Lloyd, Earl, 63, 755
Locke, Alain, 342, 599, 665
Lodge, Henry Cabot, Jr., 165,
    561
Logan, Rayford, 560
Lomax, Alan, 548
Lomax, John Avery, 302
Long, Huey, 211–12
The Long Shadow of Little Rock
    (Bates), 64, 65
Looby, S. Alexander, 460, 461
Los Angeles, 341, 384, 768, 862,
    864, 865; Watts riot (1965),
    161, 170; Zoot Suit riots
    (1943), 372, 874–75
Lott, Trent, 783
Louis, Joe, 87, 89, 272, 693, 754
Louisiana, 230, 264, 429, 479–
    82, 679; Baton Rouge bus
    boycott, 66–67, 757–58, 759;
    black Catholics in, 125; Black
    Codes in, 82, 83; black
    migration from, 429, 430;
    blackness defined in, 607; black
    voting rights in, 799; Dixiecrats
    in, 234, 236, 782; free blacks
    in, 573; Grambling University
    in, 309, 378; grandfather clause
    in, 466, 544; Haitians in, 356;
    Huey Long in, 211–12;
    lynchings in, 487, 490; Native

Americans in, 583; poll tax in,
    631, 632; prisons in, 636, 637,
    640, 641; Republican Party in,
    847; school desegregation in,
    261, 872–73; segregation law
    in, 623, 797; sharecropper
    union in, 729; suffrage
    amendment in, 846; UNIA in,
    804; White Citizens Council in,
    837; white primary in, 838. *See
    also* New Orleans; *Plessy v.
    Ferguson*
Louisiana State University, 872
L'Ouverture, Toussaint, 121
Love, Emmanuel King, 324
Love v. Griffith (1924), 839
Loving v. Virginia (1967), 504,
    535, 725, 813
Lowery, Joseph, 2, 482–83, 746,
    749
Lucy, Autherine, 166, 217, 484–
    85, 509, 852
Luizzo, Viola, murder of, 747
Lymon, Frankie, 690, 697
lynching, 265, 345, 467–68, 484–
    91, 524, 865; of African
    American war veterans, 95,
    469, 647; antilynching
    activists, 77, 194, 197, 255–56,
    468, 469, 675, 679, 822, 832,
    834–35; blues music and, 86,
    99, 100; documentation of,
    326, 563; in East St. Louis,
    258; Evers and, 276; FBI and,
    294, 326; in Florida, 304;
    geography of, 487–88; in
    Georgia, 487, 489, 490, 625;
    Great Migration and, 340;
    Houston race riot and, 859;
    identity and, 490–91; of IWW
    leaders, 395; of Jews, 325,
    413–14, 444; Ku Klux Klan
    and, 266, 325, 339, 414, 489,
    532, 704; legal, 178; legislation
    against, 177, 195–97; of
    Mexican Americans, 779; in
    Mississippi, 265, 537–38; mob
    typology, 484, 488–90, 532;
    NAACP investigations (White),
    612; as punishment for
    interracial relations, 490–91,
    504, 787; rape allegations and,
    513, 523, 656, 779, 790;
    retaliation for, 568; of Sam

ABOUT THE EDITORS AND CONTRIBUTORS

Editors

Nikki Brown is an Assistant Professor of History at the University of New Orleans.

Barry M. Stentiford is an Associate Professor of History at Grambling State University.

Contributors

Carol Adams-Means is an Instructor in the Department of Communications at the University of Texas, San Antonio.

Regina Barnett is a masters student in the African American and African Diaspora Studies Department at Indiana University.

Jeffrey D. Bass is an Assistant Professor of History at Quinnipiac University in Connecticut.

Michael Beauchamp is a PhD candidate in History at Texas A&M University.

Shannon Smith Bennett is a PhD candidate in History at Indiana University.

James M. Beeby is an Assistant Professor of History at Indiana University Southeast.

Alfred L. Brophy is a Professor of Law at the University of Alabama Law School.

Thomas Brown is an Assistant Professor of Sociology at Northeast Lakeview College, Texas.

Joan C. Browning is a freelance writer.

John Russell Burch, Jr., is Director of Library Services at Campbellsville University.

Frank Cha is a PhD candidate in American Studies at the College of William and Mary.

Lauren Chambers is a PhD student in English at the University of Georgia.

Aaron Cooley is a PhD student in Education at the University of North Carolina, Chapel Hill.

Simon T. Cuthbert-Kerr is a Lecturer in American History at the University of Glasgow, Scotland.

Christina L. Davis is a PhD student in History at the University of Georgia.

Olethia Davis is a Public Law Professor at Troy University in Alabama.

Sharlene Sinegal DeCuir is a PhD candidate in History at Louisiana State University.

Rutledge M. Dennis is a Professor of Sociology/Anthropology and African American Studies at George Mason University.

James I. Deutsch is a Program Curator for the Smithsonian Center for Folklife and Cultural Heritage in Washington, DC.

Wayne Dowdy is a Senior Librarian and Archivist at Memphis Public Library and Information Center.

Carla J. DuBose is a PhD candidate in American History at the City University of New York, Graduate Center.

Shawntel L. Ensminger is a PhD student at Florida State University.

Kwame Essien is a PhD student in History at the University of Texas at Austin.

Amy Essington is a PhD candidate in History at Claremont Graduate University, California.

Marianne Fisher-Giorlando is the Acting Dean of the College of Professional Studies, Grambling State University.

Monroe Friedman is a Professor Emeritus in Psychology at Eastern Michigan University.

Julieanna Frost is an Assistant Professor of History at Siena Heights University.

Justin D. García is an Instructor of Anthropology at Temple University.

Laura Gimeno-Pahissa teaches U.S. History and Literature at the Universitat Autonoma de Barcelona.

Ivan Greenberg is an independent scholar writing on civil liberties and social movements.

Skylar Harris is a PhD candidate in History at the State University of New York.

Danielle C. Heard is a PhD candidate in English at Cornell University.

Emily Hess is a PhD student in History at Case Western Reserve University.

Karlos K. Hill is a PhD candidate in History at the University of Illinois at Urbana-Champaign.

Arthur Holst holds a PhD in Government from Temple University.

Marilyn K. Howard is an Associate Professor in the Departments of Social and Behavioral Sciences and the Humanities at Columbus State Community College.

James Ivy is an Instructor in the Department of English of Trinity University, San Antonio.

Eric R. Jackson is an Associate Professor and Assistant Chair of the Department of History and Geography at Northern Kentucky University.

Sherita L. Johnson is an Assistant Professor of African American Literature at the University of Southern Mississippi.

George H. Junne, Jr., is a Professor and Chair of Africana Studies at the University of Northern Colorado.

Gregory Kaliss is a PhD student in History at the University of North Carolina at Chapel Hill.

Stephen C. Kenny is a Lecturer in History at the School of History, University of Liverpool, England.

Steven E. Knepper is a PhD student in English at the University of Virginia at Charlottesville.

Karen Kossie-Chernyshev is an Associate Professor of History at Texas Southern University.

Jeffrey Kraus is a Professor of Government and Politics and Associate Provost at Wagner College in New York.

Anthony A. Lee is an Adjunct Professor of History at West Los Angeles College.

Jennie Lightweis-Goff is a Graduate Instructor in the College Writing Program at the Rush Rhees Library in Rochester, New York.

James W. Loewen is a Professor Emeritus of Sociology at the University of Vermont.

J. Vincent Lowery is a PhD candidate in History at the University of Mississippi.

Angie Maxwell is a PhD candidate in American Studies at the University of Texas in Austin.

Louis Mazzari is an Assistant Professor of History and English at Bogazici University in Turkey.

Barbara McCaskill is an Associate Professor of English and General Sandy Beaver Teaching Professor at the University of Georgia.

Douglas Milford is the Associate Director of Academic Services for Professional MBA Programs at the University of Illinois at Chicago.

Mark Edwin Miller is an Assistant Professor of History at Southern Utah University.

William A. Morgan is a PhD candidate in History at the University of Texas.

James Newman is an Assistant Professor of Political Science at Idaho State University.

Yusuf Nuruddin is a Visiting Assistant Professor in the Africana Studies Program, University of Toledo.

Barbara A. Patrick is an Assistant Professor of Public Administration at Mississippi State University.

Mika'il A. Petin is Associate Director of African American Studies and the African American Studies Research and Resource Center at George Mason University in Virginia.

Brian Piper is a graduate student in American Studies at the College of William and Mary.

Michelle A. Purdy is a PhD student in Educational Studies at Emory University.

Sanjeev A. Rao, Jr., is an Adjunct Professor of History at Monmouth University in New Jersey.

Alyssa Ribeiro is a PhD candidate in History at the University of Pittsburgh.

Natalie J. Ring is an Assistant Professor of History at the University of Texas at Dallas.

Mario Marcel Salas is an Assistant Professor of Political Science/Government at Northwest Vista College in San Antonio.

Mark Schultz is an Associate Professor of History at Lewis University in Illinois.

Donald Scott is a history journalist and columnist.

Dorsia Smith teaches English at the University of Puerto Rico at Río Piedras.

John Matthew Smith is a PhD student in History at Purdue University.

Mary Stanton is a writer and independent scholar.

Kevin Strait is a PhD candidate in American Studies at George Washington University.

Gregory S. Taylor is an Assistant Professor of History at Chowen College.

Jack A. Taylor III is an Adjunct Instructor of Ethnic Studies at Bowling Green State University in Ohio.

Gabriel H. Teninbaum is an Assistant Professor of Legal Writing at Suffolk University Law School in Boston.

Jennifer Jensen Wallach is an Assistant Professor of History at Georgia College and State University.

Katherine Kuehler Walters is a PhD student in History at Texas A&M University.

Thomas J. Ward, Jr., is an Assistant Professor of History at Rockhurst University in Missouri.

Melissa F. Weiner is an Assistant Professor of Sociology at Quinnipiac University in Connecticut.

Gregory Wood is an Assistant Professor in History at Frostburg State University in Maryland.